Cosmopolitan Sydney

Explore the world in one city

Jock Collins
and
Antonio Castillo

Pluto Press Australia
HTTP://WWW.SOCIALCHANGE.NET.AU/PLUTO

with

Comerford and Miller

First published in August 1998 by Pluto Press
Pluto Press Australia Limited
Locked bag 199, Annandale NSW 2038
In conjunction with Comerford and Miller Publishers
36 Grosvenor Rd, West Wickham, Kent, BR4 9PY. United Kingdom.

Copyright © Jock Collins and Antonio Castillo

Printed by Alken Press Pty. Ltd
128 Long Street, Smithfield NSW 2164

Cover and design by Tracey Baglin
Typeset and layout by John Chan

Transport maps courtesy CityRail and Sydney Ferries

Cover images courtesy Carnivale by Effy Alexakis, Andrew Jacubowicz, Bangarra Dance Theatre – Frances Ring photographed by Greg Barrett, Tourism NSW.

Inside Images:
Andrew Jacubowicz Making Multicultural Australia CD Rom Project
Joe Lafferty
State Library of NSW, Brian Bird, p.158; Ronald H. Armstrong, p.166
University of Sydney Archive
Kenneth N Soovoroff
Canterbury-Bankstown Migrant Resource Centre
Tourism NSW

Australian Cataloguing In Publication Data

Australian ISBN 1 86403 040 2
United Kingdom ISBN 1-871204-11-9

Collins, Jock, 1949-.
Cosmopolitan Sydney: explore the world in one city.

1. Sydney (N.S.W) – Description and travel – 1990-. 2. Sydney (N.S.W) – Social Life and customs – 1990-. I. Castillo, Antonio, 1961-. II. Title

International Destinations
Written for World Travellers and Serious Tourists

Cosmopolitan Sydney
Explore the world in one city

Cosmopolitan Sydney required the assistance of numerous people to bring it to fruition. We would like to thank the many people who contributed to its production. Ric Sissons was publisher of Pluto Press when the idea for the book was conceived. He was enthusiastic about the book and encouraged the authors on their long road ahead. Sean Kidney was also very supportive of the project, despite his constant jokes about when the manuscript would finally be completed. Our publisher Tony Moore, from our first meeting at Bar Italia, was instrumental in driving us to the finishing line. Tony has been a great source of encouragement and inspiration, with the final book a testimony to his vision and commitment to the project.

Acknowledgments

Cosmopolitan Sydney is a highly designed book. We would like to thank Tracey Baglin and John Chan for their imaginative work on the look and production. Tracey conceived and produced the overall design feel and the cover, while John's task was to bring the various chapters to fruition. John Chan's contribution was herculean: his good spirit never failed despite constant "final" changes. We also thank Melinda May who helped with the design of the book in its early stages. And thanks to Ingrid Urh whose wonderfull ethnic precinct maps have added an extra artistic touch to this book.

A book of this length needs a lot of research. Along with the authors own research, we thank Michael Banks, who became an unlimited source of information. At the beginning of the project we also had the research assistance of Basundhara Dhungel, Glen Nole and Mohammed Rashtia. The editing of the final manuscript was done by Michael Wall – with the exception of the Italians, which was done by Alison Cowan. The book was proofread by Virginia Muzik.

More than 200 photos and images illustrate the text. We are indebted to all those who contributed to this aspect of the book production. Our most important source was Andrew Jakubowicz's *Making Multicultural Australia CD Rom project*. Photographer Joe Lafferty spent lots of day on the road shooting for the book, while Helen Velissaris provided some wonderful photos of Sydney's *Koorie* community. Russian-born photographer Kenneth N Soovoroff provided us with great shots for the Russian chapter, while the Italians chapter is enlivened by the images from the NSW State Libraries' 1995 exhibition, *La Dolce Vita? Italo – Australians of NSW*. Linda Mastronado and Tina Platonia also provided family photos for this chapter. The Canterbury-Bankstown Migrant Resource Centre kindly provided photos for the Koreans chapter. We also thank our friends at the Bangarra Dance Theatre for their cover photo and Carnivale for the use of Effy Alexakis' evocative cover images. We also thanks NSW CityRail and Sydney Ferries for the transport maps we reproduce in the book.

The Australian Tourist Commission and Tourism NSW also provided help and advice on the project. Victor Boulos of the Multicultural Education Unit of the NSW Department of Education and Training, and Nada Spasojevic and her team from EMD gave important assistance at a critical moment of the book. We would like to thank Frank Panucci and Lex Marinos from Carnivale for helping us organise the book launch. Finally, we would like to thank our partners, Carol Reid – who also wrote the chapter on Indigenous Sydney – and Jenny Kingham. Their support and critical input never flagged.

Contents

Cosmopolitan Sydney 1

How to use Cosmopolitan Sydney as a guide 3

A snap shot of Cosmopolitan Sydney 5

The world in a street-some of Sydney's
key cosmopolitan precincts 14
    Bondi Road, for a quick Hungarian and Russian fix. MAP 15
    Cleveland Street, Turkish pizzas and Lebanese delights. MAP 17
    Marrickville, at the heart of Australian multiculturalism. MAP 21
    Newtown, multi-ethnic, eccentric and grungy. MAP 25
    Bankstown, from *baklawa to pho*. MAP 30
    Oxford Street, explore the world in one drag. MAP 33
    Glebe, from Ireland to China. MAP 37

INDIGENOUS SYDNEY 40

BRISTISH AND IRISH SYDNEY 55
    The Rocks. MAP 56

The English 59

The Scots 63

The Irish 69

EUROPEAN SYDNEY

The Austrians 77

The Croatians 82

The Czecs and Slovaks 89

The Danes 94

The Dutch 96

The Estonians 105

The French 109
The Germans 120
The Greeks 132
The Hungarians 149
The Italians 155
   "Little Italy," Leichhardt. MAP 158
   Stanley Street, the CBD's unofficial "Little Italy". MAP 160
The Latvians 175
The Lithuanians 179
The Macedonians 183
The Maltese 187
The Poles 195
The Portuguese 203
   Petersham, Sydney's "Little Portugal". MAP 205
The Russians 213
The Serbs 225
The Spanish 230
   Liverpool Street, Sydney's " Little Spain". MAP 232
The Swedes 237
The Swiss 243
The Turks 246
   Auburn, Sydney's "Little Turkey" MAP 248
The Ukrainians 254

ASIAN SYDNEY

Getting to know Asian Sydney 260
   Cabramatta, Sydney's Southeast Asia Capital. MAP 263
The Burmese 267
The Cambodians 271
The Chinese 275
   Sydney's Chinatown. MAP 279

The Filipinos 298
The Indians 305
    The Hindus 316
The Indonesians 319
    Kingsford, Jakarta along Anzac Parade. MAP 325
The Japanese 329
    Buddhist Sydney 343
The Koreans 347
    Campsie, Sydney's "Korea Town". MAP 350
The Laotians 357
The Malaysians 360
The Nepalese and Tibetans 364
The Pakistani 369
The Thais 371
The Vietnamese 377

MIDDLE EASTERN SYDNEY

The Afghans 384
The Armenians 386
The Assyrians 389
The Egyptians 392
The Jews 396
    Bondi: kosher, sand and kites. MAP 406
The Lebanese 411
    Lakemba, "Little Lebanon". MAP 416
    The Sydney Muslim Community 422
    The Arabic-speaking community 424
The Iranians 425
    The Sydney Baha'i Community 428

ISLANDER SYDNEY

The Fijians 429

The Papua New Guineans 432
The Mauritians 434
The Samoans 437
The Tongans 440

AFRICAN SYDNEY
Getting to know African Sydney 443
The Ethiopians 449
The Ghanaians 451
The Nigerians 453
The Sierra Leoneans 455
The South Africans 456
The Sudanese 460

AMERICAN SYDNEY
The North Americans 462

LATIN AMERICAN SYDNEY
Getting to know Latin American Sydney 467
The Argentinians 473
The Brazilians 475
The Chileans 477
The Mexicans 480
The Peruvians 483

THE NEW ZEALANDERS 485

Transport
CityRail Suburban Network 489
Sydney Ferries 490

Readers' Feedback 491

Cosmopolitan Sydney

When most people from other countries think of Sydney they imagine the Opera House, the Harbour Bridge and Sydney's magnificent harbour. Sydney's beaches, such as Bondi and Manly, are also well known internationally. Others might also conjure up other international symbols of Australia: kangaroos, koalas and boomerangs. But cities are much more than physical beauty or flora and fauna.

Cities are also about people and places. Or, more correctly, people in places. The most significant feature of Sydney is its people. The indigenous people of Sydney and its surrounds have witnessed more than two centuries of immigration to their shores. This makes Sydney first and foremost a cosmopolitan city whose multicultural character derives from people who have come from over 180 nationalities. Sydney can claim to be the world in one city, a claim that few contemporary cities can make.

Sydney's cosmopolitan city and suburbs

Sydney's cultural diversity shapes the sights, smell, tastes and sounds of daily life in the city and the suburbs in a profound way. This fact will surprise many visitors and new settlers to Sydney probably more than the physical beauty of our city. While most tourists and other visitors are prepared for – and expectant of – the brilliant sights of Sydney, they don't expect the cosmopolitan character of Sydney: it is our city's greatest international secret.

Sydney reflects this cultural diversity in its people and its places. In the precinct of downtown Sydney – or the central business district (CBD)- this ethnic diversity is reflected in the faces of the people you pass in the street, in the many languages you will hear or in the people who sell you goods and services. It is also reflected in the restaurants of Sydney and in the diversity of cultural, community and family events which map contemporary life in the city.

Sydney's famous 'Coat'-hanger', the Sydney Harbour bridge.

Some restaurants are clustered in ethnic groups – Chinatown near Dixon Street (see page 283), Little Spain around Liverpool Street (see page 233), the Italian restaurants in Oxford Street (see page 35), the Lebanese and Turkish eateries around Cleveland Street (see page 19). In other places, restaurants of diverse ethnic background mix and match to provide the casual tourist with a smorgasbord of gastronomic choice and delight as they stroll along the city's many streets and alleys. Around the fringes of downtown Sydney, exciting pockets of cultural life are to be found in King Street in Newtown (see page 27), Glebe Point Road in Glebe (see page 38), and Darling Street in Balmain. With a variety of foods, prices and reputations, these restaurants provide Sydneysiders with great access to brilliant, exciting and imaginative food from all corners of the globe. Yes, in one city.

Most tourists, sadly, miss Sydney's suburbs. Yet it is in the suburbs where the Sydney people live, and in suburban neighbourhoods where Sydney's cosmopolitan character is most evident. If you don't visit one of Sydney's cosmopolitan suburbs, you are missing out on gems such as Leichhardt, Sydney's Little Italy (see page 159), with its vibrant inner-west café society along Norton Street. You'll miss Bar Italia, famous for the gelato, coffee and relaxed cool. Or you will miss the sounds and smells of Asia along Cabramatta's Johns Street (see page 265), with traders like the BKK Supermarket advertising their goods and services in many languages and scripts. Or the Arabic community centred on Auburn railway station and nearby mosques (see page 248), where the diversity of shop owners reflects the diversity of the community. You will miss the experience of a Korean barbecue in Campsie (see page 350), or a *pho bo* in a Vietnamese restaurant in Bankstown or Marrickville (see pages 31 and 22), or the Mediterranean taste of Lisbon in Sydney's Little Portugal (see page 207). You won't see the churches of many denominations that stand proudly amid the pigeon droppings as a testimony to religious diversity in Sydney. You will miss the snake man and Aboriginal boomerang throwers at La Perouse. Or the other monuments and relics to the history of so many different ethnic groups. In other words, you will miss the heartbeat and cosmopolitan magic of Sydney.

Sydney's people are as 'exotic' as our flora and fauna.

How to use Cosmopolitan Sydney as a guide

This is the first edition of *Cosmopolitan Sydney*. The authors and Pluto Press aim to provide a guide to the cultural diversity of Sydney's people and places. We aim to help you to understand, find and explore the world in one city.

Cosmopolitan Sydney offers a history of Sydney's immigrant communities. Most chapters are based on different birthplace groups, despite the fact that many people from the same birthplace – for example, Vietnamese-born of Vietnamese or Chinese ethnicity – are of a very different ethnic, cultural or religious background. This is a consequence of the way in which the Australian Bureau of Statistics collects population data.

The chapters give a brief history of each major birthplace group in Sydney, providing a profile of key individuals, institutions and festivals. Information is provided to enable the international or interstate visitor to link up with different ethnic communities through foreign language media, consulates, organisations, churches, events, landmarks and places of interest. We would like to warn that some telephone numbers – especially of community organisations – may change. We have made every effort to ensure that the numbers provided are the most updated and accurate. Information on key festivals and events that mark the calendar of Sydney's myriad ethnic communities are also included in these chapters. Throughout, information is provided on Sydney's cosmopolitan places: how to get there, what to expect, where to eat, where there is a good cup of coffee. Some of these are in the downtown part of Sydney. These are the most likely to be discovered by international or national visitors. But other ethnic precincts are found in the suburbs from the inner-city areas on the fringes of the CBD to those on the distant outer-urban fringes of the city.

One of the most obvious manifestations of Sydney's cultural diversity is the great variety of foods that are available in restaurants and shops. You can find food from almost every cultural tradition in restaurants in downtown Sydney and the suburbs. Some areas are centres for particular food types. Like any city, the restaurant food varies in terms of price and

Most of our telephone numbers are Sydney numbers. If you are ringing from interstate add the prefix 02 before the number. If ringing from overseas put 61 (country code) and 2 (area code for Sydney and NSW) before the number you ring.

Cosmopolitan kids are the happy face of Sydney.

quantity, but most of it is good and, by international standards, relatively cheap. Throughout this guide - in almost every chapter – we suggest some good eating experiences praised by the experts and by those friends we made from different ethnic communities during the preparation of this book. They generously shared their tips with us. For a specific eating guide we recommend *The Good Food Guide* edited by Sydney Morning Herald's food experts Terry Durack and Jill Dupleix, the *SBS Eating Guide to Sydney* by Maeve O'Meara and Joanna Savill (Allen & Unwin), and *Cheap Eats*.

Note that many of Sydney's restaurants are BYO, which means that you can bring your own wine to the restaurant, sometimes at the cost of a small cover charge. This provides a great opportunity for having good, cheap wine with your food. Australia produces great red and white wines, so explore Australian wines as you sample Sydney's cosmopolitan food. The restaurant prices supplied – in Australian dollars – are based on individual orders, they are approximate and should be treated as a guide only. Along with our eating guide, we have also included the names of shops – from antiques to souvenirs, from butcheries to bakeries - were you can also experience the ethnic flavour of our city.

Pacific Islanders who have made Sydney their home.

The book also tries to induce you to experience the "other" Sydney: the suburbs. We would encourage you to make the effort to see some of Sydney's cosmopolitan suburbs. We include maps of suburban centres that have become ethnic enclaves. These are mostly in the inner-West, West and South West of Sydney, where most of Sydney's immigrants from a non-English-speaking background live. Maps of Sydney's key multicultural suburban centres such as Marrickville, Leichhardt, Auburn, Bankstown, Campsie and Cabramatta are provided as your guide to getting there, eating, sight-seeing and shopping.

The one problem of doing a book about a city with such cultural diversity is that is not possible to do justice to the many smaller, but no less important, communities. In future editions of the book we will expand to include those not yet given their appropriate place among Sydney's cosmopolitan communities. We would encourage community leaders and individuals to send in information that can improve our coverage for the second edition. As we go to press much of the 1996 census data on Sydney's Cosmopolitan communities is not fully available. In some places we report 1991 census data.

A snap shot of Cosmopolitan Sydney

Despite the great desert interior of the island continent, Australia is one of the most urbanised of nations. Most Australians live in large cities along the coastline. Sydney is the first and the largest of Australian cities. Australia has 18.5 million people, and about one in six of all Australians – or 3,245,225 people – live in Sydney, over half of the population of the State of New South Wales.

One in three Sydneysiders – just over 1 million people – are born overseas or are first generation immigrants. They come from all corners of the globe: 16.5 per cent were born in the UK and Ireland, 15.9 per cent in Southern Europe, 15.1 per cent in South East Asia, 12.5 per cent in North East Asia, 8.4 per cent in the Middle East and 5.6 per cent in New Zealand. Taken together with their Australian-born children – the second generation – immigrants comprise more then half of Sydney's population today. As Australia approaches the end of the millennium, the centenary of Federation and wanders inevitably towards a Republic, cultural diversity is one of the key characteristics of Australian national identity.

First generation immigrants have contributed enormously as workers, professionals and business owners to wealth and employment creation in Australia. They were changed by the Australian immigration experience and at the same time changed Australian society. In the city and the suburbs, immigrants have played a vital role in rebuilding and revitalising cityscapes. In the last four decades, dead, dull and boring neighbourhoods have been transformed to vibrant and energetic suburban centres bristling with life and energy. Immigrant shopkeepers were the vanguard of this process of urban renewal in Sydney. Their Australian-born children continue to fundamentally challenge and change what it means to be an Australian today.

And, of course, Sydney is now associated with the Olympic symbol of the five concentric rings, testimony to the fact that Sydney will stage the 2000 Olympic Games. One of Sydney's selling points for the games was the cultural diversity of Sydney itself. During the Sydney 2000 Games, the world's athletes and their supporters will come to Sydney. Most of

> In the city and the suburbs, immigrants have played a vital role in rebuilding and revitalising cityscapes. In the last four decades, dead, dull and boring neighbourhoods have been transformed to vibrant and energetic suburban centres bristling with life and energy.

these Olympic visitors will be surprised that there is a community of their people living in our city. Their culture is already established in Sydney through ethnic organisations, foreign-language newspapers, religious facilities, monuments, cultural events and culinary influences. They will find enthusiastic supporters among these Sydneysiders from their "old" country.

Indigenous Sydney

Sydney's cultural diversity is not just a product of immigration. Sydney's indigenous peoples have a long history which predates white invasion 210 years ago. The Eora tribe kept watch and care of the land that is now Sydney for some 40,000 years. They have shown great resilience to survive the first two centuries of white settlement against the odds. There are 28,754 Sydneysiders who are Aboriginals or Torres Strait Islanders, or 0.9 per cent of Sydney's population. They have come from many tribal groups from across NSW and other Australian states. Though small in numbers, Sydney's Aboriginal population has increased by 75 per cent since 1986. Sydney's indigenous minorities are the spiritual heart of the city, although they are often relegated – in spatial and socioeconomic terms – to the marginal fringes. Today, indigenous cultural images and political issues are one of the most visible features of our country, and Aboriginal Sydneysiders profoundly shape the past, present and future of our city. Many of Sydney's suburbs carry Aboriginal names.

Sydney indigenous minorities are the spiritual heart of the city.

Australian indigenous peoples are fighting for recognition and for reconciliation. Aboriginal artists, authors, academics, lawyers and doctors are challenging negative stereotypes and demanding a place for their people in the mainstream of our history. They demand land rights, self-determination and reconciliation. The songlines of our nation will remain discordant to many national and international ears until reconciliation between white and Aboriginal Australia is achieved.

Aboriginal settlement in Sydney is today concentrated in a number of suburban clusters. These include the inner-city suburbs of Redfern, Waterloo, Woolloomooloo and Glebe, La Perouse on the southern shores of Botany Bay, Bidwell, Shalvey, Willmont, Tregear and Mount Druitt in Sydney's outer west and Airds in the outer southwest. Sydney's indigenous peoples are often called *koories* to distinguish them from their compatriots from the mid north NSW coast, the *goories*, or those in the north west of NSW and Queensland, the *murries*. Traditional and modern indigenous cultural sites and events are an important part of Sydney's cultural diversity. They are outlined in detail in the chapter on Indigenous Sydney page 40.

Sydney is a global city

Sydney is the archetypical global, post-modern city. And Sydneysiders are proud of it. The world-wide attention that the 2000 Games has brought Sydney merely entrenches this fact. Sydney is home to virtually all the peoples of the globe. If the post-modern world is about globalisation, internationalisation and diversity of culture, politics and economics, then Sydney represents the city of the future. Our city has one of the greatest levels of cultural and linguistic diversity of any other metropolis in the world. At a time when, internationally, cultural diversity is associated with conflict and trouble, Sydney's very successful experience of very different peoples living in relative harmony and prosperity is a great achievement.

It has not all been smooth sailing. It is true that until the 1970s, Australian immigration laws were racist. The White Australia policy is an example. It is also true that some Sydneysiders today still hold attitudes of prejudice towards Sydney's ethnic and indigenous communities. But Sydney has not seen the violence that so often characterises ethnic diversity in other places. Racists here are swimming against the unstoppable stream of our history. They are a nonsense minority. Each and every day tolerance is found on the street corners, on public transport and in the public spaces of Sydney's communal and family life. Sydney's achievement of producing social harmony out of cultural diversity is perhaps the greatest of Sydney's many achievements.

Sydney's characteristics and its charm, its challenges and its opportunities, increasingly stem from its multicultural makeup. Sydney is a global city. This means that Sydney and its people are shaped by the increasing internationalisation of culture and communications, of economics and finance, of daily life itself. Sydney has recently been chosen as the site for multinational corporations such as American Express to establish regional Asian headquarters because Sydney provides a multicultural and multilingual workforce. There is a neat fit between the cosmopolitan nature of Sydney and the globalisation that is shaping all aspects of economics, politics and culture in contemporary society. And, of course, Sydney has a great climate and great people, enhancing its attractiveness to globetrotting corporate executives.

One of the features of globalisation is that the opportunities for international travel are increasing dramatically. Every day the streets of Sydney are swelled by temporary visitors - tourists, international students and business people - for whom Sydney is home for a day, a week or more. These short-term visitors in turn add to the cosmopolitan flavour of Sydney, since the number of temporary entrants annually far outweighs the permanent flow of immigrant settlers.

> As part of the run to the 2000 Sydney Olympics, four yearly cultural festivals -called Sydney's Cultural Olympiad - have been organised. The first, held in 1997, was the *Festival of the Dreaming*. It celebrated the arts of Australia's indigenous peoples and of other indigenous peoples around the world. More than 700 indigenous artists participated in this very successful series of events. At the launch of the *Festival of the Dreaming* in the forecourt of the Sydney Opera House, the original site of their dispossession, Aboriginal people performed a cleansing ceremony through the ritual of burning eucalyptus leaves.

Sydney already attracts nearly 4 million tourists annually, and expects some 6 million in the year 2000. They come from all corners of the globe: New Zealanders are the largest in number, followed by the United Kingdom, Asia, Europe and North America. Until the recent Asian economic collapse, the largest growth in Sydney's tourism was from Asian countries, particularly China, Japan, Korea, Philippines, Sri Lanka, Taiwan and Thailand.

Sydney has also become an intellectual hub for the Asia-Pacific region. Sydney's universities and other educational institutions are attracting increasing numbers of foreign students, particularly from Asian countries. China, Hong Kong, Malaysia, Indonesia, Japan and South Korea supply the greatest number of these students. Other foreign students come from other parts of Asia, Europe, the Americas, Africa and the Pacific. They add to the cultural diversity in Sydney's CBD and suburbs during their stay. Many return later as permanent immigrants.

Sydney's successful bid to host the 2000 Olympic Games has excited Sydneysiders from all backgrounds.

The multicultural face of Sydney's people

The United Kingdom and Ireland are – not surprisingly – the origin of the largest groups of Sydney's first generation immigrants, comprising 211,000 people or about 20 per cent of all foreign-born Sydneysiders. These immigrants came from England, Scotland, Ireland and Wales to become the dominant cultural group in Australian society, and are generally referred to as Anglo-Celts despite the cultural differences among these peoples.

British immigrants shaped many aspects of Australian life, particularly the institutions of parliament and law. The Irish started horseracing, and would like to claim drinking in pubs as their cultural legacy on Australian life. The English taught us capitalism and cricket. The Scots are still proud of their heritage, and regularly meet in Sydney to celebrate their Scottishness, tossing the odd caber to enthusiastic bagpipe music. The Welsh are fewer, and less visible in public life. These immigrants are relatively invisible because their culture is the mainstream.

The next largest group of immigrants are our neighbours – the New Zealand born– including people of Maori or Pacific Islander background. Unlike all other people, they can come and settle in Australia at will. All other potential immigrants must apply with the other 1 million applicants for about 70,000 places annually.

Southern Europe was a key source of Australian immigration in the

1950s and 1960s and immigrants from this region today comprise 6.1 per cent of the Sydney population and 21.1 per cent of Sydney's immigrant community. Nowadays there are 49,923 Italians living in Sydney, the largest ethnic group from a non-English-speaking background. A similar number, 49,564, of Sydneysiders are born in the countries that comprised the former Yugoslavia, while there are 36,917 who were born in Greece. Southern European immigrants exhibit highly concentrated settlement patterns in Sydney. Most live in the suburbs in Sydney's inner-west and south west, while there are also large concentrations west of Liverpool.

Since the mid-1970s, the Sydney immigration net has focused increasingly on the Asian region. Today Sydney has 163,086 people who were born in Southeast Asia. They comprise 5.2 per cent of the total Sydney population and 15.1 per cent of the total overseas born in Sydney. Of these, 59,174 were born in Vietnam, 41,254 were born in the Philippines and 15,854 were born in Indonesia. Most of these immigrants live in the Fairfield and Cabramatta regions in Sydney's western suburbs, while others settle in western suburbs like Lidcombe, Bankstown and Marrickville that are closer to the city centre. Many Asian students settle into areas near Sydney's universities, with large settlements in Camperdown, Haymarket, Kensington and Randwick. More than half of all Southeast Asian immigrants arrived since 1986.

Another 135,078 immigrants living in Sydney were born in Northeast Asia. They comprise 4.3 per cent of Sydney's population and 12.5 per cent of all overseas-born. The majority of these were born in China (61,274 people) followed by Hong Kong (36,651 people), the Republic of Korea (20,486 people) and Japan (8,977 people). Most immigrants from Northeast Asian countries live in a radius of suburbs 5 km to 25 km from the city centre where public transport and high to medium density housing exists. Suburbs of high Northeast Asian settlement include Auburn, Strathfield, Burwood and Ashfield in the inner-west, Campsie in the south west and Rockdale and Hurstville in the south. Unlike most other immigrant minorities, Northeast Asian immigrants also have centres of settlement on Sydney's north shore, centred around Chatswood in the north and Meadowbank, Eastwood and Epping in the north-west. Some also live in Chinatown and the centre of the city.

Other large ethnic communities in Sydney include about 50,000 immigrants from Lebanon, 21,000 from Germany, 18,000 from India, 16,000 from Poland and 14,000 from the Netherlands. There are many other ethnic communities of more than 6,000 first generation

Many foreign-born students attend Sydney's six universities

immigrants. They include the birthplaces: Ireland, USA, Chile, Turkey, Sri Lanka, Hungary, the former USSR, Portugal, Cyprus, Cambodia, Uruguay and Canada. In addition to these ethnic groups, many other immigrant groups live in Sydney and are covered in this book.

Religious diversity in Sydney

With cultural diversity comes religious diversity. Just as Sydney is home to most peoples on earth, it is also home to most of the world's religions. Under the policy of multiculturalism, the cultural, linguistic and religious heritage of Australia's immigrants are welcomed and respected. This is one of the reasons that cosmopolitan Sydney works: difference is valued and respected, and not seen as shameful and "un-Australian". Immigrants bring with them a feast of religions, and feel free to celebrate their beliefs. Their cathedrals, churches, synagogues, mosques and temples which dot the downtown and suburban Sydney landscape stand as monuments to Sydney's rich religious diversity.

Sydney's religious profile reflects the dominant Christian religions of the Anglo-Celtic majority of Sydney's population. Catholicism is the most popular religion with over 1 million Catholics in Sydney. St Mary's Cathedral in the city is the centre for Sydney's Catholics. Most Catholics are born in Australia, with others have come from Italy, the Philippines, England, Yugoslavia, Lebanon, Malta, Poland and New Zealand. The next largest religions are also Christian denominations: Anglican, the Uniting Church and Presbyterian.

Other Christian religions practised in Sydney include Baptist, Lutheran, Pentecostal, Oriental Christian, Jehovah's Witness, Salvation Army, Seventh Day Adventist, Churches of Christ and the latter Day Saints, Brethren and Congregational.

Just as Sydney is home to most peoples on earth, it is also home to most of the world's religions.

But there are other religions in Sydney, the largest being Greek Orthodox, followed by Islam. Sydney's Muslim community comprises a diverse range of ethnic groups, with most Australian-born or born in Lebanon, Turkey, Indonesia, Iran, Pakistan, Fiji, Afghanistan, Cyprus and Egypt. Both major branches of Islam – Sunni and Shi'a – are represented in Australian's Muslim community (see page 422).

Other Eastern religions practised by Sydney people include Buddhism (see page 343) and Hinduism (see page 316). There are about 75 Buddhist temples in Sydney. Both religions draw on followers from a diverse range of ethnic backgrounds. There are more Buddhists born in Vietnam than Australia. Most of the others are immigrants from Asian countries, including Cambodia, Laos, Thailand, Malaysia, China, Japan and Sri Lanka. Most of Sydney's Hindus were born in Fiji and India, with the Australian-born the next largest group. Immigrants born in Sri Lanka, South Africa, Malaysia, England, Singapore, New Zealand and Indonesia also adhere to Hinduism.

Sydney has a rich spiritual diversity. The Jewish community has a long history in our city. Those who follow Judaism in Sydney are mostly Australian-born, often children of immigrants who arrived from Europe as refugees in the late 1940s (see page 396). Other smaller religions are also present. They include Antiochian, Armenian, Assyrian (Church of the East), Baha'i World Faith (see page 428), Coptic, Macedonian Orthodox, Russian Orthodox (see page 221) and Sikh.

Multilingual Sydney

About one half of Sydney's immigrants are from non-English-speaking countries. The diversity of cultural backgrounds of Sydney's immigrants has produced a rich linguistic diversity that is the soundtrack of daily Sydney life. In the shops, on the trains and buses, and in the homes of Sydney, many languages other than English are spoken. The most common non-English language spoken at home is Chinese. It's spoken by 148,771 people, or 5.1 per cent of Sydney's population. Two thirds of these people speak Cantonese, and one third Mandarin. With 110,377 people, Arabic is the second most common non-English language in our city. Of these mainly Arabic speakers, who comprise 3.8 per cent of the Sydney population, most were born in either Lebanon or Australia while 7.7 per cent were born in Egypt. This is followed by Italian (spoken by 90,975 people at home), Greek (88,037), Spanish (41,465), Vietnamese (38,004), Filipino (25,371), German (23,517), and Croatian (18,992). These languages make the "top ten" languages, other than English, found among Sydney's peoples.

Other languages spoken in Sydney's homes by less than 10,000 people include Maltese, Portuguese, Polish, Macedonian, French, Korean, Turkish and Hindi. The greatest growth in recent years has been in the number of Filipino, Vietnamese. Korean and Hindi speakers at home.

Sydney's cultural diversity has a very long history.

A SNAP SHOT OF COSMOPOLITAN SYDNEY

Ethnic Media

The cultural, religious and linguistic diversity of Sydney's people provides both the opportunity for – and the need for – a diverse, multicultural and multilingual media. There is a thriving ethnic media in Sydney. One of the unique products of Australian multiculturalism has been the establishment of the Special Broadcasting Service (SBS Television & Radio). In Sydney a diverse range of languages are broadcast on SBS Radio, while the free-to-air SBS Television brings the world to our city through high quality documentaries, movies, sport, current affairs and news.

Sydney hosts newspapers and magazines in almost every language to serve its cosmopolitan community. These papers give coverage about sport and politics in the "home country" as well as Australian news. In this way, international visitors can keep up news of home affairs, often impossible to find in other countries of the world. Many of these newspapers are available at newsagents and bookstores. At the same time, the Internet, global cable television and the mainstream media provide outlets in Australia for news of international events and for glimpses of international cultures.

The most common non-English language spoken in Sydney is Chinese; with Cantonese-speakers outnumbering Mandarin-speakers two to one.

Explore the world in one city

Sydney, a world of music, dance and food

Carnivale. September in Sydney has a name – "Carnivale" – Sydney's biggest celebration of multi-ethnic talent and diversity. With more than 200 events held throughout the month – from film festivals, music concerts, theatre, art exhibitions and of course the culinary traditions of the world – Carnivale is the most eclectic and broad-based festival of our city. Carnivale is celebrated in public parks, museums, theatres, art galleries and community centres. It's a festival bursting with colours, smells and sounds, and where there is something for everyone- from Scottish Pipers to Chinese Lion Dance, from Afghan to French cuisine, from Argentinean tango to Irish dance.

For further information: Carnivale Infoline 1800 064 534.

Festival of the World Dance. Part of Dance Week, this feast of dance and music, held at the end of April, features dancers from, among other countries, Scotland, Hungary, Greece, Poland, US, India, Rumania and Ireland. It is usually held at Tumbalong Park, Darling Harbour kicks off at around 11am and it's free.

For additional information: Darling Harbour Visitor Information Centre on 9286 0111.

Festival of Nations. Organised by the Australia Chinese Charity Foundation, this Festival is a celebration of the multi-ethnic and diverse nature of Sydney. It's generally celebrated mid-October at Tumbalong Park, Darling Harbour. It features music, food, games, song, dance and art from just about every corner of the world. Free.

For additional information: Darling Harbour Visitor Information Centre on 9286 0111.

Lex Marinos, the artistic director of Carnivale, Australia's premier multi-ethnic celebration.

The world in a street – some of Sydney's key cosmopolitan precincts

Wave after wave of immigrants of different nationalities have been attracted to the same urban precincts over time, each wave leaving its own unique traces in the streetscape, restaurants, faces, festivals and churches of these suburbs, mingling with the other waves. As well as being interesting vibrant places to live, suburbs like Newtown, Bankstown, Marrickville, Darlinghurst, Bondi Beach and Glebe offer the visitor an array of ethnic tastes, sensations and activities – all in close proximity to the city centre and public transport. The following precincts are built around a landmark high street replete with historical buildings and eccentric characters, pubs and clubs, bookshops and record stores, restaurants, and cafes. As well as reflecting Australia's cosmopolitan heartland, main drags like Oxford Street, Darlinghurst, King Street, Newtown and Campbell Parade, Bondi Beach are where the locals go to have fun. We advise you to join them.

Sydney attracts many immigrants, students and tourists from Asia.

Bondi Road
for a quick Hungarian and Russian fix

Before diving into hip Bondi Beach (see The Jews, page 396), have a quick stroll along Bondi Road. Amidst the Russian presence you will find the Hungarians – including the legendary (no-Hungarian name) Wellington Cake Shop. A quick Hungarian fix - such as the deliciously *kugelhopf* (a cake filled with runny chocolate) is our decadent tip.

1: Ogala Portuguese Style Chicken. Portuguese take away.
235 Bondi Road (tel: 9365 7043)

2: Krinsky's. Supermarket where you can find a huge array of kosher products, including cereals, meats, sweets and chocolate.
Monday-Thursday 8am-6pm (till 5pm on Friday),
Sunday 8.30am-1.30pm.
175 Bondi Road, Bondi (tel: 9386 9021)

3: Eilat Kosher Butcher. Right next door to the popular Krinsky's. In this full line *kosher* butchery you'll find zesty salami, fresh corned beef and a good selection of cold meat.
Open Monday-Friday 6am-2pm (till 6pm Tuesday-Thursday),
Sunday 6am-1pm.
173 Bondi Road (tel: 9389 1793).

Bondi Road is the place to get delicious Jewish food.

4: Wellington Cake Shop. From *dobos* to *bon vivant* and from hazelnut cakes to the friendly service, this Bondi Road cake shop is Hungarian to the bone. Open Monday-Friday 7am-6pm, Saturday-Sunday 7am-5pm.
157 Bondi Road (tel: 9389 4555).

5: Kemeny's Supermarket. This Hungarian deli - whose well stocked shelves are a gourmet European tour - sells Hungarian wines to spicy salami. Open Monday-Saturday 8am-9pm, Sunday 9am-8pm.
141 Bondi Road (tel: 9389 6422).

GETTING THERE

Bus 380, 382, L82 from the city.

6: Russki's. (see The Russians, page 213). Russian deli.
89 Bondi Road (tel: 9387 2015)

7: Skazka. (see The Russians, page 213). Russian restaurant.
140 Bondi Road (tel: 9369 2133).

USEFUL NUMBER FOR VISITORS

Bondi Visitors Information Centre, Bondi Beachside Inn, corner of Campbell Parade and Roscoe Street, Bondi Beach

Tel: 9130 5311

Opening hours: Monday-Friday 9am-5.30pm

BONDI ROAD

1. Ogala Portuguese Style Chicken.
2. Krinsky's.
3. Eilat Kosher Butcher.
4. Wellington Cake Shop.
5. Kemeny's Supermarket.
6. Russki's.
7. Skazka.

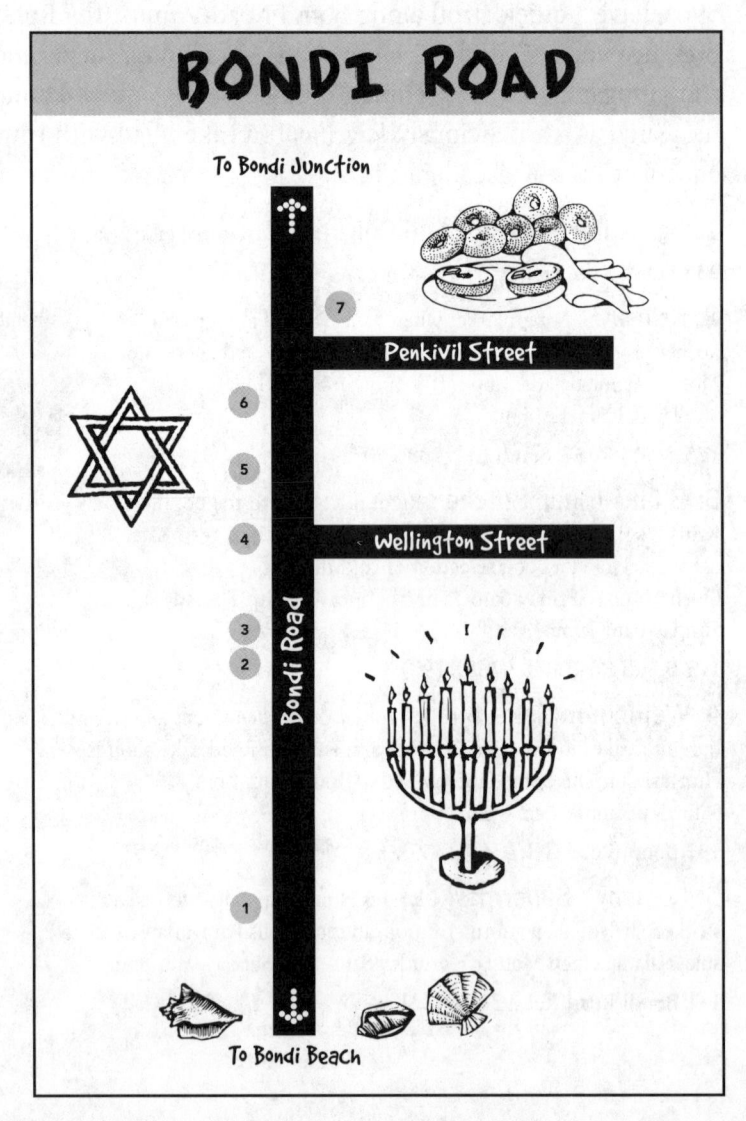

BONDI ROAD

To Bondi Junction

Penkivil Street

Wellington Street

To Bondi Beach

Explore the world in one city

Cleveland Street
Turkish pizzas and Lebanese delights

Located where Surry Hills meets Redfern, Cleveland Street has its own borders – the bottom end of the street is dominated by Indian eateries, Turkish pizza and kebab salons, while the top end is an unmistakable enclave of Lebanese restaurants, including the pioneering Abdul's which opened in 1963.

Before the Turks arrived with their pizza and sweet shops, the Lebanese pioneered the area as early as the 1890s. They were Christians from the Bekaa Valley, and were wrongly called 'Syrians'. These early Lebanese worked as street hawkers, small merchants and importers. Whilst many Lebanese moved away towards Campsie and Punchbowl in southern Sydney in the 1970s, the eateries and some shops remained, and years later were joined by Turkish, Thai, French, Indian, Pakistani, Japanese and Nepalese restaurants and shops.

3: Maya Indian Sweets Centre. Arguably the best known Indian sweet shop in Sydney. The delicious desserts - including the traditional dumplings in syrup are addictive. Monday-Friday 9am-9pm. Average $8.
470 Cleveland Street, Surry Hills (tel: 9699 8663).

4: Mehr'ay Da Dhaba. The first Indian eatery in the street. The North Indian cuisine features the timeless and delicious tandoori chicken. Open Wednesday-Sunday lunch noon-3pm, Sunday-Saturday dinner 5.30-11pm (till midnight on Friday and Saturday). Average $10, BYO.
466 Cleveland Street (tel: 9319 6260).

7: Emads & Salindas Lebanese Restaurant. Consistent with its food and ambience. Make yourself comfy in one of the cushioned rooms, and enjoy the Friday and Saturday night belly dancing (from around 9pm). Average $15, BYO. Open Monday-Sunday noon-midnight.
298 Cleveland Street (tel: 9698 2631).

8: Fatimas Lebanese Restaurant. Another pioneer, established approximately 25 years ago - has been reported as having the most famous *falafel* rolls in the street. Cushion room and belly dancing on Friday and Saturday nights. Open Monday-Sunday 10am-till late.
294 Cleveland Street (tel: 9698 4895).

The Lebanese and Turkish restaurants along Cleveland Street provide an oasis from the busy traffic.

GETTING THERE

By car or bus, Cleveland street is only minutes from the CBD. If you elect to take a bus, catch the **301, 302, 303** from Bourke street. Also **372, 393** and **395**. A taxi will set you back about $8-$10.

11: Almustafa. This in an Irish-Lebanese conspiracy. Ian Ballingou and Salwa Lghji have made a damn good job with Almustafa. The food is good and the portions generous. Average $15, BYO.
Open Monday-Saturday 5pm - late, Sunday noon-10pm.
276 Cleveland Street (tel: 9319 5632).

12: The Prophet Lebanese Restaurant. The sublime Lebanese cuisine makes The Prophet one of the best in the neighbourhood. Average $15, BYO. Open Monday-Sunday noon-midnight.
274 Cleveland Street, Surry Hills (tel: 9698 7025).

13: Omar Khayyam's Lebanese Restaurant. To recreate home style Lebanese flavour is always the ultimate goal and Omar Khayyam's achieves it. Average $15, BYO.
Open Monday-Tuesday lunch noon-3pm, dinner 5-11pm, Wednesday-Sunday noon-midnight.
272 Cleveland Street (tel: 9699 3546).

14: Nada's. It has been around for more than 15 years and that says a lot. Average $15, BYO.
Open Monday-Sunday noon-midnight.
Corner Elizabeth and Cleveland Street (tel: 9690 1289).

18: Abdul's. Pleasant and inexpensive, Abdul's opened in the 1960s making it the longest running Lebanese restaurant in the street. "Customers are mainly Anglo-Celtic, very few Lebanese customers," explains the waiter. Average $15 (set menu), BYO.
Open Monday-Sunday 10am-midnight.
Corner Elizabeth and Cleveland Street, Surry Hills. (tel: 9698 1275).

21: Erciyes Pizza Pide and Kebab Saloon. Reportedly one of the best Turkish eateries in the neighbourhood, it was established in 1984 and info tells us that despite the stiff competition it has maintained a solid and loyal clientele. Don't pass by without trying the delicious sucuklu – a folded pizza with Turkish sausage, eggs and spices.
Friday and Saturday live belly dancing. Average $12, BYO.
Open Monday-Sunday 11am-midnight.
409 Cleveland Street (tel: 9319 1309).

23: Girne Pide. The great range of pizzas are cheap, big and good. Average $8, BYO. Open Monday 5-11pm, Tuesday-Sunday 11am-midnight.
427 Cleveland Street, Redfern (tel: 9319 4307).

Explore the world in one city

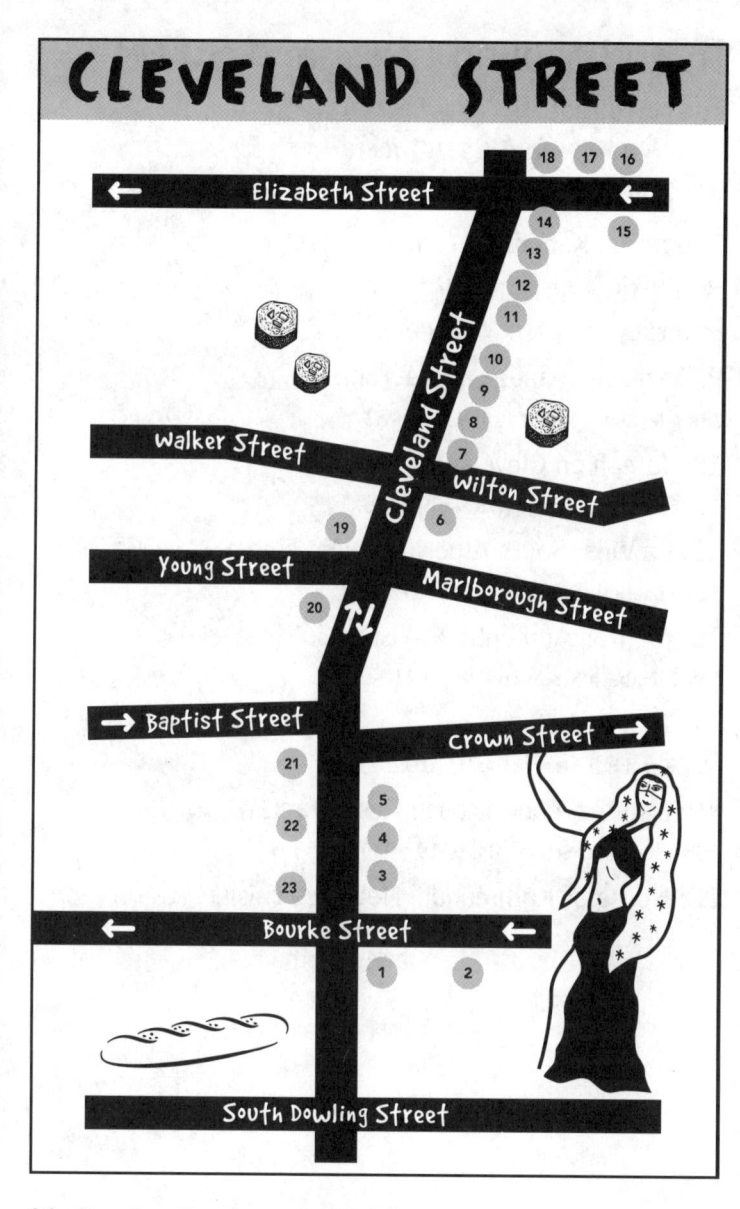

CLEVELAND STREET

CLEVELAND STREET, IN AND AROUND

1. Golden Pide.
2. Greek Orthodox Church.
3. Maya Indian Sweets Centre.
4. Mehr'ay Da Dhaba.
5. Samsun Kebabs and Pizza.
6. Turkey Redfern Mosque.
7. Emads & Salindas Lebanese Restaurant.
8. Fatimas Lebanese Restaurant.
9. Gazals Lebanese Restaurant.
10. Joseph on Cleveland.
11. Almustafa.
12. The Prophet Lebanese Restaurant.
13. Omar Khayyam's Lebanese Restaurant.
14. Nada's.
15. La Viña, South American night club.
16. Mehron Authentic Pakistan Cuisine.
17. Thai Taste.
18. Abdul's.
19. L'Aubbergade French Restaurant.
20. Persian Carpet and Gift Store.
21. Erciyes Pizza Pide and Kebab Saloon.
22. House of Kathmandu, Nepalese cuisine.
23. Girne Pide.

20: Persian Carpet and Gift Store. For over 10 years this shop has operated always filled to the rafters, trading in good quality Persian rugs, household gifts, Arabic scarves and other attractive stuff from the Middle East. Open Monday-Sunday 9am-6pm.
357 Cleveland Street.

AND NEARBY...

DIVAN TURKISH PIZZA AND KEBAB SALON.
From the *sucuklu* Turkish pizza to the tabouleh salad, the "salon" has made good. You can eat in or take it away. Average $20, BYO. Open Monday-Sunday 10am-midnight.

577 Crown Street,
Surry Hills
(tel: 9698 4434).

In and around Cleveland Street

1: Golden Pide.
500 Cleveland Street (tel: 9319 0706).

2: Greek Orthodox Church.

5: Samsun Kebabs and Pizza.
462 Cleveland Street (tel: 9319 4213).

6: Turkey Redfern Mosque.

9: Gazal's Lebanese Restaurant.
286 Cleveland Street (tel: 9318 1982).

10: Joseph on Cleveland.
280 Cleveland Street (tel: 9699 5096).

15: La Viña, South American night club. See page 467.
504 Elizabeth Street (tel: 9319 0423).

16: Mehron Authentic Pakistan Cuisine. See page 370.
557 Elizabeth Street (tel: 9690 2109).

17: Thai Taste.
559 Elizabeth Street (tel: 9310 5232).

19: L'Aubbergade French Restaurant. See page 111.
353 Cleveland Street (tel: 9319 5929).

22: House of Kathmandu, Nepalese cuisine. See page 365.
423 Cleveland Street (tel: 9319 2170).

Marrickville
at the heart of Australian multiculturalism

More than half the population of Marrickville come from non-English speaking countries, while the local schools educate children from more than 50 different ethnic backgrounds. It's a polyglot community. More than 60 languages other than English are spoken – Arabic, Mandarin, Greek, Portuguese and Vietnamese are the five most common that you'll hear while wandering along the multi-ethnic Marrickville and Illawarra Roads.

Located 8 km south-west of the CBD, Marrickville was once home to a handful of Cadigal Aborigines, before they had to relinquish their land in the 1790s to the first European settlers in the area, the English, Scots, Irish and Welsh. They were later followed by a smaller number of German, Chinese and American immigrants. Between the 1880s and 1945, Marrickville underwent a significant social and ethnic change. From a sparsely rural area it became a densely populated industrial zone, where working class Irish and Italian immigrants began pouring in.

Greeks, Maltese and a new wave of Italians began settling in the area after World War II. In the 1960s the local Greek community was reinforced with the arrival in the neighbourhood of Greeks from Rhodes (who originally were entrenched in Surry Hills) and Greek Macedonians, who were originally living in Chippendale. The Greek influence in the neighbourhood was at its height by the 1970s when around 13,000 Greek-born were living here. This was the same period when the suburb witnessed a significant Islamic presence with the growth of Muslim Allawis from Lebanon and Turkey. In the following years, especially in the 1980s, the cosmopolitan nature of the area was enriched with the strong presence of South-East Asians – notably Vietnamese – whose most visible presence is felt in several restaurants and shops dotted along Illawarra Road.

Marrickville prides itself as an example of ethnic peaceful coexistence which is showed off annually at the wonderful Marrickville Multicultural Festival (tel: 9335 2151). Held on the third Saturday of September, the festival is massively celebrated along Marrickville and Illawarra Roads. It is a showcase of tolerance and understanding.

ILLAWARRA AND MARRICKVILLE ROADS

1. Loi Phat Sieu Thi.
2. Hellenic Bakery.
3. D&A Danas Continental Delicatessen.
4. Athena Cake Shop.
5. Old Thanh Huong.
6. Thanh Huong 2.
7. Nhat Tan.
8. Bac Lieu.
9. Corinthian Rotisserie Restaurant.
10. Van Long.
11. Tang Hong Phat.
12. Bay Tinh.

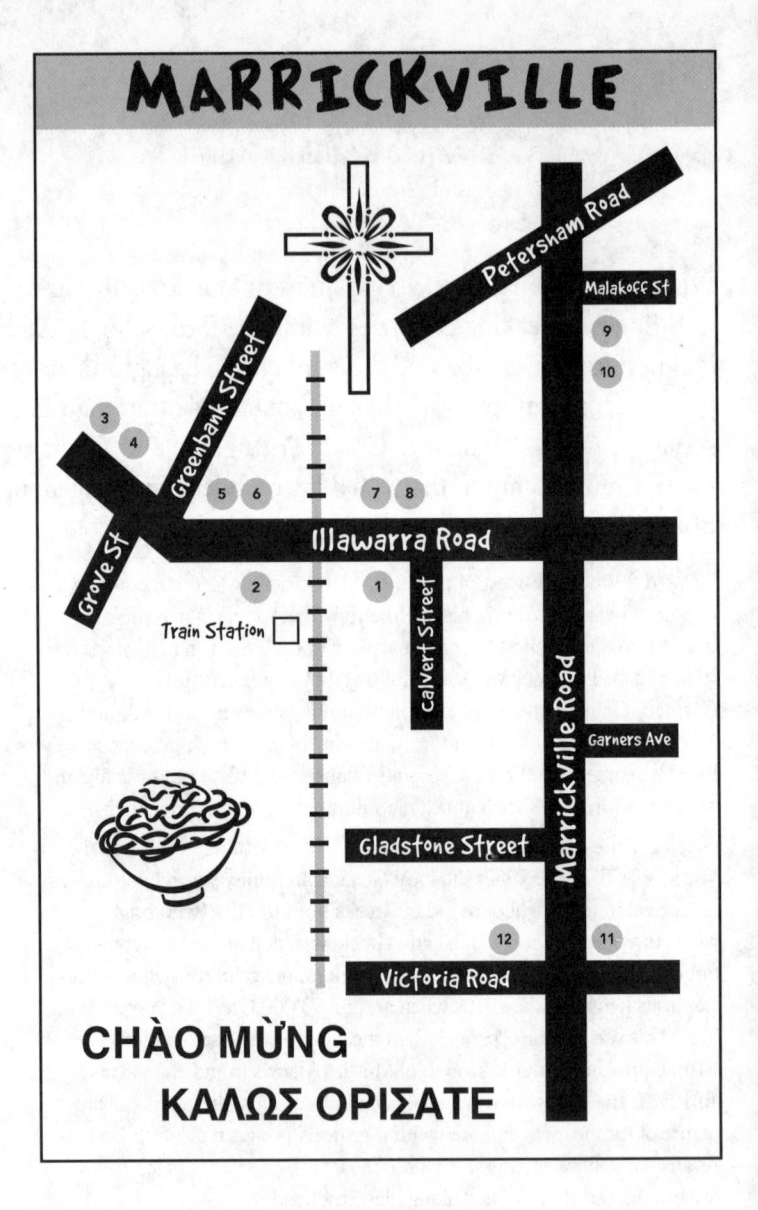

MARRICKVILLE

CHÀO MỪNG

ΚΑΛΩΣ ΟΡΙΣΑΤΕ

Explore the world in one city

Restaurants

6: Thanh Huong 2. An eclectic interior of round and square tables, Vietnamese families and inner-city alternative artists, this is the place where the exquisite mint-tasting steam rolls run out quickly – we got the alternative, the last three "money bags" of the night (a moist filling of minced pork, carrots and celery in a deep fried pastry). They're good and if you carry on with the rest of the menu you won't be disappointed either.
Open Thursday-Tuesday (closed on Wednesday) 10am-9pm. Average $12, BYO.
356 Illawarra Road (tel: 9558 0863).

8: Bac Lieu. Run by the whole family, this Vietnamese restaurant has already earned a good deal of praise from the critics. Average $15, BYO. Open Monday-Saturday 9m-9.30pm.
302 Illawarra Road (tel: 9558 5788-check the number).

9: Corinthian Rotisserie Restaurant. No frills, just traditional Greek hospitality, good and abundant food. Average $25, licensed. Open Monday-Sunday lunch noon-3pm, dinner 6pm-1am.
283 Marrickville Road (tel: 9569 7084).

12: Bay Tinh. The owner isn't only a celebrity for being a former chef of the South Vietnamese prime minister, but also for knowing how to transform a modest suburban restaurant into a highly recommended eatery. You can check what the experts have said about Bay Tinh in the newspaper cuttings glued to the front window. Average $15, BYO.
Open Monday-Friday lunch 11am-2pm, Monday-Sunday dinner 6-10.30pm.
318 Victoria Road (tel: 9560 8673).

5: Old Thanh Huong. Vietnamese restaurant.
358 Illawarra Road (tel: 9558 0650).

7: Nhat Tan. Vietnamese take away.
310 Illawarra Road (tel: 9558 4309).

GETTING THERE

By bus from the City **423** and **426**. By train City/Marrickville station.

NOT FAR...

MINH.
One of the success stories of the noodle bars, Minh has achieved quite a reputation for its sensational beef *pho* noodles, mint, onion, chilli and bean sprouts. $6 a generous bowl, BYO and licensed. Open Monday-Sunday 10am-10pm.

508 Marrickville Road, Dulwich Hill
(tel: 9560 0465).

Shopping

1: Loi Phat Sieu Thi. Large, and one of the best stocked Vietnamese supermarkets in the area. Expect to find a wide range of products imported from Vietnam. Newspapers and magazines in Vietnamese are also available. Have a look at the freezer section storing – among other things – dried fish, plastic bags of noodles and exotic tinned fruit. Open Monday-Sunday 8am-8pm.

307 Illawarra Road (no telephone).

11: Tang Hong Phat. The small Vietnamese enclave in Marrickville wouldn't be complete without this grocery, fruit and vegetable corner store (corner of Victoria and Marrickville Roads). Inside you'll find a disparate mix of things such as vegetables, bags of noodles and sandals. Open Monday-Sunday 8am-7pm.

127 Marrickville Road (tel: 9568 3552).

2: Hellenic Bakery Greek bakery. (see The Greeks, page 132).

371 Illawarra Road (tel: 9559 2701)

3: D & A Danas Continental Delicatessen Greek store and delicatessen. (see The Greeks, page 132).

416 Illawarra Road (tel: 9558 3573).

4: Athena Cake Shop. Greek bakery.

412 Illawarra Road (tel: 9558 1276).

10: Van Long. Vietnamese supermarket.

281 Marrickville Road (tel: 9560 6096).

Newtown
multi-ethnic, eccentric and grungy

Located 4 km south-west of the CBD, Newtown is one of the most ethnically diverse and colourful areas of Sydney, especially along its main drag – King Street. Now a hub of commercial activity, an ethnic eatery paradise and an enclave of alternative art, Newtown began as a farming community that has come a long way since its dwellers in 1838 were "877 Protestants, 364 Roman Catholics, one Pagan and one Jew."

The ethnic diversity of Newtown is nothing new. In the early years of this century a number of Italian and German shopkeepers established their businesses along King Street, while the significant Eastern European Jewish community made a statement of community consolidation with the completion in 1918 of the Western Suburbs Synagogue at 18 Georgina Street.

Nowadays, the congested King Street boasts a huge range of eateries and shops offering the cuisine and the extravagances of the world. Chinese, Vietnamese, Indian, Greek, Italian, Spanish, Middle Eastern, African, Polish, Serbian and Sydney's highest concentration of Thai eateries are on the street's menu, while exotic gifts, souvenirs, music and clothing can be found as you stroll along the drag.

Sydney's fruit and vegetable shops offer a wide range of produce.

King Street is one of the few streets in Sydney where you can explore a full African experience while dropping at Le Kilimanjaro for a quick bite, shopping at the best African music store – Blackstarr Records – or getting an exotic hairbraid at Afrique Ali. Now if you fancy a "Pacific experience", you should head to the far south end of King Street, where there is a small but very vibrant Fijian/Polynesian quarter.

King Street is also the central stage for the very popular Newtown Festival held around October 9 (tel: 9516 4755). Displays of visual art in galleries and shops, free performances in Newtown Square, film and theatre festivals are some of the many activities during the two week event. Not to be missed if you are in town about this time.

GETTING THERE

By bus the trip goes smoothly till you hit the first few yards of King Street. From there it's faster to stroll than drive, since the traffic has a well deserved infamous reputation, especially on weekends. So, ask to be dropped off early and from there... be ready to roll. **Bus 422 423, 426, 428** from Circular Quay via Castlereagh Street and City Road or train to Newtown Station.

Many newly-arrived immigrants initially lived in inner-city suburbs like Newtown, where rent was cheap. Today rents have escalated with gentrification.

Restaurants, Cafes & Take Away

2: Ban Thai. Hot- fiery Thai food gets a kind of break here, maintaining though, its full flavour and taste. It's also a good place for vegetarians. Average $25, BYO and licensed.
Open Monday-Sunday lunch noon-3pm, Sunday-Wednesday dinner 5.30-10.30pm (till 11pm Thursday-Saturday).
115-117 King Street (tel: 9519 5330).

3: Asakusa. Where sushi and sashimi meets – a resounding thumbs up to this Japanese eatery. Average $15, BYO.
Open Monday-Friday lunch noon-2.30pm, Sunday-Thursday dinner 6-10pm (till 11pm on Friday and Saturday).
119 King Street (tel: 9519 8530).

5: Indian Fantasy. Featuring cooking from North and South India, it has earned the kudos with King Street folk for its vegetarian (not exclusively) based menu. Average $15, BYO.
Open Monday-Sunday 5.30-10.30pm.
169 King Street (tel: 9519 1925).

10: Africa Feeling Cafe. Good coffee, inexpensive desserts, cakes and soups. Average $10, BYO.
Open Tuesday-Friday 6-10pm, Saturday-Sunday noon-10pm.
1/501 King Street (tel: 9516 3130).

19: Thai Pothong. Fitting up to 280 people, this traditional King Street Thai spot specialises in group bookings – so expect to see a whole class from nearby University of Sydney eating there. The menu is extensive and the food is good. Average $25, BYO and licensed.
294 King Street (tel: 9550 6277).

20: Le Kilimanjaro. One of the most recognisably African eateries in Sydney. You can't miss it – it's the one with the yellow and red tiled facade and a giant map of Africa on the side of the building. Following an African tradition, the aromatic food is steamed in clay pots and then served in wooden platters. Average $10, BYO.
Open Monday-Sunday noon-till late.
280 King Street (tel: 9557 4565).

Explore the world in one city

NEWTOWN

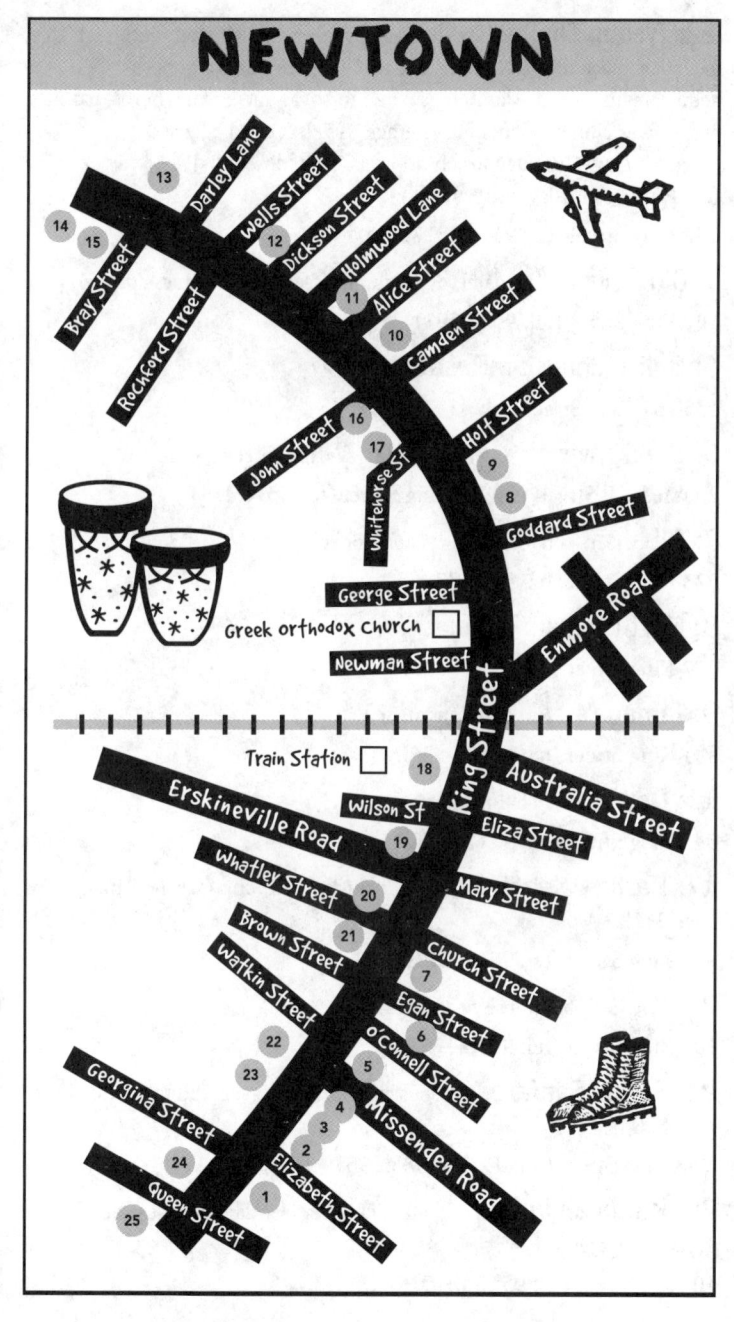

KINGS STREET

1. Old Saigon.
2. Ban Thai.
3. Asakusa.
4. Bali Indonesian Restaurant.
5. Indian Fantasy.
6. Steki Taverna.
7. Elbahsa.
8. North Indian Flavour.
9. Tamana's. North Indian cuisine.
10. Africa Feeling Cafe.
11. Doy Thao.
12. Island Food.
13. Fiji Markets.
14. Maya.
15. Vinayak.
16. Made in Japan.
17. Pasha's Kebab House.
18. Afrique Ali.
19. Thai Pothong.
20. Le Kilimanjaro.
21. Kims. Vietnamese restaurant.
22. Tycoon Thai.
23. Blackstarr Records.
24. Safari Seafare.
25. Kathmandu Ma.

NEWTOWN 27

NOT FAR FROM KING STREET...

NETTEYS AFRIKA.
Planing some "alternative" music tuition? - here you'll find a complete range of African drums such as djembe and dundun. At Netteys you can get those masks, fetish figures that you were planning to get in your next African expedition. African processed food is also available. Open Tuesday-Saturday 10am-5pm.

Shop 40 Enmore Road (tel: 9557 8883).

BETTA MEAT.
(see The Poles, page 195). Polish butchery.

407 King Street (tel: 9557 3354).

HOT BUREK.
(see The Serbs, page 225). Serbian burek shop.

484 King Street (tel: 9557 2951).

22: Tycoon Thai. When it's time for your regular Thai food treat, this is a good place to go. Nicely decorated, Tycoon offers a superb achievement – grilled lamb marinated in soya sauce, wine, herbs, garlic and honey. Not to be missed. Average $15, BYO and licensed. Open Sunday-Thursday lunch noon-2.30pm, dinner 5-10.30pm (till 11pm on Friday and Saturday).

152 King Street (tel: 9516 2817).

1: Old Saigon. Vietnamese restaurant. (see The Vietnamese page 377).

107 King Street (tel: 9519 5931).

4: Bali Indonesian Restaurant.

135-137 King Street (tel: 9557 3441).

6: Steki Taverna. Greek taverna. (see The Greeks, page 132).

2 O'Connell Street, just off King Street (tel: 9516 2191).

7: Elbahsa. Lebanese sweets and coffee.

233 King Street (tel: 9557 3886).

8: North Indian Flavour.

377 King Street (tel: 9550 3928)

9: Tamana's. North Indian cuisine.

441 King Street (tel: 9519 0439).

11: Doy Thao. Thai restaurant.

543 King Street (tel: 9517 1051).

17: Pasha's Kebab House. Turkish restaurant. (see The Turks, page 247).

490 King Street (tel: 9519 3139).

21: Kims. Vietnamese restaurant.

194 King Street (tel: 9550 4752).

24: Safari Seafare. Indonesian restaurant. (see The Indonesians, page 320).

22-8 King Street (tel: 9557 4458 or 9519 1249).

25: Kathmandu Ma. Nepalese cuisine. (see The Nepalese and Tibetan page 365).

10 King Street (tel: 9557 1425).

Explore the world in one city

Shopping

12: Island Food. Located in the Fijian/Polynesian quarter of King Street, Island Food has a fantastic range of Fijian and Indian fresh vegetables.
Open Monday-Sunday 9.30am-7.30pm.
565 King Street (tel: 9519 1141).

13: Fiji Markets. Equally in the far south of King Street, it's probably the most diverse and the best scene for Indian, Fijian, Sri Lankan, Pakistani, Samoan, Tongan and Cook Islander products – spices, powders, rice, magazines, music and much more.
Open Saturday-Wednesday 9.30am-7pm (till 8pm on Thursday and Friday).
591 King Street (tel: 9517 2054).

23: Blackstarr Records. Arguably Sydney's number one home of black music. Monday-Wednesday 10am-9pm, Thursday-Friday 10am-8pm, Sunday noon-5pm.
128 King Street, Newtown (tel: 9557 6013).

14: Maya. Indian sweets and pastries.
642a King Street (tel: 9550 6681).

15: Vinayak. Indian gifts, videos, music.
634 King Street (tel: 9550 6681).

16: Made in Japan. (see The Japanese, page 336).
502 King Street (tel: 9360 6979).

Hair & Beauty

18: Afrique Ali. It's great to think that a dull hairdo can be transformed into a groovy-alternative African design. Here is the place to do it - Coolio dreads, weaves, hair extensions, afros.
Open Monday-Saturday 9.30am-6pm (till 9pm on Thursday).
Shop 7, 324 King Street, Newtown (tel: 9557 3574).

CHECK THIS OUT...

NOONOOS. Specialises in tribal gifts and musical instruments. Here you'll find talking drums from Nigeria and thumb pianos from Kenya and Zimbabwe.
Open Monday-Wednesday 9.30am-6.30pm, Thursday-Saturday 9.30am-9.30pm, Sunday 10am-6pm.
238 King Street (tel: 9516 4368).

FATOU'S HAIR ARCHITECTS. Senegalese-born Fatou is a kind of hair architect in the hairy field of braiding, dreadlocks, twists and hair extensions. Warning, the rate goes from $150.00 – up and not down – no pain no gain.
Open Monday-Sunday 10am-7pm.
109 Enmore Road (tel: 9519 5546).

Bankstown
from *baklawa* to *pho*

Known during World War II as "Yankstown" – due to the large presence of US Air Force personal accommodated at the local Aerodrome – Bankstown is located approximately 20 km to the south-west of the CBD, and not far from the 2000 Olympics site.

Named in honour of the botanist Sir Joseph Banks, Bankstown has developed a name for itself as the one of the most cosmopolitan centres of the western suburbs – more than a quarter of its 16,000 residents were born overseas. Bankstown is where the fragrance of the Vietnamese *Pho* competes head to head with the sweetness of the Lebanese *baklawa* and with the welcoming European experience at the local Lithuanian, Latvian and Polish clubs – while at 54 Northam Avenue, the St. Brendan's Catholic Church (tel: 9790 2859) organises regular services in Filipino, Samoan and Vietnamese. Bankstown was also home of the Olympic swimming champions, John and Ilsa Konrad, cricket stars, the Waugh brothers, and of course Paul Keating, former Australian Prime Minister.

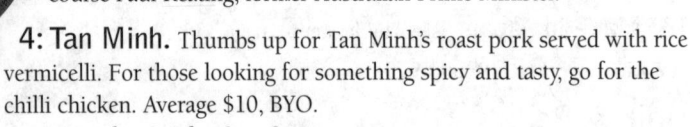

Bankstown is the fragrance of the Vietnamese Pho and the sweetness of the Lebanese Baklawa.

4: Tan Minh. Thumbs up for Tan Minh's roast pork served with rice vermicelli. For those looking for something spicy and tasty, go for the chilli chicken. Average $10, BYO.
Open Monday-Sunday 9am-9pm.
317 Chapel Road (tel: 9790 7129).

5: Pasteur. There is nothing assuming here, the simple and well prepared menu includes chicken and beef noodles. Average $10, BYO.
Open Monday-Sunday 7am-8pm.
295 Chapel Road (tel: 9790 2900).

6: The "Old Town Centre." For a full-tilt ethnic experience, stroll around the mall where there are some good restaurants, well-stocked shops and well-priced dress fabrics.

8: An Restaurant. According to the savvy, An offers the best pho around town. Average $10, BYO.
Open Monday-Sunday 7am-8pm.
29-31 Greenfield parade (tel: 9796 7826).

Explore the world in one city

BANKSTOWN

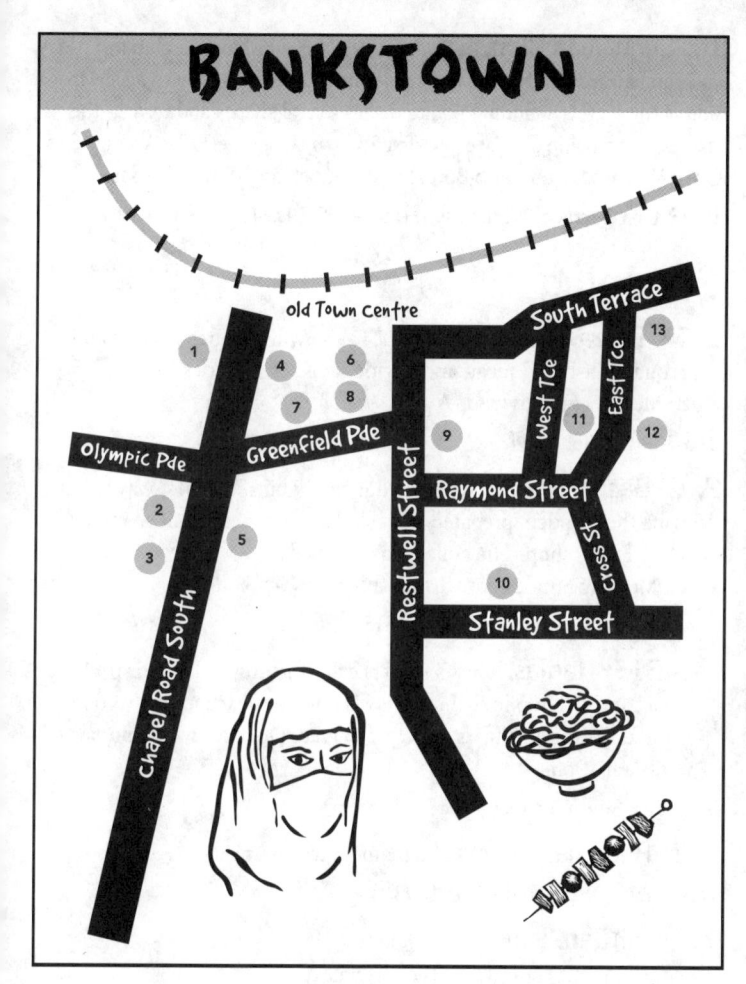

IN AND AROUND BANKSTOWN

1. TK Plaza.
2. El Basha Sweets.
3. Pho Thang Long.
4. Tan Minh.
5. Pasteur.
6. The "Old Town Centre."
7. Thanh Tan.
8. An Restaurant.
9. Golden Nights.
10. D.V. Latvian Club.
11. Bankstown Polish Club.
12. Lithuanian Club.
13. Hadlas.

9: Golden Nights. Described by some Sydney Lebanese as the venue for the "who's who," Golden Nights delivers what its name promises. Great restaurant service, a fun and friendly clientele makes this place highly recommended for a Friday and Saturday Lebanese night out (see also, The Lebanese page 411).
Open Friday & Saturday 9pm-4am.

10-12 Restwell Street, Bankstown (tel: 9790 5555).

10: D.V. Latvian Club. Traditional Latvian homecooked food on weekends (see also The Latvians, page 175). Average $15, licensed.
Open Saturday-Sunday noon-4pm.

49 Stanley Street (tel: 9790 1140).

GETTING THERE

Long gone are the days when in 1866 the New South Wales Gazette wrote "Bankstown is an isolated town, where only one coach per day runs to Sydney, starting out at 7.30am in the morning and returning at 7.45pm at night." As a major centre, the train service from the city now runs regularly and efficiently.

Bankstown's many Vietnamese restaurants offer good cheap food.

12: Lithuanian Club. In this only registered Lithuanian club in Sydney you can help yourself to the most authentic Lithuanian food treats on this side of the world, including potato dishes - in all shapes and forms - the staples of the Baltic diet (see also The Lithuanians, page 179). Average $15. Open Wednesday dinner 6-8pm, Sunday lunch and dinner 1-9pm.
16-18 East Terrace, Bankstown. (tel: 9708 1414).

Shopping

1: TK Plaza. Under one roof, at TK you will find fresh vegies and fruit, quality fish and meat, and a wide range of groceries.
Open Monday-Sunday 8am-7pm.
316-324 Chapel Road.

2: El Basha Sweets. Highly addictive. This is the best way to describe the wonders prepared with skill and savvy at this Lebanese sweet and cake shop. The coffee isn't half bad.
Open Monday-Sunday 8am-10pm (till 11pm on Saturday).
288 Chapel Road (tel: 9796 4818).

B13: Hadlas. This is real special - the only Lebanese specialist ice-cream shop in Sydney. The ice-cream is exceptionally good and the thumbs up is widely deserved. Open Monday-Sunday 10am-10pm.
222 South Terrace (tel: 9790 6886).

3: Pho Thang Long. Vietnamese restaurant.
284 Chapel Road (tel: 9796 4393).

7: Thanh Tan. Vietnamese restaurant.
4-5/307-311 Chapel Road (tel: 9790 7346).

11: Bankstown Polish Club.
15 East Terrace (tel: 9708 2433).

Check these out at the "Old Town Centre":

Thai Ki Butchers, Shop 1, Phong Hung Butchers, Shop 37; Thai Sun Butchers, Shop 53; Hai Yen Vietnamese restaurant, Shop 61; Nhut Tan Grocery store, Shop 59; Phuong Minh (tropical sweets and great fresh sugar cane drinks), Shop 57; Ben Ngu Chinese – Vietnamese and Thai Restaurant, Shop 43; Hung Nyugen (fashion fabrics), Shop 64.

Oxford Street
explore the world in one drag

There was a time, at the beginning of the century, that the main attraction in Oxford Street was a German band that performed sacredly every Monday in Taylor Square – the area's heart and main point of reference. War paranoia put that to an end. Last century, around the 1880s, Taylor Square was an Aboriginal reserve named Eastern Hill, and in the 1840s the area was chosen to build Darlinghurst Gaol. A French citizen, John Videle – perpetrator of a nasty murder – was the first person hanged publicly there.

During World War II, the brothels along Oxford Street were the magnet for American soldiers stationed in Sydney – except for black servicemen to whom the area north of the street was off limits. Instead they were accepted into the bars and brothels of Surry Hills because – as the story goes – "Riley Street knew an underdog when it saw it."

Located 2 kilometres east of Sydney's CBD and running south-east from the southern end of Hyde Park, Oxford Street is today one of Sydney's most lively, dynamic and famous thoroughfares. There is plenty to do and see. The annual Gay and Lesbian Mardi Gras is one of the main events along the street, while the strip of Oxford Street between Crown and South Dowling Street – with a plethora of fine and non-expensive restaurants covering a broad range of world cuisine – is the ethnic contribution to this fascinating drag. While in the area you should pay a visit to the wonderful Jewish Museum at the corner of Darlinghurst Road and Burton Street (see The Jews, page 396).

Oxford Street, where Sydney's gay community merges with the "indy" film scene and assorted artists, designers and musicians.

Restaurants

3: Bach Hy. A Vietnamese favourite of the inner-city dwellers, it has received the thumbs up from the specialists. As entree try *goi guon* (prawn rolls with dipping sauce). Average $15, BYO.
Open lunch Monday-Saturday 11.30am-3pm, dinner 5pm-till late, Sunday dinner 5-till late.
139 Oxford Street, Darlinghurst (tel: 9331 1363).

GETTING THERE

Many buses run along Oxford Street, such as **378, 311** from Railway Square and **338, 327, 380 or 382** from Circular Quay. Get off in Taylor Square and then you're in the heart of Oxford Street.

The world really is your oyster when dining along Oxford Street.

6: Silver Spoon. This Thai spot is a good place to have dinner after strolling around cosmopolitan "Darlo". From the menu try the seafood, it's highly recommended. Average $15, BYO. Open Monday-Sunday lunch noon-3pm, dinner 6-10pm.

203 Oxford Street, Darlinghurst (tel: 9360 4669)

7: Balkan Continental. An old-timer along Oxford Street, Balkan is Croatian to the backbone. You can choose from a good variety of meat and seafood dishes such as grilled octopus or cevapcici (a little and very tasty spicy sausage). Average $25, BYO. Open Wednesday-Monday, 11am-11pm (till midnight on Friday and Saturday).

209 Oxford Street, Darlinghurst (tel: 9360 4970).

8: Balkan Seafood and Adriatic Restaurant. Run by the same owners as the Balkan Continental, it specialises in char-grilled seafood. The portions are large and wholesome. Average $25, BYO.

215 Oxford Street, Darlinghurst (tel: 9331 7670).

9: Rockerfellers. Inside this colour purple spot, the American accent is as heavy as the New York Giant – a luscious and towering burger. The char-grilled seafood plate is thoroughly recommended. Average $20 (burger prices from $10.90 up), BYO and licensed. Open Monday-Thursday 6pm-midnight (till 1am on Friday and Saturday), Sunday 6-11pm.

225 Oxford Street (tel: 9361 6968).

10: Angkor Wat. If you're not in the mood to do the long train trip from the City to Cabramatta (the heart of the Cambodian community), this is the place to try authentic Cambodian cuisine. The beef dishes with fresh vegetables are excellent. Average $15, BYO and licensed. Open dinner Tuesday-Sunday 5.30-10.30pm.

227 Oxford Street, Darlinghurst (tel: 9360 5500).

12: Kim. By the look of things, the owners of this small Vietnamese restaurant have put a lot of work into transforming it into a charming and friendly spot. The large menu offers the likes of sweet and sour squid and a delicious asparagus soup with chunks of crab. Average $15, BYO. Open Wednesday-Monday 7-10.30pm.

235 Oxford Street, Darlinghurst (tel: 9357 5429).

13: Thai Nesia. The spicy and tasty cuisine of Indonesia and Thailand plus the pleasant ambience keeps customers coming back. Average $20, BYO. Open Monday-Sunday 6-10.30pm.

243 Oxford Street (tel: 9361 4817).

Explore the world in one city

OXFORD STREET

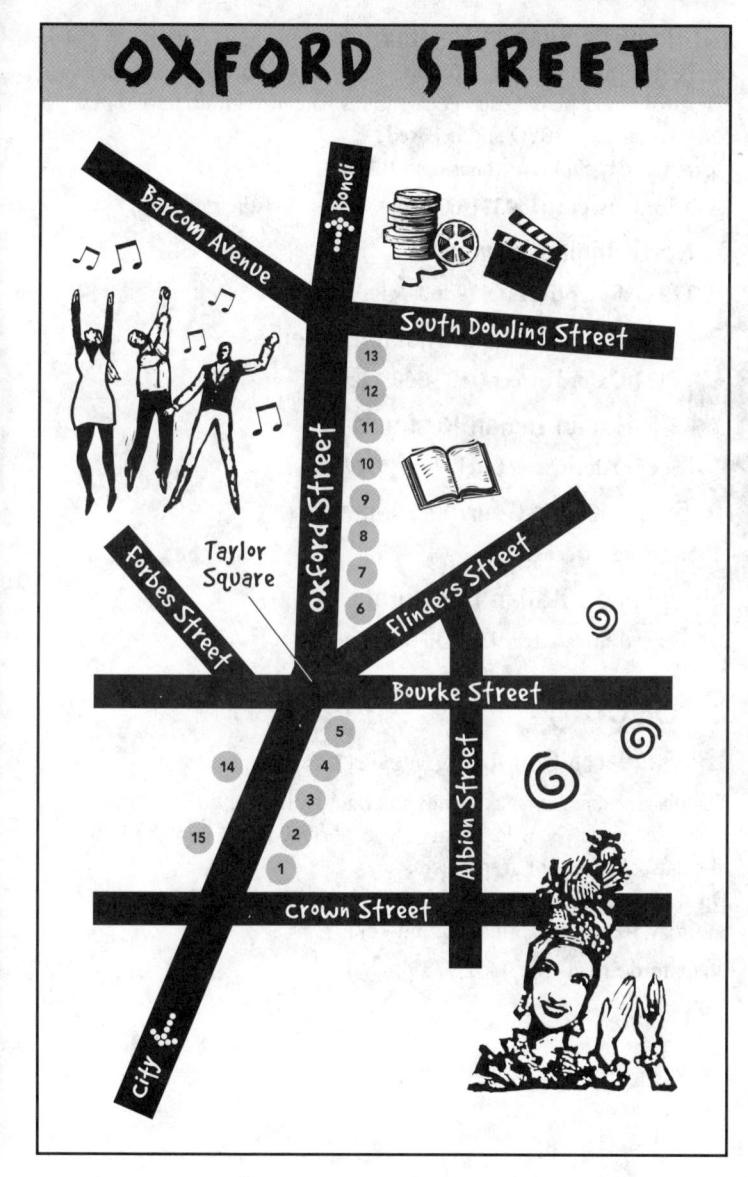

OXFORD STREET

1. North Indian Flavour.
2. Tamana's North Indian Dinner.
3. Bach Hy.
4. Habibi Indian Restaurant.
5. Emperor's Gourmet.
6. Silver Spoon.
7. Balkan Continental.
8. Balkan Seafood and Adriatic Restaurant.
9. Rockerfellers.
10. Angkor Wat.
11. Juliano's Italian Restaurant.
12. Kim.
13. Thai Nesia.
14. Raquel's Spanish Restaurant
15. Pandarra Country & Western.

14: Raquel's Spanish Restaurant. At the heart of Darlo, Raquel's can be defined as a simple, non-pretentious and affordable restaurant. The great guitar player Paco Peña and his flamenco group have dined here. Average $20, BYO and licensed.
Open Monday-Sunday dinner 6pm-till late.
98 Oxford Street (tel: 9331 6806).

1: North Indian Flavour.
129 Oxford Street (tel: 9360 9388).

2: Tamana's North Indian Dinner.
131 Oxford Street (tel: 9360 7229).

4: Habibi Indian Restaurant.
147 Oxford Street (tel: 9361 5527).

5: Emperor's Gourmet. Asian eatery.
185 Oxford Street (tel: 9360 4547).

11: Juliano's Italian Restaurant.
229 Oxford Street (tel: 9380 5646).

Oxford Street pubs offer a range of interesting experiences.

Shopping

15: Pandarra Country & Western.
The place where city slickers buy the right stuff from the American far-west to conquer the wild urban prairie – from cowboy boots to Dallas-like hats, all the right gear is here.
Open Monday-Friday 10am-5.45 (till later on Thursday),
Saturday 10am-6pm, Sunday 11am-4pm.
96 Oxford Street (tel: 9361 5785).

Explore the world in one city

Glebe
from Ireland to China

A Sunday afternoon of Irish ballads at the The Friend in Hand pub, a bite at Yak & Yeti – the local Nepalese eatery – and a cultural visit to the Buddhist Sze Yup Temple, an historical landmark of the Sydney Chinese community (see The Chinese, page 275), are some of the ethnic experiences to enjoy at this very charming inner-western suburb, 3 kilometres from the CBD.

Glebe Point Road, the main strip, is an aesthetic delight amid the eclecticism of its residents: artists, yuppies and old working class dwellers. Once a week this diverse scenario comes to life at the wonderful Saturday market (9am-4pm). Glebe is also proud of celebrating – since 1983 – one of the longest and most cosmopolitan neighbourhood fiestas – The Glebe Street Festival (tel: 9552 1546) in mid November. It's a time to dance along Glebe Point Road, to hunt through the dozens of stalls and to eat in the many ethnic eateries installed along the thoroughfare.

Restaurants

2: Dakhni. The menu captures the essence of Indian cuisine - plenty to choose from the extensive menu: tandoori, korma, vindaloo, tikka. Average $25, BYO.
Open Thursday-Sunday lunch noon-2.30pm, Monday-Sunday dinner 5.30-10.30pm.
65 Glebe Point Road (tel: 9660 4887).

9: Flavour of India. On the corner of Glebe Point Road and Bridge Road, this Indian restaurant features a reliable and simple menu. Beef coconut fry is one of the achievements of the house. Average $25 (lunchtime buffet $12), BYO.
Open Tuesday-Saturday lunch, noon-3.30pm, Monday-Sunday dinner from 6pm.
142a Glebe Point Road (tel: 9692 0662 or 9692 0322).

Glebe Point Road, the main strip, is an aesthetic delight amid the eclecticism of its residents: artists, yuppies and old working class dwellers.

GLEBE POINT ROAD

1. Yak & Yeti.
2. Dakhni.
3. Nissaki Greek Restaurant.
4. Japanese Bookshop Arts and Crafts Centre.
5. Bogart.
6. Thai Intra.
7. Lien Vietnamese & Malaysian Restaurant.
8. Lilac Chinese Restaurant.
9. Flavour of India.
10. Broadway Cellar.
11. Mukunghwa.
12. Tanjore.
13. Ryoma Japanese Restaurant.

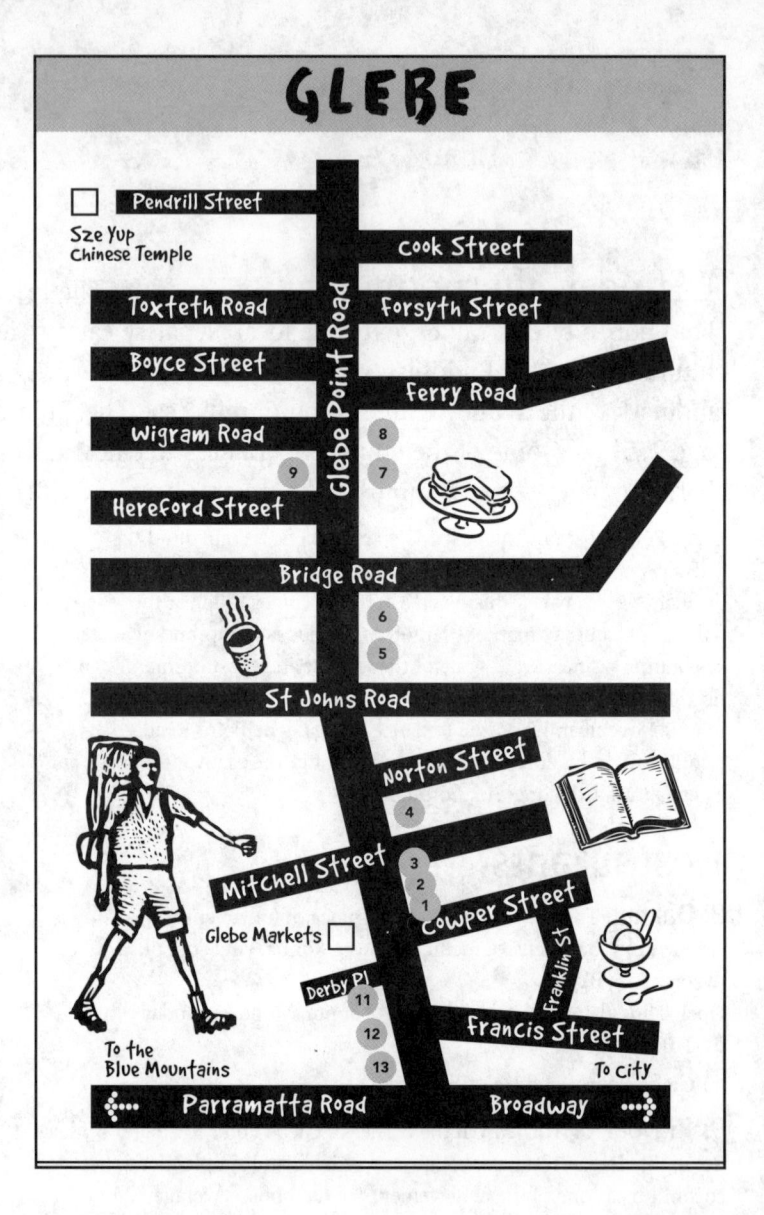

GLEBE

Sze Yup Chinese Temple
Pendrill Street
Cook Street
Toxteth Road
Forsyth Street
Boyce Street
Glebe Point Road
Ferry Road
Wigram Road
Hereford Street
Bridge Road
St Johns Road
Norton Street
Mitchell Street
Glebe Markets
Cowper Street
Derby Pl
Franklin St
Francis Street
To the Blue Mountains
Parramatta Road
Broadway
To city

Explore the world in one city

5: Bogart. A pleasant ambience, attentive service and Italian food cooked *al dente* speak of a place worth visiting. Average $35, BYO and licensed.
Open Monday-Sunday 6-10.30pm.
199 Glebe Point Road (tel: 9692 0936).

1: Yak & Yeti. Nepalese restaurant. (see The Nepalese, page 364).
41 Glebe Point Road (tel: 9552 1220).

3: Nissaki Greek Restaurant.
101 Glebe Point Road (tel: 9660 3906).

6: Thai Intra. Thai cuisine.
207 Glebe Point Road (tel: 9660 4149).

7: Lien Vietnamese & Malaysian Restaurant.
331 Glebe Point Road (tel: 9566 4385).

8: Lilac Chinese Restaurant.
336 Glebe Point Road (tel: 9660 5172).

11: Mukunghwa. Korean restaurant. (see The Koreans, page 347).
36 Glebe Point Road (tel: 9660 0744).

12: Tanjore. Indian restaurant. (see The Indians, page 305).
34 Glebe Point Road (tel: 9660 6332).

13: Ryoma Japanese Restaurant.
22 Glebe Point Road (tel: 9660 7464).

Shopping

10: Broadway Cellar. The world's wines in one cellar – including a superb selection of Chilean and Spanish wines.
Open Monday-Sunday 9am-9pm.
96-98 Glebe Point Road (tel: 9660 3908).

4: Japanese Bookshop Arts and Crafts Centre.
(see The Japanese, page 329).
Shop 6, 131 Glebe Point Road (tel: 9552 4930).

GETTING THERE

By buses such as **431, 433 and 434** via George Street and Railway Square. The trip from the City takes around 15 minutes.

OFF AND NOT FAR...

THE MIXING POT.
Reflecting the diversity and gastronomic "know how" of traditional and modern Italian cuisine. If I were you I'd definitely go for the fresh seafood or fish of the day. Average $35, BYO and licensed. Open Monday-Friday lunch, noon-2.30pm, Monday-Saturday dinner from 6pm.
178 St Johns Road, Glebe (tel: 9660 7449 or 9692 9424).

THE FRIEND IN HAND HOTEL.
The Irish nostalgic flavour in the area. Drop by on Sunday afternoon for the all-Irish band time.
58 Cowper Street, Glebe (tel: 9660 2326).

Indigenous Sydney

By Carol Reid

"On Saturdays we went shopping on Botany Road [Redfern] for the weekend vegetables and groceries. It was an outing we looked forward to, browsing through the shops, and there were a lot of koories there, in our area".

(the late Ruby Langford, Aboriginal author of *Don't Take Your Love to Town*, Penguin Books, 1988)

Aboriginal people have always been part of Sydney life. They watched, from the shores of Botany Bay, the arrival of the first Europeans from James Cook's "voyage of discovery" in 1770. They witnessed the arrival of the "First Fleet" in Sydney Cove in 1788. They are the first Sydneysiders. Since then, Sydney's Aboriginal peoples have seen a progression ships, planes and cars bringing people to our city from all points of the world. 210 years ago, Aboriginal peoples vastly outnumbered the European invaders. Today, they comprise less than one per cent of our city's population.

Despite the marginalisation and racism that shaped so much of their life, Sydney's Aboriginal peoples have survived. Aboriginal Sydneysiders nowadays make their mark in the arts and media, at universities and other educational institutions, in law, in the sporting arena, in community welfare, in business, and in public service.

Aboriginal Day Redfern Primary School, early 1990s.

Sydney's indigenous peoples are often called koories to distinguish them from their compatriots from the mid north NSW coast, goories, or those in the north west of NSW and Queensland, the murries. Today many of Sydney's suburbs carry Aboriginal names. They include Parramatta, Cabramatta, Yagoona and Woolloomooloo.

Torres Strait Islanders are also indigenous Australians who come from the islands that separate the north of Australia from Papua New Guinea. They have distinctive cultures which are continued through some networking in the Fairfield area of Sydney. They are fewer in number than Aboriginal people in Sydney.

Explore the world in one city

Invasion and resistance

If you stand at Circular Quay and look towards the Opera House, you are looking at Bennelong Point. This place was named after an Aboriginal man kidnapped by the first Governor of New South Wales, Arthur Phillip (and it's not only the name of the upmarket restaurant now found there, as many still think). Bennelong became a kind of 'go-between', utilising the English he had learned while living with the Governor for six months. Bennelong's new lifestyle, and a trip to England, set him apart from his group of people, the Cadigal. He was finally killed in a 'tribal' fight in 1813.

The Eora people were the original Aboriginal inhabitants of the area currently known as Sydney. Their presence in the Sydney basin has been dated at around 20,000 years, however the earliest stone tools found in the region go back more than 45,000 years. When the First Fleet arrived in 1788 there were approximately 3,000 Aborigines with three main languages and several dialects. Within 12 months small pox wiped out so many Aboriginal people that those left ill had no time to bury the dead. Coupled with influenza and measles – to which they had no immunity – and the odd gun shot, the Eora were virtually wiped out. A period of resistance and survival began.

Detail from the reconciliation poster 'Learning Together'.

The famous Aboriginal leader Pemulwuy – also known as the 'rainbow warrior' – led a series of attacks against expanding settlers along the Georges, Hawkesbury and Parramatta Rivers in the 1790s. The guerrilla tactics employed by him and those he led were largely aimed at preventing the take-over of traditional lands and hunting grounds. For example the yam fields on Dharug land by the Hawkesbury River were ripped up by white settlers to make way for the crops which eventually dominated the rich alluvial banks. Local Aboriginal groups had little access to traditional crops and estuarine food. Eventually, in 1802, two settlers shot Pemulwuy and his head was removed and sent back to "mother" England for "classification" purposes.

As the colony spread further from Sydney Cove to the base of the Blue Mountains disruption to traditional life-styles of Aboriginal people was relentless. Areas of land that were fire-stick farmed were taken over as rich grazing lands for the settlers sheep and cattle. This particularly affected the Gundungarra and the Tharawal peoples around south and western Sydney. Fire-stick farming had maintained open expanses of grassed land to attract game, while controlled bush fires assisted the germination of native plant life, such as the banksia. A cave with restricted access at Minto in Sydney's south-west records in red ochre the coming of strange animals with the painting of a bull. It was also in this part of Sydney, at the base of the Blue Mountains on Gundungarra land, that a French explorer first heard the Aboriginal bush call "coo-ee".

Displaced from their traditional land by the colonisers, different cultural and linguistic groups of Aboriginal people in NSW were rounded up and moved from place to place, as white settlements grew higgledy-piggledy throughout and beyond the Sydney basin. Yet the Aboriginal groups remaining did not die out, as was expected. Despite their smaller numbers and less effective weapons, Aboriginal groups continued to struggle for their land and for basic civil rights. People from Tharawal and groups from the south coast had set up homes at Perouse on the southern shore of Botany Bay to maintain traditional kinship and ceremonial links. The Gundungarra also survived and began their call for Land Rights in the 1860s.

Land has always been a central concept in Aboriginal life, linking religion, economy, kinship and traditional stories that characterise Aboriginal identity. In contemporary times, land rights is about cultural survival, economic independence and social justice. At the time of invasion, colonialists viewed land in terms of individual ownership: as something to be fenced in and tilled. Given that land was not used in the same manner by the existing indigenous peoples it was conveniently considered by the British government to be a wasteland and therefore 'empty'. It was this doctrine of *terra nullius* that was successfully challenged by the late Eddy Mabo in the Australian High Court in June 2, 1992 in the now famous Mabo decision.

By 1838 white settlers had crossed the mountains and were occupying land up and down the coast of New South Wales. This was a monumental year in the history of the treatment of Aboriginal people in this State. The Myall Creek Massacre in the northwest of NSW occurred in early June, 1838. Twelve stockmen tied up 28 Aboriginal men, women and children before butchering them and burning their bodies. This act of brutality brought about the first conviction against white men for treatment of Aboriginal people. Throughout the nineteenth century Aboriginal people continued to argue for their rights, though with limited success. In 1888, for example, Aboriginal people boycotted the Centenary celebrations in Sydney, but this was hardly noticed in reports of the events in Sydney's newspapers.

Throughout the 1800's missionaries involved themselves in Aboriginal affairs to 'civilise' them. The result was often cultural genocide through the denial of Aboriginal cultural and linguistic practices. From 1883, when the Aborigines Protection Board was set up, Aboriginal people were separated based upon colour. This racist policy and practise

Redfern Cup day,
Redfern Primary School.

preached that 'full-bloods' were to live on reserves along with 'half-castes' over the age of 34, while the others with less Aboriginal blood were expected to assimilate. This was the beginning of the period of the Stolen Generations. Aboriginal children of 'mixed-blood' were taken from their parents and placed in institutions, many never seeing their parents again and many having their names changed so that finding them became impossible. In recent years, Aboriginal people formed an association called Link Up to help those looking for families.

Important chapters of Aboriginal resistance have occurred in Sydney. On January 26, 1938 – Australia Day – non-Aboriginal Australia celebrated the 150th anniversary of white settlement in Sydney. At the same time 100 members of the Aboriginal Advancement League and the Aboriginal Progressive Association organised a Day of Mourning in the Australian Hall (near the Mandolin Cinema, 150 Elizabeth Street). The aim was to draw attention to their claims for citizenship rights. This day, and the historical venue – currently under the threat of our voracious developers – is regarded as a landmark in Aboriginal political history. In 1965 Aboriginal and white Freedom Riders set out from Sydney University and travelled by bus to towns in rural NSW to challenge the existing discriminatory laws. These laws prevented Aboriginal workers earning wages equal to whites, prevented them from consuming alcohol in public bars, banned their children from swimming in local pools, and led to the roping off of sections in movie theatres for Aboriginal people. Two years later, in 1967, a national referendum gave all Aboriginal people citizenship rights for the first time and transferred legal powers to the Commonwealth Government to act on behalf of Aboriginal people throughout Australia. Prior to this, Aboriginal people were not even counted in the Australian census.

Koorie boys.
Redfern Primary School, early 1990s.

After this period, new Aboriginal organisations appeared in the Sydney suburb of Redfern to fight for medical, legal, education, welfare and housing rights for Aboriginal peoples in Sydney. The inner-city suburb of Redfern became the symbolic and organisational centre of the contemporary struggle for Aboriginal rights during the 1970s and consolidated the role of Redfern as a key centre of Aboriginal settlement in our city. In 1971 the Aboriginal Legal Service was founded here. It was followed fairly quickly by the Aboriginal Housing Company and Aboriginal Medical Service. Later, other services such as the Aboriginal Children's Service were opened to fight against the practice of removing Aboriginal children from Aboriginal families and placing them in 'white' homes. A period of cultural revival gave birth to the National Black Theatre and the Aboriginal and Islander Dance Theatre (now housed temporarily on Windmill Street in the Rocks). The Murawina Preschool was formed by Aboriginal people in Redfern to challenge the assimilationist tendencies of conventional schooling.

On Australia Day, January 26th, 1988 a march in Sydney meandered through the city streets to celebrate the survival and diversity of Aboriginal and Torres Strait Islander cultures in Australia. At the head of the procession were elders who had travelled all the way from desert areas of central Australia. Their slow dance and chanting was a marked contrast to - and held in direct opposition to – the official bicentennial celebrations on Sydney Harbour. The elders were followed by indigenous youth, children and dance groups in a moving moment that reaffirmed indigenous identity while celebrating diversity. These indigenous Australians were joined in the march by more than 10,000 people united in their affirmation of Aboriginal Torres Strait Islander cultures and their demand for justice. Many of the marchers were Australians from successive waves of immigration, many who had fought their own struggles for cultural respect, recognition and social justice.

Aboriginal Sydney Today

Aboriginal resistance has a history as long as white settlement. Indigenous people have survived 210 years of marginalisation and dispossession to be the spiritual heart of Sydney's cultural diversity today. Today there are 28,754 Sydneysiders of Aboriginal or Torres Strait Islander origin.

Indigenous people are more likely to live in rural areas than other peoples are. Slightly less than one in three (28.3 per cent) of Aboriginals and Torres Strait Islanders in New South Wales live in Sydney. While small in number – only 0.9 per cent of Sydney's total population – this number is up by 50 per cent compared to a decade ago, when Aboriginal people comprised only 0.6 per cent of the population. This increase is partly explained by the fact that Sydney's indigenous population is relatively young compared to the population as a whole: 38.4 per cent of indigenous people are aged less than 15 years, compared to only 20 per cent of the total population. It is also explained by the fact that Sydney is a magnet for Aboriginal people across the nation, just as it is for all Australians seeking better employment prospects.

Aboriginal settlement in Sydney is today concentrated in a number of

Koorie girls from the Mundine and Coe families, Redfern Primary School.

Explore the world in one city

suburban clusters stretching west and south-west from the inner-city suburbs of Redfern, Waterloo, Woolloomooloo and Glebe. Key Aboriginal concentrations are also found at La Perouse on the southern shores of Botany Bay, in suburbs like Bidwell, Shalvey, Willmont, Tregear and Mount Druitt in Sydney's outer west, and Airds in the outer south-west.

When most people think of Aboriginal Sydney they think of Redfern, just one stop on the western train line from the CBD. Redfern was the site of earlier attempts to establish welfare, legal, health and education rights for Aboriginal peoples. Many of the Aboriginal activists in the 1970s were based in Redfern, as were most of the Aboriginal organisations established during this period. In recent years, Redfern has been at the centre of another struggle with attempts to move existing Aboriginal residents to other Sydney suburbs. These moves followed a series of clashes between Aboriginal youth and police near Redfern Station and Eveleigh Street, or the Block as it is called by locals. High unemployment rates among Aboriginal youth and problems related to youth drug culture lay behind these events. Today Aboriginal people in the Block are struggling to keep out the demolishers' bulldozers. On this issue, like many others, the Aboriginal community – like the non-Aboriginal community – have diverse opinions.

Sydney's Koories are proud of the Aboriginal flag.

La Perouse is another Sydney suburb with strong Aboriginal historical symbolism. It sits on Botany Bay, the original landing site for Captain Cook. La Perouse has a thriving Aboriginal community that has survived periodic war and economic crisis and consistent neglect. Until 1997, La Perouse was the site of the annual Aboriginal Survival Concert on Australia Day, January 26. Its locals still do a trade in crafts (especially on Sundays) and there is a fine museum displaying Aboriginal art (see page 49). The La Perouse Bushtucker Walkway – a short historic walk where a guide names and explains the uses of traditional food, medicine and weapons – is a great way to get to know local Aboriginal history and culture.

All of Sydney's metropolitan universities have Aboriginal centres attached to them, while all universities have programs in place to increase Aboriginal access to tertiary education. Universities such as the University of Technology, Sydney (UTS), Macquarie University and the University of Western Sydney (UWS) have specially designed programs for Aboriginal peoples to get professional skills in teaching, adult education, management and welfare. Another key site of Aboriginal education in Sydney is Tranby College, in Glebe, run for years by Aboriginal stalwarts such as Jack Beetson and Kevin Cook. Aboriginal people are now graduating as doctors, lawyers, social workers, teachers and managers.

INDIGENOUS SYDNEY

Influential Aboriginal Sydneysiders

Aboriginal people have made their mark on Sydney life since the earliest days, despite the circumstances that constrained their lives and opportunities. One arena most accessible to Aboriginal people is sport. Great Aboriginal sporting champions such as former Wimbledon tennis champion Evonne Cawley (nee Goolagong), former world boxing champion Lionel Rose or current 400 metre world champion athlete, Kathy Freeman, may not be Sydneysiders but they have won the hearts of all of Sydney for their courage and skill. Aboriginal people have also made their mark in other facets of Sydney life. Some have reached high office in the public service, law, education, welfare and politics. Others have been quiet achievers within their communities.

Over the decades, Aboriginal men and women have made their mark on Sydney's sporting fields. The legendary Ella brothers, Mark, Garry and Glen, grew up in La Perouse and played rugby union for their local Matraville high school before graduating through the ranks to play for Randwick, New South Wales and Australia. Mark Ella was the first Aboriginal captain of the Wallabies, the Australian national team, and is generally thought to be Australia's greatest ever player. Glen Ella is currently involved with planning for the 2000 Games with SOCOG (Sydney Organising Committee of the Olympic Games).

People like the legendary Tony Mundine, a former world boxing champion and his son, Anthony Mundine, who plays for the Sydney rugby league club, St. George, and is one of the most exciting rugby league footballers playing today, are proud of their Aboriginal heritage. Many other Aboriginal footballers have been attracted to live and play in Sydney, including the great Arthur Beetson, who came to the Sydney Balmain Tigers club from Queensland in the 1960s and is perhaps the best forward ever to play for Australia. Current Aboriginal players who star in Sydney rugby league clubs include Andrew Walker from Sydney City and Darrell Trindall from South Sydney. But teams in Sydney's other major football codes also include key Aboriginal players. The Sydney Swans Aussie Rules team has built a success around current Aboriginal players such as Michael O'Loughlin, Troy Cook, Robbie Arhmat and former ones such as Dereck Kickett.

There are many other notable Aboriginal people in Sydney, some with high profiles in education, the arts, social justice and Aboriginal politics related to the key contemporary issues of Land Rights and Reconciliation. Pat O'Shane was the first female Aboriginal barrister who lived and gained her law degree in Sydney. She then became the first

Cathy Freeman silver medalist at the 400m at Atlanta, is not from Sydney but hopes that she wins gold at the Sydney Olympics. She is pictured here with Melinda Gainsford, Australia's other female track star.

Aboriginal to head a government department, and is now a magistrate and Chancellor of the University of New England. She has continued to use her position to fearlessly promote Aboriginal issues and she played a very prominent role in the discussions about an Australian republic at the recent Constitutional Convention. Other prominent Aboriginal people include Nancy De Vries, who was the first Aboriginal person to address the New South Wales parliament in 1997. Linda Burney, until recently the president of the Aboriginal Education Consultative Committee and now chair of the State Reconciliation Committee, is also a prominent Aboriginal activist and a Sydneysider. Mick Dodson is a barrister who was – until recently – the Aboriginal and Torres Strait Islander Social Justice Commissioner with the Human Rights and Equal Opportunity Commission. Dodson has been recently appointed as the director of the Indigenous Law Centre at the University of New South Wales. Bob Morgan is the head of the University of Technology, Sydney (UTS) indigenous unit, Jumbanna, and was a key organiser of the 1993 World Indigenous Peoples Education Conference, held in Wollongong, NSW.

People like Tiger Bayles and Garry Foley were key Aboriginal activists in Sydney in the 1970s and 1980s. And how could we forget the late Burnum Burnum, the internationally known Aboriginal rights campaigner who rose to prominence through his involvement in the Aboriginal tent embassy outside the Federal Parliament during the 1970s and 80s. Burnum Burnum planted an Aboriginal flag on top of England's white cliffs of Dover during the Australian Bicentennial celebrations in 1988 and claimed England for Aboriginal people in an attempt to gain international publicity for the cause of his peoples.

Other Aboriginal people, particularly the younger generation, are playing an exciting role in the Sydney and national arts scene. They include David and Stephen Page, from the internationally acclaimed Bangarra Dance Theatre, and Rhoda Roberts, who was the Artistic Director for the 1997 Festival of the Dreaming, the first of the four Sydney Cultural Olympiads. Others include film maker Tracey Moffatt, television personality Ernie Dingo, artist Bronwyn Bancroft and actors Arron Pederson and Lydia Miller.

But there are other Aboriginal people who are notable for their important and selfless work within the Sydney Aboriginal community. There is the late Mum Shirl who worked tirelessly for the Aboriginal communities in Redfern and Waterloo. She visited many Aboriginal prisoners in jail, and helped out all those – black and white – who called on her in their desperation. Mum Shirl was buried after a ceremony in St Mary's Cathedral, Sydney's main Catholic Church, which was packed to overflowing.

Comedians H.G. Nelson and Roy Slaven Show support for Aboriginal Reconciliation, Sydney 1998.

Aboriginal History, Art & Culture

Aspects of the rich history, art and tradition of one of the oldest cultures of the world are displayed in all Sydney's major public museums. Here we list some of the best places to explore Aboriginal culture in Sydney.

Art Gallery of NSW's Yiribana Gallery.

With a collection of more than 200 works, Yiribana has one of the most complete and extensive selections of Aboriginal and Torres Strait Islander art in Australia. This interesting collection – including dot paintings, sand stone carvings and paintings on bark and card – is a wonderful celebration of traditional and contemporary Aboriginal art. Free admission to the gallery; exhibitions between $7 adults, $4 concession. Open Monday-Sunday 10am-5pm.

Art Gallery Road, The Domain, City (tel: 9225 1744).

Aboriginal Section, Australian Museum.

Aboriginal Australia – located on the ground floor – is a good place to be introduced to the history and cultures of Aboriginal people, from the Dream Time to present days. Here you'll find a fine display of Aboriginal artifacts and a superb example of rock painting, and if you want to deepen your knowledge of Aboriginal Australia call in at the museum book shop. Admission $5 adults; $2-$3 concession; $12 family. Open Monday-Sunday 9.30am-5pm.

6 College Street, City (tel: 9339 8111).

National Maritime Museum.

With an excellent video and audio visual program, the Maritime Museum introduces visitors – in Level 1 – to the history and sea culture of Aboriginal Australians. Admission $7 adults; $4 concessions; $18.50 family. Open Monday-Sunday 9.30am-5pm.

Darling Harbour, City (tel: 9552 7705).

Museum of Sydney.

One of the newest museums in Sydney (opened in 1995) and located on the site of the colony's first Government House, the Museum of Sydney has already earned the praise of locals and tourists alike for the section – on Levels 2 and 3 – dedicated to the history and culture of the Eora people. A central part in this display is played by contemporary Aboriginal people who introduce visitors to the many tales of one of the oldest societies on earth. Very impressive also is the Edge of the Trees sculpture, located outside the Museum, that consists of 29 pillars made

The Aboriginal flag is red on the bottom half (representing the red earth), Black on the top half (representing the people). In the middle is a yellow circle, the Sun.

Explore the world in one city

of sandstone, wood and steel symbolising the early contact between Aborigines and Europeans. Admission between $6-$15 (family). Open Monday-Sunday 10am-5pm.
37 Phillip Street, City (tel: 9251 5988).

Aboriginal Art Dealers

Traditionally, Aboriginal art was once developed under an almost exclusively sacred or religious context. Today, however many Aboriginal artists are exploring not only different media and artistic techniques but also motifs, including the way in which land is depicted. Many Aboriginal artists use their art to make political statements about the past and the present. In the last few years, the art specialists have considered Aboriginal art as the most vital area of contemporary Australia art and it seems that the Western world of art has agreed with this. Private and public art collectors have embraced the vibrant works and diverse styles emerging from Australian Aboriginal art with great enthusiasm in the last two decades. This popularity has seen well established art dealers and galleries in Sydney displaying and selling works produced by urban and rural Aboriginal artists. The following are some recommended galleries.

Aboriginal and Pacific Art Gallery.

It has a fantastic display of Aboriginal arts, including rare barks, carvings and other artifacts. Check out the temporary displays of the likes of Mirrima Marawilli, Kitty Kantilla and Declan Apuatimi. Free admission.
Open Tuesday-Friday 10am-5.30pm, Saturday 10am-2pm.
8th Floor, Dymocks Building, 428 George Street (tel: 9223 5900).

Boomali Aboriginal Artists' Co-op.

A well reputed venue for traditional and contemporary Aboriginal art and artists. The works of prominent urban Aboriginal artists such as Rea exploring the way in which Aboriginal people have been perceived in terms of banal cultural cliches is an example of new art techniques and themes in Aboriginal art. Free admission.
Open Tuesday-Friday 10am-5pm, Friday 11am-5pm.
27 Abercrombie Street, Chippendale (tel: 9698 2047).

Utopia Art Sydney.

This is a highly acclaimed art gallery with a strong commitment to Northern Territory's Aboriginal artists from Utopia and Papunya Tula. Some of the most well known Australian-Aboriginal artists – such as the

NATIONAL ABORIGINAL CULTURAL CENTRE
Responding to the growing interest in Aboriginal culture, especially from tourists, the National Aboriginal Cultural Centre was open to the public in July 1998. The Centre brings to one place many of the over 200 tribal nations which make up Aboriginal Australia. At the Centre you will have the opportunity to admire Aboriginal dance, performed four times every day, a wide range of Aboriginal art including didgeridoos, boomerangs and woven mats, and a photo gallery showing how white folk saw Aboriginal people a hundred years ago. Admission, general entry $2, refunded with any purchase.
Open Monday-Sunday 9.30am-8pm.
Darling Walk, 1-25 Harbour Street, Darling Harbour
(tel: 9283 7477).

late Emily Kame Kngwarreye – have displayed their art work here. Free admission. Open Wednesday-Friday 10am-4pm, Saturday noon-5pm.

50 Parramatta Road, Stanmore (tel: 9550 4609)

Hogarth Galleries Aboriginal Art.

With a solid tradition of showing the best of Aboriginal commercial art, Hogarth houses a fine collection of contemporary Aboriginal art and crafts, including some fascinating desert paintings by artists from Yuendumu and Haasts Bluff in the Northern Territory.
Free admission. Open Monday-Sunday 10am-5pm.

7 Walker Lane, off Brown Street, Paddington (tel: 9251 2455).

La Perouse Aboriginal Art Gallery.

Located in one of the most significant Aboriginal areas in Sydney, La Perouse, the Gallery displays and sells some beautiful pieces of Aboriginal art and craft. A suggestion, call in to this art gallery on Sunday afternoons when the area is full of activity, including the presence of craft stalls where you can purchase beautifully designed boomerangs and get some quick lessons on how to throw them. Open Monday-Sunday 10am-4pm.

Old Cable Station, La Perouse (tel: 9661 2765).

Aboriginal and Tribal Art Centre.

An eclectic gallery displaying fascinating contemporary and traditional artwork, including wooden instruments, sculptures, desert paintings, pottery, furniture and body decorations made by Aboriginal art co-operatives. Open Monday-Sunday 10am-5pm.

Level 1, 117 George Street, The Rocks (tel: 9247 9625).

Aboriginal Artists Gallery.

It has a fine showing of Aboriginal art ranging from musical instruments to carvings. Open Monday-Friday 10am-5.30pm, Saturday 10am-1.30pm.

477 Kent Street, City (tel: 9261 2929).

Jinta Desert Art Gallery.

A well established gallery that provides a programme of national and international exhibitions and events focussing on recent developments in contemporary Australian Aboriginal art. It has one of the largest collection of Aboriginal painting and artifacts in Australia.
Open Monday-Saturday 10am-6pm; Sunday 1-6pm.

154-156 Clarence Street, City (tel: 9290 3639).

Many Sydneysiders have supported their Aboriginal brothers and sisters' demands for reconciliation.

Explore the world in one city

Aboriginal Gifts and Souvenirs

With increasing local and international interest in Aboriginal culture, there is a strong interest in Aboriginal cultural artifacts. This provides work for local Aboriginal peoples as well as business opportunities for Aboriginal and non-Aboriginal entrepreneurs. We recommend that you check out the following:

Gavala Aboriginal Art & Cultural Education Centre.

Owned and operated by local Aboriginal people, Gavala has a large selection of paintings, boomerangs, didgeridoos, handmade ceremonial artifacts, music, clothing and jewellery.

Shop 321 Harbourside Darling Harbour (tel: 9212 7232).

Coo-ee Aboriginal Emporium and Art Gallery.

The upstairs Gallery exhibits Aboriginal bark and desert paintings, sculpture, artifacts and the largest selection of limited edition prints in Australia. There is a shop downstairs which carries souvenirs, didgeridoos, boomerangs, Aboriginal books and music. The profits from sales go back to the authors of the works displayed.
Open Monday - Saturday 10am-6pm, Sunday, 11am-5pm.

98 Oxford Street, Paddington (tel: 9332 1554).

While visiting the Sydney Opera House don't miss out on the opportunity to admire the Detail of The Possum Dreaming, the wonderful dot painting mural located in the Opera Theatre foyer. Its author is Michael Nelson Tjakamarra, an Aboriginal artist from the central Australian desert.

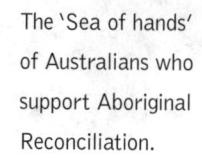

Aboriginal Sites

Just as a blank page is an invitation so were expanses of rock for Aboriginal people. Through art rock carvings and paintings, they told their history to the next generations. Depictions of the arrival of the first Europeans, of Aboriginal resistance and daily life are evident in many sites around Sydney. Representations of themselves, animals and mystical figures are recurrent features of Aboriginal rock engravings. Some of these examples of Aboriginal art go back thousands of years and it's estimated that in Sydney alone there are around five hundred thousand of them.

Aboriginal rock carvings can be found at several sites in Sydney. The most remarkable are those found in Ku-ring-gai Chase National Park to the north of Sydney and the Royal National Park to the south. One of the expressions of rock carving closest to the City is a short walking distance north of Bondi Beach (in the grounds of the Bondi Golf Course). There is also a great collection of rock carvings and paintings in

The 'Sea of hands' of Australians who support Aboriginal Reconciliation.

> **WARNING:**
>
> Do not touch any traditional Aboriginal art sites because the grease and dirt from your fingers will hasten the process of natural erosion. Also remember that all Aboriginal relics are fully protected by the National Parks and Wildlife Service. The maximum penalty for destroying or damaging a relic is $1000 and/or six months imprisonment.

the Gumbooya Reserve in the northern Sydney suburb of Allambie Heights; in the Balls Head Reserve, on Sydney's north shore; and at Dharug National Park, Wisemans Ferry, 80 km north-west of Sydney where some of the rock engravings are around 10,000 years old.

Ku-ring-gai Chase National Park.

Located about 30 km from the Sydney CBD, this national park possesses arguably the richest and most fascinating collection of Aboriginal rock art from representation of marine animals to images of spiritual deities. Aboriginal engravings are located 1.5 km along on the left hand side of the Bobbin Head Track. It has been estimated that the oldest sites in the park predate the Roman temples, the Athenian Acropolis and even the Egyptian pyramids.

(For more information contact the Pittwater Information Centre on 9979 8717). For a guided tour contact the well established Walkabout Tours, 83 Stafford Street, Paddington (tel: 9332 2611).

Royal National Park.

Located 34 km south from the Sydney CBD, you will find some fascinating and interesting Aboriginal rock carvings in the vicinity of the Jibbon Lagoon. It has been estimated that some of the rock carvings are around 5,000 years old.

(More information can be obtained from the National Parks & Wildlife Service Visitors' Centre on 9542 0648).

Red Hands Cave, Blue Mountains.

The Daruk and the Gundungara tribes were two of the main Aboriginal group that occupied the valleys of the northern Blue Mountains before the arrival of the first Europeans. The testimony of their presence in the area - the very impressive red hand stencils on the rocks painted using natural red ochre and dating between five hundred and fifteen hundred years old – can be appreciated in the Red Hands Cave Nature Track. Other art sites and axe grinding grooves occur in several places in this area.

For further information contact the Blue Mountains Visitor Information Centre on 047 396 266.

Getting to know the Aboriginal and Torres Strait Islander community

Events

Survival Concert.

The largest and most significant Aboriginal celebration, Survival coincides with Australia Day on January 26. La Perouse was until 1997 the traditional site for this celebration, but since 1998 this event of Aboriginal music, history and traditions has been celebrated at Waverley Oval on Bondi Road, Bondi. Survival goes from 10am to 6pm. Admission $12 adults, $5 elders and $2 kids. No alcohol allowed. There is no parking but buses run to and from Eddy Avenue, City.

For more information call 9331 3777.

NAIDOC Day (National Aboriginal and Islander Day of Celebration).

For more than 20 years, July 11 has marked the beginning of a week of Aboriginal celebrations held in all Australian capital cities and many regional centres and communities. Organised to foster awareness and understanding of Aboriginal culture and history, this event is held in art galleries, community centres and open space venues. In Sydney, two of the most important venues are La Perouse and the Cleveland Street High School, Park Road, Alexandria.

For additional information call 9286 1500.

ART ORGANISATIONS

BANGARRA DANCE THEATRE.

Formed in 1989, Bangarra is Australia's leading indigenous arts company and one of Australia's top contemporary dance companies. Drawing on the traditional dances and culture of the *Yirrkala* community in the remote area of Arnhemland in the north of Australia, under the artistic direction of Stephen Page, Bangarra has fused the traditional aspects of Aboriginal and Islander life with contemporary movement, and from this fusion has emerged an innovative, truly unique Australian style.

Ochres was the breakthrough piece for Bangarra in 1994, followed up by Stephen Page's long anticipated new piece, *Fish*, which had its world premiere at Edinburgh Festival in August, 1997.

Beginning in November 1998, as part of the City of Sydney's Streets Alive program, Bangarra will host a festival of Aboriginal and Torres Strait Islander dance each year at their home on the Wharf on Sydney's Harbour.

More information on 9251 5333.

Media

Koori Mail. The voice of Aboriginal and Torres Strait Islanders, *Koori Mail* is a must read newspaper for those looking for an accurate coverage of Aboriginal issues. This fortnightly publication hits the stands on Wednesday and can be found in major newsagencies (check the one in Town Hall). $1.50. Its current editor is Todd Condie.

PO Box 117, Lismore, NSW 2480 (tel: 66 222 666).

Radio

SBS Radio 1, AM 1107. Aboriginal news and music. Monday and Wednesday 12 noon-1 pm.

2SER FM 107.3. Aborigines in Focus. Friday 12noon-1pm.

Television

Perleeka Aboriginal Television. News, community information and music on Channel 31 Sydney's Community Television Station.

For additional information call 9262 1066.

Further Reading, Video and Film

There are a growing number of books on Aboriginal peoples and issues. We recommend Nigel Parbury's *Survival* (1986) and Heather Goodall's *From Invasion to Embassy* (1996) for historical overviews. Aboriginal author Ruby Langford's *Don't Take Your Love to Town* (Penguin Books, 1988) explores growing up in the war and post-war years. Also worth seeking out is John Pilger's film *Secret Country* (available on video), which charts the history of Aboriginal/state relations. Aboriginal film-maker Tracey Moffat's *Night Cries* explores issues related to Aboriginal identity.

Websites

Infokoori: An index of Australian indigenous affairs
http://www.slmsw.gov.au/koori

Koori Music International http://www.koori.net/koori-music.html

ATSI WWW Resource Directory
http://www.koori.usyd.edu.au/register.html

British and Irish Sydney

The word "cosmopolitan" conjures up the image of diversity and difference. Sydney is a cosmopolitan city because it counts peoples from over 180 nationalities as Sydneysiders. But difference is always relative. Or, to be more specific, this difference is defined in terms of difference from the majority. In Sydney's case, the majority is the Anglo-Celtic community that are first or later generation British or Irish immigrants.

From 1788 until 1997 the United Kingdom was the biggest source of migrants in Australian history (overtaken that year, for the first time in our history, by New Zealand) – pleasing at least partially the unfulfilled hope of Arthur Calwell who in 1946, stated his aspiration that "for every foreign migrant there will be ten people from the UK."

Today, one half of Sydney's people are third or later generation Australians, mostly of British or Irish origin. Of the other half who are first or second-generation immigrants, more than one in three are of British or Irish origin. So, it is the English, Scottish, Welsh and Irish immigrants of the last two decades or the last two centuries who became the dominant mob in terms of population, power and influence. But in doing so, this Anglo-Celtic mob became invisible. The invisibility of the most visible.

Many of Sydney's foundation institutions and arrangements are a product of this Anglo-Celtic economic, political and cultural heritage. The Westminster parliamentary system, the legal and the financial systems are products of this predominantly English colonial society that was established in the antipodes. But they are in the background, visible mainly in the sandstone monuments along Sydney's Macquarie Street. Other less establishment influences from our British and Irish peoples range from drinking in pubs and betting at the race-tracks through to playing cricket on long hot summer days. In the media, American culture has mixed with British film, television and music to shape the mainstream culture among different generations and sub-cultures. American basketball stars are of greater street credibility than cricket heroes among many younger Sydneysiders. But this Americanisation of Australian culture merely reinforces the invisibleness of the Anglo-Celtic majority.

GETTING THERE

Sydney Explorer and bus routes **431, 432, 433** and **434** run regularly, while most of the City buses go to Circular Quay. By train just catch any train that goes to Circular Quay and then walk.

Because it is numerically the largest and the most dominant cultural group, Anglo-Celtic Sydney is harder to spot than the presence of, or impact of, minority cultural groups from non-English-speaking backgrounds. The impact of the Anglo-Celts is not so visible. There are few English, Scottish or Welsh restaurants. Imported newspapers keep many up with happenings in the old country, though most are catered for by the mainstream press in Australia. Moreover, the broad dispersal of British and Irish immigrants throughout Sydney's regions has prevented a Little England or Little Scotland emerging. This relative invisibility does not mean impotency. Precisely the opposite is true. The cultural institutions of the English in particular have become the institutions of power, part of the establishment.

Of course, while we talk in terms of British immigrants we must acknowledge the great differences between English, Scottish, Welsh and Irish cultures. And within each birthplace group, differences related to class background, regional dialect and religion combine to produce many differences, highlighting the need for caution about cultural stereotyping or simplification.

The Rocks

While the Irish are much dispersed today in the vastness of our city, The Rocks becomes for St. Patrick's Day - on March 17 or the Sunday before – the meeting point for Sydney's Irish. The streets of The Rocks welcome the enthusiastic Irish parades, while the local pubs draw the boisterous Irish, sipping Guiness and green beer.

Referred to often as the birthplace of white Australia, at The Rocks you can feel, see and taste the sights and atmosphere of Sydney's colonial heritage, including some of the oldest pubs in the country.
Contact The Rocks Visitors Centre, 106 George Street, The Rocks, tel: 9255 1788).

But The Rocks is not only about pubs and Irishness, it's also where at different times, some of the best Latin American bands perform their sensuous rhythms, and where you can – along with visiting the many historic places – purchase your souvenirs, antiques and exotic gifts at **The Rocks Market (under the Harbour Bridge) that operates Saturday-Sunday 10am-6pm (tel: 9255 1717).**

Explore the world in one city

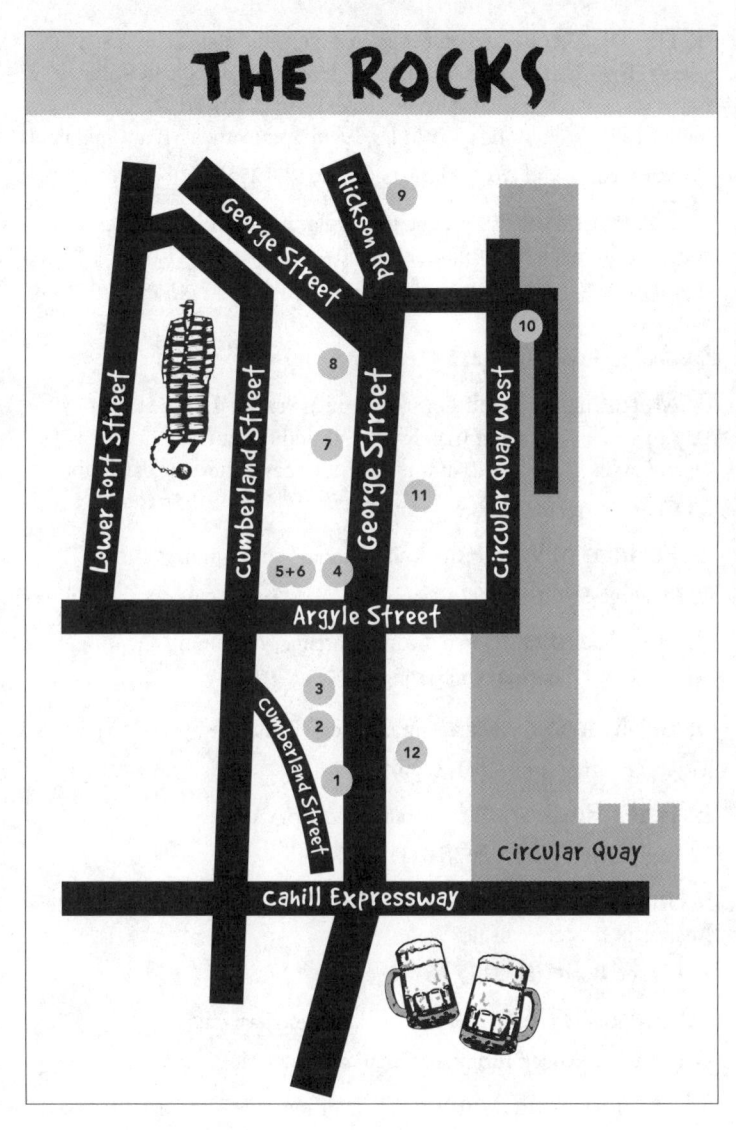

THE ROCKS

IN AND AROUND THE ROCK

1. Fortune of War Hotel.
2. The Rockpool.
3. Phillips Foote Hotel.
4. The Orient.
5. Bel Mondo.
6. Reds. Restaurant.
7. Observer Hotel.
8. Mercantile Hotel.
9. Number 7 at the Park.
10. Bilson's. Restaurant.
11. Sailors Thai
12. MCA Fish Cafe. Seafood restaurant.

3: Phillips Foote Hotel. Regarded as one of the best Sydney garden restaurants and pubs, this spot sends the tasty smell of its sizzling steaks to every corner of The Rocks.
Open Monday-Saturday 12noon-12am, Sunday 12noon-10pm.
101 George Street (tel: 9241 1485).

WILDLIGHT PHOTO AGENCY

Established in 1985, Wildlight sells and exhibits many of Australia's leading photographers, including David Moore. Check out Wildlight's stunning images.

**87 Gloucester Street, The Rocks
(tel: 9251 5857).**

BRITISH AND IRISH SYDNEY

AROUND AND HIGHLY RECOMMENDED...

LORD NELSON BREWERY HOTEL. In a historic sandstone building, Lord Nelson is a place for those looking for a "beer experience" of the highest quality. Open Monday-Sunday 11am-11pm.
Corner Kent Street and Argyle Street (tel: 9251 4044).

THE HERO OF WATERLOO HOTEL. Built in 1844, this is one of the oldest pubs in Sydney. This is a charming spot whose sandstone walls transport you easily to a bygone era. Open Monday-Saturday 10am-11pm, Sunday 10am-10pm.
81 Lower Fort Street, Millers Point (tel: 9252 4553).

THE AUSTRALIAN. This is what you would call a haven for boutique beers brewed following the old Bavarian tradition. The bistro offers a diverse cuisine that the early pubs in Australia would never have dreamt of – Thai food to 'roo. Open Monday-Saturday 11.30am-11.30pm, Sunday 11.30am-8pm.
100 Cumberland Street, The Rocks (tel: 9247 2229).

4: The Orient. Packed on Friday and Saturday nights with party-goers, The Orient is another of the good, traditional spots in Sydney's pub scene. Live music and the well stocked four bars are the basic ingredients. Open Monday-Saturday 10am-3pm, Sunday 10am-midnight.
Corner George and Argyle Streets (tel: 9251 1255).

7: Observer Hotel. A venue for regular live Irish folk music. Bands come and go while you think of Ireland – its beauty and troubles – with a Guinness in hand. Open Sunday-Thursday 11am-11.30pm, Friday and Saturday 11am-2.30am.
69 George Street (tel: 9252 4169).

8: Mercantile Hotel. One of the main venues during St. Patrick's Day, this spot is all about Irish live music and Guinness, indeed. Open Sunday-Thursday 10am-midnight, Friday-Saturday 10am-1am.
25 George Street, The Rocks (tel: 9247 3570).

1: Fortune of War Hotel. Traditional Sydney pub.
137 George Street (tel: 9247 2714).

2: The Rockpool. One of Sydney's premier restaurants.
107 George Street (tel: 9252 1888).

5: Bel Mondo. Italian restaurant. (see The Italians, page 155).
12 Argyle Street (tel: 9241 3700).

6: Reds. Restaurant. Australian modern cuisine.
12 Argyle Street (tel: 9247 1011).

9 Number 7 at the Park Restaurant. Australian modern cuisine.
7 Hickson Road (tel: 9256 1630)

10: Bilson's. Restaurant. Australian modern cuisine.
Overseas Passenger Terminal, Circular Quay (tel: 9251 5600).

11: Sailors Thai Canteen. Thai cuisine. (see The Thais, page 371).
106 George Street (tel: 9251 2466).

12: MCA Fish Cafe. Seafood restaurant.
140 George Street (tel: 9241 4253).

Explore the world in one city

The English

It has been said that contemporary Sydney still bears the birthmarks of its beginning as a Georgian town, not just in its surviving Georgian architecture – at The Rocks, for example – but in the lifestyle of its people.

While Melbourne might be characterised as a staid, respectable Victorian city, Sydney began and remains raucous, flashy, bawdy, hedonistic – with a passion for gaming and drinking.

The English were the rulers of early colonial Australia. England provided the governors, the soldiers, the finance (and the criminals) that launched white settlement at Sydney Cove in January 1788. In later decades, English immigrants provided an important pool of labour and capital that was critical to the establishment and consolidation of white settlement in Sydney. Most of the remaining colonial buildings in our city – Macquarie Street and The Rocks boast the most spectacular examples – are a product of this. London was the benchmark for Australian economics, politics and culture. Fleet Street was the model for Australian newspapers, just as the BBC was for Australian radio and television. Australia's 'high culture' society – the opera, ballet and orchestras – were also slavishly modelled on English institutions. In politics Australia took its institutions from the Westminster model, while Australian trade unions – formed from the late 1830s – followed the model of English craft unionism.

From England we also embraced the Christmas tradition of tucking into a hot roast dinner and hot plum pudding and custard – on a sweltering summer day. We drink beer in public houses and we eat meat pies with sincere appetite. Like the English, we drive on the left-hand side of the road, indulge ourselves with Devonshire teas, and celebrate – with one day off – the Queen's Birthday. From the English – especially from the working class – we have embraced egalitarianism and a resentment of the rich and powerful. We view intellectuals with suspicion and see ourselves as politically pragmatic. In 1803, in Hyde Park, we played our first game of cricket – a noble game invented by the English.

While the largest contingent of English immigrants have arrived in search of better economic and social opportunities, it's undeniable that the attractiveness of more benevolent weather has also been an important factor. The images of Aussie soapies such as *Neighbours* and *Home & Away,* and the thousands of English backpackers in Bondi are no lesser magnets to English 'weather exiles'.

From convicts to backpackers

Since 1788, when James Cook hoisted the flag in Sydney Cove proclaiming the land a British possession, the English have been the largest of the immigrant groups from the United Kingdom to arrive on our shores. They have come in different numbers and at different times. However, they have followed a simple criterion: when London needed to find a quick solution to an immediate problem, Australia was the answer. Australia was the way out of the increasing problem of overcrowded English jails, exacerbated after the American War of Independence brought transportation of convicts to a halt. The English transformed Sydney (apparently called Albion originally but then named after Lord Sydney, the man credited with devising the idea of Australia as a penal colony) into a large and open prison that for the first 30 years of its existence relieved the pressure on England's prisons. From the time of the arrival of the First Fleet until 1868, it is estimated that about 160,000 convicts where shipped to Australia. Around 56 % of them, mostly thieves, were English.

The first free settlers – five single men and two women – arrived in the colony in 1793. They were very much part of the plan to find, in the new colony, the solution to the English 'land problem', an issue at the core of British politics until the eve of World War I. A similar idea was behind the 1830's 'shovelling out paupers' principle whereby England's poor were sent to Australia at public expense. In the latter years of that

> The English transformed Sydney into one large, open prison, that for the first 30 years of its existence, relieved the pressure on England's prisons.

Jaslyn Hall
RADIO BROADCASTER

A trained teacher who has worked in schools in England, East Africa, Barbados, Canada and Australia, Jaslyn Hall is one of Australia's most respected radio broadcasters. She is producer and host of The World Music Show on Triple J, and writes a regular column on multicultural issues and popular culture for the *Sydney Morning Herald*. A permanent Australian resident since 1981, Jaslyn has actively supported the work of a number of overseas aid agencies, in particular Community Aid Abroad and AUSTCARE, through a number of radiothons on Radio National and Triple J. And for several years she has been the Sydney MC for CAA's Walk Against Want concerts. In 1995 she launched *Tilting Cages,* a book of prose and poetry by writers in the Kakuma refugee camp in Kenya.

century, English immigrants continued leaving from Liverpool, Plymouth and London in search of a better life Down Under.

In the twentieth century Australia maintained its role as a quick solution to this problem. With the onset of the recession following World War I, with wages falling and inflation rising, the London government implemented – between 1919 and 1922 – an immigration scheme for ex-servicemen wanting to settle on our shores. They were later followed by thousands who came to Australia after War World II under the £10 passage scheme (the so-called '£10 Poms'). The economic and social problems in Britain continued into the 1950s and the 'sunny Antipodes' again provided the way out.

The unemployment level of the 1980s, during the savage years of the Thatcher era, and the inability of the Conservative government to lower the level of unemployment (which reached more than 13% by 1986) was another of those crucial factors in pushing English immigrants to look at Australia. A record high of 896,355 English-born people in Australia was recorded in the 1991 Census.

While the largest contingent of English immigrants have arrived in search of better economic and social opportunities, it's undeniable that the attractiveness of more benevolent weather has also been an important factor. The images of Aussie soapies such as *Neighbours* and *Home & Away*, and the thousands of English backpackers in Bondi (especially on New Year's Eve) are no lesser magnets to English 'weather exiles'. Despite the almost ritual 'pommy bashing' – which, according to a historian, goes back to the 1920s and is related to the Gallipoli campaign, as well as the 1932 'Bodyline' cricket furore – the English, be they immigrants or just temporary visitors, are welcome in Australia. They feel, to use a line from the current Prime Minister, John Howard, 'relaxed and comfortable'.

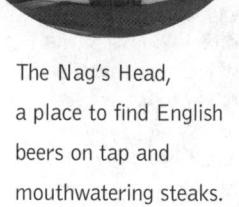

The Nag's Head, a place to find English beers on tap and mouthwatering steaks.

Restaurants

Carey Cottage. Located in Hunters Hill – Sydney's 'French Village' – Carey Cottage has a definitive English atmosphere, both in the architecture of the building and in the selections on the menu, which goes from roast lamb with mint sauce to apple crumble. BYO, fixed priced dinner $36. Open Wednesday-Friday for lunch 11am-4pm, Monday-Sunday for dinner 7pm-midnight.

18 Ferry Street, Hunters Hill (tel: 9817 3643).

Robin Hood Bistro. This is clear evidence that good British cuisine – ModBrit in this case – is still possible. A real find in the small Sydney English restaurant scene. Average $35, licensed.
Open Tuesday-Saturday dinner from 6.30pm.

203 Bronte Road, Waverley (tel: 9386 0674).

USEFUL NUMBER FOR VISITORS

UK CONSULATE,
tel: 9247 7521 or 9247 9731

SHOPPING

ENGLISH CHINA FACTORY SHOP. Under an unimaginative name, this small space is devoted to a huge and eclectic range of English stuff – from English canned drinks to English China. We were told that expats drop by to buy the sorely missed Pease pudding, Paxo, Bisto gravy granuals, Tizer, and Irn bru. Some Irish gifts are also available, including the Irish Paddy hat. Open Monday-Friday 9am-6pm (till 7pm on Thursday), Saturday 10am-4pm, Sunday noon-4pm.

Shop 26, Town Hall Arcade, City
(tel: 9267 9720).

English pubs

Lord Dudley. Close enough to the traditional English pub – decorated with English memorabilia – this welcoming spot has built up the core of its clientele among Brit expats with home withdrawal symptoms. Darts and English beer are part of the attraction. Downstairs you'll find a highly recommended restaurant. Open Monday-Wednesday 11am-11pm, Thursday-Saturday noon-midnight, Sunday noon-10pm.

236 Jersey Road, Woollahra (tel: 9327 5399).

The London Tavern. This is what you can call with confidence 'an old English-style pub'. A good bistro, two well-stocked bars and a pool comp on Wednesdays and Sundays set the scene. Nothing exotic, just English. Open Monday-Wednesday 11am-11pm, Thursday-Saturday 11am-11.30pm, Sunday noon-10pm.

Corner Underwood and William Street, Paddington (tel: 9331 1637).

The Nag's Head. The charming dark-wooded ambience – generated by clever decoration and a well-designed bar – will help you excuse the strong presence of inner-city yuppies who take this spot by storm, especially on Fridays after work. At The Nag's Head you will find English beers on tap and mouthwatering steaks. Open Monday-Saturday 11am-midnight, Sunday noon-10pm. Live music Wednesday-Sunday.

162 St John's Road, Glebe (tel: 9660 1591).

Getting to know the British community

Events

Britfest.

Proving how flawed is the idea that the English are unsociable people, more than 6,000 British expats and their friends gather at this annual event, hailed as the biggest British party thrown in Sydney. From Cornish pasties to bitter beer, and with the Union Jack waving proudly in defiance of the Australian republican mood, this is an event not to be missed. Held mid-October at the Blacktown Showground, Richmond Road, Blacktown, Britfest kicks off at 10am and finishes at 4pm. All are welcome. Admission: adults $5, children $3.

Further information, tel: 9689 1980.

The Scots

Sydney's Scottish heritage is most visible in the phone book. In Sydney's 1997-98 White Pages, 70 pages are devoted to Mac's and Mc's. It's also found in the sound of the bagpipes in military bands every Anzac Day, and during the annual Sydney Highland Gathering, a traditional festival that was first held on New Year's Day in 1869 on the Albert Ground in the inner-city suburb of Redfern.

Currently there are over 150,000 Scottish-born people living in Australia, of which more than 46,000 have settled in New South Wales. The Scottish presence on our shores goes back in history to Australia's first Scotsman – John Hunter – who arrived with Arthur Phillip in 1788 and became his successor as Governor of New South Wales in 1795. Until at least 1975 the Scots were the third largest immigrant group in Australia, after the Irish and English.

There were few Scots among the convict population – of the 160,000 convicts transported between 1788 and 1868 only 8,700 were Scots. Among them were a small number of Scottish rebels who were involved in the uprising of 1794-1800. The small number of Scottish convicts is explained by the more humanitarian Scottish penal system whereby only the most ferocious criminals were deported.

From the early years, especially from the 1820s when Scottish free settlers began arriving in large numbers, until today the Scots, who are largely Presbyterian and imbued with the Calvinist work ethic, have been extremely influential in government, agriculture, education, finance, industry, media and the arts. Scots in Australia are seen as synonymous with moral righteousness, educational achievement and financial know-how. They are discreet, industrious and very proud of their traditions.

Three of the first six governors in New South Wales – John Hunter, Lachlan Macquarie and Thomas Brisbane – were Scots, likewise Alexander Macleay, the first Colonial Secretary. The Scottish role in public affairs continues today, a good example being Ian Sinclair, the

Is it the Presbyterian ethos of hard work and saving – and the desire to become financially successful – that have made Scottish immigrants leading figures in finance, banking and industry?

John Anderson
PROFESSOR OF PHILOSOPHY

Maverick Professor of Philosophy at the University of Sydney from the late 1920s into the 1960s, John Anderson attracted controversy through his ideas about 'free thought' and exposure of what he saw as 'illusions' such as religion and nationalism. Anderson arrived at Sydney University from Glasgow in the late 1920s's to take up the Chair of Philosophy and immediately caused ripples with his criticism of sacred cows like God, King and country. Anderson was an inspiring teacher and defender of the university and in the finest traditions of Scottish philosophy he developed his own system of realism. He nurtured a Sydney school charactersised by inquiry, independence and a committment to philosophy as a way of life. Far from being an ivory tower pedagogue, the young Scotsman became a controversial public figure, opposing all forms of censorship and indoctrination and outraging Sydney's clergy and conservative politicians. He was twice censured by the NSW Parliament.

Anderson's pluralism and criticism of the status quo inspired generations of students. Always a moving target, Anderson journeyed from Marxism in the late 1930s to being an opponent of communism in the 1950s. But he is best remembered for shaking up Sydney's intellectual life and starting a 'Free Thought Society' that splintered into the Quadrant of Donald Horne and Peter Coleman on the Right and on the Left, the libertarian 'Sydney Push', a crucible of local bohemian life in the post-war decades.

Based in a series of downtown pubs, the 'Push' (slang for delinquent larrikin youth gangs who terrorised Sydney streets in earlier times) was a loose network of philosphers, free thinkers, anarchists, artists and film makers who drank, argued and partied together over a couple of generations from the late 1940s into the early 1970s. The Push became a magnet for youthful iconoclasts on their way to notoriety and fortune, including expats Robert Hughes, Germain Greer and Clive James, newspaper commentator Paddy McGuiness, journalist Wendy Bacon and writer Frank Moorehouse.

Chairman of the historic Republican Convention in 1998 and now Speaker of the House of Representatives.

Sinclair – a country man with Scottish blood, whose expertise moderating the Convention was applauded by just about everyone – is also a good example of the strong Scottish connection with the land. Since the early years, when New South Wales Scottish officers were granted land, Scots began pioneering irrigation, and the pastoral, beef and dairy cattle industries. They were so influential in agriculture that the first professor of Agriculture at the University of Sydney – Sir Robert Dickie – was a Scot. The wine industry in the Newcastle Hunter Valley was also developed, in the 1830s, by an entrepreneurial Scottish immigrant, James Busby.

The appointment in 1997 of the Scottish-born Gavin Brown (born in Largo, Scotland) as vice-chancellor of the University of Sydney confirms the commanding role of the Scots in education. At that same university, they were responsible for the foundation of a large number of schools, including chemistry, philosophy and veterinary sciences. It is almost redundant to add that the prestigious Scots College was founded, in the 1890s, by Presbyterian Scots (note: the students still wear kilts).

Was it the Presbyterian ethos of hard work and saving – and the desire to become financially successful – that made Scottish immigrants leading figures in finance, banking and industry. They were behind the establishment of AMP and Colonial Mutual, the Colonial Sugar Refining Company (CSR) and one of the Australian icons, biscuit giant Arnotts, the highly successful family business started by William Arnott in 1865.

In the media, there is no better example than Rupert Murdoch, whose father Sir Keith, a Presbyterian from Aberdeen, was the founding father of News Ltd. In the arts the Scottish blood flows in such talented Australian heroes as opera singers Nellie Melba and Joan Sutherland, and poet Les Murray.

More than 125 years have elapsed since the first Sydney Highland Gathering was celebrated in Redfern, and since then there has only been one year that this wonderful festival was not celebrated – that was in 1962, a turning point for the Sydney Scottish Community. It was the year when the most important Scottish organisation in Sydney was founded – the Combined Scottish Society. The Society – which unites more than 40 Clan Societies – has made possible the continuation (from 1963) of one of the most traditional cultural and social celebrations of our city.

"To any questions about what is worn under your kilt: avoid responding with the cliche 'Nothing is worn under my kilt. Everything is in fine working order." Similarly, do not offer any demonstration of what is worn under your kilt.

"And an offer such as 'I'll show you mine if you'll show me yours' can be misconstrued as the opening salvo in an ever escalating series of challenges and exhibitions which may be illegal in public, even between consenting adults." ('Kilt Etiquette' by Colin Wallace, *The Scottish Banner*)

PUBS

SIR WILLIAM WALLACE HOTEL.
Well... it may or may not be a Scottish pub, but with that name and the huge poster of a kilted Mel Gibson as William Wallace in the epic *Braveheart*, who could argue against it. According to the Hotel's regular patrons, 'Mad' Mel Gibson used to drop by here when he lived in the area, and it seems that with a schooner in hand he knew that one day he would play the role of the Scottish rebel.

31 Cameron Street, Birchgrove
(tel: 9555 8570).

Shops

Havelock Meats. 'A wee bit o' Scotland near ye...' – this is what this butchery (and bakery) is all about. The Scottish meat pies and the hearty potato scones are more than a quick fix. Now if you want to get to know Scottish cuisine you should start with *haggis* – the Scottish national dish made, according to the dictionary, 'from sheep's or calf's offal, oatmeal, suet and seasoning boiled in a skin made from the animal's stomach (origin unknown)'. Drop by at Havelock Meats and check for yourself if the description is accurate.
Open Monday-Friday 8am-7pm, Saturday 7am-2pm.
7 Havelock Avenue, Coogee (tel: 9665 1390).

Scottish Clan Tartan. The Scottish-born Jonathon Fowler established his business 11 years ago and it's getting better and better. And his accent is more Aussie than ever: 'nobody understands a Scottish accent, mate', he jokes. His huge range of Scottish gear including superb kilts, clan crests (large and small), kilt pins, sporrans, clan ties and clan jewellery – from Anderson to Wallace. You can even hire a kilt for your Scottish party. Imported food – shortbreads of course – and music from Glasgow keep Scots coming.
Open Monday-Sunday 9.30am-5.50pm.
Shop 18A, Birkenhead Point, Drummoyne (tel: 9819 7208).

Getting to know the Scottish community

Events

Robbie Burns Night.

On January 25 the Sydney Scottish community gets together to celebrate the memory of Robert Burns, Scotland's national poet. His poems and songs, strongly inspired by traditional Scottish music, help to preserve folk songs and ballads from Scotland. The evening includes a special toast in his honour.

Further information: Scottish Society & Burns Club (tel: 9949 1417).

Bundanoon Highland Gathering.

Only two hours drive south from Sydney, Bundanoon ('a place of deep gullies') is Scottish from top to bottom. It's a town where men walk down the streets in 'skirts' and the sound of bagpipes breaks the silence of the Southern Highlands. Annually, in April (the week after Easter) Bundanoon receives thousands of visitors attracted by one of the most authentic Highland gatherings in the antipodes. Started in 1978 to raise funds for local charities and community groups, the gathering – which attracts 20,000 spectators – features street parades of massed bands, dancing displays, a highland dress competition, haggis hurling and a program of cultural activities. Trains to the Southern Highlands depart from Sydney's Central Station regularly every day (call the Public Transport Infoline 13 1500).

For further information on the Festival, where to stay and how to get there: Southern Highlands Visitor Information Centre, Winifred Park West, Old Hume Highway, Mittagong (4871 2888 or 1800 656 176).

Scottish Week.

Organised by the Scottish Australian Heritage Council, this historical, cultural and religious event is celebrated annually at the end of November in Rawson Park, Gross Street, Mosman. The week of activities includes a gala day with more than 40 stalls packed with traditional Scottish food, bagpipe performances, highland dancing and woodchopping displays.

Further information: Scottish Australian Heritage Council (tel: 9220 6126).

Annual Highland Gathering.

This one-day Scottish festival plays an important part in keeping alive the ancient traditions of the Scots in Australia. Celebrated on November 30 in Drummoyne Park, Drummoyne, it includes dancing contests, pipe band championships, a display of Scottish country dancing, and 'heavy events championship' (a boat pull, plane pull and truck pull, hammer and caber throwing). So don't miss the opportunity to shake the hand of David Huxley – our Scottish Heavy Events champ – who a few years ago pulled the Concorde a few inches! Activities start at 10am; all welcome.

Further information: Combined Scottish Societies of NSW, 80 Menzies Road, Eastwood (tel: 9869 1499).

Whenever Sydney's Scottish Clans gather the kilt and the bagpipe colour the moment.

Community organisations

The Combined Scottish Societies of NSW Inc.

Founded in 1963, the Society is made up of various clan societies, local district societies such as Drummoyne Scottish, Eastwood Scottish, Orkney and Shetland, or specific groups such as the Burns Club or the Scottish Country Dancers. All the constituent groups of the Society promote Scottish culture through music, dance and language, and in particular by upholding the tradition of the Highland Gathering.

Further information: Combined Scottish Societies of NSW (tel: 9869 1499).

Scottish Australian Heritage Council.

Formed in 1981, the Council promotes the role played by Scottish migrants and their descendants in the growth and development of Australian society. The Council is behind the organisation of the annual Sydney Scottish Week.

55 Cronulla Street, Cronulla (tel: 9523 6877).

Scottish heritage is in the bones of many of Sydney's institutional pillars.

Media

Newspapers

The Scottish Banner. Claims to be the largest Scottish newspaper in the world outside Scotland. Published in North America, this 21-year-old publication covers the Scottish community in USA, Canada, New Zealand and Australia. It produces a calendar of Scottish events in the above-mentioned countries, and for those searching for their 'Scottishness' there is a section dedicated to information on the Clans. It also covers issues happening back in Scotland. The paper is published monthly and can be found in most Sydney newsagencies at a cost of $2.50.

Further information: contact the paper's Australian correspondent Bob Brian (tel: (03) 9874 4757).

The Australasian Highlander. Published since 1970, this is a magazine for those interested in Scottish cultural community activities. Published in English, it covers news and community information from all over Australia. Quarterly; cost $2.

The current editor is C. McEwan (tel: (02) 4952 6533).

Explore the world in one city

The Irish

When the Irish spilled onto Australian shores, first as convicts and later as free settlers, they brought with them the *craic* – the sense of fun, even in the face of adversity. Many would say that in pursuing the *craic*, Irish immigrants were responsible for the amazing growth of corner pubs that dotted the Sydney urban landscape, and also were behind the establishment of the first racecourse in Sydney.

They brought with them those elements that many claim as essential to the Australian character – independence, anti-authoritarianism, a love of fun and freedom, generosity and a good dose of larrikinism. In the history of Australia, Irish have been involved whenever God and politics were on the agenda.

Irish convicts were in the first Fleet in 1788, and it's estimated that about 23 per cent of the estimated 160,000 convicts shipped to the Australian colonies between 1788 and 1868 were Irish. While the largest majority were simply criminals, there were also a significant number of political prisoners from the 1798, 1848 and 1867 Irish uprisings. They were Irish rebels seen with apprehension and distrust, and a threat to the British establishment. It was not groundless: in 1804, 300 Irish led by Philip Cunningham rallied menacingly on Parramatta on March 4. This early uprising – the Castle Hill rebellion – was violently crushed and some of the agitators were hanged, including Cunningham.

Nowadays around seven million Australians claim direct Irish background, ranking second only behind the English.

Although Irish immigration has continued right through till today, it was heavily concentrated in the nineteenth century – especially between the 1850s and 1892. Behind this influx was the Great Hunger that began with the potato blight of 1847, when two million Irish died and another two million emigrated. Even though the majority made their way to the US and Canada – the fare was cheaper – a considerable number came to Australia under an assisted passage scheme. At their arrival, Irish immigrants suffered ethnic prejudice, hostility and anti-Catholic phobia from the English rulers. They were the early "wogs" of our history.

IT WAS AN IRISH SCULPTOR – John Hughes – who made the massive bronze sculpture of Queen Victoria, located outside the magnificent Queen Victoria Building on George Street, in the heart of Sydney. Created in 1908, this familiar Sydney sculpture was installed originally at Leinster House in Dublin. In 1948 it was removed and sent to a storehouse where it spent almost 40 years – until the 1980s – when the dust was removed and a new location was found, here in Sydney.

It's estimated that half a million Irish emigrated to our shores in the nineteenth century. Interestingly enough, a large proportion of them were young Irish single women (in the later part of that century there were six Irish women immigrants for every Irish man) who found work as servants. In the hostile environment that Irish women and men found they felt the need to assert the value of their culture, so the first Irish associations – such as the Shamrock and the Irish National Club – emerged at the end of the century. They were venues for solidarity, and also where the *craic* – drinking, dancing and singing – was found. These venues – especially the Irish Club – were also good places to find single Irish girls – it was not for nothing that the club was better known as the "Irish marriage bureau."

By the end of the century the inner-city areas of Chippendale, Redfern and notably Surry Hills – especially along Devonshire Street, where the Irish National Association is still found – were where Sydney's Irish community life flourished. Irish residents of these areas made substantial contributions to the growth and strengthening of Sydney's Catholic inner-city parishes through membership, priesthood and support of Catholic primary schools – a system developed in Australia by the Irish.

By the 1891 Census, just a year after the date when historians mark the "alliance" between Irish Catholics and the Australian Labour Party, Irish immigration reached its peak to a total of 227,698. From that year onward the number of Irish-born began a steady decline, reaching a low point of 44,813 in the 1947 Census. Incidentally, the relationship between the ALP and Irish Catholics, already strained by Catholic opposition to the Communist presence in the unions, was brought to an end in 1964 when a Liberal government under Menzies began funding private schools – an aspiration long felt by the very militant Irish-born Cardinal Daniel Mannix.

Even though the Irish immigration has declined significantly since the early years of this century, by 1991 there were still more than 50,000 Irish-born living in Australia. Nowadays around seven million Australians claim Irish background, ranking second behind the English. It's a question of pride – just take a look at the streets of Sydney on St Patrick's Day when everyone from the clerk at the post-office to the underground cable construction worker (a sector dominated by Sydney Irish since the 1960s) – reaffirms their profound Irishness with a shamrock attached to their clothing, a hearty Guinness in their hand and with a misty and evocative Irish ballad issuing from their throats.

Restaurants

Mulligan's. This place gains an entry for two major reasons. Firstly, it's the best place to discover Irish cuisine without spending 24 hours on a plane, and secondly it's the only place in town where Tony Moore – the Pluto Press publisher – can order bread and butter pudding "like the one cooked by Mum". Mulligan's, located on busy Cleveland Street, is all about Irish tradition – stew, cabbage and bacon. Live Irish music on Friday & Saturday from 8.30pm. Average $25, BYO. Open Wednesday-Saturday dinner 6pm-till late.

137 Cleveland Street, Chippendale (tel: 9319 5582).

Berowra Waters Boatshed. A visit to this self-proclaimed 'seafood restaurant with a touch of Irish' involves a trip out of town. Located at Berowra Waters, in the lower reaches of the Hawkesbury River and about 12 km from Sydney, this picturesque restaurant, in the heart of a National Park, offers some interesting dishes. A tip: try the flamed garlic steak with Irish whiskey and the Irish curd cheese. Don't miss the Sunday lunch fixed price deal, three courses at $35 per person. Average $25, BYO. Open lunch Wednesday-Sunday; dinner Friday-Saturday (opening hours vary, according to demand).

Berowra Waters Road (right beside the ferry), Berowra Waters (tel: 9456 1025).

A glass of Guinness is very much part of the Irish *craic*.

Irish Pubs

When the *craic* is what you're looking for, Sydney is well stocked with a profusion of Irish pubs scattered across the city and the suburbs. If you're looking for a glass of Guinness, Irish whiskey, or just Irish music, these pubs are the places to go. Be they up or down market – most of them feature live traditional and modern Irish music performed by some of the dozen Irish bands existing in Sydney. As a general rule in terms of trading hours, most of the Irish pubs open between 10am and close after 11pm on weekdays (a few of them past midnight) and – as expected – till very late on weekends. The following is just a selected list. For very comprehensive information on the Sydney Irish *craic*, get the *Irish Echo* ($2.50), which is sold in most newsagencies.

Brendan Behan Hotel. Formerly known as the Brittania Hotel, this relatively new Irish spot has been named after the (in)famous Irish playwright Brendan Behan. However there isn't anything infamous about this place. The live music – Thursday to Sunday – and the friendly atmosphere make the Brendan a good place to have a good time. Drop by on Sunday for a traditional Sunday roast ($8.00).

103 Cleveland Street, Chippendale (tel: 9699 5315).

Bridie O'Reilly's. In three locations – we vote for the one located next to the Capitol Theatre, just across the road from the Czech deli Cyril's. This a good spot to have a cold beer after strolling around nearby Chinatown.

Corner George and Hay Streets, Haymarket (tel: 9212 2111).
Located also at Corner Kent and Erskine Streets, City (tel: 9279 3133).
and at "Star City" Casino Complex, Pyrmont Bay (tel: 9660 9777).

Hero of Waterloo Hotel. This historic and picturesque old inn makes space for live Irish music from Friday to Sunday.
Open Monday-Saturday 10am-1am, Sunday 10am-10pm.

81 Lower Fort Street, Millers Point (tel: 9252 4553).

Kitty O'Shea's. Named after the legendary pub in Dublin, this is one of the most recognisable and busy Irish pubs in Sydney. Kitty O'Shea's claims to have the highest Guinness sales in Australia. There's live Irish sports via satellite and live Irish music six nights a week.

384 Oxford Street, Paddington (tel: 9360 9668).

O'Malley's Hotel. Very, very, very crowded with backpackers staying in the nearby hostels. Sydney bands, playing traditional and modern Irish music, are one of the main attractions of this spot.

228 William Street, Kings Cross (tel: 9357 2211).

Saint Patrick's Tavern. One of the best known Irish nightclubs in Sydney. Live Irish music from Tuesday to Sunday. Check the daily happy hour from 4pm.

66 King Street, City (tel: 9262 3277).

Siobhan's Irish Bar. At the Cock'n'Bull Hotel, it's a good place to listen to live traditional and modern Irish music every Friday and Sunday, with performances from some of the best known Sydney Irish bands such as Celtic City Sons and Molly Rasher. Guinness and Killian's on tap. Open till 2am on Thursday-Saturday and till midnight on Sunday.

89 Ebley Street, Bondi (tel: 9389 3004).

The Illinois. Home of Aisteoiri Irish Theatre and of the well-reputed Celtic Kitchen Bistro, The Illinois is Irish to the bone. On Monday you can get Irish music lessons, on Thursday everybody gets misty-eyed with a session of Irish ballads, and the craic doesn't fade on Saturday or Sunday either. Open Monday-Sunday 10am-1.30am.

15 Parramatta Road, Five Dock (tel: 9797 9822).

As Irish as a glass of Guinness.

SCRUFFY MURPHY'S.
The dim lit music venue in this Irish city pub has live entertainment seven days a week, with the likes of Molly Rasher, The Kid and Rattle & Hum.
On Monday, after 8pm, there is an international backpackers night gathering featuring Irish live music, giveaways and beer promotion. Guinness on tap.

Corner George and Goulburn Street
(tel: 9211 2002).

Explore the world in one city

The Mercantile Hotel. One of the most popular and renowned Irish venues in Sydney. At the Mercantile the Irish music and the Guinness on tap guarantee a good time. Live music Monday - Sunday with the best Irish bands in Sydney, including Hooley Band and Blind Mary. Open Sunday-Thursday 10am-midnight, Friday-Saturday 10am-1am.
25 George Street North, The Rocks (tel: 9247 3570).

The Friend in Hand. See "Glebe" page 37. Open Monday-Saturday 10am-midnight, Sunday 12noon-10pm.
58 Cowper Street, Glebe (tel: 9660 2326).

Shops

McDonagh's Irish Butchers. Sydney Irish know that here they have the certainty that the boiling bacon is fresh, the black and white pudding is tasty and the Irish pork sausages are irresistible. Open Monday-Friday 6am-6.30pm, Saturday 6am-2pm.
294 North Road, Eastwood (tel: 9874 6879).

Emerald Meats. Considered by the specialists as one of the best butchers in Sydney, Emerald Meats is as Irish as the extensive selection of food available here – including boiling bacon, Irish sausages, home-cooked hams and white and black pudding.
Open Monday-Friday 5am-7pm, Saturday 5am-2pm.
18 Lawrence Street, Harbord (tel: 9905 3224).

Irish Design Centre. Located in the tourist area of The Rocks, this tiny and charming Irish-owned shop sells just about everything related to Ireland and Irish – Bewley's tea and coffee, china, jumpers and hats, books on Irish history, CDs, videos and more. Open Monday-Sunday 10am-5pm.
111 George Street, The Rocks (tel: 9247 3233).

The Irish Shop. At this gift, souvenir and deli shop – all in one – you'll find a small but good selection of traditional Irish teas, jams and marmalades (check out also the much sought after Irish mustard). Also available is Irish music, videos, history and recipe books. When tweed is making a come back with a vengeance, this shop imports quality clothing, including wool jackets, chunky turtlenecks, scarfs and hats. Now, if you have in mind an audition for Riverdance, the Irish Shop has a basket full of hard shoes to choose from (no optional colour, just black).
Open Monday-Saturday 9am-5.00pm (till 8pm on Thursday), Sunday 10am-4pm.
Glasshouse Shopping Centre, 5th Floor, Pitt Street Mall (tel: 9231 1600).

CLUB

GAELIC CLUB. At the Gaelic Club – located in what was years ago one of the traditional Irish enclaves in Sydney – you can expect anything from a nationalist speech to a simple invitation to enjoy a gigantic glass of Guinness. Entertainment every Saturday night (free admission). Irish classes are also held at the club every Tuesday at 8pm. Fully licence. All welcome.
64 Devonshire Street, Surry Hills
(tel: 9212 1587).

USEFUL NUMBERS FOR VISITORS

IRISH TOURIST BOARD,
tel: (02) 9299 6177

tel: (02) 9299 6177

Landmark

Irish Monument at Waverley Cemetery

This very impressive marble, bronze and mosaic monument, standing in the centre of Waverley Cemetery, is arguably the most significant Irish monument in Australia. Built in 1898, the monument is a memorial to those who participated in the 1798 Irish rebellion. It contains the bodies of Michael Dwyer – one of the leaders of the uprising – and his wife Mary. At the back of the monument, where the leaders of the 1798 uprising are listed, there is one blank space. This is the memorial to Robert Emmet, who insisted after his capture by the British: "Let no man write my epitaph... until Ireland takes its place among the nations of the world." In 1948 the names of 17 Irish men who participated in the 1916 Easter Uprising in Dublin were added on the wall of the lower part of the monument. The memorial, funded by the Irish and their descendants in Australia and New Zealand, is about to be proposed for World Heritage Listing. 'People of Ireland, treasure the memory of the deeds of your ancestors. The warriors die but the true cause lasts for ever' reads an inscription in the Irish language on the memorial's east wall facing the sea. You can find more information about the history of this monument at Waverley Library, 14-26 Ebley Street, Waverley (tel: 9389 1111).

Waverley Cemetery, bordered by Trafalgar, St Thomas and Boundary Streets, Bronte (tel: 9369 8193).

Getting to Know the Irish Community

Events

St. Patrick's Day.

The Rocks, where there are pubs are on every block is the focal point for St Patrick's Day, the most important celebration in the Irish calendar. Usually held on March 17, this festival of Irish pride features the best of the Irish craic – drinks, food, music and dance. The Parade, with bands, pipers and dancers, is the climax of this traditional celebration. The legend tells that 1,600 years ago more or less, St Patrick was able to convince every single snake existing in Ireland to get into tiny wooden boxes which he chucked into the sea. Just a tale. The real reason for St Patrick's sainthood is that he converted Ireland's pagans to Christianity. The Guinness bit of the celebration is surely the 'pagan' side. The key areas to be for this celebration are Town Hall and Hyde Park south below Elizabeth and Bathurst streets. Also check out the music and dance concert - from 1-9pm - generally held in Prince Alfred Park near Central Station. Entry is free.

For additional information call the Irish National Association (tel: 9211 3410).

1916 Easter Sunday Uprising Mass.

Celebrated for the first time on Easter Sunday 1900 and held at the Waverley Cemetery Irish Monument, this Catholic service commemorates the Easter Uprising in Dublin in 1916. The service begins at 3pm.

For further information contact the Irish National Association (tel: 9211 3410).

Yulefest.

Although a bit away from Sydney – in the Blue Mountains – and not uniquely Irish, this June-August Christmas celebration is notable as it was initiated around 17 years ago by a group of Irish tourists longing for a winter Christmas. Hotels and restaurants offer special Christmas fare at this time.

For further information contact the Blue Mountains Tourism Authority, Great Western Hwy, Glenbrook, Echo Point Road, Katoomba (tel: 047- 39 6266).

Community Organisations

Irish National Association.

An umbrella organisation for Sydney Irish community organisations, it provides social assistance, advice and organises cultural and social activities.

64 Devonshire Street, Surry Hills (tel: 9212 1587).

Sydney Irish Welfare Bureau & Resource Centre.

Provides advice and support to Irish immigrants, with special emphasis on young and elderly Irish living here. A drop-in centre functions on Tuesdays between 10am-2pm.

64 Devonshire Street, Surry Hills (tel: 018-433 661).

SYDNEY IRISH BANDS

CEILIDH.
It performs traditional and contemporary Irish folk music. Contact Malcolm (tel: 9632 7144).

IRISH DROVERS.
Irish folk and acoustic. Contact Myles (tel: 9599 1793).

TRIPPIN' ON TRAD.
Traditional Irish music. Contact Brian O'Kelly (tel: 9314 5942).

WAXIE'S DARGLE AND THE DARGLE RIVERDANCERS.
Irish folk music with traditional Irish dance. Contact Ted King (tel: 9529 8852).

Media

Newspaper

Irish Echo. Established originally in 1988 as *The Irish Exile*, the *Irish Echo* took on its current name in 1992. Published fortnightly, the *Irish Echo* covers contemporary Irish issues, sports, community news and the supplement – 'The Craic' – is without any doubt the definitive Irish Australian guide to arts and entertainment. By the way, in the current Australian constitutional change debate, *Irish Echo* has, not surprisingly, thrown its support in with the republican cause. $2.50. The current editor is Sue Bromley. PO Box 285, Balmain, NSW 2041 (tel: 9555 9199).

Radio Programmes

SBS Radio 1, AM 1107. Community information, news and music from Ireland, Wednesday 10-11pm.

WOW, FM 88.3. A Touch of Ireland, Sunday 10am-12noon.

2RDJ Radio, FM 88.1. Ireland Calling, Saturday, 6-10am.

2GLF, FM 89.3. Shades of Green, Wednesday 7.30-9pm.

2SER, FM 107.3. Sydney Irish Radio Programme, Sunday 7.30-9am.

2WKT Highland, FM 107.1. The Craic with Mac, Monday 6-8pm.

2NBC, FM 90.1. The Craic with Mac, Friday 12noon-1.30pm.

Television

Channel 31. Irish programme (Siamsa).

For further information contact the Celtic Television Productions (tel: 9686 3678).

The Austrians

International Modernism was not well known in Australian architecture until the Viennese-born Harry Seidler made his way to Australia in 1948. 'A Bauhaus emissary', a 'Messiah of Modernism' – there are many tags for Harry Seidler. He is not only one of the most influential Australian post-war architects, but also one of the most controversial.

Stroll the Sydney CBD and gaze up at his creations – the imposing MLC Centre in Martin Place; the highrise Australia Square, one of the world's tallest lightweight concrete office towers; Grosvenor Place, with its reptilian skin; the amazing Capita Building, with gardens on the 20th floor; and the highly controversial Blues Point Tower, standing in less-than magnificent solitude on McMahons Point. Harry Seidler is also the designer of the Australian Embassy in Paris. The earliest work in Australia by this Austrian-Australian (or is it the other way round?) was the house that he built for his mother, Rose, in the late 1950s. A celebration of modernism, the design received the prestigious Sulman Prize. The Rose Seidler House is now a museum open to the public (see page 81).

The same year in which Harry Seidler came, another Viennese-born, a 13-year-old girl named Eva, arrived in Sydney. Soon she was attending Bondi Beach public school, where she was instantly dubbed a 'reffo'. This girl was Eva Cox – now one of Australia's most lucid social commentators. Her essay *A Truly Civil Society* has become compulsory reading for those concerned with the future of our society.

The earliest arrival of Austrians in Australia goes back to the early 1880s when the botanical artist, Ferdinand Lukas Bauer, was appointed to accompany Matthew Flinders on the investigator's voyage to Australia. He was followed by his fellow countryman, John Lhotski, who arrived in Sydney in 1832 and carried out botanical and geological studies.

One of the first Austrians to settle in Sydney was a Viennese accountant, Emil Hansel, who arrived in 1889. He worked in an Austrian import firm, then went gold-digging in West Wyalong in western NSW before

Many post-World II War Austrian refugees ('reffos' - as they were called) settled initially in Kings Cross. Here the proximity of the city and the cosmopolitan lifestyle reminded them of the life that they left behind.

HARRY SEIDLER, Australia's most famous architect was born in Vienna in 1923 and emigrated to Australia in 1948. Seidler's designs in Sydney include Australia Square, the MLC Centre and the Blues Point Tower, Grosvenor Place. Check out also, his latest work: the impressive and contemporary design of The Horizon towers - at the William Street end of Darlinghurst.

finally working for the Austrian-Hungarian Consulate. He married an Australian woman and returned to Austria in 1905.

More substantial Austrian immigration to Australia, in terms of its impact in a wide range of fields, occurred at the end of the 1930s, after Hitler annexed Austria, and again after World War II. From the thousands of Austrians who fled the country – a large percentage of them Jews – some of them made it all the way Down Under. Arriving in Sydney loaded with their beloved belongings (including their trademark long winter raincoats that denounced them as 'reffos') the Austrians settled in Kings Cross. Here, the proximity of the city and the cosmopolitan lifestyle reminded them of the life that they left behind. However, the Cross was only temporary. Gradually they left their rented flats and moved to houses in the eastern suburbs of Double Bay, Vaucluse, Bondi and Coogee. Others moved to the lower North Shore suburbs of Lindfield and Roseville. Always they found ways to keep in touch, particularly through the coffee shops they established in Sydney. One of the most popular of that time was Claridge's, in George Street.

Two marvellous Austrian sculptors chose to come to Australia at that time, Herbert Flugelman and Arthur Fleischman. Flugelman, who arrived in Sydney in 1938, is one of Australia's best-known artists. His works include 'The Pyramids', the stainless steel sculpture situated in Martin Place. Fleischman arrived in Sydney the year after, in 1939. He designed the magnificent bronze doors of the New South Wales State Library that depict the early Australian explorers. He also made the relief sculptures of David Scott Mitchell and Sir William Dixson located at the same library. Other works of this talented Viennese-born artist can be seen at the Conservatorium of Music (the bust of Dr E. Baiton) and in the Royal Botanic Gardens.

The year 1939 also saw the arrival of a seven-year-old boy called Gustav Nossal, with his parents and two elder brothers. He would become Sir Gustav Nossal – one of Australia's greatest scientists. With a career spanning more than 50 years, Dr Nossal has been behind some outstanding scientific research projects, including work for the World Health Organisation on tropical diseases and immunisation for people in the Third World.

The same year of his arrival, an exiled Viennese viola player called Richard Goldner also started a new life here. A man with an agile mind and brilliant teaching skills, he gave Sydney that wonderful and most revered institution, Musica Viva. British author Norman Lebrench writes: "The best success story of musical regeneration in modern times took place in Australia where, on December 8, 1945, an exiled Viennese viola player called Richard Goldner put on a chamber music concert with money he earned from inventing a clothes fastener. Whipping sixteen fellow refugees into weekly rehearsals for three months, the zip maker stunned an unsophisticated audience in a half blacked out conservatory hall with a performance that was the best rehearsed of any given in Sydney in the memory of the oldest critic". (*When the Music Stops*, Simon & Schuster, 1996). Musica Viva is now the largest chamber music organisation in the world.

The outbreak of War World II was a turning point for the Austrians living here. Many of them were declared 'enemy aliens' and lost their refugee status. It was not until 1944 that they were reclassified as 'friendly aliens', mainly through the efforts of one of the first Austrian organisations in Sydney, the Free Austrian Committee, founded in 1940. Another organisation that played an important role in establishing the loyalty of the local Austrians was the Free Austria League, which was set up in 1944.

The years following the end of the conflict saw a large number of Austrians arriving under the Assisted Passage Scheme. Between 1947 and 1954 the Austrian immigrant population increased from around 4,000 to nearly 11,000. By 1961 this number had doubled. Like the post-war German immigrants, Austrians who worked in skilled trades settled in the western suburbs of Sydney, where cheap house-land packages were available in the 1950s and early 1960s.

As in the pre-war period, the post-war Australia boasted some very talented Austrian immigrants. Dr Eric Gross, for example, arrived in 1952 and developed a successful career as a composer and academic, while Rudi Komon – one of the best-known art gallery proprietors in Sydney – arrived a year later (his portrait, painted by Eric Smith, won the 1981 Archibald Prize).

Following the arrival of a large number of Austrian immigrants, community life began taking shape with the establishment of several cultural and community organisations and the foundation of several newspapers. In 1946, prominent Austrian journalist, Wilhelm Krieger, started the first Sydney Austrian newspaper, *New Citizen*. In 1958, a theatre company, Die Kammerspiele, was founded. One of the all-time favourite spots of the Sydney Austrian community, the Austrian Club, was founded in 1961 at 20 Grattan Crescent, Frenchs Forest. It was followed in 1963 by the Austrian-Australian Cultural Society, begun by the tireless Gery Felser. Austrian restaurants and coffee shops began popping up around Sydney. One of the best-known Austrian venues, Una's Coffee Lounge (formerly Una's Continental) opened its doors about this time, at 340 Victoria Street, Darlinghust.

EVA COX, one of the most influential social commentators, remembers being called 'reffo' at Bondi Beach public school were she was enrolled soon after arriving in Sydney in 1948. Australia was the final stop for Eva Cox and her family in a journey that began when they escaped from Nazi occupied Austria at the end of the 1930s. One of the most influential and astute social commentators in the country, Eva Cox is also a respected academic at the University of Technology, Sydney (UTS). A member in the 1950s of the bohemian underworld of the Sydney Push, she's the author of *A Truly Civil Society*, an essay presented for the ABC Boyer Lectures, that deals with the central issues of tolerance, acceptance, social participation and the ability to debate.

After the 1970s, Austrian immigration began to decline. With a solid improvement in the Austrian economy less Austrians tended to emigrate. From 24,000 in 1961, the Austrian-born population decreased to 23,000 in 1981. This tendency continued over the following years, accelerated by the numbers returning to Austria. Currently, there are about 5,700 Austrians living in Sydney. This number increases substantially, though temporarily, with enthusiastic tourists, creative artists and modern adventurers eager to have glance at the country whose name is constantly mistaken for that of their own.

Restaurants and Cafes

Kaiserstub'n. The accent is very definitely Austrian – herring salad, meat dumplings and sauerkraut are specialities. Average $30, licensed and BYO. Open Wednesday-Sunday, lunch noon-2.30pm and dinner 6pm till late.

205 Mona Vale Road, Mona Vale (tel: 9450 0300).

Una's. Owned by the Austrian-born Anne Helbling and established in the early 1970s, Una's has been consistently reviewed as one of the best (and largest) breakfast spots in Sydney. If you're really hungry go for the Big Breakfast of bacon and eggs and fried tomato plus two sausages ($7.60). Average $9, BYO.
Open Monday-Saturday 6.30am-11pm, Sunday 8am-11pm.

340 Victoria Street, Darlinghurst (tel: 9360 6885).

Clubs

Austrian Club. Established in 1961 with the support of Professor Gery Felser, the Austrian Consul of the time, the Austrian Club holds regular cultural, social and sporting events, and the Club's restaurant is where you'll find the most authentic Austrian food in the antipodes. The restaurant opens for dinner Friday-Saturday 6-11pm, lunch and dinner Sunday noon-8pm. Average $30, licensed.

20 Grattan Crescent, Frenchs Forest (tel: 9452 3304).

See also The Germans, page 125

Landmarks and places of interest

Rose Seidler House.

Built between 1948 and 1950 for his parents Rose and Max, this is the first house that Austrian-born architect Harry Seidler designed in Australia. Shockingly modern, it was an immediate sensation. Imitators soon followed, and the early admiration for Harry Seidler in architectural circles soon became veneration. The house is basically a box suspended on steel columns with glass walls, sandstone and strong primary colours sitting amid the luxuriant vegetation of the North Shore bush. It's widely told that even though the house was built for his parents, Harry Seidler wouldn't allow them to decorate it with their old European furniture because that didn't suit the modernism of his masterpiece. The capriciousness of a genius? You can visit this museum on Sundays 10am-4.30pm or by appointment at other times. If travelling by public transport take a 575 bus. Admission $5 adults and $3 children.

71 Clissold Road, Wahroonga (tel: 9487 1771).

USEFUL NUMBERS FOR VISITORS

AUSTRIAN CONSULATE:
tel 9567 1008.

AUSTRIAN NATIONAL TOURIST OFFICE:
tel 9299 3621.

Getting to know the Austrian community

Events

Austrian National Day.

On October 26 the Austrian community commemorates the passing of the 1955 law that ensured Austria's permanent neutrality. The law was passed immediately after the last of the Allied forces left Austria in 1955. Special celebrations are held at the Austrian Club.

Further information: tel 9452 3304.

The Croatians

He's so good that the Croatian president himself, Franjo Tujman, came here to secure his signature for his beloved club Zagreb, in 1995. In soccer circles this is what you probably would be told about Mark Viduka – hailed today as one of the most talented soccer players in Australia.

From a Croatian background, Viduka is a $1 million-a-season player who was courted by the wealthiest soccer clubs in the word, including the English Premier League champions, Manchester United and the Spanish League's glamour team Real Madrid. 'A proud Australian' – in his own words – Mark Viduka is scoring goals and more goals for his club, Croatia and making President Tujman a very happy man.

The very talented and controversial Croatian-Australian sculptor Drago Martin Cherina came to Australia in 1975 to do a bust of the then Prime Minster, Gough Whitlam. He liked the country and decided to stay. His sculptures can be seen in the world's major capital cities. His bronze sculpture of the former Soviet Union dissident Alexander Solzhenitsyn can be seen in the National Gallery in Canberra.

Early days

The gold rushes of the mid-1880s brought the first Croatian immigrants to Australia – Nick Antikovic and Nicholas Milovic. Antikovic came from the Ballarat goldrush to settle in Sydney where he married an Irish woman and worked as a wharf labourer. Among the Croatian immigrants arriving in Sydney in the late 1880s was Baldo Kunic. He moved to Young and became known as the 'Cherry King' due to his early contribution to cherry production in that district. Many Croatians arriving in Australia during that period moved to Broken Hill to work in the mines. The first Catholic priest appointed to Broken Hill, Father P Zundolic, spoke Croatian. The Croatian miners played an important role in the strike of 1919 which reduced the miners' working week from 40 to 35 hours.

In Sydney, the Croatian community did not expand significantly until the 1930s, when many miners lost their jobs in the Broken Hill mines. Some of them moved to Sydney and many of these set up market gardens in the northern beaches suburb of Warriewood; by 1940 there were 1,500 glass houses in the suburb. Later Croatian market gardeners spread to the western suburbs of Cabramatta, Blacktown and Leppington.

During this period numerous clubs were established, such as the Orijen and Club Zora. These clubs were all affiliated with the FYIA (Federation of Yugoslav Immigrants in Australia), which was initially established as the Yugoslav Progressive Workers Association in Broken Hill. When the Association moved its headquarters to Sydney, it developed a lending library and produced its own newspaper, *Napredak* ('Forward').

The war and beyond

When World War I broke out, many Croatian immigrants were interned as enemy aliens because they had travelled to Australia with Austrian passports. One of the internment camps was at Liverpool, in western Sydney, where approximately 1,000 internees, including Croatians, were held.

The period following the Second World War saw great changes in the Croatian community due to large-scale immigration. Many immigrants arrived as 'displaced persons' who had to accept one or two-year work contracts in Australia in logging camps, farms, mines or construction camps before being allowed to settle in this country. At the end of their contracts most settled in Sydney, Melbourne, Wollongong and Whyalla. The peak year for immigration was 1958, in what became known as the 'great wave' of Croatian immigration. In the late 1950s between 20,000 and 30,000 Croatian immigrants arrived.

The large post-war immigration saw the establishment of many community associations which reaffirmed a specifically Croatian character, emphasising both sporting and cultural activities. The first Australian Croatian Association was founded in the eastern suburb of Maroubra in 1951, and it was followed by Croatia House in inner-city Surry Hills in 1957. Croatian Catholic congregations were organised in the 1950s and today have a very strong presence in Summer Hill and in the western suburbs of St John Park and Blacktown. A welfare association – Croatian Caritas – was set up in Sydney in 1952, and a co-operative of Croatian farmers was founded on land near Liverpool in 1958.

> The first Sydney-Croatian folkloric group was Koleda, founded in 1967 by the Croatian Club of Sydney. It was around this time, at the beginning of the 1970s that arguably the best-known Croatian club in Sydney-the King Tomislav Croatian Club – was built.

Sydney Croatians today

The first wave of Croatians mainly worked on labour-intensive schemes such as the Snowy Mountains Hydroelectric Scheme. The second great stream of Croatian immigration occurred in the 1960s and 1970s. They came from diverse backgrounds, with a mix of unskilled labourers and professionals.They often set up their own businesses once they became financially independent.

CLUBS

KING TOMISLAV.
One of the greatest achievements of the Sydney Croatian community, the King Tomislav Club is a venue for sport, cultural and educational activities. The restaurant offers affordable and typical Croatian dishes. Average $20, licensed. Open for lunch Monday-Friday 11am-3.30pm, dinner Friday 6pm till late, lunch Saturday 12.30pm-3.30pm.
223 Edensor Road, Edensor Park
(tel: 9610 6111).

THE CROATIAN CLUB.
Established in the mid-1950s, the original premises were located at Buckingham Street in inner-city Surry Hills. In 1983 it moved to its current location in the western suburb of Punchbowl. At the time of writing the Club was due to move to an even newer premises, so check before dropping by.
Canterbury Road (corner Punchbowl Road), Punchbowl
(tel: 9708 4699).

The 1960s saw the creation of folkloric groups and clubs, and the strengthening of Fairfield, in the west, as the main suburb for the Sydney Croatian settlement. The first folkloric group was Koleda, founded in 1967 by the Croatian Club of Sydney. It was around this time, at the beginning of the 1970s, that arguably the best-known Croatian club in Sydney – The King Tomislav Croatian Club – was built. The Club's park is the current home ground of the other central institution of the Sydney Croats, Sydney United (former Sydney Croatia). Established in the 1970s, it remains one of the most successful soccer clubs in Australia – so successful, that the former leader of the Liberal Party, John Hewson, accepted in 1996 the offer to become chairman of the Club, an institution based in the Labor heartland of the outer western suburbs. 1983 was also an important year for the Sydney Croats as it was the year that the Centre for Croatian Studies at Macquarie University was established.

Sydney Croatians are proud not only of Mark Viduka but also of the sporting achievements of the Australian weightlifting gold medallist in the 1984 Los Angeles Olympic Games, Dean Lukin, and of Australia's brightest gymnastic prospect for the 2000 Sydney Olympics, Katarina Frketic. In many other arenas Croations manage to shine: academia, where Luka Budak, current Director of the Centre for Croatian Studies has made his mark; politics, with Australian Democrat Pero Lukunic playing a prominent role in society; and in the arts where sculptor Drago Marin Cherina has become – according to the critics – one of the greatest (and controversial) Australian sculptors of modern times.

Restaurants

Balkan Continental. Excellent grilled octopus and *cevapcici* (a little spicy sausage). Average $25, BYO. Open Wednesday-Monday 11am-11pm.
209 Oxford Street, Darlinghurst (tel: 9360 4970).

Balkan Seafood and Adriatic Restaurant. Grilled seafood is the speciality here. Average $25, BYO.
215 Oxford Street, Darlinghurst (tel: 9331 7670).

Shopping

Croatian Books. "We used to have more books, but we still have some," says the apologetic shop assistant at Croatian Books. Luckily, it also sells Croatian newspapers – ones published in Australia and ones from Croatia – magazines and lots of CDs of Croatian music.
5/8 The Crescent, Fairfield (tel: 9728 6207).

Ivan's Butchery. Established at the end of the 1970s and located in the multicultural Addison Road, Marrickville, Ivan's butchery is a feast of fresh meat and traditional Croatian smallgoods. Open Monday-Thursday 7.30am-5.30pm, Friday 6am-5.30pm and Saturday 6am-1pm.
220 Addison Road, Marrickville (tel: 9569 7751).

Getting to know the Croatian community

Events

Croatian National Day.
Held on May 30, this is a celebration of national pride, culture and tradition. The main activities are held in the Sydney Croatian clubs. For further information, ring some of the clubs listed in page 84.

Croatian Independence.
On 15 January 1992 Croatia was formally recognised as an independent state. Since 1994 a massive celebration has been held at the Sydney Town Hall, with local and federal politicians as regular attendants. The event includes a well-organised cultural program featuring folkloric music and dance.

Further information: Croatian community organisations (See page 87) or newspapers (See page 87) (we also suggest contacting Franjo Harmat, editor of *New Croatia*, 9212 3623).

Croatian Festival.
Organised by the Consulate General of the Republic of Croatia and the Australian Croatian Community this festival, which runs from April 21 to May 4, is an annual celebration of Croatian history, culture and tradition. Activities include a Croatian food festival, lectures, art exhibitions and a fashion parade.

Further information: 9299 8899.

Croatian Australian Literature Competition.
Run by the Croatian Australian Literature and Art Association, this is an annual event designed to highlight writers from the Croatian community, but it is also open to non-Croatian residents. "The award is modest but

USEFUL NUMBER FOR VISITORS

CROATIAN CONSULATE:
tel: 9299 8899

OTHER CROATIAN CLUBS IN SYDNEY

BOSNA ST. MARYS
(tel: 9670 4282).

BRACA RADIC SCHOFIELDS
(tel: 9627 2145).

DALMACIJA TERREY HILLS
(tel: 9450 1807).

I STRA LIVERPOOL
(tel: 9606 6996).

JARDRAN HAJDUK ST JOHNS PARK
(tel: 9610 1189).

ART AND CULTURE

ASSOCIATION OF CROATIAN FOLKLORIC GROUPS IN NSW.

The Association is responsible for organising concerts and festivals, and also develops workshops for educators of Croatian music and dance.

Further information:
Charlie Butkovic, the current president,
(tel: (042) 84 3402),
1 Elnathan Parade,
Mt Pleasant.

CROATIAN-AUSTRALIAN LITERATURE AND ART ASSOCIATION.

Established in 1991 this has become an important space for bilingual writing (English and Croatian). Each year it organises a short story and poetry competition (see Events, page 85). Membership open to everyone, for a modest $22.

Further information:
Anna Kumarich
(tel: 9588 4146),
PO Box 122,
Punchbowl 2196.

with the possibility of being published," explains Anna Kumarich, the current secretary of the Association. During the year, this organisation also holds evening readings of poetry and essays at various locations. Since the literary competition and the reading evenings don't have set days, contact Anna Kumarich for **further information** (tel: 9588 4146).

Religious organisations and places of worship

In the 1980s Croatians celebrated 13 centuries of Croatia's conversion to Christianity. Since these early times the Catholic Church has played a central role in the history and life of Croatian people. It is seen as the bastion of Croatian identity, responsible for the preservation and maintenance of its culture, language, traditions and customs. The first Croatian Catholic congregations in Australia were established in the 1950s, and every four years a bishop from the homeland visits Croatian Catholic centres in Australia. It is a time of great celebration.

Saint Nikola Tavelic Croatian Catholic Church.

Established in 1985, this church holds Croatian-language masses on Friday and Saturday at 6.30pm and on Sunday at 8.30am and 10.30am.

86-90 Brisbane Road, St Johns Park (tel: 9610 6770).

Croatian Catholic Centre.

Croatian-language masses are held here from Monday to Friday at 7pm, on Saturday at 9pm, and on Sunday at 9am and 10.30am.

15 Prospect Road, Summer Hill (tel: 9798 5220).

Our Lady's Church.

Croatian-language masses are held here from Monday to Friday at 7pm, on Saturday at 6pm, and 11am.

70 Douglas Road, Blacktown (tel: 9836 1792).

Education

Centre for Croatian Studies.

Part of the School of Modern Languages at Macquarie University, the Centre was established in 1998. It offers a program of 15 Croatian units, including language, art and history. This continues a 15 year history of Croatian Studies.

Further information: 9850 7049.

Community organisations

One of the first community organisations established in Sydney was the Croatian House in Surry Hills, in 1957. The Australian Croatian Association was first established in Maroubra.

Croatian Australian Welfare Centre.

Founded in 1980 by members of the king Tomislav Club. It provides social and welfare assistance to individuals and groups.

86-90 Brisbane Road, St Johns Park. (tel: 9610 1146).

Croatian Intercommittee Council of NSW.

Established to provide information and support to members of the Croatian community, the Council develops social and community projects in conjunction with government and non-government institutions. Its current president is Tomislav Beram.

PO Box 175, Punchbowl 2196 (tel: (047) 35 5513).

Media

Newspapers

Nova Hrvatska (New Croatia). 'Independent from any political party' is the way in which Franjo Harmant, the current editor, describes this weekly newspaper. It hits the stands on Tuesdays, has a circulation of 10,000 and costs $2.

PO Box K530, Haymarket, Sydney 2000 (tel: 9212 3623).

The Croatian Herald. Established in 1983, this is a national weekly based in Melbourne. Its current editor is Tom Starcevic.

PO Box 109 Clifton Hill Victoria, 3068 (tel: (03) 9481 8068).

Kloklan. An English-language Croatian paper covering a wide range of issues, including politics, sport, art and culture. The editor is Sime Dusevic.

PO Box 512, Bankstown 2200 (tel: 015 466 110).

SPREMNOST Established in 1957, it is the oldest Croatian Weekly in Australia. (tel: 9150 4074).

Radio

SBS Radio 1, AM 1107. News, current affairs, music and community anouncements. Monday 3-4pm, Tuesday 9-10pm, Wednesday-Saturday 8-9am.

CROATIAN CHARLES BILLICH is the official artist of the Australian Olympic team for the Sydney 2000 Games. He has two galleries at the Rocks in George Street.

2SER, FM 107.3. Music, sport and community news. Saturday 5pm-6pm and 9pm-10pm.

Croatian programs can also be heard on the following Sydney Community radio stations. Timeslots vary, so call for the latest information.

2RDJ FM, 88.1 (tel: 9744 32840)

2RRR FM, 88.5 (tel: 9816 2988)

2RSR FM, 88.9 (tel: 9550 9552)

Television

31 VHF Sydney's Community Television Broadcasts. A Croatian language program on Tuesdays 7.30-8.30pm. For further information: 018 975 128.

Facts and figures

The Sydney Croatian community is most numerous in the western suburb of Fairfield.

The exact number of Croatian immigrants is difficult to determine since the censuses haven't made distinctions in the birthplace data and Croats are frequently shown as Yugoslavs. However, a rough idea can be gained from the number of those who speak Croatian – currently 24,596 only in New South Wales.

Most Croatian immigrants have found work as skilled or semi-skilled labourers in the manufacturing industries, as well as in the community services sector.

According to the 1991 Census, 62.7 per cent of New South Wales Croatian immigrants held no qualifications. This lack of qualifications plus a low level of English proficiency is mirrored in the low level of income: 43 per cent have a household income of less than $40,000 per year and 22.1 per cent are in families with an income of less than $25,000 per annum.

Croatians are predominantly Catholic – 95.4 per cent – and the main language spoken is Croatian, which uses the Latin alphabet.

Explore the world in one city

The Czechs & Slovaks

The old Czechoslovakia, which arose from the remnants of the old Austro-Hungarian empire in October 1918, came to an end in 1992. Although the two groups have a history of violent struggles, the split of Czechoslovakia between the Czech Republic and Slovakia was done peacefully and with plenty of hope for the future. "We're still good friends, and fortunately we didn't go the way of the former Yugoslavia," says George Matysek, editor of the Sydney Czech's newspaper *Desedilede*.

A great number of citizens from the former Czechoslovakia arrived in Australia between 1948 and 1952 as post-war refugees. One of those Czechoslovakians who made his mark on history was the late Dr Karel Koenig, the oldest survivor of the wartime voyage to Australia of the infamous ship SS *Dunera*. Dr Koenig was a lawyer who had escaped to Britain, and was then forced to join 2,000 other refugees from Nazi persecution aboard the *Dunera*. On arrival, after a 57-day voyage, Dr Koenig was interned as a possible subversive! After his release, he resumed a law career and settled in North Sydney and later at Lindfield.

Currently there are about 5,800 migrants born in the former Czechoslovakia living in Sydney. Though census information does not differentiate Czechs and Slovaks, it is estimated that about three-quarters of these are Czechs. They tend to concentrate in the eastern suburb of Waverley and in the western suburbs of Blacktown, Fairfield and Penrith.

It was around July 1957 that Cyril's Delicatessen opened its doors. Located today on its original site at 183 Hay Street, Haymarket, it is a piece of Sydney Czech community history.

Czechs

"When people asked where I come from, I tell them that a true scientist belongs to the world, not a particular nation," the unforgettable Albrecht Adalbert (John) Racek used to say. He came to Australia as a penniless refugee in 1950 and went on to become a world authority in marine biology and geology. The first Czech to come to Australia was also a scientist. He was Tadeas Haenke, a botanist from Bohemia, visited our shores as part of a Spanish expedition that landed in Port Jackson in 1793.

As with the Czechs, the tragic events of 1948 and 1968 ('Prague Spring') led thousands of Slovaks to leave their country. Between 1948 and 1955 around 3,000 migrated to Australia mainly as refugees.

The first Czech resident was a convict, Mark Blutcher, who had been living in London and was transported to Australia in 1830, sentenced for seven years for stealing some lace. Two years later a fellow countryman, John Lhotsky, made his way to Australia. A scientist (another one!), he spent six years in Australia collecting minerals, plants and insects and visiting Aboriginal communities. He also explored the Australian Alps and left an account of this experience in his book *A Journey from Sydney to the Australian Alps*, published in 1835.

Although several Czechs came to Australia before and after the 1850s goldrush – such as Joseph Jilek, who owned a butchery in Sydney, and Cenek Paclt, a gold-digger who spent some time in New South Wales – it was not until the 1902 census that Czechoslovak-born people were counted, and there were only 264 counted at this time. This number increased in the years prior to War World II when a group of Czechs, some of them escaping from Nazism, arrived here. Among them was dancer and choreographer Edouard Borovansky, who came in 1939 and later become an influential figure in the development of Australian ballet.

When Cyril Vincenc, a native of Brno, came to Australia in 1949 as a displaced person he wasn't alone. Hundreds of his fellow Czechs left their country in the wake of Soviet occupation and a destroyed economy. After working four years part time in a Sydney smallgoods shop Cyril took the risk and established his own business; it was around July 1957 that Cyril's Delicatessen opened its doors. Located today still in its original place in the Haymarket, Cyril's Delicatessen is a living piece of Sydney Czech community history.

Cyril's Delicatessen of Czech delights in the heart of Sydney.

Czech immigrants have left their solid imprint in a wide range of fields. In arts several names come to mind, among them painter Paul Partos, violinist L Jasek, and gallery owner Rudy Kormos, whose Paddington art gallery exhibited the most acclaimed Australian artists between the 1950s and 1970s. Continuing the great scientific tradition begun way back in 1793, Dr George Rubinstein, the chief health officer of the NSW Department of Health, and Professor Paul Korner are two Czech immigrants whose work has had an enormous impact on our society.

Slovaks

Father Jakub Longa, a Jesuit, was the first Slovak to arrive in Australia. Sent by his Order in 1888, he tried without success to establish an Aboriginal mission at Daley Waters, Northern Territory. In 1910 another Slovak, scientist M R Stefanik, stopped briefly in Sydney while travelling to Tahiti to observe Halley's comet.

The first group of Slovak migrants, a group of 160 on board the German ship *Kvln*, arrived in Australia at the end of the 1920s. Ninety of them stayed in Sydney but soon after, because of a lack of work, they went to work in the bush. From then up to the outbreak of the War World II the local Slovak population grew steadily to about 350.

As with the Czechs, the tragic events of 1948 and 1968 ('Prague Spring') led thousands of Slovaks to leave their country. Between 1948 and 1955 around 3,000 migrated to Australia. At the end of 1950s about 4,000 new refugees entered the country, with another 1,200 arriving at the end of the 1960s.

Responding to the wave of post-war refugees, the Sydney Slovaks established the Australian Slovaks Association in December 1949, which, along with the Slovak Art Association and the Slovak Catholic Community, still plays an important role in keeping the Slovak spirit alive.

Restaurants and cafes

Czechoslovakian Country Club. Established in 1973, the Club is the main centre for Sydney Czechs and Slovaks. Cultural and social activities, including the celebration of the national day on October 28, are held here. The Club's restaurant is a charming country-style spot where the dumpling is king. Go for the hearty portions of traditional Czech foods, such as duckling, and pork with lots of dill gravy. Average $25, licensed. Open Saturday and Sunday noon-midnight.

30 Devonshire Road, Kemps Creek (tel: 9606 0904).

Slovak Catholic Community. This take-away stand operates on the premises of the Saints Cyril & Methodius Church on the first Sunday of each month. Come here to taste cheap, fresh and authentic Slovak food, cooked by members of the community. The potato dumplings are a must. Average $10. Open 8am-4pm.

Corner Olympic Drive and Vaughan Street, Lidcombe.
Further information: Maria Hupka (tel: 9604 2668).

Quaint. "It's the best place to have authentic Slovak food" says Maria Hupka, President of the Australian Slovaks Association. Quaint's owner, Eva, has done a good job with this unpretentious place. Try *kropova* (beef in dill gravy) or the timeless *svickova* (beef strogonoff). Average $20, BYO. Open Monday-Sunday, 7am-8pm.

195 Bondi Road, Bondi. (tel: 9387 4558)

CAFE PRALINKA.
A charming little cafe in Sydney's red light area. Try the delicious chicken *paprika* with rice.
Main courses around $8.
Open Tuesday-Saturday 11am-9pm.

4B Roslyn Street, Kings Cross (tel: 9358 1553).

USEFUL NUMBERS FOR VISITORS

CZECH AIRLINES:
tel 9247 6196

CZECH AND SLOVAK CONSULATE:
tel 9371 8878

Shopping

Cyril's Delicatessen. As you step into this Sydney icon you will not be able to take your eyes from the displayed delicacies, such as the exquisite goose liver, and the stock of jars with the best Czech goodies in town. Open Monday-Friday 6am-5.30pm, Saturday 6am-1pm.
183 Hay Street, Haymarket (tel: 9211 0994).

Kulhan Butcher. The hams, salami and sausages available here go best with rye bread and beer, we're told. Heavy stuff!
Open Monday-Friday 7am-5.30pm, Saturday 7am-1pm.
47 Sutherland Street, St Peters (tel: 9557 4076).

Getting to know the Czech and Slovak communities

Events

St Venceslao's Day Pilgrimage.

St Venceslao is the patron saint of the Czechs and his name has strong assocations, as the St Venceslao Square in Prague was the scene of the heroic 'Prague Spring' uprising. This annual event, held at the end of September, is run by the Australian Czech Orel and consists of a pilgrimage to the Schoenstatt Retreat Centre at 230 Fairlight Road, Mulgoa.
Further information: George Matysek (tel: 9918 0826).

Czechoslovakia Independence Day.

Observed on or about 28 October, this event is celebrated with music, dance and a lot of traditional food. The activities are held at the Czechoslovakian Country Club, 320 Devonshire Road, Kemps Creek.
Further information: Hana Gerzanic, Club president (tel: 9606 0904 at the Club, or 9607 8883 at home).

Slovak Day.

A celebration of national identity and pride, this event is celebrated by Sydney Slovaks on the last Sunday of November with a special mass held

at the Saints Cyril & Methodius Church, followed by a picnic. The celebration is organised by the Australian Slovaks Association.
Corner Olympic Drive and Vaughan Street, Lidcombe.
Further information: Maria Hupka (tel: 9604 2668).

Czech's Christmas Fair.

Organised by the Consulate General of the Czech Republic, the Czech-Australian Artspectrum Association Inc. and Sokol Sydney, it's a wonderful Czech Christmas celebration – including traditional songs, dance, food and colourful costumes. Approximately, November 29 from 11am-5pm. All welcome at the Sokol National House.
16 Grattan Crescent, Frenchs Forest (tel: 9452 5617).

Community organisations

Sokol National House.

The Sokol movement began in Czechoslovakia in 1862 in order to promote physical, intellectual and mental wellbeing of people. This old tradition has been continued by this important Sydney Czech organisation.
16 Grattan Crescent, Frenchs Forest (tel: 9452 5617).

Australian Slovaks Association.

Founded in December 1949, the Association develops a wide range of social and cultural activities for the Sydney Slovak community. It also publishes a very informative newsletter, the *Slovak Shield*.
PO Box 142, Lidcombe 2141.
Further information: Maria Hupka, President (tel: 9604 2668).

Media

Newspapers

Slovak Shield. A monthly newsletter, published by the Australian Slovak Association, which covers mainly community news. It's delivered by mail to subscribers, with a circulation of 600 to 1,000.

Its current editor is Mr Hupka, who can be contacted on 9649 2135 or at home on 9604 2668.

Radio

SBS Radio 2 FM 97.7. Czech news, current affairs and music, Sunday 9pm-10pm. Slovak news, current affairs and music, Sunday 10pm-11pm.

PLACES OF WORSHIP

ST FRANCIS DE SEILES.
A mass in Czech is celebrated here on the second or third week of each month, Sunday 11.30am.
Albion Street, Surry Hills (tel: 9212 2145).

SLOVAK CATHOLIC COMMUNITY (SAINTS CYRIL & METHODIUS).
A Catholic service in Slovak is celebrated every Sunday at 10.15am.
Corner Olympic Drive and Vaughan Street, Lidcombe
(tel: 9649 2153).

The Danes

"UTZON QUITS OPERA HOUSE. Danish architect Joern Utzon resigned yesterday as designer of the $50m Sydney Opera House." This story made the front page of the *Sydney Morning Herald* on 1 March 1966. Unbelievably, the creator of Australia's greatest architectural icon has never seen his masterpiece. In the flesh, Utzon departed from Sydney in April 1966, after nine turbulent years, and never returned. Thanks for the Sydney Opera House, Joern, but sorry about the manners.

Thanks for the Sydney Opera House, Joern.

The earliest Danes to visit Australia were sailors with Dutch fleets navigating the Australian coast. The first name recorded is that of Peter Petersen, a native of Copenhagen, who was on board Abel Tasman's *Zeehaen* in 1642. In the 'multicultural' early convict groups there were also some Danes – one of them was Samuel Wolff who was transported to the new penal colony in 1838.

With the exception of a group of young and adventurous Danes who came during the goldrush period, a substantial Danish immigration only occurred in the last decades of the nineteenth century. From the 4,744 counted in Australia in 1881 the number rose to 6,403 by 1891. This was the same year when the first Danish community organisation, Thor, was established in Sydney. This period also saw the arrival of some Danish dairy experts who would become pioneers in the development of the first butter factories in New South Wales and Victoria in the 1890s.

During the twentieth century, Danish immigration declined dramatically, and it was not until the end of the World War II that Danes, financially assisted by the Australian government, began again arriving on our shores. From this generation several community initiatives sprang up, including the foundation of the *Scandinavian Herald* (now defunct), in Sydney in 1984, and the consolidation of the cultural, social and welfare role of the Danish Church in Sydney.

Getting to know the Danish community

Events

St. Hans Festival.
Held on June 23, this is a mid-summer festival in Denmark, and a winter one here. It's a tradition to build a bonfire with a mock witch placed on top – they are set alight to expel the evil from the community. It's a very old and popular tradition where there is no shortage of food or beer.

Further information: 9874 6047.

Queen Margarette II's Birthday.
The Queen has the distinction of being one of the few popular modern monarchs, and her birthday is celebrated on April 16. A generous and traditional dinner and an animated evening of dancing are part of the celebration.

The Danish Club, 3 Grattan Crescent, Frenchs Forest (tel: 014 965 533).

Marton Evening.
Roast duck is the main fare at this traditional festival at the Danish Club. Held in November, the event remembers Marton, a national Danish hero who saved the country from being invaded by the bellicose Swedes.

Further information: 041 965 533.

Religious organisations and places of worship

Danish Lutheran Church in Sydney. Apart from the regular religious services, the Danish Lutheran Church provides social, cultural and welfare services to the Sydney Danish community.

52 Anthony Road, West Ryde (tel: 9874 6047).

Media

SBS Radio 1, AM 1107. News and current affairs in Danish. Saturday 5pm-6pm.

USEFUL NUMBER FOR VISITORS

DANISH CONSULATE:
tel: 9247 2224.

RESTAURANTS

For authentic Danish fare drop by the Northern Lights on
188 Pacific Highway, Hornsby
(tel: 9482 7364), or the Skandic Cafi,
109 Cathedral Street, Woolloomooloo
(tel: 9361 3713).

Both places are listed in The Swedes, page 239.

The Dutch

There was a time, in the 1950s, when the Sydney northern beach suburb of Narrabeen became a kind of 'Little Amsterdam' where hundreds of Dutch post-war immigrants set themselves up in tents in the local camping area. It was a very good way to save money quickly and, eventually, buy a house. Although life in this temporary accommodation wasn't easy, the Dutch showed a strong community spirit and solidarity.

When their economic situation improved, the tents were left behind but they stayed in the Warringah area, particularly in Dee Why and Narrabeen, where today the 20,000 or so Dutch descendants are one of the most ethnic visible groups in the neighbourhood. Paul Couvret was one of these many settlers. In 1979, he became the first immigrant in the 75 year history of Warringah Council to become Shire President.

Arguably the best known Dutch immigrant is Annita Keating – wife of the former Prime Minister Paul Keating. Her multilingual presentation before the International Olympic Committee – as part of Sydney's Olympic bid - is already legendary.

Early explorations

Well before the English arrived in Australia, Dutch explorers had already been here. In 1605-6, the ship *Duyfken* ('little dove'), captained by the Amsterdam-born navigator William Jansz, landed in what is today the Cape York Peninsula. Years later, in 1642, a seaman called Abel Tasman struck a piece of land that, two hundred years later British settlers named Tasmania.

Despite this early Dutch presence it was not until the end of War World II – when the Dutch government, fearing overpopulation, forced 600,000 citizens out of the Netherlands – that a significant number of Dutch people found their way to Australia. While in 1947 there were only 2,174 Dutch living here, their numbers rose dramatically to 52,032 by 1952. "The motivation for the [emigrants] was that they wanted to see greener pastures after the war," with says Dirk Eysbere, a Dutch immigrant who along his wife developed 'Where Waters Meet', a moving exhibition celebrating the 1950s and 1960s Dutch immigration experience to our shores. And, it seems that in Narrabeen they didn't only find the 'green pastures' but also lakes and lagoons which reminded them of home. It was in the Narrabeen tent camp where the first Sydney Dutch community organisation, Neerlandia, was formed in 1952. The founding president was Jan van 't Veen. In 1977, the foundation stone was laid for a modern and well-equipped venue which is now the centre of social life for the Sydney Dutch community. Other organisations soon followed

Modern explorers

The Dutch Reformed Church, which held its first services in private homes and tents, opened its own premises in 1955. It was followed four years later by the foundation of the very popular Dutch choir and folkloric group, Dee Why. Their members still retain memories of their most significant performance, at the opening of the Sydney Opera House in 1973.

Just like the early explorers, the modern Dutch have proven to be people with a great deal of resourcefulness and ambition. Their contribution to our society is large and vast. Dutch artists such as Afra Beuken, Jet Cozin, Thea Lokkers, Johanna Geluk, Willem Paes and Chris van Otterloo are widely recognised. Paul Cox, who arrived from Holland in 1963, and Rolf de Heer, who arrived in Australia in 1959, are two of the most successful film directors in the country. The artistic director and chief conductor of the Sydney Symphony Orchestra, Edo de Waart, is Dutch-born (more about him on page 100), while Patrick Jonker, regarded as one of the best road cyclists in Australia, was born in Holland and has represented Australia in the past two Olympics. And certainly, no-one can forget the best known Australian-Dutch of them all, Annita Keating – wife of the former Prime Minister Paul Keating – whose multilingual presentation before the International Olympic Committee was a celebration of the achievements of Sydney, the multicultural capital of Australia.

Shops

't Winkeltje (The Dutch Shop).

The shelves of this wonderful 'piece of Amsterdam' store, established in the early 1980s, carry just about every single Dutch product, including matjes herring, smoked eel, a full range of Dutch cheeses plus a hundred different kinds of licorice. Wooden clogs, plain or decorated, are also available ($30 adult, $15 children). You can also find Dutch souvenirs, genuine Delft blue ceramics from 'De Porceleyne Fles', wall tiles and T-shirts (including the club strip of Ajax, arguably the best soccer team

in the world). It also has a large range of Dutch books, dictionaries, magazines, records and CDs, and in its large showroom you'll find a great selection of high-quality oak furniture.
Open Tuesday-Friday 9am-4.30pm, Saturday-Sunday 9am-4pm.
85 Market Street, Smithfield (tel: 9604 0233).

Cafes
Cafe Rinus.
Part of the Dutch Shop, this is the place to have a break after shopping in the Dutch Shop.
Open Tuesday-Friday 9am-4.30pm, Saturday-Sunday 9am-4pm.
85 Market Street, Smithfield (tel: 9604 0233).

Landmarks and places of interest
Discovery Gallery, National Maritime Museum.
This exciting gallery has a range of navy artifacts belonging to the early Dutch explorers, including Dutch shipwreck materials, spooky skeletons of unfortunate Dutch sailors and a valuable 1602 rare Dutch globe showing the Southern Cross. The Gallery's curator is Martin Terrey.
Admission $7 adults, $4 concessions, $18.50 family ticket.
Open Monday-Sunday 9.30am-5pm.
2 Murray Street, Darling Harbour (tel: Monday-Friday 9552 7777; Saturday-Sunday 9552 7500/recorded information 0055 62002).

Dutch Australian Centre.
Since its establishment in 1983, the Centre has become the most important cultural institution for the promotion, dissemination and preservation of Dutch culture and heritage in Australia. It has a permanent exhibition focused on the World War II Dutch Australian experience and covers the post-war Dutch presence on our shores in four parts – why people migrated in the first place, the journey to Australia and arrival here, the early years of Dutch migration in Australia, and contemporary Dutch-Australian life.
The Centre also holds special and temporary exhibitions showing the works of some of the most exciting Australian-Dutch artists such as the woodcarver Peter Otto, and the paintings of Afra Beuken, Jet Cozin, Thea Lokkers, Johanna Geluk and others. Other special exhibitions

Established in the early 1980s, The Dutch Shop carries just about every single Dutch product.

relate to social subjects such as the role of Indonesia in both the history of the Netherlands and in Australia's future.

There is also a reference library open to the general public. The collection of several thousands books and other documents covers language, literature, the arts, music, religion, folklore, customs, handicrafts, film and video. As an extension of the reference library facility an archive has been established to store, among other things, Dutch newspapers, letters, radio recordings, maps and the like, as well as the recorded oral histories of various individuals. Since it's a reference library there's no borrowing, so you have to rely on the photocopy machine available. The Centre opens Thursday 10am-2pm and Saturday 10am-1pm, or by request. Entry is free.

222 Waldron Road, Chester Hill (tel: 9644 7327).

USEFUL NUMBER FOR VISITORS

DUTCH CONSULATE:
tel: 9387 6644.

Getting to know the Dutch community

Events

Sydney Holland Festival.

A traditional annual event on the Sydney Dutch community calendar. Held at Fairfield Showground on the last weeked of February, the Holland Festival is a celebration of Dutch tradition, history and culture.

Further information: 9609 6765.

Sunrise Choral Society Annual Concert.

The annual performance of this superb Dutch choir society of 50 members is much anticipated, and finally is heard on the last Sunday of May. Held at the Blacktown Civic Centre, the event is attended by hundreds of loyal admirers of the Society. The concert is free and kicks off at 1.30pm-2pm.

Postal address: 39 Parkin Road, St Marys 2760. Further information: Mrs Buddeke, Secretary (tel: 9673 3317).

Sunrise Choral Society Annual Concert.

THE DUTCH

Tulip Time, Bowral (Southern Highlands).

Annual early spring event when thousands of tulips begin blooming. Held in late September, it runs over a week and two weekends. The hub of this festivity is Bowral's Corbett Gardens, and more than 30 private gardens are also opened (and stay open through spring). $3 entry to Corbet Gardens, $4 for private gardens, or four gardens for $12 and nine for $18. There are several train services to the region from Sydney's Central Station.

Book early by calling Tourism Southern Highlands Visitor Information Centre on 1800 656 176.

Edo de Waart

ARTISTIC DIRECTOR AND CHIEF CONDUCTOR, SYDNEY SYMPHONY ORCHESTRA

Born in Amsterdam, Edo de Waart studied oboe and conducting at the Music Lyceum. From this time he began a stellar career that would see him reach the very top of his field both in his homeland and on the world stage. Upon graduation, he was appointed Associate Principal Oboe of the prestigious Concertgebouw Orchestra and at the age of 23 won first place in the Dimitri Mitropoulos Conductors' Competition. It was not long before he was made Assistant Conductor to Leonard Bernstein with the New York Philharmonic.

The year 1967 saw him on the home front again as he became conductor of the Rotterdam Philharmonic Orchestra and also founded the Netherlands Wind Ensemble. In 1973, he became Music Director of the Rotterdam Philharmonic, retaining the position until 1979.

It was in 1992 that Edo de Waart was appointed Chief Conductor and Artistic Director of the Sydney Symphony Orchestra, and from the start he expressed his great ambitions for the Orchestra. In 1995 he led the SSO on its first European tour since 1974; it was an extremely successful venture with performances at the London Proms, Lucerne, Hamburg, Hanover, Leipzig, Berlin, Stuttgart and Amsterdam. In 1996 he decided to make links in Asia by taking the orchestra on its first ever tour of Japan and Taiwan, culminating in a highly acclaimed performance for the Crown Prince and Princess of Japan in Tokyo which was broadcast nationally on both Japanese and Australian television.

St Nicholas Day (Dutch Christmas).

Traditionally the Dutch have not celebrated Christmas on December 25. Rather, they have the traditional Saint Nicholas Day on December 6, a date adopted by the Dutch when Holland was ruled by Spain. In Sydney, one of the main venues for this celebration is at the Neerlandia Club, which organises special activities on the weekend closest to December 6.

Further information: 9999 2629.

Religious organisations and places of worship

Religious tolerance and freedom has been, since 1579, an important feature of Dutch society, and in the immigration experience religious affiliation is a chief structural element within the Dutch community. It is estimated that 40% of the post-War World II Dutch settlers on our shores are Catholics and also a large number of Protestant followers.

Reformed Church of St Marys.

Following a policy of the Reformed Church, services have been held for the last 20 years ago in English only. For times of services, contact Rev G. Van Schie on 9623 3151.

72 Marsden Road, St Marys.

Dutch Parish of the Uniting Church in Australia.

Holds religious celebrations and bible study sessions and provides pastoral care. It also produces a Dutch-language parish newsletter.

Further information: Rev Lange (tel: 9631 2235).

Through folk dancing and music Sydney's Dutch community keeps old traditions alive in a new country.

Arts

Folk dancing and music has been part of the cultural life of Dutch villages and towns for centuries, and Dutch immigrants have always kept the culture of Dutch costumes and traditions alive.

Dutch Folk Dancing Group.

Formed in 1951, this traditional group performs regularly, and welcomes new members of all ages and ethnic backgrounds.

69 Cobham Street, Marayong. Further information:
Theo Boelhouwer, President (tel: 9626 9672).

If you'd like to check out a fine piece of Dutch architecture, search out the Australasian Steam Navigation Company on the western side of Circular Quay (they now house the Ken Done Gallery). The warehouses and offices at 3-5 Hickson Road, designed in 1884 by the celebrated architect William Wardell, have unique Dutch-inspired gables, clock tower and heavily coloured brickwork.

Sunrise Choral Society.

Established in 1959, the Society holds regular concerts, the largest being in May (see Events, page 99). Membership is open to people from any background, as long as they pay a mere $2.50 for each weekly night rehearsal.

39 Parking Road, St Marys.
Further information: T Buddeke, Secretary (tel: 9673 3317).

Community organisations

Dutch Australian Society 'Neerlandia'.

One of the oldest Dutch community organisations in Australia, founded in 1952. The society provides a space for social, cultural and artistic events.

PO Box 2, Narrabeen 2101 (tel: 9999 2629).

Netherlands Society in the Sutherland Shire.

Organises social and recreational activities for the Dutch community.

PO Box 209, Sutherland 2232 (tel: 9521 5265).

Federation of Netherlands Societies.

The Federation has a membership of 23 affiliated clubs and societies in New South Wales promoting social and cultural activities.

22 Ambleside Street, Wheeler Heights.
Further information: J Leiseboer, Secretary (tel: 9982 2362).

Abel Tasman Village.

A retirement villa that caters for Dutch-speaking and non-Dutch-speaking elderly immigrants. The facility has 40 hostels units and 26 self-care units. Its current manager is Hans Timmers.

222 Waldron Road, Chester Hill (tel: 9645 3388).

Nederlandse Vereniging in Sydney (Netherlands Society in Sydney).

Organises social and cultural activities.

86 Lucinda Avenue, Wahroonga. Further information: Tine Vander Heyden (tel: 9487 3612).

Media

Newspapers

The Dutch-language press in Australia has been operating since the1950s. Its pioneer was Hans Mol who established a broadsheet – *Maadelijks Contacorgaan van de Nederlandse Emigranten in Australie* (Monthly Contact Paper for Dutch Migrants in Australia) – to help immigrants keep in contact after arrival. Two more publications soon followed, *Spectrum* and *Trowel and Sword*, issued by the Reformed Churches. The first secular and general information newspaper – *The Dutch Australian* – was established in 1951.

Dutch Courier. The paper provides coverage of events in the local Dutch community and in the Netherlands. Overseas correspondent Koen Reynaert provides insightful reports on Flanders, while Henri Overhoff, former celebrated journalist of *De Tijd*, shows off his extensive knowledge of the world by describing all that is curious and interesting about the Netherlands, and his articles are illustrated with his own drawings. Published monthly the *Courier* is available at selected newsagencies on the 20th of every month. It has a circulation of 14,200 and costs $1.90, or $20 per annum. The current editor is Max Leening.

PO Box 47 Frankston, Victoria 3199 (tel: 03 337 8525).

Het Compas. Published monthly, it can be found in newsagencies the first week of the month, except in January. The paper has a circulation of 1,500 issues and its current editor is Francis Veringa.

PO Box 105, Matraville 2036 (tel: 9661 8207).

Dutch Weekly. Started in 1951 as the *Dutch Australian Weekly*. While the name might suggest otherwise, the paper is published every fortnight. It has a circulation of 13,000 copies, with 80% sold through subscriptions and 20% via 900 newsagencies throughout Australia and New Zealand. The cost is $1.80 and the editor is Wade Roskam.

Suite 401, 3 Smail Street, Broadway (tel: 9281 8522).

Radio

SBS Radio 2, FM 97.7. News, current affairs, community news and music. Monday and Wednesday 10am-11am, Friday 9pm-10pm and Saturday 10am-11am.

Facts and figures

Unlike many of the other post-war immigrant group, most Dutch did not initially settle in inner-city areas but were attracted to semi-rural regions on the fringes of the larger cities.

Since 1981 the Dutch population in Australia has remained fairly steady at around 95,000. After Melbourne, Sydney is home to the largest number of Dutch immigrants, around 14,400.

The Dutch show a relatively high rate of Australian citizenship (75.1%) which is consistent with the high proportion who have been resident in Australia for a long period. Their level of post-secondary qualifications (11.6%) on the other hand, is slightly below that for the total Australian population (12.8%). A higher proportion (20%) have done skilled or basic vocational training when compared with the Australia-born population, (13.9%).

Overall, the income distribution among Dutch residents isn't very different from that of the total Australian population, although the median income of all Netherlands-born people was $13,800, about 3% lower than that for all persons aged 15 years and over in Australia. One reason for this is the relatively high median age of the Dutch immigrants. Aged persons tend to report a lower than average personal income. According to the 1991 Census 76.4% of Dutch are owners of their own house.

Dutch people have shown a great deal of commitment to their language and culture, a fact demonstrated by the large proportion of them (92.7%) who speak only Dutch at home. There also is a small proportion (4.6%) who speak only German at home. It's estimated that around 40% of the post-war Dutch immigrants to Australia were Catholics, with many of the others associated with one of the Protestant denominations.

Explore the world in one city

The Estonians

For two decades spanning this century and the last, Estonian immigrant Evan Lumme recorded with his camera the life and times of the central western New South Wales town of Mandurama and its surrounds. His Estonian eyes saw the celebration of life of a bygone era in a remote land.

When Lumme died, he left behind thousands of glass plate negatives – of young women, men in their Sunday best, pioneers of the district, and more (the National Library has collected 95 of those wonderful photographs into a book, *Faces of Mandurama*).

Early arrivals

Sydney's original Estonian settler, Alfred Julius Sickler, arrived in the city in 1853 and established a permanent residence in Dubbo in western New South Wales. He came from Tallinn, the same hometown of Australia's best-known Estonian, mining millionaire Sir Arvi Parbo, who arrived in Australia on board the migrant ship *Nelly* almost a century after Sickler's arrival.

A large group of Estonians arrived in Sydney in the early 1900s, and some of these relocated to Thirlmere, near Picton, where they established a successful poultry farming community. Years later Thirlmere – with a strong Estonian cultural and social presence – was the location chosen by the Sydney Estonian community to built an Estonian retirement village, Eesti Kula, which was completed in 1978.

Following the economic hardships faced by Estonia after Independence in 1918, a significant number of Estonians immigrants began arriving on our shores, and the majority settled in Sydney. Among them were some very talented artists whose works were displayed in the first Estonian Art Exhibition in Sydney in 1929. The chief community initiative at this time was the establishment of the Estonian Society of Sydney – which has survived to the present day – and the Estonian House in Darlinghurst. Since its establishment, the Estonian House has been the centre of Sydney Estonian cultural and social life (see page 106).

The first large group of 142 post-war Estonian refugees arrived in Sydney in November 1947 on board the General Stuart Heintzelmann. Among this first boatload of displaced persons was a group of young Estonians who founded the Estonian Mens Choir, an institution committed to cultural preservation and ethnic identity. Some of the original founders of the Mens Choir still live in Sydney.

The Estonian population experienced a peak growth in 1954 (6,549) the same year in which the tide of Estonian immigration to Australia began its dramatic decline. Even though the Estonian immigration practically ended in 1958 the community life of the Sydney Estonians continues alive and well today. The annual Estonian Cultural Festival is still celebrated – as it was from its beginning in 1954 – the Lutheran church services at North Strathfield maintain their high attendance, and they have even managed to undertake a new community endeavour – the Sydney Estonian Heritage Foundation – established in 1991, the same year in which Estonia began walking again as an independent and free nation.

Fleeing to a new land

By the mid-1940s there were more that 1,000 Estonians living in Australia. This number remained relatively unchanged until the end of the decade when the conclusion of the war and German occupation gave way to a new era, of Soviet rule. Thousands of Estonians fled. Among these was the late Aldur Kaljo, one of the best-known Sydney Estonians. Kaljo fled to the West in 1944 and shortly after arriving in Sydney he enrolled at the NSW Institute of Technology (now University of Technology, Sydney). Equipped with a diploma in engineering he found work in firms manufacturing electronic, electrical and white goods. Then he established his own business in electrical goods and went on to amass a personal fortune estimated at $65 million. After Estonia regained independence in 1991 Kaljo was made honorary Consul-General, but was only able to enjoy the role for three years until he died in 1994.

The first large group of 142 post-war Estonian refugees arrived in Sydney in November 1947 on board the *General Stuart Heintzelmann*. Among this first boatload of displaced persons was a group of young Estonians who founded the Estonian Mens Choir, an institution committed to cultural preservation and ethnic identity. Some of the original founders of the Mens Choir still live in Sydney and in 1997 the Choir's fiftieth anniversary was celebrated.

Community initiatives were undertaken very soon after the war. The first Estonian newspaper, *Meie Kodu* (Our Home) was published in Sydney in 1949. In 1952 the community came together to establish the *Australia Eesti Seltside Liit* (Council of Estonian Societies in Australia), an umbrella organisation originally established in Sydney and later based in Adelaide. It was the same year that the late Dr Hugo Salasoo started the Estonian Archives, in the garage of his Lidcombe house. At his death this valuable archive was relocated to the Estonian House.

Landmarks and places of interest
Estonian House.

Located in the inner-city suburb of Darlinghurst, the Estonian House is one of the most precious historic reminders of the Estonian immigration experience in Sydney. Its construction began in 1939 and was completed in 1940. In the 1960s, it was renovated and enlarged. The Estonian House is the main venue for a wide range of cultural and social events, including Estonian Independence Day and the annual Estonian Singing Festival. It also has a well-stocked library which holds the Estonian archive collection that was begun in 1952. The archives include Estonian publications and a massive pictorial collection. The Estonian House can be visited on Wednesdays from 10am to 4pm, though you need to call beforehand.

141 Campbell Street, Darlinghurst (tel: 9212 2373).

Getting to know the Estonian community

USEFUL NUMBER FOR VISITORS

ESTONIAN CONSULATE:
tel: 9810 7468.

Events

Estonian Independence Day.

On 24 February 1818 Estonia gained independence from Russia, after being ruled since 1721. In 1940 Russian rule was restored again by the Soviet Union when Estonia was annexed by the Red Army after an agreement with Nazi Germany. Estonia regained independence finally in 1991 following the disintegration of the Soviet Union. A celebration, with commemorative speeches, choir performances and traditional food, is held in the Estonian House, 141 Campbell Street, Darlinghurst.

Further information: Estonian Society of Sydney (tel: 9212 2373).

Estonian Singing Festival.

An annual event in which several Estonian mixed choirs perform at the Estonian House. A special presentation was held in 1997 from the Estonian Mens Choir to celebrate its fiftieth anniversary. All are welcome.

Further information: tel 9212 2373.

Estonian Cultural Festival.

Held every second year, this is the most eagerly awaited festival among Australian Estonians. A tradition maintained from 1952, the venue for this national event is shared between Sydney, Melbourne and Adelaide. The drawcard of the festival is the performance of several Estonian choirs. The event includes traditional dancing, food, and craft stalls.

Further information: tel 9212 2373 or 9212 2113.

PLACES OF WORSHIP

ESTONIAN LUTHERAN CHURCH.
Services are held every second Sunday.
11 Waratah Street, Concord West
(tel: 9743 205).

Community organisations
Estonian Society of Sydney.
Operates from the premises of the Estonian House, where a wide range of activities are held, including the Saturday Estonian Language School and the guides and scout groups.
141 Campbell Street, Darlinghurst (tel: 9212 2373).

Media
Newspapers
Meie Kodu (Our Home). Established in 1949, this is one of the oldest non-English newspapers in our city. It's published weekly and covers local and international news.

The current editor is Uino Simmul (tel: 9212 2113).

Radio
SBS Radio 2, FM 97.7. Community announcements, traditional music, local and international news. Thursday 5pm-6pm.

Explore the world in one city

The French

It has been a matter of much debate and analysis. What would Australia have been like today if the French had occupied Australia instead of the English? Even though it didn't happen of course, the French have still been around here for a very long time.

One of the first Frenchmen in Australia was Peter Paris, a convict who was sentenced to seven years in the newly established penal colony. Luckily for him, his stay was a short one, as he managed to escape in 1788 with La Perouse's crew anchored at Botany Bay. Another French lawbreaker, James Larra, who was caught stealing a five pound pewter tankard, was to stay much longer. He was transported to Sydney's Port Jackson in 1790 and seven years later was pardoned and granted a piece of land. An enterprising man, he opened an inn at Parramatta, The Freemason's Arm, and over the years became a prominent member of the Royal Parramatta Association and was the first newspaper agent in Australia. He died in his adopted homeland in 1839.

When Governor King was appointed to Australia in 1799 he employed the services of the French architect Francis Luis Barralier, who on arriving in Sydney in 1800 was appointed to the New South Wales Corps. (One wonders whether before coming he had the opportunity to see the first French play set in Australia, *Les Emigres aux Terres Australes*, written in 1792). Barralier is well remembered for his explorations. In 1801, he sailed down the southeast coast and mapped the coastline from Wilsons Promontory to Westernport. Later, he travelled north to where Newcastle is today and surveyed the harbour, and in 1802 he explored the Blue Mountains and discovered the Nattai River. It seems that Barralier was the first European to hear and popularise the Aboriginal bush call of 'coo-ee'.

Following the 1789 Revolution a handful of disaffected French turned up on Sydney's shores. One of the most flamboyant was Gabriel Louis Huon de Kirilleau, whose identity as a member of the Bourbon family was only revealed 75 years after his death. He owned 1,000 acres of land around Fairfield in western Sydney, and became an influential figure in the Australian pastoral industry. He also taught French at Parramatta and

Many French immigrants have left their mark on our society, but Sydnesiders remember with special affection and admiration the magnificent boxer Jean Pierre, 'Johnny' Femechon.

Le Courrier Australien is not only the oldest Australian French newspaper but also the oldest surviving non-English language outlet in this country. Interestingly, it wasn't founded by a French person but by a Polish immigrant, M de Wrobleski. Its first issue hit the Sydney stands on 30 April 1892 (a copy of this can be seen at the Mitchell Library). This very same year, under the initiative of the French consul, the French Benevolent Society of NSW was established to assist French immigrants in need, and in 1895, that wonderful cultural institution, the Alliance Française, opened its doors in Sydney (see more about this on page 117). By the end of the century the French population had reached 4,500, and almost half of them were living in Sydney.

was well connected with the Sydney authorities. Another refugee, Le Chevalier de Clambre, arrived in 1802 and was granted 100 acres of land at Castle Hill, which he employed in growing cotton and coffee.

Between the 1820s and 1850s a small number of French immigrants settled in Sydney. Among them was Prosper de Mestre, who arrived in 1818 and became Director of the Bank of New South Wales between 1826 and 1842. However, it was brothers Jules and Didier Joubert who are better remembered. Jules Joubert, who arrived with this brother in the 1830s, became a prominent Sydney wine and spirit merchant, while Didier pioneered the development of Hunters Hill, one of Sydney's oldest and now most exclusive suburbs. It was here in this 'French Village' as it was known then that the first French consulate was established in 1839 (for more about Hunters Hill see page 115).

Strengthening the friendship

During the second half of last century French immigration grew steadily, spurred by the goldrushes and the political upheaval in France in 1848. By the 1870s there were almost 2,500 French people living here. The economic and trade relationship between the two countries began a steady upswing at this time, and a further boost was given with the establishment of the Sydney-French Chamber of Commerce in 1889.

This was also the year when a French immigrant called Georges Frere began attempting to grow grapes on his 1,280 acres of land near the Georges River and Punchbowl Creek (Frere's Crossing was named after him – he used to keep a boat hooked to a tree by the river's edge and it was used to cross the river even after the bridge was built). Frere thought that the sandy soil – 'naturally poor' as it was described by the Department of Agriculture of the time – would grow vines resistant to phylloxera, just like vines growing in sandy soil in France were. By 1895, after a long battle against nature, he realised that the soil was indeed unsuitable and his projected vineyard failed. However, it seems that he had better fortune in politics, becoming the Mayor of Albury in 1913.

During the two world wars that clouded a large part of the first half of the twentieth century, Australia and France were allies, a factor that has contributed significantly to a close relationship between the two countries. In World War I hundreds of Australians fought on French soil, and they are remembered in France with monuments in Bretonneux, Pozihres and Mont St Quentin. In Sydney, the Archibald Memorial in Hyde Park also remembers those diggers. At the end of the war many Australian soldiers returned with French wives. World War II strengthened even further the wartime friendship between the two countries; in 1944 L'Association

Franco-Australienne was founded in Sydney by war veterans to "retain and develop the bonds of friendship and brotherhood created in the harsh conditions of war," as its current president Robert Michkine explains.

Many French immigrants have left their mark in our society, but Sydneysiders remember with special affection and admiration the magnificent boxer Jean Pierre 'Johnny' Famechon. Born in Paris in 1945, he arrived in Sydney in 1950 with his parents. Against his father's wishes he began training at Ambrose Palmer's gymnasium, and went on to win the world featherweight title in 1970. Famechon holds the record of being the only featherweight boxing champion never to be knocked out. A legend.

Nowadays there are about 4,600 French-born people living in Sydney and they tend to be concentrated in the eastern suburbs of Woollahra, Waverley and Randwick. French immigration has differed from that of most other European countries in that the French have tended to migrate more as individuals, for trade, cultural and business reasons.

Selected restaurants

Many might argue that 'La Bombe' de Monsieur Chirac led Sydneysiders to boycott French restaurants. But as far as we saw – and apart from a restaurant that had its window broken – Sydneysiders opted to walk out in the streets instead of walking out of French restaurants.

Inner-city

Abercrombies. The pork and filet with bacon and green onions are a must. Average $30, BYO. Open lunch Monday-Friday noon-2pm, dinner Monday-Saturday 6pm-10.30pm.

98 Abercrombie Street, Chippendale (tel: 9698 7730).

L'Aubbergarde. Established at the end of the 1960s, this is one of the most traditional and likeable French spots about town. $24 set menu, BYO and licensed. Open for lunch Monday-Friday, noon-2.30pm, dinner Monday-Saturday 6pm-9.30pm.

353 Cleveland Street, Surry Hills (tel: 9319 5929).

Cicada. Quite upmarket and one of the most fashionable Sydney French restaurants. This explains the bill, needless to say. Average $50, licensed. Lunch Wednesday-Friday noon-2.30pm, dinner Monday-Saturday 6.30pm-10.00pm.

29 Challis Avenue, Potts Point (tel: 9358 1353).

Claudine's. A long-running Sydney favourite. Average $40, BYO. Open lunch noon-2pm, dinner 6pm-8.30pm.

151 Macquarie Street, City (tel: 9241 1749).

Onde. A simple and easygoing bistro. We tried the pork and fennel sausages with roast onion and can only say go for it! Average $20, BYO.

346 Liverpool Street, Darlinghurst (tel: 9331 8749).

LA RENAISSANCE PATISSERIE CAFE.

Great quiches and superb cakes and pastries – one of Sydney's must-go places. Open Monday-Sunday 8.30am-6pm.

47 Argyle Street, The Rocks (tel: 9241 4878).

LA GERBE D'OR.

Established at the beginning of the 1980s and located in the very charming ambience of Five Ways, this 'boulangerie et patisserie' has been supplying Sydneysiders with a great range of pastries, bread, salads, quiches and much more for years. Open Tuesday-Friday 8am-7pm, Saturday 8am-4pm and Sunday 8am-1pm.

255 Glenmore Road, Paddington (tel: 9331 1070).

VICTOIRE FRENCH BAKERY.

It's renowned as making the best croissants and cakes in town. Open Monday-Friday 8am-7pm, Saturday 7.30am-6pm and Sunday 7.30am-4pm.

385 Darling Street, Balmain (tel: 9818 5529).

Sirocco. France meets North Africa, a great mix. Average $60, licensed. Open only for dinner Monday-Saturday 6.30pm-10.30pm.

23 Craigend Street, Darlinghurst (tel: 9332 4495).

The Little Snail. A place where you can eat very well at an affordable price. The menu is extensive and includes the old favourites such as pumpkin soup, wild mushroom creme, and of course snails in the shell and fried frogs' legs *Provençal*. Three courses for $22, BYO and licensed. Open for lunch Monday-Friday noon-3pm, dinner Monday-Sunday 6pm-11pm.

135 Broadway, City (tel: 9212 7512). We also recommend The Little Snail at Bondi Beach, 96 Curlewis Street (tel: 9365 4847).

Mere Catherine. Provincial French cuisine with a rustic ambience. Average $30, BYO. Open only for dinner Tuesday-Saturday 7pm-midnight.

146 Victoria Street, Potts Point (tel: 9358 3862).

In the 'burbs

Bistro Moncur. Ultra chic – a French spot with a strong Mediterranean accent. The onion *soufflé gratin* is one of Moncur's legendary dishes. Average $40, licensed. Open lunch, Tuesday-Sunday noon-3pm, dinner Tuesday-Sunday 6pm-10.30pm.

Woollahra, 116 Queen Street, Woollahra (tel: 9363 2782).

Le Pot De Terre. If you're a couscous fan, drop by when they cook it on the last Tuesday of each month; it's arguably one of the best in Sydney. Average $30, BYO. Open for dinner only Tuesday-Saturday 6.30pm-10pm.

344 Darling Street, Balmain (tel: 9555 1130).

Prunier's. Very classy with classically French fare (in one of the poshest Sydney locations, needless to say). Average $50, licensed. Open for lunch Monday-Friday noon-2pm, dinner Monday-Saturday 6pm-10.30pm.

65 Ocean Street, Woollahra (tel: 9363 1974).

La Goulue. We tried the favourite of just about every critic, the glorious pig's trotters stuffed with sweetbreads, chicken and cipes. They're right. It's superb! Average $50, BYO. Open for dinner only Tuesday-Saturday from 6.30pm.

17 Alexander Street, Crows Nest (tel: 9439 1640).

Maurice's. Even the name contributes to the traditional flair of this old-fashioned restaurant. Average $30, BYO.
Open for dinner only Monday-Saturday 6.30pm-10.30pm.
521 Military Road, Mosman (tel: 9960 3351).

Tetsuya's. No, it's not wrong, this wonderful restaurant is also listed under The Japanese, (see page 332). The point is that Tetsuya's isn't only Japanese, or French, it's a celebration of a multi-ethnic society. In any food guide, Tetsuya's will always be at the top. $60 fixed menu (five courses), dinner $85. Open for lunch Wednesday-Saturday noon-3pm, dinner Tuesday-Saturday 7-11pm.
729 Darling Street, Rozelle (tel: 9555 1017).

Cafes

It seems that unlike Italian cafes, where coffee is the main attraction, in French cafes we also go for their pastry and bread, and this multicultural Sydney has a few good French cafes.

Le Cafe, Alliance Française. An ideal place for those mastering the French language. You can get the latest issue of *Le Monde Diplomatique* and order one of those delicious savoury croissants or home-made quiches, and if you're around for lunch on Thursday drop by for the 'plat du jour'. Open Monday-Friday 9.30am-5pm (till 3pm on Friday).
257 Clarence Street, City (tel: 9267 1755).

La Buvette. It's not only the coffee but also the luscious pastries that make this place a favourite.
Open Tuesday-Friday 7am-6pm, Saturday-Sunday 8am-8pm.
2 Challis Avenue, Potts Point (tel: 9538 5113).

La Passion du Fruit. The good coffee, the desserts and the variety of seasonal fruits make this cafe one of the most highly recommended.
Open Tuesday-Saturday 8am-10.30pm, Sunday 11am-4pm.
633 Bourke Street, Surry Hills (tel: 9690 1894).

Le Petit Creme. You would need a whole chapter to describe the wonders of this cafe – the price is good, the coffee is great and the pastries are sensational. Don't leave the place without trying a fresh baguette – baked on the spot every half-hour – filled with chicken and home-made mayo or eggs and bacon.
Open Monday-Friday 7am-4pm, Saturday 7am-5pm and Sunday 8am-5pm.
118 Darlinghurst Road, Darlinghurst (tel: 9361 4738).

Shopping

Baguette de France. Drop by for one of the finest baguettes in Sydney, and while you're there grab a few *croissants* and *brioches*.
Open Monday-Friday 7am-7pm, Saturday 6am-5.30pm and Sunday 6am-3pm.

317 Darling Street, Balmain (tel: 9555 7745).

Croissant d'Or. A cake shop not only praised for its croissants but also for its legendary brioches and biscuits.
Open Monday-Friday 7am-6pm, Saturday 7am-5pm.

117 Macleay Street, Potts Point (tel: 9385 6014).

Délifrance. In a very short space of time, this bakery chain has been able to win a reputation as a place for buying great French bread and pastries. Délifrance can be found in several locations. If you are in the City try the one in the Queen Victoria Building. Open Monday-Friday 7.30am-7.30pm (till 9pm on Thursday), Saturday 8am-7pm and Sunday 8.30am-7pm.

York Street, City (tel: 9261 5582). Also at: 33 Victoria Avenue, Chatswood (tel: 9411 8414); 395 George Street, City (tel: 9262 2936); 605-607 Haymarket, City (tel: 9267 6744); Kiosk K, 4 Town Centre Railway, Kogarah (tel: 9588 7609); Shop 195 Westfield Shopping Centre, Liverpool (tel: 9601 5321); Shop 2076 Westfield Shopping Centre, Miranda (tel: 9524 1526); Kiosk 144, Eastgardens Westfield, Pagewood (tel: 9344 6615) and 162 Church Street, Parramatta (tel: 9687 9204).

Furniture and antiques

Provençal Furniture Design. The French craftsman and designer Jean-Christophe Burckhardt, who came to Australia in 1981, has transformed his Mittagong showroom (one-and-a-half hours from Sydney) into an exquisite French 17th century cottage where you can almost feel the ambience of the southern French countryside. You'll find a superb range of French provincial furniture – from rustic to formal designs – including tables, Louis XV-style doors, fireplaces, *armoires* and other items crafted from timber. The Mittagong showroom and workshop is open Monday-Sunday by appointment. The works of Jean-Christophe can also be seen Monday-Sunday 10am-6pm at the Woollahra Antique Centre,

160 Oxford Street, Woollahra (tel: 019 122 130).
Unit 7/11 Priestly Street, Mittagong (tel: 048 713 410).

Antiques Avignon. The two-level gallery has a great display of French (and Scandinavian) furniture and *objets d'art*. It has some beautiful pieces such as a group of 17th and 18th century porcelain resting upon a finely-coloured cherrywood buffet, from the Bourgogne region of France of circa 1800. Bronze figures and chandeliers complement the French scene. Open Monday-Saturday 10.30am-5.30pm.
120 Hargrave Street, Paddington (tel: 9362 1482).

Landmarks and places of interest

La Perouse Museum and Monument

Sydney's La Perouse is on the northern side of the Botany Bay entrance, at the site where the French explorer of that name arrived on January 24 1788, and stayed for six weeks. La Perouse sailed from Botany Bay on March 10 1788 and was never seen again. It was not until several years later that the wreck of his ship was discovered on a reef near Vanuatu. The Museum, housed in the 1882 Old Cable Station, commemorates the ill-fated voyage of this French explorer, displaying early navigation instruments and interesting old maps and drawings. There is also a monument dedicated to La Perouse, built in 1828 by French sailors searching for him. Bookings are essential for guided tours, which are available in French and English. From Circular Quay you can get there by bus – catch the 394, 398 or express L94, or from Railway Square get the 393. The Museum is open Monday-Sunday 10am-4.30pm. Entrance fee is $2.

Further information: 9311 3379.

Hunters Hill

Since it was first settled and developed by a group of French in the 1830s, this Sydney suburb between the Parramatta and Lane Cove Rivers has been a Sydney French landmark. After all, it was known as the 'French Village', and has a sister relationship with the French town La Vesinet.

Hunters Hill is one of the most historic and magnificent residential suburbs of Sydney; just strolling around its streets is an open air history lesson. Many of the early houses were designed and built by French architects, and much of the area was developed by the French brothers Jules and Didier Joubert, who emigrated to Sydney at the end of the 1830s. They brought with them a group of Italian stonemasons, from Lombardy, to build houses, mansions and cottages using the local sandstone. In his autobiographical *Shavings and Scrapes from Many Parts* (1890), Jules Joubert (who lived here until 1881 and became Hunters Hill mayor in 1861) wrote his impressions about Hunters Hill and the

---

GETTING TO HUNTERS HILL

The local Hunters Hill Museum is worth a visit. This small venue, located next to the Town Hall on the corner of Alexandra and D'Aram Streets, gives an interesting taste of local history. It opens the second and fourth Sundays of each month, 2pm-4pm
(tel: 9414 0411).
Entry is free.
From Circular Quay you can get to Hunters Hill by a **506 bus or by ferry** from the **wharf 5** to the Alexandra Street or Valentia Street wharves.

USEFUL NUMBERS FOR VISITORS

FRENCH CONSULATE:
tel: 9261 5779
(general enquiries);
tel: 9261 5799
(visa enquiries)

FRENCH-AUSTRALIAN CHAMBER OF COMMERCE AND INDUSTRY:
tel: 9251 1033.

FRENCH TOURIST BUREAU:
tel: 9231 5244.

New Caledonia Tourism:
tel: 9299 2573.

Sydney Harbour. He lived most of the time at 65 Alexandra Street, where you will find some of the most charming cottages to be seen anywhere. Equally beautiful are the French Provincial Cottages built by Joubert and standing on the corner of Campbell Street. Hunters Hill was the place selected in 1839 for the Sydney French Consulate, the first foreign diplomatic mission in the country.

Archibald Fountain

Commissioned to commemorate the alliance between Australia and France during War World I, the Archibald Fountain, located at Sydney's Hyde Park, is the work of the French sculptor Frangois Leon Sicard. This piece of neo-classicism features the images of Diana, Theseus, Apollo and Pan.

Notre Dame

It's hard to describe it: museum, entertainment park, or both? This historic house dating from Parramatta's governmental period is worth a visit mainly because of its precious collection of French antiques. Entry adults $13.50, children $7.50. Open Wednesday-Sunday 10am-4.30pm. Camden Valley Way, Narellan (tel: 9606 6266).

Getting to know the French community

Events

SYDNEY FRENCH FILM FESTIVAL.
This is one of the great film events in Sydney. It is run by L'Alliance Française. In 1997 the Festival was cancelled, but is back again in 1998. At the time of writing, there was no set date, so we suggest you contact the Alliance for details (tel: 9267 1755).

Sydney French School Annual Fete. Run by the French School located in the Sydney beach suburb of Maroubra, this annual fete cum garage sale cum school market attracts hundreds of people. It's held at the end of May and the activities go though the day from 10am to 3pm.
88 Cooper Street, Maroubra. Further information: tel 9344 8692.

Bastille Day. Several activities are organised to celebrate this important historical event. L'Alliance Fraçaise organises an annual ball on the Saturday closest to Bastille Day, which is July 14. The venue changes from year to year. The Alliance also has a 'Formal Ball, Dinner and Dancing' at its headquarters at 275 Clarence Street in the City (tel: 9267 1755). The French-Australian Association organises a special lunch spiced with French music and a few speeches, normally made by the French Consul. The venue for this event also changes. For further information, contact the president of the Association, Robert Michkine on 9929 4435. The La Perouse Monument at La Perouse is also a regular venue for Bastille Day celebrations.

For further information contact the Museum (tel: 9311 3379).

Anzac Day. Organised by the French ex-Servicemen's Association, French veterans show up annually for this day of remembrance, on April 25. The French flag and war medals are carried by the proud French war veterans. After the exercise, the celebrations continue at a chosen Sydney French restaurant.

Further information: Jean-Pierre Sourdin, president of the Association, on 9267 6930.

Cultural and educational centres
Alliance Française de Sydney.

Established in Sydney in 1895 L'Alliance Fraçaise has been a major contributor to the cultural life of our city. It's the perfect place to learn French language and culture. All French teachers are qualified native speakers who are specially trained in foreign language teaching methodology.

L'Alliance Fraçaise has a video library with over 800 French videos available for rent ($5 per week per video, with a maximum of three to be borrowed), and a selection of the newest French music in town on CD and cassettes. It is a well-organised library that holds 7,500 works, classics in French literature, essays and travel guides; and a superb bookshop where you will be able to find French newspapers and magazines (no later than five days delay from Paris), including the venerable Le Monde Diplomatique, the leftist Liberation and the glossy Paris Match.

L'Alliance Fraçaise is also behind the organisation of an important number of community and mainstream cultural festivals, including the celebrations of Bastille Day and the splendid French Film Festival. Open Monday-Thursday 9.30am-7pm; Friday 9.30am-5pm; Saturday 9am-3pm.

257 Clarence Street, City (tel: 9267 1755).

The French School of Sydney.

Founded in 1965, the School provides bilingual (English-French) primary and secondary education. It currently has about 260 students.

88 Cooper Street, Maroubra (tel: 9344 8692).

RELIGIOUS ORGANISATIONS AND PLACES OF WORSHIP

FRENCH CATHOLIC COMMUNITY.
Organises religious services in French as well as other social and religious activities.

2 Missenden Road, Camperdown
(tel: 9550 2795).

Catholic services in French are regularly held at:

CONVENT OF THE SACRED HEART,
corner of New South Head and Vaucluse Road, Rose Bay. Second Sunday of the month, 6pm.

ST THERESE CATHOLIC CHURCH,
corner The Boulevarde and Stella Street, Fairfield West. Third Sunday of the month, 6pm.

ST MICHAEL CHURCH,
26 Margaret Street, Belfield. Sunday 10.30pm.

Community organisations

L'Union des Français de l'Etranger.

Established to defend the interests of French immigrants in France and in Australia. It provides welfare and social assistance.

41 Dumaresq Street, Gordon. Further information: John MacColl (tel: 9498 4374).

French Benevolent Society of NSW.

The Society has been operating since 1896. In 1973 it opened a welfare office that provides information, referral and settlement services for the French-speaking community in New South Wales. The welfare office opens Monday-Friday 9.30am-1.30pm.

257 Clarence Street, City (tel: 9267 1849).

Association France-Australie.

Founded in 1944 by the war veterans of France and Australia, it has played a major role in developing 'the bonds of friendship and brotherhood created in the harsh conditions of the war...' The Association meets once a month and organises a wide range of social and cultural activities.

PO Box 419, Cammeray 2062. Further information: Catherine (tel: 9874 7774) or Maud (tel: 9929 4435).

Media

Newspapers

Le Courrier Australien. This is a real success story. Founded by a Polish immigrant, M de Wrobleski, the first issue of this newspaper hit the Sydney stands on April 30 1892. Looking today more like a magazine, *Le Courrier Australien* hasn't lost its appeal to Sydney French residents or those learning French. In its 32 pages, it features news from France and New Caledonia. Published monthly, it has a circulation of about 7,000 and costs $2.90. Its current editor is Jean-Pierre Sourdin.

149 Castlereagh Street, City (tel: 9267 6930).

Radio

SBS Radio 1, AM 1107. International, local and community news and music. Tuesday 1-2pm, Thursday and Friday 11am-12noon, Saturday 9pm-10pm and Sunday 4pm-5pm.

2NBC, FM 90.1. Great French music and a wide range of community news. Sunday 9pm-10am.

2RRR, FM 88.5. The latest French music hits. Tuesday 9pm-10pm.

2BLU, FM 89.1. A Katooma community radio station, it has French language news and music program every Monday 4pm-6pm.

Television

SBS Television carries the excellent daily news services of *Le Journal* (France 2), Monday -Saturday 9am-9:45am.

Facts and figures

According to the latest figures there are 17,731 French-speaking people in NSW (this includes Mauritians). Of these 4, 698 are Sydney residents. The local French community is a relatively young population of less than 40 years of age, with a medium-term residency of more than 10 years and a high level of English competency.

The French are mainly Catholics (60.7 %), and there is a small number belonging to other religions such as Judaism (2.6%) or Protestantism (6.2%).

In terms of education, 55.4% of French-speaking residents in NSW have no formal qualifications, 3.7% have a basic vocational qualification, 5.4% have an undergraduate or associate diploma, 8.6% have a post-graduate diploma or bachelor degree and 3% have a higher degree.

The French speakers' high socioeconomic status is reflected in their annual household income, as 20% earn more than 60,000 per annum and 45% earn more than $40,000 per annum.

French speakers in Australia come from a number of different countries, as well as being born in Australia. The two main source countries are Mauritius and France.

The Germans

"**It was confiscated** and they never gave it back," snorted crusty old Ted Schroeder, one of the pioneers of the reopening of the Concordia Club in 1949. Founded in 1883 by a group of Sydney German settlers, the Concordia was closed during the war and its venue was confiscated by the authorities.

The oldest German club in Sydney, it has a lot to tell about the history of the Sydney German community; it was the place of contact for all Germans arriving in Sydney and also a place where many sought and found help. Originally in Macquarie Street it is now located on busy Stanmore Rd, just across from Newington College (more about the Concordia on page 124).

Early days

Arthur Phillip, Commander of the First Fleet, was himself of German origin: his father was a teacher of languages from Frankfurt who married in London.

The German presence in Sydney stretches back to the earliest days of European colonisation. Arthur Phillip, Commander of the First Fleet, had a German father who was a teacher of languages from Frankfurt who married in London. Sydney's earliest German settler, Phillip Schaeffer, was also on board the First Fleet. In 1791 he was granted 57 hectares of land on the north bank of the Parramatta River where he developed one of the earliest vineyards in Australia. He was joined years later by six 'vine-dresser' families from Hatteheim who were brought in to improve the vineyards of the Macarthur brothers in Camden in south-west Sydney.

One of the most influential Germans to arrive on our shores in the mid-1800s was the explorer Ludwig Leichhardt. A resourceful man who always managed to get money from rich benefactors, Leichhardt (evading military service in his home country) arrived in Sydney in 1842 (his fare was paid by a close friend). Failing to find suitable work in Sydney he went to stay on the property of A Scott, a rich pastoralist near Newcastle. He spent two months there collecting botanical specimens before engaging himself in the epic exploration from the Darling Downs, in Queensland, to Port Essington, Darwin in 1844-45. This expedition was of great importance to Australia's development as it resulted in the discovery of several notable rivers and much usable land. For his work he was awarded gold medals by the Geographical Societies of London and Paris, and in Sydney his name is commemorated by the inner-west suburb of Leichhardt that years later would become known as 'Little Italy'. (By the way, Leichhardt was finally pardoned by the German Government for dodging military service).

The majority of Germans who came to Sydney during the nineteenth century were single young men who worked as tradesmen or craftsmen. There were also those who joined the goldrush, including two very politically aware young men, F Wern and E Thonen, who figured prominently in the uprising at the Eureka Stockade of 1854.

Bernhardt Holterman (who, like Leichhardt was evading military service) was another who tried his luck in the goldfields. He arrived in Sydney in 1858 and it seems that luck was on his side. In 1871 he became rich when he found a gigantic 286 kilogram nugget. It wouldn't be hard to imagine everybody talking about it! With his new-found wealth Holtermann – a photography fanatic – hired the services of the photographer Beaufoy Merlin who took a series of plates of New South Wales, including two of Sydney Harbour, which were the largest plates ever taken at the time. The photos were used to promote New South Wales abroad (the valuable collection of photographs Holtermann sponsored can be seen today at the Sydney's Mitchell Library). He was also involved in a business importing German products to Australia, including lager beer. In 1882, Holterman entered politics as the member for St Leonards with two central issues in his political platform – immigration and the development of North Sydney. He died in Sydney in 1885, just two years after his fellow countryman, Edmund Resch, established the famous Reschs Brewery.

One of the most unforgettable Germans at the end of the nineteenth century was Pastor Herbert ('Papa') Wiese. An early Lutheran minister in New South Wales, 'Papa' Wiese was in charge, between 1876 and 1900, of the parishes of Jindera, Gerogery and Burrumbuttock, near Albury. Soon after arriving in the district, the local bank manager paid him a visit to tell him that a branch was being opened in his parish and invited him to open an account. When Wiese received his cheque book he went on a shopping spree, thinking that the cheque book was a kind of divine bottomless sack. It didn't last long. The good pastor was soon summoned by the rather serious bank manager and politely informed him that his account was overdrawn – "That's fine," said the good Papa, "I will write you a cheque for the amount."

Edmund Resch, a German immigrant, established in 1895 the famous Sydney Reschs Brewery.

(The original 1895 Reschs brewery façade still stands along South Dowling Street, between Maddison and Crescent Street, just across from Moore Park).

THE GERMANS

By 1901 there were around 9,000 Germans living in Sydney. Community life developed around the social and cultural activities organised by the Concordia and some of the choir groups ('Liedertafeln') established by the musically-minded Germans. Among the young, the 'socio-gymnast' associations or 'Turnverein' were most popular. Up to 1914 it was not unusual to see proud, robust young German gymnasts marching along Sydney's streets.

Casualties of war

The coming of World War I brought considerably hostility and hardship for Sydney's burgeoning German community. Torn between their loyalty for their adopted land and sympathy for the policies of German imperialism, the Germans came under sharp attack. Leading figures were deported and thousand of others were interned in detention camps. Many of them lost their jobs. The use of German was banned from church services, while streets and towns with German names were changed (Germantown in New South Wales was renamed Holbrook, for example). Clubs such as the Concordia and other associations were closed. Immigration from Germany was prohibited until the end of 1925.

World War II also had a major impact, but for different reasons. The accession of Nazism in Germany saw the arrival of a considerable number of German refugees, nearly all Jewish and highly educated. Among them were notable artists such as Inge King, one of the Australia's leading sculptors, the painter L Hirschfeld-Mack, and the leading composer George Dreyfus, who arrived in 1939. This wave of refugees and those who arrived after the war, including the film producer Bob Weis (*Waterfront*, *Dunera Boys*, *The Petrov Affair* and other TV credits), formed the nucleus of a cultural elite who have left a strong mark in the cultural and social life of our city.

Rebuilding the community

The Australian German population experienced a dramatic growth in the decades after the end of World War II. From 14,567 in 1947 the German-born community grew to an all-time high of 114,790 in 1986. It was during these decades that the Sydney German community began flourishing again through important community endeavours such as the foundation of two newspapers, *Der Anker* in 1954 and *Die Woche in Australien* in 1957. Also important was the establishment in the 1960s of St Rapahel's Catholic Community Centre and Retirement Home in Blacktown. Instrumental in the completion of this project was Father John Krewenka, who in 1997 was awarded the Order of Australia for his service to the community. The Centre is now home to about 200 senior citizens. Other community initiatives soon followed, including the opening of the Sydney Goethe Institute in 1974.

In the 1960s there was an emerging German community in Bankstown, where a number of German-run shops and services along Chapel street served the more than 3,000 Germans living in the area. But the Germans, like so many other European ethnic groups, have moved to other areas, their places taken by newcomers, especially those from Southeast Asia. Currently there are around 21,000 German-born immigrants scattered across the eastern suburbs of Waverley and Randwick, and the western suburbs of Fairfield and Blacktown.

Restaurants and Cafes

See Clubs, page 124, for some club restaurants that offer good affordable and food in large servings. We also recommend:

Berlin Café. As soon as you've polished off the fantastic smoked pork sausages, dig into the array of German desserts. Average $15, BYO. Open Monday-Sunday noon-10pm.

249 Darling Street, Balmain (tel: 9810 2336).

Forgotten Valley. Have a break from Sydney and drop by this charming spot where the only challenge to its great food is the wonderful view of the Hawkesbury River. Average $25, licensed. Open for lunch and dinner Friday-Saturday noon-midnight, Sunday noon-10pm. You can get there by the Pacific Highway (Route 83) Hornsby, Galston Road and then the Old Northern Road.

81 St Albans Road, via Webb's Creek Ferry, Wiseman's Ferry (tel: (045) 66 4490).

Löwenbraü Keller. A piece of Munich down under – great beer, live music and traditional Bavarian cuisine at The Rocks. 'Oktoberfest' in October is a great time to drop by at this German spot. Average $15, licensed. Open Sunday-Thursday 11am-10pm, Friday-Saturday 11am-11pm.

Cnr Argyle and Playfair Streets, The Rocks (tel: 9247 7785).

Shopping

Rudi's Metzgerei (Butchery). Continental smallgoods with a great motto 'frische und qualität zu vernünftigen Preisen' - something like 'fresh and quality at an affordable price'. Open Monday-Friday 7am-5pm, Saturday 7am-noon.

167 Oak Road, Kirrawee (tel: 9521 1414).

Iseli Butchery. Germans, Swiss and Austrians emigres know this is the place to get quality meats and Swiss-style smallgoods. Open Monday-Thursday 8am-5.30pm, Friday, 6am-5.30pm, and Saturday 7am-noon.

8 Charlotte Street, Ashfield (tel: 9798 6406).

BOOKSHOPS

There is a specialised bookshop on religious literature which is part of the Lutheran Church NSW District Office. It's open Monday-Friday 9am-7pm, Saturday 9am-5pm.

15-17 Blaxland Road, Rhodes (tel: 9743 0233).

INTERNEWS.

This is a book distribution company for German language publications. Cheques and money orders accepted.

1-3 Seddon Street, Locked Bag 22, Bankstown, 2200 (tel: 9707 4577).

A piece of Munich down under – great beer, live music and traditional Bavarian cuisine.

Schwarz Conditorei Patisserie. After your Blue Mountains weekend bushwalk, have a break here and stock up with some of the locally cooked cakes and biscuits. Open Wednesday to Monday 7.30am-5.30pm.

30 Station Street, Wentworth Falls (tel: (047) 57 3300).

Social clubs

Concordia Club. "Gough Whitlam has dined here, he loves this place," says the friendly Concordia receptionist. The imagination goes wild – the big man of Australian politics digging into one of those huge schnitzels. Situated in the inner-west suburb of Stanmore, the hundred-year-old Concordia Club is a landmark of the German community and of Sydney at large. Closed during the war period, Concordia opened again in 1949. A new stage then began with the construction of new club rooms and a large hall. In 1956 Concordia was granted a liquor licence, the first ethnic club to receive one. With the massive German immigration of the 1950s, the Club began increasing its activities, eventually forming different subsections such as table tennis, soccer, gliding and skittling, chess, judo, shooting, skating and golf.

Who said that Germans don't dance? Every Wednesday, Saturday and Sunday from 8pm there is dancing at the Club and every Friday from 9.30pm-2am a disco in the Lounge Bar (on Saturday the disco keeps going till 3am). The Club, which is open seven days a week from 10am, also has a small library with German language publications – open to anyone if you call first. Membership of the Club is also open to everybody (Full Member $20, Associate Member $15, Pensioner and Special Members (overseas and country) $10, joining fee (once only) $5).

Finally, it is worth mentioning the Club's good but inexpensive restaurant and bistro service. Try *Jäger Schnitzel* (a delicious, and big, crumbed pork fillet topped with spicy hunter sauce and served with vegetables), or a succulent *schweine haxen* (pork knuckles served with potatoes and saeurkraut). Open for lunch Sunday noon-2pm, dinner 5pm-8pm; and for dinner on Saturday, Wednesday and Friday 6pm-10pm. Bistro hours are Tuesday-Saturday noon- 2pm, dinner Monday-Sunday from 6pm.

231 Stanmore Road, Stanmore (tel: 9569 5911).

Club Germania. A fully-licensed club built by a group of German settlers, this is one of the success stories of the Sydney German community. The club holds a wide range of social activities throughout the week. On Tuesday night, the male and female choirs of the German Choir Association present a repertoire of traditional music. Wednesday is

BAVARIAN BAKEHOUSE. Pity it does not open seven days a week, but it's still worthwhile to wait till Tuesday morning for your stock of bread. Open Tuesday-Saturday 7am-7pm, Sunday 6.30am-5.30pm.

9 Duneba Avenue, West Gordon (tel: 9880 2242).

the day dedicated to senior German ladies who meet for an exciting game of pool. On Thursday there is a traditional session of card games, with the best players going to international competitions. Friday is when the 'Stammtisch' Group meet for a drink and to share some good German jokes. This group meets in what they call an 'English-free zone' – when an English word is spoken the 'perpetrator' is fined 20 cents, so if you want to have a bit of German fun don't forget your German-English dictionary (or carry a lot of 20 cent coins). Lately, the Germania Club has been the venue – every second Sunday – for the French Petanque Club, a game of French bowls.

636A Northcliffe Drive, Berkeley (tel: (042) 71 5011).

Landmarks and places of interest

Sydney Lutheran Church, Goulburn Street.

'Establishment of a German Evangelical Church in Sydney' was the headline run by the *Sydney Morning Herald* on February 29 1866. Located at 96 Goulburn Street and squeezed between a noisy pub and a travel centre, the Sydney Lutheran Church is a small, charming white sandstone building reminiscent of a German town church. The peaceful feeling irradiated by the Church is very much at odds with its location in one of the busiest areas of the city.

Further information: tel 9975 5800.

German Monument at Rookwood Cemetery.

Part of a very sad chapter in the lives of the Sydney German community, this impressive monument was unveiled in memory of the 218 Germans who died in internment camps during the War World I. Even though almost all died from natural causes, it is certain that the pain of being detained contributed in many cases. The monument was built with funds donated by the Sydney German community. One of the important events held at the base of the monument is a choral concert on the second Saturday of November. For additional information about the concert, contact the President of the German Choir Melody, Wilma Stanish, on 9728 6846.

The Friends of Rookwood Cemetery holds regular tours to the cemetery, we suggest contacting them on 9499 2415.

CLUB

GERMAN-AUSTRIAN CLUB.

This is the venue in the Sydney western suburbs where long-established Germans (and non-Germans) drop by regularly. It holds a wide range of sporting, cultural and social activities the whole week round. It also runs that feast of beer and food that is the 'Oktoberfest' on 12 October. On Fridays it's the '25 and overs' dance party, admission free; on Saturday night the Club goes wild with its regular floorshow entertainment. The Club's fully licensed restaurant, the Black Forest, is also recommended. If you want to eat German food this is a great place to go (chef Erich Koenigseder is the star of the show). The restaurant opens for dinner on Fridays 6pm-12.30am, Saturdays 5.30pm-12.30 am, and Sundays noon-8pm. Average $35 for two courses. The bistro is also worth a look; it's open Monday-Friday 9am-3pm.

73-75 Curtin Street
Cabramatta
(tel: 9728 7724).

USEFUL NUMBERS FOR VISITORS

GERMAN CONSULATE,
tel: 9328 7733.

LUFTHANSA GERMAN AIRLINES,
tel: 9367 3888
(reservations and information).

Getting to know the German community

Events

Schutzenfest (Shooting Festival).

First held in 1854, this is one of the most popular annual festivals among the Australian German community. Celebrated on January 11-12 in the historic German town of Hahndorf in South Australia (OK, so it's a bit of a hike from Sydney), the Festival attracts hundred of tourists every year from all around Australia and abroad. While there, have a break from the party and pay a visit to the grave of Pastor Kavel, the leader of the first Lutheran pilgrims to arrive in Australia. It is located in the Adelaide Hills and has the historic Lobethan church as a background.

Further information: Adelaide Hills Regional Tourist Association (tel: (08) 8370 8760) or the South Australian Tourism Commission Travel Centre, Sydney office, 24 Pitt Street, City (tel: 9264 3375).

German Unification Day.

On October 3 the German community celebrates the formal unification of what until 1990 was West and East Germany. Helmut Kohl was then elected the first Chancellor of the reunited Germany. Sydney German clubs hold special events and festivities to mark the occasion. The Concordia holds an annual concert by the German Choir Melody.

For further information about other activities we suggest you contact the clubs listed on page 124.

Oktoberfest.

One of the world's best-known German events, Oktoberfest dates back to October 12 1810, when Ludwig I, King of Bavaria, celebrated his marriage to Maria of Sachsen Hildburghausen. The dukedom of Bavaria, which had only recently been raised to a kingdom, wanted to celebrate this occasion in grand style, so people of all classes in the whole country were invited to take part in this event. So great was the success and the response to this wedding celebration that Germans decided to commemorate it every year in Bavaria's capital, Munich. Nowadays the Munich Oktoberfest begins the second last Saturday in September and continues until the first Sunday in October, luring tourists from all over the world. In Sydney, Oktoberfest is celebrated every year at Fairfield Showground where a huge covered area becomes the centre for thousands of people to celebrate the festival – with music, dance, food and beer. Bars offer local and imported beers that are consumed not in glasses but litres (leave your car at home).

Further information: German-Austrian Society of Australia (tel: 9728 7724), Karl Heinz Schubert, Manager.

Aga Kahner Carnival.

Celebrated at the Club Germania on 16 November, it marks the beginning of the annual calendar of activities held regularly in the premises of the Club. The Carnival is a lavish occasion spiced with great German food, music and dance. The pick of the night is the election of a prince and a princess who will lead and represent the Club throughout the year.

Further information: tel (042) 71 5011.

Helmatabend.

A regular event held at the Concordia Club, it is an evening of song, music and – you guessed it – a lot of beers and schnapps. We have been told it's advisable to book early to avoid disappointment. The party kicks off at 8pm.

Further information: Concordia Club (tel: 9569 5911).

German Choir Melody.

Established in 1964, this choir which sings traditional and classic German music has three annual concerts. The first concert is held on 28 September at the St Christophorus German Catholic Church, 112 Edwin Street, Croydon; the second is on October 3 (for German Unification Day) at the Concordia Club, 231 Stanmore Road, Stanmore; the third is a commemorative performance held at the German Monument at Rookwood Cemetery on the second Saturday of November. You can read more about the Choir on page 129.

Further information: Wilma Stanish, President (tel: 9728 6846).

Religious organisations and places of worship

Lutheran Church NSW District Office.

Deals with enquiries about issues pertinent to the Sydney Lutheran Church.
15-17 Blaxland Road, Rhodes (tel: 9736 2366 or 9528 9331 after hours).

WINZERFEST (WINE FESTIVAL).
An annual event held at the Concordia Club around July 26. Music, dance and, of course, wine tasting are the main features of this traditional festival.
Further information: 9569 5911.

Located at 96 Goulburn Street, the Sydney Lutheran Church was established in 1866.

German Lutheran Church, City.

A historical German landmark, it holds German language services every Sunday at 11am. It is also the central venue for the Indonesian Lutheran community and for services of the Mainland Chinese Mission.

96 Golburn Street, City (tel: 9975 5800).

German Lutheran Church, Old Guildford.

Services are held here on Sundays at 8.30am.

10 Gurney Road, Old Guildford. Further information: Pastor Dr Russell Briese or Pastor Ludwig Sauer (tel: 9644 4487).

German Catholic Centre, St. Christophorus Church.

Holds a weekly German language mass on Sundays and special holy days at 9am.

112 Edwin Street, Croydon. Further information: Father Fautsch (tel: 9716 9021).

Sydney has a long history of German cultural and education centres.

Cultural and educational centres

The Goethe Institut.

This is a non-profit, publicly-funded organisation based in Munich. It plays a vital role in the promotion of the study of the German language and culture and in encouraging international co-operation. It has also been instrumental in fostering the work of German filmmakers. At present the Institute has 165 representative offices in more than 70 countries, and 17 languages centres in Germany. In Sydney the Goethe Institut offers German language courses, scholarships for further education in Germany, in-service seminars for teachers of German, and library services, plus a wide variety of cultural programs. The easiest way to get there is by train, getting off at Edgecliff Station.

90 Ocean Street, Woollahra (tel: 9328-7411).

Deutscher Schulverein Sydney.

A Saturday German-language school, it operates in the Sydney suburbs of Chatswood, Miranda and Liverpool. Classes start at 9am and finish at noon. Annual tuition is $240. The education program goes from basic to high school level.

Further information: Paul Grunwald (tel: 9452 3372).

SYDNEY GOETHE INSTITUTE.
Open Monday, Tuesday noon-3pm, 5-8pm; Wednesday-Friday, noon-3pm.

German School Johannes Gutenberg.

A private school, it is subsidised by the Federal Republic of Germany and guided pedagogically by the standing committee of the ministers of education and cultural affairs, with the aim of providing students with a German school leaving certificate. The School offers pre-school, kindergarten, primary and secondary levels, and all classes are conducted in German.

74 Belmore Street, Ryde (near Meadowbank Station) (tel: 9809 5001).

Liedertafeln – the German choir tradition

A German community without German choirs wouldn't be a German community. In the German cultural tradition, special importance has always been given to the cultivation of music and choir groups ('Liedertafeln'). Since their early settlement in Sydney, Germans have always maintained and cultivated a fine choir music tradition.

German Choir Melody.

"We need plenty more young people, please!" is the cry of the current choir's president, Wilma Stanish. She is concerned that this wonderful choir, founded in 1964, is aging. The Choir holds three well-attended concerts every year (see page 127). Membership is just $12 for an introduction to the best of the German classic and traditional choir music.

12 Handle Street, Bass Hill, PO Box 36 Canley Heights 2166 (tel: 9728 6846).

GERMAN MALE CHOIR 'SANS SOUCI'.

Established in 1963, this 20-man choir performs German folk music with some regularity at the Wollongong Town Hall and at the Club Germania, 636A Northcliffe Drive, Berkeley. Membership is open to everybody, but you need to be able to afford the $1-per-week fee. Rehearsals are held at Germania Club. 59 Beverley Avenue, Unanderra 2526.

Further information:
W Kolodzey
(tel: (042) 713635).

Community organisations

Australian-German Welfare Society.

Provides assistance, advice and support to members of the German community, especially to the elderly and people living alone. It also publishes *The Welfarer*, the official journal of the Society.

1A Leicester Avenue, Strathfield (tel: 9746 6274).

German-Austrian Society of Australia.

Organises social, sport and cultural activities. Everybody is welcome.

73-75 Curtin Street, Cabramatta (tel: 9728 7724).

ST RAPHAELS RETIREMENT VILLAGE.
One of the great achievements of Father John Krewenka, the Centre is home for about 200 people.
138 Reservoir, Blacktown (tel: 9621 3347).

ST HEDWIGS HOME FOR THE AGED.
This is a retirement village for elderly Germans.
140 Reservoir Road, Blacktown
(tel: 9622 2221),
Nursing Home
(tel: 9831 4744).

ST RAPHAELS COMMUNITY CENTRE.
A Catholic centre that organises cultural, welfare, youth and religious activities for the German community.
136 Reservoir Road, Blacktown
(tel: 9622 0631).

Allambie Lutheran Homes Inc.

Established in 1966, this retirement village for senior German immigrants has 80 units, including small apartments for married couples. It holds annual activities, including the celebration of the major Christian events.

3 Martin Luther Place, Allambie Heights (tel: 9451 2017).

Media

Concern for and consciousness of language, literacy and the importance of political, social and cultural debate were central factors in the development of German-language media in Australia. The first German newspaper in Australia, *Die Deutsche Post für die Australischen Kolonien*, was published in Adelaide in 1848. Hermann Pütman, who arrived in Australia in 1855, is considered a central figure in the development of German print journalism in Australia. A radical writer and editor in pre-revolutionary Germany, Pütman edited a number of high-quality, though short-lived, German-language publications.

Newspapers

Australien Kurier. Operating since 1982, this paper is published monthly at a cost of $2.50. It has a circulation of 5,000. The current Managing Director (and also of *Die Woche in Australien*) is Ludger Heidelbach.

1-3 Seddon Street, Bankstown, Locked Bag 22, Bankstown 2000 (tel: 9707 4999).

Das Journal. One of the new German-language publications, this is an intelligent magazine which is published every two months (with some articles in English). Its analysis of German and European current events and issues, plus a good coverage of art and culture, helps to explain the $4 cover price. Available from selected newsagancies (Town Hall Station has it for sure). Its current publisher and editor is Gerald Stewart.

28 Gilpin Street, Camperdown 2050 (tel: 9516 4543).

Die Woche in Australien. Established in 1957, it is published weekly and can be found in selected newsagencies on Tuesdays - No 4 Wharf Circular Quay; Kings Cross Newsagency, 101 Darlinghurst Road; News-Link Bookstall, Town Hall Railway Station; News-Link Wynyard, Wynyard Railway Station, George Street. It has a circulation of 8,000 and costs $2.30.

Radio

SBS Radio 2 FM, 97.7. News, music, community activities and current affairs, Monday-Wednesday 9am-10am, Thursday-Friday 8pm-9pm, and Sunday 8pm-9pm.

Television

SBS Television. From the prestigious *Deustche Welle* comes 'Das Journal', a mandatory news and current affairs program for those who love high-quality journalism. Monday- Saturday 8.30am-9 am (in German) and Monday-Saturday 11.30am-noon (in English).

Facts and figures

Based on 1991 Census figures, Germans were the fifth largest group from a non-English-speaking background in Australia. In 1986 there were 113,444 German-born immigrants but that number had decreased slightly to 111,975 by the 1991 Census. After Melbourne, Sydney (with 21,457) has the largest number of German-born residents in the country. German immigrants have a high rate of citizenship, which can be attributed to the higher proportion of them residing in Australia for a long period of time.

The proportion of German immigrants with post-secondary qualifications (12.7%) is almost the same as that for the Australian population. However, Germans have a higher number (25.5%) of people with skilled or basic vocational training compared with the Australia-born population (13.9%).

Regarding income levels, 48.8% earned an average of $16,000, which is slightly less than for the total Australian population (49.7%). The 1991 Census showed that 51% of German settlers own their own home, a proportion that is lower than that for the total Australian population.

Fifty per cent of the German-born residents speak only German at home, followed by 42.7 per cent who speak English only at home and 2.6 per cent who speak Polish. In 1991, Lutheran was the largest denomination among German immigrants (30.6%), followed by Catholic (29.6%).

Annual household income data suggests that the German-born earn more than the average Australian.

THE GERMANS

The Greeks

"**Strange that in** the native heart/of this unending summer/ there should be another land/and that this land should abide/where the mind fades/into a greyness" – wrote poet Dimitri Tsaloumas.

Greek authors and musicians, such as Dimitri Tsaloumas and Themos Mexis; film stars and opera singers, including the Carides sisters and John Antoniu; journalists, such as Helen Vatsikopoulos, John Mangos and Mary Kostakidis; architects and painters, such as Alexander Tzannes and Theo Pangelis; and the 14 elected members of Parliament of Greek descent – in both the federal and state parliaments – point to a community that has been able to maintain its cultural and religious heritage and adapt to a new environment.

For this Australian-Greek writer, as he likes to call himself, 'Conflicts' is a maudlin poem that shows the dilemma of the Greeks in foreign lands – to come to terms with the land left behind and the new land to be embraced. For some there is no way back. For others, Greece is the land of pilgrimage where – as Dimitri Tsaloumas puts it – they can go and water their roots. Home is a hard thing to determine, and Australian Greeks know about it. It's what Australian-Greek composer Themos Maxis described once so well when he said that "I still feel out of place whenever I go there. Australia's my home, but I must admit that sometimes I feel out of place here too." A Greek drama?

The beginning of Hellenism

'It's easier to discover the North Pole than to discover the beginning of Hellenism in Australia'; these words were written in 1916 in *I Zoi en Afstralia* ('Life in Australia'), the first modern Greek book that appeared in Australia. Published by Ionnis 'John' Cominos, a founder of the Sydney Greek Orthodox community, with the assistance of the Andronicus brother (patriarchs of the famous coffee brand), the book gave general information about Australia to Greeks that were planning to start a new life Down Under.

It is unlikely, however, that the first known Greeks in Australia - seven convicts transported in 1829 for piracy in the Mediterranean - had much information about the land they were sent to. In 1837 they were pardoned and all but two, Andonis Manolis and Ghikas Bolugaris, returned to Greece. Manolis worked as a gardener at Picton in Sydney's west, and Boulgaris became a shepherd in southern New South Wales and married an Irish woman.

Aikaterini Plessas is identified as the first Greek woman in Australia. She arrived in Sydney in 1835 as the wife of Major James Henry Crummer, an Irish officer posted to a British regiment in New South Wales. After the death of her husband in 1867, she spent the rest of her life at Kings Cross in the heart of Sydney, where she died in 1908.

The first free Greek immigrant to Australia was John Peters, probably from Samos, who arrived in Sydney in 1838. He preceded a stream of fellow countryman who tried their luck in the 1850s goldrush. By the 1890s, when the chain migration of families from Ithaca and Kythera (there are now an estimated 38,000 people of Kytherian descent in New South Wales alone) became significant, several hundred Greek-born migrants were counted living in Sydney. They set up small businesses – restaurants, fruit shops, fish shops and of course coffee houses, the quintessential meeting place for Greek men.

One of those early self-made entrepreneurs was Athanasios 'John' Cominos. Better known as the 'Oyster King,' he was the first Kytherian to settle in Sydney, in the 1870s. After losing his job at the old Balmain Colliery, Cominos had an 'inspirational vision' while waiting for his fish and chip order in an Oxford Street shop run by a Welshman named Hughes. Cominos was struck by the simplicity of the business – to dip the batter-covered fish into boiling oil. Easy. So, he decided to try his own culinary expertise by setting up his own fish and chip shop not far from Hughes. He did so well that he was able to afford a pioneering oyster farm on the Hawkesbury River and in 1884 he began running one of the most popular oyster bars in Sydney. Other Kytherians followed his example. Another Greek who made good in business by the end of the 1800s was Mark Maniakis, a businessman who strove to expand Greek-Australian trade and to have the customs duty on Greek currants reduced. He also was instrumental in publicising Australia in the Athens media. In 1897 he became the first Sydney Greek honorary consul.

Religious and cultural heritage matters to Greeks. Sydney Greeks haven't forgotten that. This sense of hearty pride about their history, language, culture and their membership of the Orthodox Church, and the maintenance of these elements of identity for the next generations, is what has defined Greek community life. It was with this in mind that as soon as they settled they began establishing community organisations, schools and churches – and became, with the years, the best-organised ethnic community in Sydney.

> The first Greek immigrant to Australia was John Peters, probably from Samos, who arrived in Sydney in 1838.
>
> The most important Greek organisation established by the end of the 1800s – a milestone for the Sydney Greek community – was The Holy Trinity Greek Orthodox Church, located at the corner of Bourke and Ridge Street in Surry Hills; it opened its doors for the first time in 1898 with its first priest, Father Seraphim Phokas.

Settling in

The 1901 Census counted 878 Greeks living in Australia, a number that grew substantially during the inter-war period. This period was also when the Sydney Greek community began taking shape. They established pockets of settlements in the inner-city suburbs of Redfern,

Darlinghurst and Kings Cross. Several regional community organisations, including sporting, cultural, youth and womens groups, were established, and a few pan-Hellenic organisations also began functioning. These were the years when two of the first Greek-language newspapers, the right-wing and church-supporting *National Tribune*, and the left-wing and socialist-supporting *Hellenic Tribune*, were widely read.

In 1927 a second and larger Orthodox church, St Sophia, was built in Paddington, and it was just one year after its establishment that a 17-year-old Greek, Vasilis 'Bill' Spanos, arrived full of dreams in Sydney. Years later he had established such as reputation for being able to get things done that he become known around Sydney as the 'Unbelievable Greek'. A man of many jobs, 'Bill' Spanos became proprietor of George Street and Circular Quay cafes and later went into business in another cafe in Oxford Street. His 'cafe empire' became larger when he bought the Station Cafe in Elizabeth Street, as well as the Mayflower, Quay, Lewis and Arizona cafes (for generations of Sydney bohemian artists, writers and actors in search of the exotic these cafes were affectionately known as 'The Greek's'). In the 1950s Spanos opened a US-style butcher shop in George Street and it was soon followed by the opening of similar shops in Oxford Street and in Maroubra in Sydney's east. His reputation achieved legendary status when he organised in 1949 the first airlift of Greek-Cypriot immigrants to Australia. Twenty-eight hopeful immigrants packed the 200 km/h charter. They safely landed in Sydney a week later. Bill Spanos, the 'Unbelievable Greek', died in 1997.

The post-war era was a period of community consolidation. More than 50 new regional organisations, and at least 30 pan-Hellenic societies were formed. Social clubs, such as the highly successful Castellorizian, in Kinsgford, and the centrally located Hellenic Club, in Elizabeth Street just across from Hyde Park, became popular meeting venues for the Sydney Greeks. In the 1970s the Sydney Olympic Soccer Club was formed, and in the 1980s St Andrew's Theological College, from which many future Greek Orthodox priests and theologians were to graduate, was established.

The post-war wave

In the years immediately following War World II, few Greek immigrants arrived in Australia, as Greece was involved in a bloody civil war. However, by early 1951 several factors, including high levels of unemployment, a demand for labour in Australia and the introduction of assisted passages, contributed to the rise of Greek immigration. They came predominantly from the Peloponnese, Epirus and Macedonia, as well as from Crete and Lesbos. In Sydney, Greek settlements sprang up in the inner-city suburbs of Redfern and Surry Hills and spread into Newtown, Kensington, Waterloo and Rosebery. The presence of Greeks rapidly changed the character of these areas. Greek coffeehouses, clubs, corner shops (open until late!), restaurants, picture-theatres and musicians gave them a new flavour.

Migration to Australia from Greece practically ceased by 1972, and in fact more people returned to Greece each year than migrated to Australia. However, those who have stayed form today a community that has reached the point of maturity where they assert a strong influence on the cultural, social and political life of our society. Greek authors and musicians, such as Dimitri Tsaloumas and Themos Mexis; film stars and opera singers, including the Carides sisters and John Antoniu; journalists, such as Helen Vatsikopoulos, John Mangos and Mary Kostakidis; architects and painters, such as Alexander Tzannes and Theo Pangelis; and the 14 elected members of Parliament of Greek descent – in both the federal and state parliaments – point to a community that has been able to maintain its cultural and religious identity, while maintaining a strong interest and involvement in the society that has embraced them for more than 150 years.

Restaurants

Nobody calls it 'Little Athens' – not yet – but the Greek and Mediterranean atmosphere is there. Welcome to the late-night promenade of Grand Parade in the beachside suburb of Brighton-le-Sands, 20 minutes south of the Sydney CBD. Greek street musicians, the dark sea lit by the footpath lamps and the smell of grilled seafood emanating from the Greek taverns have transformed this sector, in a very short period of time, into an emerging Sydney tourist destination. To get there by public transport take a 303 or 304 bus from Circular Quay. Check out some of the places in The Grand Parade, listed below. For other venues to eat traditional Greek food, see Social Clubs, page 138.

Mouthwatering lamb or succulent seafood. The choice is yours at Sydney's many Greek restaurants.

Eleni's. Where the legendary Peter Conistis' Cosmos was not long ago, Eleni's – owned by Peter's man Eleni – offers quality modern Greek food in a cosy Mediterranean ambience. One of Sydney's best Greek restaurants. Average $35, BYO. Open Monday-Friday lunch noon-2.30pm; Monday-Saturday dinner 6-11.30pm.

185a Bourke Street, East Sydney (tel: 9331 5306).

Diethnes. Centrally located, this is the place to try grilled calamaris and octopus, and *pastistio* (baked pasta). Average $25, licensed. Open for lunch Monday-Saturday noon-3.30pm, dinner Monday-Saturday 5.30pm-10pm.

336 Pitt Street, City (tel: 9267 8956).

Enigma 88. Traditional Greek home-made food including cheese *saganaki*, baby calamari and the highly recommended barbecued octopus. Average $20, licensed. Open Monday-Sunday noon-2am.

88 The Grand Parade, Brighton-le-Sands (tel: 9556 3611).

THE GREEKS

Le Sands. The seafood is exceptionally delicious, especially the grilled octopus. Drop by on Friday or Saturday for the live music show. Average $30, licensed. Open for lunch noon-3pm, dinner 6pm-midnight.

The Grand Parade, Brighton Le Sands (tel: 9599 2128).

Mezes Espresso Bar Restaurant. Go straight for the fresh seafood platter which, includes baby blue swimmer crab, whitebait fritters, and flatbread with *tzatziki*. Average $39, licensed. Open Monday-Sunday 8.30am till late.

36 Bayside Plaza, Grand Parade, Brighton-le-Sands (tel: 9567 2865).

Never on Sunday. The deal is tasty and affordable – you won't regret calling in. Average $25, BYO. Open Monday-Saturday 6pm-11pm.

576 Darling Street, Rozelle (tel: 9810 2411).

Nostimo. After trying the grilled pide filled with *pancetta* and *pecorino*, don't forget the Greek pastries and desserts to top it all off. Average $25, BYO. Open Monday-Friday 7am-6pm, Saturday-Sunday 7am-5pm.

Shop 2 113 Queen Street, Woollahra (tel: 9362 4277).

Perama. Regarded as one of the best in Sydney – try the tender lamb skaras marinated in herbs, lemon and garlic. Average $20, BYO and licensed. Open Tuesday-Saturday 6.30pm-10pm.

88 Audley Road, Petersham (tel: 9569 7534).

Skorpios Taverna. The homemade *tiropitta* is a must, drop by on Friday or Saturday night for the traditional Greek dance *zembekiko*. Average $25, licensed. Wednesday-Sunday 6.30pm-1am.

125 Johnston Street, Annandale (tel: 9660 7245).

Sophocles Restaurant. More than 16 years operating in the heart of Parramatta, this Greek restaurant has one of the greatest Mediterranean style fresh seafood offers in town. Average $20 BYO. Open for lunch Monday-Sunday from noon 'until you finish' as the owner says, dinner Monday-Sunday 6pm-11pm.

79 Phillip Street, Parramatta (tel: 9633 3309).

Steki Taverna. If you want a quiet dinner don't dare to drop in on Fridays or Saturdays after 11pm, as the acrobatic Greek dance and the live music rules. Average $20, licensed. Wednesday-Sunday 6.30pm-11pm.

2 O'Connell Street, Newtown (tel: 9516 2191).

The Greek Taverna Kafe Kamari. One of the most popular spots for young Greeks; the traditional *moussaka* is a must. Average $20, licensed. Open Monday-Thursday noon-11.30pm, Friday-Sunday noon-2am.

82 The Grand Parade, Brighton-le-Sands (tel: 9556 2533).

Shopping

Athenaikon Continental Cake Shop. Established in 1955, this is the oldest existing Greek cake shop in Sydney, offering great *baklava* and olive bread. Monday-Saturday 7am-6pm

409 Bourke Street, Darlinghurst (tel: 9360 4878).

Athens Cake Shop. A great range of fine cakes, pastries and biscuits baked daily on the premises. Open Monday-Friday 8.30am-6pm, Saturday 8.30am-4.30pm.

914 Anzac Parade, Maroubra (tel: 9349 5910).

D & A Danas Continental Delicatessen. The range in this deli goes from an amazing variety of olives to marinated octopus. Monday-Friday 8.30am-6.30pm, Saturday 830am-6pm.

416 Illawarra Road, Marrickville (tel: 9558 3573).

Hellenic Bakery. The fresh bread and wide range of sweets and biscuits – *paximathia, kouloria, baklava* – make this bakery one of the best in Sydney. Open Monday-Wednesday and Friday 5am-7.30pm, Thursday and Saturday 5am-8.30pm, Sunday 6am-6pm.

371 Illawarra Road, Marrickville (tel: 9559 2701).

Queen Street Deli. Call in and get a good portion of the daily prepared creamy *ricotta*. Open Monday-Friday 6am-7pm.

142 Queen Street, Woollahra (tel: 9328 7121).

St Andrews Greek Orthodox Theological College Book Centre. The best place to find specialist theological and historical publications, in Greek and English. Open Monday-Friday 10am-4pm, Thursday 9am-5pm.

242 Cleveland Street, Redfern (tel: 9698 5812).

SALAPATAS THEMELIO GREEK ART & BOOKSHOP. You can't miss dropping by at this wonderful book and gift shop, established almost 40 years ago. It has a great range of history and religious books, in English and in Greek. If you are planning an original present, have a look at the huge range of religious *objets d'art*. Greek music and movies are also available. Open Monday-Friday 9am-5pm and Saturday 9am-2pm.

251 Elizabeth Street, City (tel: 9264 7795).

Clubs

Where can you go for a good time – Greek style? "There are too many" says a loyal patron of the Hellenic Club at Elizabeth Street. Here is selected group of them.

Hellenic Club. "A coffee, sweet or medium?" is the offer from George, the tall, friendly chain-smoking waiter. This was a bit of a surprise. You would expect instead the offer of a beer in this halfway pub and *cafeneion*, on the fourth floor of this Greek Sydney club. But in the Greek tradition, when a patron enters a shop he is 'shouted' a small cup of black coffee by one of his acquaintances in the same way that other Australians shout each other a beer. In an enviable location, along Elizabeth Street and across from Hyde Park, the Hellenic Club was established in the 1950s and has a fine reputation as the favourite meeting place for Sydney Greeks. By the way, since the Club is owned by the Greek community, the profits go to a diverse range of charitable initiatives. The Club restaurant also deserves a visit – try the baked snapper, the traditional cooked lamb, and regional dishes such as *souzoukavia pilaf*. Average $25, licensed. Open for lunch Monday-Friday noon-3pm and dinner 5pm-9pm, Saturday (dinner only) 5pm-9pm.

251-253 Elizabeth St, Sydney (tel: 9264 5128).

Sydney Olympic Social Club. Traditional cuisine, á la carte restaurant, sporting facilities and Greek entertainment all week. Members and guests welcome. Open Monday-Sunday 10.30am-midnight.

64 Tennent Parade, Hurlstone Park (tel: 9558 5355).

Landmarks and places of interest

Greek Orthodox Church of The Holy Trinity.

The first Greek Orthodox church in the country, a combined effort between the Sydney Greek and Syrian Orthodox Community, was founded in 1898.

The Church lies today in the same place that it was originally erected, at the corner of Bourke and Ridge Streets in Surry Hills. Its first Greek Orthodox priest was Father Seraphim Phokas.

Further information: 9319 7504.

CASTELLORIZIAN CLUB.
Located on Anzac Parade not far from the Kingsford roundabout, the Castellorizian is one of the best-known Sydney Greek social clubs and certainly is the most popular entertainment venue for the large Greek community in Maroubra and Kingsford. The Club premises is open Monday-Thursday 10am-11.30pm, Friday-Sunday 10am-1.30am. The food from the bistro is good and affordable; it's open for lunch Monday-Sunday noon-2.30pm, dinner Monday-Thursday 6pm-10pm, Friday-Saturday 6pm-11pm, Sunday 6pm-10pm. There are some special things to take note of: the bistro lunch deal Monday-Saturday noon-2.30pm for $4, the 'Super Sunday lunch' noon-2.30pm for $5, the Taverna Night with free live entertainment Wednesday and Sunday $4, free live Greek entertainment Wednesday and Friday-Sunday 7.30pm till late.

440-444 Anzac Parade, Kingsford
(tel: 9663 3827).

St Andrew's Greek Orthodox Theological College.

In a premises formerly occupied by the Anglican Church, this College is a Sydney Greek landmark that speaks of the achievements and contributions made by the Greek community to our city. To establish this institution was a dream that goes back to the 1930s when Metropolitan Timotheos was contemplating the establishment of a centre for theological education. Several years later, in 1959 when Archbishop Ezekiel arrived, thought was given to the subject and a committee appointed, but nothing much was done. Since his arrival here in 1975, the current primate, Archbishop Stylianos, persistently reiterated the wish and desire of his predecessors in this respect, and sought ways of putting the idea into effect. At the Fourth Clergy-Laity Congress held in Sydney in January 1981, the Archbishop moved and the delegates voted for the immediate implementation of such a project. In 1986, the long-awaited dream became a reality, and the College opened its doors to the very first students in February of that year.

242 Cleveland Street, Redfern (tel 9319 6145).
Further Information: tel 9319 6145

USEFUL NUMBERS FOR VISITORS

GREEK NATIONAL TOURIST ORGANISATION,
tel: 9241 1663.

GREEK CONSULATE,
tel: 9221 2388.

GREEK GOVERNMENT COMMERCIAL OFFICE,
tel: 9247 2334.

Getting to know the Greek community

Events

Epiphany (Blessing of the Waters at Yarra Bay).

On the Sunday closest to 6 January, the Sydney Greeks get together at Yarra Bay, La Perouse, to celebrate this massive annual religious event that marks the holiest day of the Greek Orthodox calendar. The climax of the celebration is reached with a race to reclaim a silver cross which is thrown into Yarra Bay after the blessing of the water to celebrate the baptism of Christ in the Jordan River. It is a real spectacle to see around 50 Greek men, in their cossies, chaotically diving to find the holy cross. This annual event is held partly on Aboriginal land, with the local Aboriginal land council providing parking. All are welcome. You can get to La Perouse from Circular Quay (39 or express L94 buses) or from Railway Square (393 bus).

Further information: 9698 5066.

Religious and cultural heritage matters to Greeks

GREEK FESTIVAL OF SYDNEY.

The Festival, held either in March or April is a month of celebration of Greek art and culture, attracting overseas as well as local talent. Organised by members of the community, in conjuction with artists, the festival aims to reflect the ever-changing nature of the Greek-Australian community.

Further information: tel: 9740 6022.

Greek Glendi, one of the most popular community events, marks the beginning of springtime

Independence from Turkey & Day of the Assumption.

A historic and religious celebration held on 25 March. This day the Sydney Greek community honours the Greeks who rose up against the 400-year rule of the Turkish Otoman Empire and freed Greece in 1821. This same day the Greek community celebrates the Day of the Assumption. The whole day of celebrations kick off with a religious ceremony at the Cathedral of the Annunciation of Our Lady, at Cleveland Street in Redfern. The celebration is followed by a laying of wreaths at Martin Place. Immediately after, a procession of priests, teachers, students, association and organisation representatives goes to the steps of the Sydney Opera House where dancers and musicians in traditional costumes celebrate this event.

Further information: contact any of the community organisations listed on page 145.

Greek Easter.

One of the most traditional religious celebrations in the Sydney Greek Orthodox community, held at the end of April. Special festivities are held in most of the Greek Orthodox churches in Sydney. At home, traditional dishes and pastries are prepared, including melomakaroma, baclava and koulouria kourambiedies.

Further information: contact some of the churches listed in page 141-2.

St Spyridon's Ball.

Hundred of parishioners and friends from the Kingsford St Spyridon's Greek Orthodox Church meet around the end of July to celebrate their annual ball – a highlight of the parish calendar.

72-76 Gardeners Road, Kingsford (tel: 9663 5147).

Greek Glendi.

One of the most popular community events marking the beginning of springtime. A massive day out, with Greek music, food and dance, is held at Kensington Oval, corner of Cottenham Avenue, Edward Avenue and Barker Street. The festival kicks off at 11am and finishs at 5pm. Free admission. All welcome.

Further information: 9313 8868.

The Greek-Macedonian Dimitria Festival.

Celebrated annually during the second half of October at Tumbalong Park, Darling Harbour. In a tradition dating back a thousand years and originated in Byzantium, the Sydney Greek community celebrates the name day of Saint Dimitrius of Thessaloniki.

Greek National Day.

On October 28 the Greek community gets together to celebrate the driving back of the Italian army which on this day in 1940 had invaded Greece from Albania. The Greek army was led by General Alexandros Papagos. Celebrations are held in most of the Greek Orthodox Churches in Sydney.

Religious organisations and places of worship

The Greek Orthodox Church.

The principal institution of common identity for the Sydney Greek community, it will soon celebrate the centenary of its first church – the Holy Trinity – opened in May 1898 in Surry Hills, where it still stands. Its first priest was Father Seraphim Phokas.

Since 1975, the Greek Orthodox Church has been headed by Archbishop Stylianos and the Greek Orthodox Archdiocese of Australia and New Zealand is centred in Sydney. Archbishop Stylianos is a former lecturer at the University of Thessaloniki, and has been instrumental in encouraging the growth of churches in Australia, taking a strong interest in the social and cultural development of his congregation. Nowadays, the Archdiocese has over 100 priests, 105 churches and 120 community organisations.

Sydney's Greek Community remain proud of their Greek cultural heritage.

Most of Sydney's Greek Orthodox churches have their own premises, resident priests, ethnic schools (teaching children Greek language, history and culture after normal school hours), women's and youth groups. The following is a list of some Greek Orthodox churches operating in Sydney. Although most of the services are in Greek, the Archidiocese organises services in English.

For information call 9698 5066.

Cathedral of the Annunciation of Our Lady.

Has regular service on Sunday 8am-11.30am with Rev John Grylles.

242 Cleveland Street, Redfern (tel: 9698 5066).

Church of Holy Trinity.

A Sydney Greek landmark, it is the oldest Greek Orthodox church in the country. A service is held on Sunday 8am; Rev Nicholas Sergakes.

Corner Bourke And Ridge Street, Surry Hills (tel: 9319 7504).

Church of the Dormition of Our Lady.
Regular service on Sunday at 8.15am; Rev Panagiotis Baskoutas.
360 Abercombrie Street, Redfern (tel: 9319 5425).

Parish Community of Archangel Michael.
A normal srvice is held on Sunday 8am-11am; Rev John Daskalakes,
49 Holterman Street, Crows Nest (tel: 9436 1957).

Parish Community of Saint Euphemia.
Regular service on Sunday at 8am; Rev Michael Apostolopoulos.
6N 12 East Terrace, Bankstown, (tel: 9709 6908).

Parish Community of Saint George.
An English service is held the second Sunday of the month at 9.30am; Rev Miltiades Chrysavges.
90 Newcastle Street, Rose Bay (tel: 9371 9929 or 015 225876).

Parish Community of Saint Gerasimos.
Regular services on Sunday 8am-11am and Tuesday 5pm-6.30pm; Rev George Koukoulas.
21 Henry Street, Leichhardt (tel: 9560 8330).

There are many churches in Sydney for Greek religious workship.

Dr Con Costa
NATIONAL PRESIDENT OF THE DOCTORS REFORM SOCIETY

Con Costa was born in Sydney to Greek Cypriot parents. The early experience of living in a poor migrant family – where a visit to the doctor was a luxury – as well as the experiences of over 15 years practising multicultural medicine as a family GP, have shaped his views on the importance of accessible and affordable heath care for all the community.

Dr Costa has been the National President of the Doctors Reform Society for four years and prior to that was the NSW President for several years of the Doctors Reform Society – a lobby group for progressive heath reforms and a strong advocate for the public health system in Australia. He is a Master of Public Health from Sydney University, and is a Fellow of the Australian Faculty of Public Health Medicine and of the Royal Australian College of Physicians.

Explore the world in one city

Parish of Saint Sophia and Her Three Daugthers.

Normal service on Sunday 8am-11pm; Rev John Evangelinides.

411A Bourke Street, Darlinghurst (tel: 9331 5031).

Parish Community of Saint Spyridon.

Regular Greek service on Sunday 8.30am-11am and an English liturgy on Saturday 6.30pm-815pm; Rev Stylianos Skoutas.

72-76, Gardeners Road, Kingsford (tel: 9663 5147).

Art

Greek-Australians: In Their Own Image.

A travelling photographic exhibition tracing the history of Greek Australians from the early 1800s. The exhibition, consisting of some 200 photographs, is designed to challenge the stereotype of the Greek 'fish-and-chip shop owner' and offers a glimpse of Australia's early multicultural credentials. The exhibition is coordinated by social historian Leonard Janiszewski, photographer Effy Alexakis and the State Library of NSW. At the time of writing, the exhibition is being displayed in Thessaloniki, Greece and will be shown in Canberra, Sydney and Melbourne over 1998.

Further information: National Project and Touring Exhibitions, 16 Bloodwood Road, Arcadia (tel: 9656 1128).

Take Away Theatre.

A community theatre company, it dedicates itself to producing new and contemporary works by Greek-Australian playwrights as well as offering regular performances and workshops.

PO Box 210, Petersham 2049 (tel: 9744 0476).

Culture and education

Greek language and culture are taught in Sydney through a wide range of programs at all levels of education, from primary to tertiary. It is taught at government schools and colleges, ethnic schools, including the Greek Orthodox schools and colleges, Saturday schools of languages, private language centres and private tuition classes. Some 55,000 students attend Modern Greek classes in Australia today with Modern Greek retaining its popularity as the third language in Australia.

SCHOOLS

PARISH COMMUNITY OF S.E. SYDNEY SAINT SPYRIDON – SECONDARY SCHOOL.
1130 Anzac Parade, Maroubra
(tel: 9331 3340).

ALL SAINTS COLLEGE. PRESIDENT, JOHN THEODORIDES.
54 Hampden Road, Lakemba
(tel: 9740 5938).

SAINT EUPHEMIA COLLEGE.
6-12 East Terrace, Bankstown
(tel: 9796 8240).

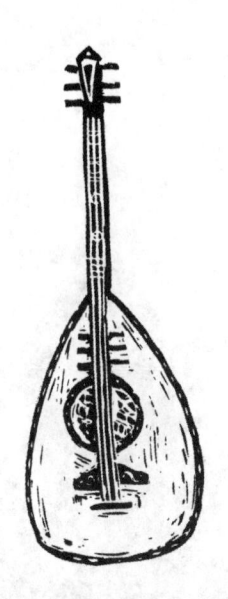

MACQUARIE UNIVERSITY, School of Modern Languages, North Ryde (tel: 9805 7111).

THE UNIVERSITY OF NEW SOUTH WALES, Faculty of Arts and Social Sciences, Modern Greek Section, Staff Contact, Dr Helen Amvrazi (tel: 9385 2188).

UNIVERSITY OF SYDNEY, Department of Modern Greek. Staff contact, Dr Antony Dracopoulos (tel: 9692 3658).

Religious education

St Andrew's Greek Orthodox Theological College. An institution dedicated primarily to theological study, in cooperation with other theological colleges. The BTh program at St Andrew's Theological College includes both academic and practical components in order to give students thorough training in Eastern Orthodox theology and the skills needed for a contemporary pastoral ministry in Australia. In addition, the College is intended to be a centre for ecumenical scholarship and interaction. It is expected that a student will undertake the program over four years full time; since 1992 part-time study has also been available. In addition, a series of evening lectures are organised every semester for members of the public.

242 Cleveland Street, Redfern (tel: 9319 6145).

University Greek studies. In the higher education system, Modern Greek language, history and culture courses have been available in the tertiary and further education sector for the past 25 years, at both undergraduate and postgraduate levels. The basic aims of the subjects offered, in terms of language, are to provide a sound reading knowledge of Greek and a command of basic conversational and written Greek. They also offer courses designed to create an understanding of Greek literature and history. Whenever possible, language course are conducted in Greek, while history lectures are mainly in English.

Libraries

St Andrew's Greek Orthodox Theological College Library. It holds some 7,000 volumes, forming the nucleus of a fine collection.

Helen Vatsikopoulos

PRESENTER OF DATELINE, SBS TELEVISION

Born in Florina, Greece, Helen Vatsikopoulos joined SBS's international current affairs program *Dateline* in 1988, and in 1997 she became its presenter. One of the most talented journalists in the country, Helen has received several awards including the prestigious Walkley Award for Best International Report in 1992 and the United Nations Media Peace Prize in 1993.

Prior to joining SBS, Helen worked for four years for the ABC on radio and television news as well as in current affairs on *Nationwide* and *The 7.30 Report*.

The Library is of special interest to students researching the history and thought of Orthodox theology and spirituality. The Library receives 105 current journals and newsletters. Another major resource is the Patrologia Graeca on microfiche. This wonderful library also has a wide collection of Byzantine music scores, along with a collection of tapes of Byzantine chanting. Approximately one-third of the monograph and serials collection is in Greek. Members of the public are welcome to use the Library. Open Monday-Friday 10am-4pm, Thursday 9am-5pm.

Further information: 9319 6145.

Community organisations and institutions

Most Greeks in Australia today belong to a Greek community, cultural, political, educational, or professional organisation. This is the way in which their commitment to the maintenance, preservation and promotion of Greek culture is carried out. After the Church communities, the earliest Greek organisations were the regional fraternities of the large groups, such as the Kytherians, Kastellorizons and Ithacans. With the massive Greek immigration of 1950s and 1960s Sydney Greek community organisations and institutions grew even further. The following is a selected list.

Hellenic Advancement Council (HAC).

Formed in 1970 when Greek immigration peaked, it has played a major role in the social and cultural development of the Sydney Greek community. Several organisations come under its umbrella.

49A Tramway Street, Rosebery. Contact George S Eleftheriades (tel: 9667 3045).

Greek Welfare Centre.

The Centre provides social and welfare assistance to Greek immigrants and also develops diverse community development projects.

116 Redfern Street, Redfern. Contact S Magdas, Director (tel: 9319 5964).

Greek Australian Professionals Association.

Plays a very important role in providing advice to Greek students pursuing a professional career. It also supports and gets involved in charitable and cultural activities.

PO Box 125, Enmore 2042. Contact George Griziotis (tel: 9587 4801).

Media

The Greek-language press began in Australia with the appearance of the weekly newspaper *Afstralia*, the first edition of which was published in Melbourne in June 1913. Soon after, in 1914, a second weekly named *Okeanis* emerged in Adelaide. The language used in the media is about one-third Greek and two-thirds a combination of Greek and English. One of the few Greek publications in English is *The Monthly Chronicle*.

There are 29 Greek language radio programs; of these 86% of the program content is broadcast in Greek and 14% in English. There are also two television programs in Greek, one on SBS Television and one on a community channel. Two television programs are also received directly from Greece, totalling 2 1/2 hours of daily broadcasting from Greece. The strong support for Greek media reflects the generally high level of Greek language retention typical of the Greek community.

Newspapers

To Bhma (Tribune). Established in 1913, it was the first Hellenic newspaper in Australia and the second-oldest non-English-language newspaper in Australia. Published three times a week, it hits the stands on Tuesday, Thursday and Saturday. It has a circulation of 19,800 and costs $1.30. Its current editor is Ikaros Kyriakous.

1-27 Princes Highway, St Peters (tel: 9557 6000).

Mary Kostakidis

PRESENTER, SBS TELEVISION WORLD NEWS

Born in Salonica, Greece, Mary Kostakidis came to Australia with her parents at the age of two. Nowadays she is considered one of the leading newsreaders on Australian television. Before joining SBS Television in 1980, Mary Kostakidis was an editor at the Ethnic Affairs Commission of NSW. Prior to that she worked as a tutor at Sydney University, a research officer for the Departments of Health and Youth and Community Services, and as a court interpreter. She has also worked for ABC Radio News. She holds a BA from the University of Sydney where she studied French, German, Italian, Modern Greek and Philosophy. Mary Kostakidis also is a member of the Republic Advisory Committee.

Explore the world in one city

Ellinikos Kirikas (The Greek Herald). It is published daily from Monday to Friday and has a circulation of 24,000, and costs $1.40. Its current editor is Michael Mystakidis.
1-9 Glebe Point Road, Glebe (tel: 9660 2033).

O Kosmos. A bilingual (English and Greek) newspaper, it's published twice a week and has a circulation of 20,000, costing $1.30. The current editor is George Messaris.
204 Canterbury Road, Canterbury (tel: 9789 4211).

The Monthly Chronicle. Established in 1994, this is a Greek-English monthly magazine. It is very well designed and offers in-depth political, economic and current affairs analysis. It also has features and art sections. It is, indeed, a welcome addition to the list of quality magazines on the local scene. It can be found in selected newagencies (try the Town Hall newsagency) at a cost of $3.50. Its editor-in-chief is Anthony Liberiu.
Postal Address, 7/460 New South Head Road, Double Bay 2028.

Radio

SBS Radio 1, AM 1107. News, music and current affairs. Monday-Sunday 7am-8am and 6pm-7pm.

2SER, FM 107.3. Hellenic Program, Sunday 1.30-2.30pm and Voice of Orthodoxy, Sunday 2.30pm-3pm.

2MM, AM 1665. Twenty-four hours of news, current affairs, music, entertainment and sport.

Greek radio programs can also be heard on the following Sydney community radio stations. Timeslots vary, so call for the latest.

2BCR, FM 88.7 (tel: 9724 7877 or 9726 8233)

2MWM, FM 92.1/93.7 (tel: 9913 8986)

2NBC, FM 90.1 (tel: 9534 2778)

2RDJ, FM 88.1 (tel: 9744 3284 or 9744 0881)

2RES, FM 89.7 (tel: 9331 3000)

Television

SBS Television carries the daily news of *Ta Nea Toy Ennea*, the most prestigious news service in Greece, Monday-Saturday 6-6.30am.

Facts and figures

Greek is the third most popular language in Australia behind Italian and English.

Since the late 1950s the Australian Greek population – just over 136,000 people – has been and continues to be, after the Italians, the second largest group from a non-English-speaking background in Australia. New South Wales has the second largest Greek community in Australia – 44,330 – after Victoria. Just over 40,000 or 91.7% of these currently live in Sydney.

Greek immigrants have one of the highest rates of citizenship, 93%. They are also very fast in deciding to take out Australian citizenship, with those arriving in 1990-91 already having a rate of naturalisation of 24.9% by the time of the Census in late 1991.

The percentage of Greek immigrants with post-secondary qualifications (3.4%) is well below that for the total Australian population (12.8%). Similarly, the proportion of Greek-born who have received skilled or basic vocational training (7.5%) is also low,

compared to the Australian-born population. However, 15% of second-generation Greeks (born in Australia with at least one Greek-born parent) had completed post-secondary qualifications, a figure considerably higher than the national average.

While the median annual income of Greek immigrants ($12,400) is below to that of the total Australian population ($14,200) they have a much higher home ownership (83.0%) than the rest of Australia.

The strong Greek commitment to culture is reflected in the generally high level of Greek language retention. In the 1991 Census, 91.3% of Greek-born people aged five years or over indicated that they usually speak Greek at home. As the church is a dominant organisation in the community, around 97% of Greek-born settlers are members of the Greek Orthodox Church.

The Hungarians

The novelist, poet and play wright David Martin was once described by the *The Times* (London) as 'Australia's outstanding literary acquisition from postwar immigration'. Born Ludwig Detsinyi in Budapest, Hungary, in 1915, he used to say that he would like to be remembered for his writings, not his life. However, his life was a tale every bit as exciting as a novel. Brought up and educated in Germany, David Martin embraced the world.

At the age of 21 he joined the Republican forces in the Spanish Civil War, and during World War II he worked as a journalist in Britain. Here he adopted the name David Martin. After the war he worked as foreign correspondent in India and Ceylon, and in 1949 he came to Australia, becoming one of the most prolific and talented of Australia's post war writers. He embraced his adopted country, and in what is probably his best novel, *The Young Wife*, (1962) he wrote about the tragedies afflicting a migrant couple torn between cultures. He passed away in 1997, more than 150 years from the time a Hungarian first set foot on Australian soil.

Early arrivals

The first Hungarian immigrant was Isaac Friedman, who arrived in Sydney in 1833 and became a merchant and a successful shop owner. In the 15 years from his arrival he was joined by about 20 other Hungarian immigrants. One of those was Maurice Birnstingl who established a jewellery shop in Bridge Street, Sydney. He was joined later by his brother Lewis, and as expert silversmiths they made some of the silverware that still decorates a number of Sydney's churches and synagogues. Ignatz and Adolphus Wortmans were another pair of brothers who came seeking their fortune. They arrived in Sydney in 1842 and made a small fortune manufacturing 'Lucifer' matches and cigar lights. These resourceful brothers began importing matchwood, boxes and chemicals from Britain and exported their finished products with very good profits.

Sydney Hungarians speak with pride and nostalgia about one of the greatest achievements of their community – the St George Budapest Social Club. Founded in 1957 and located in Victoria Street, Mortdale, it was one of the pillars of Australian soccer during the 1960s and 70s. It was in the Club, on April 5 1975, that a group of visionaries decided to form a national soccer league.

The Hungarian-born musician Jackie Orszaczky has been – since the mid-1970s – a prime mover on the Sydney music scene. A bass player and an all time legend, Orszaczky was born in Budapest and settled in Sydney in 1970 becoming – according to the specialists – one of the godfathers of the local funk and soul landscape.

The failed revolution of independence from Austria in 1848 produced thousands of refugees and political exiles. The first began arriving in 1851, and between this year and 1867 about 100 Hungarian exiles, all highly educated, reached the coast of Australia. In the 1860s they established in Sydney the first Hungarian community organisation in Australia, the Hungarian Reading Circle, which was conceived as a space for intellectual and political debate. Among those who came during these years were Albert Gustave Gyulay, a native of Transylvania, who worked as a journalist for the *Sydney Morning Herald* and was later employed by the New South Wales government; and Andrew Samuel Hollander, who in 1862 established a grocery and spirit bottle shop in George Street. He lived in the inner-city suburb of Redfern, where he died in 1885.

The 'golden age' and beyond

Political upheavals, persecutions, invasions and wars have been at the core of the Hungarian immigration experience. Following the rise of Hitler in Germany, thousands of Hungarians of Jewish origin migrated to the United States, while some, around 800, made the long way to Australia. One of these was Dr Andrew Fabinyi, a publisher who arrived in 1939 and went on to have decisive impact on the development of Australian intellectual life.

Les Murray (née Lazlo Ürge) - from SBS Television- is one of the most influential Australian sport commentators.

At the end of World War II, the destroyed Hungarian economy and a country occupied by the Soviet Union again pushed Hungarians to search for freedom and economic opportunities in foreign lands. Between 1948 and 1954 close to 17,000 displaced Hungarians settled in Australia. If you forget the refugee drama, you could say that this was the 'golden age' of Hungarian immigration to Australia. It was a generation that gave our country many very talented people: Les Murray (née Lazlo Ürge), SBS Television's high-profile sports commentator; Nick Greiner, former New South Wales Premier and influential Sydney personality; Tommy Tycho, the multitalented and popular musician; Andrew Riemer and Susan Varga, two of the most distinguished contemporary Australian writers; and Sir Peter Abeles, the former high-flying Sydney corporate business leader. The list goes on.

The Hungarian uprising of 1956 and the violent repression that followed it sent a new wave of refugees to the west. Close to 14,000 exiles came to Australia, bringing the number of Hungarians in Australia to 30,000 by the end of the 1950s. One of the 'fifty-sixers', as they were called, was Dr Nicholas Derere, who arrived in 1957, became a research agronomist for the NSW Department of Agriculture and succeeded in laying down the foundations for the prime hard wheat and cotton industries in this state. In the last few years, Dr Derera has become the driving force behind the development in Australia of the lucrative paprika market, an exclusive domain of the Hungarians for 200 years. No more, it seems.

Hungarians speak with pride and nostalgia about one of the greatest achievements of their community – the St George Budapest Social Club. Founded in 1957 and located in Victoria Street, Mortdale, it was one of the pillars of Australian soccer during the 1960s and 70s. It was here, on April 5 1975, that a group of visionaries decided to form a national soccer league. The influence of St George extended into the 1980s when Hungarian-born coach Frank Arok took the 'Saints' to their only national league title in 1983. It was a time of glory but it was also the year when the Club began its inevitable slow decline. Despite a brief period with Les Murray as president (1994-96), the Victoria Street clubhouse was eventually sold in 1997, and with that the doors of this great Sydney Hungarian institution were finally closed.

Currently there are about 9,200 Hungarians living in Sydney. Those of Jewish origin tend to concentrate in the eastern suburbs, especially in Waverley and Woollahra, while a large number of non-Jewish Hungarians have settled in the western suburbs of Croydon, Ashfield and Bankstown. Here they have established a number of very important community and religious organisations, including the Hungarian Catholic Community at Ashfield and the Magyar Social Club at Bonnyrigg. Equally important for the Hungarian community – a real landmark – is the St Elizabeth Home for Aged Hungarians, which opened in Blacktown in 1967. Instrumental in its establishment was Catholic Father Ferenc Forro who arrived in Sydney in 1951. Father Forro also was behind the creation of the Hungarian Section in Rookwood Cemetery, which has great significance for Sydney Hungarians. He was the Chaplain of the Hungarian Catholic Community until his death in 1974.

Born in Budapest, Sir Peter Abeles arrived in Australia shortly after War World II. In 1950 he founded Alltrans Pty Ltd, one of the most successful transport companies in the country. By 1967, Alltrans was taken over by TNT and Sir Peter Abeles became its managing director and deputy chairman. An important step in his corporate career was achieved in 1972 when he became a director of Ansett, an Australian domestic airlines company.

Sir Peter Abeles has been chairman of the Opera Foundation of Australia and established the Australian Cancer Foundation for Medical Research. His long and successful career as an industrialist has transformed him into one of the hundred richest men in Australia. He is now retired from business.

Restaurants and cafes

Hearty soups and *gulyás* (goulash) are what you would describe as "Hungarian national dishes". Give them a try.

Art and Cafe. No fuss – down-to-earth traditional Hungarian cuisine. Make sure you finish off your meal with one of the mouth-watering desserts. Average $30, BYO.
Open dinner Wednesday-Monday 5.30pm-10.30pm.
298 Bronte Road, Waverley (tel: 9387 8265).

FOOD

I SOOS AND CO.
A venerable bakery with a strong Hungarian accent. Open Monday-Thursday, 6am-2pm and 4pm-5pm ("I have to do deliveries to some restaurants in the city and we're short of hands," says the shop assistant Barbara explaining the temporary closure), Friday 6am-4pm and Sunday 6am-1pm.
443-5 Old South Head Road, Rose Bay
(tel: 9371 7341).

HUNTER'S LODGE.
It's not only the food that enjoyable here but also the beauty and charm of the surroundings. The *halszle* (fish soup) and the veal medallion with *paprika* cream sauce are highly recommended. Average $30, licensed. Open Monday-Sunday dinner 6pm-midnight.
18 Cross Street, Double Bay
(tel: 9363 1747).

See also Wellington Cake shop and Kemeny's supermarket, page 15

Bondi Road Brasserie. It seems that it's almost traditional that Sydney Hungarian restaurants don't like to match their names to their cuisine - this isn't an exception. The zesty Hungarian menu includes the popular tomato and capsicum stew with duck. BYO.
198 Bondi Road, Bondi (tel: 9387 1082)

Double Bay Steak House. A good tip for winter: the old and timeless Hungarian paprika fish soup - a real achievement. BYO
15 Knox Street, Double Bay (tel: 9327 1115)

Gelato Bar. Again we still think that the only thing wrong with this restaurant is its name. It does sell gelato and it's good, but the real reputation of this traditional and long-established Hungarian restaurant in Sydney has been built on its magnificent food. You cannot go wrong if you order, for example, the scrambled eggs with mushrooms and fried sausage, or the perpetual favourite, beef stroganoff. Average $30, BYO. Open Monday-Sunday, 8am-midnight.
140 Campbell Parade, Bondi Beach (tel: 930 4033).

Clubs

Magyar Social Club. The only Hungarian social club in Sydney, it was founded at the end of the 1960s but its new venue is only two years old. "It costs us one million!", the CEO of the Club ("just call me Alex" says). It operates on Friday and weekends and has frequent cultural and social activities, including a dance night. "This is the place were the old tales from Budapest are told," says Alex. At the bistro the menu is mostly Hungarian and very cheap, "you get a big portion of *goulash* or *nockerl* (dumplings) for $8," Alex explains. Imported Hungarian wines and drinks are also available. Open Friday-Sunday noon-10pm, or later depending on the functions.
706-708 Smithfield Road, Bonnyrigg (tel: 9610 6226).

Landmarks

Hungarian Section, Rookwood Cemetery.

The Hungarian section in Rookwood Cemetery, in the western suburb of Lidcombe, is a very important landmark for the Sydney Hungarian community. The Heroes' Cross Memorial here has been the site of Hungarian religious and historic commemorations. Conceived by Father Ferenc Forro, the section is maintained by Hungarian volunteers.

Getting to know the Hungarian community

Events

Monthly historical lectures.

An ongoing event run by the Hungarian Historical Society, this is one of the great community initiatives of Sydney's Hungarians. The lectures, held at the Punchbowl Senior Centre (until the refurnishing of the Hungarian House Co-op is finished), are held mid-month. "We analyse historical issues relating to mediaeval and modern history," explains Gabor Foldvary, the Society's president. The function starts with afternoon tea at 4.30pm while the lecture kicks off at 5pm and finishes at 6.30pm. All are welcome, and admission is free but a $2 donation would be appreciated.

Further information: Gabor Foldvary (tel: 9661 9007).

Hungarian National Day

A historical celebration held on March 15 involving various cultural and social activities.

Magyar Social Club, 26 Smithfield Road, Bonnyrigg (tel: 9610 6226).

Feast of St Stephen.

On August 20 the Hungarian community has a celebration in honour of Stephen ('Istvan') the First. Stephen ruled Hungary between 997 until his death in 1038, presiding over a period in which Hungary enjoyed political stability and economic growth. He was canonised in 1803. Activities are held at the

Magyar Social Club, 26 Smithfield Road, Bonnyrigg (tel: 9610 6226).

Hungary Martyrs' Day.

On October 23 the Sydney Hungarian community remembers the 1956 invasion of Hungary by troops and tanks from the former Soviet Union. The Magyar Social Club often organises cultural activities to commemorate this episode.

Culture

Hungarian Historical Society of Sydney.

Established in 1971, the Society has continued cultivating the great love

---

USEFUL NUMBER FOR VISITORS

HUNGARIAN CONSULATE,
tel: 9328 7860.

Established in 1971, the Hungarian historical society has continued cultivating the great love affairs of Hungarians with history.

RELIGIOUS ORGANISATIONS AND PLACES OF WORSHIP

HUNGARIAN CATHOLIC COMMUNITY.
The Community organises mass in Hungarian as well as various Catholic activities. Times and days of religious services may vary so it is best to call the office for information, Monday and Wednesday 9.30am-4.30pm. The office is open by appointment on Fridays.

120 Parramatta Road, Ashfield (tel: 9799 5469 or 9798 0658).

HUNGARIAN HOUSE COOPERATIVE.
Since its establishment in the early 1950s, the Cooperative has provided social, cultural and welfare services to Sydney's Hungarians.

1-5 Breust Place, corner Highclere Avenue and Breust Place, Punchbowl (tel: 9759 6974).

affair of Hungarians with history (a refreshing and encouraging activity considering some people have declared the 'end of history'). The Society also organises monthly public lecturers (see page 153) and publishes the *Hungarian Past*, an annual journal of mediaeval and modern history (it's mainly in Hungarian but the article abstracts and some complete articles are translated to English). You can purchase the journal for $10 from Gabor Foldvary, President of the Society.

267 Beauchamp Road, Matraville (tel: 9661 9007).

Community organisations

Hungarian St Elizabeth Caritas Association.

"Most Hungarians would have dealt with or know about this Association as it's the main welfare association for Hungarian people in Sydney," explains Anna Hollai, the Association's community worker.

120 Parramatta Road, Ashfield (tel: 9799 5469).

St Elizabeth Home for Aged Hungarians.

Established in 1967, the Home provides residential rooms, reading rooms, a nursery wing and other facilities for elderly Hungarians.

Richmond Road, Blacktown (tel: 9626 9254).

Media

Newspapers

Magyar Elet ('Hungarian Life'). This is the only Hungarian weekly in Australia. It has a circulation of 6,000 and can be found in selected newsagencies on Thursdays. Price $1.80. It has offices in Melbourne and Sydney; the current Sydney editor is Erika Demian Jozsa.

22 Marinella Street, Manly Vale (tel: 9907 6151).

Radio

SBS Radio 1, AM 1107. News, current affairs and a wide range of music from Hungary, Monday and Tuesday 1pm-2 pm.

A Hungarian radio program can also be heard on 2RSR, FM 88.9. Since timeslots may vary, call for the latest (tel: 9550 9552).

Television

SBS Television offers a weekly Hungarian news service on Sunday 7am-7.30am.

The Italians

"**He is a *paesano*.**" Ask Sydney Italians about David Campese, the great Australian rugby player, and that's what they'll say. This sense of community and national pride – *paesano* or compatriot – sums up the Italian Australian experience.

Italians waste no time in telling you about those *paesanos* who have forged their identity: they will tell you about the achievements of Dr Franco Belgiorno-Nettis, one of the most influential figures in the construction industry; about the paintings of Salvatore Zofrea, considered the doyen of modern Australian art; the movies starring Greta Scacchi; the political influence of MP Franca Arena; and the striking fashions designed by Carla Zampatti. And, of course, they won't forget to drop the name of Frank Sartor, Sydney's current Lord Mayor, following in the hallowed footsteps of New York's Rudy Giuliani – another Italian boy made good.

Early arrivals

Italians have been arriving on Australian shores since the early years of white settlement. The first known Italian to visit Australia was James Matra, after whom the eastern Sydney suburb of Matraville is named; drawing on his experience as a midshipman with James Cook in 1770, Matra proposed Botany Bay as a suitable place for settlement. Another Italian, Antonio Ponto, sailed with Captain Cook on the Endeavour, while Giuseppe Tusa was part of the First Fleet, which established white settlement in Sydney Cove in 1788. They were soon followed by two artists, Ferdinand Brambilla and Giovanni Ravenet, who arrived with Marchese Alessandro Malaspina's expedition in 1793, spending their time in the colony sketching scenes of convicts and free settlers. Their works constitute a valuable testimony, and can be viewed in the Mitchell Library (see page 168 for more on the Italian collection at the State Library of New South Wales).

While a handful of convicts and some of the earliest free settlers were Italian, they did not arrive in large numbers until the 1850s Gold Rush hit Eastern Australia. Among those seeking a new start was

> Italians waste no time in telling you about those *paesanos* who have forged their identity: Dr Franco Belgiorno-Nettis, Salvatore Zofrea, Greta Scacchi; Franca Arena; Carla Zampatti and Frank Sartor.

The first Australian Italian-language newspapers, the Italo-Australian, *Giornale Italiano* and the Italian *Bulletin of Commerce*, were also founded in the first decade of the century. There was no shortage of stories and the one that made headlines was the Sydney wedding of the popular soprano Toti Dal Monte, who married her leading tenor, Enzo de Muro Lomanto. More than 25,000 attended the cornucopian ceremony at St Mary's Cathedral.

schoolteacher Raffaele Carboni, who became a leading figure in the Eureka Stockade, before returning to Italy, where he played a major part in the emergence of modern Italy. Another famous Italian of the time was the artist Achille Simonetti, the sculptor of the Phillip Fountain and Statue in the Royal Botanic Gardens (see page 168).

A year after Tommaso Sani finished carving the relief figures on the Pitt Street facade of Sydney's General Post Office in 1880, a group of 317 Italian migrants arrived in Australia. They became the founding fathers of the settlement of New Italy at Woodburn, in northern New South Wales, the first and most successful attempt to transplant Italian traditions to Australia. Isolated from the mainstream, the community prospered, building houses in Friulian and Venetian styles, together with a church, a school, and a community hall.

Federation and beyond

At the time of Federation in 1901, there were nearly 6000 Italian-born immigrants living in Australia. Italian immigration increased in the early years of the twentieth century, when southern Italy was ravaged by poverty and thousands of Italian labourers replaced the Chinese, who were excluded by the White Australia Policy. By 1939 the Italian-Australian community had grown to approximately 40,000, the largest non-British group, establishing themselves as cane cutters, fruit growers, market gardeners, miners and fishermen.

Around this time, the Italian community in Sydney began to find its feet: one of the first organisations to emerge was the *Circolo Isole Eolie*, founded in 1903, which united migrants from the Aeolian Islands; other regional clubs, such as Roma, Venezia and Savoia, soon followed. They became well-attended venues where Italian immigrants – most of them with very little English – gathered to find emotional support, advice or just have a good chat.

And it's unlikely they would have passed up the opportunity to have a passionate discussion, over a shot of coffee or a glass of wine, on the political fate of Giuseppe Zani, an Italian *paesano* who in 1904 was elected mayor of Cabramatta-Canley Vale, in western Sydney.

From the late nineteenth century, the Italian presence had a profound inflence on the Sydney arts community. During the nationalist ferment of the 1890s and on into the 1920s young Sydney artists, painters and assorted bohemians worshipped at the altar of all things Italian. The immigrants' cafés were magnets for Sydney's literati, attracted to the communal lifestyle and exotic flavours. But it was more than just food and atmosphere. The Mediterraneans linked rough and philistine Sydney with a classical past and a respected artistic tradition. In the years before World War I, immigrant Datillo Rubbo formalised the connection, establishing a famous art school that was to inspire a generation of Sydney artists and kickstart post-impressionism in Australia. In 1913, Rubbo fought a duel to defend the artistic reputation of one of his students.

The golden years

During the 1950s and 1960s, Italian migration reached unprecedented levels. Most arrived by the process of "chain migration", with earlier arrivals funding the migration of brothers, cousins, wives, parents and grandparents. They came from Sicily, Calabria, the Aeolian Islands, Campania, Tuscany, the Veneto and Lombardy. Initially, these immigrants settled in the inner-city suburbs of Darlinghurst, Woolloomooloo, Redfern, Pyrmont and Ultimo – then all staunchly working-class areas – but by the 1960s, Leichhardt had consolidated itself as Sydney's "Little Italy".

Thankfully, the Italians brought their love of good food and wine with them, transforming a cuisine based on grey roasts and suspect meat pies. Zesty Mediterranean ingredients heralded a revolution in the kitchen, while espresso machines launched a thousand coffee bars. The unstoppable Sydney love affair with coffee can be traced back to a tough guy, former boxer Luigi Coluzzi, who opened the legendary Bar Coluzzi, in the inner-Sydney suburb of Darlinghurst, in the 1950s. Also vying for custom was the Piccolo Bar at Roslyn Street, Kings Cross: established by Ozzie Comati, a flamboyant Italian who arrived in Australia in 1949, this was the coffee bar of choice for entertainers such as Sammy Davis Jnr and Frank Sinatra and a longtime haunt of Sydney bohemians.

During the golden era of the 1950s, Italian immigrants would religiously gather in cafés, bars or the family home to listen to *The Italian Hour*, hosted by Mamma Lena (née Lena Gustin), the fondly remembered Italian radio broadcaster and journalist. Her popular radio programmes, including the longstanding *Arrivederci Roma* and the *Festival in Casa Contest*, a show that launched several successful entertainment careers, were a resounding success. Mamma Lena's programmes were also instrumental in assisting new settlers and organising welfare and charity appeals, and in 1967 she was honoured by the Italian government with the Croce di Cavaliere for her services to the community. Mamma Lena died in 1983, but tapes of her programmes can be found in the Italian Historical Collection at the State Library of NSW (see page 168).

Sydney's love affair with coffee can be traced back to former boxer Luigi Coluzzi, seen here with Angiolina Lorenzi, who opened the legendary Bar Coluzzi, in the inner-Sydney suburb of Darlinghurst, in the 1950s.

The next generation

Even though the number of Italians living in Sydney has dwindled in recent years, they still form the largest non-English-speaking group and second-generation Italian-Australians are vigorously injecting new life into the arts and sports scene. Here you'll find talented journalist Paola Totaro; (daugther of Paolo Totaro, the foundation chairman of the NSW ethnic affairs commission); versatile actor Salvatore Coco, of *Heartbreak High* fame; much-liked Vince Sorrenti; acclaimed comedian and director Santo Cilauro, known for ABC TV's *Frontline* and his first feature film, *The Castle*, which mercilessly lampooned Australian icons. And, of course, David Campese himself – who once wryly observed, "If I play well, I'm Australian; if I mess things up, I'm Italian". Between them, they're making sure that the Italian language (with that unmistakeable Aussie twang), culture and tradition will continue to invigorate Sydney.

Italian-Australians have changed what it means to be an Aussie, not just in terms of "Modern Australian Cuisine" (Mediterranean meets Asian meets English) but in a close-knit family life, a sense of fashion and a gregarious use of public space. Italian-Australians have led Australians out of their backyards and into the streets, proudly promenading down public thoroughfares like Norton Street in Leichhardt. By infusing our lifestyle with a Mediterranean outlook, Italian immigrants and their children have helped us feel more comfortable with Sydney's climate and landscape.

Mamma Lena's popular radio programmes, including the longstanding Arrivederci Roma and the Festival in Casa Contest, a show that launched several successful entertainment careers, were a resounding success.

"Little Italy"

Leichhardt

Leichhardt, in Sydney's Inner West, has been the home of Sydney's Italian community since the the end of the nineteenth century. Among the first Italians to settle in Leichhardt, in 1885, were a fishmonger, Angelo Pomabello, and the Bongiorno Brothers, who had a fruit shop on Parramatta Road.

But it was not until the 1920s that "Little Italy" began taking shape: the story goes that when the Capuchin priests were posted here, Italian immigrants would gravitate to them for help in dealing with those impenetrable official letters, to get a job or just to find a place to live. By 1933, around 400 Italians were living in Leichhardt, and the community was reinforced by a massive influx in the late 1950s and early 1960s; for these post-war Italian migrants, Leichhardt offered cheap housing, proximity to employers of unskilled labourers, Italian shops and other businesses. As early as 1962 there were already four Italian cafes in Leichhardt and soon they were joined by bakeries, fruit vendors, grocers, butchers, hairdressers, bookmakers, real estate agents, pharmacies, jewellers, restaurants and nightclubs, serving an Italian population of more than 4000.

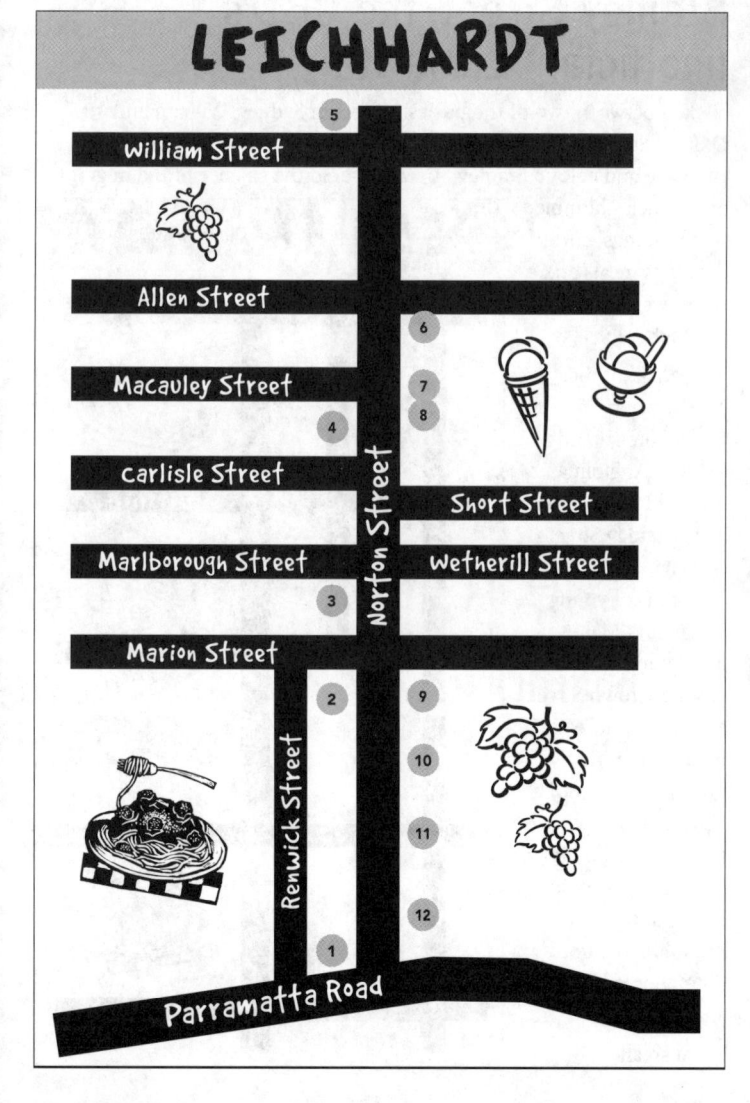

GETTING TO LEICHHARDT

The heart of "Little Italy", Leichhardt's Norton Street, is a short distance west of Sydney's CBD.

Buses 436, 438, 440, 470 and the L38 run from Circular Quay every 20–30 minutes, via George Street and Parramatta Road, taking around 20 minutes to reach Norton Street.

A taxi will set you back around $10.

LITTLE ITALY

1. Caffe Sport, see page 165
2. La Cremeria, see page 165
3. Mezzapica, see page 165
4. Portofino, see page 165
5. Castew Mola, see page 165
6. Bar Italia, see page 165
7. Numero Tre, see page 165
8. Buon Appetito, see page 165
9. Palace Norton Street Cinemas, see page 165
10. Norton Street Markets, see page 165
11. Bar Baba, see page 165
12. Anna and Aldo's, see page 165

In recent years, Leichhardt has undergone significant changes. Many Italian families have moved to other suburbs, such as Drummoyne, Ashfield, Haberfield, Concord and Burwood – a pattern of neighbourhood displacement illustrated by the latest figures, which indicate that only 2000 out of Leichhardt's population of 60,000 were born in Italy. Despite this, some things never change. Leichhardt, especially Norton Street with its outdoor cafes, restaurants and delicatessens has maintained its seductive Italian atmosphere.

A big new cinema complex, the Palace Norton Street cinemas has opened at 99 Norton Street in Leichhardt

Stanley Street, the CBD's unofficial "Little Italy"

Tucked between two of the busiest streets in Sydney, William and Oxford, Stanley Street is a tiny little corridor of Italian flavour, smell, language and colour. Stanley Street captured the essence of the migrant experience - humble surroundings, cheap delicious meals and a warm welcoming atmosphere.

At the end of the 1940s, when the late Carlo Lorenzi and his wife Angiolina opened La Veneziana at 73 Stanley Street (see map S4), hundreds of young Italian and Maltese immigrants boarding around Crown Street and nearby areas began dropping by. For most of them La Veneziana was where they received their first Italian meal in this country, and Angiolina became their adopted 'mamma'.

From small

IN AND AROUND STANLEY STREET

1. Bar Reggio, see page 163
2. Ristorante Stella, see page 164
3. The Arch Cafe (downstairs), see page 164
4. Beppi's, see page 163
5. Alife, see page 163
6. Bill and Toni's Italian Restaurant, see page 163
7. Giotto Cafe, see page 163
8. Palati Fini, see page 163
9. Giardinetto Restaurant, see page 163

Explore the world in one city

beginnings La Veneziana eventually expanded upstairs and next door. By that time it was common to see Italians lining up to get in. Carlo's passion for boxing attracted a regular contingent of Italian boxers who would fight at the nearby Sydney Stadium. Among them were Luigi Colussi and the great Rocky Marciano, who dropped by during his visit to Sydney in the 1960s. Many non-Italian Australians also began calling in to 'find out what the fuss was all about'. These were the years when Stanley Street was also known as a gambling and red light district where the 'working girls' would make the Italian and Maltese feel at home.

After La Veneziana – which closed in the early 1970s – other cafes and restaurants soon followed, and the Italian flavour of the area increased. The legendary No Names was the next. Established in the early 1950s, it was a place where a few coins would get you a gigantic bowl of pasta – and it still is. Beppi's appeared in 1956 when Beppi Polese, an adventurous Italian immigrant, transformed a rundown Yugoslav coffee shop at the corner of Stanley and Yurong Streets into a fine-dining institution.

Bill and Toni's was another pioneer of this Italian enclave. It began in 1976 and many famous people, including politicians Gough Whitlam, Bob Carr, and Michael Egan, lawyer Chris Murphy and singer Jon Bon Jovi have eaten here. It even got the thumbs up from Australia's richest man: "This is a good little business you got here" Kerry Packer once commented to its owner Toni de Santis.

GETTING TO STANLEY STREET

Stanley Street is a walking distance from the Sydney Town Hall. From Circular Quay take the **389 bus**, which goes directly past Stanley Street, or a **380 or L82 (limited stops)**, which go to Oxford Street. If you're taking a taxi from Circular Quay expect to pay between $7 and $10.

A taste of Italy

Sydneysiders have long ranked Italian as their favourite dining-out cuisine, and Italian immigrants have been instrumental in reshaping the nation's tastes.

Two men in particular broke the mould of Sydney's old eating habits: the late Ettore Prossimo, a Sicilian-born migrant who arrived in Sydney in the early 1950s, and Beppi Polese, a larger-than-life character who escaped a concentration camp on the border of Austria and Hungary during World War II. On Christmas Eve, 1956, Ettore Prossimo opened what became the most highly regarded Italian restaurant in Sydney for many years. In its heyday, the Buona Sera, on Macleay Street, Potts Point, was favoured by Frank Sinatra, Ella Fitzgerald and Rudolf Nureyev, among other international celebrities. Beppi Polese began his long-running Beppi's in 1956, after buying and transforming a rundown Yugoslav coffee shop on the corner of Stanley and Yurong Streets, East Sydney, where his restaurant still stands.

THE ITALIANS

Many other Italian restaurateurs have succesfully followed in Ettore and Beppi's footsteps, among them Armando Percuoco of Buon Ricordo in Paddington; Lucio Galletto of Lucio's, also in Paddington; and Steve Manfredi of Bel Mondo in The Rocks – all of whom have been awarded the Italian government's *Insegna del Ristorante Italiano* in recognition of their contribution to authentic Italian cooking.

Restaurants

In Sydney there are hundreds of Italian restaurants, ranging from pizzerias to elegant formal dining rooms; we've focused on critically acclaimed places within close range of inner Sydney, but you won't go far wrong if you stick to places thronged with customers. One of the greatest concentrations of Italian restaurants is in "Little Italy" (Leichhardt), a short cab or bus ride from the city centre.

When the late Carlo Lorenzi and his wife, Angiolina, opened La Veneziana in Stanley Street, this spot began its long love affair with Italy. Hundreds of Italian immigrants began dropping by, attracted by the homestyle cooking and reassured by the warm welcome.

Leichhardt and the West

Anna and Aldo's. Traditional family-run trattoria. Average $15; licensed & BYO. Lunch Monday-Saturday 11.30am-2.30pm; dinner Monday-Saturday, 5.30-9.30pm.
9 Norton Street, Leichhardt (tel: 9550 9760).

Club Marconi. A unique Sydney-Italian dining experience is offered by this cavernous complex, which boasts no less than four restaurants. The Elettra serves lunch Wednesday-Sunday 12.30-3pm, with a "La Dolce Vita" special on Wednesdays ($40, including wine), and dinner, accompanied by live music, Thursday-Sunday 6.30-10pm. For bargain pasta and gelati, make for the Trattoria, which is open for lunch Tuesday-Friday noon-3pm and dinner Tuesday-Sunday 6-10pm. Otherwise, you can always drop by the charming Cafe Piazza for *foccacia* and desserts, or fill up at the Marconi Bistro, which does $3 "special plates" for Monday-Friday lunch.
Cr Marconi Plaza and Prairie Road, Bossley Park (tel: 9823 2222).

Portofino. Chargrilled seafood to die for, plus bowls of pasta drenched in creamy sauces. Average $30; licensed & BYO. Lunch Wednesday-Saturday noon-3pm; dinner Monday-Sunday 6pm-late.
166 Norton Street, Leichhardt (tel: 9550 0782).

City and Eastern suburbs

Original No Names (Upstairs in the Arch Cafe). Cheap, gigantic

Explore the world in one city

and good quality. Average $6, BYO. Open for lunch Monday-Sunday noon-2.15pm, dinner 6pm-9.30pm.

81 Stanley Street, East Sydney (tel: 9360 4711).

Beppi's. One of Sydney's most consistently popular Italian restaurants. Not a 'fly-by-night' venue, it has built a solid base of regular customers. Average $50, licensed. Open Monday-Friday lunch noon-3pm, Monday-Saturday dinner 6pm-11.30pm.

Corner Yurong and Stanley Streets (tel: 9360 4558 or 9360 4391).

Alife – La Vita. Has been hailed as making the best wood-fired pizza around. Average $20, BYO and licensed. Open lunch Monday-Friday noon-3pm, dinner Monday-Sunday 6pm-midnight.

68 Stanley Street (tel: 9360 2347).

Bill and Toni's Italian Restaurant. There's a family atmosphere at Bill and Toni's, where *spaghetti bolognaise* and a glass of orange cordial is the standard order. You can eat here for about $10, BYO. Open Monday-Sunday for lunch noon-2.30pm, dinner 6pm-10.30pm.

74 Stanley Street (tel: 9360 4702).

Giotto Cafe. An ideal place if you like hanging around till late — let the coffee and the smell of the bacon and eggs energise you. Average $10, coffee less than $2. Open Monday-Sunday 6pm till late.

78 Stanley Street (tel: 9331 6090).

Palati Fini. Mario, the owner and waiter, is an operatic singer who may belt out a tune for you. Recommended: seafood, pastas and the *goulash*. Open for lunch Monday-Friday noon-2.30pm, dinner Monday-Sunday 6pm-10.30pm.

80 Stanley Street (tel: 9604 3948).

Giardinetto Restaurant. One of the more traditional spots in the area, where families, business people and loyal followers drop by for a plate of *gnocchi, spaghetti* or other Italian beauties. Average $15, BYO. Open Monday-Sunday for lunch noon-3pm, dinner 6pm-11pm.

113 Crown Street, corner of Stanley Street (tel: 9360 6416).

Also worth a look

Bar Reggio. One of the original cafes in the area, it was a place where many Italians would meet to have a game of cards. In the morning you can still see some elderly Italian gentlemen sitting, sipping coffee and having a good chat in Italian.

135 Crown Street, near the corner of Stanley Street (tel: 9332 1129).

COURTYARD DINING

In true Italian style, when the weather is fine, diners move outdoors.

CASTEL MOLA.
The food is homestyle Italian, complete with an authentic *pizza* oven, the decor is rustic minimalist and the courtyard is perfect for a get-together. Average $25; BYO. Dinner Monday–Sunday.

286 Norton Street, Leichhardt
(tel: 9569 8814).

NUMERO TRE.
Unpretentious place serving generous helpings of traditional dishes such as *misto di carne* (grilled meats), accompanied by steaming side-plates of potato, pumpkin and spinach. Average $25; BYO. Dinner Tuesday–Sunday.

159 Norton Street, Leichhardt
(tel: 9560 9129).

...And don't forget a post-prandial coffee in **BAR ITALIA'S** delightful courtyard.

FROM RAGAZZI TO RICHES...

BUON RICORDO. Signature dishes include casserole of rabbit with caramelised onion and sage, but make sure you leave space for the rich chocolate tart with gingered cream. Average $60; licensed. Lunch Friday-Saturday noon-2.30pm; dinner Tuesday-Saturday, 6.30-11pm.

108 Boundary Street, Paddington (tel: 9360 6729).

MEZZALUNA. Another success from the Beppi stable - rich, northern Italian dishes best enjoyed on the covered terrace with city panoramas. Average $50; licensed. Lunch Tuesday-Friday and Sunday noon-3pm; dinner Tuesday-Sunday 6-11pm.

123 Victoria Street, Potts Point (tel: 9357 1988).

Ristorante Stella. A modern restaurant serving modern Italian and Mediterranean cuisine. Open lunch noon-3pm, dinner 6pm-11pm.
Corner Crown and Stanley Streets (tel: 9331 5375).

The Arch Cafe (downstairs). Established in the early 80s, this has become a spot for young and hip costumers. A good place to play pool and to have a gelato or coffee.
81 Stanley Street. (tel: 9360 4711)

Bel Mondo. Considered the best Italian restaurant in town, with stunning views and stylish food. Average $50, but the financially challenged can settle for a taste of things to come in the Antibar for $20 or so; licensed. Lunch Monday-Sunday noon-3pm; dinner Monday-Sunday 6-11pm.
12 Argyle Street, The Rocks (tel: 9241 3700).

Grotta Capri. One for fans of kitsch: the "underwater" decor is amazing. Average $25; licensed and BYO. Lunch Tuesday-Friday, noon-3.00pm; dinner Tuesday-Sunday 6-10pm.
97–101 Anzac Parade, Kensington (tel: 9662 7111).

Cafés

Among the many gifts brought by Italian migrants to their new country was the thrill of the espresso machine – a discovery that has transformed Australia into a real café society, where the simple phrase "let's have coffee" is an invitation to friendship, debate, intrigue, or just hang out. Thanks to the Italians, Sydneysiders now order with the fluidity of a native Romano – an *espresso* (Italian for "squeeze out"); a *macchiato* ("stain"); an *affogato* ("drowned"); a *latte* ("milk"); or an *alla panna* ("with cream").

Leichhardt and the Inner West

Bar Baba. Gleaming pasticceria that's perfect for its namesake rum babas. Monday-Sunday 7am-late; the coffee machines get a well-deserved lie-in on Sundays, and is cranked up around 9.00am.
31 Norton Street, Leichhardt (tel: 9564 2044).

Bar Italia. A real institution: great coffee, *foccacia*, homemade ice cream, and a choice of well-worn formica or leafy courtyard. Perhaps it's time to retire the mugshot of Baggio in his glory days. Monday-Thursday 9am-midnight, Friday-Saturday 9am-1am, Sunday 10am-midnight.
169–171 Norton Street, Leichhardt (tel: 9560 9981).

Explore the world in one city

Caffe Sport. Friendly – and very Italian, right down to the soccer paraphernalia and signed team photos. Generous *foccacia* at bargain prices. Monday-Saturday 7am-early evening, Sunday 8am-early evening.
2a Norton Street, Leichhardt (tel: 9569 2510)

La Cremeria. Probably the best *gelati* in Syndey – and sensational coffee. Monday-Sunday 8am-10.00pm.
110 Norton Street, Leichhardt (tel: 9564 1127).

Darlinghurst, East Sydney and Eastern suburbs

Bar Coluzzi. Monday-Friday 5.30am-7.30pm. Taxi drivers, journalists, wannabe actors and tourists alike all perch precariously on tiny stools outside this quintessentially Italian coffee bar.
322 Victoria Street, Darlinghurst (tel: 9380 5420);
also at 99 Elizabeth Street, City (tel: 9233 1651).

Parmalat. The original sardine-can coffee bar – but who can resist the superb coffee and the best tuna sandwiches in the world? Monday-Friday 6am-7.30pm.
320 Victoria Street, East Sydney (tel: 9331 2914).

Tropicana. Eclectic decor, including a vintage jukebox, makes this one for the terminably hip. Monday-Sunday 5am-midnight. The café is even the hub of the annual Tropicana Short Film Festival, which takes over one of Sydney's busiest streets as crowds gaze at the work of young filmmakers on enormous outdoor screens.
227b Victoria Street, Darlinghurst (tel: 9360 9809).

The last gasp...

Caffe Italia. The parting shot, a sorrow sweetened by delicious cakes and pastries – "Arrivederci Sydney!" Monday-Wednesday and Friday 7.30am-6pm; Tuesday, Thursday and Saturday 7.30am-9pm.
Shop 23, Departure Level, Terminal C,
Kingsford Smith International Airport (tel: 9669 6434).

COFFEE HOT SHOTS

BAMBINI ESPRESSO BAR. A beacon in the caffeine-starved southern end of the city, these cafés are full of clamouring journos covering the tribunal beat. Monday-Friday 7am-5pm.

262 Castlereagh Street, City (tel: 9264 9550);
also at
60 Clarence Street, City (tel: 9299 4890).

CAFE DIVINO. Great breakfasts, *spaghetti, pizzette* and meaty meals. And, sure enough, the coffee is divine. Monday-Sunday 7am-midnight.

70 Stanley Street, East Sydney (tel: 9360 9911).

Shopping

If you're short of time or disinclined to trawl the suburbs, go straight to "Little Italy" and tempt your senses with the smell, colours and tastes of Norton Street Markets.

Leichhardt

AC Butchery. Gourmet meats – from' roo and game to organic, grass-fed beef and free-range chooks. One of the many contenders for the finest Italian sausages in Sydney. Monday-Friday 6am-6pm, Saturday 6am-3.30pm.

174 Marion Street (tel: 9569 8687).

Buon Appetito. Stock the freezer with fresh pastas and sauces, and you're all set for those impromptu suppers. Tuesday-Friday 9am-6.30pm and Saturday 9am-1pm.

141 Norton Street (tel: 9560 7564).

Italian models promoting "Italy at David Jones" in 1955.

Mezzapica. Luscious cakes to send your diet scurrying for cover. There's always tomorrow. Monday-Friday, 8am-5.30pm, Saturday, 8am-2.30pm and Sunday 8am-noon.

130 Norton Street (tel: 9569 8378).

Norton Street Markets. Behind this unassuming warehouse-like façade, is an Aladdin's Cave of Italian produce: wines, spirits, *panettones*, crusty bread, coffee, olive oils, balsamic vinegar, fresh vegetables, and everything you need to assemble stunning antipasto platters – olives, artichokes, sun-dried tomatoes, prosciutto, and delicious regional Italian salamis and cheeses. And when the time comes to cart your goodies home, you'll be relieved to know there's parking out front. What's more, you can brush up your Italian while you shop, ready for your next trip to Rome or Venice. Monday-Saturday 8am-7pm, Sundays 8am-6pm.

55 Norton Street (tel: 9568 2158).

The 'burbs

Antico's. Run by the Antico family since 1935, this fruit and veg market has an unequalled range – including 14 varieties of chillies. Monday-Wednesday 9am-6pm, Thursday 8am-8pm, Friday 8am-7pm, Saturday 7am-5pm, Sunday 9am-4pm.

24 Northbridge Plaza, Northbridge (tel: 9958 4725).

Cavallaro. You won't regret the trip to the wild west for these home-made biscuits, pastries and *gelati*. Monday-Friday 8am-5.30pm, Saturday 7.30am-1.30pm, plus Sunday 9-10am (for collection of orders only).
253 Macquarie Street, Liverpool (tel: 9602 6055).

Enzo and Marisa's. A pinnacle of the Sydney Italian delicatessen landscape. Monday-Friday 8am-6.00pm, Saturday 8am-2pm.
560 Marrickville Road, Dulwich Hill (tel: 9560 7546).

Il Gianfornaio. Among the best Italian bakeries in Sydney, with great pastries and bread. Monday-Friday 8am-7pm, Thursday 8am-9pm, Saturday 8am-4.30pm.
414 Victoria Avenue, Chatswood (tel: 9413 4833).

Libreria Italiana Bookshop. For over 40 years, the Sydney Italian community have bought their sport and fashion magazines and newspapers here. The shop also has a modest range of books in the Italian language. Monday and Wednesday-Friday 9am-1pm and 2-5pm, Tuesday 9am-1pm.
430 Parramatta Road, Petersham (tel: 9569 4514).

PAESANELLA CHEESE FACTORY. Locally made, Italian-style cheeses. Tuesday-Friday 6am-1pm, Sunday and Monday 6am-noon.
37 Gerald Street, Marrickville (tel: 9519 6181).

PARISI'S. A great variety of fruit and vegetables, and don't forget *gelati*, vegetable *lasagne*, jams and yogurts. Monday-Wednesday and Saturday 8am-6pm, Thursday 8am-7pm, Friday 8am-4pm, Sunday 9am-3pm.
15 Dover Road, Rose Bay (tel: 9371 8732).

Good times, Italian style
Club Marconi

From its original 25 members in 1958, Club Marconi has flourished to reach its current membership of over 20,000. Club Marconi is the centre of the social, cultural and sporting life of the Sydney Italian community (and of many non-Italians).

With a wide range of facilities, including restaurants, cafés, cocktail lounges, bars, shops and top-class sporting facilities, the club's pride and joy is its soccer team, which competes in the Australian National Soccer League, winning four times in recent years.

A few highlights from a typically action-packed week at Club Marconi includes live entertainment from rock bands and solo singers (Thursday, 7pm onwards in the Main Lounge) and performances by the all-time favourite Marconi Dance Band (Saturday, 7.30pm-late; free). The pace slows a little on Sunday for Cabaret at the Colosseo (from 7pm; free), with singers, bands and comedians – Vince Sorrenti performs from time to time.

Cr Marconi Plaza and Prairie Vale Road, Bossley Park (tel: 9823 2222).

Italian-born men have frequented Club Marconi for decades.

Fogolar Furlan

Tutti benvenutti! ("Everybody's welcome") is what Fogolar Furlan is all about. The history of this very popular Italian social club goes back to Giuseppe Castronini, an Italian immigrant from Udine, Friuli, who arrived in Sydney in 1949. Together with other Friulian migrants, Castronini formed a club to preserve Friulian social and cultural life. Completed in 1970, the club was called *Fogolar Furlan* – a reference to the traditional Friulian fireplace around which families gather – symbolising family unity. This family atmosphere is best appreciated on the weekends when you can drop by for an enjoyable and affordable meal, while listening to the popular sounds of Anthony Vandala and his orchestra.

Wharf Road, Lansvale (tel: 9726 4511).

IL PORCELLINO. Standing guard at the Macquarie Street frontage of Sydney Hospital, the bronze boar *Il Porcellino* is a replica of a 17th-century fountain in Florence's Mercato Nuovo. One of Sydney's best-known statues, *Il Porcellino* was donated by an Italian immigrant whose relatives had worked at the hospital. Tradition has it that *Il Porcellino* brings you luck when you rub his snout – and to spread your good fortune, throw those coins weighing down your pockets into the shallow pool that surrounds him, where they'll be gathered for the hospital's coffers.

Places of interest

The Italians in New South Wales. This is a rare and important collection of photographs and documents recording the experience of Italian individuals and families who settled in New South Wales. Their stories are brought to life through diaries, autobiographical accounts, letters from the internment camps, short stories, newspapers, books, magazines, newsletters and tapes. Monday-Friday 9am-9pm, Saturday-Sunday 11am-5pm.

Further information: State Library contact officer for the Italians in New South Wales Project, Jim Andrighetti (tel: 9273 1506).

Ravesi's Corner. Now a Bondi Beach landmark, Ravesi's Corner, at the intersection of Campbell Parade and Hall Street, was born in 1912 when an Italian fruiterer set up shop and lent his name to the crossroads. Now a time-honoured meeting place, Ravesi's boasts a first-floor restaurant, looking directly out over Bondi Beach, and well-designed and comfortable accommodation.

Royal Botanical Gardens' Phillip Fountain and Statue. Created by the famous Italian architect Achille Simonetti (1838–1900), the Phillip fountain commemorates the contribution of Governor Phillip to the founding of the colony of New South Wales. Fashioned from marble and bronze brought from Italy, construction began in 1889 and the statue and fountain were finally unveiled in 1897. While you're here, explore the lush palm groves and delightful rose garden, or just laze on the lawns, which are peppered with office escapees at lunchtime.

Getting to know the Italian Community

When you ask Sydney's Italians about their greatest moment, they'll more than likely go misty-eyed as they tell you of the day Italy won the World Cup in 1982.

The party along Norton Street went on for days. But you don't need to wait for the next Italian soccer conquest to enjoy a party in Leichhardt – you can go to the Norton Street Festival.

Events

Norton Street Festival.

Held in March or April, this is one of the major festivals in the Sydney calendar. Sponsored by Leichhardt Council, the festival is a celebration of the cultural and social contribution of the Italian community to the city of Sydney and, in particular, to Leichhardt. Lavishly decorated with the traditional green, red and white Italian colours, Norton Street hosts a multitude of activities, market and food stalls, art exhibitions and other entertainments. In 1996, approximately 60,000 people attended; in 1997 a crowd of 100,000 gave the thumbs-up to a festival that just keeps getting better and better.

Further information: 9367 9281

Viva Italia.

This week-long festival is billed as a showcase for "Italian prestige". Every year around mid-April, Maserattis, Ferraris and Lamborghinis purr along the glamorous streets of the eastern Sydney suburb of Double Bay, escorted by *Ducati* and *Laverda* motorbikes. There's also an Italian music concert at Guilfoyle Park, and plenty of opportunities to indulge in aromatic Italian coffee and food at local restaurants, many of which feature special festival menus and wines.

Further information: Cec Monkhouse, Double Bay Chamber of Commerce (tel: 9328 6419).

The Italian Song Festival.

Each August, this festival brings together musicians and singers from the Sydney Italian community in a performance at the Club Marconi's Colosseo Room.

Further information: Club Marconi (tel: 9823 2222).

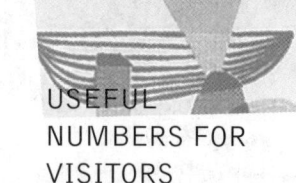

USEFUL NUMBERS FOR VISITORS

ALITALIA,
tel: 1300/653 747 for reservations;
1300/653 757 for fare enquiries;
9294 6268 for arrival and departure information.

ITALIAN CONSULATE,
tel: 9392 7900.

ITALIAN CHAMBER OF COMMERCE IN AUSTRALIA,
tel: 9262 5744.

Bar Italia is famous for its coffee and brilliant gelato.

"CAMPO", as David Campese is fondly known, is one of Australia's greatest Rugby Union players, his 100 tests and 64 tries for the Wallabies having made him an international rugby legend.

At the age of 18, Campese wore the gold jersey of the Wallabies for the first time, while touring New Zealand in 1982. Almost ten years later, he led Australia to victory in the 1991 Rugby World Cup.

Campese's father migrated to Australia from the village of Montecchio Pre, northwest of Padua, in the early 1950s. Born in Australia, Campese was taken back to his father's village, where he lived from the age of two until the family moved back to Australia. "Had I stayed [in Italy], I guess I would not have become a rugby player," he said in his autobiography.

Italian National Day.

On June 2 each year, the Sydney Italian community gathers at Circular Quay to celebrate the anniversary of the birth of the Italian Republic in 1946. Open to the public, this event is a good opportunity to enjoy Italian food, traditional music and dances. Celebrations also take place at various venues around The Rocks and at Club Marconi in the western suburb of Bossley Park.

Further information: Club Marconi (tel: 9823 2222).

The Blessing of the Fishing Fleet.

The tradition of blessing the fishing fleets goes back to the 12th century, when a wooden image of the *Madonna dei Martiri* (Our Lady of the Martyrs) was left behind by Catholic crusaders in the Italian port of Molfetta. In mid-October, Italian fishermen and their fleets gather to receive the *Madonna dei Martiri's* blessing and protection for the coming year. This colourful event begins at 9am with a mass at St Mary's Cathedral, followed by a procession to Pyrmont Point Park for the blessing ceremony, with festivities winding down around 7pm.

Further information: 9872 3493.

Religious organisations and places of worship

St Kevin's Church.

Here you will find the incredible, Father Lauro Rufo, who is fluent in Italian, Spanish, Portuguese and English, and celebrates an Italian-language mass every Sunday at 10am. The church is also the main venue for the Italian Catholic Federation of Dee Why, which organises a number of religious processions.

50 Oaks Avenue, Dee Why (tel: 9982 6536).

Italian Catholic Centre.

An Italian religious service is held every Sunday at 10am The centre publishes a weekly bulletin, *Eco di Famiglia*, and provides welfare services.

Father Raffaelle Tresca, Saint Brigids Retreat,
392 Marrickville Road, Marrickville (tel: 9559 4909).

San Francesco Catholic Italian Association.

Formed in 1945, the association has an active program of religious, cultural, social and sporting activities.

96 Catherine Street, Leichhardt (tel: 9481 9793).

Cultural and education centres

Dante Alighieri Society.

Established in Sydney in the early twentieth century in the heart of Sydney's CBD, the society is a gateway to the rich and intriguing world of Italian civilisation and culture – art, fashion, architecture, literature, cuisine and travel. The language school offers three levels of courses for beginners, and the society maintains a library and multimedia resource centre (membership fee $20.00). Monday-Friday 10am-6pm.

Level 5, 72 Pitt Street, City (tel: 9231 0691).

Italian Institute of Culture.

An agency of the Italian Ministry of Foreign Affairs, the institute is the official link between Italy and Australia in the field of culture, sponsoring lectures, exhibitions, concerts and film screenings. The institute is one of the best places to learn Italian, with fully qualified, native Italian teachers.

Level 45, Gateway 1, Macquarie Place, City (tel: 9392 7939).

Italian 500 Italian Centre for Language and Cultural Studies.

Language courses for students at different levels of proficiency. Monday–Friday 10.30am–8.30 pm.

Level 2, 203 Castlereagh Street, City (tel: 9261 1795).

Italian Language and Culture Centre.

Established in 1992, the Italian Language and Culture Centre is a private educational institution where anyone can study Italian language and culture – so don't be surprised if you find opera singers in your class. The centre also organises educational trips to Italy.

Level 8, 428 George Street, City (tel: 9232 7055).

Community organisations and institutions

Along with the massive influx of Italian immigrants in the 1950s and 1960s, new community organisations emerged in the suburbs where Italians tended to settle.

The trail was blazed by the Italo-Australian Welfare Centre, which was established in Leichhardt on May 1, 1950, on the initiative of Father Anastasio Paoletti of the Capuchin Friars.

CATHOLIC SERVICES IN ITALIAN

ST THERESE'S CHURCH,
Sutherland Road, Mascot
(tel: 9667 3040).
Sunday 8am.

OUR LADY OF LOURDES CHURCH,
286 Homer Lane,
Earlwood
(tel: 9558 1254).
Sunday 10.30am.

ST JOSEPH'S CHURCH,
13 Parker Street,
Rockdale
(tel: 9567 3088).
Sunday 11am.

SCALABRINI VILLAGE,
34 Harrow Road, Bexley
(tel: 9597 1333).
Sunday 9:45am and
Wednesday 11am.

Some selected Italian organisations and institutions in Sydney are given below.

Federation of Italian Migrant Workers and their Families (FILEF).

Established in 1972 in the Inner Western suburb of Leichhardt, FILEF aims to defend and promote the rights of migrant workers and their families, and to foster an appreciation of Italian culture. It publishes *Nuovo Paese* magazine, found in libraries and trade union offices.

157 Marion Street, Leichhardt (tel: 9568 3776).

Italian Association of Assistance (Co.As.It).

Since its establishment in 1968, Co.As.It has been providing welfare, social assistance and education to the Sydney Italian community. A staff of 160 Italian language teachers, and an advice and referral service deal with an annual average of 3000 clients, fulfilling a vital role.

Level 4, 2 Holden Street, Ashfield (tel: 9798 7222).

Scalabrini Villages.

A great achievement of the Sydney Italian community, these villages (in Austral and Bexley) provide welfare, care and accommodation to aging Italian people. The central plaza of the Scalabrini Village at Austral has a magnificent bronze statue of St Francis of Assisi that's worth seeing if you're in the area. Corner Fifth and Edmondson Avenues, Austral.

For further information, contact Father Nevio Capra (tel: 9606 0477).

Italian cultural organisations helped new immigrants to settle in Sydney and fought for their rights and needs.

The Media

The Sydney Italian community is well catered for by quality newspapers, and radio and television programmes broacast in Italian, which give direction to the community and help preserve its identity.

Newspapers

La Fiamma. One of the oldest ethnic newspapers in the country, *La Fiamma* was established by Capuchin interests in 1947. Published Mondays and Thursdays, it has a circulation of 35,000. Its current editors are G. Montagna and D. Morizzi. Cost:$1.20

92-94 Norton Street, Leichhardt (tel: 9569 4522)

Il Globo. Founded in 1959, *Il Globo* is a weekly broadsheet that hits the stands on Mondays. It has a circulation of around 50,000 and is edited by Armando Tornari. *Cost:$1.50*

92-94 Norton Street, Leichhardt (tel: 9560 1707)

Nuovo Paese. Published monthly by the Federation of Italian Migrant Workers and Their Families (FILEF), *Nuovo Paese* contains bilingual articles and provides an alternative view to the mainstream Italian-language press on social and labour issues. Widely distributed through trade unions and in university libraries, its co-ordinator in Sydney is Cesare Giulio Popoli.

157 Marion Street, Leichhardt (tel: 9568 3776).

Radio programmes

SBS Radio 2, FM 97.7. News in Italian. Monday–Sunday 8–9am and 6–7pm.

Radio Uno 2, AM 1620. News and current affairs. Monday and Friday 6–10pm.

Italian radio programmes can also be heard on the following Sydney community radio stations. Timeslots vary, so call for the latest.

2MWM, FM 92.1/93.7 (tel: 9913 8986)

2RDJ, FM 88.1 (tel: 9744 3284 or 9744 0881)

2RSR, FM 88.9 (tel: 9550 9552)

Television programmes

SBS carries the daily news of Telegiornale Italiano (RAI), Monday-Friday 7-7.30am and Sunday 10-10.30am, and broadcasts the Italian "Serie A" – arguably the best Soccer League in the world – on Sundays 10.30–11.30am.

TeleItalia also broadcasts Italian programmes. Call 1800/651 692 for information.

One of the oldest ethnic newspapers in the country, *La Fiamma* was established by Capuchin interests in 1947.

The Italians in figures

The Italians are a splendid example of immigrants who have maintained the best elements of their homeland, yet who have also enthusiastically embraced their life in Australia.

Senator Bolkus, *former Minister of Immigration and Ethnic Affairs.*

According to the 1991 census, the Italian-born population of Australia numbered 253,332.

The majority migrated here in the 1950s and 1960s as young adults, with Italian migration diminishing considerably in the 1970s and 1980s.

Currently in Sydney, there are around 56,828 Italian-born Australians, and it is definitely an aging community.

Italian immigrants have shown a strong desire to become Australian citizens, with around 77 per cent taking out naturalisation.

Despite having an educational level below the national norm (43.6 per cent leaving school before the age of 15, compared with a national average of 15 per cent), and with a below-average income (55 per cent earn $16,000 or less), Italians are more likely to own their homes (77.4 per cent) than other Australians.

Italians have made an enourmous contribution to this country, yet they have also retained their Italian identity, culture, religion and language.

Almost 90 per cent of the community speak Italian at home and, even among the second generation, nearly half speak Italian at home.

In terms of religion, 93 per cent of Italian immigrants profess a strong link with Catholicism.

The Latvians

"**Working together** to purchase a collection of worthy books, newspapers and magazines, and, as far as possible, promoting the moral and spiritual development of both members and non-members. Any Latvian-speaking person living in Sydney or its environs can become a member."

These were the very lofty aims of the *Sydnejas Latweeschu Pulzinch* (Latvian Circle), the first Latvian community organisation in Australia. It was founded in June 1913, 48 Argyle Place in The Rocks. This Latvian organisation, equipped with a good library, was at the heart of the social and cultural life of the first large group of Latvians who arrived in Australia in the early twentieth century. They were mainly left-wing intellectual exiles from the abortive Russian 1905 revolution.

The Latvian Circle existed until 1926, when political disagreements and differences of opinions about its purposes forced a split into two groups. In 1928, due to the efforts of a new arrival, Karlis Nicis, a Latvian opera singer and actor, the two groups held a joint St John's Day celebration, a traditional Latvian event. This led to the establishment of the Latvian Club, which has survived until today and is located in the south-western suburb of Bankstown.

It seems that the first Latvian in Australia was a convict – a man of Jewish background who was transported to Sydney in 1829 for the theft of 14 gold watches. The first free Latvian settler, whose name has not been recorded, arrived in 1849. It is estimated that by the end of the nineteenth century there were around 160 Latvians living in Australia.

A large number of Latvian refugees arrived on our shores after the end of World War II. The first group of 262 displaced persons arrived in Australia in November 1947. The vast majority settled in Sydney and found work – under the two-year contract program – on the Chullora Railway, in Bankstown, where they established a well-organised and very cohesive community. One of the most well known Latvians who arrived during this time was John Konrads, who, with his sister Ilsa, is considered among the greatest legends in Australian swimming. Konrads – whose family had come from Riga, Latvia, in 1949 - became

> It seems that the first Latvian in Australia was a convict – a man of Jewish background who was transported to Sydney in 1829 for the theft of 14 gold watches.

BOOKSHOPS

LATVIAN SOCIETY BOOKSHOP.
Established in 1952, this is one of the oldest ethnic bookshops in Sydney. It has a wide range of Latvian-language publications, including newspapers and magazines, and also tapes and CDs. Open Monday-Friday 2pm-6.30pm, Thursday 10am-noon and Sunday 9am-noon.

**32 Parnell Street, Strathfield
(tel: 9745 1435).**

Australian coach Don Talbot's first pupil when he was only 11 years old. He reached his peak as a swimmer in 1958. From then on he went on to break 14 individual world records and became the first to hold every record from 200 to 1500 metres at the one time.

With the massive number of new arrivals in the following years, the Sydney Latvian community life (put on hold during the years of the Second World War) was resurrected. In 1947 the Australian Latvian Welfare Society was founded, in 1949 a weekly newspaper, *Australijas Latvietis* ('The Australian Latvian') was begun, and in 1952 the Latvian Society of Sydney was formally registered. Community festivals, social gatherings and cultural functions began flourishing again. It was around this time that the most important event on the Sydney Latvian calendar, the Australian Latvian Cultural Festival, was first held. Since 1951, the Festival has been celebrated uninterrupted.

Imant J Ronis, who arrived as one of the 'reffos' as he puts it, recalls that in those years the most interesting and well-attended Latvian community function was a monthly literary afternoon held at the old Deaf & Dumb Society's Hall, located then in Elizabeth Street in the City. "The attendance at these literary afternoons, where we read the latest works of TS Eliot, Eugene O'Neill and others, never fell below an average of 60 people. The first session was held in May 1951 and the last in November 1959," he remembers with nostalgia. Mr Ronis is to this day an active member of the Latvian Press Society in Australia.

Nowadays there are little more than 2,100 Latvian-born living in Sydney, and even though their contribution to Australia have been made in a wide range of activities, it is in the area of arts that the Latvians have undoubtedly had the greatest impact. Jean Senbergs, the acclaimed Riga-born painter and printmaker, is just one example.

Restaurants

DV Latvian Society. The equivalent of the Australian RSL, the Society was established in the 1950s and has a large membership. There is a restaurant that operates on weekends and this is the place to taste the traditional Latvian cuisine. For the adventurous there is a wealth of Baltic drinks, cakes and soups. Average $15, Licenced. Open Saturday-Sunday noon-4pm.

49 Stanley Street, Bankstown (tel: 9790 1140).

Getting to know the Latvian community

USEFUL NUMBER FOR VISITORS

LATVIAN CONSULATE:
tel: 9744 5981.

Events

Most of the following events are held at the Sydney Latvian Society's Hall, 32 Parnell Street, Strathfield.

For further information call 9744 8500.

Independence Day.

Latvia was invaded by the former Soviet Union's Red Army on June 16 1940. On May 4 1991 independence was finally achieved, and the Sydney Latvian community celebrates the occasion on this date each year.

Anniversary of 1941 Soviet Deportation.

On June 13 the Latvian community, along with the Estonians and Lithuanians, remembers the forced deportation to Siberia of thousands of Latvians following the 1940 Soviet occupation of their country.

Latvian National Day.

Every November 18 the Latvian community gets together to commemorate Latvian independence from Czarist Russia, an occupation that lasted from the end of the eighteenth century to 1818. The original declaration of a Latvian republic was made on that day.

Sydney Latvian Theatre Festival.

This is a national cultural event for Australian Latvians. It is held each year during the long weekend in June, featuring the best of the Latvian theatre tradition.

Australian Latvian Cultural Festival.

This is the most important event on the Sydney Latvian calendar. The Festival, which is the culmination of the entire community's activities for that year, has been annually held since 1951, and takes place between Christmas and the New Year. Two central features of the Festival are the massed choir concert, a tradition that began in Latvia last century, and a week dedicated to the works of Latvian writers.

RELIGIOUS ORGANISATIONS AND PLACES OF WORSHIP

The large majority of Latvians are Lutherans, but also there is a sizeable Catholic community.

LATVIAN EVANGELICAL LUTHERAN CHURCH.
This is the largest Lutheran Church in Sydney.
30 Bridge Road, Homebush
(tel: 9746 1934).

STRATHFIELD LUTHERAN CHURCH.
Corner The Boulevarde and Lyons Street, Strathfield
(tel: 9670 3330).

LATVIAN CATHOLIC CONGREGATION.
123 The Crescent, Flemington
(tel: 9826 1288).

Community organisations

Most Latvian organisations belong to the Latvian Federation of Australia and New Zealand. This is an umbrella organisation which plays a central role in coordinating various activities across Australia. It belongs to the World Federation of Free Latvians, which plays a similiar role on a global scale.

Latvian House.

Established in 1954, this is a cultural and social space for Sydney Latvians. It has a choir, a folk-dancing group and a theatre group.

32 Parnell Street, Strathfield (tel: 9744 8500).

Sydney Latvian Folk Dance Group.

This group performs traditional Latvian dance and organises dance workshops. Its current director is Dr J Rungis.

21 Margaret Street, Roseville (tel: 9417 8286).

Media

The Latvian community is catered to by a number of bulletins to which writers and journalists from the Latvian Press Society in Australia are contributors.

More information on the Latvian Press Society can be obtained on 9438 4653 (NSW representative).

Newspapers

Australijas Latvietis (Latvian News). Based in Melbourne, it is published weekly and hits the Sydney news-stands at the end of the week, or on the following Monday. Its current editor is E Delans.

Further information: (042) 67 4824 (NSW contact).

Radio

SBS Radio 2, FM 97.7. News and current affairs, Wednesday 4pm-5pm, Saturday 5pm-6pm.

The Lithuanians

From the geographical centre of Europe to Down Under – it was a long way to go. They left behind the fertile valleys and rich forests of Lithuania and went searching, in a faraway land, for political freedom and economic opportunities.

Lithuanians began arriving in Australia in large numbers after 1940, when their homeland became an incorporated state of the Soviet Union. Without knowing it, they were following the immigration experience of Antanas Lagogenis, who in 1836 was the first Lithuanian to migrate to Australia. Not much is known about him, except that he was a naturalised British citizen when he arrived.

When Lithuanian refugees arrived in Sydney at the end of the 1940s they found a small but cohesive community of no more than 240 people. They were well organised under the guidance of the Australian Lithuanian Society in Sydney, founded in 1929. Renamed as Australian Lithuanian Community of Sydney years later, it became the centre of the cultural and social development of Sydney Lithuanians. One of the original founders of the Society, Anna Bauze, 97, still lives in Sydney. She is the wife of the late Antanas Bauze, one of the first presidents of the organisation.

Between 1947 and 1953 just under 10,000 Lithuanians came to Australia. They were highly educated professionals and among them there were an amazing number of prominent artists who have made a significant contribution to Australian culture. The sculptor Teisutis Zikaras, whose works in aluminium have been highly acclaimed, is one of them, as is the painter Leonas Urbonas, who arrived in 1948. Henrikas Salkauskas and Eva Kubbos, whose graphic works and paintings have been displayed in all major Australian art galleries, also deserve a mention; these two were the principal initiators of the Sydney Printmakers Society.

The Lithuanians who arrived in Sydney at the end of the 1940s and went to work at the Chullora Railway depot founded an informal 'Little Lithuania' along Horton Street in Yagoona, and still today this neighbourhood has a distinctive Lithuanian presence. Nearby Bankstown

Sydney artist Henrikas *Salkausakas* belongs to the fertile generation of Lithuanian graphic artists and painters who arrived in Australia at the end of the 1940s. *Salkausakas* whose paintings and graphic works have been exhibited in all main Australian cities and in exhibitions overseas, has won 60 awards in Australia alone and his works are displayed in several state art galleries. At the Art Gallery of New South Wales a Salkauskas Contemporary Art Purchase Awards was established.

The Lithuanians who arrived in Sydney at the end of the 1940s and went to work at on the Chullora Railway yards founded an informal 'Little Lithuania' along Horton Street in Yagoona, and today this neighbourhood still has a distinctive Lithuanian presence.

was the place chosen by the community to build the Lithuanian Club. With offices for the Sydney Lithuanian Consulate and for the newspaper *Musu Pastoge*, the Lithuanian Club has become the main venue for Sydney Lithuanian social and cultural festivities.

There was a great party in the Club when, a few years ago in 1994, Soviet troops finally left and the long-awaited and elusive freedom knocked on the door of Lithuania. It was time.

Clubs

Lithuanian Club.

The only registered Lithuanian club in Sydney, it is an important cultural and social place for the small Sydney Lithuanian community. In the Club's bar you can order imported Utena beer and traditional *krupnikas* – a delightful spirit mixed with honey. In the restaurant you can help yourself to the most authentic Lithuanian food treats on this side of the world, including potato dishes – which are, in all shapes and forms, the staple of the Baltic diet. If it's available try *kugelis*, the timeless spud with meat tucked inside, or just go for the dumplings and pancakes. Average $15, licensed. Open for dinner Wednesday 6pm-8pm, lunch and dinner Sunday 1pm-9pm.

16-18 East Terrace, Bankstown (tel: 9708 1414).

Getting to know the Lithuanian community

Events

Lithuanian Independence Day.

On February 16 1918 the Lithuanian National Council proclaimed the restoration of Lithuania's independence. To commemorate this date the Lithuanian Club holds an annual celebration at its premises.

16-18 East Terrace, Bankstown (tel 9708 1414).

Kaziuko Muge (St Casimir's Day).

In Lithuania the annual St Casimir celebration marks the beginning of Spring. St Casimir, the patron saint of Lithuania, was born in 1458 in

Krakow, Poland. Sydney Lithuanians honour him on March 4 with a special religious celebration at the St Joachim Church, Mills Street, Lidcombe.

Further information: Australian Lithuanian Community of Sydney (tel: 9795 1210).

Australian Lithuanian Cultural Festival.

This festival is celebrated every two years – the last one was in 1996 in Melbourne and it will be held in Geelong in 1998 and Sydney in the 2000. The week-long festival, run by the Federal Lithuanian Council, features traditional food, a choral festival, folk dancing, art, literature and other artistic activities.

Further information: Australian Lithuanian Community of Sydney (tel: 9795 1210).

Black June, or Black Ribbon.

On June 13 1941 thousands of Lithuanians were forcibly deported to Siberia and to the Arctic region of the former Soviet Union. It is estimated that by 1953 one in five Lithuanians had been deported. Sydney Lithuanians, along with the Latvians and Estonians, get together on this day in commemoration of these events.

Further information: Australian Lithuanian Community of Sydney (tel: 9795 1210).

Art

When Lithuanians arrived in Australia they brought with them their rich traditional folk dances and songs.

Lithuanian Folkloric Ensemble *'Sutartine'*.

A bastion of traditional Lithuanian music, it performs in many community events.

16 East Terrace, Bankstown (tel: 9543 1001).

Sukurys.

This group organises dance and choir performances in traditional Lithuanian costume.

57 Cedarwood Drive, Cherrybrook (tel: 9484 6276, Marina Cox).

USEFUL NUMBERS FOR VISITORS

LITHUANIAN CONSULATE:
tel: 9498 2571.

CONSULAR SERVICES also are available from the Lithuanian Club, Monday-Friday 1pm-2pm (tel: 9708 1414).

Lithuanian folkloric ensemble *'Sutartine'*, a bastion of traditional Lithuanian music.

LEONAS URBONAS
Painter and graphic artist Born in 1925 in Zarasai, Lithuania, Leonas Urbonas arrived in Australia in 1948. His abstract surrealist paintings and graphic works have been displayed in the most well-known art galleries throughout Australia, including the Leveson Street Gallery in Melbourne, the Woollahra Gallery and Macquarie Galleries in Sydney. His awards include the 1959 Mosman Prize, and the Australian Fashion Design Gold Medallion in 1965.

Community organisations

Australian Lithuanian Community of Sydney.

This is the peak organisation for the Lithuanian community, with branches in all state capitals. It deals with a broad range of cultural, social, political and other issues. The current president is Vytas Juska.

31A Parsonage Road, Castle Hill (tel: 9795 1210).

Lithuanian Co-op Credit Society Talka.

Its main purpose is to finance the activities of the Lithuanian cultural groups.

16 East Terrace, Bankstown. (tel: 9796 8662).

Lithuanian Village.

A retirement village for Lithuanian senior citizens. It also acts as a community and cultural centre.

23 Laurina Avenue, North Engadine (tel: 9602 6358 or 9520 3908).

Media

Newspapers

Musu Pastoge. A monthly publication which appears on the first Monday of the month, with a circulation of 1,200. The paper has a strong focus on community and world news. Its current editor is Bronius Zalays.

16-18 East Terrace, Bankstown (tel: 9790 3233).

Radio

SBS Radio 2, FM 97.7. Community news and a summary of news from Lithuania, plus a good selection of traditional music. Tuesday 5pm-6pm.

The Macedonians

One prominent Sydney Macedonian is Bill Saravinovski, who was first elected to Rockdale Council in 1983 at the age of 21, the youngest counsellor ever. In 1995, Bill became the first Macedonian person to be elected to the position of mayor. Not to be typecast, Bill is also Vice-President of the Chinese Association of Rockdale!!.

While it is likely that Macedonians visited Sydney in the late nineteenth century, the first Macedonian recorded is Krste Malik – known in Australia as Chris Maalek and Dedo Maluko (old Maluk). Malik worked as an ice-cream vendor before drowning in the Edwards River at Deniliquin, south western New South Wales.

It is estimated that there were only 50 Macedonians in Australia in 1921 but by 1947 this had grown to 1900. The Macedonians who came during these years were mostly from the Aegean part of Macedonia. They were from a peasant background, though many bought or rented land to set up a market garden, grow tobacco and eucalyptus or milk cows.

Determining numbers of Macedonians is difficult since statistics are collected on country of birth, not ethnicity and Macedonians were born in a number of countries: Greece, Albania, Turkey, Bulgaria and countries of the former Yugoslavia. Macedonians of a Slav background have been arriving in Australia since the late nineteenth century century, but did not arrive in large numbers until the end of War World II. The last wave of migration from the Republic of Macedonia began in the late 1980s and was due to the lack of political stability and economic security back home.

While Melbourne is a centre for Macedonians born in Greece, most Sydney Macedonians are from the former Yugoslavia. There are over 25,000 Macedonians in New South Wales and they make up a relatively young community, with two in three less than 40 years of age. Nearly all Macedonians are of Macedonian orthodox religion. They have tended to settle in the St George area of Sydney in suburbs such as Rockdale (by the way, Rockdale is where you will find some Macedonian bakeries and delis widely recommended by the food buffs), Bankstown and

> Macedonians have tended to settle in the St George area of Sydney in suburbs such as Rockdale (by the way, Rockdale is where you will find some Macedonians bakeries and delis widely recommended by the food buffs).

Marrickville. There are also large Macedonian communities in the large towns of Newcastle and Wollongong, north and south of Sydney.

In socioeconomic terms, Macedonians suffer a higher unemployment rate (25.5%) than the average of about 8 per cent. More than half of Macedonian families have an income below $40,000. But many Macedonians set up successful businesses, particularly noticeable in the dry cleaning business in Sydney and the citrus fruit and fish trade in other parts of Australia. Macedonians have established an extensive community infrastructure in Sydney. Some 40 Macedonian community organisations have made their mark on Sydney, and one of the most important is the Macedonian Australian Welfare Association of Sydney established in 1982. They have set up soccer clubs, ethnic schools, cultural, literary and drama societies, welfare organisations and churches. There is also a significant Macedonian media presence in Sydney, with many radio programs and newspapers in Macedonian.

Tapestry 'image of home' produced by Macedonian Women's group 'Dobro Utro' Rockdale.

Shopping

Makedonska Prodavnica. Macedonians have an original varied and hearty cuisine and here you'll find some of its basic ingredients. Imported products from Romania and Bulgaria are also available.
Open Monday-Friday 6am-6pm, Saturday 6am-4pm.

King's Court, King Street, Rockdale (tel: 9567 1627).

Macedonian Hot Bread. A neighbourhood institution for the large Macedonian community living in Rockdale. Fresh *burek* baked daily. Macedonian language newspapers and music are also available.
Open Monday-Friday 6am-5.30pm, Saturday 6am-3pm.

34 Walz Street, Rockdale (tel: 9567 6659).

Getting to know the Macedonian community

Events

Macedonian Cultural Week.
A Festival of Macedonian culture, art, theatre, poetry readings, folk dancing and concerts. The festival, organised by the Macedonian Cultural Week Committee of NSW, lasts one month and occurs every two years.

Contact the organisers for detail on venues and calendar or activities on 9558 9595

St Elias Day.
Celebrated on August 2, it commemorates the *Ilinden* uprising of 1903 for national liberation from the Turkish rule. It also celebrates the formation of the Macedonian State. For further information on activities and venues contact some of the organisations listed below.

Macedonian Independence Day.
Celebrated on September 8, it commemorates the 1991 Referendum when Macedonians from the Republic of Macedonia decided to break up from Yugoslavia. For further information on activities and venues contact some of the organisations listed below.

Cultural and education centres

Macedonian Australian Theatre *'Vojdan Chernodrinski'*
Established in 1991, it organises regular Macedonian theatre productions and visual arts exhibitions.

c/- St George Migrant Resource Centre, 554-556 Princes Hwy, Rockdale (tel: 9597 5455).

RELIGIOUS ORGANISATIONS AND PLACES OF WORSHIP

94.9% of Macedonians are Macedonian Orthodox that broke away from the Serbian Orthodox Church in 1967. There is also a substantial number of Macedonians who have adopted Islam and Catholicism. There is also a small numbers of Jews.

Macedonian Orthodox Church *'Sv Kiril i Metodij'*

Established in 1970, it provides church activities and regular religious services.

18 Dalmeny Avenue, Rosebery
(tel: 9667 1962).

Regular services are also held at the Macedonian Orthodox Church *'Sv Nikola.'*
79 Cabramatta Road, Cabramatta;

and at the Macedonian Orthodox Church *'Sv Petka'*
65 Railway Street, Rockdale

LIBRARY

Macedonian Library
'Grigor Prlichev.'

Founded in 1978, the library maintains a good selection of Macedonian books, magazines and a community archive open to the public. Open Friday 6.30-8.30pm.

5 Belmore Street,
Arncliffe
(tel: 9597 7362).

COMMUNITY ORGANISATION

MACEDONIAN AUSTRALIA WELFARE ASSOCIATION OF SYDNEY (MAWA).

Established in 1982, MAWA operates from the St George Migrant Resource Centre in Rockdale and employs a Community Development Worker who provides welfare and social assistance to Sydney Macedonians. Meetings are held at 12noon on the first Monday of the month.

c/-St George Migrant Resource Centre, 552 Princes Hwy, Rockdale
(tel: 9597 5455).

Macedonian School Council of NSW.

Since its establishment in 1978 it has been responsible for coordinating and assisting all Macedonian Ethnic & Saturday Schools in NSW
PO Box 164, Rockdale 2216 (tel: 9521 3778).

Macedonian Studies, Macquarie University

Based at the School of Modern Language, it teaches and coordinates Macedonian studies at tertiary level. The current head is Dr. Ilija Casule. Office hours, Monday-Friday 9am-5pm.

c/-School of Modern Languages, Balaclava Road, North Sydney
(tel: 9805 7030).

Media

Newspapers

Voice of Macedonians. A magazine published monthly, its current editor is Angele Vretoski. it provides a wide range of cultural and educational information.

Further information: 9567 7344.

Radio

SBS Radio 1, AM 1107. News and current affairs, Tuesday 10-10.45pm, Thursday & Friday 4.45-5.30pm, Sunday 8.30-9.15am.

Macedonian Radio Panorama, FM 88.7. Community announcements, music and news, Sunday 6-8pm.

2RES, FM 89.7 Macedonian Voice, Saturday 4.30-8pm, Sunday 8.30-10am.

2RES, FM 89.7. *'Gerdan'*, Macedonian radio program, Sunday 7.30-8.30am.

2SER, FM 107.3. *Pej Makedonijo*, Saturday 6.30-8.30pm

2NBC, FM 90.1. Macedonian Community Radio Program, Sunday 6.30-8pm.

2NBC, FM 90.1. *Sydney Makedonija*, Sunday 10.30am-1.15pm

The Maltese

"I thought he was Italian!," confesses with awe our researcher Michael Banks – a self-taught musicologist. Joe Camilleri, one of the best-known names in the Australian entertainment scene is not from an Italian background, he's Maltese. Spanish, Greek, Lebanese or Italian are usually suggested when discussing the ethnicity of quite a number of prominent Australians. But Maltese? – hardly.

Let's get this straight. John Aquilina, the NSW Education Minister, isn't Spanish; Paul Zammit, another New South Wales politician (and member of the Liberal Party who resigned short time ago) isn't Greek and Jeff Fenech, the former triple boxing world champion, isn't Lebanese. Yes, they're all from a Maltese background.

The first Maltese free and independent immigrant, Antonio Azzopardi, arrived in Australia in 1838, and two years later he married a Scottish woman, Margaret Sandeman. However it was only in the early years of the twentieth century that the Maltese began arriving as a group, the first being a bunch of 50 men who arrived in Sydney in 1912. They suffered prejudice – without any knowledge of English and no government assistance on their arrival they faced the racist hostility of the Australian Worker's Union (AWU). In those unenlightened times these cheap non-white labourers were considered a threat to Australian workers.

By the 1920s and 1930s, Maltese began forming pockets of settlement in Sydney's west where they established market gardens, small dairy and poultry farms and, with the steady growth of the community, diverse organisations and associations emerged. When the first Maltese organisation, the Sydney Melita Social Club, was founded in 1922 there were around 1,000 Maltese living in Sydney.

After World War II Malta began experiencing a rapid rise in its population, a process that was accompanied by the downgrading of the activities in the British naval dockyard, the main employment source for the locals. With unemployment soaring, immigration was encouraged, not just by the government but also by the very influential Catholic Church. With the signing of the 1948 assisted passage agreement with

> Let's get this straight. John Aquilina, the NSW Education Minister, isn't Spanish; Paul Zammit, another New South Wales politician (and member of the Liberal Party who resigned a short time ago) isn't Greek and Jeff Fenech, the former triple boxing world champion, isn't Lebanese. Yes, they're all from a Maltese background.

Twenty knockouts and three weight-class world championships make Jeff Fenech a true sporting legend. Born in the multicultural inner-city suburb of Marrickville in 1965, Jeff Fenech won his first title — the IBF Bantamweight Championship — in 1985, knocking the Japanese fighter Satoshi Shingaki out in the ninth round. The second title came in 1986 when he defeated Daniel Zaragoza, and in March 1988 Jeff stopped Victor Callejas in the tenth round to win his third title, the WBC Featherweight Championship. Wearing the white and red colours of the Maltese flag — alternating with the Australian sporting colours of green and gold — Jeff Fenech made an unambiguous statement about his Maltese-Australian legacy. His famous words sum it up: "I love youse all."

Malta, the first made with any country other than Britain, Maltese immigration to Australia reached a new high, and most of them came to Sydney. It was around this time that a small Maltese community sprang up in the inner-city suburb of Woolloomoolo, where many Maltese men found work with the sea-going fishing fleet or on the waterfront. During these years it was common to see whole Maltese families having a *passiggata* (walking along the main street or the sea front), chatting animatedly on street corners or just sitting in front of their houses sipping coffee or playing cards. They were mainly Catholic, and attended the nearby St Mary's Cathedral Sunday mass. Unfortunately, over the years this Maltese enclave has almost completely disappeared.

Overall, approximately 12,000 Maltese migrants settled in Sydney between the end of the war and 1960. Being unskilled or semi-skilled, and coming from rural villages or dockyard cities in Malta, they found work in the Sydney construction and manufacturing industry. A large number became involved in the small agricultural settlements of Blacktown, Penrith and Hawkesbury in the outer west of Sydney, and even now the Maltese still constitute Sydney's largest group of migrants employed in agricultural activities.

More Maltese in Australia than in Malta

Most of the current Sydney Maltese community, religious and cultural organisations and clubs were established by these post-war immigrants. The popular Melita Eagles Soccer Club and the Maltese Guild, in Evelyn Avenue in Concord, were founded in 1953. The Maltese Community Council, an umbrella body for the community, was established 10 years later, and La Valette Social Centre, an important social and recreational venue, was founded in 1964 (it was originally known as the Maltese Community Western Suburbs Association); it is currently located at Bankstown. The only licensed Maltese club in Sydney, and a landmark of the Sydney Maltese community, is the Phoenician Club on Broadway in the inner city.

The first half of the 1950s saw the arrival in Sydney of one Joe Forace. He migrated to Australia in 1954 and during the humble first years found work as a ticket-collector at Central Station, a postman, and a clerk before joining Hooker Real Estate. He became an active member of the Maltese Sydney community and in 1971 was appointed Maltese High Commissioner in Australia and an Ambassador to China. A close friend of the former Chinese leader Chou En Lai, Forace passed into history as the colourful diplomat who managed to bring the first Chinese table-tennis team to Australia, and incidentally helped to normalise the Australian-Chinese relationship. He was the pioneer of what was called 'ping-pong diplomacy'.

"More Maltese in Australia than in Malta", is a myth that persists today "and for a while I mistakenly helped to promote this myth," confesses historian Barry York, an authority on Australian Maltese history. The author of *The Maltese in Australia* (AE Press, 1986) Barry admits that he personally experienced the fervour of many local Maltese who opted for the biggest population figure on offer to prove that the Maltese community was among the biggest in Australia. But, as Barry puts it, "The Maltese in Australia stand proudly as a medium-sized ethnic community whose achievements have consistently been disproportionately greater than their numerical strength."

Shopping

When the Maltese arrived in Sydney they brought with them the old recipes of ravjul and pastizzi. Nowadays, is there an end-of-year cocktail party without *pastizzi*? Try the selected shops listed below.

Gato's Pastizzi.

This is the place to find fresh, cooked and frozen *pastizzi*. Open Monday-Sunday 8am-5.30pm.

Shop 4/46-66 The Horsley Drive, Carramar (tel: 9724 3861).

Mario's Pastizzi.

Ready-to-cook and frozen *pastizzi*, savoury and sweet. Open Monday-Friday 7am-4pm.

Shop 2 Parklawn Place, North Street, St Marys (tel: 9673 3255).

Meno's Pastizzi.

Get them fresh or frozen – it doesn't matter, they always they taste delicious. While there, stock up on traditional Maltese *ravjul*. Open Monday-Saturday 9am-5pm, Sunday 9am-2pm.

33 Irrigation Road, Merrylands (tel: 9631 1660).

The Maltese Cheese Factory.

Established in 1989 by Polly and Charlie Vella, this factory on 5 acres of land in Sydney's west is becoming an institution among Sydney cheese lovers. "You can get a good idea of our variety by getting the $3 packets of 6 different cheeses," says Polly, who advises trying the pepper and dry cheeses. Open Monday-Friday 7am-5pm and on weekends by request.

Lot 235/2555 Lincoln Road, Horsley Park (tel: 9620 1465).

CAFES AND RESTAURANTS

L-EWWEL (THE FIRST).

Authentic Maltese food with a blend of Maltese and Italian tastes. Average $25, licensed. Open for lunch Tuesday-Friday noon-3pm and for dinner 6pm-10pm, Saturday only dinner 6pm-till late.

108 Station Street, Wentworthville (tel: 9688 1785).

THE MALTESE CAFE.

Hailed as cooking the best *pastizzi* (savoury cheesecakes) and *ravjul* (ravioli) in town. And it's very affordable; if your budget is limited go for a *macaroni* plate at less than $3. Open Tuesday-Sunday 7am-8pm.

310 Crown Street, Darlinghurst (tel: 9361 6942).

Social clubs

Sydney Maltese know how to have fun. Although they can hardly wait for the Maltese entertainers who tour Sydney from time to time, they know that the popular Phoenician Club always has its door wide open.

Phoenician Club.

Along with the Hellenic Club in Elizabeth Street, the Phoenician Club is a fascinating ethnic venue in Sydney. With cabaret, dances, concerts and a number of Maltese community festivals, this is the place to go for the real Maltese experience. Until a few years ago this building on busy Broadway housed the Sydney office of the Maltese consul. Open Monday-Sunday 9.30am-9.30pm (on weekends open till late, depending on activities).

173 Broadway, Sydney (tel: 9212 5955).

Landmarks

Maltese Bicentenary Monument.

This monument is the most important landmark for the Sydney Maltese community. Built for the Australian bicentenary, it celebrates Maltese immigration and its contribution to Australian society. This bronze monument, depicting the eight arms of the Maltese cross, was built with the financial assistance of the Maltese Government, the NSW State Government and members of the Maltese Sydney community. This little piece of Sydney Maltese history is located at Civic Park, Pendle Hill.

For further information contact Oreste Aquilina (tel: 9481 8324).

Getting to know the Maltese community

Events

For one of the most Catholic communities in Sydney (93% of Maltese migrants identify themselves as Catholic) a *'festa'* is a very Maltese affair. A tradition brought from Malta, this ceremony of commemoration to a patron saint features a solemn high mass followed by a street procession with a statue of the saint. A parish music band accompanies the procession playing traditional marches, then the festa ends with a display of fireworks. Currently, the Maltese Sydney community celebrates several festas during the year.

Festa of Our Lady of Victories (il-Vitorja).

Held on September 8 this festa commemorates the lifting of the blockade of Malta by the Turks in 1565, and by the axis forces in 1942. The event begins with a religious celebration at St Mary's Cathedral in town, and is then followed by a social night at the Phoenician Club.

Further information: 9360 6672.

Festa of Our Lady Queen of Peace.

Held on the long weekend in October, this event takes the form of a feast in traditional Maltese customs. A religious ceremony is followed by a day of entertainment including marches and music by a 60-strong band; a fireworks display finishes proceedings. The festa is held at Our Lady of Peace Church, Old Prospect Road, Greystanes.

Further information: 9636 7767.

Other Festivals

Maltese Cultural Award.

Organised by the Maltese Cultural Association, this award is celebrated – as the former president of the Association, Frank Zammit, explains – "to honour those individuals who are actively contributing to the development of Maltese culture in Sydney". The award is held in different locations in western Sydney.

Contact the Association for additional information (tel: 9772 3164).

Karnival Malti (Maltese Carnival).

A historical and cultural event held in the second weekend of October, this is the largest event for the Sydney Maltese community. It features traditional songs, fancy dress and costumes, Maltese food and drinks, and a colourful parade of decorated floats. In good weather the main festival events are held at the Melita Stadium, Everley Road, Granville.

Further information: 9579 7026.

Religious organisations and places of worship

Historically, the Maltese have had strong links with Christianity dating back to the time of St Paul's shipwreck, as mentioned in the Bible. The Catholic Church is a central pillar of Maltese culture and society and Maltese, whatever their social class, tend to participate actively in parish organisations. The Maltese Catholic Church was instrumental in advising

USEFUL NUMBER FOR VISITORS

MALTESE CONSULATE: tel: 9267 3363.

FESTA OF ST PETER AND ST PAUL. Held at the end of June (around the 29th). This *festa*, run by the Maltese Cultural Association, is celebrated at the hall of the Pennant Hills Catholic Church, 20 Boundary Road. The venue may change, so if you're planning to attend this traditional Maltese festivity contact the Association beforehand on 9772 3164.

FEAST OF SAINT GAETANO. Organised by the Harum Association, this religious celebration – held the last weekend of August – is held in front of the statue of Saint Gaetano at St Patricks Catholic Church, 51 Allawah Street, Blacktown. All welcome.

Further information, tel: 9622 1125.

BOOKS AND MUSIC

THE MALTESE HERALD. Although there are no Maltese bookshops in Sydney, you can purchase Maltese-language publications, including newspapers and books, from the office of The Maltese Herald. It also has a great selection of Maltese music, with many old-time favourites, including Enzo Gusman (who isn't Spanish!) and Joe Apap. Open Monday-Friday 10.30am-4pm and on Saturday by appointment.

195 Merrylands Road, Merrylands.
(tel: 9637 9992).

and encouraging Maltese to look to Australia as a place to start a new life.

At the moment of writing the old Maltese National Chaplain's House at 19 Stanley Street, East Sydney, is under reconstruction and extension. We were informed that it would become, in the near future, the main centre for Maltese cultural and religious activities. Currently Catholic services in Maltese are held at Walter Street, Blacktown, Saturday at 5pm and 6pm, and on Sunday at 7am (tel: 9622 5850).

Art and culture

Our Lady Queen of Peace Parish Band.

Established in 1976, this was the first traditional Maltese-oriented concert band formed in Australia. The band of 50 musicians playing piccolos, drums, saxophones, clarinets and other instruments is a real institution among Sydney's Maltese.

"We perform at various festas and whenever else we are invited," says the founder and now musical conductor Joe Darmanin. This well-known musical institution has regularly performed as part of the Sydney Festival. And, Mr Darmanin points out, you can hire the band (he isn't sure about the fee but he says it's cheap for what you get!).

8 Lance Street, Pendle Hill. Further information: Joe Darmanin (tel: 9631 7748).

Maltese Cultural Association of NSW.

One of the key Maltese cultural institutions in Sydney, it organises various cultural activities, including the annual Maltese Cultural Award. The Association is also responsible for organising the traditional Festa of St Peter and St Paul at the end of June.

Further information: 9772 3164.

Community organisations

Sydney Maltese community life is primarily located in areas of greatest Maltese concentration, mainly in the inner and outer western suburbs.

Maltese Community Council of NSW.

This is an umbrella organisation which coordinates the activities of several Maltese community associations in New South Wales and plays a major role as a mouthpiece for the Maltese community. It provides an information service in the west, at Blacktown and Fairfield, and also in the inner-city. It also has a weekly radio program on Radio 2SER FM.

11 Lincoln Street, Stanmore (tel: 9519 7026).

La Valette Social Centre Inc.
A social and educational centre, it provides social welfare services.
175 Walters Road, Blacktown (tel: 9621 2151).

Maltese Welfare.
Provides advice, information and referrals on welfare issues affecting the Sydney Maltese community.
3 Hillary Crescent, Greystanes (tel: 9631 9295).

Media

The first Sydney Maltese newspaper, the biweekly *Lehen il-Malti* (Maltese Voice) hit the stands in 1958 and was followed a year later by the *Malta News*. They were both short-lived. The only existing Sydney Maltese newspaper, *The Maltese Herald* appeared in 1961. Maltese radio programs, widely appreciated by their loyal listeners, have been a feature of Sydney's airwaves since the mid-1970s.

Most of the current Maltese Sydney community, religious, cultural organisations and clubs were established by the 1950s. The very popular Melita Eagle Soccer Club was founded in 1953.

Newspapers

The Maltese Herald. The only weekly Maltese newspaper in Australia – with offices in Sydney, Melbourne, Adelaide, Brisbane and Perth – is a matter of pride for its current editor Lino C. Vella. It has a circulation of 6,500 issues and covers a wide range of issues, with a strong emphasis in reporting the various festas celebrated throughout the country. It costs $1.50 and comes out on Tuesday.

195 Merrylands Road, Merrylands (tel: 9637 9992).

Radio

SBS Radio 2, FM 97.7. News, community announcements and a good dose of soccer results. Monday-Thursday and Saturday noon-1pm; Friday 5pm-6pm.

2SER, FM 107.3. The Maltese Hour. Sunday 11am-noon.

Television

SBS Television. Maltese news, Sunday 6-6.30am.

Facts and Figures

90 per cent of the Maltese-speaking community live in the Sydney metropolitan area, with concentrations in the suburbs of Blacktown, Holroyd, Fairfield, Botany and Liverpool.

By the 1991 Census there were 53,858 Maltese immigrants living in Australia; Sydney (with 19,315) had the second largest concentration, after Melbourne. In common with a number of other post-war immigrant groups, the Maltese are an aging community, and current immigration from Malta has diminished considerably.

The proportion of Maltese with educational or vocational qualifications (25%) is well below the 38.8% figure for the total Australian population. According to the 1991 Census, 3.3% of Maltese immigrants have post-secondary qualifications, again far below the figure for the total Australian population (12.8%). However, it's comparable to other Mediterranean immigrants, such as Italians (3.3%) and Greeks (3.4%).

The Maltese median annual income of $14,300 is similar to that of the total Australian population ($14,200). Maltese are highly likely to own they own house (84.3%), which is a considerably higher figure than the national average (68.2%).

Maltese immigrants, like others from Commonwealth countries such as the United Kingdom and New Zealand, do not always become Australian citizens. A total of 59.8% of them have become naturalised, compared to 72.1% of all people from non-English speaking countries.

The Catholic Church is a central foundation of Maltese culture and society and this is mirrored by the great majority of Maltese (92.8%) identifying themselves as Roman Catholic. In terms of language, 67% of Maltese-born people aged 5 years old speak only Maltese at home, while 31.2% speak only English.

The Poles

A perpetual pronunciation and spelling challenge, Mount Kosciuszko is not only *the* geographical icon as Australia's highest peak (2,228m), but also a reminder of the Polish immigration experience on our shores. Discovered and climbed by the renowned Polish explorer Sir Paul Edmund de Strzelecki in 1840, Mount Kosciuszko was named after the eighteenth century Polish hero, Tadeusz Kosciuszko, who fought in the American Revolution and led the 1794 Polish independence struggle.

Although in Australian maps since 1840 and then in textbooks, it was not until 1996 that we got the spelling of Mount Kosciuszko right! In a careless historical mistake Australia's early surveyors messed up the transcription and what should have been Mount Kosciuszko went down on maps and textbooks as Mount Kosciusko. The missing 'z' has been added and the spelling is now correct. However it seems that it will take a bit longer to get the pronounciation right. Or it may be never, as Agnieszka Morawinski, Poland's ambassador to Australia admitted when she conceded that, extra 'z' or not, Australians could not pronounce the name properly; "I'm afraid they will never be able to," she says.

Michael Klim – nowadays Australia's most successful swimmer at any world championship – has been in Australia since his family moved here from Poland when he was 11.

Small beginnings

A convict, Joseph Potaski and his wife and child – who arrived in 1803 – were the first known Polish settlers in Australia. They were followed several years later by a group of political exiles, mainly army officers and members of the nobility, from the 1830s Polish-Russian War. One of them was a nobleman by the name of Plater, whose remains are now buried at Parramatta cemetery. Around this time, in 1840, a bushranger on the loose – a 'native from Poland' – was apprehended near Sydney, prompting hysterical headlines.

The 1848 rebellion against the Austrian Hapsburgs and the 1863 uprising against czarist Russia in Poland sparked a new stream of political refugees to Australia, and it is estimated that by the 1870s there were about 1,000 to 1,250 Poles living here.

In 1882 a group of Sydney Polish labourers established *Stowarzyszenie Polskie*, one of the first Polish community organisations in the country. Fifty years later, as the local Polish population passed the 3,000 mark, the organisation changed its name to the Polish National Alliance of Australia. It was followed in 1940 by the creation of the Polish Democratic Society in Sydney which played an influential role in disseminating Polish art, culture and music.

The war and beyond

The occupation of Poland by Nazi Germany in 1939 resulted in a new wave of refugees entering Australia, many of Jewish background. A large number of intellectuals and highly educated emigres, including such people as Richard Krygier, the founder of the influential political and cultural magazine *Quadrant*, came at this time.

In the aftermath of World War II, Australia, as a signatory to agreements with the International Refugee Organisation (IRO), received around 60,000 Polish refugees. Among them were ex-servicemen, veterans of the Tobruk siege, and a large contingent of Polish pilots who had courageously fought in the Battle of Britain. The largest number of the post-war immigrants, however, was made up of peasants and working-class people. Their adjustment was extremely hard since they were unskilled, had little knowledge of English and no formal education. They found jobs in railway workshops, road buildings and water and sewerage maintenance, while others were recruited to work on the Snowy Mountains Hydroelectric Scheme. Many highly trained professional Poles worked there as labourers. Since professionals were specifically excluded from entry to Australia, they chose not to reveal their qualifications. By the year when the man hailed as the father of Australian multiculturalism, the Krakow-born Jerzy Zubrzycki, arrived in 1956, the Polish community was made up of well over 50,000 people.

Reaching for the top

Through the 1960s and the early years of the 1980s, the Polish community stabilised itself in terms of number, and the community – fanned across the western suburbs of Bankstown, Fairfield and Blacktown – continued flourishing, with the creation of educational institutions, Saturday schools, folkloric groups, theatrical associations and discussion societies. One of the great community achievements of this time was the inauguration, in 1966, of the Polish War Memorial Chapel at Marayong in western Sydney (see page 198). Three years later, in 1969. the now acclaimed Krakow-born filmmaker Yoram Gross came to Sydney (see page 200).

During the height of the 1982-1983 Solidarity Movement crackdown a large group of Poles arrived at Sydney Airport fleeing repression. Members of the professional class and arts community came here to start a new life. It wasn't easy. They were forced to accept menial employment, cab driving, cleaning other people's houses or scrubbing the floors of city buildings – at least at the beginning. More than a decade has elapsed since then and the 'big break' for some of them has finally come up. Gosia

Dobrowolska, for example, has become one of Australia's best actresses, starring in films such as *The Surfer*, *Phobia* and *A Woman's Tale*, by Paul Cox (a Dutch-born immigrant). Bogdan Koca, the Warsaw-trained actor, writer, director and composer, is another of the Australian Poles who has made good. After an emotionally and financially tough time, as he describes it, Bogdan Koca has finally carved out a niche for himself with his critically acclaimed productions at the Pilgrim Theatre – *Sparring Partner*, *Annette & Annette* and *Gunter's Wife*. Deserving a very special mention is the multi-gold winner Michael Klim - nowadays Australia's most successful swimmer at any world championship - he has been in Australia since his family moved here from Poland when he was 11. Living in Australia has been an exhausting challenge, but in many regards the Australian Poles of today have only done what their fellow countryman Strzelecki did more than 150 years ago – reach the top of the mountain.

Social clubs and restaurants

The Polish Club. In the 1960s the premises of this club were subdivided into a community centre and social club. The jewel of the Club is the Warsaw Restaurant, where you can try the very 'corpulent' *Zywick* beer (as it was called by one of the regular patrons of the Club) or the traditional *flaczki* (tripe soup). Average $20, licensed. Open for dinner Wednesday-Friday 5-10pm, Saturday-Sunday 1pm-10pm.

73 Norton Street, Ashfield (tel: 9798 7469).

Shopping

Asquith Bakery. The only place in Sydney where you can find the kind of bread most likely to be found at Warsaw's bakeries. Open Monday-Friday 7.30am-7pm, Saturday-Sunday 7am-5pm.

401 Pacific Highway, Asquith (tel: 9477 3786).

Betta Meats. A deli/butchery with a great range of Polish (and also Macedonian, Croatian and Hungarian) smallgoods. Open Monday-Thursday 8am-5.30pm, Friday 6am-6pm, and Saturday 6am-1pm.

407 King Street, Newtown (tel: 9557 3354).

Tatra Smallgoods and Butchery. The smoked and fresh Polish sausages and pork chops are glorious. Open Wednesday 8am-5pm; Thursday 8am-7pm, Friday 8am-5pm, and Saturday 8am-1pm. 81 The River Road, Revesby (tel: 9774 2894). The shop also operates on Thursdays from 6pm at an upstairs room of the Polish Club in Ashfield,

73 Norton Street (tel: 9798 7469).

BOOK AND GIFT SHOPS

POLISH CENTRE.
A cross between a bookshop and travel agency, the Polish Centre has a great range of Polish merchandise, including history books and guide books, Polish newspapers and magazines and a wide range of gifts.
Open Monday-Friday 9am-5pm and Saturday 9am-12noon.

84 Wentworth Avenue, Surry Hills
(tel: 9212 5077).

During the height of the 1982-1983 Solidarity Movement crackdown large group of Poles arrived at Sydney Airport fleeing repression. Members of the professional class and arts community came here to start a new life.

USEFUL NUMBER FOR VISITORS

POLISH CONSULATE:
tel: 9363 9816.

Landmarks

Polish War Memorial Chapel. This chapel at Marayong is a significant landmark for the Sydney Polish community. Opened in 1966, the Polish War Memorial has played an important role in the settlement process of recent Polish immigrants. The Memorial Chapel, built in Australia by Poles themselves, commemorates the millennium of Christianity in Poland.

116/132 Quakers Road, Marayong (tel: 9626 7268).

Getting to know the Polish community

Chopin Birthday Concert.

Held in February or March and run by the Polish Cultural Association, this popular annual concert celebrates the music of Chopin. "Until eleven years ago, the concert was held at the Sydney Conservatorium, but now the premises haven't been made available," explains Iwona Kower, President of the Polish Cultural Association. So in the last two years the event has been held in the premises of the Sydney Polish Consulate. Tickets are $10.

At the time of writing they are looking for a more adequate venue for the next concert in 1998 so if you are interested in attending call beforehand Mrs. Kower on 9527 3564.

Three out of every four Polish immigrants living in Sydney are Catholics.

Poland Constitution Day (Feast of Our Lady of Czestochowa).

A cross between history and religion, this event is held on May 3. There are social gatherings and a dinner and dance at various venues, including the Polish Club.

Further information: Polish Club (tel: 9798 7469).

Sir Edmund de Strzelecki Annual Dinner.

A formal evening held on May 18 to commemorate the birth of this great Polish explorer who discovered and named Mount Kosciuszko.

Contact the Polish Club (see above) for further information.

Monte Casino Battle. Organised by the Polish Club, this event brings together ex-servicemen and Polish residents in general to remember the heroic Battle of Mount Casino in 1944, where the Polish Second Corps defeated the mighty German army and opened the path to Rome. A lot of Polish food, drinks and the old songs collude together to give a nostalgic touch to this special celebration. Contact the Polish Club again for information.

The Polish community also celebrates many Catholic religious festivities, especially Easter, Christmas and All Soul's Day (November 2). Between May and November the community celebrates the figure of Virgin Mary, regarded as the religious Queen of Poland.

Further information: Polish War Memorial Chapel (tel: 9626 7268) or the Polish Catholic Chaplain (tel: 9796 7775).

Arts

Polish Performing Arts Theatre Inc. "Call in any time and I'll be waiting with a bottle of Chardonnay" is the tempting invitation of Jozep Drewniak, director and administrator of this theatre company established in 1973. The Company stages plays in various venues throughout Sydney – "we bring the show to church halls, soccer fields, town halls, it doesn't matter the venue, the play is what matters," says Jozep, who arrived as a refugee in 1948 and has a theatre career spanning more than 40 years. Call Jozep for information on the productions (you might even get a glass of Chardonnay!)

452 Pitt Street, City (tel: 9212 5491).

Polish Cultural Association. Established about 20 years ago, the Association organises art exhibitions and musical concerts, including the annual Chopin Birthday Concert. Membership of the Association is open to all.

182 Liverpool Road, Ashfield. Further information: Iwona Kower (tel: 9527 3564).

Community organisations

Polish community organisations date back to the latter half of the nineteenth century (the Polish Association of New South Wales, founded in the 1880s, for example) but none of these survived very long. A Polish National Association was established in 1931 with branches in Sydney, Brisbane and Ipswich, and nowadays the Polish community has an extensive structure of organisations with at least one Polish Centre in

RELIGIOUS ORGANISATIONS AND PLACES OF WORSHIP

THE ROMAN CATHOLIC CHURCH has been an integral part of the Polish nation since 966 AD, when the Polish prince Miesko I married the Bohemian princess and accepted Christianity for himself and his people. In Australia, Polish immigrants are overwhelmingly Catholic (75.7%) and they still retain fresh in their memory the 1995 visit to Sydney of the 'Polish Pope' John Paul II.

POLISH WAR MEMORIAL CHAPEL. Polish language services are held Monday-Friday at 7.30pm, Saturday 7pm and Sunday 9am, 11am and 6.30pm

116/132 Quakers Road, Marayong.
(tel: 9626 7268).

POLISH CATHOLIC MISSION IN AUSTRALIA.
The Mission has religious services Monday-Friday at 7pm and Sunday at noon.

4 Little Road, Bankstown
(tel: 9796 7775).

every state. The Polish Centre is the focal point for a wide range of organisations, such as educational and discussion societies, theatrical and music groups and the ex-servicemen's league. The following are two of the most important organisations.

Polish Welfare & Information Bureau of NSW. Provides social and welfare support and information to members of the Sydney Polish community. It covers the area of Ashfield, Blacktown and Liverpool.

182 Liverpool St, Ashfield (tel: 9798 4005).

Polish Association in NSW (Cabramatta Branch). Better known as the White Eagle House, it was established at the end of the 1950s. It organises social, religious, women's and children's activities. It also promotes and develops cultural and educational initiatives. Its current president is Jan Knopek.

White Eagle House, Corner Bareena and West Streets, Canley Vale (tel: 9724 5738).

Yoram Gross

FILMMAKER

Born in Krakow, Poland, Yoram Gross graduated from the prestigious Polish Film Institute, then gained his experience in filmmaking as an assistant to the Polish film directors Cenkalski and Buczowski, and to the famous Dutch director Yoris Ivens.

In 1968 Yoram migrated to Australia, with his wife Sandra and young family, and has since then lived in Sydney. Yoram and his wife established the very successful Yoram Gross Film Studio whose first animated feature film, *Dot and the Kangaroo* (1977) was described by the legendary ABC film critic, John Hinde, as a "brilliant technical success and the best cartoon film originated in Australia".

Since 1977, Yoram has produced, directed and scripted a total of sixteen feature films for children, including *Blinky Bill* (1992) -- based on the Australian children's classic by Dorothy Wall. This film introduced the popular Australian koala to an overseas market and Blinky became Australia's 'animated ambassador' to millions of children around the world. In recognition of his achievements and contribution to the film industry, Yoram Gross was awarded the Order of Australia in 1995.

Media

Newspapers

In the years 1928-33 there were several attempts to establish a Polish press in Australia. The English-language monthly *Polish and Central European Review* was launched by the Polish consul in Sydney in 1942 and ran for three years. Also in 1942 the *Polish News* appeared in Sydney. It stayed and in the process began the development of Polish language newspapers throughout Australia. The post-war and post-1980s waves of Polish immigration kept the Sydney Polish press alive.

Wiadomosci Polski (Polish News). With a strong readership base, this 20-page weekly has a circulation of around 2,800-3,500. It appears on Thursdays; its current editor is Jan Dunin-Karwicki.

3rd Floor, 32 York Street, City (tel: 9299 1248).

Polish Catholic Review. The Review began in 1965 when the *Polish Weekly* became a secular paper. It's published monthly and has a circulation of over 2,000. The current editor, Rev Antoni Dudek, describes the magazine as an "outlet for Polish social history and religion". It costs $2 and can be found at the Polish churches listed on page 199.

4 Little Road, Bankstown (tel: 9626 7268).

Radio

SBS Radio 1, AM 1107. Polish-language news, current affairs and music, Monday-Sunday 1pm-2pm.

2SER, FM 107.3. Music, arts and community news, Saturday 7pm- 8pm.

Television

SBS Television. *Oto Polska* offers news and current affairs, Monday noon-12.30pm and Sunday 8.55am-9:30am.

Facts and figures

The largest numbers of Sydney Poles are found in the western suburbs of Bankstown, Fairfield and Blacktown, where displaced Poles were able to rent, and later buy, cheap land-house packages in the 1950s.

The 1991 Census showed more Polish immigrants (68,496) were living in Australia than at any previous time. Sydney, with around 16,300, has the second largest number of Polish settlers in the country, after Melbourne. The Census shows that Sydney is the favourite city for the post-1980s immigrants. The establishment of solid roots and the succesful settlement of the Polish post-war arrivals in Australia is reflected by the high rate of citizenship (86.1%).

The proportion of Polish settlers with educational and vocational qualifications is high (47.1%). The high proportion of tertiary-qualified Poles is due mainly to the post-1980s and Jewish-Pole immigration.

The medium annual income, $10,000, is considerably lower than that of the total Australia population, which is at odds with their high level of qualifications. This is explained by the low level of English in the community, which makes it very difficult to find suitable jobs. Nevertheless, the economic hardships haven't deterred them from having a dream, possessing their own homes. Polish immigrants have a higher rate of house ownership (73.8%) than the total Australian population (68.2%).

Census figures show that 82.6% Poles speak languages other than English at home. This includes 72.4% who speak Polish, 4% who speak German and 3.2% who speak Yiddish. Most Polish settlers (75.7%) identify themselves as Catholic.

Explore the world in one city

The Portuguese

Two hundred and seventy years before the British set foot on *Terra Australis*, the Portuguese had already been around the Western Australian Kimberley coast and established a small settlement. African slaves were brought to Australia at this time and when the Portuguese abandoned this area they were left behind.

It has been argued that these slaves eventually mixed with local Aborigines and generated a group of descendants that lived in the area until the 1930s, speaking a kind of Portuguese-Aboriginal creole. Of this early settlement in Australia's north-west coast almost no historical evidence is left.

Two convicts, Antonio Rodriguez and Jose Barbose are recorded as the earliest Portuguese presence in Sydney. Sentenced to 14 years, Rodriguez and Barbose arrived in the penal colony in 1810 where they were assigned to work as stockmen on the property of William Cox, in Bathurst, western New South Wales. "Very honest, hardworking man and very fit for this country," wrote Cox about Antonio Rodriguez who was later freed and given 20 hectares of land.

A family of three, Emmanuel and Ana de Freitas Serrao and their daughter Selena, were among the earliest Portuguese immigrants here. From Madeira, they arrived in 1824 and found work in the experimental grape farm of Dr William Redfern in Parramatta. Emmanuel later joined the police force while his daughter married another immigrant from Madeira in 1847. Emmanuel died in 1880.

Until the mid-twentieth century, immigration from Portugal continued with the pattern of the nineteenth century – sporadic and limited to a few individuals. In the 1950s, a group of Portuguese from Madeira arrived in Perth, establishing a very successful fishing community in Fremantle.

"The Portuguese community life in Sydney dates back to the 1960s," explains Tony Martin, the new proprietor of the oldest Portuguese newspaper in Australia, *O Portuguese na Australia*. "Most of the Portuguese immigrants arriving in Sydney at this time settled, initially, in the eastern suburbs of Darlinghurst and Paddington," he says. When the

Presently, the Sydney Portuguese community numbers about 30,000 (including the second generation). They have established an energetic enclave in the Sydney inner-western suburbs of Marrickville and Petersham.

OPORTO TAKE-AWAY.
This is a success story of owner Tony Cerqueira who arrived in Sydney at the end of the 1970s. In 1986 Tony opened his now legendary Portuguese-style charcoal chicken take-away named after his home town, Oporto. His mini take-away empire began in Bondi and has spread to Newtown, Maroubra, Crows Nest, Kings Cross, Brighton-le-Sands Broadway and Balmain. Why? The Oporto chickens are not what you would call ordinary fast food. The chicken has been flattened, spiced with home-made chilli sauce and char-grilled – mouth watering! Whole chicken $8.80, half $4.80, quarter $2.70. Open Monday-Sunday 10am-9pm.

1/37 Campbell Parade, Bondi (tel: 9365 1177). Also at 331 Darling Street, Balmain (tel: 9810 1555); 126 Willoughby Road, Crows Nest (tel: 9906 6050), 944 Anzac Parade, Maroubra Junction (tel: 9314 1002); 1-19 Enmore Road, Newtown (tel: 9557 6160); 3c Roslyn Street, Kings Cross (tel: 9368 0257).

newspaper moved to its current premises in Petersham, and other Portuguese businesses – including a Portuguese real estate agent – did the same, the community soon followed.

A pivotal Portuguese community institution that also recently moved to this area is the Portuguese Community Club. Tony Martin remembers that back in the 1960s, the activities organised by the Club were held at Paddington Town Hall, because it lacked its own premises. It then began renting a place in the eastern suburb of Rosebery. By the beginning of the 1990s, the Club, under the presidency of Luis Coelho, finally fulfilled its dream, when the crumbling Frazer Park in Petersham was transformed into a marvellous venue for the Club.

Petersham was also the birthplace of two of the oldest Portuguese folkloric groups in Sydney, *Aldeias de Portugal*, founded in 1976, and *Assim i Portugal*, founded in 1988. Today, Petersham's New Canterbury Road, lined by Portuguese coffee and pastry shops, restaurants, delicatessens and bottle shops give this area of Sydney a truly Portuguese flavour. It truly earns the name 'Little Portugal' (see page 205-208).

Restaurants

El Captain Balmain. Unpretentious Portuguese eatery offering a superb speciality, *carne de porco a Alentejana* (pork with clams and fried potatoes cut in cubes). Average $15, BYO and licensed. Open dinner Monday-Sunday 6pm-10.30pm, lunch only on Sunday noon-3pm.

390A Darling Street, Balmain (tel: 9555 8551).

Numero Uno. Randwick residents still miss this charming and delicious restaurant since it moved to Newtown not long ago. Suckling pig is one of its real wonders. Average $15, (Saturday any three courses $25), BYO and licensed. Open Monday-Sunday noon-11pm, later on Friday and Saturday.

33 Enmore Road, Newtown (tel: 9557 8999).

Shopping

Sunshine Meats. It has a loyal clientele looking for the very Portuguese *piri piri* sauce, salamis and smoked meat. Other Portuguese delicacies are also available. Open Monday-Friday 8am-6pm, Saturday 8am-2pm.

253 Wardell Road, Dulwich Hill (tel: 9559 7309).

Fernando and Joe's Bakery. Portuguese bread rolls are one of the rising stars in Sydney and this bakery is one of the best places to find them. Open Monday-Friday 6am-5.30pm, Saturday 6am-1pm, Sunday 7am-noon.

455 Marrickville Road, Dulwich Hill (tel: 9560 5214).

Clubs

Portugal Madeira Club. A long-time hangout for the Sydney Portuguese. It holds weekly social and cultural activities, and on Friday and Saturday the dance party is on with some of the Sydney's best Portuguese bands. It also has a fully licensed restaurant. Open Monday-Wednesday 9am-10.30pm (till midnight on Thursday), Friday-Saturday 9am till late.

1-3 Denby Street, Marrickville (tel: 9569 9015).

Petersham is the centre of Portuguese cuisine in Sydney.

Petersham's New Canterbury Road, Sydney's "Little Portugal"

At first glance, the busy intersection of New Canterbury Road and Stanmore Road, in Petersham, seems an unlikely place to recreate in Sydney the Mediterranean atmosphere of Portugal.

Yet, if you ignore the fumes of the cars and follow instead the succulent fragrance of the charcoal-grilled Portuguese chicken, the sweet aroma of the *pasteis* (Portuguese pastries), and the strains of *fado* (the traditional Portuguese ballad) you will find here Sydney's Little Portugal.

7 km southwest of the CBD, Petersham – bounded by Stanmore and Lewisham – was a farm community in the early years of the penal colony, a retreat spot, and the kingdom of bold Jack Donahue, the bush ranger who in the 1800s terrorised its early residents.

Petersham began filling with Portuguese in the 1970s. They left behind their first home in Sydney, Paddington and Darlinghurst, and followed a

SYDNEY PORTUGAL COMMUNITY CLUB. One of the most traditional Portuguese venues in Sydney, it makes room for a huge array of community activities, including the annual Portuguese beauty contests. It also has a library with Portuguese publications, while on weekends the 'till-late dance parties' take over. For a full taste of Portugal you should drop by the restaurant. Average $20, licensed; opens Monday-Sunday, lunch noon-2.30pm, dinner 6pm-9.30pm (till 10.30 Friday and Saturday).

Frazer Park, 100 Marrickville Road, Marrickville (tel: 9550 6344).

GETTING THERE

The City/Petersham train will get you there in around 10 minutes. New Canterbury Road is to the South of the railway station.

number of Portuguese business and community organisations that began operating in Petersham. Currently, 38 per cent of the 10,000-odd Portuguese-born living in Sydney have settled in the Municipality of Marrickville – where the inner-suburb of Petersham is located. Here, the Portuguese, with their traditional restaurants and cafes, mouth-watering cake shops, congested delicatessens, retail and grocery stores have shaped New Canterbury Road and placed it in more than one tourist brochure. A place to visit.

Restaurants, Cafes & Take Away

P3: Cafe Restaurante Portugal. Typical of the area's dining spots, Cafe Portugal brings to Sydney the style and taste of one of the great European cuisines. We tried the highly recommended *bacalhau* (dried salted cod served with tomato and a sauce made of capsicum, topped with fried potato) and it's a must. Average $20, BYO and licensed. Open Wednesday-Monday 11.30am-9pm (till 10.30pm on Friday and Saturday).

102 New Canterbury Road (tel: 9564 1163).

Gloria's cafe restaurant provides cheap traditional Portuguese food and genuine Portuguese coffee.

4: Restaurante Costa do Sol. A friendly environment and the extensive Portuguese traditional menu – including the very fresh and not overpriced seafood fare (cooked with rice) – makes this a spot to visit. Average $20, BYO and licensed. Open Monday-Wednesday and Thursday 11am-10pm, Friday-Sunday 11am-11pm.

144 New Canterbury Road (tel: 9569 2319).

9: Portuguese Charcoal Chicken. In the last few years Sydneysiders have become familiar with the traditional Portuguese recipe of charcoal-grilled chicken brushed with a sauce of chilli-hot *piri piri*. This is the place to get it. Open Monday-Sunday 9am-8.30pm.

45 New Canterbury Road (tel: 9569 5335).

14: Gloria's Cafe Restaurant. Gloria's is a traditional and friendly restaurant of the kind you find in some of the most charming streets of Lisbon. At least the *bica* (a short-black coffee) is very much the same as found back in Portugal. At Gloria's the atmosphere and reasonable prices complement the superb home-cooked fare. Don't go past without trying the hearty bean casseroles. Average $15, BYO and licensed. Open Monday-Saturday 10am-10pm, Sunday 10am-7pm.

82 Audley Street (tel: 9568 3996).

Shopping

1: Honeymoon Patisserie. His *pasteis* - Portuguese pastries- have made Luis Santos, the owner and pastry chef, a famous Sydneysider. Here you will find, among others, the *folares* (a traditional oval-shaped Eastern cake), the *ninhos de pascoa* (almond sponge decorated with chocolate butter cream and sugar almonds) and the *pasteis de feijao* (almond and sweet bean tart). They are irresistible. No wonder that the Art Gallery, the Opera House and the Powerhouse Museum have decided to purchase Santos' "masterpieces" for their foyer cafes.

96 New Canterbury Road (tel: 9564 2389).

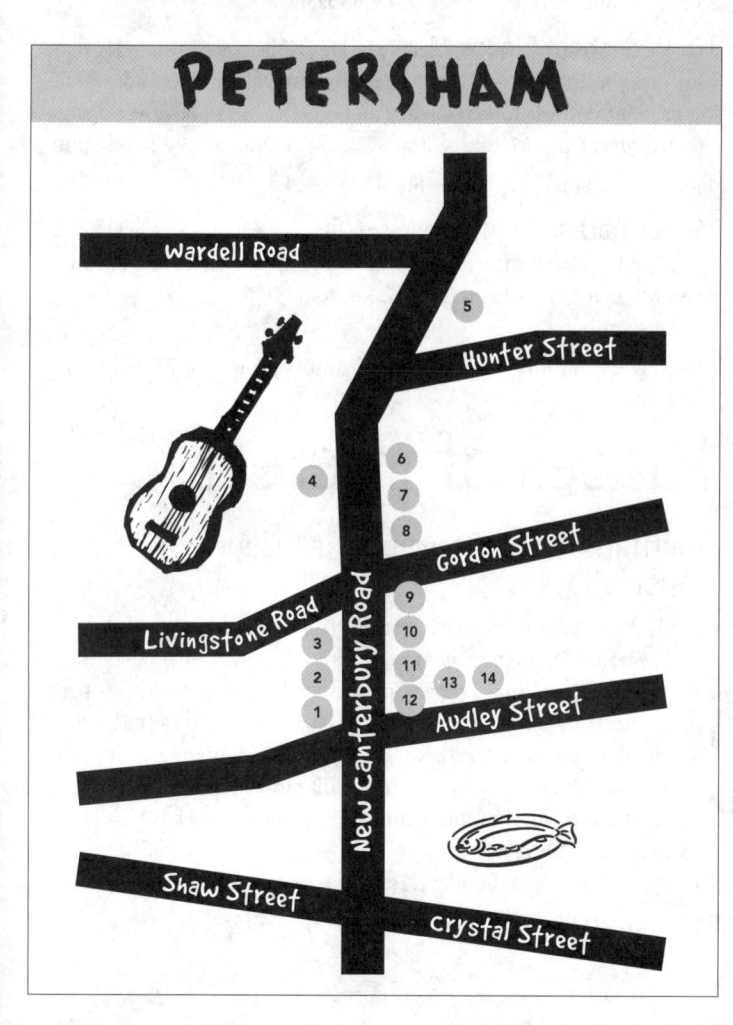

PETERSHAM

LITTLE PORTUGAL

1. Honeymoon Patisserie.
2. Petersham Charcoal Chicken.
3. Cafe Restaurante Portugal.
4. Restaurante Costa do Sol.
5. Portuguese Radio.
6. George's Continental Deli.
7. Talho Portuguese.
8. The Spanish Portuguese Butcher.
9. Portuguese Charcoal Chicken.
10. Petersham Liquor Market.
11. Charlie's Delicatessen.
12. La Patisserie.
13. Da Silva Haircutter & Portuguese Barber.
14. Gloria's Cafe Restaurant.

THE PORTUGUESE

5: Portuguese Radio. Sydney's Portuguese language radio headquarters is so diversified that they even sell magazines, newspapers and the latest from the Portuguese music scene.
Open Monday-Friday 9am-7pm, Saturday-Sunday 9am-3pm.
133 New Canterbury Road (tel: 9569 8333).

7: Talho Portuguese. Established in the area for over 20 years, Talho, is arguably the most popular deli and butchery among Sydney Portuguese (and also Brazilians). Check out the black beans, *bacalhau* and fresh sausages. Open Monday-Wednesday 8am-6pm (till 8pm on Thursday), Friday 6am-6pm, Saturday 6am-4pm.
95 New Canterbury Road (tel: 9569 5552).

10: Petersham Liquor Market. This is the place to shop for that wine that you tried on your last holiday in Portugal. Products from Chile, Russia, South Africa, Turkey, Croatia and other corners of the world are also available. Open Monday-Saturday 8am-8.30pm, Sunday 10am-6pm.
43-41 New Canterbury Road (tel: 9560 2414).

12: La Patisserie. Reported as the oldest Portuguese cake shop in Sydney, it has a well earned reputation for its divine cakes and pastries.
Open Monday-Friday 8am-5.30pm, Saturday 8am-4.30pm,
Sunday 8am-noon.
350 New Canterbury Road, corner of Audley Lane (tel: 9569 1107).

Places of interest

Portuguese Ethnographic Museum of Australia.

"It's an attempt to establish a bridge between the history of the Australian Portuguese community and the wider society," says journalist Antonio Sampaio, public relations officer of this superb community initiative. The Museum, which opened in June 1997, highlights personal testimonies on Portuguese immigration to Australia. It also houses painting, sculpture and photographic exhibitions by local or international Portuguese artists. Highly recommended. Entry $2.50.
Open Saturday 1-5pm, Sunday 11am-5pm or by appointment.
24A Australia Street, Camperdown (tel: 9633 4548).

Portuguese Historical Collection, State Library of NSW.

Don Diego de Prado y Tovar's manuscript diary about his voyage through the Torres Strait in 1606 – the earliest documented account of European discovery of Australia – is one of the most precious pieces in this collection of 250 works by some of Portugal's most eminent writers. It was donated in 1997 by the departed Portuguese Consul-General, Jose Costa Pereira who assembled this superb collection with the assistance of the Institute of National Libraries and Books in Lisbon. Open Monday-Friday 9am-9pm, Saturday-Sunday 11am-5pm.

Macquarie Street, City (tel: 9230 1414).

USEFUL NUMBERS FOR VISITORS

PORTUGUESE CONSULATE:
tel: 9326 1844.

INFORMATION SERVICE 24 HOURS:
tel: 1902 261 171 or 1902 261 172.

Getting to know the Portuguese community

Events

Festival da Cerjeva (Festival of Beer).

A celebration where your car has to be left at home. It's held at the beginning of May at the Portuguese Madeira Club.

1 Denby Street, Marrickville (tel: 9569 9015).

Our Lady of Fatima.

A religious celebration held on May 13 to commemorate the miraculous appearance of the Virgin Mary in the Portuguese village of Fatima. It's also observed by the East Timorese community. Special masses are organised by the diverse Sydney Portuguese religious organisations.

Further information: contact some of the Catholic Parishes listed on page 210.

Portugal Day and Day of Portuguese Communities.

Celebrated on June 14, this is the year's most important event for the Sydney Portuguese community. Usually a massive celebration is held at either the Sydney Portugal Community Club at 100 Marrickville Road, Marrickville (tel: 9557 4130) or at the Portugal Madeira Club at 1-3 Denby Street, Marrickville (tel: 9569 9015). Celebrations last all day and

Information on other communities events such as the *'Feira Regional'* (Regional Fair) and the Folkloric Festival can be obtained by ringing the Portuguese Community Club, Frazer Park,

100 Marrickville Road, Marrickville
(tel: 9550 6344 or 9557 4130).

TALKING ABOUT SOCCER...

13: DA SILVA HAIRCUTTER & PORTUGUESE BARBER.
This is a kind of hang out for the local folks. It's not only a scissor and combs affair... it's also where the latest in Portuguese music can be found, and the scarves, patches and flags of Portuguese soccer teams are treasured – particularly the flags of 'Benfica' – one of the most popular football clubs in Portugal. Open Monday-Friday 9am-6pm, Saturday 8am-2pm.
78 Audley Street (tel: 9569 0027).

2: PETERSHAM CHARCOAL CHICKEN.
98 New Canterbury Road (tel: 9560 2369).

6: GEORGE'S CONTINENTAL DELI.
103 New Canterbury Road.

8: THE SPANISH PORTUGUESE BUTCHER.
83 New Canterbury Road (tel: 9569 3573).

11: CHARLIE'S DELICATESSEN.
Traditional Portuguese products.
37 New Canterbury Road (tel: 9569 3573).

feature traditional food, music and speeches delivered by Portuguese community leaders, the Consul and the Mayor of Marrickville – the Sydney municipality where Portuguese have settled in large numbers.

Dia de St Joao (Saint Joao's Day).

An important religious celebration held on June 21 at Frazer Park, Marrickville.

Further information: 9789 4339.

Procession of Our Lady of Monte.

An annual Catholic religious celebration held on August 17.

Further information: St Pius Church, 256 Edgeware Road, Enmore (tel: 9565 1385).

Religious organisations and places of worship

St Pauls Church.

A regular mass is held here on Saturday at 5pm.

Further information: Father A Alves, Gurney Road, Villawood (tel: 9674 2531).

St Pius Church.

Father Julio Ago celebrates a mass on Saturday at 7pm and on Sunday at 10am. During weekdays regular services are at 7pm.

256 Edgeware Road, Enmore (tel: 9565 1385).

St Thomas Catholic Church.

Religious services are held on Saturday at 7pm and on Sunday at 8.30am. The parish priest Father Josi Bairos also has a weekly religious radio program – *'Momento de Reflexao'* – every Saturday at 1pm on Portugal Noticias Radio FM, 89.7.

3 Thomas Street, Lewisham (tel: 9560 2384).

Catholic services in Portuguese are also held at:

Sacred Heart Church.

Darlinghurst Road, Darlinghurst (tel: 9331 2147). Sunday 10am

St Peter's Church.

243 Devonshire Street, Surry Hills (tel: 9698 1948). Sunday 11am.

St Agnes Church.
509 Bunnerong Road, Matraville (tel: 9311 1909).

Art and culture

Banda de Mzsica Portuguesa.
A Portuguese celebration would not be complete without a performance from this traditional group. It performs at festivals, concerts, religious celebrations and other community events.
PO Box 471, Petersham, NSW 2049 (tel: 9663 1742 or 9557 4614).

Portuguese Folkloric Dancing Group 'Aldeias de Portugal'.
Performs Portuguese dances in traditional costumes.
31 Albert Street, Petersham (tel: 9558 0545).

Media

Newspapers

Jornal Portugues. Has a good coverage of Sydney Portuguese community events. It appears in the news-stands on Friday each week and costs $1.80. The editor is Filipe Azedo.
PO Box 1012 Castle Hill, NSW 2154 (tel: 9651 2286).

O Portuguese na Australia. Established in 1971, this newspaper is published weekly and has a circulation of 8,000. There is a special section dedicated to the East Timor freedom cause. The paper appears in selected newsagencies on Wednesday and costs $1.50. The editor is Manuel Gaspar.
1st Floor, 47 New Canterbury Road, Petersham (tel: 9568 5911).

COMMUNITY ORGANISATIONS

PORTUGUESE WELFARE CENTRE.
A key community welfare organisation, the Centre provides information and social assistance to Portuguese-speaking immigrants. It also organises free English classes.
24 Gordon Street, Petersham
(tel: 9569 2367 or 9568 3095).

Radio

SBS Radio 2 FM, 97.7. News, music and community announcements, Monday and Wednesday 9-10pm; Thursday-Saturday 11am- noon.

Portugal Noticias Radio FM, 89.7. News, music and entertainment 24 hours a day. For further information call 9331 3000.

Portuguese language radio programs can also be heard on the following Sydney community radio stations. Call for information about the timeslots:

2RES, FM 89.7 (tel: 9331 3000)
2RRR, FM 88.5 (tel: 9816 2988)
2RSR, FM 88.9 (tel: 9550 9552)

Facts and Figures

The Portuguese community is relatively young with 67 per cent of the population younger than 40 years of age, a long-term residency of more than 10 years (43.2 per cent) and a moderately high level of English competency (69.9 per cent).

In New South Wales there are approximately 14,000 Portuguese speaking residents, forming a young and middle-aged community. The great majority of Portuguese speakers come from Portugal, of which there are currently just over 10,000 living in Sydney. This is followed by Portuguese speakers from Brazil (about 1,000) and Indonesia (about 400) and small numbers from the Azores, Macau, East Timor, Cape Verde, Mozambique, Angola and Goa.

Of Portuguese speakers there is a very high percentage with no qualifications (77%), with Brazilians generally having a higher level of education than the Portuguese. In terms of income, 21.2% of Portuguese speakers earn $25,000 or less, while only 12.9% earn $60,000 or more.

Approximately 90% Portuguese speakers are Catholic, with a smaller percentage (around 3%) belonging to other Christian churches, including the Anglican and Orthodox.

The Russians

"Evgeniya who?" Evgeniya Senitsina! – well, the receptionist at the Australian Council of Trade Unions (ACTU) is excused if the name doesn't ring a bell. Try Jennie George (née Evgeniya Senitsina), the first and only woman ever to be elected president of the powerful ACTU.

Jennie George belongs to the main wave of immigrants from the former Soviet Union, mostly post-war displaced refugees, who arrived on our shores between 1948 and 1952. A passionate defender and promoter of Australian workers' rights, Jennie George has established herself as one of the most influential personalities in the country.

Jennie George is part of an uninterrupted, though episodic, string of Russians arriving at our shores dating back to the early years of the 1800s, when Russian ships used to call at Neutral Bay for reconditioning. For a long time, the peninsula was referred to as 'Russian Point', and it was only years later that it became known as Kirribilli, Sydney's home of the Prime Minister and Governor General (by the way, you can enjoy a wonderful view of this area by taking the ferry on the Mosman route). It seems that the first Russian settler in Sydney was a sailor who, in 1832, jumped ship from the vessel *Amerika*. Nothing is known about his name, even less about his fortunes in Australia.

Arguably the best-known Russian to visit Australian in the 1800s was Nicholai Nikolaevich de Miklouho-Maclay, a scientist and explorer who lived in Sydney from 1878 to 1886 and married Margaret Robertson, daughter of NSW Premier Sir John Robertson. Born in 1846 into a hereditary baronetcy created by Catherine the Great, he became an explorer, artist and humanist, and the first serious anthropologist to work in Papua New Guinea. On arriving in Sydney he soon became a fierce advocate of Aboriginal rights. He also started Australia's first marine biological research station, at Watsons Bay. Two grandsons, Paul Maclay, a former ABC radio announcer, and Kenneth Maclay, a solicitor, are the 'living memorial' of his presence in Sydney, while a bust and his personal collection – donated to the Macleay Museum at Sydney University – stand as a tribute his work (see page 218).

The first major Russian settlement in Sydney sprang up in the late 1880s and was located in what was once the thriving area of Eckersley, on the site of the Holsworthy military reserve near Liverpool in Sydney's west.

Early settlement

The first major Russian settlement in Sydney sprang up in the late 1880s and was located in what was once the thriving area of Eckersley, on the site of the Holsworthy military reserve near Liverpool in Sydney's west.

There, a group of thirteen Russians under the orders of De Liski, a Russian nobleman, settled on 640 acres of land and planted almonds, figs, olives and vines. By the end of the nineteenth century there were around 2,800 Russian immigrants living in Australia.

Before World War I, especially after the failed 1905 revolution, a considerable number of political exiles, mainly intellectuals from the left, found a safe haven in Australia. They were the founders of the first Russian community organisation, the Union of Russian Emigrants, with branches in Sydney, Melbourne and Broken Hill. It was in Broken Hill that the radical Russians began strong political action in the local trade unions. One of the most colourful Russian activists of the time was FA Sergeev, a close friend of Lenin, who made his way to Australia in 1911. He was an active member of the Australian Socialist Party and a leading campaigner for free speech. He went back to Russia in 1917 and died in 1921 at the age of 38.

Following the 1917 Revolution, the expansion of the Sydney Russian community gained new momentum. Ideologically, the post-1917 emigres were diametrically opposed to their predecessors – they supported the Tsarist regime and were strongly anti-communist. Their community life was profoundly shaped by the presence of the Russian Orthodox Church, whose first services were held in private homes or in the Greek Orthodox Church of The Holy Trinity in Surry Hills.

The first priest to begin regular church services was Father Innocento Serishev, a Russian Orthodox priest who arrived in Sydney in 1926. However, it wasn't until 1942 that the first Sydney Russian Orthodox Church, St Vladimir at Centennial Park, would open its doors for the first time.

A place for the displaced

In the years immediately following the end of War World II, Russian immigration to Australia reached an unprecedented level. Thousands of 'displaced persons', as they were called, began arriving in 1947 from the refugee camps of Europe. Those who settled in Sydney established pockets of Russian settlement in the western suburbs of Lidcombe, Ashfield, Blacktown, Bankstown and Strathfield. An important role in Russian community life was played by the newspaper *Edinenie*

(Unification), the weekly publication that from its foundation in 1950 has been instrumental in keeping the community informed about issues happening back in the old country as well as in the new one. It also played an important role in preserving Russian language and culture.

The overriding concern of the Russian community – one held in common with many ethnic communities in Sydney – was the loss of language and cultural traditions among the second generation. With this in mind the *Vitiaz* ('Knight') Association was founded in 1959, with a commitment to providing cultural, sporting and educational activities for children, including an annual summer camp. This time also saw the foundation of the very popular *Balalaika Song and Dance Ensemble*, a string musical group whose regular performances attract Russians and non-Russians alike who want to enjoy the melodic sound of the *balalaikas* and the *domras*.

But life in the 1950s was not all *balalaikas* and summer camps. In 1954, at the height of the Cold War, the community was rocked by what is known as the 'Petrov Affair'. In a cloak and dagger operation straight out of a Le Carré thriller, Vladimir Petrov, Third Secretary at the Russian Embassy in Canberra, was persuaded to defect to Australia. Within days there were volatile protests by Sydney's Russian community at Sydney Airport as Soviet security men escorted his wife, Evdokia Petrov, onto a Moscow-bound plane. The show of public disapproval for such strongarm tactics persuaded the government to offer Mrs Petrov asylum, and she came over to Australian officials at Darwin. (Years later in 1979 a similar incident occurred when a young woman, Lilliana Gazinskaya, climbed out of the porthole of a Soviet ship and sought asylum. As soon as the papers learned what she had been wearing when she escaped they had a field day – the Red Bikini Girl became a sensation overnight!)

Sydney Russian Orthodox community life began taking shape in the mid-1920s.

2000 here we come

Amidst these sensational events the Sydney Russian community continued to expand, particularly in the mid-1950s and early 1970s with the arrival of a group of the 'White Russians', a generation of Russians who had settled in China after the 1917 Revolution. This group contained a select number of scholars and writers, including the author and naturalist N.B. Baikov, and the historian I.I. Gapanovich. To this era also belonged Harry Triguboff, who years later would become one of the most successful and wealthy Sydney property developers (see page 220).

When in the early 1970s Russian authorities relaxed their Jewish immigration policy, a significant number of Russian Jews also made their way to Australia. Among those looking for a new start were world-class

Born Evgeniya Senitsina, Jennie George – the current President of the influential Australian Council of Trade Unions (ACTU) – belongs to the generation of Russians who arrived in Australia as post-world War II 'displaced persons'. Nowadays she is one of the most influential social and political figures in Australia.

artists such as violinist Nelli Shkolnikova, pianist Efim Stesin, and composer Elena Kats-Chernin, who arrived in Australia at the age of 17 and was once dubbed 'little Mozart'.

When Kostya Tszyu, the sensational Russian-born World IBF Junior Welterweight boxing champion, arrived in Sydney in 1992 he reaffirmed that, after the fall of the Soviet Union, Australia has become the favourite destination for a select group of very talented Russian sports people. With a large contingent of elite coaches – and with the 2000 Sydney Olympic Games just up ahead – they have been warmly welcomed. They are among the best in rowing, track and field, figure skating, boxing, fencing, swimming and gymnastics, and the names of – among others – Gennadi Tourestski (swimming), Sergei Shakhrai (figure skating), Dimitri Zorine, Vladimir Zakhariv and Andre Rodionenko (gymnastics) and are becoming familiar to Australians. Some of them have already marched under the Southern Cross in Barcelona and Atlanta. Sydney is next.

Restaurants

Skazka (Fairy Tale). Russian music, food and Bondi – what else could you ask for? It's BYO and you can expect to pay between $30-$40, though you can eat as much as you can. Open Friday-Sunday 8pm till past midnight, except on Sundays when is open 4pm-9pm. Russian music kicks off at 8pm.

140 Bondi Road, Bondi (tel: 9369 2133).

The Russian Coachman. Portions so large they could feed a batalion of Cossacks, and on weekends it is wild stuff – music, dance and vodka, all at once! Average $40, licensed. Open for lunch Tuesday-Friday noon-3pm, dinner Wednesday-Saturday 6pm till late.

763 Bourke Street, Surry Hills (tel: 9319 7705).

The Russian Lodge. A la carte dinner with traditional Russian music (from Friday to Saturday). Open for dinner Thursday-Sunday 6pm till late (on Saturday open from 4pm). BYO.

113-115 Hall Street, Bondi (tel: 9365 1997).

Russian Accent. Russian taste at the heart of Darlo. At the Russian Accent the fare is hearty and warming. *Pelmeni* dumplings are recommended. Average $20, BYO. Open Monday-Sunday 6-till late.

379a Bourke Street, Darlinghurst (tel: 9331 3605).

Social clubs

The Russian Club. Established in 1924, this is a Sydney Russian institution. It's open from Monday to Sunday from 11am till late. On weekends the action is in full swing – discos, floorshows and a Russian orchestra keep the Russian spirit alive. The Saturday night dance is free and always well attended. The Club restaurant opens for lunch Monday-Sunday noon-3pm, dinner 5pm-9.30pm. Average $15, licensed.

7 Albert Road, Strathfield (tel: 9746 8850).

The Russian Social Club. Social and cultural activites are regularly held here on weekends, and the Club restaurant is highly recommended to those purists looking for 'real' Russian food Down Under. Average $15, no alcohol allowed. Open for lunch only on Mondays noon-2pm.

1/3 William Street, Lidcombe (tel: 9646 3354).

Shopping

Russki's Deli. Close your eyes and think of a Russian treat that you would like to taste – yep it's here! Open Monday-Friday 9am-9pm, Saturday-Sunday 8am-8pm.

89 Bondi Road, Bondi (tel: 9387 2015).

Roman's Deli. Well if you didn't find that delicacy at Russki's, drop by here – they will surely have it. Open Monday-Friday 8.30am-9pm, Saturday-Sunday 8.30am-8pm.

78 Hall Street, Bondi (tel: 9365 7042).

Geniza Judaic Books and Gifts. Notable for its small section of Jewish prayer publications in Russian. Open Monday-Thursday 9.15am-5pm, Friday 9.15am-3pm, and Sunday 9.15am-2.15pm (it also opens by request).

70 Hall Street, Bondi Beach (tel: 9365 5783).

Gold Book and Judaic Gift Company. Has a good selection of Jewish literature in Russian. Open Monday-Thursday 9.30am-5.30pm, Friday 9.30am-3.30pm.

16b O'Brien Street, Bondi Beach (tel: 9300 0495).

USEFUL NUMBERS FOR VISITORS

RUSSIAN CONSULATE:
tel: 9326 1866.

RUSSIAN ETHNIC COMMUNITY COUNCIL OF NSW.
This is the peak Russian organisation in Sydney.
PO Box 157, North Strathfield 2137
(tel: 9747 1865).

For a large selection of great Russian (and Oriental) carpets and other rugs we recommend you drop by the Persian Carpet Gallery (formerly located at 352 Kent Street). "They may go from $50 to half a million," said one of the shop assistants.
Open Monday-Sunday, 9am-5.30pm (on Thursday till 8.30pm).

Shop 1N, Supa Centa, South Dowling Street, Moore Park
(tel: 9748 0212).

Landmarks and places of interest

Bust of Nikolai Miklouho-Maclay.

"You were the first to demonstrate beyond question by your experience that man is man everywhere, that is, a kind, sociable being with whom communication can and should be established through kindness and truth, not guns and spirits," wrote the great Russian author Leo Tolstoy to Miklouho-Maclay in 1886.

Miklouho-Maclay (the Maclay in his name is explained by his Scottish ancestry), a national hero in Russia, was born on July 17 1846. He lived in Sydney between 1878 and 1886 and while here married Margaret Robertson, daughter of NSW Premier Sir John Robertson. They went back to Russia in 1887 and he died one year later. In 1996 a bust – built in and brought from Russia – was unveiled and located at Sydney University to commemorate the memory of this man whose explorations, scientific achievements and Aboriginal advocacy have left a strong mark on Australian history. Miklouho-Maclay also established Australia's first marine biological station, at Watsons Bay; the building still stands there and bears a commemorative plaque.

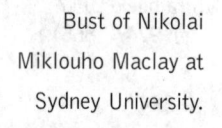

Bust of Nikolai Miklouho Maclay at Sydney University.

MACLAY COLLECTION AT UNIVERSITY OF SYDNEY'S MACLEAY MUSEUM.
Attractively organised, it holds the vast and valuable historical and anthropological items collected by Miklouho-Maclay during his explorations in Australia and in the Asia Pacific. It also includes rare autographed photographs of the Russian royal family. After his death they were donated to the Museum by his wife.

Free admisssion.
Open Tuesday-Friday 10am-4.30pm. University of Sydney, Parramatta Road, Camperdown (tel: 9351 2274).

St Peter and Paul Russian Orthodox Cathedral.

This impressive Orthodox Cathedral had its origins in the mid-1920s when the church life of the small Sydney Russian community began taking shape. A permanent place of worship was needed, as at the time either houses or existing Greek Orthodox churches were being used. World War II put this ambitious plan on hold, and instead a church, St Vladimir Church in Centennial Park, was established. With the appointment of Bishop Theodor Rafalsky in 1948, the project was back on the agenda – funds were raised, the site in Vernon Street Strathfield was selected, and in 1950 the design work began under the control of prestigious architect RJ Mahoffin. The first stone was laid on a rainy day in October 1951 by Archbishop Rafalski at a ceremony attended by hundreds of people, including prominent politicians such as Dr Clive Evatt. Construction began immediately, was completed in August 1953 and the Cathedral was consecrated just after Christmas of that year – a dream come true after so many years.

For further information contact the Australian and New Zealand Diocese of the Russian Orthodox Church Outside of Russia (tel: 9747 5892).

Getting to know the Russian community

Annual Ball.

Held in June, August or sometimes October at the Sydney Russian Club, this annual event is organised by the Vitiaz Association and the parents of children attending the Russian Saturday schools in Strathfield and Homebush, which are the main beneficiaries of funds raised at the Ball. The night includes performances by traditional Russian dances and choirs, and of course there's an assortment of delicious Russian food.

Further information: The Russian Club (tel: 9746 8850) or the Vitiaz Association (tel: 9487 2621, Anatole Zacroczymski, Director).

Summer Camp.

This is run by the Vitiaz Association and is held in January in the Blue Mountains. The camp's activities program includes Russian language, history and religion. Even though it is largely attended by children from a Russian background, organiser Anatole Zacroczymski informs us that it is open to everybody. It is a great opportunity for those studying or interested in Russian culture, language and history.

Children's Concerts.

This is another well-attended community event run by the very active Vitiaz Association. It has been traditionally held in the hall of the Cathedral of St Peter and Paul, 3-5 Vernon Street, Strathfield, on June 20. It's open to the public and well recommended for those who want to listen to traditional Russian songs.

Contact Mr Zacroczymski for details.

Sydney Russians celebrating Saint Nicholas' Day.

Saint Nicholas Day.

Held twice a year, on May 19 and December 22, to commemorate the memory of Saint Nicholas, the National Saint of Russia, who was a Greek bishop of Myra in Asia Minor in the fourth century. It is one of the major religious celebrations, and features a solemn liturgy and traditional Orthodox Church chants. The main celebration is held at the St Nicholas Orthodox Church, 13 Barbara Street, Fairfield.

Further information: 9724 3061.

Russian School of St Alexander Nevsky Dance Ball.

Held around July or August, it has been usually celebrated at the University of New South Wales' Roundhouse. An estimated 700 people attend this popular annual event featuring Russian music, dance and food. All are welcome.

Further information: Constantine Sulimovsky (tel: 9797 9486).

Russian School of St Alexander Nevsky Children's Concert.

Held on September 20, this is a two-hour feast of music, poetry, theatre and traditional Russian dances all performed by the students of this Russian School. "It is an important part of our educational program, a great way to learn the Russian language," – say the organisers. Held at the Russian Club, 7 Albert Road, Strathfield, this event welcomes everybody.

Further information: Constantine Sulimovsky (see above).

Russian School of St Alexander Nevsky Graduation Ceremony.

This long-established Sydney Russian school holds its graduation every year on December 13. It is a very special moment for parents and

Harry Triguboff

PROPERTY DEVELOPER

Among the 200 richest men in Australia, Harry Triguboff built his fortune of over $1 billion selling cheap, mass-produced housing units developed by his Meriton Group in the inner-city suburbs of Sydney and on the Gold Coast. Triguboff belongs to the generation of White Russians who settled in China after the 1917 Revolution. He came to Australia with his parents at the age of 14 and attended Sydney's Scots College, and then Leeds University in England, where he studied textile science. Triguboff is a well-known benefactor whose donations to charities and research projects are estimated at $25 million each year. In 1990 he was awarded the Order of Australia.

students alike. The graduation is celebrated with music and food (what else?). All are welcome, tickets are $40.

Call Constantine Sulimovsky for information, (tel: 9797 9486).

Balalaika Song and Dance Ensemble Concerts.

To attend a performance by this wonderful string ensemble (between eight and ten musicians wearing traditional Russian costumes) is a great way to be introduced to the richness of traditional Russian folk and classical music on *balalaikas, domras* and piano. Not to be missed.

Further information: Mrs W Jongejans (tel: 9580 5687).

Religious organisations and places of worship

Cathedral of St Peter and Paul.

Services are held on Saturday at 6pm and 9pm and on Sunday 9am-11am. There also is a Saturday school for Russian children where they are taught scriptures, language, literature, history and geography.

3-5 Vernon Street, Strathfield. Contact Dean Rev John Stukacz (tel: 9874 1947).

Russian Orthodox Benevolent Association.

Linked to the Moscow Patriarchate, the Centre organises a complete program of religious, educational, cultural and social activities. It also operates a Russian Language School for children on Saturdays.

135-137 Kildare Road, Blacktown. Contact Father Vladimir Makeev (tel: 9622 5322).

Russian Orthodox is the main religion among Russian Australians.

Russian Orthodox Diocese of Australia and New Zealand.

Established in Sydney in 1949, it holds services in Russian on Saturday at 6am and on Sunday at 9am. An English service has recently been tried and it seems that it is going to be held regularly. Everybody is welcome to attend the service, but remember: "show respect, be quiet, don't sit on the floor, and women cannot wear trousers inside the church," says the lady from the Diocese information office.

20 Chelmsford Avenue, Croydon (tel: 9747 5892).

St George.
Services, only in Russian, are held on Saturday at 6pm and Sunday at 9am. Everybody is welcome.
15 Garfield Street, Carlton (tel: 9587 1100).

St Vladimir.
The oldest Russian Orthodox church in Sydney, it has services in Russian every Sunday between 9am and noon.
31 Robertson Road, Centennial Park (tel: 9663 3341).

St Michael the Archangel.
Services are held every second Sunday at 9am.
9a Kemsey Street, Blacktown (tel: 9621 3431).

Cultural and educational centres

St Alexander Nevsky Russian School Inc.
Established in 1973, this is, according to its president Constantine Sulimovsky, "the largest single Russian school outside Russia".
It operates in the premises of the Homebush Primary School, Rochester Street, Homebush (tel: 9764 4472), and the classes are held every Saturday between 8.30am-1.15pm. The program, approved by the Department of Education, includes Russian language, literature, geography and history. Monthly fee: $37 one child; $56 two children; $60 three children or more; there also is an annual enrolment fee of $22.
PO Box S130, Homebush South 2140. Further information: Constantine Sulimovsky (tel: 9797 9486).

Library of the Russian Orthodox Diocese of Australia.
Has one of the most valuable and extensive collections of Russian books in Sydney. Pre and post-Revolution publications include Russian studies, literature, history and theology. The library is open Tuesday 10am-2.30pm and books can be borrowed.
20 Chelmsford Avenue, Croydon (tel: 9747 5892).

Australia-Russia and Affiliates Friendship Society.

Organises regular seminars, lectures and discussion programs about social, cultural and political issues in Russia. It has also been involved in welfare and humanitarian projects.

15 Crystal Street, Petersham. Further information: Betty Bloch (tel: 9564 2866).

Media

The first Sydney Russian-language newspapers date back to the 1920s and 1930s. Then, in a profoundly ideologically divided community, Russian periodicals were ferociously pro or anti-communist – no middle ground. They also were short-lived. Legendary in these years were the ferocious exchange of words between *Chuzhbina* (Foreign Land) and *Dal'ny Yug* (The Far South).

Newspapers

Edinenie (Unification). This paper was founded in December 1950 and since then has been an important medium for the dissemination of news to the Russian community. Published weekly and found in selected newsagencies on Fridays, it has a circulation of over 4,000. Its current Managing Director is EM Prokopiev.

PO Box 79, Penshurst 2222 (tel: 9586 0587).

Vzgliad (A Glance). It is a weekly publication of 64 pages with full colour cover. It hits the stands on Thursday and costs $3. Established in 1993, *A Glance* has a circulation of 5,000 issues. Its current editor is Mr. Anatoly Rubinstein.

Postal Address: Suite 604/35 Spring Street, Bondi Junction 2022 (tel: 9369 3739).

Gorizont (Horizon). Published weekly, it hits the stands on Tuesdays at a cost of $2.50.

197 Old South Head Road, (PO Box 105) Bondi Junction 2022 (tel: 9311 3763).

Radio

SBS Radio 2 FM (97.7). News, current affairs and a very good coverage of Russian community events held in Sydney. The voice of Alexi Ivacheff is unmistakeable. Monday and Tuesday 11am-noon, Wednesday 5pm-6pm, Saturday and Sunday 4pm-5pm.

Television

SBS Television, Sevodnia. Daily news services with a great coverage of Russian news and sports events such as soccer and ice hockey. Monday-Saturday 9.30am-10am.

Facts and figures

In Sydney Russians are concentrated in the eastern suburbs, Strathfield and on the North Shore, with smaller numbers in the western suburb of Fairfield.

Currently there are almost 10,500 Russian-speaking residents in New South Wales; most have come here from the former Soviet Union, China and some of the countries that until recently formed the Soviet Union, while almost 2,000 of them were born in Australia.

At the 1991 Census, 55.2% of Russian speakers stated they have no qualifications, while 8.7% have degrees; 4.4% have an undergraduate qualification or an associate diploma and 7.3% have received some vocational training. Around 5,500 (61.5%) of Russian speakers are in families with an annual income of less that $60,000. The largest proportion (28.2%) are in the range of $25,000 or less.

Explore the world in one city

The Serbs

Australia has never quite taken soccer to its heart, but every four years, at World Cup qualifying time, no other sport gets a look in. And every time there is tragedy, none more so than at the unbelievable draw with Iran that put the Socceroos out of France 1998.

Always tragedy? No. Back in 1974, Serbian-Australian Rale Rasic achieved soccer's ultimate goal, and with nothing like the array of international players Australia has to choose from these days. Having come to Australia from soccer-mad Serbia in 1962, Rasic took over the Australian national team in 1970 and took only four years to gain his team a place in the World Cup in Germany, and himself a place in Australian footballing history.

Although there were a few Serbian immigrants living in Australia by the beginning of the twentieth century – 1,000 according to the 1901 Census – the largest influx of Serbs to Australia ocurred at the end of War World II, especially from 1948 to 1955. The vast majority of them came from the resettlement camps in Germany, Austria and Italy, and upon their arrival they began their new life in Australian migrants camps at Mildura and Bonegilla. As government-assisted immigrants the Serbs were obligated to work for two years on jobs and at locations determined by the Australian authorities, but as soon as they were freed of this arrangement most moved to the main cities, especially Melbourne and Sydney.

An important chapter in the 1940s and 1950s Serbian immigration story was the arrival of Archpriest S Sekulic. He became, in 1949, the founder of the first Serbian Orthodox parish in Australia. The parish was originally located in Vineyard Street in the northern suburb of Mona Vale, but in 1954 the Saint Sava church was built in the central-western suburb of Flemington and it soon became the focal point of Serbian community life. Equally important was the creation in 1951 of the National Defence Council, a Serbian patriotic organisation which had been originally formed in the USA at the turn of the century. The Council has its premises in Bareena Street in the western suburb of Canley Vale.

The first wave of Serb immigrants arrived in Australia in the period between 1948-1955. The Serbs from this period constitute the largest group of Serbs presently living in Australia. The vast majority of them came from resettlement camps in Germany, Austria and Italy.

SHOPPING

HOT BUREK.
Established about 25 years ago, this is unchallenged as the place to get *bureks* – the traditional Serbian filled pastry. Open Monday-Friday 9am-5pm, Saturday 9am-1.30pm.
**484 King Street, Newtown
(tel: 9557 2951).**

> The 1960s were the years when Serbian immigrants began transforming the Municipality of Fairfield, Sydney west, into their main area of settlement.

It was also in Sydney that the first Serbian community organisation was established – the Serbian Cultural Club – founded in 1949. Its name was taken from an organisation founded in Yugoslavia in 1937 to defend Serbian interests against the so-called 'Yugoslavist' policies of the government of the time. A large number of the early members of the Club were former clandestine guerrilla fighters and war prisoners. The Club went through a period of decline between the early 1950s and the 1960s until a new wave of Serbian immigration gave it a new breath of life.

The early 1960s saw a stream of mostly unskilled or semiskilled Serbian labourers (though among them there were also a number holding secondary and even tertiary qualifications) looking for better economic conditions. These were the years when Serbian immigrants began transforming some of suburbs the Municipality of Fairfield – Sydney west – into the main area of settlement. One of the most important achievements of these years was the construction of the Saint George Serbian Orthodox Church in Cabramatta, completed in 1965.

The importance of Fairfield Municipality as an enclave of Sydney Serbian settlement was shown in 1985 with the building of the imposing Australian Serbian National Centre in the suburb of Bonnyrigg.

It is very difficult to ascertain the current number of Serbs in Australia – the large number of Serbs coming from Bosnia Herzegovina and Croatia makes it very difficult to calculate – but a figure of 30,000 to 40,000 is most likely. It is also likely this has grown as the recent dramatic conflict in the Balkans has pushed a large number of Serbian refugees to our shores in search of the peace so elusive in their own land.

Restaurants

A typical Serbian menu includes *peccena jagnjetina sa Kupusom* (steamed lamb with cabbage), *pecceno prase* (roast suckling pig), *sarma* (stuffed cabbage), *govedja supa* (boiled beef soup), and *svinjski paprikas sa povrcem* (vegetable stew with pork). And this is just what you'll get at the two most traditional Serbian restaurants in town.

Riverside. Make sure to also order the speciality, seafood. Average $30, licensed. Open Wednesday-Sunday, 7pm till (very) late – 3am is not an unusual time to close we're told.
4 Newbridge Road, Moorebank (tel: 9824 1333).

Village Grill. Go for the cabbage rolls and the marinated pork. Average $30, BYO and licensed. Open Monday-Sunday 5pm till late.
3 Short Street, Double Bay (tel: 9362 4942).

Landmarks and places of interest

St George Serbian Orthodox Church.

Located in Cabramatta, St George Church was built in 1965 in a traditional Byzantine style, and its altar is a showcase of the beauty of traditional Orthodox adornment. This beautifully designed Church was consecrated in January 1967, becoming the seat of the diocese and soon the centre for a large number of social and cultural activities. A children's orchestra was founded under its auspices and a drama group operates on its premises. In 1972 the Saturday School was established, and the first Sydney Serbian school building was here consecrated in 1983. It was named Vul Karadzich after the great Serbian linguistic reformer of the nineteenth century.

348 Cabramatta Road, Cabramatta (tel: 9821 3374).

Getting to know the Serbian community

Events

Krsna Slava.

The celebration of the Patron Saint's Day (Slava or Krsna Slava) is a uniquely Serbian custom in which all members of the same family or community set aside a day to honour their saint or protector. This celebration originated in pre-Christian times, when each family had its particular family god. Later, when the Serbs became Christians, they transferred this observance to the Christian saints, selecting a saint with special meaning to the family or the saint whose celebration day was nearest the day when the family accepted Christianity. St Sava, in his reformatory work, abolished blood sacrifices and established the Christian symbols of Krsna Slava, which are the candle (*voshtanica*), wheat (*koljivo*) and bread (*kolac*). The most common way of celebrating this event is by attending the holy liturgy, and Serbian Orthodox churches are the main venues for this festival (see page 228).

Uskrs (Easter).

This is one of the most important holidays celebrated by Serbs. There is great preparation for this day – on the Thursday before Easter, eggs are

CLUBS

SERBIAN CULTURAL CLUB.

Forget the ugly sound of the poker machines, this Club has a lot of history – as a matter of fact, established in 1949, it was the first Serbian community organisation created in Sydney. During the 1950s, the Club suffered a period of decline, but in the 1960s it received a new breath of life with new immigrants. In 1975 a huge hall was opened at Hoxton Park, near Liverpool, and it became the main venue for Serbian community celebrations, social events, dance – and, yes, the poker machines arrived. The Club also maintains an excellent folkloric dance group and Serbian language and cultural Saturday school. Open Monday-Friday noon-midnight, Saturday noon-11pm and Sunday 1pm-11pm (warning, we were told the Club trading hours vary depending on the number of patrons).

256 Cowpasture Road, Hoxton Park (tel: 9607 3304).

RELIGIOUS ORGANISATIONS AND PLACES OF WORSHIP.

Serbs have not always been strongly religious people but the fierce persecution suffered by the Serbian Orthodox Church during World War II and the Cold War prompted them to see the church with new eyes. The first Serbian priest to arrive in Australia, in 1948, was Father S Sekulic.

ST GEORGE SERBIAN ORTHODOX CHURCH.
Established in 1958, it has a mass on Sunday at 10am.
348 Cabramatta Road, Cabramatta
(tel: 9821 3374).

ST LAZARUS SERBIAN ORTHODOX CHURCH.
Founded in 1954, it was a focal point for Serbs who arrived during the 1960s and 1970s.
Renwick Street (corner Dibbs Street), Alexandria
(tel: 9516 1811).

dyed, and on Good Friday the family observes a strict fast and attends church. Even fish and oils are omitted from the menu on Good Friday and only nuts, fruits and vegetables are eaten. On Saturday, traditional dishes for the Easter meal are prepared – a typical menu includes lamb, lamb soup, *sarma* (stuffed cabbage), salad and cakes. Special religious services are held in Sydney's Serbian Orthodox churches.

Saint Sava Celebration.

Honouring the patron saint of the Serbian Orthodox Church, this festivity is annually held on January 27. Saint Sava, whose brother Stefan Menanja (1114-1200) was the founder of the Nemanjic dynasty, played a central role in converting Serbian people from Christianity to Orthodoxy. Saint Sava also played an important role in Serbia's mediaeval educational development. The main activities for this day are held at Serbian Orthodox churches.

Commemoration of the Battle of Kosovo (Vidovdan or St Vitu's Day).

On June 28, the Serbian community remembers the battle on the Plain of Kosovo in which Serbian independence was lost to the Turks in 1389. Remembrance activities are held at Serbian Orthodox churches and community centres.

For further information contact the Serbian National Centre on 9610 5749.

Victory Day.

Each year on November 26 the Serbian community celebrates the day on which Serbian people from Montenegro declared their union with Serbia. This event, held at the main Serbian community centres, is celebrated with a range of social activities such as choral concerts, folkoric dance performances and "a lot of long speeches" as one Serb we spoke to puts it. Contact the Serbian National Centre on 9610 5749.

General Mihailovic's Death.

The Serbian community commemorates annually the death of General Drajoljub Mihailovic, a hero of the Serbian resistance movement against German occupation during War World II. The commemoration involves a number of cultural events.

Further information: 9610 5749

Bozic (Serbian Orthodox Christmas).

Held on January 6, this is a very important festivity for the Serbian community. A special Christmas dinner consisting of roast suckling pig and other festive dishes, and of course Christmas cake (*Chesnica*), is brought to the table. The host says a prayer and everyone else sings a Christmas hymn, and after the Christmas cake is served the meal begins. The whole celebration continues for three days and centres around the family and the church. Information about special religious services can be obtained by calling some of the churches listed on page 228.

Community organisations

Most of the early Sydney-Serbian community organisations – especially during the years of the Cold War – had a strong emphasis on political activism. Nowadays there has been a shift more to social and cultural concerns.

Serbian National Centre.

The Centre's imposing venue opened in 1985 in Elizabeth Drive, Bonnyrigg just a few metres from the Croatians' King Tomislav Club. The Centre organises a wide range of cultural and social activities.

Elizabeth Drive, Bonnyrigg (tel: 9610 5749).

Media

Individual Serbian editors have been instrumental in the development of an Australian Serbian print media. The first Serbian language newspaper published in Australia, *Sloga* (Harmony), started in 1950.

Newspapers

Novosti (The News). Published three times a week – on Monday, Wednesday and Friday – it's the largest Serbian newspaper in Australia. It costs $1.30 and has a circulation of 20,000.

The current editor is Vladimir Srnic.
7 Garners Avenue, Marrickville
(tel: 9562 0500).

Radio

SBS Radio 1, AM 1107. News and current affairs presented by the experienced journalist Ken Gavrilovic. Monday, Wednesday and Friday 8am-9am; Tuesday and Thursday 3pm-4pm.

NJEGOS LIBRARY.
This library holds a rich collection of Serbian publications and archives. Its president is Dr Milan Djukanovic.
Room 6, 348 Cabramatta Road, Cabramatta
(tel: 9610 4063).

SERBIAN NATIONAL DEFENCE COUNCIL.
Established in Sydney in 1951, it has roots in the USA and has become a symbol of Serbian nationalism. Currently the largest single Serbian community organisation, its premises in Canley Vale were built by voluntary labour and opened in June 1965. It offers a wide range of activities, include theatrical and folkloric presentations.
56-58 Bareena Street, Canley Vale
(tel: 9728 6767).

Serbian radio programs can also be heard on the following community radio stations. Timeslots may vary, so call to get the latest.

2RRR, FM 88.5
(tel: 9816 2988).

2RSR, FM 88.9
(tel: 9550 9552).

The Spanish

Myth and reality combine to trace the early Spanish presence in Australia. It has been said that in 1595 a group of Spanish sailors from the ship Santa Isabel, commanded by Lope de Vega, were the authors of the rock carving at Murriverie, North Bondi, showing coats of arms and Spanish galleons.

It has also been suggested that the Sydney suburb of Dee Why was named after Lope de Vega, after some rocks were found carved with what may be his initials (DV). What is certainly not a myth is that Australia owes its name to navigator Pedro Fernandez de Quiros, who in 1606 took possession of what he named '*Austrialia del Espiritu Santo*', in honour of King Phillip III of the House of Austria. For more than 300 years Australia was considered a Spanish possession.

The first Spanish immigrant to come to Australia was JBL De Arrieta, who settled in Sydney's Morton Park in July 1822 where he received 2,000 acres of land. Around 1829 Adelaide de la Thoreza, a Spanish convict woman, was transported to Australia. Probably one of the first Spanish women in Australia, she was put to work under the responsibility of De Arrieta.

Bishop Rosendo Salvado was another early Spanish immigrant. He arrived in 1845 and was behind the establishment in 1847 of the Spanish missionary settlement and monastery of New Norcia in Perth. In 1848 Bishop Salvado visited Sydney and described the city as a very cosmopolitan place with people from 'everywhere'. Five years after Bishop Salvado's visit, Sydney saw the first Spanish Consulate open its doors. Antonio Arron was the first consul.

The last decades of the nineteenth century saw a few other Spanish immigrants. One of the best known was Joseph Merrey Vasquez who arrived in the late 1870s. After working as a gold digger in Queensland he moved to Sydney and lived in Greenwich Point, becoming a well-known Justice of the Peace and an occasional Spanish interpreter. By 1891 there were about 500 Spaniards who had also chosen to call Sydney their home.

Sydneysiders are not just great consumers of paellas and tapas; we have also been seduced by the passionate flamenco, and nobody more so than Diana Reyes, arguably the best exponent of this traditional Spanish art in Sydney.

Although Spanish immigration to Australia in the twentieth century has increased substantially, the Spanish community it is still one of the smaller Mediterranean communities in Australia. The Spanish Civil War generated thousands of refugees but very few of them came to Australia. It was only at the end of 1950s, with the assisted passage system, that substantial Spanish immigration began. The peak was reached in the early 1960s when more than 6,000 – largely semi-skilled labourers – turned up on Australian shores. Since the 1970s the Australian Spanish population has remained stable at around 15,000.

About 4,600 of these live in Sydney, and the colour and the flavour of their culture – food, music and dance – has spread across our city. Sydneysiders are not just great consumers of *paellas* and *tapas*; we have also been seduced by the passionate flamenco, and nobody more so than Diana Reyes, arguably the best exponent of this traditional Spanish art in Sydney.

Spaniards have tended to settle in the inner and outer western suburbs of Sydney, though the most visible face of Sydney Spaniards is at Liverpool Street in the heart of the city. Since the 1950s, this area between George and Sussex streets, has been known as 'Little Spain' (see page 232). Eusebio Morales, a journalist and well-known member of the Spanish community explains that the foundation, in 1962, of the Spanish Club in Liverpool Street was central to the consolidation of this area as a Spanish enclave.

Cafes and restaurants

Cafe Hernandez. This is not just a cafe, it's a Sydney landmark. Open 24 hours a days, the patrons are as diverse as they are loyal – yuppies, intellectuals (and pseudo-intellectuals), artists, taxi drivers, ambulance paramedics and people suffering from insomnia. The amazing range of coffee blends from New Guinea, Spain, Kenya, Colombia and many more makes this cafe one of the best in town. Try also the fresh tortillas and empanadas. Open Monday-Sunday 24 hours.

60 Kings Cross Road, Potts Point. (tel: 9331 12343).

Raquel's Spanish Restaurant. Raquels is a simple, non-pretentious and affordable restaurant right in the heart of Darlo. The great guitar player Paco Peña and his flamenco group has dined here. Average $20, BYO and licensed. Open for dinner only Monday-Sunday 6pm till late.

98 Oxford Street, Darlinghurst (tel: 9331 6806).

BOOKSHOPS

THE HISPANIC CULTURE CIRCLE.
This is home business affair established about three years ago, so don't drop by without calling beforehand. The selection of books and CDs is good and wide. A complete catalogue is available and you can order over the phone.

4 Jarvis Place,
Hebersham.
(tel: 9835 1222).

Liverpool Street, Sydney's 'Little Spain'

Squeezed into 100 metres of Liverpool Street – between George and Sussex Streets – has been since the early 1960s Sydney's undisputed 'Little Spain'.

The history of this Spanish enclave is closely linked to the establishment of the Spanish Club in 1962. "The first president of the Club was a multi-millionaire shipping tycoon called RD De Lasala. He purchased the original premises and donated it to the Spanish community of Sydney," says Rudolf Dominguez, the Spanish Club's assistant manager. He also remembers that in the 1950s the Spanish quarter was located in the same street, but closer to Oxford Street, when early Spanish immigrants used to live in the nearby East Sydney. The Club was the catalyst. Soon other restaurants and shops followed.

Plans to transform the Spanish Quarter into a kind of *Barcelona Gran Via*, with tables outside where you could have a glass of red wine or *sangria* and a few *tapas*, have been announced by Sydney Council. Hopefully the plans are not going to be postponed until '*mañana*'.

Little Spain is a short walk from Town Hall station. If you are at Circular Quay and in a non-walking mood, a cab will set you back $6 or $8. Alternatively, take a 339 bus, or any bus beginning with 4, and get off at the corner of George and Liverpool Streets.

In downtown Sydney the Spanish heart is found along Liverpool Street between George and Sussex Street.

Recommended to drop by

1: Spanish Club. Founded in 1962, this is where the history of Sydney's 'Little Spain' began. "The Club treasures the memories of very illustrious visitors including the King and Queen of Spain and the tennis superstar Arantxa Sanchez Vicario," says Rudolf Dominguez with pride. The facilities of the Spanish Club includes a lounge with noisy poker machines competing against the sound of the cable Spanish television. The restaurant upstairs is done in 18th century Spanish style – leather chairs, Spanish paintings and armour on the walls. The food? It's good and inexpensive.

88 Liverpool Street, Sydney (tel: 9267 8440).

2: Don Quixote. Don't think too much about what to order – the roast suckling pig has been making this restaurant, located in an historic 1856 premises, famous since the 1970s. Rustic decor, Spanish memorabilia and Spanish live music on Friday and Saturday add an extra touch. Average $40, licensed. Open lunch Monday-Friday noon-2.30pm, dinner Monday-Saturday 6-11pm.

7 Albion Place, City (tel: 9264 5903).

LITTLE SPAIN

1. Spanish Club.
2. Don Quixote.
3. Spanish Terrazas.
4. Torres Travel Centre.
5. Miro Tapas Bar.
6. La Campana.
7. Capitan Torres.
8. Torres Cellars & Deli.
9. Casa Asturiana.
10. Sir John Young Hotel Spanish Bistro.

THE SPANISH

5: Miro Tapas Bar. With Miro paintings on the wall and floors, this is a successful attempt to bring to Sydney the traditional *'tascas'*, the Spanish taverns where conversation is made an art while devouring tapas and drinking red wine. The *sardinas a la plancha* are also recommended. Average $30, licensed, wine by glass. Open lunch Monday-Friday noon-2.45pm, dinner Monday-Sunday 6pm till late.

76 Liverpool Street (basement level), City (tel: 9267 3126).

6: La Campana. One of the best known Sydney Spanish night clubs, La Campana (The Bell), is the spot for Latin and Spanish music and dance. On Fridays and Saturdays the party goes till 5am (after that, do the right thing and head to Cafe Hernandez – a coffee and a few pastries will start the long recovery process). Now, if you're planning to dance as a real *Latino*, drop by on Wednesday or Thursday for the free lambada, salsa and cumbia classes with Jose Prates, *'El Professor'*. La Campana also has a good tapas bistro, 'Costa Brava'.

52-55 Liverpool Street, City (tel: 9267 3787).

7: Capitan Torres. Established in 1975, this is the oldest remaining Spanish restaurant in the Spanish Quarter. Its 16th century Spanish decor, the spicy Iberian cuisine, and its well known *paellas* make this spot a must-go place. Private function rooms available. Average $30, licensed. Open lunch Monday-Sunday, noon-3pm, dinner 6-11pm.

73 Liverpool Street, City (tel: 9264 5574).

9: Casa Asturiana. A real winner, it has been considered by the specialists the best Spanish restaurant in Sydney. At Casa Asturiana you will have a bit of trouble deciding what to order. Suggestions: *tapas*, spicy barbecued *chorizo*, fried calamari or the magnificent *fabada*. Average $30, BYO and licensed. Open for lunch Tuesday-Friday and Sunday noon-3pm; dinner Tuesday-Sunday, 5:30-10:30pm.

77 Liverpool Street (tel: 9264 1010).

10: Sir John Young Hotel Spanish Bistro. Busy, busy all the time busy. The superb *paellas* and *tapas* make it worthwhile spending the time to grab a spot on those long wooden tables. Open lunch Monday-Saturday noon-3pm; dinner Monday-Wednesday 5.30-10pm and Thursday-Saturday 5.30-11pm.

557 George Street, City (tel: 9267 3608).

The Spanish Club was established in 1962.

3: SPANISH TERRAZAS.
A tapas bar. Open lunch Monday-Friday noon-3pm, dinner Friday Saturday 5.30-11pm.

541 Kent Street, City (tel: 9283 3046).

4: TORRES TRAVEL CENTRE.
Spanish travel agency.

Shopping

8: Torres Cellars & Deli. There aren't many Spanish delis in Sydney, but this one makes up for the lack of numbers. Here you will find the aromatic and strong *jamon serrano*, the tempting *chorizos* and *morcilla* sausages – especially for cooking a *fabada* (the renowned sausage and bean stew). Bread rolls, wines, spirits and beers are also available. Open Monday-Friday 9am-6pm (till 8pm on Thursday), Saturday 9am-4pm.

75 Liverpool Street, City (tel 9264 6862).

Getting to know the Spanish community

Events

Dia de la Hispanidad.

On October 12 the Sydney Spanish community commemorates the arrival of Christopher Columbus in America, by organising a range of sporting, artistic and cultural activities. In recent years various attempts have been made to bring together the Sydney Spanish and Latin American communities with the objective of having a common celebration. The Spanish Club, in Liverpool Street, is one of the main organisers for this annual commemoration (and supplies a venue as well).

Further information: The Spanish Club (tel: 9267 8440).

Concurso Literario del Club Español (The Spanish Club Literary Award).

This is a prestigious event that coincides with the October 12 celebrations. The Sydney Spanish-speaking community has a great tradition of fiction writers, including a few exponents of the Latin American 'Magic Realism'.

For further information, contact the Spanish Club (see above).

USEFUL NUMBERS FOR VISITORS

SPANISH CONSULATE:
tel: 9261 2433.

SPANISH GOVERNMENT COMMERCIAL OFFICE:
tel: 9362 4212.

SPANISH OFFICIAL CHAMBER OF COMMERCE:
tel: 9362 3168.

Sydney's Spanish community keeps the dance tradition alive and kicking.

Art and education

Flamenco Studio Newtown. The Artistic Director is the well-known flamenco *'bailaora'* Diana Reyes. Classes are available for beginners, intermediate and advanced students at a cost of $105 for nine sessions.

1-3 Gladstone Street, Newtown (tel: 9557 1825).

Amigoss. An educational institution offering Spanish language classes at an affordable cost. Beginner, intermediate and advanced levels are available. $100 a term which consists of eight sessions of two hours of duration.

102-106 Glebe Point Road, Glebe (tel: 9660 8813).

Community organisations

The Spanish Migrant Coordinator.

Established in 1980, it provides social assistance and organises cultural activities.

88 Liverpool Street, Sydney (tel: 9267 8822)

Media

Television

SBS Television offers *Telediario*, the main daily news service of the public owned Television Española. It has a very long segment dedicated to sporting news, which in Spain (and Latin America) means soccer. Monday-Saturday 10.15am-10.45am.

The Swedes

"**Slightly tongue-in-cheek** Sydney Swedes enjoy the fact that the sail-like roof tiles of the Sydney Opera House are of Swedish manufacture!" laughs Birgitta Sharpe – editor of the small but very informative *Kvintessen*, the Sydney Swedish newsletter.

She is also the chairperson of the Swedish Church Council and an endless source of information. "Every Swede in Sydney knows that the ceramic tiles were manufactured and supplied by the Sweden Hvgands group," she says. And every Australian-Swede is also aware that one of their compatriots – the botanist Daniel Solander – was on board Captain Cook's *Endeavour* in 1770.

A hard life

Among the convicts arriving in Sydney in the early 1820s were some Swedes; one of them was Anders Nyman, who was sentenced to 14 years for burglary in England. Nyman arrived in Sydney in 1826 and became naturalised 25 years later. A Swedish trading vessel, the *Edward*, carrying a cargo of timber, iron, steel and paint, among other things, arrived in Sydney in 1842. On board there were also nine Swedish immigrants. They were the first free Swedes to establish permanent residency in Sydney.

Life was hard in Sweden in the 1860s. It was an agricultural society unable to keep up with the massive population growth experienced in the nineteenth century. Immigration was the way out. Hundreds boarded the boats in the port of Gvteborg and went in search of a new land. The largest group went to the US while a few made the long journey to Australia. William Kopsen arrived in Sydney in 1868 at the age of 21. After a brief spell in Sydney, Kopsen tried his luck in Fiji where he became the first Swedish Consul and the Mayor of Suva. In 1889 he returned to Sydney where he opened a successful chandler's business. In 1890, this unstoppable Swede hopped on his pushbike and made his way to Kiandra – where Canberra is situated today. There, amazed by the strength and elasticity of the local mountain-ash timber that he found, he envisioned the possibility of manufacturing wooden oars and paddles.

One of the first Swedish community organisations in Sydney was the Valhalla Society, established in 1877. In its short life it gained the reputation of holding some of the wildest parties in Sydney – interrupted very often by the forces of the law.

A total success. Kopsen went on to establish what is considered Australia's first wood-processing plant and his wooden oars and paddles were sold in Fiji and other South Sea islands. Kopsen was also very active in the early twentieth century Sydney Swedish community. He was involved in the Swedish Chamber of Commerce, and in 1923 was appointed Sydney's Swedish Honorary Consul. He died in 1930, but his business in Sydney is still very much alive under the direction of his grandson.

The Swedish Society, founded in 1925, was the favourite venue for working-class Swedes, while the Sydney Swedish Chamber of Commerce, founded in 1911, was where Sydney Swedish businesspeople used to meet.

One of the first Swedish community organisations in Sydney was the Valhalla Society, established in 1877. In its short life it gained the reputation of holding some of the wildest parties in Sydney – interrupted very often by the forces of order. In 1883 another short-lived community organisation was founded, the Vikingen Society. By the 1890s the centre of the social and intellectual life of the Swedes was the mechanic workshop of Andreas Ringdahl. Here the generous consumption of drinks were soon followed by well-known songs. It was also here that the first Swedish publication in Australia appeared – the evocatively named *Sillsaladen* (Herring Salad). Other organisations soon followed.

Part of modern society

The Sydney Swedish population experienced a steady increase with the General Assisted Passage Scheme in 1952. Along with the new arrivals, new organisations sprang up. One of these was the Swedish Ladies' Association, which is still active today. Formed in 1961 by a group of Swedish ladies (as the name implies), it functions as a supportive network for newly arrived Swedes.

Under the leadership of the late Dr Gullan Kjellgren, the Linnia Folk Dancers was formed in 1977, and a large number of its founding members are still active. The *Svenska Skolan Sydney* (The Swedish School in Sydney) was founded in the early 1980s, offering Swedish-language studies, history and culture in various areas of Sydney – Cremorne, St Ives, Epping, Waverley, Narrabeen and Tempe.

Sydney's Swedish community retain traditional costumes and folk dance.

In 1982 the Swedish Club opened its doors, thanks to the initiative of a tireless Sydney Swede, Kjell Hermansson. The Club organises the National Day Dinner Dance in June, and in early December a well-attended *smörgasbord* (a Swedish word, needless to say). Following the division in 1987 of the Scandinavian Church in Sydney (into Danish and Swedish churches), the *Svenska Kyrkan i Sydney* (Swedish Church in Sydney) was formed. A very recent community initiative has been the establishment of The Swedish Council of NSW. Apart from being the 'Swedish voice' in Sydney, it publishes the already mentioned newsletter *Kvintessen*

Swedes have enriched our city in many aspects. Gustaf Mauritz Lindergren, for example, was the long-standing Secretary of the Swedish Chamber of Commerce (1920-1947) and played a substantial role in strengthening business relations between Australia and Sweden. Sir Edward Hallstrom (of Swedish descent) became a multi-millionaire in the refrigeration industry and also held the position of Director of Taronga Zoo, while Nils Josef Jonsson, a seaman and well-known personality in Kings Cross bohemian circles, became one of Sydney's most celebrated cartoonists.

Restaurant and cafes

Northern Lights. Fish is a mainstay in the Scandinavian diet, and the Northern Lights knows how to prepare it. You can enjoy a traditional Scandinavian meal of herring, or try the salmon marinated in salt and dill accompanied by a mustard sauce (gravlax). Top the dinner off with Swedish pancakes served with lingonberries or fruit preserves. Average price is $20 for a group of 12 or more having a traditional Swedish menu it costs only $16 per person. BYO and licensed (wine only).
Open for dinner Tuesday-Saturday from 6pm.

188 Pacific Highway, Hornsby (tel: 9482 7364).

Miss Maud of Sweden. A cafe where Sweden, Norway and Finland meet. Great open sandwiches and cakes in the largest shopping centre in the Southern Hemisphere. Open Monday-Friday 8am-5.30pm (till 9pm on Thursday), Saturday 8am-5pm, Sunday 9am-4pm.

Shop 11, Westfield Miranda (tel: 9540 5022).

Skandic Cafe. The place to get those delicious open Swedish sandwiches – on white, black or cracker bread they are just perfect. Accompany them with the good coffee and tea served here.
Open Monday-Saturday 7am-3pm.

109 Cathedral Street, Woolloomooloo (tel: 9361 3713).

Shopping

Inne (Swedish for 'inside'). In a very short period of time – it opened only in 1996 – Inne has made a name for itself selling contemporary furniture and home accesories from the Swedish design greats. Here you will find ceramics, chairs, glassware, and even Scandinavian slippers to plod around in.
Open Monday-Friday 10am-5pm, Saturday 11am-4pm.

47 Queen Street, Woollahra (tel: 9362 9900).

SCANDINAVIAN TRADITION. An old-fashioned Scandinavian deli. No frills, just lots of good food for sale. Anchovies, biscuits, bread, remoulade, sauces, sausages, coffee, *mackerel, marzipan* and *clogs*! A mail-order catalogue is available. Open Tuesday-Friday 10am-5pm.

216 Parramatta Road, Stanmore
(tel: 9564 6453).

Swedish restaurants are hard to find in Sydney but worth the effort.

USEFUL NUMBERS FOR VISITORS

SWEDEN CONSULATE:
tel: 9262 6433.

SWEDISH CHAMBER OF COMMERCE:
tel: 9262 1077.

Funkis. Distinctive contemporary Swedish furniture is the staple of this friendly space in Bondi. Recently Funkis has branched out with another shop right next door – *Mvbler* – ('furniture') devoted to an elegant and inexpensive range of Swedish chairs, tables, glassware and ceramics. Make sure you drop by Funkis and then Mvbler (or the other way round). Funkis is open Monday-Friday 10am-5pm (till 7pm on Thursday), Saturday 10am-4pm. Mvbler opens Thursday 11am-7.30pm, Saturday 11am-4pm.

23a Curlewis Street, Bondi (tel: 9130 6445).

Landmarks and places of interest

Daniel Solander Bust and Monument. Daniel Solander, the first Swede to visit Australia, stepped ashore at Botany Bay on April 19 1770 as a member of Captain Cook's first voyage on board the *Endeavour*. The Daniel Solander bust is located at the Sydney Botanical Gardens and was unveiled in 1982 by the King of Sweden – Carl XVI Gustaf – while visiting Australia. A monument to Solander was erected in 1914 at Captain Cook's Landing Place in Kurnell. This monument, built from a two-tonne block of Swedish granite, was the initiative of a group of Swedes led by the businessman William Kopsen.

Getting to know the Swedish community

Events

Midsummer's Eve Celebration.

On June 24 (the event actually takes place on the Sunday nearest to this date), the Sydney Swedish community celebrates this festival whose centrepiece is the midsummer pole (or maypole), which is dressed with leaves and flowers earlier in the day. The Festival includes traditional dancing, singing and games. It's organised by The Swedish Ladies Association.

Further information: 9996 9979.

St Lucia Festival.

On December 13 (or on the Saturday closest to this date) Sydney Swedes gather to celebrate what has been described as the only festival typically and uniquely Swedish. After failing to take root as a part of the Christmas celebrations, the tradition of the seventeenth and eighteenth century of representing the Christ child with a girl (dressed in a white tunic and with a candle wreath in her hair), was transferred to Lucia Day. Early on this day, according to tradition, Swedes eat and drink up to seven breakfasts in a row! – to prepare themselves for the Christmas fast which begins at sunrise on the morning of December 13.

Further information: The Swedish Ladies' Association (tel: 9996 9979).

The National Day Dinner Dance.

On June 6 (actually on the Saturday night nearest to that date), this event celebrates the day that has become – since 1983 – the official national day of Sweden. Until then, Sweden was perhaps the only country in the world with no official national day. Held at the Sydney Hilton Hotel, it is a formal occasion usually attended by the Ambassador and the Consul General. The event is organised by the Swedish Club.

Further information: 9819 7681.

Christmas Platter.

A more recently established event held in early December. It consists of an evening smorgasbord which gathers members of the Swedish community for the traditional Swedish buffet-style meal. For the last three years this event has been held at the American Club.

131 Macquarie Street, in the City. This event is organised by the Swedish Club (tel: 9819 7681).

Art and culture

The Linnia Folk Dancers.

Established in the 1970s and based in the beach suburb of Newport, this group takes part in a diverse range of cultural and artistic events, such as the Sheel Folkloric Festival. They also perform at the National Day, Midsummer and St Lucia Festival. Weekly rehearsals are held at St Andrew's Anglican Church's Hall, Roseville.

Further information: 9918 2966.

RELIGIOUS ORGANISATIONS AND PLACES OF WORSHIP

SVENSKA KYRAN I SYDNEY (SWEDISH CHURCH IN SYDNEY).

This is an Evangelical-Lutheran congregation which works in collaboration with the Swedish Church in Melbourne, whose resident Pastor travels to Sydney to hold services in Swedish. They are offered ten times a year, always on the second Sunday of the month, except in January and July. The services are held at St Mark's Lutheran Church.

56 Norfolk Road Epping. Further information: 9858 5335.

COMMUNITY ORGANISATIONS

THE SWEDISH COUNCIL OF NEW SOUTH WALES.
Founded in 1994, this is the main organisation for Swedes living in this state.

Further information:
Linda Petterson
(tel: 9799 7375).

THE SWEDISH LADIES' ASSOCIATION.
Formed in 1961, the Association organises the Midsummer's Eve Celebration and the St Lucia Festival. It also functions as a supportive network for newly arrived Swedish women, whether on temporary contracts or as permanent migrants.

2/2 Munsgrave Street, Mosman
(tel: 9996 9979).

Education

Svenska Skolan Sydney (Swedish School in Sydney).
Founded in the early 1980s, it offers teaching of Swedish language, history, geography and culture in weekly sessions to groups of students from 6-16 years. It operates in various areas of Sydney, including St Ives, Epping, Waverley, Narrabeen, Tempe and Cremorne.

Further information: 9449 2269.

Media

Newspapers

The Sydney Swedish community does not have any local newspapers but it has a newsletter, *Kvintessen*, published and edited by the Swedish Council of NSW. In English and Swedish, it covers mainly community news. It appears six times a year and has a circulation of 350 distributed among Sydney's Swedes. Its current editor is Birgitta Sharpe.

Further information: 9858 5335.

Radio

SBS Radio 1, AM 1107. News and current affairs in Sweden, Saturday 4pm-5pm. SBS Radio also has a Danish language program on Saturday 5pm-6pm and a Norwegian radio service on Monday 11am-noon

The Swiss

From John Webber to Joe Felber, the most distinctive feature of the Swiss presence in Australia is its artistic talents. John Webber – likely the first Swiss to touch Australian soil – was an illustrator who accompanied Captain Cook to record his third voyage, in 1777. His best-known work is 'The Death of Captain Cook' – showing the English navigator being killed by a group of Hawaiians.

Joe Felber, on the other hand, is the latest Swiss artist to arrive in Australia. A self-taught painter, he came in 1980 and since then has developed a solid reputation through the fusion of his Australian and Swiss experience.

Yet the most influential Swiss artists in Australian painting are Louis Buvelot and Sali Herman. Buvelot – who arrived in 1865 – is considered the father of Australian landscape painting. He brought to Australia the tradition of the French Barbizon School and introduced the practice of painting *en plain-air* which was fundamental to what became Australia's Heidelberg School. Sali Herman – who arrived at the beginning of 1937 – made an important contribution to the modern movement in Australian art (he still does so from his Avalon studio). Herman carved a niche in twentieth century Australia through his painting of the humanity and the spirit of Sydney's inner-city of the 1940s – he brought to the canvas the old terraces and the lively streets of Potts Point, Paddington and Balmain (well before they became the gentrified domains of well-off 'yuppies').

The first large Swiss immigration to Australian occurred during the 1850s when more than 2,000 Italian-speaking Swiss tried their fortune during the goldrush. By the 1870s, when the first Swiss social organisations were founded, the number of Swiss was no more than 2,500 and the majority were living in Victoria. Since then immigration from Switzerland suffered a long decline lasting until the 1950s, when a group of Swiss turned up on our shores. Like many of their fellows, they stayed temporarily. The second largest group of immigrants from Switzerland – 3,000 – arrived from 1969-1971 under the assisted passage program.

> The first large Swiss immigration to Australia occurred during the 1850s when more than 2,000 Italian-speaking Swiss tried their fortune during the goldrush.

FROM SWITZERLAND WITH A PAINTBRUSH

The works of Swiss artists John Webber, including 'The Death of Captain Cook' (painted 1781-1783), can be seen at the Dixson Library, State Library of New South Wales, Macquarie Street, City (tel: 9230 1414). Open Monday-Friday 9am-9pm, Saturday-Sunday 11am-5pm. Admission is free.

The paintings of at Louis Buvelot, Nicholas Chevalier, Sali Herman, and Paul Haefliger are displayed at the Art Gallery of New South Wales, Art Gallery Road, The Domain, City (tel: 9225 1700 or 9225 1744). Open Monday-Sunday 10am-5pm. Admission free (gallery), $7 adults (exhibitions).

SWISS CLUB OF NSW.

Organises social and cultural functions. It meets every Monday from 7pm onwards at the Ox on The Rocks Restaurant, 135 George Street. Contact Peter Pluess for details.

GPO Box 3713, Sydney 2001 (tel: 9416 6190).

Nowadays it's estimated that there are approximately 4,700 Swiss in New South Wales, where community life is encouraged by a small number of associations, including the Swiss Australian Society, established in the 1970s, and the very active Swiss Club.

Restaurants

En guete, bon appetit, buon appetito, bien appetit! In any of the four national languages – Swiss-German, French, Italian, Romansh – it all means the same 'Enjoy!'

Chez Rene. Listed in The French, page 109, Chez Rene is the work of Swiss-born Isidor Burch, who for over 17 years has been creating wonders at this well-known restaurant specialising in Swiss and French cuisine. Average $20, BYO. Open Monday-Sunday from 6.30pm.

537 Willoughby Road, Willoughby (tel: 9958 0547).

Eiger. Make sure you drop by on Swiss National Day (August 1) when a good time and special menu are guaranteed. Eiger has an excellent variety of quality meats and chicken-based dishes. Try the boneless chicken in mushroom wine sauce with rice – and the veal *cordon bleu* with potato salad isn't half bad. Average $20, BYO. Open for lunch Wednesday-Monday noon-2pm, dinner from 6pm.

552 Parramatta Road, Petersham (tel: 9564 1160).

Le Petit Savoyard. It's petit, full of charm and the Swiss-French menu is good – but the *fondues* (cheese, beef and chocolate) are just awesome. Average $20, BYO. Open Tuesday-Saturday 6pm-10pm.

55 Ridge Street, North Sydney (tel: 9923 2336).

Lurline Cottage. A little out of town, but if you're planning a weekend retreat in the Blue Mountains put this down on your list of things to do (or rather, eat). This charming restaurant and tearooms has a wonderful cheese fondue. Open Thursday-Saturday from 6pm. Average $20, BYO.

132 Lurline Street, Katoomba (tel: (047) 82 2281).

Zurich Restaurant. From Zurich with love. Chris and Debbie Hani have done a good job here – Swiss from top to bottom. Average $20, BYO. Open Tuesday-Saturday from 6pm.

282 North Road, Eastwood (tel: 9858 2251).

Shopping

Iseli Swiss Butcher. This butchery is just right for the purists – those looking for the essential Swiss-style smallgoods needed for an authentic meat fondue. Open Monday-Friday 8am-5pm, Saturday 9am-noon.
8 Charlotte Street, Ashfield (tel: 9798 6406).

Spiess Australia. The fine-quality meat and smallgoods of Spiess-Schiers have been renowned in Europe for more than 75 years, and now they have arrived here. The recently opened Sydney factory has combined the Swiss techniques and technology with Australian premium-grade meat to produce a superb range of tasty small goods. The factory outlet opens only on Thursday 9am-5pm.
103 Percival Road, Smithfield (tel: 9757 2255).

Viktor's Swiss Patisserie. For the past 17 years Viktor has been making mouth-watering Swiss cakes, including the diet-threatening *zugerkirsh*, *linzer torte* and *nussgipel*. Open Monday-Saturday 8am-1pm.
403 Guildford Road, Guildford (tel: 9632 3518).

Getting to know the Swiss community

Events

Swiss National Day.

The anniversary of the foundation of the Swiss Confederation is celebrated every year by the Swiss Club with a dinner and dance. The venue changes but not the regular crowd of 200 people. The Sunday after August 1, the Swiss Yodlers and Alphorn Group hold a traditional picnic at 200 Jersey Road, Plumpton. This big celebration kicks off at midday and features Swiss traditional food, music, yodling and games for children.

Further information: The Swiss Club (tel: 9416 6190) or The Swiss Yodlers Group (tel: 9871 3676).

Yodlers' Gathering.

An annual folkloric dinner and dance gathering held on October 25. Each year this celebration features a Swiss regional theme – in 1997 it was dedicated to the Swiss mountain people.

Further information: 9871 3676.

USEFUL NUMBERS FOR VISITORS

SWISS CONSULATE: tel: 9369 4244.

SWISSAIR: tel: 9232 1744.

SWISS DELI. A well-established Sydney deli chain, it carries a huge range of Swiss and European products. Recently, Swiss Deli began selling the long awaited Schwob's Swiss Farmer breads (long established in Melbourne, this bakery was founded by the Swiss Schwob family in 1954). So, you now have an additional reason to drop by Swiss Deli. Open Sunday-Friday 7am-7pm, Saturday 7am-9pm.
273 George Street, City (tel: 9247 8599). Also at 330 New South Head Road, Double Bay (tel: 9363 0629), 239 Oxford Street, Bondi Junction (tel: 9369 2805) and other locations.

The Turks

A short quiz – where is the most likely place to find the world's biggest Turkish delight? In Auburn, of course. Bill and Eddy Pektuzun from the Real Turkish Delight Shop spent a week cooking two tonnes of the sweet and gigantic *lokum* (one of the most traditional Turkish sweets) to crack the *Guinness Book of Records*.

The NSW Fair Trading Minister Faye Lo Po was there to prove it, and the Sydney Turks made their little enclave of Auburn – western Sydney' famous among the suburbs of the world. (see page 248).

"The Turks have been around in considerable numbers since 1968," explains Burlent Borluk, co-ordinator and social worker at the Turkish Welfare Association. Until then Turkish immigration to Australia was small (in 1947 there were only 116 Turks in the whole of Australia). The first large group of Turkish immigrants arrived in Australia under the Turkish Australian Agreement in 1968. Most of them came from Anatolia and were Muslims. Being mainly unskilled workers, they settled in the inner-city industrial suburbs and found work as labourers or process workers in the manufacturing industry.

The 1970s and 1980s saw the foundation of a number of community and educational organisations. In 1972 the NSW Turkish Associations Federation was formed, and in 1978 the Sydney Turkish Peoples House was established to assist Turkish migrants with legal, social and welfare difficulties. Other organisations, such as the Turkish Welfare Association and the Australian Turkish Social and Cultural Trust Inc, soon followed. Islamic and Koran studies started being offered by schools, based in some of the Sydney mosques in Redfern and Auburn.

Nowadays there are nearly 28,000 Turkish-born people living in Australia. A third of them have established permanent residency in Sydney, especially in the western suburb of Auburn, where most of the Turkish associations have established their headquarters, and the local shopping centre has become an urban kaleidoscope of Turkish restaurants, sweet shops, groceries and cafes. Auburn is also where the Camii Mosque is located.

> Nowadays there are nearly 28,000 Turkish-born people living in Australia. A third of them have established permanent residency in Sydney, especially in the western suburb of Auburn where most of the Turkish associations have established their headquarters, and the local shopping centre has become an urban kaleidoscope of Turkish restaurants, sweet shops, groceries and cafes.

Explore the world in one city

Restaurants and take-aways

If you drop by Cleveland Street or Crown Street, where Redfern meets Surry Hills, you will find some of the most exciting, affordable and friendly Turkish eateries around (see page 248). Alternatively, you can get the train from the City and get off at Auburn. Sydney's unofficial 'Little Turkey', Auburn provides some great places for a healthy and cheap Turkish pig-out (see page 248). You can also have a go at the ones listed below.

Pasha's Kebab House. A well-established Turkish restaurant with a superb selection of *mezes* (hors d'ouvres), including *pastirma* (pressed beef) and the ever-popular *humus*. Average $15, BYO. Open Tuesday-Saturday 11am-11pm, Sunday 3pm-10.30pm.

490 King Street, Newtown (tel: 9519 3139).

Pide Fez. This is where the super-cool Bondi surfers recover their carbohydrate level. Superior *pide* bread and fantastic Turkish delight. Open Monday-Sunday noon-midnight.

Shop 20, 180-186 Campbell Parade, Bondi Beach (tel: 9130 3131).

Landmark

Camii Mosque.

Located at Auburn, the lavish and dramatically beautiful Camii Mosque was built in traditional Turkish Islamic architectural style. David Evans, the architect and designer of the Mosque, was sent to Turkey in 1985 to visit historic sites and mosques, including the wonderful Blue Mosque, to get inspiration for his work here in Sydney. The construction began in 1986 and is just now coming to and end. This superb piece of architecture, covering 4,000 square metres, is surrounded by well-maintained rustic gardens. The Mosque is visited daily by around 200 people and on Fridays this number increases to approximately 1,500. You can get there by train, getting off at Auburn station.

15-17 North Parade, Auburn.
Further information: Sydney Turkish Islamic Cultural and Mosque Association (tel: 9516 3039 or 9558 0360).

The lavish and dramatically beautiful Camii Mosque was built in traditional Turkish Islamic architectural style.

Auburn, Sydney's "Little Turkey"

GETTING THERE

By train from Central, Town Hall or Wynyard.

Auburn is also the host of one of Sydney's most colourful street festivals. On September 19 (or the Saturday closet to this day), the main drag – Auburn Road – is closed to the traffic, giving way to a huge array of cultural activities. These include traditional, contemporary and classical dance, music and performances, while the food stalls along the street are a celebration of the culinary tradition of the countries of the world. Free and everybody welcome.

For additional information call 9649 5559.

In the first post-war decades Auburn was a dormitory suburb for working class Australians of Anglo-Celtic background. They worked in local factories and on the railways. However in the last decades, many local industries have shut their doors. New immigrants have moved in so that today Auburn is a vibrant place. Thanks to the vitality of its people who come from more than 54 countries. Immigrants from Turkey, Lebanon, Vietman, Bosnia, African and from other corners of the world have transformed this suburb into one of Sydney's most polyglot, though distinctive communities.

Despite the cosmopolitan nature of Auburn, the suburb has achieved notoriety as the heartland of the Turkish community. The local Turks have even made Auburn a celebrity when two local folk, Bill and Eddy Pektusun – owners of the Real Turkish Delight shop – cracked in 1997 *The Guiness Book of Records* with the world's biggest Turkish sweet ever made. Auburn is the address of one of the most beautiful mosques in Sydney – the Turkish Camii Mosque – whose lavish presence rises above the booming Turkish restaurants, sweet shops, markets and community organisations. The suburb is renowned as home to the best Turkish pizzas in town.

Restaurants & Take Aways

2: Bosphurus Reception Lounge and Centre. The homestyle Turkish fare at the reception lounge is good, tasty and addictive – while the live entertainment provides a damn good time. By the way Bosphurus is a great place to have a wedding with a difference – think about it. Dinner and show $40, licensed. Open every second Saturday only.

7 Station Road (tel: 9649 5666).

11: Ali Baba's Charcoal Chiken. There are more than forty reasons to drop by this *halal* spot – one it's friendly, second it's inexpensive and third the fare is very tasty – after eating here you'll be able to work out the remaning thirty seven reasons to visit Ali Baba's. Average $8, no alcohol. Open Monday-Sunday 8am-1am.

1 Civic Parade (tel: 9649 7320).

AUBURN

LITTLE TURKEY – AUBURN

1. Turkish Mosque
2. Bosphurus Reception Lounge and Centre.
3. Afghan Market.
4. Serdar Akturk Video.
5. Pasa Meat Market Halal Meat.
6. Ben Da Vietnamese Restaurant.
7. Buket Cake Shop.
8. Arzum Market.
9. Real Turkish Delight.
10. Elif Market.
11. Ali Baba's Charcoal Chiken.
12. Marathon Kebab House and Restaurant.
13. Dilek Gida Pazari.
14. Halal Meat Market.
15. Anjum Spice Centre.
16. Auburn Lebanese Bakery.
17. Sofra Pide Kebab House.
18. Arab Bank of Australia.
19. Merhaba Restaurant.
20. David's Asian Food Store.
21. Golden Crown BBQ Food Centre.
22. Xuan Hao Grocery.

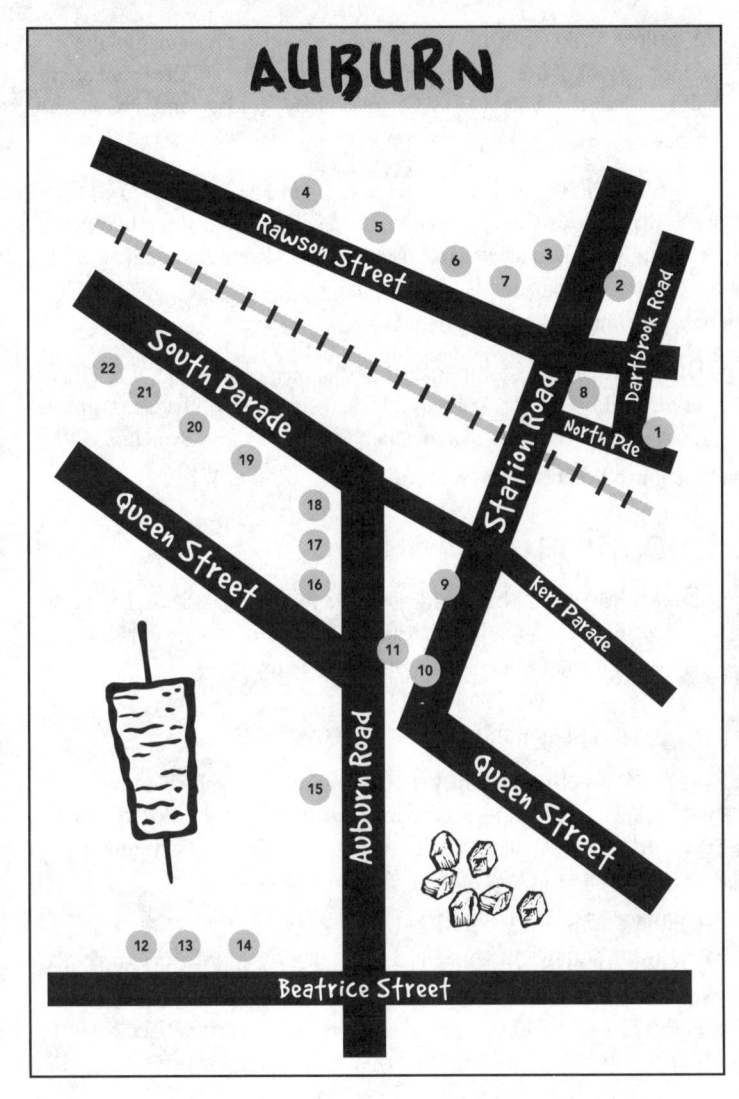

12: Marathon Kebab House and Restaurant. A local landmark, this is the place recommended by the local folks for a succulent Turkish pizza and a solid cup of coffee. It's a bit more expensive than the average Turkish eateries but it's worth it. Average $20, BYO. Open Monday-Sunday 7am-11pm.

22A Auburn Road (tel: 9649 3036).

THE TURKS

7: Buket Cake Shop. A quiet achiever with an imaginative and wide spectrum of fresh Turkish pizzas. The biscuits and the bread aren't half bad. Eat in or take it away. Open Monday-Sunday 7am-7pm.
67 Rawson Street (tel: 9643 2135).

17: Sofra Pide Kebab House. Expect to find a crowded and friendly place patronised by a cosmopolitan clientele tucking into the delicious Turkish food available from this friendly and unprententious spot. Open Monday-Sunday 7am-till late.
39 Auburn Road (tel: 9649 9167).

19: Merhaba Restaurant. The halal menu is so good, it can make you forget the wine. Try the roast chicken and some of the various pide pizzas. Average $10, no alcohol. Open Monday-Sunday 9am-1am.
15 Auburn Road (tel: 9649 1166).

Shopping

3: Afghan Market. A little gem of a food store – the Afghan-born Raz Rashtia who did some research for us drops by here regularly to get the right spices for his Agfhan cooking.
Open Monday-Sunday 9am-9pm.
1/2-4 Station Road (tel: 9749 2009).

8: Arzum Market. In this transplanted and charming Ankara market, expect to find everything from Turkish coffee to dried fruit. Make sure to save some space for the tasty Turkish *sucuk* sausage. Open Monday-Sunday 7.30am-11pm.
61 Rawson Street (tel: 9649 9327).

9: Real Turkish Delight. The record holder, it has some of the most exquisite and decadent hand-made chocolates in town. The rose and almond Turkish delight – covered in chocolate – is just perfect. Open Monday-Saturday 8am-6pm, Sunday 9am-4pm.
Shop 1, 3-5 Station Road (tel: 9649 9787).

10: Elif Market. This smart grocery has earned a well deserved reputation for the quality and variety of its products. Check out the imported *halva*, cheeses and breads. Open Monday-Sunday 8am-9pm.
6 Civic Road (tel: 9749 9365).

Many Turkish families have moved into the Auburn area in the last two decades.

13: Dilek Gida Pazari. Another superb market with a strong Turkish theme. The imported products include cheese, soups, olive oil, and the tempting and tasty *sucuk* (Turkish sausage). Open Monday-Sunday 7am-10pm.

9B Beatrice Street (tel: 9649 675).

1: Turkish Mosque

4: Serdar Akturk Video.

115 Rawson Street (tel: 9649 2804)

5: Pasa Meat Market Halal Meat.

75 Rawson Street (tel: 9649 7686)

6: Ben Da Vietnamese Restaurant.

71 Rawson Street (tel: 9649 5657).

14: Halal Meat Market.

9A Beatrice Street (tel: 9649 7571)

15: Anjum Spice Centre.

3 Beatrice Street (tel: 9649 7017)

16: Auburn Lebanese Bakery.

91 Auburn Road (tel: 9749 7142)

18: Arab Bank of Australia.

19 Auburn Road (tel: 9749 9400)

20: David's Asian Food Store.

80 South Parade (tel: 9649 2202)

21: Golden Crown BBQ Food Centre.

128 South Parade (tel: 9649 9622)

22: Xuan Hao Grocery.

148 South Parade (tel: 9649 7513)

The shop signs of Auburn reflect the culture.

USEFUL NUMBER FOR VISITORS

TURKISH CONSULATE:
tel: 9328 1155.

Getting to know the Turkish community

Events

Australia Turkish Day.

October is Turkish in Sydney – this is a month of great significance for Sydney Turks, when the first large group of Turkish immigrants arrived on our shores in 1968. Rather than a day it is a month-long celebration which features a hefty array of cultural activities held in Auburn and in the City, where the Opera House becomes the backdrop for a massive, joyful and colourful Turkish parade. One of the most significant activities of this month is the planting of a pine tree – brought from Gallipoli – in the Auburn Botanical Gardens, to symbolise friendship between Australia and Turkey.

Further information: Australian Turkish Social and Cultural Trust (tel: 9649 6279).

Turkish Republic Day.

This is celebrated on October 29 with a wide range of cultural and social activities. There are several locations, and Auburn is of course one of them.

Further information: tel 9649 6279.

Mustafa Kemal Ataturk Remembrance Day.

The memory and legacy of Kemal Ataturk – the founder of modern Turkey – is widely celebrated by Sydney Turks on November 10. Cultural activities, including seminars and talks about the life of Kemal Ataturk, are held usually in some of the community halls in Auburn.

Further information: 9649 6279.

Youth and Sport Day.

Parramatta Park in Sydney's west is the main venue for this celebration – an annual sporting and cultural festival which gathers together hundreds of Sydney Turks. It's free and everybody is welcome.

Further information: 9643 1666.

Turkish dance and traditional dress help establish continuities between The 'old country' and the new.

Community organisations

Turkish Welfare Association.
Provides welfare and social assistance to the Sydney Turkish community. It operates in Auburn, Marrickville and Botany.

Hut 35, 142 Addison Road, Marrickville (tel: 9569 1943).

Australian Turkish Social and Cultural Trust.
Provides information and assistance to the Turkish community.

2/102 South Parade, Auburn (tel: 9649 6279).

Media

Newspapers

Dunya. Edited by Dursun Candemir, this is a fortnightly publication that appears in newsagencies (and also Turkish shops and take-aways) every Friday. It has a balanced coverage of local and international news. It's free and has a circulation of 2,000.

PO Box 444 Auburn 2144 (tel: 9724 7447).

Yeni Vatan. Published weekly, this paper comes out on Fridays and has a good coverage of Australian political affairs. It has a circulation of 9,000 and can be picked up for free in some of the shops and restaurants scattered around Surry Hills and Redfern. The editor is Sedat Yilmazoc.

PO Box 206 Auburn (tel: 9646 3039).

Radio

SBS Radio 2, FM 97.7. News, comment and traditional and modern Turkish music. Monday 5pm-6pm, Tuesday-Sunday 3pm-4pm

Religious organisations and places of worship

SYDNEY TURKISH ISLAMIC CULTURE AND MOSQUE ASSOCIATION.
13 John Street, Erskineville
(tel: 9516 3039).

SYDNEY TURKISH ISLAMIC MOSQUE.
14 Barrena Street, Canley Vale
(tel: 9727 2447).

TURKISH ISLAMIC CULTURAL MOSQUE.
15-17 North Parade, Auburn
(tel: 9516 3039 or 9558 0360).

The Ukrainians

"I... listened enraptured by your overwhelmingly beautiful music," wrote the great Dmitri Shostakovic in a letter to the Ukrainian composer and now Sydney resident Myroslav Skoryk. Considered one of the most talented composers in his native Ukraine, Skoryk is the composer of a large number of symphonic, chamber and orchestral works.

Sydney Ukrainian community life dates back to the late 1940s when Ukrainians began arriving in large numbers from the refugee camps of West Germany and Austria.

He has also written music for some 40 movies, and is at home with jazz and contemporary music as well. "It's extremely hard to be an artist in Ukraine at the moment. Four years ago it wasn't that bad but in the last two the situation has worsened," comments Myroslav, who came to Sydney in 1995. While mastering his English and establishing networks, he is waiting with great patience for the opportunity to show us what he does best – "to create beautiful music," as he says with humility.

His artistic input will be much appreciated after the literary scandal that has left a bad taste in the mouths of Ukrainians in Australia – yes – the Demidenko affair. It is only a few years since a young 'Ukrainian' Australian writer with a shock of white-blond hair caused a stir with her book *The Hand that Signed the Paper*, concerning a 'true' account of Ukrainian persecution of Jews during the war. It was not enough that her book was perceived as anti-semitic; what really caught the media and public attention was her revelation that her Ukrainian family background, which was used to give authenticity to the book, was itself a complete fiction – Helen Demidenko was in fact plain Aussie Helen Darville. "This Demidenko affair was negative – Ukrainians were portrayed in the wrong light as anti-semitic," remembers Jaroslav Duma, the president of the Council of the Ukrainian Association. But the affair did open up a good level of debate with the local Jewish community. "We even wrote some joint communiques. That was the positive aspect," says Mr Duma.

Members of the Ukrainian community believe that their number in Australia is somewhere between 30,000 and 35,000. According to the 1991 Census there are about 2,230 Ukrainian-born people living in Sydney, forming a strong and cohesive community in the outer western

Myroslav Skoryk.

suburbs such as Bankstown, Blacktown and Lidcombe. This community dates back to the late 1940s when Ukrainians began arriving in large numbers from the refugee camps of West Germany and Austria. Among them was Wolodymyr Shumsky; shortly after arriving in 1948 to the refugee camp in Cowra and witnessing the lack of community support and information, he began editing *Wilna Dumka* ('Free Thought'), one of the first Ukrainian newspapers to be published in this country. The newspaper still exists and Wolodymyr Shumsky is still behind the editing desk.

It has been argued that centuries of life under foreign occupation in Ukraine explains the tendency of Ukrainians to establish community organisations. They represent either a means of resistance to oppression or a means to maintain their culture, history and tradition. Either way, the publication of *Wilma Dumka* was the trigger for the development of other community initiatives, including the founding of the Ukrainian Society of Sydney and the Ukrainian Association of Sydney. In the early 1960s the first Ukrainian *Hromada* – an association consisting of a central representation and affiliates in country towns – was established in Australia. The *Hromada* played an important role in developing community organisations, particularly by raising money to purchase or build large community centres.

To stay and to succeed is firmly in the mind of Atlanta Olympic medallist Rustam Sharipov. One of the most talented world gymnasts in the world today, Sharipov arrived in Australia in June 1997 after a long battle in which his immigration application was continually blocked by Ukraine's gymnastic federation. After two years of permanent residence Sharipov will be able to take out Australian citizenship, and he is already looking forward to 2000 and to giving Australia its first gymnastics medal. The Australian men's head coach Warwick Forbes summed it up when he said recently: "It's such a bonus to have him. It's part of Australia's multicultural makeup to have people like Rustam coming in and bringing their highly prized skills."

Philologist, journalist, poet and writer, **YURI MIKHAILIK** is regarded as one of the most important Ukrainian writers of his generation. Born in the Ukrainian port of Odessa in 1938, Mikhailic has been living in Sydney since 1993 with his family. He is the author of ten books of poetry, five plays and several critical essays.

Religion is a central part in the life of Ukrainian people, and church activity began in 1948 with the arrival of the first priests. Ukrainians are either members of the Ukrainian Orthodox Church, if they come from the eastern side of the country, or followers of the eastern rite of the Catholic Church if they're from the western side. After worshipping in small and modest venues, Sydney Ukrainians began in the early 1960s to build solid churches. It was symbolic – Ukrainians had come to stay, and succeed.

Restaurants

Ukrainian Cultural and Social Club. One of the main centres of Sydney Ukrainian activities, it has dining and social activities on weekends plus sporting and cultural events. The restaurant is nothing fancy; it just offers good, traditional food – and lots of it. Try the *borscht* soup (based on beetroot) or the *holubtsi* (cabbage rolls). Average $10, licensed. Open Friday and Saturday, 5.30pm-11pm, lunch and dinner on Sunday 11.30am-8.30pm.

11-15 Church Street, Lidcombe (tel: 9649 2285).

PLACES OF INTEREST

ST ANDREW'S UKRAINIAN CATHOLIC CHURCH.

Located in the western suburb of Lidcombe – the hub of the Sydney Ukrainian community – St Andrew's was built during the years 1959-61 as a memorial to Ukrainians who lost their lives in World War II. Designed to hold a congregation of 600, St Andrew's was opened for use in 1961 and was consecrated on April 1971.

The interior of this beautiful building, adorned with magnificent murals, has – in the Byzantine tradition – an Iconostasis (wall of Icons) separating the Sanctuary from the main nave. The Icons – representing the meeting of the Divine and the mortal on earth – are made of cut coloured glass set in fibreglass in aluminium frames, and they bear colourful designs painted by the Ukrainian artist Myron Levytsky, of Toronto, Canada, who is also the creator of all pictures and murals in the church.

57 Church Street, Lidcombe
(tel: 9649 9957)

Ukrainian Community School. A Ukrainian take-away operates here every weekend, offering down-to-earth Ukrainian traditional dishes such as *varenyky* (dumplings), *kovbassa* and *kapustka* (Ukrainian sausage with a mild sauerkraut) and *kartpolyanyk* (potato pancakes). Open Saturday 1pm-5pm, Sunday 9am-4pm.

2nd Floor, Ukrainian Community School, 57 Church Street, Lidcombe

Getting to know the Ukrainian community

Events

The majority of community events are held in the hall of the Ukrainian Association of Sydney, at 59-63 Joseph Street, Lidcombe. For further information call 9749 1912. Religious festivals are celebrated at various Ukrainian churches in Sydney (see this page and next).

Christmas.

Celebrated on January 7, the Sydney Ukrainian Catholics celebrate Christmas. An important feature of this celebration is the separation of present giving from the religious ceremony. Gifts are given and received on St Nicholas Day, December 6. One of the main venues for this celebration is the Ukrainian Catholic Church of St Andrew, 57 Church Street, Lidcombe.

Further information: 9649 9975.

Remembrance Day.

On January 22, the Sydney Ukrainian community celebrates gaining its independence from Russia in 1918. Though it had only a brief period as an independent nation – six months – it is one of the most important events on the Sydney Ukrainian calendar.

Anniversary of Lesya Ukrainka.

This well-known Ukrainian poet, thinker and dramatist was also a celebrated fighter for the rights of women. Her birth is commemorated every year with a music concert and a literary festival held in February at the Ukrainian Hall. All are welcome.

Ukraine Heroine's Day.

This is a major celebration held the last Sunday of February where Ukrainians pay their respects to all women who fought and died for the independence of Ukraine.

Further information: Nonna Iwasyk, Ukrainian Women's Association (tel: 9642 7702).

Taras Shevchenko Festival.

In the first weekend of March the Ukrainian community remembers the memory of Taras Shevchenko, Ukraine's greatest poet, who championed the independence movement at the expense of his own personal freedom. Shevchenko was exiled to Siberia for his beliefs, but his memory is preserved with this annual celebration. The main feature of the event is a choir and music ensemble concert held at the Lidcombe Ukrainian Hall. Entry is free and all are welcome.

Independence from the Soviet Union.

On August 24 1991, following the downfall of the Soviet Union, the Ukrainian people finally regained that elusive independence and freedom they held so briefly in 1918. Cultural and social events are held on the day closest to March 24.

Religious organisations and places of worship

Ukrainian religious denominations need to be understood against a historical background. Apart from a brief period, the Ukraine was for centuries dominated by foreign powers. Its eastern lands were under Russian rule – first by the czarist and later by the communist regime – and followed the Ukrainian Orthodox Church. Western Ukraine was part of the mighty Austro-Hungarian Empire, coming under Polish rule after World War I, and follows the Eastern rite of the Catholic Church. No musical instruments are used in the services in the Ukrainian Catholic Church, while all services are in dialogue form between the celebrant and the congregation. When passing his church, a Ukrainian will raise his hat or make the sign of the Cross.

Ukrainian Autocephalic Orthodox Church, St Aphanasius Parish.

A regular service is held here on Sunday at 9am.

35 Killdara Road, Blacktown, Rev Czerwaniw (tel: 9627 1838).

EDUCATION

UKRAINIAN CENTRAL SCHOOL IN SYDNEY.

The School prides itself on preparing Ukrainian children to become fully integrated into Australian society without losing their rich cultural background. Subjects taught include Ukrainian history, geography, language and culture. Its current Director is Mr. Ivan Shestowsky. Operates Saturday 9am-1.30pm.

59-63 Joseph Street, Lidcombe (tel: 9707 1820).

Art

The Sydney Ukrainian community is one where art – painting, singing and dancing – occupies a central part. Ukrainian choirs and dance groups regularly take part in such multicultural events as the Carnivale and the Festival of Nations.

Ukrainian Artists Society of Australia.

A cultural organisation that supports Ukrainian artists living in Australia. It also aims to promote Ukrainian artistic expression in the wider community, and generally "to give inspiration to creative minds," its current secretary Peter Kravchenko puts it. The Society has a major involvement in the events listed on page 256.

57 Georges Avenue, Lidcombe (tel: 9649 3014).

Ukrainian Bandura Ensemble 'Lastivka'.

A cultural ensemble which plays the Ukrainian national instrument the 'bandura', which is used both as a solo instrument and for accompaniment. Formed over 20 years ago, the Ensemble promotes the rich Ukrainian heritage and traditions.

Further information: Edward Kulcycki, Musical Director (tel: 9939 6274).

Ukrainian Musical Society 'Boyan-Surma'.

Established in 1951, this group of 45 male and female voices is a fine exponent of the best of the Ukrainian choir tradition. It has regular performances and an annual concert. All are welcome to join, as the group's secretary Paul Chudakewycz explains: "A few years ago we had a member from New Zealand who had a wonderful voice and learnt to pronounce Ukrainian quite well, although she didn't speak the language." Rehearsals are held every Thursday at 1.30pm at the Ukrainian Youth Hall.

11 Church Street, Lidcombe. Further information: 9533 5817.

Community organisations

The main Ukrainian community body is the Federation of Ukrainian Organisations in Australia whose executive – at least at the time of writing – is located in Melbourne. It's a non-political umbrella organisation covering 32 member organisations. The Sydney Ukrainian community has developed an extensive network of community organisations whose main venue is the premises of the Ukrainian Association of Sydney in Lidcombe.

Ukrainian Association of Sydney.

This is one of the oldest Ukrainian organisations in Sydney. Founded in 1950, it covers a wide range of activities, such as cultural, welfare and entertainment activities. Its premises is the main venue for a large number of Sydney Ukrainian associations and community festivals.

59 Joseph Street, Lidcombe (tel: 9749 1912).

Council of Ukrainian Association in NSW.

This is the peak umbrella body that coordinates the Ukrainian community and represents it to the wider community. It was established in 1949 and its first Chairman was Dr EJ Pelensky. An important part in the history of the Association was played by Jurij Dechnicz, who was involved in the Council from 1975 until 1992. The current president is Jaroslav Duma.

59-63 Joseph Street, Lidcombe (tel: 9749 2859).

UKRAINIAN CENTRAL INFORMATION SERVICE. Provides information and undertakes research on issues affecting the Ukrainian community. It also provides assistance regarding business contacts between Australia and Ukraine.

11-15 Church Street, Lidcombe (tel: 9749 2859).

Media

Newspapers

Wilna Dumka ('Free Thought'). This paper has been running uninterrupted from 1949, when recent immigrant Wolodymyr Shumsky brought out the first issue in Nowra. Mr Shumsky is still behind the editing desk, making him probably the longest-standing ethnic newspaper editor in the country. His son and assistant, Marko Shumsky, is making sure of the continuing success of this valuable publication. *Wilna Dumka* includes news from Ukraine along with Sydney Ukrainian community information. It is published weekly, has a circulation of 2,000 and can be found in selected newsagencies on Fridays.

PO Box 101 Lidcombe, 2141 (tel: 9649 1489).

Radio

SBS Radio 2 FM 97.7. Ukrainian news and music. Tuesday and Thursday 4pm-5pm and Sunday 2pm-3pm.

Television

SBS Television. Ukrainian news service. Sunday 7am-7.30am.

Getting to know
Asian Sydney

Around 10 years ago Campsie was a neglected Sydney suburb. A dump. Then the Koreans arrived with their businesses and fixed it up, and today Campsie is a success story. Kingsford, in eastern Sydney, was until a few years ago a dull lifeless suburb. The Indonesians and Malaysians settled there and Kingsford is on the rebound – Indonesian restaurants and Asian shops along Anzac Parade abound, while the thousands of Asian students at the nearby New South Wales University has given a fresh, young and cosmopolitan face to the suburb. Cabramatta, Marrickville, Chinatown, Bankstown – the list goes on. Asians – with their vitality, hard work and self-reliance – have embraced Sydney in all aspects of its life, making our city a far better place to live in.

> Asian migrants make up the fastest-growing ethnic group in New South Wales, and Asian communities are likely to continue to expand into the next century.

Asian migrants make up the fastest-growing ethnic groups in New South Wales, and Asian communities are likely to continue to expand into the next century. In 1947 only 0.3% of New South Wales residents were born in Asia; in 1976 this had increased to 1.1%, and by 1991 the rate had skyrocketed to 5.2%. The largest group of Asian-born people comes from Vietnam (49,222), though the number born in China (44,714) is rapidly approaching it.

The Asian experience in Sydney fans across the vastness of the city. Southern Asians – especially Indians and Sri Lankans – tend to be concentrated in Ryde and Hornsby on the North Shore. Southeast Asians – Vietnamese, Laotians and Cambodians – have settled in the western suburbs, especially Fairfield and Cabramatta. Pockets of Malaysians, Indonesians and Singaporeans are found in the middle and high-income northern and eastern suburbs – chiefly in Kensington, Kingsford and Randwick. The residential distribution of people from Northeast Asia – China, Hong Kong, Korea, Taiwan and Japan – shows a strong preference for the middle and high-income northern suburbs – especially Chatswood – though there is also a considerable presence in the areas of Parramatta, Fairfield and Blacktown. And we already know that Koreans feel very much at home in the Sydney south west suburb of Campsie.

Explore the world in one city

Asian festivals

Festival of Asian Music and Dance.

Organised by the Australian Institute of Eastern Music, the festival was held for the first time in 1994. Since then, it has become a showcase of Australia's best talent in Asian music and dance, running for four days in October. Tickets are $15-$60 and bookings are available from the Belvoir Theatre and Ticketek (tel: 9266 4800).

Belvoir Street Theatre, Belvoir Street, Surry Hills (tel: 9699 3444).

Asian Theatre Festival.

Held for the first time in 1992, the festival – run by the Australian Institute of Eastern Music and Company B Belvoir – is held during the first two weeks of September. These two weeks bring to Sydney the rich and growing talent of Asian-Australian artists. A unique Australian experience, it features performances in storytelling, music and dance, comedy and drama, plus a series of workshops and forums. Tickets go from $12 to $20 and are available from the Belvoir Theatre and Ticketek (see above).

Sydney Asian Festival.

Organised by the Chinese Youth League, this event is part of the annual Carnivale, Sydney's most significant multicultural festival. The Asian Festival is usually celebrated at the end of September and features music and dance concerts. Chinatown's Dixon Street and Darling Harbour are the main venues.

Further information: 9251 7974.

Art galleries

Art Gallery of New South Wales.

The third floor of this magnificent gallery is home to one of the finest Asian art collections in Australia. Here you will find a chronological exhibition of Chinese art from the pre-Shang dynasty (c.1600-1027) to the twentieth century, a magnificent Japanese painting collection and an extensive display of Indian ceramics and sculptures. Open Monday-Sunday 10am-5pm. Admission to the Gallery is free, exhibitions are $7 for adults.

Art Gallery Road, The Domain, City (tel: 9225 1700 or 9225 1744).

AUSTRALIAN INSTITUTE OF EASTERN MUSIC (AIEM). Founded in 1985, the Institute supports, promotes and develops the rich musical tradition of Asia. Currently, it is under the guidance of Ashok Roy, a leading exponent of the Indian *Sarod*. The AIEM offers regular concerts (approximately every two months), lectures and appreciation classes. It also organises the highly acclaimed annual Sydney Asian Theatre Festival. Membership is open to everybody – $20, $15 concession, $30 family, $50 community organisations.

Further information: (tel: 9310 0694).

ASIAN DANCE & MUSIC CENTRE OF AUSTRALIA.
This Centre has a solid reputation in providing a wide range of Asian art workshops. Here you can have either private or group classes in *tabla*, *pakhawaj* and *kathak* dances. The Centre is also available for lectures and demonstrations.
154A Stacey Street, Bankstown.
Further information: Pandit Ram Chandra Suman (tel: 9796 7401).

Gallery 4A.
Run by the Asian Australian Artists Association, this is an exhibition space displaying a wide range of contemporary and experimental art forms. The Association is a non-profit organisation which fosters cultural ties between Australia and Asia. Open Thursday-Saturday noon-6pm.
Room 3, Third Floor, 405-411 Sussex Street, City (tel: 9211 2245).

Quadrivium Gallery.
Located in the Queen Victoria Building the Gallery has regular exhibitions of contemporary Asian (and Aboriginal) art.
Open Monday-Saturday 10am-6pm (till 8pm on Thursday), Sunday 11-5pm
Level 2 (Town Hall end), Queen Victoria Building (tel: 9264 8222).

Shopping

Chosun Gallery.
When it's time to change the old furniture, this is the place to do it. Chosun sells smart Korean secret drawer chests, Korean hat boxes, Korean headside chests, Japanese *mizuyatansu* and much more.
Open Monday-Sunday 9.30am-5.30pm.
993 Pacific Highway, Pymble (tel: 9488 9298).

Lynette Cunnington Asian Art.
A tasteful selection of Chinese, Japanese and Korean art, plus magnificent classic Chinese furniture.
Open Monday-Saturday 10am-6pm, Sunday noon-5pm.
92 Queen Street, Woollahra (tel: 9326 2227).

Raymond & Victoria Tregaskis.
This gallery specialises in Asian and Oriental antiques. You can find a wide range of Chinese furniture, stone pedestals and even Buddhist lions (to protect your home from evil spirits).
Open Monday-Saturday 10.30am-5.30pm (or by appointment).
120 Hargrave Street, Paddington (tel: 9362 1582).

Cabramatta, Sydney's Southeast Asia Capital

GETTING THERE

Located 30 km south-west Sydney, by private car the busy Hume Highway will take you there in around 40 minutes. From Central Station, the train on the Liverpool line will get you there in 45 minutes.

"Land where the cobra grub is found" – is the Aboriginal meaning of Cabramatta – home to 250, 000 Vietnamese, the largest community – among the 109 nationalities currently living here.

Every Sunday "Vietnamatta" – as it's popularly known – receives more than 15,000 visitors, encountering a fascinating collage of ethnic sights, sounds, and smells.

Cabramatta's first settlers were Irish political prisoners. It was a long time ago. It was once also the home of the 'big man' of Australian politics, the former Prime Minister Gough Whitlam. That wasn't long ago. 'Vietnamatta' acquired its distinctive southeast Asian character when thousands of Vietnamese, Cambodian and Laotians refugees poured into the migrant hostels established around this area, following the bloody conflicts in Southeast Asia in the 1960s and 1970s .

Nowadays Cabramatta is a showcase of authentic and cheap Vietnamese and Cambodian eateries, exotic fruit and vegetable markets, fascinating alley-bargain shops. It's fair to say also that Cabramatta has its own problems. Drugs – controlled by the infamous Asian 5T gang – is the major one. However, the uniqueness of this Sydney Asian enclave shouldn't be missed.

Cabramatta has become the centre for Southeast Asian immigrants living in Western Sydney. It is well worth a visit.

1: Vinh Phat. It has made a damn good reputation for its well prepared seafood. Average $15, BYO.
Open Monday-Sunday lunch 9am-3pm, dinner 5-9pm.

Shop 7/8 40 Park Road – don't get confused, it's actually in Hughes Street, see the map – (tel: 9726 2720).

3: Tan Thach Hong. A palace of exotic, tropical and fresh desserts and juices. On a hot Cabramatta summer day, this is the place to cool down with a *durian* or lychee juice or fruit salad.
Open Monday-Sunday 8am-9pm.

Shop 17/24-32 Hughes Street (tel: 9724 1813).

4: Dong Son. Not a very flash interior but Dong Son delivers with its authentic and cheap Cambodian cuisine. Average $10, BYO. Open Monday-Sunday 7.30am-9pm

2/44 Park Road (tel: 9724 4551).

7: Won Kee. The Cambodian section of the extensive menu – covering Thai and Chinese cuisine – is worth a look. Average $10, BYO. Open Monday-Sunday 9am-10pm.

19-20 Arthur Street (tel: 9728 6718).

9a: Pho Ga Tau Bay. Inside the Arcade, it's not easy to find but the effort is worth it: try the generous and superb *Pho*. Average $10, no alcohol. Open Monday-Sunday 7.30am-7.30pm.

Shop 16/107 John Street (tel: 9724 7162).

16: An Lac. This top-to-bottom vegetarian restaurant is run by holy people – the members of the nearby Vietnamese Buddhist temple. Not just to enhance your flesh but also your spirit. It has great achievements such as the steamed spring rolls or *bun rieu* – a tomato and vermicelli soup mixed with Asian basil, lemons and bean sprouts. Average $10, no alcohol. Open Monday-Sunday 10am-10pm.

94b John Street (tel: 9727 5116).

19: Thanh Binh. One of the most well known Vietnamese eateries in the 'hood. Not unexpectedly, the food is great and reasonably priced. Mains could well be the amazing *chao tom* (sugar cane prawns). Average $15, BYO. Open Monday-Sunday 9am-9pm.

52A John Street (tel: 9727 9729).

Shopping

C6: Asian Imperial Centre. Tucked at the rear of the Cabramatta Arcade at 46 Park Road, this is a Laotian heaven of fresh and zesty spices and vegetables. Rice, sweets and some pretty handy cooking pots are also available here. Open Monday-Sunday 9am-7pm.

3/50 Park Road (tel: 9726 6889).

8: BKK Supermarket. This astonishing place crosses the border of just about every Asian corner and brings to Sydney all those goodies that you must expect to find in Asia. Noodle bars, vegetable and groceries shops, butcheries and even colourful bazaar of clothes and jewels are all here. Open Monday-Sunday 8.30am-9pm.

53 Parl Road (tel: 9727 8222).

CABRAMATTA

IN AND AROUND CABRAMATTA

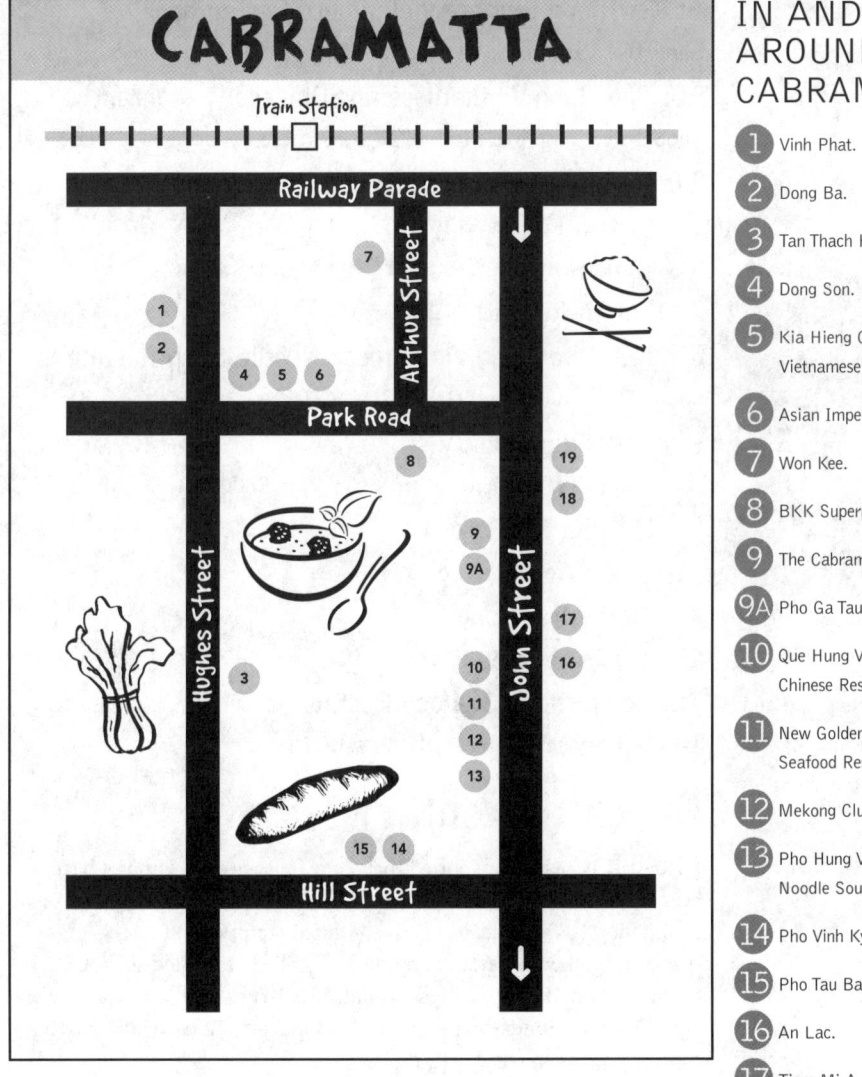

1. Vinh Phat.
2. Dong Ba.
3. Tan Thach Hong.
4. Dong Son.
5. Kia Hieng Chinese Vietnamese Restaurant.
6. Asian Imperial Centre.
7. Won Kee.
8. BKK Supermarket.
9. The Cabramatta Arcade.
9A. Pho Ga Tau Bay.
10. Que Hung Vietnamese and Chinese Restaurant.
11. New Golden Court Seafood Restaurant.
12. Mekong Club.
13. Pho Hung Vietnamese Noodle Soup Restaurant.
14. Pho Vinh Ky.
15. Pho Tau Bay.
16. An Lac.
17. Tiem Mi A Dong.
18. Long Phung Seafood Restaurant.
19. Thanh Binh.

9: The Cabramatta Arcade. An alternative to the BKK – it has an astonishing range of groceries, vegies and spices shops. Good quality and inexpensive. Open Monday-Sunday 8am-7pm.

107 John Street.

2: Dong Ba. Next to Vinh Phat.
(tel: 9755 0727).

ASIAN SYDNEY

5: Kia Hieng Chinese Vietnamese Restaurant.
Shop 1/44 Park Road (tel: 9726 5081).

10: Que Hung Vietnamese and Chinese Restaurant.
Shop 4/117 John Street (tel: 9725 7680).

11: New Golden Court Seafood Restaurant.
1st Floor/117 John Street (tel: 9725 1140).

12: Mekong Club.
117 John Street (tel: 9724 6688).

13: Pho Hung Vietnamese Noodle Soup Restaurant.
7/117 John Street (tel: 9726 7442).

14: Pho Vinh Ky.
Shop 10/11-117 John Street (tel: 9724 2800).

15: Pho Tau Bay.
117 John Street (tel: 9726 4583).

17: Tiem Mi A Dong.
92b John Street (tel: 9726 2853).

18: Long Phung Seafood Restaurant.
1st Floor 64a John Street (tel: 9724 3057).

Cabramatta has so many cheap and good restaurants that it is difficult to choose just one for your bowl of delicious Pho.

Check this out...

Pho 54. It has been reported that some inner-Sydney yuppies have been seen around Cabramatta's Freedom Plaza. This miraculous act of exploration has a name, *bun bo xao* – the masterpiece of Pho 54 – rice vermicelli with a salad of marinated, grilled beef, fried shallots, peanuts, cucumber and leaves of mint. $10, BYO.
Open Monday-Sunday 8am-7pm (till 7.30pm on Thursday and Friday).
254 Park Road (tel: 9726 1992).

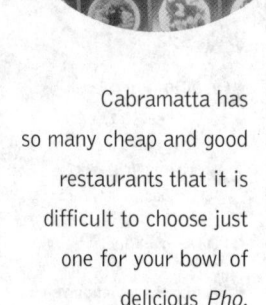

The Burmese

The Burmese in Australia have shown a strong commitment to the restoration of political freedom in their homeland through diverse political actions organised by the very active Committee for Restoration of Democracy in Burma, the All Young Burmese League, and the Australia Burma Council – a political lobby group established in 1992 – one year after Aung San Suu Kyi, the remarkable Burmese democracy fighter, was awarded with the Nobel Peace Prize.

When Myanmar, formerly Burma, gained its independence in 1948, the British left behind a distinctive group – the "Anglo-Burmese". They were the offspring of the British colonial staff and their Burmese wives. When racial and employment obstacles faced after independence pushed them to emigrate, those Anglo-Burmese with British passports went to the United Kingdom while others opted to come to Australia.

Between 1947 and 1959 about 3,500 Anglo-Burmese settled here.

Presently there are around 9,100 Burmese immigrants in Australia, with most having settled in Perth, Western Australia. This was mainly due to two very practical reasons: the air fare from Burma was cheaper and the weather was similar. In Sydney, there are about 1,000 Burmese-born, and a considerable number of them are ethnic Burmese who fled the dictatorial military regime that has run Myanmar since 1962.

The Burmese are largely Therevada Buddhists. In Sydney they worship in the Burmese Buddhist Monastery, established in 1987 and located at 121 John Street in the western suburb of Marylands.

The Burmese are largely Therevada Buddhists. In Sydney they worship in the Burmese Buddhist Monastery at 121 John Street, Marylands.

Getting to know the Burmese community

USEFUL NUMBER FOR VISITORS

EMBASSY OF MYANMAR (CANBERRA),
tel: (06) 9273 3811

Events

Water Festival.

One of the main religious events in the Burmese calendar, the Water Festival is celebrated during the last three days of the old year (according to lunar calendar). During this time, the Burmese symbolically wash the old year away with water and get ready to receive the new year. Special celebrations are held at the Sydney Burmese Buddhist Monastery at 121 John Street, Marylands.

Further information: 9637 8334.

Light Festival.

Around October or November, the Burmese celebrate the Buddha's enlightenment and his journey to earth. In Burma it's traditional to light candles outside the home. In Sydney the Light Festival is celebrated in various Buddhist temples, including the Sydney Burmese Buddhist Monastery at Merrylands.

Further information: 9637 8334

For other Buddhist events celebrated by the Sydney Burmese see Buddhist Sydney, page 343.

Myanmar (Burma) Independence Day.

On January 4, 1948, the Burmese saw the end of British colonial administration. Due to the current political situation in Burma this day is not so much celebrated. However, members of the All Young Burmese League use this date to stage a day of political protest in Sydney against the ruling dictatorship of the SLORC (State Law & Order Restoration Council).

Further information: All Young Burmese League (tel: 9632 7215).

Senior Citizens Festival.

One of the hallmarks of *banahsan chin* – the standard of ideal behaviour expected from Burmese – is showing respect for elders, and this is what the Senior Citizens Festival is all about. This event is celebrated in a variety of ways by several of the Sydney Burmese organisations. The Burmese Friendship Association holds a senior citizens' luncheon where food is provided and small gifts are given. The Burmese Buddhist community celebrates this event with various special ceremonies.

Further information: Sydney Burmese Buddhist Viahara (tel: 9637 8334) or the Burmese Friendship Association (tel: 9819 7999).

Religious organisations and places of worship

Sydney Burmese Buddhist Viahara (Burmese Buddhist Monastery).

The Monastery has been serving the religious needs of the Sydney Burmese Buddhist community since its foundation in 1987. The Abbot is the Venerable Sayadaw Jagara.

121 John Street, Marylands (tel: 9637 8334).

Burmese Buddhist Centre.

This is a centre for worshipping and the studying of Burmese Buddhism. The Venerable Sayadaw Ashin Sandar Thuriya is Abbot here.

26 Vickliffe Avenue, Campsie (tel: 9789 5904).

Community organisations

Australia Burma Council.

Founded in 1992, the Council is an umbrella political organisation that plays an important role in lobbying for the restoration of democracy in Burma.

15 Barbara Boulevarde, Seven Hills (tel: 9620 7007).

Committee for Restoration of Democracy in Burma.

Like the Council, the Committee is a political organisation that fights for democracy and human rights in Burma.

Orhadleigh Street, Yennora. (tel: 9632 7215).

All Young Burmese League.

This is another very active Burmese organisation involved in political and human rights issues.

21 Kerrs Road, Lidcombe (tel: 9746 2101).

RESTAURANTS

Burmese cuisine is basically a blend of Burman, Indian, Chinese and Mon influences. An essential part of any Burmese meal is rice *(htamin)* eaten with a curry dish *(hin)*.

NEYPEDAW RESTAURANT.
An unpretentious Chinese-Burmese eatery, this is the place to sample a good range of Burmese cuisine, including a traditional chicken with noodles. Average $15, BYO and licensed. Open for lunch Monday-Saturday 11.30am-3pm, dinner Monday-Sunday 5pm-10pm.

Woodville Lane, 330 Forest Road, Hurstville (tel: 9570 3331).

SHOPPING

AMY'S ORIENTAL GROCERIES.
Specialises in a wide range of Burmese products. Open Monday-Friday 9am-6pm, Saturday 9am-3pm, Sunday 9am-1pm.

16 Portico Parade, Toongabbie (tel: 9896 0531).

Burmese Friendship Association.

Assists Burmese immigrants with information on employment and also plays a role as an advocacy organisation.

28/2 Beattie Street, Balmain (tel: 9819 7999).

Newspapers

Lokanat Bulletin. This newsletter is published every month by the All Young Burmese League. Its current editor is Kenneth Oo, who can be contacted on 9746 2101.

Radio programs

SBS RADIO 2, FM 97.7. News, current affairs and music. Wednesday 2pm-3pm.

2SER, FM 107.3. Burmese community program. Sunday 7am-7.30am.

SBS Radio 2, FM 97.7. News, current affairs and music. Wednesday 2pm-3pm.

2SER, FM 107.3. Burmese community program. Sunday 7am-7.30am

Facts and figures

Between 1947 and 1959 about 3,500 Anglo-Burmese settled in Australia.

It is estimated that there are 9,000 Burmese immigrants in Australia, of which only about 1,000 have settled in Sydney. It's apparent that immigration from Burma has been educationally selective, with some 23.7% of adults having degrees or diplomas, compared to 12.7% for the adult Australia-born population.

Burmese have a similar proportion in the highest income categories to the Australian average. 48.3% earns $16,000 or less, and 9.6% earns $35,000 or more. A slightly smaller proportion of Burmese (68.2%) own their own home, compared to the Australian average, (68.8%).

Explore the world in one city

The Cambodians

It was called 'Year Zero'. In 1975, the same year that the Vietnamese Communists took over Saigon, Pol Pot's Khmer Rouge army captured the Cambodian capital of Phnom Penh. Pol Pot's insane 'Year Zero' policy tried to create a classless society based on agriculture, and in the process erased an entire culture.

Cities and towns were emptied, two million Cambodians were killed, and around 500,000 fled the country to refugee camps.

Refugees to Australia at this time were not the first Cambodians to come to these shores. It seems that the first Cambodians to set foot in Australia were a family of nine, possibly of French or Chinese ancestry, who arrived during the 1940s. In 1954 a Cambodian student, the first in Australia, was enrolled at the University of Adelaide. Later, after graduating, he returned to his homeland. On October 12, 1961, six Cambodian students, under the Colombo Plan, arrived in Sydney. After living with Australian families for a few months they boarded at Trinity Grammar School, in the inner-western suburb of Summer Hill.

Eventually, two of the six obtained university degrees while the remaining four studied technical courses. By 1975, the number of Cambodian students under the Colombo Plan had risen to 68.

In 1976 a mere 241 Cambodian refugees were resettled in Australia. However it was not until 1978, when a substantial resettlement program was in place, that a larger number of Cambodians began arriving. Between 1975 and 1981 almost all of the 4,000 or so Cambodians who entered Australia were refugees. In the last few years, they have been joined by parents, brothers, wives, husbands and children who were left behind.

Like the Vietnamese, the Cambodians have begun rebuilding their lives and in doing so they have established community and religious organisations. Since 1976, the Khmer Community of New South Wales (the name was changed to Khmer Community Inc in 1986) has provided greatly needed welfare, educational and settlement assistance to Sydney Cambodians. Since the 1980s, the Cambodian Cultural Centre has also played an important role in bridging the cultural gap experienced by new Cambodian immigrants. Equally central to the community life of

The Sydney Cambodian community, like the Vietnamese, with whom it has shared so much pain in their recent history, has developed its community social and cultural life in the Sydney western suburb of Cabramatta. There, the fragrant smell of *Korko*, the Cambodian national dish, competes with the warm smell of *Pho*, coming from the Vietnamese eateries.

RESTAURANTS

Cambodian cuisine is closely related to that of neighbouring Thailand (though without the spices) and Laos. In Cabramatta you can get authentic, cheap Cambodian food (see Cabramatta, page 263, which also covers Cambodian shops).

ANGKOR WAT.

If you're not in the mood to do the long train trip from the city to Cabramatta, this is the place to try authentic Cambodian cuisine. The beef dishes with fresh vegetables are excellent. Average $15, BYO and licensed. Open for dinner Tuesday-Sunday 5.30pm-10.30pm.

227 Oxford Street, Darlinghurst
(tel: 9360 5500).

the Sydney Cambodian community is the Cambodian Buddhist Society whose *wat* (temple) is in the western suburb of Bonnyrigg. The *wat* replaced a house in Fairfield which had been converted, in 1985, into a Buddhist pagoda. The establishment of this temple was an important step towards the future.

The Cambodian community, like the Vietnamese, with whom it has shared so much pain in their recent history, has developed its community social and cultural life in the Sydney western suburb of Cabramatta. There, the fragrant smell of *Korko*, the Cambodian national dish, competes with the warm smell of *Pho*, coming from the Vietnamese eateries.

Getting to know the Cambodian community

Events

Songkran (Cambodian New Year).

On April 13 approximately, the Sydney Cambodians hold a three-day celebration to welcome the new year. The main venue for this event is the Vat Khemarangsaram, located on the corner of Bonnyrigg Avenue and Tarlington Parade, in the western suburb of Bonnyrigg. The celebration includes chanting, offering food to the monks, and listening to the monks' teachings.

Vesak (Buddha's Birthday).

Apart from a traditional ceremony held at the Bonnyrigg Buddhist Temple, the Cambodian Buddhist community, along with Thai and Laotian Buddhist followers, attends a larger ceremony on the first Sunday in June at the Wat Buddha Dharma in Wiseman's Ferry.

Further information: Cambodian Buddhist Society (tel: 9604 2807)

Christmas and New Year are mainly celebrated by the Cambodian Baptists (more information from the South Granville Cambodian Baptist Fellowship on 9632 8398). Another important event among Cambodians is Independence Day, celebrated on November 9 (for further information on activities we suggest you contact some of the community and cultural organisations listed on page 273).

Religious organisations and places of worship

Cambodian Buddhist Society.
The Society aims to develop and maintain Cambodian religious and cultural traditions.

Corner Tarlington Parade and Bonnyrigg Avenue, Bonnyrigg (tel: 9604 2807or 9823 6404).

Vat Dhamma Sameaky.
Concerned with the maintenance and promotion of Buddhist teaching.

Further information: Abbot, Venerable Long Sakkhone, 13 Melville Avenue, Cabramatta (tel: 9724 1194).

Vat Khemarangsaram.
Organises cultural and religious activities.

Corner Bonnyrigg Avenue and Tarlington Parade, Bonnyrigg (tel: 9823 3479).

South Granville Cambodian Baptist Fellowship.
The Fellowship provides welfare and community services and holds religious and cultural events.

228 Excelsior Road, Guildford (tel: 9632 8398).

Khmer Krom Cambodian Temple.
For activities contact the current Temple president Cheng Thach.

114 Broomfield Street, Cabramatta (tel: 9727 4426).

Community organisations

Australian Cambodian Association of NSW.
Information, welfare and educational services for the Sydney Khmer community.

4 Moorine Close, Greenfield Park (tel: 9610 4876).

Cambodian Welfare Centre.
A key welfare organisation, providing counselling and referral.

232 Railway Parade, Cabramatta (tel: 9728 4411).

Media

Newspapers

Smaradey Khmer. This paper gives a good coverage of local activities. Published fortnightly, it has a circulation of 3,000 issues. The current editor is Leo Ung.

1 Bernadette Place, Fairfield; PO Box 187 Villawood 2163 (tel: 9728 1731).

Radio

SBS Radio 1, AM 1107. Local news and news from the homeland. Monday and Thursday 9pm-10pm, Wednesday 11am-noon.

Facts and figures

Of the State and Territory capitals in Australia, Sydney has the largest Cambodian-born population.

Though Cambodians constitute one of the smaller ethnic communities in Australia, their community is one of the fastest growing. In just a ten-year period, 1981 to 1991, the Cambodian population grew approximately 400 per cent; of the 17,629 Cambodians counted in the 1991 census, 43.3 per cent, around 7,600, were living in Sydney.

Consistent with other recent arrival groups, predominantly refugees, Cambodians have an above average rate of Australian citizenship, 79 per cent. The high percentage of Cambodians who have entered in Australia as refugees helps to explain the hard economic situation in which they live. Their median annual income ($8,600) is well below that of the median annual income of the total Australian population ($14,700), while only half own or are purchasing their homes, compared with the Australian average of 71.3 per cent.

Religious practice plays a central role in the lives of the Cambodians. The main religions are Buddhism (62.8%), Christianity (11%) and Islam (0.1%). Around 97% of Cambodians speak a language other than English at home: 62% speak Khmer, 29% speak a Chinese language, including Cantonese and Mandarin, and 3.5% speak Vietnamese.

The Chinese

"Not passers-by, we came to Australia with the intention of throwing ourselves into the embrace of this great land. My foreign friends! Don't look at me with such strange cold eyes. We're all the same, Ha Ha, people who have come down in the world."

In these simple words, with a healthy dose of humour in the sadness, Australian Chinese writer Lawrence Wong captures the alienation of living in a foreign land. Wong, author of *Footprints on Paper* (Robyn Iassen Productions, 1996), from which the poem comes, belongs to a group of Chinese writers, artists, academics, actors and filmmakers who arrived on our shores just before or just after the Tiananmen Square massacre in 1989. With him are artist Guan Wei, writer Leslie C. Zhao, and author Li 'John' Wu, whose book *He Married a Foreign Woman* has sold nearly a quarter of a million copies and was number one on Beijing's non-fiction list.

The adjustment of this very talented bunch of Chinese artists and writers to their new country hasn't been easy, but they have shown a great desire to succeed, just like the many from their country before them who have made their mark on Australian history.

Fair dinkum Aussies

Unbelievable as it sounds, some Chinese historians think the first Chinese may have visited Australia as far as back as 2600 years ago, while others believe the great fifteenth-century explorer Ch'eng Ho might have 'discovered' Australia. A more likely scenario, though still unproved, is that a cook on the First Fleet in 1788 was the first Chinese person in Australia. Shirley Fitzgerald, author of *Red Tape, Gold Scissors* (State Library of NSW Press, 1997), believes that the first Chinese in Sydney was Mak Sai Ying, who was born in Canton and arrived in our city in 1818. He purchased a block of land at Parramatta, changed his name to John Shying and, in 1823, married an Englishwoman, Sarah Thompson. By 1829 Shying had the licence for the Lion Inn at Parramatta, where his descendants live to this day.

In all walks of life, Australians of Chinese descent have made their mark: in medicine, there is the recently retired chief executive of Sydney's New Children's Hospital, Dr. John Yu, and the late Dr. Victor Chang who attracted international attention with his pioneering cardiac research; in entertainment, there is the world renowned guitarist John Williams, and the television presenter Annette Shun Wah; even in sport there is the cricket player Richard Chee Quee, the first ethnic Chinese to play for New South Wales.

The Sydney Chinese community began taking shape in the 1890s around Gipps Ward (west of the central business district), where Chinatown was then located. Many set up small businesses as grocers, vegetables hawkers and cabinet makers. Others worked as wharf labourers, craftsmen and street vendors (more about Chinatown on page 279).

Whatever the exact facts, it is clear that the Chinese have been a part of Australia's history for a long time. As early as 1783, James Matra (of Matraville fame) argued for the introduction of Chinese labourers to Australia, but it was not until many years later, in 1848, that the first group of 123 Chinese indentured workers disembarked at Sydney's Millers Point wharf. They were from the southern Chinese provinces of Guandong and Fujian.

Within three years about 900 Chinese immigrants had arrived in Sydney, but it took a goldrush to really get the ball rolling. During the 1850s and 1860s thousands of Chinese flocked to the goldfields of Victoria and New South Wales. They actually gave rise, it is believed, to that most Australian of expressions, 'fair dinkum' (true or trustworthy) – '*din kum*' is Cantonese for 'real gold'. 'Dinkum! dinkum! dinkum! was the cry heard by the Chinese when one of their countryman was lucky enough to find a nugget. (Among these hopeful fortune seekers was Kwong Chee, from the Chinese province of Guangzhou, who tried his luck at the goldfields of Kiandra, near Cooma. He settled down and established a family whose present-day members include the current New South Wales Ombudsman, Irene Moss, née Chee.)

From church to joss house

When the gold finally dried up, the Chinese began moving to the cities. In Sydney, these mainly single men found work in businesses owned by other Chinese, and lived in modest accommodation scattered along George and Goulburn Streets. Sydney's George Street was also where many Chinese set up their small businesses and where so many success stories began. One of the best-known tales is of Quong Tart, who was not only an immensely successful merchant and owner of the Queen Victoria Building's Elite Tearooms, but also a respected philanthropist. He was a member of the Church of England and a ferocious campaigner against opium.

The first Chinese community organisations were also formed at this time. One of the earliest was the Chinese Presbyterian Church, which established two premises in 1882, one in Foster Street and the other in the inner-city suburb of Waterloo. With the financial support of the Chinese community a third church was built in Wexford Street in downtown Sydney. The attendance at Christian churches was periodically challenged by those who frequented joss-houses or Chinese Temples dedicated to gods such as *Cai Shen* (God of Wealth), *Guan Yi* (Goddess of Mercy) and *Guan Di* (the symbol of loyalty and devotion to duty). One of the first joss-houses established in Sydney was the *Sze Yup* Temple, built in the Sydney-inner suburb of Glebe in 1898. Still standing, the *Sze Yup* Temple has been recently renovated (see page 289). A second worship place – Yiu Ming Temple – was built in 1908 in the inner-suburb of Alexandria by the Chinese market gardeners living in Botany Bay (see page 289). Both temples are major historical Sydney Chinese landmarks.

At this time, a variety of organisations started appearing in the city, such as social clubs, whose objectives were to promote friendship, mutual support and protection. Secret societies, imported from China, also began emerging, like the *Loon Ye Tong* society, dedicated to illegal gambling.

Several Chinese newspapers were founded around the turn of the century. The first regular paper, the *Chinese Australian Herald*, was founded in 1894 and operated for more than 30 years. (None of these early efforts survived past the mid-twentieth century, however, and it wasn't until the 1980s that a new wave of locally published Chinese papers began appearing back in Sydney's newsagencies.)

In 1908 a Federation-style temple – *Yiu Ming* – was built alongside a row of terraces at Retreat Street, off Botany Road, in the inner Sydney industrial suburb of Alexandria.

Federation and discrimination

By 1900 there were 3,500 Chinese in Sydney, nearly all men from the Pearl River Delta area of Guangzhou province but the introduction of the *Immigration Restriction Act* in the Federation year of 1901 stemmed the tide of Chinese immigration for the next fifty years. Life under the racist 'White Australia Policy' was not easy for those who were already here, but they showed an unparalleled desire to overcome prejudices.

The many restrictive rules and regulations which governed their lives failed to quench their entrepreneurial spirit. Take for example Sydney tycoon Daniel Chen who, after arriving from Shanghai with £5, built a textile and property empire that today is valued at $65 million. Equally successful were Thomas Yee and Ping Nam, who established the China-Australia Mail Steamship Line, which operated between 1917 and 1924.

An important role in promoting and encouraging Chinese business in these difficult times was performed by the Chinese Merchants' Defence Association of Sydney, established in 1904, and by the Sydney Chinese Chamber of Commerce, founded in 1913. No less important was the part played by the Chinese Consulate, which moved from Melbourne to Sydney in 1928.

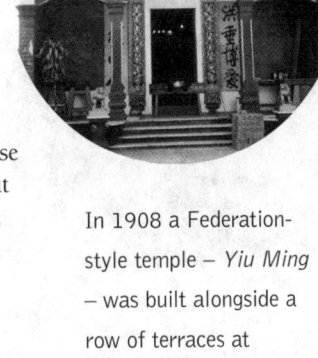

Chinese Sydney today

Following the abolition of the 'White Australia Policy' in the late 1960, Chinese immigration began a new phase. In 1961 there were almost 15,000 Chinese-born people in Australia and by 1991 more than 75,000.

This wave of Chinese immigration has seen a large number of Chinese arriving from places outside Guandong and Fujian provinces – Hong Kong, Singapore, Malaysia, Papua New Guinea and the former Indochina became the new sources of immigration. From the 1980s immigration from China itself also shifted, from the Cantonese-speaking regions of the south to the Mandarin-speaking cities of the north, including Beijing.

Needless to say, the long-established southern and the newly arrived northern Chinese have cultural and linguistic differences. Southerners have good business acumen and are often associated with a strong history of entrepreneurship, while northerners bring with them strong academic backgrounds but little experience in the free-market system. This shift also brought with it the earthy Northern Chinese cuisine challenging the long supremacy of the Cantonese style.

All this time, Sydney's Chinatown was steadily growing and prospering. From a collection of old buildings and dirty streets, limited to Dixon and Campbell streets, Chinatown has expanded to incorporate commercial activities, offices and shopping complexes. It is now a strong attraction for tourists from all over the world.

While Chinese Australians have traditionally channelled their energies and money into business and work, they are slowly getting involved in the political arena – among them Helen Sham-Ho, Member of the Legislative Council, and Sydney's Deputy Lord Mayor, Henry Tsang. In the last few years the Australian Chinese Forum (ACF) has been prominent as a political lobby group to articulate and represent views on social and political issues affecting the Australian Chinese community.

In all walks of life, in fact, Australians of Chinese descent have made their mark: in medicine. They include the recently retired chief executive of Sydney's New Children's Hospital, Dr John Yu, and the late Dr Victor Chang, who attracted international attention with his pioneering cardiac research; in entertainment, such as the world-renowned guitarist John Williams, and in television the presenter Annette Shun Wah; even in cricket Richard Chee Quee has become the first ethnic Chinese to

The Sydney Chinese community will continue to make the best of their varied backgrounds without forgetting the Confucian virtues that they have learnt so well: hard work and humility.

play for New South Wales. They are proud Australians and proud about their Chinese heritage. The Sydney Chinese community will continue to make the best of their varied backgrounds without forgetting the Confucian virtues that they have learnt so well: hard work and humility.

Facts and figures

Today, Australia's ethnic Chinese population is estimated at between 260,000 and 400,000, and is drawn from a dozen countries; it is estimated that some 650,000 Australians have Chinese ancestry. Sydney is home to more than 40,000 Chinese-born people, and this number grows to over 200,000 when Chinese who were born in countries other than China are included.

In Sydney, Chinese people are scattered over several suburbs, mainly in those located in the western areas of Canterbury, Fairfield and Parramatta. In Strathfield there is also a small Chiu Chow Chinese community, while in inner-city Surry Hills there is a strong Chinese Christian community. In the last few years, the Chinese community has been expanding on the North Shore, particularly to Chatswood where this stronghold of affluent Anglo-Saxon Australia is making space for a thriving and dynamic Chinese community.

Chinatown is a major tourist attraction that has come a long way from its humble beginnings in the 1890s.

Sydney's Chinatown

Described once as a "winding dragon with its head in Campbell Street, its body climbing up Ultimo Road and its tail in Dixon Street," Chinatown is a major tourist attraction that has come a long way from its humble beginnings in the 1890s in Gipps Ward – west of the CBD.

There, many Chinese immigrants set up small businesses as grocers, vegetable hawkers and cabinet makers. Others worked as wharf labourers, craftsmen and street vendors. In the 1940s, the residential concentration of Sydney Chinese moved to Campbell Street and eventually Dixon Street. "Crowded, noisy and dirty" – such are the fading images of Chinatown that linger in the memory of its older dwellers. Then, very few Australians would venture down Dixon Street.

In the last few years, with the steady entry of wealthy, entrepreneurial and skilled Chinese – following fairer immigration policies and the hand

GETTING TO CHINATOWN

Hop on the enviromentally friendly Sydney Light Rail and get off in Haymarket to explore the exotic flavour and colours of Sydney's Chinatown.

For more information call: 9660 5288

Along the lantern spruced Sussex Street that has taken over as the main thoroughfare of Chinatown the flurry of activity starts from the early hours of the day. The scene is vibrant with business people closing deals on their mobiles, tourists hunting for bargains, grannies doing the grocery shopping and an increasing number of young Australian Chinese hanging out around the newest and grooviest fashion shops in the quarter. Now if you prefer a more gentle and quiet day's start, head to Belmore Park (near Central Station), where every weekday from 11am a group of Chinese Australians meet for an hour of loug tong (callisthenics). All are welcome and it's free.

over of Hong Kong to the mainland – Sydney's Chinatown has become the focus of a growing wave of investment in real estate, shopping centres and restaurants. And they keep coming, as Market City – Chinatown's biggest retail space with 15,000 square metres of floor space and 92 outlets over the flea-market of Paddy's Market – has shown. Chinatown has also expanded in urban geography. From the original Campbell and Dixon Streets, it has now extended to the east as far as Elizabeth Street, as far north as Liverpool Street, to Broadway in the south, and Ultimo in the west.

Visitors to Sydney's Chinese quarter encounter a fascinating kaleidoscope of sights, sounds and fragrances. Here you will find some of the most imaginative Chinese restaurants in the world (long gone are the days of the exclusive fare of sweet and sour pork and dim sims), and the grocery stores are stacked to the ceilings with exotic Asian spices, fruit and herbs.

Chinatown is not merely about business. More importantly – Chinatown is a historical testimony of the Chinese diaspora to our city – from their humble beginnings, to the discrimination suffered along the way and to their untold contribution in making Sydney a far better city. When soil, sand and rocks from Guandong province were buried not long ago around the gates of Chinatown in Dixon Street, Sydney's Chinese symbolically reaffirmed that Australia is now home.

Restaurants and Take Away

(See map, page 283)

9: Fuji-san. No, it's not a token non-Chinese spot in Chinatown, as a matter of fact Fuji-san – a corner take-away – has developed a name for itself as a highly recommended Japanese eatery.
Open Monday-Saturday noon-6.30pm.
76 Ultimo Street (tel: 9211 1764).

10: Marigold. One of Sydney's top Chinese restaurants, Marigold is an action-packed spot on a panoramic screen. This huge restaurant – where Cantonese cuisine rules – has a large, imaginative but "non backpacker" bill. Drop by at lunch time for the more affordable and equally fantastic yum cha. Average $50, licensed.
Open Monday-Sunday lunch 10am-3pm, dinner 6-11pm.
Levels 4 & 5, 683-689 George Street (tel: 9281 3388).

11: Silver Spring. The deal here is very straight forward, queuing for the superb yum cha by day, a relaxing stroll for dinner by night. Either option gets our thumbs up. A tip? The suckling pig and the tender duck

roast (warning: the latter is expensive). Average $25, licensed.
Open Monday-Friday 10am-11pm, Saturday-Sunday 9am-11pm.

191 Hay Street (tel: 9211 2232).

18: Marigold. Midday (or a bit earlier) is yum cha time, be patient and respect the queue. If you aren't, call in for dinner. The specialists like to use words like "consistent" or "solid" to explain the superior quality of Marigold's Cantonese cuisine (it has been reported that Sydney's Lord Mayor Frank Sartor is one of the well known customers here). Average $40, licensed. Open Monday-Sunday lunch 10am-3pm, dinner 5.30-11pm.

299 Sussex Street (tel: 9264 6744).

19: The Regal. Sublime yum cha and one of the most authentic Cantonese menus in town. Owned by Hong Kong's Chung family – The Regal is a good place to try the prawn dumplings and vegetable menu. Average $30, licensed.
Open Monday-Sunday 10am-3pm, dinner 5.30-11pm.

347-353 Sussex Street (tel: 9261 8988).

20: Golden Century. The fish tanks are part of the decor and its occupants – lobsters, king crabs, morwong, abalone and the like – are part of the menu. If you're an all out animal liberation militant, skip this place. Average $30, licensed. Open Monday-Sunday noon-4am.

393 Sussex Street (tel: 9281 1598).

Visitors to Sydney's Chinese quarter encounter a fascinating kaleidoscope of sights, sounds and fragrances.

25: Golden Harbour. At the heart of the original Chinatown, the Golden Harbour is an old time favourite of *dim sim* lunch patrons. Average $25, licensed. Open Sunday-Thursday 10am-11pm, Friday-Saturday 10am-1am.

31-33 Dixon Street (tel: 9211 5160).

27: Kam Fook. If you're looking for company, this "new kid on the block" is the place to go – the 800-seat monumental Kam Fook will guarantee you the massive company of those inside and the hundreds lining up outside. What is all this about? – *yum cha* – fan-tas-tic!!

Level 3, Market City, 9 Hay Street (tel: 9211 8988).

26: Superbowl Chinese Restaurant.

41 Dixon Street (tel: 9281 2462).

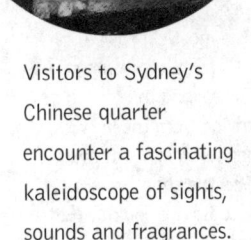

TEA SHOP

LIVE CRAFTS CENTRE. Located in the old Kwong Wah Ching shop, it opened in 1995, and it is Australia's first and only specialist Chinese tea shop. This is the place where you can enjoy the fresh fragrance of more than 200 or more varieties of tea. All are imported from mainland China and Taiwan. Be warned, they are not cheap, expect to pay $52 a tal (one tal= 37.5g) of *juen shan* silver needle (the most expensive) or $15 for a tal of *lung chin*. For a good mix of tea ask advice from the very helpful Alice or Lawrence Cho, the shop owners. Also have a look at the beautiful clay teapots, sold from $10 to $150. Open Monday-Saturday 10.30am-6.30pm, Sunday 2-6.30pm.

84 Dixon Street (tel: 9281 2828).

Barbecue Outlets

1: Emperor's Garden Barbecue and Noodles. Eat in or take away, as its name indicates, the forté of this Cantonese cuisine place is the superb barbecue menu extending to delicacies such as barbecued pork, noodles and Peking duck. Average $30, licensed and BYO. Open Monday-Sunday 9.30am-11pm.

213-15 Thomas Street (9281 9899).

16: BBQ King. If the aristocratic title were conceded for services to gastronomy, this place deserves it – the barbecued pork and duck is the best around town. Average $18, licensed. Open Monday-Sunday 11.30am-2pm.

18-20 Goulburn Street (tel: 9267 2433).

3: Wong's Barbecue.

4/37 Ultimo Street, Haymarket (tel: 9211 3359).

12: Wing Hing.

12 Campbell Street (tel: 9212 1481).

13: Wai Wong Barbecue & Butcher.

20 Campbell Street (tel: 9211 1808).

Eating on a shoestring

21: Sussex Food Centre. On the 1st floor – reached by a mechanical escalator there is huge range of hawkers offering cheap and tasty Chinese and South-East Asian dishes. Prices range from $4.50 to $8.

401-403 Sussex Street. Open Monday-Sunday 9am-10pm.

23: Dixon House. Located at the corner of Dixon and Little Hay Streets, this food centre is the smallest among its equals, but the prices are similarly good. The court house opens Monday-Sunday 10.30am-8.30pm.

24: Chinatown Food Centre. Arguably the best hawker centre, it's located on the corner of Dixon and Goulburn Streets, at the basement. With stall-holders offering Chinese, Singaporean, Malaysian, Vietnamese, Thai and Korean dishes – all at bargain basement prices, between $4.50 with few above $6, this is a good place to keep your budget under control. Open Monday-Sunday 10.30am-10.30pm.

CHINATOWN

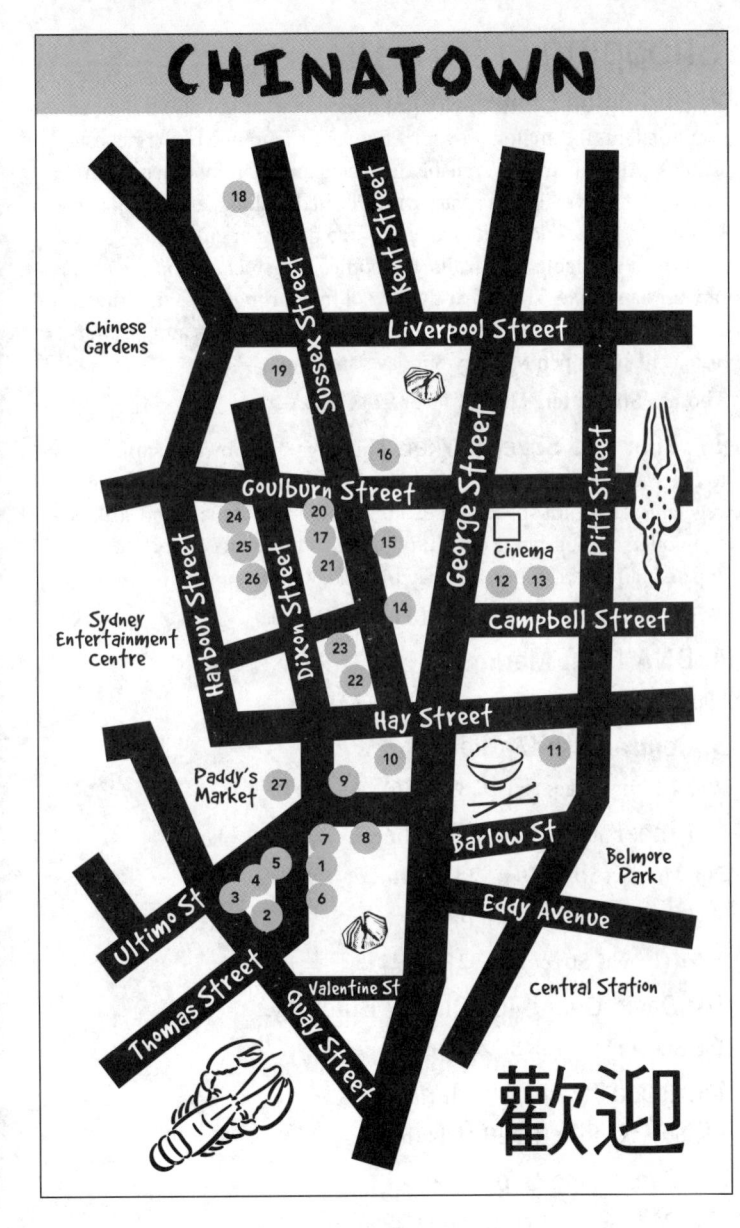

SYDNEY'S CHINATOWN

1. Emperor's Garden Barbecue and Noodles
2. Burlington Centre.
3. Wong's Barbecue.
4. DNA Meat Market.
5. Central Fish Market.
6. Emperor's Garden Butcher.
7. Dong Nam A Grocery.
8. Chinese Ginseng & Herb Co.
9. Fuji-san
10. Marigold
11. Silver Spring
12. Wing Hing.
13. Wai Wong Barbecue & Butcher.
14. David Duong Top Quality Butchery.
15. China Town Fish Market.
16. BBQ King.
17. Thai Kee Supermarket.
18. Marigold.
19. The Regal
20. Golden Century
21. Sussex Food Centre.
22. Everspring Supermarket
23. Dixon House.
24. Chinatown Food Centre.
25. Golden Harbour
26. Superbowl Chinese Restaurant.
27. Kam Fook

THE CHINESE

CINEMAS

CHINATOWN CINEMA. From *Once Upon a Time in China* to the saucy. *Sex and Zen*, all films have English subtitles. This is a great place to catch up with the oldest and latest blockbusters from Hong Kong.
Open Monday-Sunday, the earliest session starts at 2pm and the latest at 9.50pm. Adult $11, children (under 14) $16, concession $7.
27 Goulburn Street (tel: 9211 4546).

AUSTRALIAN CHINESE CINEMA. Located a few blocks up along the same street as Chinatown Cinema, the Australian Chinese Cinema also shows daily action packed blockbusters. Earliest session at 1.40pm, latest sessions at 10.45.
59-63 Goulburn Street (tel: 9281 2883).

Shopping

2: Burlington Centre. Not just a supermarket but also a sight and scent delight, Burlington – own by Bernand Chan, one of the richest Chinese Australians – is arguably the best pan-Asian food market in Sydney. Inside you'll find a vast array of dried seafood, and ready to eat barbecued pork, duck and chicken. While the green grocery is stacked with fresh vegetables and fruits, the bottle shop stocks a good selection of wines and sake. Located at the rear of the Burlington Centre there's an amazing herbalist section. Newspapers, cooking utensils and tea seats are also available. Open Monday-Sunday 9am-7pm.
Thomas Street (tel: 9281 2777 or 9211 2353).

17: Thai Kee Supermarket. This large overcrowded store bursts to the seams with Thai and South-east Asian imported products, fresh vegetables, fragrant spices and exotic herbs. The butchery and seafood shop offers a good range of quality products from cuts of pork to appetising prawns. Open Monday to Sunday 9am-8pm.
393 Sussex Street, Chinatown (tel: 9281 2202).

4: DNA Meat Market.
Shop 5, 37 Ultimo Street (tel: 9281 1773).

5: Central Fish Market.
9/37 Ultimo Street (tel: 9281 3086).

6: Emperor's Garden Butcher.
211 Thomas Street (tel: 9281 2206).

7: Dong Nam A Grocery.
215a Thomas Street (tel: 9211 1927).

14: David Duong Top Quality Butchery.
438 Sussex Street (tel: 9281 4685).

15: China Town Fish Market.
396 Sussex Street (tel: 9121 1118).

22: Everspring Supermarket.
421-425 Sussex Street (tel: 9211 2980).

Herbalists

8: Chinese Ginseng & Herb Co.
75 Ultimo Street (tel: 9212 4397).

Explore the world in one city

Restaurants

The best place to sample 'traditional' (ie southern-style Cantonese) Chinese food is, of course, Chinatown (see page 280), and it's hard to find a part of Sydney (or country towns) that doesn't offer something similar. However, after the long dominance of the southern cuisine, the northern fare from the People's Republic has come to town, and the challenge from the earthy and robust Pekinese and Szechuan dishes is fiery. To taste it you'll have to look beyond Chinatown as the northerners have opted to move to the 'burbs'.

Chinese Sydney cuisine has also experienced another revolution brought about by the local talent of Australian-Chinese chefs. It's an exciting fusion of Australian and Chinese products – and the results have to be seen (and eaten!) to be believed. You will find Tasmanian king crab or barramundi in black bean sauce, or kangaroo tail in a Chinese herb soup.

The following is a selected list of some of the best restaurants offering Chinese food of various types. And remember, when you finish your meal tap the two middle fingers on the table – it's the traditional Chinese way to say thanks for the service.

Chinese entrepreneurs have transformed the North Shore suburb of Chatswood – regarded in the past as a dormitory suburb – into one of the most dynamic commercial areas in Sydney.

Chatswood BBQ Kitchen. For a quick, exquisite and affordable won ton noodle fix, this is the place to go. A bowl of noodles costs $5-$8.
Open Monday-Sunday 10.30am-10pm.
377 Victoria Avenue, Chatswood (tel: 9419 6532).

Eastern Sea Chinese Restaurant. Opened in 1959, this restaurant has seen the growth of Coogee as a serious challenge to Bondi. The Mongolian lamb and honey king prawns are the all-time favourites of the loyal clientele. Average $15, BYO.
Open Monday-Sunday for lunch noon-3pm, dinner 5pm-9pm.
254 Coogee Bay Road, Coogee (tel: 9665 4935).

Imperial Peking. One of the top Chinese Sydney restaurants, it features more than 180 different dishes. The view and the food are just sensational. Average $30, licensed.
Open Monday-Sunday for lunch noon-3pm, dinner 6pm-11pm.
15 Circular Quay West, The Rocks (tel: 9724 7073).

Imperial Peking (at Blakehurst). Located far away from the Cantonese stronghold of Chinatown, this is where the northern Chinese experience is lived to the full. The timeless Peking duck is just legendary. Call in on weekends for *yum cha*. Average $25, licensed. Open for lunch Monday-Saturday 11am-3pm and Sunday 10am-3pm, dinner Sunday-Thursday 5.30pm-10.30pm and Friday-Saturday 5.30pm-11.30pm.
979 King Georges Road, Blakehurst (tel: 9546 6122).

Peking Inn. You don't need to be a food critic to guess that the north rules in any of the 'Peking' restaurants in town. This one isn't an exception. It's charming and the house trademarks, Peking duck and beggar's chicken, are magnificent. Average $30, BYO and licensed. Open for lunch Tuesday-Sunday noon-3pm, dinner Monday-Sunday from 5.30pm.

390 Pacific Highway, Lindfield (tel: 9416 3509).

Szechuan Garden. A great place to explore the northern cuisine of Szechuan and Hunan. Average $20, BYO and licensed. Open for lunch Monday-Friday noon-3pm, dinner Monday-Saturday 6pm till late.

1/56-62 Chandos Street, St Leonards (tel: 9438 2568).

Superbowl Seafood Restaurant. One of the members of the well-known Chinese restaurant chain, it features superb suckling pig and a bill that will make you smile. Average $15, BYO.
Open Monday-Sunday 11am-11pm.

4 Spring Street, Chatswood (tel: 9419 7833).

The Cleveland. Downstairs it's a superb vegetarian kingdom, while upstairs you'll find the wonderful taste of Szechuan. Average $30, licensed. Open for lunch Monday-Sunday noon-3pm, dinner 6pm-11pm.

63 Bay Street, Double Bay (tel: 9327 6877).

The Original Peking Restaurant. A very straightforward deal: Pekinese, Szechuan and Shanghai fare. Also offers great noodles and dumplings. Open for lunch Monday-Sunday noon-3pm, dinner Monday-Sunday 6pm-midnight. Average $20, BYO and licensed.

23 Pelican Street, Surry Hills (tel: 9264 6210).

Wockpool. If you are looking for ModOz-Chinese cuisine this is *the* place to go. Average $40, licensed. Open Monday-Saturday for dinner 6.30-11pm, Sunday 6.30pm-10pm.

155 Victoria Street, Potts Point (tel: 9368 1771).

Yum Cha (outside Chinatown)

Yum cha ('drinking tea' in Cantonese) gives you the chance to sample a wide – make that huge – variety of Chinese foods, and Sydneysiders are loving it. *Yum cha* is a traditional Cantonese way of eating *dim sum* dumplings and other delicacies accompanied by Chinese tea, and it seems immigrants from Hong Kong were the ones who brought it to these shores. *Yum cha* is as varied as it is delicious. The hard part is knowing what to select from the hundreds of bamboo baskets on carts rolling out of the kitchen. The following is a selected list of places that have gained praise for their *yum cha*. See also Chinatown, page 280.

Pearl Chinese Restaurant. If you want to avoid the hyper-crowded Chinatown, drop by on a Sunday for an excellent *yum cha* deal. Open Monday-Sunday for lunch 11am-3pm, dinner 6pm-11pm (Saturday from 10am). Average $15, licensed.
Level 3, 169 Dolphin Street, Coogee (tel: 9665 3308).

Chequers. The choice here is large and the dishes attractive. The *ngor mai guy* (glutinous rice with minced chicken, pork and vegetables wrapped in lotus leaf) is a must. Try also the shark fin dumplings. Average $15, licensed. Open Monday-Sunday 11am-10.30pm (*yum cha* till around 3pm).
Shop 220-222, Mandarin Centre, 65 Albert Avenue, Chatswood (tel: 9904 8388).

Fook Yuen. From Hong Kong with love – one of the best and busiest *yum cha* places on the North Shore. The *daan tart* (flaky pastry tarts filled with sweet egg custard) is amazing. Average $15, licensed. Open Monday-Sunday for lunch 11am-3pm, dinner 6pm-11pm.
Level 1, 7 Help Street, Chatswood (tel: 9413 2688).

Hung Cheung. Located in the stronghold of the Greek and Vietnamese community, this is an unpretentious place to eat cheaply and well. Average $10, BYO. Open Monday-Sunday for yum cha and lunch 9am-11pm (till 10pm on Sunday).
388 Marrickville Road, Marrickville (tel: 9560 4681).

Sea Treasure. A many-times awarded restaurant, it offers the full gamut of yum cha, including the much sought-after *har gow* (prawn dumplings). Open for yum cha and lunch Monday-Friday 11am-3pm, dinner 5.30pm-11pm; Saturday-Sunday for *yum cha* and lunch 9.30am-3pm, dinner 6pm-11pm. Average $20, licensed.
46 Willoughby Road, Crows Nest (tel: 9906 6388).

Bookshops (outside Chinatown)

China Publication Centre Beijing. Has a wide range of magazines, medical books and Chinese-language teaching texts. Open Monday-Friday 10am-6pm, Saturday-Sunday 10am-4pm.
81 Enmore Road, Enmore (tel: 9557 2701).

For *yum cha* first-timers. Bring along friends and your extended family or, if you're a tourist bring the whole bus. In a yum cha place the variety of dumplings that you can try increases exponentially with the number of people who share the table. By the way, the bill comes before you eat – everything that you order will be stamped in there. At the end, hand it in to the cashier.

CLUBS

MANDARIN CLUB.
Here you'll have a full-tilt Chinese-Australian cultural experience. The three floors of the Club feature several bars and restaurants, a dance floor and carpeted corridors with state-of-the-art poker machines and TAB betting facilities. Open Monday-Sunday till 3am.

Corner Goulburn and Pitt Street, City (tel: 9211 3866).

Art & Gifts

Taylors Chin Hua Galleries.

The three floors of this shop cum gallery have one of the largest displays of Chinese (and other Asian) objects in Sydney. You will find an amazing range of pieces, such as antique taoist scroll paintings, ceremonial swords, a large collection of Chinese jade, porcelain, bronze and ceramics and much more. Open Monday-Sunday 9am-4pm.

385 Pacific Highway, Crows Nest (tel: 9957 2558).

Tai Chi

Australian Academy of Tai Chi.

If you're planning to get into this wonderful art, we suggest contacting this academy that organises *Tai Chi* classes all throughout Sydney – it's just matter of calling to ask where the nearest classes are being held. The basic course consists of 10 sessions and they are held every Thursday 6.30-7.30pm. The cost for the 10 sessions is $79.

Further information: 9797 9355.

Places of interest

Chinese Garden of Friendship.

Winding pathways, waterfalls, lakes and pavilions combine to form this tranquil oasis in the heart of Sydney. Located at the south-eastern end of Darling Harbour, near the Sydney Entertainment Centre, the Chinese Garden of Friendship was designed in China by the Guandong Landscape Bureau (Guandong is the sister province of NSW) to celebrate the Australian bicentenary.

It was opened on January 17 1988. It's the biggest such garden outside China. Designed in the traditional southern Chinese style, the Chinese Garden – covering 10,000 square metres – is a celebration of 'yin' and 'yang' or the achievement of the balance of the opposites – the softness of the waterfall cascades edged by the hardness of the rocks. Many of the decorative features were especially made by Chinese craftsmen and sent from China.

After wandering around, drop by the teahouse balcony and have a cup of *shui hsien* tea. On weekends expect to see lots of brides being photographed against the decorative backgrounds. Admission, $3.00

Sydney's Chinese Garden – designed by the Guandong Landscape Bureau to celebrate the Australian Bicentenary – was opened on January 17, 1988.

adults; $1.50 concessions; $1.50 children, $6.00 families, free for disabled in wheelchairs. Open Monday-Sunday 9.30am till sunset.

Darling Harbour (tel: 9281 6863).

Sze Yup Temple.

This temple, or joss house as it was originally known, was built in 1898 and has become an important historical landmark in Sydney. It was established by the Chinese immigrants who came during the mid-nineteenth century gold rush. The Sydney Sze *Yup* Temple is dedicated to *Cai Shen*, the God of Wealth; *Guan Yin*, the Goddess of Mercy; and *Guan Di*, the God of Justice. *Guan Di* is the most popular of the Gods worshipped at the Temple. He was a general who worked for one of the warlords in China; his figure is particularly important for the Hong Kong police.

Every year, on June 24, the Temple is the main venue for the *Guan Di* Festival, and in 1998 the centenary of the *Sze Yup* Temple will coincide with this festival. The Temple is open to the public but remember that it's a holy place, so show respect. At the Temple visitors can pray to the gods and try their fortune. Open Monday-Sunday 8.00am-5pm. The maintenance of the place is based on donations, so please be generous.

Edward Street, Glebe. For information contact the Sze Yup Society of Sydney (tel: 9281 6640).

Yiu Ming Temple

This is one of the most fascinating pieces of the history of the Sydney Chinese community. In 1908 a Federation-style temple – *Yiu Ming* – was built alongside a row of terraces at Retreat street, off Botany Road, in the inner Sydney industrial suburb of Alexandria. It was conceived by the Chinese market gardening community that used to live in Botany Bay (expect to have a cultural and enticing shock while walking through the alley of Retreat Street leaving behind noisy truck-filled Botany Road and heading to the main gate of this remarkable place). A row of terraces occupied by Chinese dwellers is the first sight after crossing the Chinese-style gate.

Following the tradition of the Chinese cosmology, the Temple is not placed at the end of the alley but beside it. The *Yiu Ming* Temple – xone of only nine surviving in Australia – belongs to the Guandong and Hong Kong building tradition combined with Australian Federation style. Within the visually rich and stimulating interior you will find an immense and wonderful collections of objects of the early twentieth century craftsmanship from Guandong province – wooden carvings, textile banners, sculptures, traditional ceremonial furniture, and a magnificence altar table.

Further information: 9211 1945.

Chinese calendar years are named after the 12 animals that were called together by Buddha: Rat, Rabbit, Horse, Rooster, Ox, Dragon, Sheep, Dog, Tiger, Snake, Monkey and Pig.

A 'typical' celebration of the Chinese New Year starts between January 21 and February 21. On the 16th day of the year's last month, businesspeople close their accounts and thank the gods for a successful year. Customers celebrate by paying their debts so the new year can begin with a clean slate. On the 24th day of the last month, households honour the Kitchen God, who returns to heaven each year to report on the family. Before he returns on New Year's Eve the house is cleaned by every member. A new statue is placed in the kitchen and a feast is held. Children receive new clothes and spend New Year's Day playing and eating 'forbidden' sweets.

USEFUL NUMBERS FOR VISITORS

CHINESE CONSULATE:
tel: 9698 7929.

CHINA NATIONAL TOURIST OFFICE:
tel: 9299 4057.

CHINA EASTERN AIRLINES:
tel: 9290 1148.

CHINA AIRLINE:
tel: 9321 9121.

Getting to know the Chinese community

Events

Yuan Tan (Lunar Chinese New Year).

This is the most important festival in the Chinese year. Because the coming New Year signifies the end of winter, the festival is also known as the Spring Festival. Festivities are held over a three-day period between January 21 and February 21. Apart from the noisy firecrackers (to drive out any evil spirits of the old year), one of the most significant symbols of this celebration is the 'kumquat', a small, evergreen plant. The *kumquat* fruit, which lasts for a long time, is a symbol of prosperity and is given as a gift. During the New Year it is very common to see many Sydney Chinese houses displaying a potted *kumquat* plant.

Sydney's Chinatown, which remains flush with red – the colour of good fortune – during the festivities, is the most popular venue for this very important event. The New Year features a three-day flower market throughout Chinatown, sedan races along the track of the light rail in Haymarket, outdoor concerts in Martin Place, lion dances to chase away bad luck, sword dances, Chinese opera performances, food stalls, drum dances and a display of lanterns along the streets. Also, during these days traditional *hong bao* (red packages filled with money) are given to unmarried people and children. Chinese bakeries – from Cabramatta to Chatswood – sell traditional fare such as sticky rice cakes, sweets such as dragon whisker, dragon snow and dumplings. Restaurants offer *fat choy ho shi*, a dish featuring seaweed and oysters, which is the equivalent of the western Christmas turkey. The highlight of the event is the final, very noisy, dragon dance.

Chinese New Year's celebrations are also held at Cabramatta, Chatswood, Ashfield, Parramatta and Bankstown.

Call the Sydney Chinese Events Committee on 9809 1088, 9893 9088, 9391 3000 or 018 404 496, or call the Dixon Street Chinatown Chinese Committee on 9211 5651.

Yuen Siu (Lantern Festival).

Falls on the 15th day of the month of the Chinese New Year (Lunar Calendar), and it is very similar to the western St Valentines Day

Explore the world in one city

celebration, but without the chocolates or the flowers. Instead, Chinese lovers celebrate their day by going to the lantern fairs. (Thousands of years ago young Chinese women were not allowed into town by themselves except during the Spring Festival, during which time they would have the chance meet young men. They would be carrying traditional lanterns to light up the night and also to symbolise a bright future.) The event, organised by the *Independence Daily Newspaper* is held at Darling Harbour's Tumbalong Park. It features food stalls, dance, music, martial arts demonstrations and various competitions.

Further information: 9211 4611.

Sydney Dragon Boat Festival.

This is one of the best known and most popular events in the Sydney calendar, and it's not just limited to the Chinese community. It is held on May 5 (lunar calendar) which usually falls in June. Boat teams from within and beyond Australia compete in this colourful two-day regatta at Darling Harbour's Cockle Bay. The idea of organising a Dragon Boat Carnival in Sydney, similar to those in South-East Asia and Hong Kong, was proposed for the first time in 1983 by the proprietor of the Sydney press group the *Sing Tao Newspapers*. The first Sydney Dragon Boat Carnival was officially held on April 8 1984, and since then it has become a major annual event. In April 2000, Sydney will host the Third World Cup of dragon boat racing, to be held at Penrith.

The Sydney Dragon Boat Festival commemorates the death of 4th century Chinese poet Chu Yuen, who threw himself into a river.

The origin of the Dragon Boat Race is found in a tale of a humble poet who was an adviser to a powerful warlord. The adviser expressed the view that the warlord's territory was in decline but his advice was not heeded by his master. In despair the adviser – who was well liked by the people of the territory – jumped into a lake. Upon witnessing this some people got into a boat and raced into the centre of the lake, beating drums on the boat to keep the marine animals away. Other people dumped rice puddings to draw the animals away so they would not feed on the advisor's body. Many Chinese believe it is bad luck to die with parts of the body missing.

Further information: Rev Brown, **Dragon Boats (NSW)** (tel: 9525 2893).

Ching Ming.

Celebrated around April 5, it is a traditional annual day when Chinese families go together to pay homage to family ancestors. The family will take incense, flowers, fruit and wine for the graves in the cemetery where there ancestors lie. This event usually coincides with the 'rainy season' and it's said that the mood of the people during Ching Ming is similar to that of the season.

AUSTRALIAN CHINESE DAY.
Celebrated on May 17, this is a day of music and dance organised by the Australian Chinese Community Association; it is held at Darling Harbour's Tumbalong Park. The event is designed to give all Australians an opportunity to be exposed to and appreciate Australian Chinese history and culture.
Further information:
Australian Chinese Community Association (tel: 9281 1377).

The Weaver Maid Festival.

This festival, held on July 7 could best be described as a 'sad Valentines Day'. The Cantonese version of this festival concerns the legend of a young weaver woman married in heaven to a cowherd. The weaver woman began neglecting her duties, and as punishment the Emperor of Heaven sent her and her husband to earth to experience the toil of human life. The weaver woman and the cowherd could only ever meet on July 7. Both the cowherd and weaver woman were reborn seven times and each time they fell in love, but each life time ended unhappily as they could never marry. Thus, seven stories were created based on their sad experience. Old Chinese people say that young Chinese should remember this day in order to learn from the mistakes of the weaver maid and the cowherd, and they also believe that if you celebrate this day then you will have a good partner and a happy marriage.

Henry Tsang

DEPUTY LORD MAYOR OF SYDNEY

Born in 1942 in the Chinese province of Kiangsi, Henry Tsang arrived in Australia in 1960 after living for several years in Hong Kong as a refugee with his family. In Sydney he attended Vaucluse Boys' High School and the University of New South Wales, where he received his Bachelor of Architectural Science. As a principal of Tsang & Lee architectural practice, he has been involved in a number of projects, including the Dixon Street Chinatown Mall and the Cabramatta Mall Oriental Plaza. He was also the head consultant for the Chinese Garden at Darling Harbour.

As a strong believer in multiculturalism, Henry Tsang has participated extensively in ethnic affairs. From 1984 to 1990 he was Vice-Chairman and, subsequently, Senior Vice-Chairman of the Ethnic Communities Council of the New South Wales. In 1994 Counsellor Tsang was appointed to the Prime Minister's Multicultural Advisory Council, which will advise the Government on the cultural diversity dimension of the Sydney 2000 Olympics and the Centenary of Federation in 2001.

In 1991 Henry Tsang was elected to Sydney City Council, becoming the first Asian-Australian ever to be elected to the Council and then to the office of Deputy Lord Mayor. In September 1995 he was re-elected to both positions.

Explore the world in one city

Chinese Moon Festival or Mid-Autumn Festival.

This festival, held in mid September, celebrates the 'Autumn Harvest'. The Cantonese legend of this festival tells of a cruel emperor who obtained a medicine that would make him live forever. His beautiful wife, knowing her husband's cruelty, did not want him to live forever, so she swallowed all the medicine. She became so light that she floated to the moon where a rabbit kept her company. She stayed on the moon forever but was happy in the knowledge that her husband would not live eternally.

The Moon Festival is also related to a more real piece of history. It recalls the resistance movement of Piu Pe against the despotic rule of the Yuan Dynasty (1260-1368), in which the revolutionaries used cakes containing messages as a means of communicating. The uprising was planned for the night when the harvest moon would be at its brightest. 'Mooncakes', round pastries filled with egg yolk, fruits and preserves, continue to be a feature of the present-day festivities. They are passed around among friends and relatives and eaten in the moonlight. Lanterns are also used on this day, usually in the shape of a fruit or a rabbit.

In Sydney, one of the traditional features of this day is a spectacular Moon Festival Parade in Darling Harbour's Chinese Garden, which includes dragon dancers, acrobats and a martial arts performance. The Australian Chinese Community Association (ACCA) organises some events for the festival, such as a lunch for senior citizens from both inside and outside the Chinese community.

Further information: ACCA (tel: 9281 1377).

Mooncakes, round pastries filled with egg yolk, fruits and preserves are a feature of the very colourful Chinese Moon Festival.

Community organisations

Chinese Australian Union Inc.

A peak Chinese political lobby organisation, it plays an important role in the area of public relations.

Level 1, 32 Carrington Street, City (tel: 9299 6700).

Chinese Youth League of Australia.

Founded in 1939, the League is very active in promoting social and cultural activities.

10 Dixon Street, Haymarket (tel: 9267 3166).

AUSTRALIAN CHINESE BUDDHIST SOCIETY.
Provides Chinese Buddhist education and religious services.
654 Cabramatta Road, Bonnyrigg
(tel: 9823 3622)

HWA TSANG MONASTERY.
The monastery holds Buddhist religious services and also provides a space for cultural activities.
29 Mackenzie Street, Homebush West
(tel: 9746 6334)

Chinese Australian Services Society (CASS).

Formed in 1981, CASS provides welfare and social services to the Sydney Chinese community, fosters and develops multicultural activities, promotes the teaching of Chinese language and cultural traditions, and fosters and promotes multicultural activities.

44-48 Sixth Avenue, Campsie (tel: 9789 4587).

Australian Chinese Community Association of New South Wales.

Provides a wide range of social, welfare and information services to the Sydney Chinese community.

2 Mary Street, Surry Hills (tel: 9821 1377).

Chinese Migrant Welfare Association.

The Association provides social welfare and information assistance to migrants from the People's Republic of China.

Suite 3, Level 1, 388 Sussex Street, Sydney (tel: 9264 6448).

Irene Moss

NEW SOUTH WALES OMBUDSMAN

Born in 1948 in Dixon Street, Chinatown, Irene Moss became, in 1995, the first woman Ombudsman to be elected in NSW. Prior to that, she worked as a magistrate for the New South Wales Government, the first Asian woman magistrate in the state. For a period of eight years Irene was the Federal Race Discrimination Commissioner at the Human Rights and Equal Opportunity Commission (another first for women), and during that time she chaired the National Inquiry into Racial Violence.

Irene Moss was a Senior Conciliation Officer for the Anti-Discrimination Board (NSW) from 1983-1986. She is also a former Chairperson of the former National Breast Cancer Centre, a former member of the Fullbright Commission, and a former committee member reviewing the Australian honours and awards system. She is currently on the board of SBS. Irene was admitted as a Solicitor to the Supreme Courts of NSW and ACT in 1974 and to the High Court of Australia in 1975. In 1995 she was appointed an officer of the Order of Australia.

Sydney Chinese Events Committee.

Organises diverse social and cultural events relevant to the Sydney Chinese community.

29 Arinya Street, Kingsgrove (tel: 9809 1088, 9893 9088, 9391 3000 or 018 404 496).

Art and culture

Chinese Folk Dancing School.

The School has a well-deserved reputation for its commitment to the maintenance and fostering of Chinese folk dancing. It performs regularly in multicultural and Chinese festivals.

53 Australia Avenue, Bass Hill (tel: 9644 1191).

Sydney Drama Playhouse.

A Chinese community theatre company, the Playhouse stages plays by local playwrights.

PO Box K105, Haymarket 2000 (tel: 9281 1018).

Australian Chinese Performing Artists Association.

Develops a wide range of cultural and artistic activities in the field of drama, dancing, video and literature.

3/9 Parry Avenue, Narwee. (tel: 9584 2869 or 9744 8969).

Religious organisations

Chinese Presbyterian Church.

The church claims to be the biggest and oldest surviving Chinese congregation in Australasia. The services – in English and Mandarin, with a translation service into Cantonese – are attended by more than 800 people each week.

Corner Albion and Crown Streets, Surry Hills. (tel: 9331 4459).

Chinese Christian Church.

A fast-growing interdenominational church, it has regular services in Cantonese, Mandarin and English.

Further information: Rev Charles Cheung; 100 Alfred Street, Milsons Point (tel: 9955 2800).

CHINESE MEDICINE

LIU LILY. At one of the most traditional and few authentic Chinese herbal medicine practices still existing in Sydney – you will be in the good and wise hands of the Liu Lily herbalists. Here you'll be told – by monitoring your pulse and checking you tongue – whether your 'chi' energy level is 'ok'. Exotic and rare herbs and roots – the solution to your malaise – are brewed while you wait. Open Tuesday-Friday 9am-6pm.

473 Crown Street, Surry Hills (tel: 9310 1685).

THE SYDNEY COLLEGE OF TRADITIONAL CHINESE MEDICINE. The College provides accredited courses in areas such as Acupuncture, Chinese Herbal Medicine and Chinese Massage.

92-94 Norton Street, Leichhardt (tel: 9550 9906).

Media

The Chinese media began in 1894 when the *Chinese Australian Herald* was founded. Soon after others followed – including the *Tung Wah News* – but in general they were short-lived; by the end of War World II most of them had disappeared, and the following decades didn't see any new Chinese locally published papers on the market. It was only in the 1980s that a new generation of Chinese language newspapers began appearing in the Sydney newsagencies.

Newspapers

Sing Tao. The pioneer of the new generation of Chinese language newspapers in Australia, *Sing Tao* was founded in 1982. It offers great

Facts and figures

By 1993, the China-born population was the ninth-largest overseas-born group in Australia with 91,500 people, and the second-largest Asian birthplace group after the Vietnamese.

Today, Australia's ethnic Chinese population is estimated at about 400,000 and is drawn from a dozen countries. Of the 78,000 people born on the Chinese mainland and living in Australia, about 70% have arrived since 1980. Sydney's Chinese community of more than 200,000 is the largest in the country.

Of those Chinese who had been in Australia since before 1976, 94.8% had taken up Australian citizenship. In terms of education, while the proportion of Australian Chinese aged over 15 and holding some type of educational or occupational qualification is marginally higher (41.9%) than for the total population (38.8%), the proportion with post-secondary qualifications (18.9%) is substantially above that of the Australian average (12.8%).

The median annual income of the Chinese-born community ($12,200) is lower that the national average ($14,200), and, given that a majority of China-born people have been residing in the country for a short period, their house ownership (34.4%) is below that of the total Australian population (41.0%).

Around 22.5% of Chinese-born Australians identify themselves as Christians, while 7.8% are Buddhists. There is also a proportion (4.9%) who belong to the Russian Orthodox Church (these are mainly the White Russians who settled in China after the Soviet Revolution). Cantonese is the most common language among Chinese-born (43.6%), followed by Mandarin (24.5%) and Russian (6.0%).

coverage of local and international news and has a strong influence on the Chinese community. The coverage on the market ups and downs gives valuable information for Chinese entrepreneurs. It's published Monday-Friday and Sunday and costs 80c. It has a circulation of 24,000 on weekdays and 28,000 on weekends. The current editor is Patrick Poon.

Level 1 545 Kent Street, Sydney (tel: 9261 4466).

Chinese Herald Daily News. This paper went to print for the first time in 1986 and currently is published four days a week, Tuesday-Thursday and Saturday, at a cost of $1. It has a circulation of 14,000 on weekdays and 15,000 on Saturday. Raymond Deng is the editor.

Level 2/83 Foveaux Street, Surry Hills (tel: 9281 2966).

The Independence Daily. Apart from its good coverage of national and international affairs, *The Independence*, established in 1994, has become a very valuable channel for publishing the writings – especially poetry – of many very talented Chinese writers. It's published from Monday to Saturday and has a weekly circulation of between 12,000 and 15,000, which jumps to 18,00 on weekends. It costs 80c on weekdays and $1 on Saturday. The current editor is Vincent Ho.

141 Broadway, Ultimo (tel: 9211 4611).

Radio

SBS Radio 1, AM 1107. Cantonese program featuring community news, international events and music. Monday and Tuesday 10am-11am and 8pm-9pm, Wednesday and Thursday 10am-11am, Friday and Saturday 8pm-9pm, Sunday 10am-11am. Programs in Mandarin are on Wednesday and Thursday 8pm-9pm, Friday and Saturday 10am-11am, and Sunday 8pm-9pm.

2AC Sydney Australian Chinese Radio

2AC Channel 1: Cantonese

2AC Channel: Mandarin

Further information: 9281 9011.

Television

SBS Television. News services in Cantonese, Tuesday-Saturday 7.35am-7.55am, and in Mandarin Monday-Saturday 7.55am-8.30am.

SING TAO NEWSPAPERS

You can catch up with Jackie Chan or John Woo's latest Hong Kong blockbusters in Chinatown's Cinema or on SBS Television's cult movies on Saturday night

The Filipinos

One writer, a painter and two singers. Four very talented Filipino Australian women. Arlene Chai – the writer – is the author of the highly acclaimed *The Last Time I Saw Mother*, a book that sold more than 33,000 copies, and *Eating Fire and Drinking Water*, where she explores life during the Marcos dictatorship.

Maria Cruz – the painter – is the creator of the compelling self-portrait 'Maria', awarded the 1997 Portia Geach Memorial for the best portrait painted by an Australian woman. And the singers, Kate Ceberano, one of the leading voices in the Australian music scene; and Chita Conway, Australia's first Asian country-rock singer. Four women. The pride of the Filipino-Australians.

Filipino is the name given, since the nineteenth century, to the Christianised Malays who live in what we know as the Phillipine archipelago. During the 300 years of Spanish rule the term was applied to people of Spanish descent born in the Philippines. As a mainly Christian and significantly English-speaking nation, the Philippines has often been labelled as the most westernised country in Asia.

In the last fifteen years, Filipinos have emigrated en masse. It is estimated that each year 600,000 leave their country searching for a better life. The first Filipinos arrived in Australia in the second half of the nineteenth century. They settled in Western Australia and Queensland and helped to develop the local pearl shell and other maritime industries. By 1901 there were no more than 689 Filipinos in Australia, mostly men.

The 1901 Immigration Restriction Act decreased even further the number of Filipinos in Australia. Until the 1960s, only a few skilled Filipinos, family units and some Filipino boxers managed to gain entry to Australia. One of the most famous cases of racial prejudice involved a Filipino-born US army sergeant, Lorenzo Gamboa, who was based in Australia during World War II. When he was discharged from the army at the end of war, he was not allowed to stay in Australia despite having married an Australian woman and acquired US Citizenship. It was not until 1952, after a relentless struggle by his wife, Joyce, that Lorenzo Gamboa was

The Filipino community began taking formal direction in the early 1970s, when several community, religious and welfare organisations were established. Currently there are approximately 28 Filipino community organisations in Sydney, and, as it is a mainly Catholic group, community life revolves around colourful processions and religious festivals held in Sydney.

allowed to rejoin his wife and their two children. Little wonder that by the 1947 Census only 147 Filipinos were recorded in Australia.

With the end of the infamous 'White Australia policy', the period from the late 1960s to the late 1980s saw a new tide of Filipino migration, mainly highly skilled professionals. Among the 1960s group there were also a number of some relatively wealthy migrants. They form what is now the core of the Australian Filipino community.

The Filipinos are today the second fastest-growing group in Sydney after the Chinese. Between the 1986 and 1991 censuses it rose 125%, topping 40,000. The dominant feature of Filipino immigration is the large presence of women. They come largely as spouses or fiancees of Australian men (in 1991 there were almost 20, 000 Filipino women compared with fewer than 14,000 men).

In Sydney, the Filipinos are widely dispersed across the western suburbs of Blacktown, Fairfield, Canterbury, Penrith and Parramatta. The Filipino community began taking formal direction in the early 1970s, when several community, religious and welfare organisations were established. Currently there are approximately 28 Filipino community organisations in Sydney, and, as it is a mainly Catholic group, community life revolves around colourful processions and religious festivals regularly held in Sydney.

Restaurants

Bridging the East and West, the Filipino cuisine – or 'native' food as it's called – is a celebration of flavours ranging from sweet to sour, and bitter to salty. The national dish is *adobo*, which consists of stewed chicken, pork or squid pieces.

BM Express. A small restaurant with good and generous portions. Try the chicken *adobo*. Average $10, BYO. Open Monday-Sunday 10am-6pm.
9 Ware Street, Fairfield (tel: 9724 0350).

Fiesta Filipina. Possibly the best-known Filipino restaurant in Sydney. The house speciality is *adobo* but you should try also the *arroz caldo* (boiled rice with chicken, garlic, ginger and onions). Don't forget to order a bottle of 'San Mig' – the Filipino San Miguel beer. Average $25, licensed. Open Monday-Saturday lunch 11.30am-4pm, dinner 6pm-10.30pm (till 3am on Friday).
1st Floor, 316 Elizabeth Street, Surry Hills (tel: 9211 1946).

Filipino Food Bar. A place where portions are generous and one of the other national dishes *kare-kare* (oxtails and honeycomb tripe cooked in a peanut sauce with eggplant, green beans and other vegetables) is a

NIGHTCLUBS

FILIPINO CLUB & RESTAURANT.
The Filipinos are very keen on their nightlife and at the Club there is plenty to do. On Friday and Saturday there is live entertainment, karaoke and disco, and a very good restaurant service (try the *lechon*, it's sensational). On Friday and Saturday the action rolls on from 6pm till 3am. On Sunday the Club opens 11am-midnight and you can drop by for lunch and dinner plus more live entertainment and, yep, more karaoke.
95-97 Main Street, Blacktown
(tel: 9831 3411).

must. You also can't go wrong if you order *lechon* (roast baby pig with liver sauce) or *pinangat* (vegetable dish laced with very hot peppers). Average $10. Open Monday-Friday 11am-6pm.

Shop F24, Hunter Connection, 7-13 Hunter Street, City (tel: 9233 8785).

Sans Rival Food Service. Try the very Spanish *longaniza* (spicy pork sausage). Average $10, BYO. Open Monday-Sunday 9.30am-7.30pm.

13/52-68 The Crescent, Fairfield (tel: 9727 3146).

Shopping

Bayanihan Asian Groceries. Stocking plenty of imported and fresh Filipino food items. Open Monday-Sunday 10am-8pm.

42 Railway Parade, Granville (tel: 9897 1850 or 9718 8724).

Filipiniana Food Mart. A grocery store that also has Filipino videos available for rental. Open Monday-Friday 9am-7pm, Saturday-Sunday 9am-5pm.

Shop 5, George Street, Plaza Corner George and Moore Streets, Liverpool (tel: 9821 2503).

Kate Ceberano

SINGER

Kate Ceberano, who was born in Australia of an Australian mother and Filipino father, is one of Australia's most celebrated female artists. Soul, jazz, funk, contemporary new sounds and a bit of reggae are all a part of her versatile talent.

Her successful career began as lead vocalist with the funk band I'm Talking, which had three top 10 singles, a gold album and the award for Best Debut Group at the Countdown Awards. Kate's solo career began with her first album, *Brave*, which stormed the charts and sold triple platinum. At 25 she impressed Australian audiences with her powerful performance as Mary Magdelene in the concert version of *Jesus Christ Superstar*, playing to more than one million people. In 1996 her career reached a new high with the release of the album *Blue Box*, for which she wrote nine of the thirteen tracks. She is married to Lee Rogers, director of the film *Dust off the Wings*, in which Kate made her big screen debut.

Maligaya Filipino & Asian Foodstore. Imported canned and fresh products from the Phillipines. Open Monday-Sunday 10am-8pm.
8 Butler Road, Hurtsville (tel: 9580 6837).

Manila Foodtown. A grocery and take-away shop with a strong Filipino accent. Open Monday-Sunday 9.30am-7pm.
253 Parramatta Road, Annandale (tel: 9564 3367).

Melchrishel Bakery. A good alternative to your everyday boring bread is the authentic Filipino *pan de sal* (crusty salty bread), and this is the place to get it. $2.20 a dozen. Monday-Friday 8.30am-6.30pm, Saturday 8.30am-5.30pm, Sunday 9am-noon.
23 Rooty Hill Road North, Rooty Hill (tel: 9832 4555).

Rhoshell Food Products. A grocery and bakery where you can find just about everything from Manila. Try the Filipino cakes and the soft bread. Milkfish (*bangos* in *Tagalog*) is also available. Open Monday-Friday 24 hours a day (closes at 4pm on Friday).
6 Kerry Road, Blacktown (tel: 9831 3295).

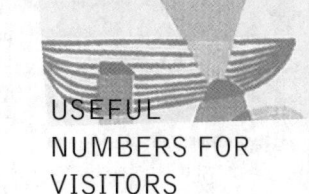

USEFUL NUMBERS FOR VISITORS

PHILIPPINE CONSULATE:
tel: 9299 6633.

PHILIPPINE DEPARTMENT OF TOURISM:
tel: 9299 6815.

PHILIPPINE TRADE OFFICE:
tel: 9267 7500.

PHILIPPINE AIRLINE:
tel: 9262 3131.

Getting to know the Filipino community

Events

The Filipino Talent Quest.

This is an immensely popular annual musical event organised by the *Philippine Community Herald* newspaper for Australian-Filipino local artists. Lately the event has been held at Burwood RSL Club.

96 Shaftesbury Road, Burwood. Further information: 9725 7722.

Independence Day.

On June 12 Filipinos remember the end of 300 years of Spanish colonial rule. The event is celebrated with an Independence Ball at the Sydney Hilton Hotel along with a Philippine Independence Presentation held at Bowman Civic Centre, Campbell Street, Blacktown.

Further information: Philippine Consulate (tel: 9299 6633).

CINEMAS

If you have been in Manila you may have noted that cinemas are always packed. Movies are a popular and inexpensive pleasure, and leading actors such as Sharon Cuneta and Cesar Montano have rabid admirers. A few Sydney suburban cinemas make space from time to time for the latest Filipino cinema releases, and the oncoming movies are regularly advertised in *The Philippine Community Herald*. The most popular screening venues are the Fairplex Cinema, in Fairfield, the Mt Druitt Hoyts and the Dumaresq Cinema at Campbelltown. Tickets are available from Filipino shops (call some of the ones listed).

Flores de Mayo (Santa Cruzan).

A significant Catholic religious event, held on May 4, which celebrates the figure of the Virgin Mary. Several local organisations hold events, including a procession and a mass. One of the venues for this celebration is the All Saint's Church.

Corner Elizabeth and George Streets, Liverpool (tel: 9602 8466).

The following are Catholic religious events organised by the very active FILCOS Parramatta. For additional information, speak to Ver Bernardo, the FILCOS's Public Officer (tel: 9897 5724 or 9897 3961).

Feast of St. Joseph, Patron of Migrants.

A religious feast celebrated at any Catholic Church in the Parramatta area. St Joseph is the patron saint of migrants and the Filipino community celebrates his feast day on the third Sunday of March every year. St Joseph is honoured with a mass and a cultural program after the feast, to which prominent figures are normally invited.

Christmas Carolling.

In December during Christmas time, members of the Catholic community visit nursing homes and households to sing carols. The carollers in return receive a gift from the household.

Simbang Gabi (Dawn Mass).

In the Philippines it is a tradition for Filipinos to prepare themselves spiritually for the coming birth of Jesus by getting up early in the morning to attend mass. Following this tradition early masses are celebrated in Sydney for nine consecutive days, December 16-24.

Novena to our Mother of Perpetual Help.

This is a weekly religious celebration. An image of Our Mother of Perpetual Help is brought to the chosen household. Petitions and thanksgiving offerings are placed in a box for the Novena intentions. The Novena is recited every day and on the seventh day the image of Our Mother of Perpetual Help is transferred to another household.

Religious organisations and places of worship

FILCOS Parramatta Inc. This is a non-profit religious and charitable organisation which plays an active role in developing a culturally pluralistic society in Australia. It also promotes unity among Filipinos as well as their development within the context of Christian values.

41 William Street, Granville (tel: 9897 5724 or 9897 3961).

Word for the World Christian Fellowship.

An evangelical congregation, it has regular worship services on Saturday at 5.30pm at 5 Hereward Highway, Blacktown, and on Sunday at 10pm at Croydon Park Public School, Georges River Road, Croydon Park.

Further information: 9831 8641 or 018 255 570.

Community organisations

Philippine-Australian Community Services. Provides welfare and social assistance to Filipino migrants. It puts a strong emphasis on youth, women and the aged.

1st Floor/93 Main Street, Blacktown (tel: 9672 3738).

Australian Philippine Association. The Association organises a wide range of cultural and social activities for the Filipino community.

359 Eastern Valley Way, Castle Cove (tel: 9417 2892).

Media

Newspapers

The Philippine Community News. A monthly freebie (look for it in some Asian shops), this is the oldest running Filipino newspaper in the country (established in 1985). Published in English, it mainly covers community news and the Sydney Filipino cultural and entertainment scene. It has a circulation of 3,000 and hits the stands in the second week of the month. The current editor is Sennie Masian.

PO Box 667, Granville 2142 (tel: 9637 6474 or 0411 398 058).

The Philippine Community Herald Newspaper. A monthly publication, it has an excellent coverage of community life from the different Australian States. It also has an impressive number of columnists analysing cultural and social justice issues.

Although the paper is largely in English, it has a section in Tagalog. It appears on the 20th of every month and costs $1. It has a circulation of 6,000 and its current Managing Editor is Evelyn Zaragoza.

PO Box 785, Fairfield 2165 (tel: 9725 7722).

PASSION PLAY OF JESUS CHRIST.

A reenactment of the passion of Jesus Christ held at the Sacred Heart Parish, Westmead, on Good Friday. Back in the Philippines observance of Holy Week is a serious event – there is a *Pabasa* (the reading of Christ's life) and a *Cenaculo* (a theatrical play of Christ's life) where some persons are genuinely nailed on the cross! Don't expect to see this here.

Radio

SBS Radio 2, FM 97.7. Tagalog language service covering local events and news from the Phillipines. Tuesday, Thursday and Friday 10am-11am, Wednesday 11am-noon, Saturday 9am-10am.

2CC Radio, FM 90.5. Music and entertainment with 'Manila Sound.' Saturday 5-8pm.

For further information contact Tony Concha on 9686 3888.

Facts and figures

The main Filipino population in Sydney is found at Blacktown, Fairfield, Canterbury, Penrith, Parramatta, Marrickville, Auburn and Campbelltown.

The number of Phillipines-born people in Australia is estimated to be around 70,000. They form a community that is among the five largest migrant groups from non-English-speaking backgrounds. The largest concentration of Filipinos, more than 33,000, is found in Sydney. Settlers born in the Phillipines have been quicker than average to take up Australian citizenship (67.7%).

The proportion of the Phillipines-born migrants with some form of educational or occupational qualifications (58.3%) is considerably higher than the national average (38.8%). It's also higher in terms of post-secondary education (32.8%) in comparison to the Australian population (12.8%). This also helps to explain the higher median annual income of Filipinos ($16,400) compared with that of the total Australian population ($14,200).

At the 1991 Census, 12.2% of Filipino immigrants were living in their own house, compared with 41.0% of the Australian population. Nevertheless, the rate of Filipinos purchasing their own house (32.5%) is higher than the national average (27.1%).

The Philippines is unique for being the only Christian country in Asia. Over 90% of the population claims to be Christian, and in Australia over 86% of Filipinos are Roman Catholics. (The Spanish certainly did a thorough job in their 300 years of ocuppation.)

In the Philippines there are a large number of local languages and dialects, but the three main indigenous languages spoken are Tagalog, Cebuano and Ilocano. In the Australian census they are grouped under the term of Filipino Languages. In Australia, over 75% speak a Filipino language, around 20% speak English and there is also a small proportion (1.6%) who speak Spanish.

The Indians

You wouldn't be blamed for a moment for thinking that you are queuing to get into one of the many Calcutta cinemas to catch up with the new 'Bollywood' box office hit. No, you aren't in Calcutta. You are queuing in the Fairplex Cinema, in Fairfield, western Sydney, for the Friday night session of Indian movies.

Sydney Indians have long been awaiting the Sydney release of *Daud* (with one of India's leading actors, Sanjai Dutt), and the Fairplex quickly starts filling up with enthusiastic Indian teenagers, adults and even whole families. We are told that the three sessions every Saturday and Sunday and the reduced price session on Mondays are always full. "Get there early or make a booking" is wise advice. There is a lot to learn from the Sydney Indian community. They have been able to find an balance between their Indian way of life and their commitment to their new country.

Even though Indian immigration in large numbers has occurred only recently, their presence on our shores goes back a long way. A group of Indian convicts were brought to Sydney as labourers at the beginning of the 1800s while the first group of free Indian settlers, from Calcutta, made their way to Sydney in 1816. In 1837, John Mackay, an Englishman, recruited 40 Indians to work for him when he moved from India to Sydney. Similarly, a number of Indians, including women and children, were recruited as domestic workers by P Friell, who settled in the new colony in 1844. Two years later, in March 1846, a group of 51 Indians, who were privately recruited, arrived in Sydney on board the *Orwell*. Around this time there was also a group of Anglo-Indians – of European and Indian parentage – who were brought to work as compositors for Henry Parke's printing press.

> Even though there has not yet emerged a readily identifiable Sydney Indian community, Indians have established small pockets of settlement in the western suburbs of Blacktown and Penrith.

Ethnic Indians, mainly Sikhs and Muslims from Punjab, began arriving during the second half of the nineteenth century. They settled in some small rural areas in New South Wales and worked as agricultural labourers, hawkers and pedlars. A number of them found work as cane cutters in the New South Wales north coast districts of Richmond and Clarence. It was around this region, at the beginning of the twentieth century, that a group of Indians laid the foundations for the present-day communities of Punjabi Sikhs and Muslims in Woolgoolga and Coffs Harbour.

With the *Immigration Restriction Act* in 1901, there was virtually no further Indian immigration to Australia for the next fifty years. Following the independence of India in 1947, a number of Indian-born British citizens and Anglo-Indians entered Australia. Other Indians, however, were not allowed to enter Australia until 1966, with the relaxation of the racist immigration policy towards non-white people. Unlike the earlier settlers, this new wave of immigrants were drawn from many regions of India and many religious, linguistic and cultural groups. A large number of them were highly educated – doctors, engineers, university teachers and computer experts who have been able to succeed professionally in Australia.

Even though there has not yet emerged a readily identifiable Sydney Indian precinct, Indians have established small pockets of settlement in the western suburbs of Blacktown and Penrith. Community life revolves around a large number of regional, religious and cultural associations where Indians with the same language and cultural background meet periodically. Until recently they mixed little with others, though things are changing. The United Indian Association (UIA), one of the few Pan-Indian organisations in Sydney, is achieving (with events like the Indian Fair) what until recently was unthinkable – a space where Indians from all regions and language backgrounds could get together. Drop by the festival in July and you will know what we are talking about.

When you ask local Indians about the moment they treasure the most during their time in Sydney, they will probably tell you about the day in which the magnificent Sri Venkateswara Temple was formally opened on June 30 1985. For many Sydney Indian immigrants, whose adjustment to their traditional ways of life without losing their cultural and religious identity has not been easy, the opening of the Temple's doors was also a statement – Sydney is now "home".

Sydney has 18,000 Indian-born residents many of whom have professional qualifications.

Restaurants

Abhi's. Especially for curry followers; try the chicken *tikka* (fillet). Average $20, BYO. Open for lunch Monday-Friday noon-3pm, dinner Monday-Sunday 6pm-10pm.

163 Concord Road, North Strathfield (tel: 9743 3061).

A Flavour of India. One of the best in town. Average $25, BYO and licensed. Open for lunch Wednesday-Friday noon-2.30pm, dinner Monday-Sunday 6pm-11pm.

120-128 New South Head Road, Edgecliff (tel: 9326 2659).

Andy's. A good place for Indian Muslim food (*halal*). Average $20, BYO. Open for lunch Saturday-Sunday noon-3pm, dinner Tuesday-Sunday 6pm-10.30pm.

658 Bourke Street, Redfern (tel: 9319 6616).

Bombay Tandoori. Great food surrounded by colourful Indian murals. Average $15, BYO. Open for lunch Monday-Friday noon-3pm, dinner Monday-Sunday 6pm-10pm.

231 Oxford Street, Darlinghurst (tel: 9361 3014).

Geronimo. While you are there also try the cuisine from Bangladesh, Pakistan and Afghanistan. Average $15, BYO. Open Tuesday-Sunday 5.30pm-10.30pm.

106 Curlewis Street, Bondi (tel: 9930 2756).

Indian Empire. Food complemented with a fantastic view of the harbour. Average $30, BYO. Open for lunch Monday-Friday noon-3pm, dinner Monday-Sunday from 6pm.

5 Walker Street, North Sydney (tel: 9923 2909).

Manjit's. Specialises in northern Indian cuisine. Average $15, BYO. Open for lunch Monday-Friday noon-2.30pm, dinner Monday-Sunday 5.30pm-11pm.

360 Darling Street, Balmain (tel: 9818 3681).

Minar. Offers a good vegetarian menu. Average $15, licensed and BYO. Open for lunch Monday-Friday noon-2.30pm, dinner Monday-Saturday 5.30pm-11pm.

15 Wenworth Avenue, Surry Hills (tel: 9283 4634).

Oh! Calcutta. Only for trendies (just joking), north-west Indian cuisine. Average $20, BYO. Open for lunch Thursday-Friday noon-3pm, dinner Monday-Sunday 6.30pm-10.30pm.

251 Victoria Street, Darlinghurst. (tel: 9360 3650).

Tanjore. A charming spot with a fantastic menu. Average $20, BYO. Open for lunch Tuesday-Sunday noon-2.30pm, dinner Sunday-Wednesday 5.30pm-10.30pm.

34 Glebe Point Road, Glebe (tel: 9660 6332).

Finally, Sydney is catching up with the fine London curry tradition. If you happen to be around in early November, don't forget the traditional Diwali Festival where the Sydney Hindu community celebrates *Laksmi*, the goddess of wealth (see page 317), and Sydney Indian restaurants put on special banquets to celebrate this festival.

Touch of India. Specialises in Northern and Southern Indian dishes, very affordable. Average $15, BYO. Open for lunch Tuesday-Friday and Sunday 12noon-3pm, dinner Monday-Sunday 5.30pm-midnight.
334 Pacific Highway, Crows Nest (tel: 9438 2811).
See also Silver Spoon, page 34.

Shopping

Indo-Australian Caterers. A great range of products from the Indian subcontinent. Open Monday-Sunday 10.30am-7.30pm.
23 Scott Street, Liverpool (tel: 9821 3080).

Maya Indian Sweets Centre. See page 17.
470 Cleveland Street, Surry Hills (tel: 9699 8663).

Krishan Spice Center. The shelves of this place are just packed with those spices needed for your Indian recipe – go for the curry-pastes, *dal* and rice and sweets. It has also an extensive range of CDs and tapes from India (and the UK). Open Monday-Friday 10am-7pm, Saturday 10am-6pm and Sunday 10am-4pm.
5/71 Edgeworth David Avenue, Waitara (tel: 9489 5012).

Nizam's Indian Food. This is one of the main suppliers of a wide range of Indian spices and other products to Indian stores.
43-45 Burns Bay Road, Lane Cove (tel: 9428 5557).

Fashion shops

The attraction of Indian clothing, with its exotic designs and vibrant colours, have long extended beyond India. "We have many, you know, kind of 'trendies' or 'alternatives', young non-Indian people searching for Northern India clothing which is very easy to use; pants or blouses are the most popular," says the owner of one of the many Sydney Indian shops. The shops below are worth a look.

Soshu's Gallery. A new good excuse to go to Palm Beach, this store sells superb woodblock printed traditional Indian clothing – including block printed *kurta* (tunic dress) and attractive *pareos* (sarongs). All made and imported from India. For your cool Sydney summer outfit, this is the place to go. Open Monday-Sunday 10am-5pm.
Shop 4, 1105 Barrenjoey Road, Palm Beach (tel: 9974 1573).

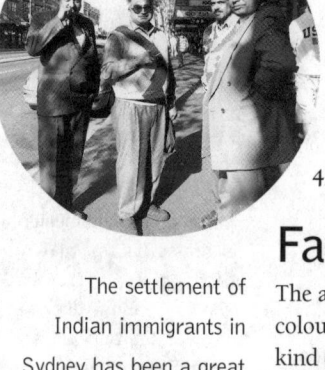

The settlement of Indian immigrants in Sydney has been a great success. Today the Indian-born have an average income 30% higher than the average for all Sydnesiders.

DGM Fashions. It boasts having the latest in Indian fashion, and it's true. Drop by there and you will find everything from *sarees* to men's *sherwani*, casual *salwar kameez*, poly silk, *kashmiri*, *kurta* pyjamas and *chokers*, and if you really want to go Indian don't forget to explore the jewellery section. Open Monday-Sunday 10am-7pm.

48 Joseph Street, Lidcombe, near the station (tel: 9749 4102).

Roshan's Fashion. *Shalwar kameez*, *sarees* (from $20 to an easy $500), sandals, *ghagra cholis* and a good selection of fashion jewellery. Open Monday-Saturday 10am-6.30pm (till late on Thursday), Sunday 11am-5pm.

15/281 Beamish Street, Campsie Mall (next to station), Campsie (tel: 9718 3251). Also at 24 Darcy Street, Parramatta, opposite the station (tel: 9687 9776).

Sydney's 'Bollywood'

If you want to catch up with the latest films from 'Bollywood', including box offices smashes such as *Jai Ganja*, *Daud*, and *Safari*, call in to the Fairplex Cinema, Station Street (corner Cunningham Street), Fairfield. Indian movies (in Hindi and Tamil, no English subtitles regrettably) are screened Monday-Thursday at 7.30pm, Friday at 7pm and 10pm, Saturday at 4pm, 6pm and 10pm, and Sunday at 2pm, 4pm and 6pm. Fridays and weekends, $10 adult; $5 children. On weekdays, $7 adult and $5 children.

Further information and bookings: tel: 9755 7733.

Getting to know the Indian community

Events

For Hindu Events and Festivals see Sydney Hindu Community, page 316

Indian Fair.

"It is not just a fair. It represents unity in a foreign land," wrote Prerna Badhwar in *The Indian Down Under*. Held the last weekend of July, it is arguably the most important cultural and community event of the year for the Sydney Indian community. Run by the United Indian Association (UIA), this festival is a true celebration of Indian unity in a community

USEFUL NUMBERS FOR VISITORS

INDIAN CONSULATE:
tel: 9223 9500.

THE INDIAN TOURIST OFFICE:
tel: 9264 4860.

NIGHTCLUBS

AASHIQUI INDIAN NITE CLUB.
This is Sydney's only club where Indian (and non-Indian) party goers go "wild in the west with the speed of Bhangra – the wild Punjabi music from the UK," as Michael Narayan, one of the organisers of the Club, explains. It operates in the premises of the Ermington Hotel, corner Silverwater and Victoria Roads, in the western suburb of Ermington. The disco starts at 8pm, but, as Mr Narayan put it, "the fun begins at 11pm and goes till 3am". $10 cover. Contact Michael Narayan on 9635 8935 or Renu on (015) 270 943, and if you can't get through just give a ring to the Ermington Hotel on 9638 0277.

with a tradition of linguistic and cultural diversity. For the last three years, an estimated 10,000 Sydney Indians have flocked to the Parramatta Park Amphitheatre for the day of activities. What you may see there is beyond our ability to summarise, but let's try. There are around 50 stalls with an enticing and wide range of dishes – *sarson ka saag, makki di roti, pakoras, dosas, papadi chat* and many more. It also has a great display of Indian fashion and traditional Indian music and dances. Prominent local, state and federal politicians usually can't resist to drop by – with more than 10,000 potential votes, who could blame them?

Further information: *The Indian Down Under* (tel: 9875 2713).

Holi (the North Indian Colour Festival).

A spring festival, this is one of the most colourful events in the Indian annual calendar. It is held on March 5 and has been described as a 'festival of mirth and merriment'. In India it is celebrated after harvest has been completed and winter has ended. For further information on activities in Sydney, please contact some of the community organisations and institutions listed on page 312-313.

Music Nite.

This is great stuff! If you really want to hear the best of Indian music in Sydney, performed by local Indian artists such as Vany Mysore, Arvind Ranjarajan, Uma Ayyar, plus Hindi film songs from 'Bollywood' don't miss this annual event organised by the Sydney Tamil Manram. In 1997 it was held on August 23 at Bankstown Town Hall, Chapel Road, in the western suburb of Bankstown. Tickets are $25 family, $10 adult, $5 children. Dates and venues may change from year to year, so we suggest contacting **Anbu Jaya of Sydney Tamil Manram Inc, PO Box 229, Strathfield, NSW 2135 (tel: 9825 4279).**

Sydney Music Circle Concerts.

Sydney has a fairly large South Indian community and there are a number of very talented local artists whose performances attract a large audience. Run by the Sydney Music Circle the concerts are held the last Saturday of each month at The Veteran Car Club Hall, 134 Queens Road, Five Dock. Programs usually commence at 7.15pm and last for two hours. They are free but each program is sponsored by two or more families to cover the costs. More information about the Sydney Music Circle is given on page 000.

Further information: Hari Subramaniam (tel: 9689 1409), B Ramkumar (tel: 9876 8545) or S Ramswamy (tel: 9878 2911).

About 60% of Sydney's Indian-born people are Christian. Another 18% are Hindus while 6% follow the Sikh faith.

Pallavi Indian Classic Music Concerts.

This is a series of about eight annual concerts by Indian classical musicians, brought to Australia by Pallavi, a non-profit cultural organisation established in 1995 (more about Pallavi on page 312). These concerts are a unique opportunity for Sydneysiders to be introduced to the best exponents of Southern Indian classical music.

Further information: Mohan Ayyar (tel: 9831 5295), VV Ramesh (tel: 9872 6479), or V Ramnath (tel: 9871 9169).

Navrang.

It means 'colourful' and this is what this event is all about. "We celebrate the colour of a multicultural society, the different skin colours, the colourful dressings and even the colour of Indian food," says Lalli Sethuram, vice-president of the Sri Mandir Association, which runs this event every year (more about this organisation on page 313). Navrang is held the third month of August and you must not miss this celebration under any circumstances. Plenty of Indian food available and a very attractive cultural program. It starts at 3pm and the cultural programs kick off at 6pm. Venues change every year, so contact

Lalli Sethuram on 0418 642 923 or 9748 4355 for details.

Mahatma Gandhi Jayanti (Birth of Mahatma Ghandi).

This day is usually celebrated at the end of September or in the first week of October. Several activities are organised; one that has become a tradition is a 'blood donation day' organised by Vishwa Hindu Parishad Australia and the NSW Red Cross Blood Bank – what a great way to celebrate the memory of Ghandi!

Further information: Virenddra Kumar Patel (tel: 9580 9231).

Indian Bazaar.

Annual event hosted by St Ignatius College, Riverview on September 12. The event helps to raise funds for the Australian Jesuit Mission in India, providing education and health support for the extremely poor in Hazaribag, India. From 9am to 5pm.

Further information: 9955 8585.

For Hindu religious organisations and places of worship see Sydney Hindu Community, page 317.

INDIAN NATIONAL DAY.

August 15 1947 marked the end of English rule in India and the beginning of India's existence as the world's largest democracy. Special celebrations, including the superb 'India: Dancing to the Flutes' art exhibition at the Art Gallery of NSW, were held in 1997. For additional information, contact either the Sydney Indian Consulate on 9223 9500 (Monday-Friday 9.30am-12.30 pm), the newspaper *The Indian Down Under* on 9875 2713, or any of the Indian organisations and institutions listed on page 312-313.

INDO-AUSTRALIAN CULTURAL SOCIETY.

A non-sectarian association whose aims are to promote multiculturalism through a diverse range of cultural, social and sporting activities. Its current General Secretary is Monika Bhatia.

10 Barnetts Road, Winston Hills (tel: 9692 4381).

Community organisations

The following is a selected group of Indian community organisations operating in Sydney.

United Indian Association.

A cross-regional and linguistic umbrella organisation representing a considerable number of local Indian organisations and associations. It runs the Indian Fair (see page 309).

PO Box 698, Strathfield NSW 2135 (tel: 9871 4947).

Sydney Indian League.

A non-profit umbrella body of Indian organisations throughout NSW.

48 Mintaro Avenue, Strathfield (tel: 9642 2195).

Pallavi ('New Beginning').

Established in 1995, this is a non-profit cultural organisation dedicated to staging Indian classical music concerts in Sydney by professional musicians from India. One of the latest concerts was the performance by the internationally famed saxophone maestro Kadri Gopalnath.

Further information: Mohan Ayyar (tel: 9831 5295).

Rubi Pesini

FASHION DESIGNER

Her designs, a blend of bright and vibrant colours where East meets West, have transformed Rubi Pesini into one of Sydney's best known fashion designers. "Exotic!!" – is how she describes her very much sought after creations.

A former model, Rubi Pesini moved to Sydney in 1977 with her businessman husband Pesi Irani, equipped with a Masters Degree in Organic Chemistry, but it was fashion designing that finally seduced her. From her beginning – a Rose Bay boutique – Rubi has grown to become a major importer and exporter in the fashion business. Over 5,000 selected boutiques and major department stores in Australia – including the prestigious, Myers, Grace Bros and David Jones – carry on her designs. She has also gone on to conquer on the international scene. Rubi Pesini's name can be found in London and New York.

Vedanta Centre of Sydney.

Established in Sydney in 1985, the Centre organises public lecturers and discourses, twice a month, about Vedanta religion and philosophy. "The central theme of Vedanta is that every individual is potentially divine, and the purpose of religion is to realise the divinity within by controlling nature – external and internal, either by work (*Karma yoga*) or by worship (*Bakthi yoga*) or by control of mind (*Raja Yoga*) or by spiritual discrimination (*Jnana yoga*). Realisation may be achieved by practising one or more or all the Yogas" (extract from the Vedanta Centre of Sydney Booklet). Admission is free and all are welcome.

27 Rickard Road, Strathfield, V Sarathy, secretary (tel: 9642 2160).

Sydney Tamil Manram Inc.

Organises educational and cultural activities and runs the very successful Music Nite (see page 310).

PO Box 229, Strathfield 2135.

Sydney Tamil Sangam.

Founded in 1977, this group organises social and cultural activities to raise funds for charity.

117 Moverley Road, South Coogee (tel: 9344 0802).

Sri Mandir.

A cultural and religious organisation established in the early 1970s. It runs the immensively successful *Navrang* festival (see page 311) and also has a Hindu temple at 286 Cumberland Road, Auburn, the oldest in the country (see also Sydney Hindu Community, page 318).

Further information: Lalli Sethuram (tel: 0418 642 923 or 9748 4355).

Punjabi Language and Cultural Society.

Started in 1985, its main objective is to maintain language and cultural traditions of the Punjabi region. The Society also organises a number of concerts featuring local as well as invited artists from India.

10 Vaughan Street, Lidcombe (tel: 9749 4140).

Media

Newspapers

The Indian Down Under. Published in English, this is an institution among the Sydney Indian community. Founded in 1987, it is the oldest Indian newspaper in the country. It's crammed with community and international news, sport, lifestyle and well-written feature stories. It is published the first week of the month at a cost of only $1 and has a circulation of 5,000. The current editor is Nina Badhwar. *The Indian Down Under* is not only a newspaper but, as Mrs Badhwar explains, is "the first place where many new Indian immigrants call to get information about jobs, education, housing and community organisations." No wonder it is so well regarded by the Indian community.

THE INDIAN Down Under
Bringing India closer to Australia

23 Barkala Place, Westleigh (tel: 9875 2713).

Other popular print outlets among the Sydney Indian community are *Samachar* (tel: 9639 4654, Monika Bhatia, Editor) and the *Indian Link* (tel: 9235 0900).

Radio

SBS Radio 2, FM 97.7. News and current affairs. Monday 3pm-4 pm, Sunday 9pm- 10am.

2RRR, FM 88.5. '*Mahak*' Hindi program, Sunday 2pm-3pm. Plays top 10 songs every first Sunday of the month, has special presentations on popular film personalities, news summaries from India, community announcements, special talks on Indian culture, interviews with visiting dignitaries and local personalities. It also has very popular give-aways every Sunday.

For sponsorships and promotions contact Sukhdev Jaswal (tel: 9795 5395) or during program time on tel: 9816 2938.

Indian Radio programs can also be heard on the following community radio stations:

2BCR FM, 88.7 (tel: 9726 8233).

2GLF FM, 89.3 (tel: 9601 4489).

2RES FM, 89.7 (tel: 9331 3000).
2RSR FM, 88.9 (tel: 9550 9552).

Television

Every Wednesday on Channel 31 you can get informed on what is on in the Sydney Indian community. It has also a selection of news from India, 8pm-9pm.

Facts and figures

Currently there are around 70,000 Indian-born people living in Australia, of which almost 18,000 are Sydney residents. Indians immigrants have shown a solid pace of settlement in Australia, which is demonstrated by the high number (67.7%) taking up Australian citizenship.

One of the most striking aspects of the India-born population is the very high level of education. According to the 1991 census, 59.4% held some educational or trade qualifications, which is a considerable higher proportion than that of the total Australian population (38.8%). Considering their high level of education and the large number of Indian-born people employed in professional, technical and white collar occupations, it is not surprising that their median annual income, $18,600, is 31% above the median income for the total Australian population. At the time of the 1991 Census, the proportion of India-born immigrants who owned or were purchasing their home was 67.0%, which is slightly lower than the proportion of the total Australian population (68.2%)

The 1991 Census shows that 32.8% of Indian immigrants speak a language other than English – mostly Hindi (9.8%) and Tamil (3.3%) – while 67% of them indicated that they speak only English, which is explained by the large proportion of Anglo-Indians who left India after independence in 1954. This also explains the large number of Christian India-born immigrants, 62.2%. Among the non-Christian denominations, 18.6% practice Hinduism and 6.3% follow the Sikh faith. There is also a small proportion of Indian Muslims.

Indian-born persons speak a range of languages, including English. Bengali, Gujarati, Hindi, Komkani, Kannada, Malayalam, Marathi, Punjabi, Tamil and Telegu.

The Hindus

Among the four major non-Christian groups – Muslims, Buddhists, Jews, and Hindus – the Hindus constitute the fastest-growing group in Sydney.

The major source of Hindu immigration to Australia continues to be Asia (53.8%), but there is also a significant proportion of Hindus born in Oceania (37.2%), many of whom are Fijian Indians. Sydney Hindu immigrants have mainly established pockets of settlement in the western suburbs of Blacktown, Canterbury, Parramatta and Strathfield.

Community events

The following are some of the main Hindu festivals held in Sydney every year. Although they are celebrated in the majority of the Hindu temples scattered around Sydney, the main venue is the Sri Venkateswara Temple at Helensburgh. We recommend you contact the Sri Venkateswara Temple Association on (042) 94 3232 and obtain its calendar for information on the main Hindu festivals and other celebrations held at the Temple during the year. Other important venues are the Sri Mandir Temple at Auburn and the Shiva Temple at Minto.

Hindus constitute the fastest-growing group in Sydney.

Ganesha Visarjana Festival.

Hindus have been celebrating this festival for thousands of years. In 1893 Lokmanya Tilak, from the state of Maharastra, called upon Hindus to celebrate this festival as a way to bring people together to build a united and strong India. The Ganesha Visarjana Committee was formed in Sydney in 1990 to celebrate this festival every year – around September 7 – as a joint effort between all the religious, cultural and linguistic organisations from the Indian subcontinent. The main venue for the festival is the Sri Venkateswara Temple.

Further information: tel (after hours) 9388 7380 (Dr A Balasunramaniam); 9637 4509 (Bhagwat Chauhan); or 9680 1120 (Kirti Bhima).

Deepavali (Festival of Lights).

Around the end of October members of the Sydney Hindu community celebrate this event by exchanging presents and greeting cards with relatives and friends. During the festival it is traditional that Hindus decorate their homes with lights.

Diwali Festival.

The inner-city suburb of Glebe is one of the main locations for this traditional event held November 1-3. This is a community celebration of the traditional Hindu ceremony dedicated to *Laksmi*, the goddess of wealth, and features a spice market, dancing, yoga demonstrations, a Hindu bookstall and a sari display. It has now become tradition that Indian restaurants in Sydney put on special banquets to celebrate this festival.

Dussehra.

A traditional festival held October 19-21. '*Dussehra*' means the tenth day and marks the end of *Navratri*, which is a nine-night event in certain parts of India. It commemorates the victory of Sri Rama in North India and the triumph of good over evil in South India.

Krishna Jayanti (Krishna's Birthday).

As with other divine human heroes, the Hindu deity *Krishna* is said to have had a miraculous birth. He is often portrayed as a plump baby, full of vitality. Although of noble heritage, the young *Krishna* dwelt among the cowherds of *Vrindaban*, where he could remain safe from the threat of his cousin *Kasma*, an evil oppressor whom *Krishna* had been born to destroy. *Krishna Jayanti*, held at the end of August, is a large celebration to which all are welcome.

Sri Radha-Krishna Temple, 180 Falcon Street, North Sydney (tel: 9959 4558).

Religious organisations and places of worship

Sydney's Hindu community have built new temples to allow them to continue their religious worship.

The worship of Hindu deities in temples is central to the practice and maintenance of Hindu faith. The following are some of the main Hindu Temples in Sydney. All are welcome, only you must show respect and follow the rules.

Sri Venkateswara Temple.

Services on weekdays are usually held after 5.30pm, although some can be celebrated in the morning around 10am. On weekends services are held through the day, starting as early as 7.00am.

Temple Road, Helensburg (tel: (042) 94 3224).

GOVINDA'S.
It's not a Hindu monument, or a temple, or a park – it's a *Hare Krishna* restaurant. The modest $12.50 you pay for the all-you-can-eat vegetarian fare also allows you to access the Movie Room (above the restaurant) which shows arthouse, mainstream and classic movies. There are two daily screenings from Monday to Sunday. Govinda's is open from 6pm till late.

112 Darlinghurst Road, Kings Cross (tel: 9380 5162).

Sri Mandir.

For information on services, contact the Sri Mandir Society on 9624 2255 (Lalli Sethuram).

286 Cumberland Road, Auburn.

Shiva Temple.

Established in 1989, the Temple has daily services 8am-10am and 5pm-8pm.

201 Eagle View Road, Minto (tel: 9820 1094, Temple, or 9600 7815, reception).

Places of interest

Sri Venkateswara Temple.

Dedicated to Sri Venkateswara – the main deity in the Temple – this magnificent Hindu shrine opened in Sydney on June 30 1985. Located at Temple Road in western suburb of Helensburgh, it was the first traditional Hindu temple in Australia and each year attracts thousands of visitors from around the country and overseas.

The Temple also has shrines consecrated to other Hindu deities, including *Sri Ganesha, Sri Mahalakshmi, Sri Andal, Sri Parvati, Sri Durga, Sri Muruga, Sri Rama, Sri Hanuman, Lord Shiva* and the *Navagrahas*.

At present a cultural hall is also being built at the site, to be used for religious discourses, marriage ceremonies, cultural programs and other functions. The construction of this impressive building was undertaken by the Sri Venkateswara Temple Association at the beginning of the 1980s, relying on money from its many fundraising campaigns and the individual generosity of Australian Hindus.

For further information about this fascinating Temple and its festivals, contact the Association on (042) 94 3224.

The Indonesians

By the time that Captain James Cook 'discovered' Australia, Indonesian seamen had already been sailing to the north Australian coast for something like 800 years. On board frail 'prahu' vessels, these adventurous fishermen were collecting the much-prized sea slug, a Chinese delicacy and aphrodisiac.

In the 1870s Indonesian divers, mainly from Kupang, were recruited to work in the Australian pearling industry and by 1885 they were followed by Javanese recruited to work in the sugar cane plantations of Queensland. The beginning of the twentieth century saw approximately 1,000 Indonesians living here, mainly in Western Australia and Queensland.

Following independence from the Netherlands in August 1945, Indonesian students, sponsored under the Colombo Plan, began attending Australian universities and technical colleges. However, it was not until the racist 'White Australia policy' was scrapped, in 1973, that Indonesians began emigrating and settling permanently here. In 1961 there were around 6,000 residents in Australia from Indonesia (mainly of Dutch origin), a number that rose to more than 30,000 by the 1991 census. In contrast to the early immigrants, the later arrivals were of mixed ethnic origin, including Javanese, Sumatrans and Sulawesi people, as well as Indonesians of Chinese and Arabic descent.

Sydney, with around 14,500, has the largest Indonesian community in the country, with the eastern suburbs of Kensington, Kingsford and Randwick being the main suburbs of Indonesian settlement (see 'Jakarta along Anzac Parade' page 325). Around these suburbs, Indonesian and Malay (Indonesian or Bahasa Indonesian is the *lingua franca* of Indonesia, while Malay, officially known as Bahasa Melayu, is Indonesia's national language) have become the fourth most spoken languages. In the last few years, a wide range of services, including restaurants, grocery stores, and Indonesian-speaking doctors, accountants and hairdressers have been established in these suburbs. In Kensington and Kingsford you can find the only Indonesian-run *halal* butcher shops in Sydney. A large Indonesian Presbyterian community exists in Randwick whose

Since its beginning in the mid 1950s, Sydney Indonesian community life has revolved around various cultural and religious organisations. One of the first was the Persatuan Pelajar Indonesia Australia, formed in 1956.

religious life revolves around the Indonesian Presbyterian Church. And, responding to this growing Indonesian presence in the area, the Indonesian Consulate established its headquarters in nearby Maroubra.

Indonesians have established pockets of settlement in other parts of the city, though in much smaller numbers. For example, Indonesians from west Sumatra (Minangkabau community) and Islamic Indonesians are mainly found in the inner-western suburbs of Marrickville, Dulwich Hill and Tempe.

Nominally a Muslim country, Indonesia enjoys great religious diversity and tolerance. There is the Indonesian Presbyterian Church, for Presbyterians logically enough, and Indonesian Uniting Church, whose followers are predominantly Minahassan; for the Buddhist community there is an Indonesian Buddhist Association, while for Muslim Indonesians the largest organisation is the NSW Centre for Islamic Dakwah and Education. And despite the fact that the Sydney Indonesian community is dispersed and consists of a large number of *sukubangsa* (ethnic groups), every year the community gets together to celebrate the two most important events on the Indonesian calendar, Independence Day and *Idul Fitri* (the end of Ramadan), which attracts not only Muslims but the Indonesian community at large.

Since its beginning in the mid 1950s, Indonesian community life has revolved around various cultural and religious organisations. One of the first was the *Persatuan Pelajar Indonesia Australia*, formed in 1956. Until recently, the peak Sydney Indonesian organisation was the *Perhimpunan Indonesia NSW*; however in 1995 it suffered a split resulting in the establishment of the *Perhimpunan Masyarakat Indonesia*. Both bodies organise cultural activities and play a major role in dealing with the Australian and Indonesian governments.

Restaurants

Sati (pieces of meat served with a spicy peanut sauce), *gado gado* (vegetables with spicy peanut sauce), and *nasi goreng* (fried rice with egg) are the national dishes of Indonesia, and in this multicultural Sydney you won't need to fly to Jakarta to taste them. In general, Indonesian restaurants are cheap and the food is tasty. Below we recommend two inner-city places, but if you really want to have a meal Jakarta style, take a 390 or 391 bus along Anzac Parade and get off at Sydney's Indonesian enclave – Kingsford (see page 325).

Gado Gado. A pleasant, low-key spot. Try the *gado gado* – the portions are generous and the quality gets a thumbs-up. Average $10. BYO. Open Friday lunch; Monday-Sunday dinner.
57 Bayswater Road, Kings Cross (tel: 9331 1577).

Safari Seafare. Seafood is the highlight at this restaurant, which has a strong West Sumatran accent. Average $10, BYO.
Open Monday-Sunday dinner 6pm-10.30pm.
22 King Street, Newtown (tel: 9557 4458).

Getting to know the Indonesian community

Events

Indonesian Independence Day.

On August 17 1945 Indonesia declared its independence from the Netherlands. Each year the Indonesian community gets together to celebrate this event, traditionally organised by the *Perhimpunan Indonesia*, NSW (Indonesian Association of NSW). The activities include a cultural evening featuring performers brought from Indonesia, an Indonesian Night concert at the Sydney Town Hall and a two-day bazaar, concert and disco night at the Marrickville Community Centre, 142 Addison Road, Marrickvile. Call 9878 4450 for details.

Pesta Makanan Indonesia (Indonesian Food Fair).

This is part of the Indonesian Independence celebrations. Organised by the Indonesian Community Association, the event is held on July 26 at the Marrickville Community Centre, 142 Addison Road, Marrickville.

Further information: Herman (tel: 9718 8286) or Lexie Tangka (tel: 9661 7086).

Idul Fitri.

The end of the Muslim fasting month of Ramadan, *Idul Fitri* is the most important date on the Indonesian Muslim calendar. Back in Indonesia, the tradition is that those working or living away from their families are obliged to return home, so each year 25 to 30 million urban Indonesians jostle for space on any bus, boat, train or plane they can get to their home villages to celebrate the event. In Sydney this festival has been traditionally held at the Marrickville Community Centre Hall,

142 Addison Road, Marrickville. Further information: Indonesian Islamic Mosque (tel: 9216 2721), Rayan Bashit, Secretary.

USEFUL NUMBERS FOR VISITORS

INDONESIAN CONSULATE:
tel: 9344 9933.

INDONESIAN TOURIST PROMOTION OFFICE:
tel: 9233 3630.

PLACES OF INTEREST AND LANDMARKS

SEKAR AMAN, AUSTRALIAN MARITIME MUSEUM.
Sekar Aman is a replica of one of the traditional Indonesia fishing *prahu* vessels that have been sailing to the north Australian coast for hundreds, even a thousand, years. The vessel is on daily display at the Museum wharves at Darling Harbour, along with a display of artifacts, models and artworks of early maritime contact between Australia and Indonesia. The Museum opens Monday-Sunday 9.30am-5pm. Admission $7 adults, $4 concession, $18.50 family ticket.

2 Murray Street, Darling Harbour (tel: 9552 7777 Monday-Friday; 9552 7500 Saturday-Sunday; 0055 62002 recorded message).

Religious organisations and places of worship

Indonesian Buddhist Association.
Organises regular Sunday services and also holds Dharma discussions.
20 Victoria Street, Lewisham (tel: 9893 8932).

Indonesian Christian Fellowship Centre.
Religious services and bible studies are held on Sunday at 8am and 6pm. It also runs a Sunday school.
93 Audley Street, Petersham (tel: 9890 1660).

The NSW Centre for Islamic Dakwah and Education (CIDE).
Founded in the mid-1980s, this is the major Indonesian Islamic organisation in Sydney. It holds Islamic celebrations and offers Quran reading classes and youth and women's groups.
45 Station Street, Tempe (tel: 9216 2721).

Gereja Presbyterian Indonesia (Indonesian Presbyterian Church).
One of the main Indonesian Christian churches in Sydney, it holds religious services and bible studies Monday 8am and 7pm, Thursday and Friday 7pm, and Saturday 4pm and 5pm.
Corner Alison Road and Cook Street, Randwick (tel: 9744 1977).

Gereja Bethel Indonesia di Australia (Indonesian Bethel Church).
Holds regular religious services at Gardeners Road Public School, corner Gardeners and Botany Roads, Rosebery on Saturday at 7pm.
Further information: 9838 9370.

Gereja Katolik (Indonesian Catholic Church).
Indonesian-language masses are held at St Joseph Church, Lennox Street, Newtown on Sunday at 11.30am, and at St Michael's Church, Banks Avenue, Daceyville on Sunday at 6pm.
Further information: 9869 0619.

Explore the world in one city

Community organisations

Perhimpunan Indonesia NSW (Indonesian Association of NSW).

This is an umbrella organisation which organises the annual celebrations for Indonesia Independence Day.

31 Lucinda Road, Eastwood (tel: 9878 4450).

Australia Indonesian Association of NSW.

The Association promotes cultural exchange between Australia and Indonesia.

PO Box 802 Sydney 2000 (tel: 9635 4186).

Australia Indonesia Contact.

Assists Indonesian immigrants and organises social and cultural meetings.

221 Cope Street, Waterloo (tel: 9787 6678).

Media

Newspapers

Citra. A freebie that you can pick up from some of the Indonesian shops in Kingsford, it has a strong Indonesian student focus – a lot of advertisements for educational institutions and student accomodation. The editors are Siennie Kurniadi and Lili Yunus.

PO Box 830, Spit Junction 2088.

Warta Berita Aquila. A free monthly publication, it covers a wide range of community events and news from Indonesia. It has a circulation of 1,200 issues. The editors are Lanny Karamoy and Leonel Loreto.

PO Box 372, Petersham 2049 (tel: 9560 8510).

Radio

SBS Radio 2, FM 97.7. Music, news and community announcements, Tuesday and Friday 2pm-3pm, Thursday 10pm-11pm.

Television

SBS Television carries an Indonesian news program (with a special hearing-impaired service), Monday-Saturday 11am-11.30am.

Facts and figures

The Indonesia-born population of Australia comprises a number of disparate elements. Some members of this group are of European (mainly Dutch origin), born to parents posted to the Netherlands East Indies during colonial times.

Between the 1980s and the 1990s the Indonesian population in Australia grew from 16,400 to 35,400 – its current number. In Sydney, there are now more than 14,000 Indonesians, and it is estimated that more than 50% of Indonesian immigrants in Australia have taken up Australian citizenship.

In terms of qualifications, 15.8% have a degree or diploma, while 7.5% have received some skilled or vocational education. The median annual income is $14,100, very similiar to the Australian average of $14,200. On the other hand, 52% of Indonesians own or are purchasing their own place, a rate substantially lower than the Australian average (68.2%); this is partly explained by the arrival of a large number of Indonesians in the last few years.

The majority of Indonesians living here are Christians (56.6%), followed by Muslims (17.2%) and Buddhists (7.9%). New South Wales has the largest number of Indonesian and Malay speakers in the country (59.6%).

Explore the world in one city

Kingsford, Jakarta along Anzac Parade

Nobody said it was at a slow pace. In a matter of five years or so, Kingsford – especially the section of Anzac Parade nestled between the University of New South Wales and the ridiculously risky roundabout, shifted from a dull, lifeless area (for many, the roundabout's Red Tomato – almost demolished by this time – was the only point of reference) to a thoroughfare dotted with good Indonesian and Malaysian restaurants, coffee shops, take-aways and by some of the best stocked Asian shops in Sydney.

Students from all over Asia attending the University of New South Wales (and they're one of the main sources for the ailing uni coffers) have settled in Kingsford, a suburb not far from the city and with excellent public transport.

This is the deal. Organise a visit to La Perouse Museum (see The French, page 115) and on the way back get off in Kingsford, at the bus stop immediately after the roundabout and have a quick fix in one of the Indonesian or Malaysian eateries around the sector. Alternatively, you may like to have a look at the National Institute of Dramatic Arts, NIDA – not that it's a building worth of looking at – but it's the alma mater of Mel Gibson and Judy Davis.

GETTING THERE

A cab from the City to Kingsford will charge you approximately $12-$15, and there are several buses to take you there: **390, 391, 392, 394, 396, 398, 399 and L94** (limited stop). Get off at the main entry of the University of New South Wales or at the bus stop immediately before the roundabout.

Restaurants (See page 326)

4: Ratu Sari. Like most of the restaurants in Kingsford, it's the quality of the food and the friendly service that makes this place highly recommended. According to the owner, the place is attended by 60 per cent Indonesians and 40 per cent of what he called "Anglo-saxons". Average $15, BYO. Open Tuesday-Sunday lunch noon-6pm, dinner 6-10pm.
476 Anzac Parade, Kingsford (tel: 9663 4072).

5: Pondok Buyung. The specialists have praised this place as having the best *nasi Padang*-style food in town. Average $10, BYO.
Open Thursday-Tuesday 11.30am -10.00pm. Average $15, BYO.
124 Anzac Parade (tel: 9663 2296).

8: Andalas Indonesian and Asian Food. More of a cafe than a restaurant. Andalas is an informal meeting place for the large contingent of Indonesian students, and a cheap take away offering the all time favourites of Indonesian cuisine – *nasi foreng, laksa, gado gado*, etc

JAKARTA ALONG ANZAC PARADE

1. Warung Surabaya.
2. Randwick Oriental Supermarket.
3. Everearn Trading Company.
4. Ratu Sari.
5. Pondok Buyung.
6. Golden Miles Cafe.
7. Mekong Asian Food.
8. Andalas Indonesian and Asian Food.
9. Nasi Uduk Jakarta.
10. Ryanni Hair & Beauty.
11. Pataya Thai Restaurant.
12. White Lotus.

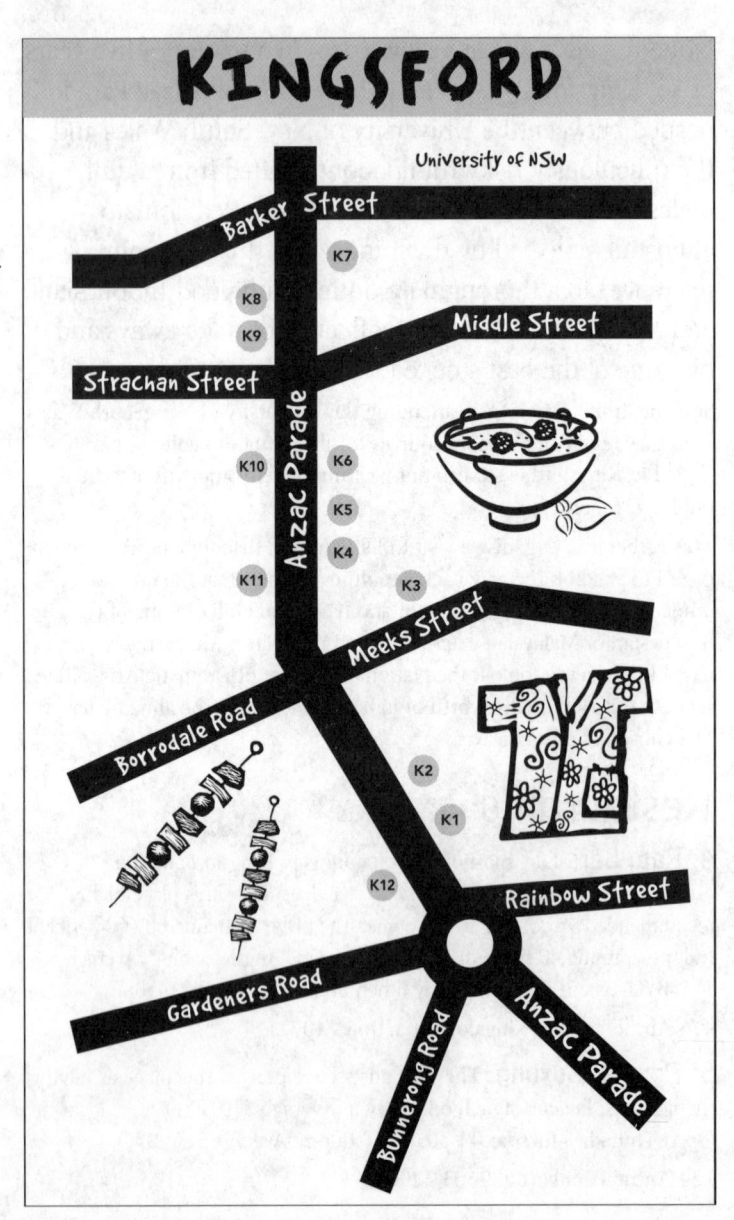

Explore the world in one city

(you can also eat in). Open Wednesday-Monday. Average $10, BYO.
Open Monday-Saturday 11.30am-9.30pm.

273 Anzac Parade (tel: 9662 2220).

9: Nasi Uduk Jakarta. On a steamy hot Sydney night, this kind of back-alley restaurant will take you straight to Jakarta. From the one sheet menu provided, tick what you fancy – have a taste of the *sayap ayam goreng* (fried chicken wing) and *ayam goreng mentega* (fried chicken with butter soya sauce). The endless cold tea is free. Average $10, no alcohol. Open Monday-Sunday 11am-10pm (close on Thursday).

275 Anzac Parade (tel: 9663 4430).

Beauty

10: Ryanni Hair & Beauty. The speciality here is the *Pijat Urut Minyak Zaitun* - the Indonesian traditional body massage with olive oil. "Uplifting, rejuvenating and relaxing", according to regular attendants. Half body massage $25; full body massage $40. Open Monday-Friday 9.30am-6pm (till 7 pm on Thursday), Saturday 9am-5.30pm.

301-303 Anzac Parade (tel: 9663 2781).

12: White Lotus. As shown by the number of Indonesian newspapers and magazines (including *Tempo*) displayed, White Lotus is a food and grocery store with a strong Jakarta accent, however the shelves are big enough to store imported products from other (and many) corners of Asia. Open Monday-Friday 9.30am-8pm.

379 Anzac Parade (tel: 9662 7736).

Restaurants

1: Warung Surabaya. Indonesian cuisine.

508 Anzac Parade (tel: 9663 2518).

6: Golden Miles Cafe. Chinese and Malay cuisine.

30 Anzac Parade (tel: 9313 8098).

7: Mekong Asian Food. Thai and Malaysian food.

394 Anzac Parade (tel: 9662 4006).

11: Pataya Thai Restaurant.

321 Anzac Parade (tel: 9662 7904).

Shopping

2: Randwick Oriental Supermarket.
500 Anzac Parade (tel: 9313 7053).

3: Everearn Trading Company. Asian general store.
6 Meeks Street, Kingsford (tel: 9662 8037).

And not far from Anzac...

Betawi. In spite of the unlikely location, this super-suburban restaurant surprises you with the good, simple food. The prawns fried in butter and sweet soya sauce (*udang goreng sauce mentega*) are highly recommended. Average $20, BYO. Open Monday-Saturday lunch 11.30am-2.30pm, dinner 5.30-10pm.

65 Bunnerong Road, Kingsford (tel: 9314 1166).

Ria Sari. Plenty of praise for its traditional and authentic fare – also packed with "eating machine" uni students. Average $10, no alcohol. Open Monday-Sunday 11am-10pm

142 Barker Street, Randwick (tel: 9399 6101).

The New Orient. More of a shop than a restaurant, The New Orient's Indonesian fare has already earned the praise of the experts. Average $10, no alcohol. Open Monday-Friday 11am-9pm, Wednesday 5-9pm. Sunday-Saturday 10am-9pm.

36 Clovelly Road, Randwick (tel: 9398 6929).

The Japanese

"My sporting dream is to make the Japanese National Cricket Team." Don't laugh. Rick Tanaka is serious about it. Presenter of the long-running and popular Nippy Rock Shop on Radio 2JJJ back in the 1980s, Rick Tanaka definitely doesn't fit the image of the strict, conservative Japanese pursuing success in the highly competitive and stressful Japan Inc.

He is laid back, humorous and thinks his flat ('with a great harbour view') should be included in a Japanese tourist guide. Rick Tanaka – whose curriculum includes the very successful book *Higher than Heaven* – belongs to a new generation of Japanese immigrants who have settled in Sydney in search of space and freedom for their artistic creativity. For Akira Isogawa, one of the most talented Australian fashion designers today, Sydney is the place where he was "finally able to breathe," while for the celebrated Japanese-born ceramicist Mitsuo Shoji, Australia has been the place where he has found the freedom needed for the development of his art. And Tetsuya Wakuda, considered the most brilliant of all Sydney chefs (the creator of the incomparable blue cheese *bavarois*) would surely agree with his fellows.

From pearls to paddies

The first Japanese immigrant to settle permanently in Australia was Toranosuke Kitamura. He is considered a pivotal figure in transforming Japan into one of Australia's major export markets. Kitamura arrived in Sydney in 1890 to manage the local branch of the Kanematsu Fusajiro trading company. Soon the astute Kitamura discovered a lucrative Japanese market for processed sinews, hooves and leg-bones. He also began exporting wool to Japan, which became by the 1930s Australia's second largest market. Under his direction the company, renamed Kanematsu Australia PTY, established the Kanematsu Memorial Institute of Pathology and Biochemistry at Sydney Hospital. Kitamaru died in 1930.

> The first Japanese immigrant to settle permanently in Australia was Toranosuke Kitamura. He is considered a pivotal figure in transforming Japan into one of Australia's major export markets.

Rick Tanaka.

The first group of Japanese migrants to Australia were mainly pearl divers who, from 1884, went to work in the pearling regions of Thursday Island, Darwin and Western Australia. They were single men and the largest number of them came from the prefectures of Wakayama, Hiroshima, Yamaguchi and Kumamoto. It seems that the first Japanese man to work in Australia's pearling industry was Nonami Kojiro, who in a few years became a highly regarded diver on the town of Thursday Island, popularly known as 'Yokohama Town' because of the large number of Japanese. The Japanese dominance of the Australia's pearling industry lasted until World War II.

Queensland's sugar industry was another important destination for early Japanese migrants. During the period 1892-1902 a group of 2,651 Japanese workers was brought to work in some of the local sugar plantations and mills. They were mostly from the prefectures of Kumamoto, Wakayama and Hiroshima. It was the increasing number of Japanese in the area that led the Japanese government to open in Townsville the first consulate in Australia in 1896. One year later it was transferred to Sydney and in 1901 it became the consulate-general.

Isaburo ('Jo') Takasuka was one of the few non-Europeans allowed to enter Australia during the Immigration Restriction Act period, under the infamous 'White Australia Policy'. A son of a Samurai and a politician himself, Jo Takasuka arrived in March 1905. A methodical man, he was soon able to prove the viability of commercial rice growing in Australia, introducing rice paddy farming to New South Wales. As a consultant for the early Australian rice industry, he convinced the local agricultural authorities that rice could be grown on a large scale like wheat, using the same harvest machinery. One of his legacies can be seen today in the extraordinary success of the Murrumbidgee Irrigation Area (MIA), south-west of NSW, where the 2,000 rice-growing families have helped to forge a strong cultural and social relationship between the Leeton district and Japan. It is estimated that around 5,000 Japanese tourists visit the area each year.

A small start in Sydney

By the first years of the twentieth century there were 3,593 Japanese residents in Australia, and the Sydney Japanese community, with only 70 people, was one of the smallest in the country. The early Sydney Japanese community consisted of former workers in the pearling and sugar industries who had moved to Sydney and established small businesses, especially laundries, and of Japanese officers working in the Sydney offices of Japanese companies such as Takashima-Lida, Mitsui, Mitsubishi, Nihon Menka and Iwai Shoten.

In 1909, the Japanese community established a *Nihonjin-Kai*, one of the first Japanese community organisations in Sydney. An information and social centre for the local Japanese community, the *Nihonjin-Kai* regularly held cultural and social events such as film nights and talks. In 1927, on the inspiration of the Japanese consul-general, several Japanese local laundrymen established a '*Dooshi-kai*' (Kindred Spirits Club) to promote cooperation and friendship among long-time Japanese settlers. In 1928 the Japan-Australia Society was formed in Sydney and it was followed a few years later by the establishment of the Japanese Chamber of Commerce.

Dark days

The events that followed the Japanese attack on Pearl Harbour in December 1941 changed forever the life of the Australian Japanese community. Almost without exception the Japanese population was interned. In Sydney, the doors of the Japanese consulate were sealed – most of those arrested were employees of Japanese companies operating in Australia. On Thursday Island, the township of Yokohama was surrounded by barbed wire, with machine-guns on each corner. Single men were sent to the Hay internment camp in south western New South Wales, while families and single women went to Camp No 4 at Tatura, Victoria.

A prisoner-of-war camp was also built in the New South Wales country town of Cowra. In 1944, over 1,000 Japanese prisoners staged an escape – known as the 'Cowra breakout' – from the camp. In the event 231 Japanese and four Australians died. The Japanese who died in the breakout were buried in Cowra and their graves were looked after by the local RSL. In 1962, the Japanese Embassy approached the Cowra Council with the idea of building a cemetery for all Japanese who died on Australian soil during the war years. Two years later, a Japanese War Cemetery, designed by Shigeru Yura, was built and now it contains the remains of all Japanese nationals who died in the Cowra breakout, in the attack on Darwin and in all Australian internment and POW camps.

The Japanese Garden in Cowra is the most popular venue for the traditional *Sakura Matsuri* Festival.

At the end of the war the Japanese, with very few exceptions, were deported to Japan, and their assets were forfeited and made part of a fund to compensate Australian prisoners of war. In 1947 a complete ban was placed on the entry of Japanese to Australia. By this year the Australian Japanese community was reduced to no more than 330 people. It was not until 1952, when the ban was lifted, that Japanese people began entering Australia again. The first group of the post-war generation of Japanese immigrants were mainly 'war brides'.

Starting again

Currently there are about 25,900 Japanese people living in Australia. In Sydney the Japanese community consists of more than 10,000, scattered across the suburbs but with emerging communities on the North Shore and in North Sydney. A distinctive characteristic of the current Australian Japanese community is its very high socioeconomic status, due to the large number of Japanese business people who have played a major role in strengthening the Australian-Japanese economic relationship.

The Sydney Japanese community that existed before the war has largely disappeared and those still alive have few links with the current Japanese community that began flourishing in the 1950s. One of the first post-war Sydney Japanese organisations was the Japanese Society of Sydney, founded in 1957. It was soon followed by the Japan Society of NSW, established in 1968. These were the years in which Japanese television programs such as *The Samurai* on ABC were taking Australian children audience by storm. When the Japanese actor from *The Samurai* visited Sydney on a promotional tour he was mobbed at Sydney Airport by hundreds of Australian kids dressed up as 'ninjas'. For many Australian kids of the 1960s and 1970s, Japanese cartoons and programs were seen to be very cool, just like the Japanese 'manga' videos are today, being big sellers among Anglo, Chinese and Vietnamese Australian youth alike.

With the development of more permanent Japanese immigration to Australia in the last few decades, new Japanese institutions and organisations have been established. One of the most important was the creation of the Sydney Japanese School, a combined initiative of the Sydney Japanese Society and the Japanese Consulate. This unique institution began operating, with 33 students, from a modest church hall in the North Shore suburb of Lindfield before moving at the beginning of the 1970s to its current location in Terrey Hills. It now has around 390 students who enjoy a truly cross-cultural education. However, the most important contribution to the promotion and appreciation of Japanese culture was the opening of the Japan Cultural Centre in 1992 (see page 337).

Restaurants

Sushi is among the few Japanese dishes that all of us know, but it seems that recently Sydneysiders have been broadening their orders, discovering and enjoying the wonderful diversity of Japanese cuisine. This has a lot to do with Sydney's wonder chefs Kimitaka Azuma, Takeo Ono and the French-trained Tetsuya Wakuda. Here is a list of selected Japanese restaurants praised by the critics and not far from the Sydney CBD. By the way, while visiting some of these restaurants our knowledge of the Japanese language increased. Check this out: '*chekku puriizu*' – 'the bill please'

Tetsuya's. For the specialists, the public and the critics alike this is the best restaurant (of any sort) in town. Average $85, BYO and licensed.

Open for lunch Wednesday-Saturday noon-3pm, dinner Tuesday-Saturday 7pm-midnight.
729 Darling Street, Rozelle (tel: 9555 1017).

Ginza Isomura. Highly praised by its loyal clientele. Average $30, licensed. Open Monday-Sunday 11.30am-10.30pm.
Ground floor, St Martin's Tower, 31 Market Street, City (tel: 9267 4552).

Raw Bar. Japanese treats mixed with the Bondi's sea breeze. Average $30, BYO. Open for lunch and dinner Monday-Sunday noon-midnight.
Corner of Warner and Wairoa Avenues, Bondi (tel: 9365 7200).

Azuma. Since it is an 'English-free zone', bring your English-Japanese dictionary (or your Japanese soccer mate, as we did). Average $30, BYO. Open for dinner Wednesday-Monday 6pm-11.30pm.
125 Falcon Street, Crows Nest. (tel: 9955 3316).

Sakana-ya. The name – House of Fish – saves further explanation. Average $15, BYO. Open for lunch Monday-Friday noon-2.30pm, dinner Monday-Sunday 6pm-10.30pm.
336 Pacific Highway, Crows Nest (tel: 9438 1468).

Yamakasa. Friendly service and terrific food. Average $25, BYO and licensed. Open for lunch Monday-Friday noon-2.30pm, dinner Monday-Saturday 6pm-10pm.
155 Miller Street, North Sydney (tel: 9957 4895).

Isaribi. The *sushi* and the *tempura* are good but the barbecue section on the menu is a must. Average $25, licensed. Open for dinner Wednesday-Monday 6pm-11pm.
41 Elizabeth Bay Road, Kings Cross (tel: 9358 2125).

Suntory. You can enjoy not only the food but also the landscaped garden. Average $50, licensed. Open for lunch Monday-Friday noon-2pm, dinner Monday-Sunday 6.30pm-10pm.
529 Kent Street, City (tel: 9267 2900).

Fuuki. Average $25, BYO. Open for lunch Wednesday-Friday noon-2pm, dinner Tuesday-Sunday 6pm-10pm.
417 Pacific Highway, Crows Nest (tel: 9436 1608).

Matsukaze. Good food in a very upmarket setting. Average $45, licensed. Open for lunch Monday-Friday noon-2.30pm, dinner Monday-Friday 6pm-10pm.
Level 1 Chifley Plaza, Chifley Square, City (tel: 9229 0191).

JIYU NO OMISE, MYO ('make your own' sushi). Average $15, BYO and licensed. Open for dinner Monday-Sunday 6.30pm-11pm.
342 Darling Street, Balmain
(tel: 9818 3886).

SUSHI-GEN. Drop by to see a real novelty, a sushi-making machine! Average $20, BYO. Open Monday-Sunday 11.30am-10.30pm.
330 Victoria Street, Darlinghurst
(tel: 9332 7454).

GION. Superb *sushi* and spicy *negimaki* (shallot-wrapped beef). Average $30, BYO and licensed. Open for lunch Tuesday-Friday noon-2.30pm, dinner Tuesday- Sunday 6.30pm-10.30pm.
129-135 Military Road, Neutral Bay
(tel: 9908 2522).

TOKYO JOE'S. It's so close you can drop by after or before a visit to the Opera House. Average $20, licensed. Open for lunch and dinner Monday-Friday 10.30am-9.45pm, dinner only Saturday 5.30pm-10pm.
5 Loftus Lane, corner of Young Street, Circular Quay
(tel: 9252 1608).

NOODLE BARS

Everybody's talking about them. Sydneysiders, adventurous as they are, have been attracted to an affordable and quick Japanese bowl of noodles. Try these ones that have been recommended by the experts.

Edosei. It's considered the best *sushi* and *sashimi* bar in town. Average $45, licensed. Open for lunch Monday-Saturday, noon-2pm, dinner Monday-Saturday 6pm-10pm.

22 Rockwall Crescent, Potts Point (tel: 9357 3407).

Yutaka 1. A very popular spot offering great hand-made *sushi*. Average $25, BYO and licensed. Open lunch Monday-Friday noon-2pm, dinner Monday-Friday 6pm-10.30pm.

200 Crown Street, Darlinghurst (tel: 9361 3818).

Hananoki. A good noodle-based menu. Average $25, BYO and licensed. Open for lunch Wednesday-Monday noon-3pm, dinner Wednesday-Sunday 5pm-9pm.

7 Cambridge Street, The Rocks (tel: 9241 1364).

Sushi Suma. Good food in the middle of the Sydney's Lebanese quarter. Average $25, BYO. Open lunch Tuesday-Friday noon-2pm, dinner Tuesday-Sunday 6-10pm.

412 Cleveland Street, Redfern (tel: 9698 8873).

Unkai. Superb food with a view to die for. Average $60, licensed. Open for lunch Sunday-Friday noon-2.30pm, dinner Monday-Sunday 6pm-10pm.

Level 36, ANA Hotel, 176 Cumberland Street, The Rocks (tel: 9250 6123).

Himegami. Informal and friendly with a wide range of dishes. Average $20, BYO and licensed. Open lunch Monday-Friday noon-2.30pm, dinner Monday-Saturday 6pm-10pm.

258 Pacific Highway, Crows Nest (tel: 9439 1494).

Fish Markets Sushi Bar. Eat Japanese in one of the most multicultural spots in Sydney. Average $15, BYO. Open lunch Monday-Sunday 11am-3pm.

Blackwattle Bay, Pyrmont (tel: 9552 2872).

Azabujuban. The *soba* noodle dishes and noodles in *miso* soup are terrific. Average $10, BYO. Open Monday-Saturday 11am-9pm.

163 King Street, City (tel: 9232 6985).

Shimbashi Soba. The wheat noodles and slender *soba* are highly recommended. Average $20, licensed. Open for lunch Monday-Saturday noon-2.30pm, dinner Monday-Saturday 6pm-9pm.

Shop 1, 24 Young Street, Neutral Bay (tel: 9908 3820).

Soba Restaurant Shimbashi. One of the most popular Japanese noodle bars in town. Average $20, BYO. Open for lunch and dinner Monday-Sunday 11.30am-10.30pm.
Shop 1, 24 Young Street, Neutral Bay (tel: 9908 3820).

Tampopo Japanese Noodle House. *Ramen* noodles (wheat flour and egg noodles) are the house trademark. Average $10, BYO. Open for lunch Monday-Sunday 11.30am-3pm, dinner 5.30pm-9.30pm.
12 Gray Street, Bondi Junction (tel: 9369 2516).

Ten-Sun. A great and crowded, fast-paced noodle bar. Average $10, BYO. Open for lunch Monday-Sunday 11am-3pm, dinner Monday-Sunday 5.30pm-8.45pm.
103 Willoughby Road, Crows Nest (tel: 9906 2956).

Selected shops

Tokyo Mart. It seems that everybody agrees that this is the best place to buy whatever you need – fresh noodles, seafoods, meat and more – to follow your Japanese recipe book. Open Monday-Friday 9.am-5.30pm, Saturday 9am-5pm, Sunday 10am-4pm.
Shop 27, Northbridge Plaza, Northbridge (tel: 9958 6860).

Anegawa Trading. Recommended not only for its wide range of Japanese products, including fresh fish, sauces and sweets, but also for its well-prepared take-away food. Open Monday-Saturday 9am-6.30pm, Sunday 10am-4pm.
16A Deepwater Road, Castle Cove (tel: 9417 5452).

7-Eleven (North Rocks). Too late, everything closed? This 7-Eleven style *Nipponya* at the Rocks stocks packets of instant noodles and *miso* for a quick nibble. Open daily 24 hours.
340 North Rocks, North Rocks (tel: 9872 4940).

Bookshops and gifts

Japan Book Plaza. In this well-stocked Japanese bookshop (formerly located at Martin Place) you can find magazines, newspapers and a wide range of Japanese language teaching materials including, videos, tapes, and dictionaries. It also has a section dedicated to Japanese history. Open Monday-Friday 9am-7pm (till 8pm on Thursday), Saturday 10am-6pm, Sunday 10.30am-5.30pm.
30 Carrington Street, City (near Wynyard station) (tel: 9294 3733).

SOCIAL CLUBS

INTERNATIONAL NIPPON AUSTRALIA NEW ZEALAND CLUB.

First open in 1977, this is a favourite of Japanese and non-Japanese Sydneysiders. It has an affordable and highly recommended fully licensed restaurant – average $15 – complete with pocker machines and a generous bar. The Club, with a daily average attendance of around a hundred people, is also a regular venue for Australian and Japanese music groups. The restaurant only opens for lunch from Monday to Friday between noon and 3pm, while the Club has more extended trading hours.
229 Macquarie Street, City (tel: 9232 2688).

JAPAN CLUB OF SYDNEY.

Provides a wide range of social and cultural activities for Japanese citizens who are settling in Australia. It runs a Japanese-language school and publishes a very informative newsletter.
GPO Box 4735 (tel: 9411 4677).

MADE IN JAPAN.
An exciting homewares shop, it sells simple things at affordable prices — ceramics in watery glazes, lacquerware tea sets, merchant chests and bamboo chopsticks. It also has a great range of timber furniture predominantly from the Meiji era (1868-1910), from tiny sewing boxes to futon storage wardrobes and kitchen cabinets. Open Monday-Sunday 11am-7pm (till 8.30pm on Thursday).

502 King Street,
Newtown
(tel: 9517 9531).
Also at
437 Oxford Street,
Paddington
(tel: 9360 6979).

Japanese Bookshop Arts and Crafts Centre. This is a charming place where you can find smart hand-made toys, Japanese prints ($4 to $100), newspapers from Japan and even *kimonos* ($75 to $500). Also has Japanese art and craft books in English. Open Tuesday-Saturday 10.30am-5.30pm, Sunday-Monday noon-5pm (you can visit the shop by appointment after trading hours).

131 Glebe Point Road, Glebe (tel: 9552 4930).

Japanese Language Institute Book and Multimedia Supercentre. Centrally located, this store has an amazing variety of texts to help your take your first steps in Japanese. It also has a translation service available and a comprehensive Japanese language course program.

109 Pitt Street, City (tel: 9369 3800).

Modeller's World. A great selection of the latest Japanese animation, models and gifts. Open Monday-Sunday 11am-7pm.

Shop 15, Dixon House, 413-415 Sussex Street (tel: 9212 7838).

Tansuya Ya. In the leafy and super-chic Queen Street, Tatsu Ya is well known as a place to find fine Japanese antiques. Open 10am-5pm except Wednesday and Sunday.

90 Queen Street, Woollahra (tel: 9363 4954).

Art and places of interest

Japan Cultural Centre Art Gallery.

Holds regular exhibitions of Japanese art, including ceramic paintings, contempary Japanese films and music. Open Monday-Friday 10am-4.30pm, Saturday 10am-1pm.

Level 13, Japan Culural Centre, 201 Miller Street, North Sydney (tel: 9954 0111).

Andrew Stuart-Robertson Gallery.

Specialises in Japanese works of art and porcelain. It also displays Chinese, Australian and European art works, including paintings and works on paper. Open Wednesday-Saturday 11am-5.30pm, or by appointment.

6 Goodhope Street, Paddington (tel: 9332 1653).

Japanese Garden and Cultural Centre.

Located in Cowra, just four hours west of Sydney, the five hectares of the Japanese Garden displays over 110 types of trees, flowers and shrubs and is home to over 120 species of birds. In early October, the spring blossoms celebrate the beginning of the Sakura Matusi, Cowra's annual Japanese Cherry Blossom Festival. The Japanese Garden, designed by the internationally renowned landscape architect, Ken Nakajima, features a traditional Japanese tea house, a lantern temple, a *bonsai* house with *bonsai* displays, two miniature lakes brimming with *koi*, a cultural centre with three Japanese art galleries, and a restaurant. Open seven days a week 8.30am-5pm.

Further information: PO Box 248, Cowra, NSW.
(tel/fax: (063) 411 875, International 61-63-411875).

Japan Cultural Centre, Sydney.

Sponsored by the Japan Foundation, the Centre opened in Sydney in 1992 with the primary goal of fostering and encouraging an appreciation of Japanese culture. The Centre has an art gallery on Level 13 where diverse art exhibitions are displayed; also located in this area is the Japanese-style room complete with *tatmi* and *shoji* screens. On Level 11 there are regular screenings of popular Japanese feature and cultural films (admission is free). On Level 12 is the Sydney Language Centre; its aims are to assist Japanese language education in Australia and New Zealand, especially at the secondary level. On Level 13 there is a very well-resourced library with a wide range of materials, including books, music tapes, slides and videos. The Gallery is open Monday-Friday 10am-4.30pm, Saturday 10am-1pm. The Library opens Monday-Friday 10am-4.45pm, Wednesday 10am-7.45pm, and every first and third Saturday of the month 10am-1pm.

The Japanese Garden in Cowra.

201 Miller Street, North Sydney (tel: 9954 0111).

Auburn Botanic Gardens (Japanese section).

The Gardens, which comprise 12 separate open areas, contains a magnificent Japanese section. The Gardens are open every day to the public and have picnic and BBQ facilities available for visitors. Since the Japanese section can also be hired, it has become a very popular venue for special occasions, especially weddings. The Gardens, located on the corner of Chiswick and Chisholm Roads, Auburn, are administered by the Auburn Council. Open 9am-5pm.

Further information: Auburn Council (tel: 9735 1222).

Campbelltown City Art Gallery's Japanese Garden.

Located in the corner of Camden and Appin Roads, the Japanese Garden, with its traditional tea house, is a delightful place to give yourself a break after visiting the great art collection on display at the

USEFUL NUMBERS FOR VISITORS

JAPANESE CONSULATE:
tel: 9231 3455.

JAPAN CHAMBER OF COMMERCE AND INDUSTRY:
tel: 9267 3377.

JAPAN AIRLINES (JAL).
tel: 9272 1111.

JAPAN NATIONAL TOURIST ORGANISATION,
tel: 9232 4522.

JAPAN TRAVEL BUREAU,
tel: 9510 0100.

Gallery. The Garden and Gallery are open from Wednesday to Friday 10am-4pm and on weekends and public holidays noon-4pm.
Further information: (046) 28 0066.

Getting to know the Japanese community

Events

Oshogatsu (New Year's Holiday).

Held on January 1-3 this is Japan's most important holiday, with families getting together to welcome the new year. Special foods are served at home including *mochi* (pounded rice cakes), *zoni* (rice cake stew), and *osechiryori* (red beans, kelp, fish roe and other items). For those interested to learn of any possible activities celebrating this event, contact some of the communities and cultural organisations listed below.

Japan Festival.

Held at the end of August and supported by the City of Sydney, the Festival offers a week of activities showing Japanese culture and traditions. The main events are held at the Sydney Opera House, Queen Victoria Building, Town Hall and Martin Place and include a variety shows, *taiko* drums, modern and traditional dance, *koto*, *kimono* shows,

Akira Isogawa
FASHION DESIGNER

In Japanese 'akira' means 'all things bright', and this is just right for Akira Isogawa. Born in Kyoto, Isogawa – who always considered himself an outsider in Japan – arrived in Sydney in 1986 penniless, with no English and nothing but a working holiday visa.

After humble beginnings as a kitchenhand, tour guide and waiter, Isogawa enrolled in 1988 in East Sydney Tech's fashion course. That was the beginning. Since then, the reputation of his designs, a cross-cultural influence of East and West, has grown with the years. Today he is one of Australia's freshest and most innovative creators in the world of fashion.

choruses, special exhibitions, music and song performances. It also displays attractive demonstrations of *origami*, Japanese calligraphy and Japanese flower arrangements.

Further information: Ron Beeldman (tel: 9954 4824).

Sakura Matsuri (Cherry Blossom Festival).

In Japan this is a celebration of spring as cherry blossom trees bloom throughout Japan and the warmer season approaches. In October, the Japanese Garden in Cowra (see page 336) is the most popular venue for this festival that includes a wide range of activities, including tea ceremonies, *bonsai*, calligraphy, *origami*, pottery making and lots more. The Japanese Society of Sydney organises a bus trip to Cowra where weekend-long activities are held. For more information about this trip, contact the Society on 9267 3380.

Further information on the festival: 6341 2233.

'MIDORI NO HI' (JAPAN CONSTITUTION MEMORIAL DAY), held on May 3 to commemorate the promulgation of Japan's post-war peace constitution.

Matsuri Fiesta.

This traditional Japanese cultural festival, held mid-November, features a colourful street parade – with more than 600 participants – commencing at the steps of Sydney Town Hall. A cultural festival, featuring Japanese cuisine, arts and crafts, is held in Tumbalong Park, Darling Harbour. The Fiesta ends with a Fireworks Spectacular over Sydney Harbour. Highly recommended.

Kodomo no Hi (Children's Day).

Formerly called Boy's Day, this event is held on May 5 to celebrate good health for children.

Tenno Tanjobi (Japan Emperor's Birthday).

Held on December 23. In Japan this is a day when the impressive Imperial Palace is opened to the public.

Religious organisations and places of worship

Hongwanji Buddhist Mission of Australia.

The Mission was established in Sydney in 1993. It holds a service in Japanese every Sunday at 11am, and a Buddhist religious service in English at 11am and 2pm every second Sunday of the month. If you are interested in learning about aspects of Japanese culture, such as tea ceremonies, calligraphy, and Japanese Buddhism, this is the place to go. For further information speak to the very gentle Rev Kosho Inamoto.

4/36 Bydown Street, Neutral Bay (tel: 9904 1843).

Buddhist Society of NSW (Karuna Foundation).

The Society belongs to the Mahayana Buddhist tradition.

PO Box 89 North Sydney NSW 2060 (tel: 9929 8643).
Further information: Malcolm Pearce.

JAPANESE CULTURE ACADEMY. Located at the heart of the Sydney Japanese community, it offers a program of Japanese language and culture. Note that sometimes it's not easy to get through on the phone, so make an effort and try to understand the Japanese recorded message (part of your first lesson!)

1 Ellis Street, Chatswood (tel: 9415 1830).

Culture and education

Sydney Japanese School.

'One school two countries' is the motto of this unique school that provides classes in both the New South Wales and Japanese primary curricula. The school was started in 1969 on the combined initiative of the Sydney Japanese Society and the Japanese Consulate with the objective of providing education for the children of Japanese business people who were temporary residents in Australia. In the mid-1970s, the school decided to extend its program and offer the NSW curriculum to primary students, integrating the two strands of the school in extra-curricula areas such as art, music and sport. Open to everybody, the Sydney Japanese School offers the opportunity to combine the benefits of Australian schooling with the chance to learn Japanese language and culture.

112 Booralie Road, Terrey Hills (tel: 9450 1833).

Tokyo Language & Culture Centre.

Offers part-time courses in Japanese from beginners to proficiency Level 1. It has also a full-time program on Japanese language and hotel

Mitsu Shoji

CERAMICIST

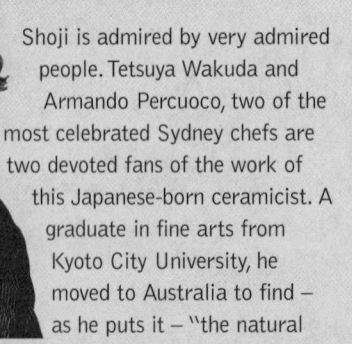

Shoji is admired by very admired people. Tetsuya Wakuda and Armando Percuoco, two of the most celebrated Sydney chefs are two devoted fans of the work of this Japanese-born ceramicist. A graduate in fine arts from Kyoto City University, he moved to Australia to find – as he puts it – "the natural life and a greater freedom for my craft". His work, based upon "our universal existence," has been exhibited at the Australian National Gallery and at the prestigious Faenza International Ceramics Museum in Italy. Shoji has also developed a successful career in teaching, at such prestigious institutions such as the California State University and The University of Sydney's College of Arts.

skills which includes work experience in Japan. For those wanting to get into business, the Centre holds seminars on how to 'understand your Japanese clients' expectations'.

97 Pacific Highway, North Sydney (tel: 9957 5050).

Community organisations and institutions

Japan Cultural Centre (The Japan Foundation).

The Japan Cultural Centre opened its doors in Sydney in 1992 with the aim of fostering and encouraging the knowledge and appreciation of Japanese culture in Australia (for details of activities, see page 337).

Level 14, 201 Miller Street, North Sydney (tel: 9954 0111).

Japanese Society of Sydney.

Founded in 1957, the Society is one of the oldest Japanese institutions in Sydney, and since its establishment has played a major role in promoting art, cultural and social activities in the community. It also organises an annual trip to the Cherry Blossom Festival in Cowra (see page 339).

29th Floor, 1 Market Street, Sydney (tel: 9267 3380).

Australia-Japan Society of NSW.

Established in 1968, the Society organises social and cultural activities in order to promote a better understanding between Japan and Australia. It also runs Japanese language classes.

Level 5, 225 Clarence Street, Sydney (tel: 9299 2242).

Japan International Senior Society of Australia.

The brainchild of Mr Yamaguchi, a Japanese who decided to retire in Australia, the Society was established in 1987. It organises social activities for Japanese people (or those married to a Japanese man or woman) over 55 years old. The membership fee is $25 for singles and $35 for couples. It meets once a month at Cherrybrook Community Centre.

Shepherds Lane, Cherrybrook (off Shepherds Drive).
Further information: Mr Yamaguchi (tel: 9484 2802).

Media

Newspapers

Nichigo Press Newspaper. This successful paper appeared for the first time in October 1977. Published monthly and issued at the beginning of each month, Nichigo Press is free of charge and is distributed through government bodies, travel agencies, hotels, restaurants, duty free shops, information centres, tour desks, grocery shops and schools. It claims a circulation of 20,000 per month and its 80 pages (sometimes 92) carry Japanese, Australian and world news, special features, sport and general events.

27 Boundary Street, Double Bay (tel: 9360 2280)

Radio

SBS Radio 2 FM, 97.7. Has a weekly hour-long program with local and international news and current affairs. Ideal for those mastering the Japanese language. Tuesday 10pm-11pm.

Television

SBS Television broadcasts the latest news from NHK Japanese Television, Tuesday-Saturday 6am-6.30am.

Facts and figures

Japanese settlement has a long history in Australia, going back to their significant presence in the north and northwest of the country early in the century. However, the most spectacular increases have come in the 1980s, with 11,195 being counted at the 1986 Census and 25,984 at the 1991 Census.

Japanese-born people constitute a relatively small immigrant group by Sydney standards, but one whose number have increased in recent years. In the 1991 Census there were around 25,984 Japanese living in the country, with Sydney having 9,587 of these.

As a substantial number of Japanese in Australia are business-related travellers, there is a large number (21.3%) in the highest income category, which compares with 11.1% for the national average. On the other hand, the temporary nature of the residency of Japanese people is reflected in the fact that only 37.5% own or are purchasing their own home, while 48% are renting privately.

Over 17% have a degree or diploma (the average is 12.7%). On the other hand only 4.7% have skilled and basic vocational qualifications, reflecting a low level of involvement in manual or vocational training.

Buddhist Sydney

In our frenetic society many people find meditation a means of calming the mind and coping with daily life. Many Australians are becoming attracted to Buddhism for this and other reasons.

Buddhism is in fact Australia's fastest-growing religion – currently there are almost 200,000 Buddhists across the country. This is a rapid increase from around 140,000 in 1991, and makes Buddhism the second largest non-Christian religion in the country, after Islam. If current trends continue, there will be more Buddhists than Muslims in Australia by 2001, when the next census will be conducted.

In Sydney all traditions of Buddhism are represented. The Chinese, Japanese, Korean and Vietnamese communities have established temples in the Mahayana tradition, while the Cambodian, Khmer Krom, Laotian, Sri Lankan and Thai communities have erected Theravada temples. One of the smallest ethnic groups, the Tibetans, has one of the largest number of Buddhist organisations; this is largely due to "western" followers being attracted to the Vajrayana teachings.

In Sydney – where there are 75 Buddhist temples – Buddhists tend to concentrate in the western suburb of Fairfield, a sector with a high degree of Indochinese refugee settlement, based around the Villawood Migrant Hostel. Other areas of Sydney with a strong Buddhist presence are the inner city areas of South Sydney, and Randwick in the eastern suburbs.

In Sydney all traditions of Buddhism are represented.

Events

These are some of the most important festivals celebrated by Sydney Buddhists. For specific information contact the Buddhist Council of New South Wales on 9669 3053 or relevant organisations in the chapters listed above.

Light Festival.

Held on the last weekend in October and beginning of November, this is one of the most popular Buddhist festivals. It commemorates the enlightenment of Lord Buddha and his subsequent descent to earth. Buddhist temples are the main venues.

FOR SPECIFIC INFORMATION on Buddhist temples, organisations, activities or other information see The Cambodians, page 273; The Chinese, page 293; The Japanese, page 339; The Koreans, page 354/5; The Laotians, page 358/9; The Thais, page 374; The Tibetans, page 368 and The Vietnamese, page 382.

Thingyan (Water Festival).

One of the high points of the Buddhist calendar, it marks the Buddhist New Year. This is a very spiritual occasion when Buddhists symbolically wash away – with water – the old year and get ready to receive the new one. It's also a time of feasting in which special meals are prepared.

Vesak Day.

In the Lunar Calendar, the month of *Vesak* usually corresponds to May in the Gregorian Calendar, and this is the time when the Theravadan Buddhists from Cambodia, Thailand, Sri Lanka, Burma and Laos celebrate the birth, enlightenment and death of Buddha. Temples scattered around Sydney are the main venues of this very significant festival. In the last few years, one of the most traditional places for this celebration has been the wonderful Chinese Garden at Darling Harbour. The festivities include a vegetarian food fair, free medical consultation and exhibitions of the traditions of Buddhism. The Buddhist Council organises a combined *Vesak* Celebration each year with diverse ethnic groups. In the past, *Vesak* has been celebrated at the *Nan Tien Temple*, in Wollongong. For further information call the Council on 9669 3053.

Saga Dawa.

This is the celebration of the birthday, enlightenment and *Parinirvana* of Lord Buddha by Buddhists from the Tibetan tradition. *Saga Dawa* falls on the 15th of the fourth month of the Tibetan Calendar.

Places of interest & landmarks

Nan Tien Buddhist Temple.

The biggest Buddhist temple in the southern hemisphere, the *Nan Tien Temple* (in Chinese it means "Paradise of the Southern Hemisphere") is located at Berkeley – a suburb of Wollongong – just two hours from Sydney. It's one of the branch temples of *Fo Kuang Shan*, which has over 120 branches worldwide. The Temple is today a major touristic attraction.

The Main Gate, which is the major gateway to the Temple, is also called the Mountain Gate. There are three openings to the gate, each with a meaning: liberation, wisdom, compassion. In the Front Shrine, also known as the Great Mercy Hall, you can see the statue of Kuan Yin, which – according to the Buddhist faith – helps release the sufferings of the people. Here a chanting service is held each weekend from 11:30am-noon. Meditation courses are held each Saturday afternoon and evening in the the Meditation Room – a very peaceful

The biggest Buddhist temple in the southern hemisphere, the Nan Tien Temple (in Chinese it means "Paradise of the Southern Hemisphere") is located at Berkeley – a suburb of Wollongong – just two hours from Sydney.

space which seats around 60 people. The Temple Museum also deserves a visit. Exhibitions are changed on a regular basis, and the works come from overseas, mainly China and Taiwan but not restricted to Buddhist artists. Nan Tien Temple is open to the public Tuesday-Sunday 9am-5pm.

Further information: 042 72 0600.

Education & Culture

There is no shortage of places to study Buddhism in Sydney. Several centres – many with well-resourced libraries – have been established. The following is a select list; see also the relevant chapters as mentioned above. For a more comprehensive directory of Buddhist centres contact the Buddhist Council of New South Wales on 9669 3053.

Buddhism Information Centre.

The Buddhist Council of New South Wales' Buddhism Information Centre is located at Eastlakes. The Centre has a large range of high quality Buddhist books, in both English and Chinese, which are distributed free of charge to Buddhist organisations and the public. At the Centre Buddhist organisations or *Dharma* teachers also run education programs, which are open to the public. Buddhist classes are held on the first and third Friday of the month at 7pm. All are welcome, for free, but donations are accepted.

Shop 82, BKK Shopping Centre, Evans Avenue, Eastlakes (tel 9669 3053).

Buddhist Library & Education Centre.

With its non-sectarian tradition, the Education Centre is a good place to explore Buddhism. It has introductory courses on Buddhism, given by very experienced teachers. The courses are free but donations are very welcome (say, $5). Contact Michael Dash and Justine Lee for information. The Centre also has a library with a wide range of Buddhist publications that can be borrowed by members only. Library membership is $30. The library is open Monday-Friday 10am-5pm, Saturday-Sunday 2-5pm.

90-92 Church Street, Camperdown (tel: 9519 6054, Hot Line 9519 8329).

There is no shortage of places to study Buddhism in Sydney.

Publications

Buddhism Today.

The journal, published quarterly, contains articles, news items and information on upcoming events. Its editor is Dr LS Ong. You will find articles by Master Sheng-yen, Apichato Bhikkhu, Abhinyana, Petr Karel Ontl and others. The cost is $3 per issue or $10 for a year's subscription.

Further information: 9498 8201.

Organisations

Buddhist Council of New South Wales.

Established in 1985, this umbrella organisation became a Regional Centre of the World Fellowship of Buddhists in 1992. Since its establishment, the Council has worked closely with the Department of Immigration in creating better understanding of the specific needs of the local Buddhist community, and the result has been easing of visa restrictions for Buddhist teachers. Due to growing media exposure, the Council has also become an important source of information and opinion for journalists. In 1995, the Council set up the Buddhist Council's Buddhism Information Centre at Eastlakes.

The Koreans

There are two unmistakable truths about the Sydney Koreans. First: around 15 years ago, Campsie – in Sydney's south west – was an unappealing suburb, and a symbol of urban decay. It had potential, however as it was on the railway line, not far from the City, and property in the area was cheap.

Don Moon, one of the first Koreans to migrate to Sydney – and now a millionaire – foresaw the potential. He moved there and encouraged his fellow Koreans to follow him. They did, and Campsie is now a different tale – the streets bustle with commercial activities and its vibrant urban kaleidoscope well deserves the unofficial name of 'Korea Town' (see Campsie, Korea Town, page 350).

Second: from the 1970s no other ethnic group has established as many churches as Koreans have during this period. Koreans are three times more likely to attend church than the average Australian, and currently there are more than 100 Korean congregations. In Sydney there are at least 14 Korean Protestant churches, one Catholic church and various Buddhist temples. The largest are the Presbyterian, the Uniting and the Yoido Full Gospel Churches (a brand of Pentecostal faith). The biggest Korean Uniting Church congregation is the Sydney Cheil Uniting Church in the suburb of Concord, with an average Sunday attendance of 1,500.

Religion was in fact the first point of contact between Australia and Korea. It dates back to 1885 when Australian-Protestant missionaries began visiting Korea. Years later, between 1921 and 1941 a handful of Koreans were brought into Australia by some of those missionaries (Presbyterian and Uniting Church) for study or training.

But it was only in the mid-1980s that Koreans began turning up on Australian shores in large numbers. By 1991, the number of Koreans in Australia had increased substantially to more than twice the 1986 figure. Like the Japanese, a large number of the Koreans living here are associated with business, trade and investment, so Sydney – Australia's centre of international commerce – has been the focus of Korean settlement.

Credited with turning Sydney's once run-down Campsie into the bustling 'Korea Town' of today, Don Moon (who anglicised his name Dong to Don) began running one of the first Korean shops in Sydney. He also worked in wool-buying houses and then went into business with his company Sunmoon Pty Ltd. Don now lives on the North Shore and is the owner of a multi-million dollar textile retailing and duty free empire.

One of those Koreans is Choi Chang Gurl, Korea's biggest single investor in Australia. But Choi, with his $2 billion zinc mining company, operates just one of several Korean businesses in Australia. Each week, around 2,000 Hyundais, Daewoos and Kias reach our ports. Students and tourists are also coming in. It is estimated that each year some 10,000 Korean students enrol in Australia universities and every week around 3,800 Korean tourists visit the country. Korea is the second largest market for Australia's products, after Japan, and there is no doubt that Korean immigrants, with their demonstrated entrepreneurial skills, are an important asset for Australia's profitable relationship with Korea.

Restaurants

In many aspects Korean cuisine is a combination of Japanese and Chinese food traditions, though it tends to be spicier than either of these. The hotness comes chiefly from chilli, and other common spices are sesame and ginger. The staple food of Koreans is rice (*bap*), and rice noodles (*chapche*) and bean curd (*duboo*) are also consumed daily. One of the most distinctive aspects of Korean cuisine is its way of pickling instead of cooking vegetables – it's called *kimchi*. Koreans are likely to eat *kimchi* every day of the year, commonly for breakfast, lunch, and dinner. The following is a group of selected Korean restaurants outside Campsie.

Mukunghwa restaurant at 36 Glebe Point Road, Glebe.

Central Court Restaurant. At the heart of the growing Crows Nest Japanese community, this is a key place for *bulgogi* (beef marinated in soy sauce, garlic and onions) and *bibimbap* (an eclectic mix of vegetables, grilled beef and bean shoots topped by an egg). Average $15, BYO. Open for lunch Monday-Saturday 11am-3pm, dinner Monday 5pm-11.30pm.

382 Pacific Highway, Crows Nest (tel: 9966 8855).

Il Mee. The decor is not fancy but the friendly ambiance and the quality of the food make this place highly recommended – just try the *bulgogi*. Average $15, BYO. Open for lunch Monday-Friday noon-3pm, dinner Monday-Sunday 5pm-10.30pm.

306 Penshurst Street, Willoughby (tel: 9417 1363).

Jingogae. A generous portion of *kimchi* welcomes you while flicking the pages of the extensive menu. Try either the marinated beef, pork or seafood fares. Average $10, BYO. Open for lunch Monday-Friday 11.30am-2.30pm, dinner Monday-Sunday 6pm till late.

57 Ridge Street, North Sydney (tel: 9955 1484).

Mukunghwa. When we went here a friendly Mexican waiter (a traveller, so we're not sure whether he's still there) picked up that we spoke Spanish and advised us in Spanish what to order. How's that for a cultural mix? (He suggested the *bibimpap*, by the way. The portions of *kimchi* are also very generous). We suggest you sit in the charming back courtyard. Average $15, BYO and licensed. Open for lunch and dinner Friday-Sunday 11am-11pm, Saturday 8am-11pm.

36 Glebe Point Road, Glebe (tel: 9660 0744).

Yeodo. Where Korea meets Japan (Koreans rely less on fish and seafood), this is a well-established place with an extensive array of seafood, noodle dishes, marinated and grilled beef, and spare ribs. Average $20, licensed. Open for lunch Monday-Friday noon-3pm, dinner Monday-Sunday 6pm-11pm.

197 Military Road, Neutral Bay (tel: 9953 8979).

Shopping

Asian Savour Grocery. A North Shore grocery stocking a wide range of Korean products, including *kimchi* and prepared dishes. Open Monday-Sunday 8.30am-8pm (till 8.30pm on Thursday).

468-470 Victoria Avenue, Chatswood (tel: 9419 4748).

City Grocery & Video. The Sydney CBD's first Korean mini-supermarket, it stocks a huge range of Korean products, including snacks, spices, fresh vegetables and kimchi. Check out the fridge packed with fresh Korean take-away salads. Open Monday-Sunday 10am-9pm.

389 Pitt Street, City (tel: 9267 4217).

Chosun. The Korean-born Young-ah Rose, one of the owners of Chosun Gallery, and her husband Noel have made this charming place a doorway to appreciating traditional Korean furniture and artefacts. It also has Chinese and Japanese furniture. Open Monday-Sunday 9.30am-5.30pm.

993 Pacific Highway, Pymble (tel: 9488 9298).

For more shopping see Campsie: Korea Town, page 350

RELAXATION CENTRE.

You wouldn't be blamed for thinking otherwise at the sight of a sauna house in Kings Cross – but believe it or not it's genuine. This traditional Korean bath-house is a great place to drop in to alleviate those aching muscles and stressed mind. Here you can get good skin scrubs, body massages, wet and dry saunas. Complete the treat with a delicious Korean soup in the dining area. Massage with facial costs $40 per half hour, Shiatsu massage $40 per half hour, body exfoliation $25. Open Monday-Sunday 10am-10pm.

Hotel Capital,
11 Darlinghurst,
Kings Cross
(tel: 9358 2755).

GETTING THERE

By train, City/Campsie (on the Bankstown line).

Campsie, Sydney's "Korea Town"

Known as "Korea Town," Campsie – 13 kms southwest of the Sydney CBD – was until not long ago an unlikely place to visit. Until the area began filling with Koreans in the early years of the 1980s.

Most were following the advice of Don Moon, one of the earliest and most financially successful Sydney Koreans. A man with vision, Moon saw the many good things of Campsie – then a dilapidated suburb – it was close to the city, on the train line and the property was cheap.

The advice was heard and the entrepreneurial and resourceful Koreans began buying commercial properties along Beamish Street – the main drag – that today bustles with the activities of restaurants, supermarkets, groceries, commercial and financial offices. It's estimated that Campsie (named after the hilly district of Campsie in Stirlingshire, Scotland) is home to around 3,000 Koreans a number that rises – although temporarily – with the arrival of regular tour buses carrying dozens of Korean tourists. It's here that they purchase gifts and souvenirs. Campsie is also an immaculately clean suburb, and a lot is due to the "grannies" – a group of Korean elders who every Thursday at 2pm, dressed in a hat, blue aprons and equipped with rubbish bags clean up the streets of the 'hood with admirable commitment.

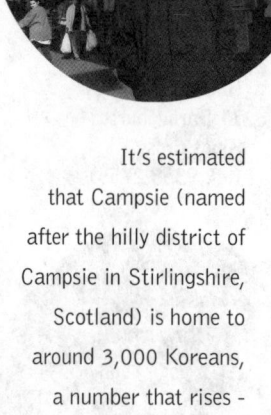

It's estimated that Campsie (named after the hilly district of Campsie in Stirlingshire, Scotland) is home to around 3,000 Koreans, a number that rises - although temporarily – with the arrival of regular tour buses carrying dozens of Korean tourists.

Restaurants

1: Pojan Macha. Always with a busy, lively and bustling night atmosphere. Pojan Macha is where the local Koreans hang out eating, talking and drinking. A real experience. Average $15, licensed. Open Monday-Sunday 5pm- 2am.
Unara Lane (tel: 9787 1811).

2: Cha San Hi Cool Noodle House. This small and unpretentious Korean spot has developed a good reputation through its delicious *bulgalbi* (marinated beef) and noodles in beef broth. Average $15, BYO. Open Monday-Saturday 11am-pm (close on Tuesday), Sunday 1-9pm.
347 Beamish Street (tel: 9718 6969).

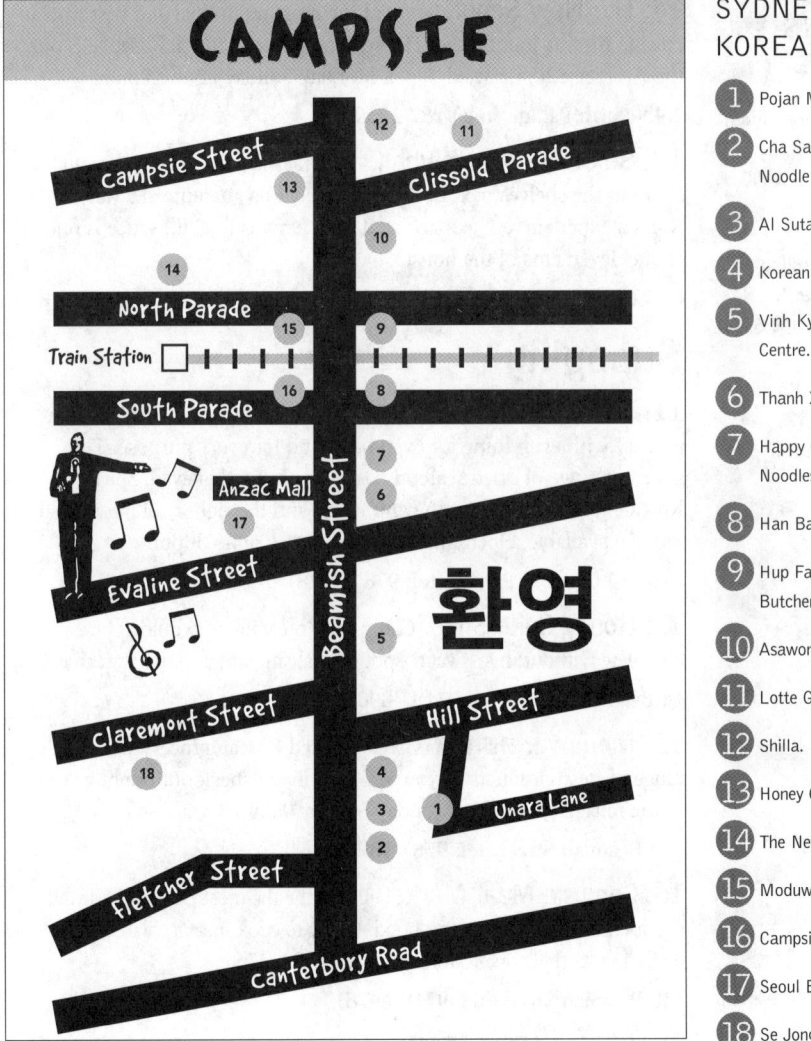

CAMPSIE

SYDNEY'S KOREAN TOWN

1. Pojan Macha.
2. Cha San Hi Cool Noodle House.
3. Al Sutan Halal Meats.
4. Korean Village.
5. Vinh Ky Asian Food Centre.
6. Thanh Xuan.
7. Happy Chef Seafood and Noodles Restaurant.
8. Han Bat Restaurant.
9. Hup Fatt Groceries and Butchery.
10. Asawon.
11. Lotte Groceries.
12. Shilla.
13. Honey Cake Shop.
14. The New Seoul.
15. Moduwa.
16. Campsie Meat Market.
17. Seoul Ban Jan.
18. Se Jong Hwai Kwhan.

10: Asawon. One of the longest running Korean eateries in Sydney, Asawon has a solid and well deserved reputation - *bulgogi* is one of the highlights. Average $20, licensed. Open Monday-Sunday 11am-10pm.
179 Beamish Street (tel: 9718 7132).

12: Shilla. This is one of the favourite night hang outs for Sydney Koreans, the atmosphere created by the interrupted buzz of conversation, the good food and the Karaoke which make Shilla a fun place to visit.
161 Beamish Street (tel: 9718 1029).

CHECK THIS ALSO OUT...

Mi Rak. Who cares about the decoration!! – the bottom line is you want good and generous portions of food, nice people and a "smiling" price. This is what Mi Rak is all about. Average $10, BYO.

371 Canterbury Road (tel: 9718 0120).

14: The New Seoul. Some of the most traditional and best Korean cuisine is to be found here. The seafood platter with chilli sauce is our tip. Average $20, licensed. Open Monday-Sunday noon-10pm.

2/43 North Parade (tel: 9787 3259).

18: Se Jong Hwai Kwhan. After taking off and leaving your shoes in the shelves next to the entry, you'll be guaranteed a fully-Korean experience. The marinated king prawns in chilli sauce is one of the achievements of the house.

68-72 Evaline Street (tel: 9718 4039).

Shopping

11: Lotte Groceries. A well stocked and highly praised Korean grocery with everything for everybody and for every purpose. The amazing range of dried seafood has to be seen to believed. Spices, Korean soft drinks, ready to cook meals and the right cooking utensils are also available. Open Monday-Sunday 8.30am-9.30pm.

115-117 Clissold Parade (tel: 9787 3128).

13: Honey Cake Shop. Campsie "Korea Town" wouldn't be complete without this "sweet" spot specialising in tempting Korean cakes.

74 Beamish Street (tel: 9718 3090).

15: Moduwa. This is very well stocked Korean grocery with a full range of fresh products. If you're a *kimchi fan*, check out the huge range in the refrigerator. Open Monday-Sunday 9am-8.30pm.

156 Beamish Street (tel: 9787 1886).

16: Campsie Meat Market. By far the the most popular and well regarded butcher shop in the 'hood. Ready to cook meat available, yep including *bulgogi*. Open Monday-Saturday 8am-7pm.

158 Beamish Street (tel: 9718 1478).

3: Al Sutan Halal Meats.

343 Beamish Street (tel: 9718 0025).

4: Korean Village.

341 Beamish Street (tel: 9718 7059).

5: Vinh Ky Asian Food Centre.

321 Beamish Street (tel: 9787 3757).

6: Thanh Xuan. Vietnamese and Chinese cuisine.

269 Beamish Street (tel: 9718 2427).

7: Happy Chef Seafood and Noodles Restaurant.
233 Beamish Street (tel: 9718 8516).

8: Han Bat Restaurant.
201 Beamish Street (tel: 9787 2546).

9: Hup Fatt Groceries and Butchery.
199 Beamish Street (tel: 9787 4932).

17: Seoul Ban Jan. Korean restaurant and take away.
Anzac Mall off Beamish Street (tel: 9789 4566).

Getting to know the Korean community

Events

Korea Independence Movement.

On March 1 Koreans commemorate the beginning of the Independence Movement against the Japanese occupation (1904-1945) led by a small group of Christians. Over the years, the Independence Movement has held peaceful ceremonies and demonstrations to remember the violation of civil and human rights during the years of Japanese rule. From a small group, the movement has grown to now include the majority of the Korean population. In Sydney, most Koreans celebrate this day in informal events. The Korean Parish of the Uniting Church, at 98-102 Albert Road, Strathfield, celebrates this day with a memorial service followed by a small informal gathering for refreshments.

Further information: Rev Dr Sang Taek Lee (tel: 9642 3518).

Korea Day is celebrated on September 9.

Children's Day.

This event is designed to celebrate children and wish them future happiness. It takes place on May 5 and is organised by the Korean Parish of the Uniting Church.

For information, contact the Parish on the number given above.

LIBERATION DAY.
August 15 is a day when Koreans remember the end of the Japanese occupation in 1945. An annual memorial service is held at the Korean Parish of the Uniting Church. Other Korean community organisations also have diverse activities.

We suggest contacting the Korean Society of Sydney (tel: 9718 2288) for further information.

Sydney has over 14,000 Korean-born residents.

Korea Day.

Usually celebrated in Korea on October 3, in Sydney it is celebrated on September 9. The Korean Society of Sydney holds a celebration at Gough Whitlam Park in Arncliffe, near Tempe Station. The celebration features food stalls, information sessions, and traditional dancing, music and songs.

Further information: Korean Society of Sydney (tel: 9718 2288 or 9718 8297).

The following are Buddhist events organised by the *Won* Buddhism of Australia Association and held at the *Won* Buddhist Temple, 474 Burwood Road, Belmore. For further information, contact the Association on 9750 5669 (Cassie Lee is a lawyer who plays the role of public relations officer for the Association and we can guarantee that she is extremely helpful in providing information about *Won* Buddhism).

Dae Gak Ge Gyo Jul (Festival of Great Enlightenment).

This festival is held on April 28 to celebrate the enlightenment of the Great Master and creator of Won Buddhism, *Sotaesan*. It is the most important annual event for Won Buddhists and this occasion is also used to celebrate the birth of *Sotaesan* as well as the birthday of all members of the Won Buddhist faith.

Dae Jae (June the First Commemoration Day).

Sotaesan passed away on June 1 1943. Every year on this date a religious service is held to honour his memory and also that of all Won Buddhists and their ancestors and family members, as well as all other lives.

Shin Jung Jul (New Year's Day Festival).

Every year on January 1, Won Buddhists celebrate *Shin Jung Jul* by paying their respect to *Dharmakaya* and their teachers, exchanging best wishes with their fellows, reviewing the past year, making plans for the new year, and offering prayers for future prosperity.

Religious organisations and places of worship

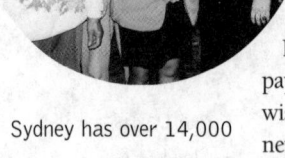

In contrast to the religious profile in Korea – where Confucianism, *Mahayana Buddhism*, ancestor worship, *Shamanism* and *Ch'ondogyo* are practised by the majority of the population – in Australia most Koreans identify themselves as Christians and fewer than 3% as non-Christians (mostly Buddhists).

Korean Uniting Church. Holds a regular service in Korean on Sunday at 11am. Contact Rev Dr Sang Taek Lee for further information.

75 Wallis Avenue, Strathfield (tel: 9642 3518).

Korean Catholic Community Church.

6 Asquith Street, Silverwater (tel: 9748 0712).

Korean Central Presbyterian Church.

72 Burwood Road, Belfield (tel: 9642 3149).

Korean Sydney Evangelical Holiness Church. Religious services are held on weekdays and weekends. Call for additional information.

15 Cowells Lane, Ermington (tel: 9874 9111).

Korean Buddhist Society of Australia. Provides religious and welfare services.

538 Woodville Road (tel: 9892 1190).

Community organisations

Korean Society of Sydney. Provides information and support for members of the Sydney Korean community. It also advocates and lobbies on behalf of the Korean community.

7 Wairoa Street, Canterbury (tel: 9718 2288).

14 First Avenue, Campsie (tel: 9787 4969).

Korean Welfare Association. The Association provides welfare and social assistance to Sydney Koreans.

85 Concord Road, Concord (tel: 9746 9001).

Media

Newspapers

Dae Yang Chu News (Korea-Oceania Business Review). This monthly publication began in Canberra in 1989 and moved to Sydney one year later. It covers community and business news, and information for Korean immigrants. With a circulation of 8,000, this free paper can be picked up in most of Sydney's Korean shops and restaurants. The publisher is Chung-Yup Kim.

PO Box 77A, Strathfield 2135 (tel: 9744 7997).

KOREAN BUDDHIST TEMPLES

BO MOON SA TEMPLE.
In the Mahayana tradition. Abbot: Bop Il Sunim.
40 Norval Street, Auburn (tel: 9643 2216).

BO MOON SA TEMPLE.
Abbot: Bop Il Sunim.
30 Meredith Street, Bankstown
(tel: 9790 0919).

JONG BOP TEMPLE.
Abbot: Ven. Ki Hu Sunim.
2 Elliott Street, Belfield
(tel: 9642 7672).

KWANEUM TEMPLE.
Abbot: Venerable Jeong Oh Sunim.
50 Highclere Avenue, Punchbowl
(tel: 9750 8033).

Ho ju Dong-A. The only daily Korean newspaper in Sydney, it offers a very good coverage of news from Korea (the stories are filed from Seoul), and is a must-buy paper for those eager to get in touch with the Sydney Korean scene. It has a circulation of 2,000 issues on weekdays and 7,000 issues on Saturday, and can be found in most of Sydney's Korean shops and restaurants at a cost of $2. The editor is Seng Kim.

Suite 201/418a Elizabeth Street, City (tel: 9281 8000).

Radio

SBS Radio 1, AM 1170. News, current affairs and community announcements in Korean. Tuesday and Friday 10pm-11pm, Thursday 2pm-3pm, Sunday 3pm-4pm.

For more information on Korean-language radio programs contact Korean Broadcasting Australia, Suite 101/388 George Street, City (tel: 018 602 449).

Facts and figures

Almost all Koreans who have chosen to settle or study in Australia are from South Korea (Republic of Korea). According to the 1991 Census only 45 persons in Australia reported their birthplace as North Korea (Democratic People's Republic of Korea)

Since the mid-1980s, Korean immigration to Australia has increased substantially. In 1981 there were 4,514 Korean immigrants — a number that stretched to 20,997 by the 1991 Census. Sydney, with 15,109, is the focus of the Australian Korean settlement. Only about 41% of Korean immigrants have taken up Australian citizenship, a rate relatively low when compared to the percentage for all overseas-born people (61.4%).

Koreans have a lower proportion of income earners in the highest category than the Australia-born population and a greater representation in the lower income range. Their median annual income is $11,100 which is much lower than the Australian average ($14,200). However, Koreans do have a higher rate with a degree or diploma (14.4%) than the Australia-born (12.7%). Around 47.1% of Koreans own or are purchasing their own home, which is substantially lower than the national average. The socioeconomic disadvantage of Koreans — their relatively high unemployment, lower annual income and house ownership — is explained to a large extent by the fact that it is the youngest immigrant community in the country.

The 1991 Census showed that 15,245 Korean-born persons older than five speak a language other than English at home. Of this number, 92.5% speak Korean, 0.3% speak Mandarin and 0.2% Japanese.

The Laotians

Laos is a country whose fate has been closely linked to that of its neighbours – China to the north, Vietnam to the east, Cambodia to the south, Thailand and Burma to the west. Until the mid-1970s, when Indochina was taken over by communist rulers, Laotians hardly ever emigrated overseas. But that situation rapidly changed.

Prior to 1976 – when a group of 200 Laotian refugees arrived in Sydney – there were only 188 Laotians in Australia, all studying here under the Colombo Plan. In the years that followed, the Laotian community experienced a steady growth. Currently there are almost 10,000 in Australia, and Sydney is by far the most popular place to begin a new life, with about 5,700 living here. In Sydney they have fanned out across the western suburbs of Liverpool and Fairfield where migration hostels and public housing are located and private rental costs are low.

The Laotian community, the smallest of the groups from the former Indochina in Australia, is made up of several groups, including ethnic Chinese, ethnic Vietnamese, ethnic Cambodians, *Tai Dam*, *Khmu* and a small *Hmong* community based in the western suburb of Bonnyrigg. They have tended to establish community enclaves sharing religious beliefs and family or ethnic ties. Sydney Laotian community organisations include several welfare and religious associations. The oldest organisation in Sydney is the Lao Community Advancement Co-operative in Cabramatta. Most Laotian immigrants, like the Thai, are Buddhists of the Theravada sect. For a long time Laotian Buddhists relied upon the premises of the already-established Sydney Thai Buddhist *wats* (temples) for their ceremonies, but in 1989 when their own temple – the *Wat Prayot Keo* – was built at Edensor Park in Sydney's west, one of the long-held dreams of this small community came true.

> The Laotian community, the smallest of the groups from the former Indochina in Australia, is made up of several groups, including ethnic Chinese, ethnic Vietnamese, ethnic Cambodians, *Tai Dam, Khmu* and a small *Hmong* community based in the Sydney western suburb of Bonnyrigg.

Restaurants

Lao Refreshment II. For an authentic Laotian cuisine experience try this place located at the heart of the Sydney Vietnamese and Cambodian community. Try the very tasty spicy *laap* (beef salad with generous portion of chilli, mint leaves, onion and lime juice). Average

USEFUL NUMBER FOR VISITORS

LAOS EMBASSY:
tel: (06) 286 6933.

There is a lot of similarity between Laotian and Thai cuisine – fresh vegetables, meats and seafoods are ever-present. All meals are eaten with rice or with the typical Laotian *furr* (noodles) prepared as a soup flavoured with pork, garlic and a number of herbs – including leaves of marijuana! (don't get excited, it's not used in Australia).

$10 (no alcohol allowed). Open Monday-Sunday 11am-9pm (we're told that sometimes it opens at noon).
148 Cabramatta Road, Cabramatta (tel: 9727 2563).

Song Fang Khong. Here alcohol is allowed and the menu is authentically Laotian (don't forget the tradition of grabbing a small fistful of sticky rice, rolling it into a ball and dipping it into the side dish sauce). Average $10, BYO. Open Monday-Sunday 11am-9pm.
7 Anzac Parade Avenue, Fairfield (tel: 9728 4552).

Getting to know the Laotian community

Events

Back in Laos most festivals are related to agricultural seasons and Buddhist religious celebrations. In Sydney the Laotian community celebrates the majority of Buddhist festivals (see page 343), including the following:

Magha Puja.

Celebrated on May 5, it commemorates a speech given by Buddha to more than 1,000 enlightened monks. Main events are held at the Laotian Buddhist temples, and activities include chanting and lighting of candles inside the wats. For further information contact the wats listed below.

That Luang Festival.

This is a colourful event that takes place in November when Laotians monks receive donations and floral gifts. The festival – held in the Sydney Laotians temples – features music and candles. For further information contact the wats listed below.

Religious organisations and places of worship

Buddhism is deeply ingrained in the cultural and social fabric of Laotian people. Most Laotians are Therevada Buddhist, but the *Khamu* and *Hmong* Laotians practise animism and ancestral worship.

Wat Prayotkeo (Temple).

711-715 Smithfield Road, Edensor Park (tel: 9823 7338).

Wat Lao Buddhist Society of NSW (Wat Prayortkeo).
Abbot: Ven. Chanti Souphanthavong.
442 Smithfield Road, Bonnyrigg (tel: 9823 7338).

Wat Buddhalavarn Forest Monastery. A meditation and retreat centre. Abbot: Ven. Thongsoun Phantaoudom.
Lot 12 Minerva Road, Wedderburn (tel: (046) 341 200).

Wat Lao Buddhametta. Abbot: Ven. Souroth Vongcharath.
1 Fitzroy Close, St. Johns Park (tel: 9610 3608).

Media

Newspapers

Khao Lao. Published monthly on the sixteenth of the month, it has a small circulation of 400. The current editor is Nina Long.
PO Box 517 Cabramatta 517 (tel: 9823 1227).

Radio

SBS Radio 1, FM 97.7. News, music and community announcements. Monday 10am-11am.

COMMUNITY ORGANISATIONS

LAO COMMUNITY ADVANCEMENT.
The main community body of Sydney Laotians, it provides social, welfare and cultural assistance.
24 Lovoni Street,
Cabramatta
(tel: 9724 1951).

Facts and figures

The Laotians form in Australia the smallest community from the former Indochina. By 1986 there were 7,438 Laotians living here, and the number grew to 10,800 by 1993. Currently Sydney has a population of 5,697 Laotians.

In terms of education, Laotians show a low level of qualifications — only 5.9% have a diploma or degree compared to the Australian average of 12.7%, and only 3.4% have some skilled or basic vocational training compared with 13.9% for the whole population. The economic profile of Laotians clearly shows this lack of qualifications. Very few Laotians are in the highest income category (2.2% earn $35,000 or more) and they're disproportionately represented in the lowest income bracket (59.8% earn $16,000 or less). This situation is also mirrored by the substantially lower rate of house ownership among Laotians (51.5%) when compared with the Australian average (68.2%).

The majority of Laotians living in New South Wales are Therevada Buddhists (76.8%), and there is also a small Catholic community (5.3%). Of Laotian immigrants living in New South Wales, 90.7% speak the official language of their homeland, Lao.

Laotian migration to Australia started towards the end of 1975 following the Vietnam war and the communist victory in Vietnam, Cambodia and Laos. In Sydney, the Laotian community is concentrated in the south-western suburbs of Fairfield, Liverpool and Campbelltown.

The Malaysians

It was the great American comedian Bob Hope who said "every time I think of going to Australia, I think of one man, Kamahl." For nearly four decades Malaysian-born Kamahl has been one of the most loved recording stars in Australian music history. To use a phrase Kamahl himself coined, he has "done alright for an FBA" (foreign-born Australian) in a country reluctant to accept Asian entertainers.

Sydney Malaysians have established a youthful and vibrant community in the eastern suburbs of Kensington and Randwick, around the University of New South Wales.

Malaysians are not new to Australia. They have been visiting our shores for nearly 300 years, coming mainly to the northern and north-western coasts to work in the pearling and trepang industries. Temporary communities of Malaysians living from pearling were found in Port Darwin, Thursday Island and Broom, and it was here where one of the first mosques in Australia was established, just after World War II. By 1947 there were 1,768 Malays living in Australia.

The first significant experience that Malaysians had of Australia was as overseas students under the Colombo Plan. As a matter of fact, the largest single group of the 17,000 overseas students who came during 1959 and 1976 were Malaysians. The Colombo Plan marked the starting point for the permanent presence of Malaysian students attending Australian educational centres – one very welcomed by cash-strapped local universities. Today, it is estimated that 120,000 Malaysian students have completed their studies here and 12,000 are currently enrolled in Australian educational institutions.

At the end of the 1960s the Malaysian government introduced a social program called the New Economic Policy (NEP). This policy of affirmative action in favour of the ethnic Malays and indigenous groups tended, however, to marginalise many Chinese Malaysians. They opted to immigrate. As many as 80% of Malaysian immigrants in the past fifteen years have been ethnic Chinese.

Currently, there are around 84,000 Malaysians living in Australia and about 17,000 have settled in Sydney, where they have established a young and vibrant community in the eastern suburbs of Kensington and

Singer and humanitarian Kamahl

Explore the world in one city

Randwick (along with the Indonesian community). In Randwick, Malay and Indonesian are the most spoken non-English languages and the largest number of Asian students at the nearby University of New South Wales are from Malaysia.

Malaysians constitute one of the most economically well off ethnic communities in Sydney, and this reflects the general Malaysian immigration experience in Australia. Many are highly educated professionals and highly motivated to succeed (witness the wonderful restoration of the Queen Victoria Building by the Malaysian company Ipoh Garden, which was also responsible for the superb restoration of the Capitol Theatre).

Restaurants

'Inexpensive and diverse' best describes Sydney's Malaysian restaurants. *Satay, char kway teow* (flat rice noodles stir-fired with garlic and seafood) and the timeless curry *laksa* are some of the treats that you will find in Sydney's Malaysian eateries.

Andy's. Basic decor – nothing whatsoever to distract you from the inexpensive and excellent food. Average $20, BYO. Open for lunch Saturday-Sunday noon-3pm, dinner Tuesday-Sunday 6pm-10.30pm.

658 Bourke Street, Redfern (tel: 9319 6616).

A Taste of Malaysia. Here you can order from the basic dishes displayed in a bain-marie or from the extensive menu. The food is good and you can eat in or take it home. Average $10, BYO. Open for lunch Tuesday-Sunday 11.30am-2.30pm, dinner Tuesday-Thursday and Sunday 5.30pm-10pm, Friday and Saturday 5.30pm-11pm.

142 Avoca Street, Randwick (tel: 9399 3309).

Jalan Sehala. From curry *laksa* to *nasi goreng* (fried rice with bits of meat, prawns, egg and vegetables), the menu is extensive, authentic and tasty. Average $15, BYO. Open Wednesday-Monday from 5.30pm.

194 Enmore Road, Enmore (tel: 9516 2129).

Malay. Patronised by an eclectic clientele of business types and some loyal academics from the nearby University of Technology, Malay has one of the best prawn *laksas* around town – wash it down with a chilled Tiger beer. Average $15, licensed. Open for lunch Monday-Sunday
noon-3pm, dinner 5pm-10pm (till 9pm on Sunday).

761 George Street, Broadway (tel: 9211 0946).

KAMAHL TRACES

his ancestary back to Sri Lanka and began calling Australia home as a teenager. Apart from his musical achievements, Kamah has been strongly involved in humanitarian causes recognised with the Order of Australia.

Kamahl's success story has been followed by his daughter Rani and his son Rajan. Rani is one of the emerging singer/songwriters in the country. Nominated in the "best new talent" category in the 1997's ARIA awards, Rani made her singing debut aged five when she ran on stage while Kamahl was performing at the Opera House.

Rajan Kamahl is one of Australia's most talented young composers and has written music for countless television commercials. Most recently, he has been studying in Los Angeles with Emmy Award winning composer Mike Post.

Getting to know the Malaysian community

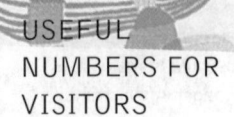

USEFUL NUMBERS FOR VISITORS

MALAYSIAN CONSULATE:
tel: 9327 7565.

MALAYSIA TOURISM PROMOTION BOARD:
tel: 9299 4441.

Seri Nonya. It features a mouthwatering array of authentically prepared Malaysian cuisine. Average $20, BYO. Open for lunch Wednesday-Sunday 11.30am-2.30pm, dinner Tuesday-Sunday 5.30pm-10pm.

561 The Kingsway, Miranda (tel: 9525 0036).

Temasek. Here you will find a range of Malaysian dishes – from spicy and savoury to sweet – to tantalise your tastebuds. Average $15, BYO. Open for lunch Tuesday-Sunday 11.30am-2.30pm, dinner 5.30pm-10pm.

The Roxy Arcade, 71 George Street, Parramatta (tel: 9633 9926).

To's Malaysian Gourmet. Don't be discouraged by the take-away and the low-key look, the quality of the food is what matters here. Average $10, BYO. Open Monday-Wednesday 11am-6pm, Thursday-Friday 11am-7pm, Saturday 11.30am-3pm.

181 Miller Street, North Sydney (tel: 9955 2088).

SHOPPING

RANDWICK ORIENTAL. Like most of the shops scattered along Sydney's eastern suburbs of Kingsford, Randwick and Kensington, this place has an impressive display of fresh and imported products from Malaysian, Indonesian and neighbouring Asian countries. Open Monday-Saturday 8.30am-7pm (till 8.30pm on Thursday), Sunday 8.30am-6pm.

61 Belmore Road, Randwick
(tel: 9398 2192).

Events

Food Fair.

Sydney's Malaysian and Singaporean communities host this annual food fair in September or October. Recently it has been held at Don Moore Community Centre, corner of North Rocks Road and Farnell Avenue, Carlingford. Expect to taste treats such as satay, *laksa*, *roti*, *chania* and *kueh*.

Further information: 9299 4441.

Malaysia Fest.

This is a very colourful festival held each year in September. Among the program and activities visitors can look forward to are handicraft demonstrations, cuisine of Malaysia's different regions and traditional music. Recently the event has been held at Tumbalong Park, Darling Harbour. Entry is free.

Further information: 9399 9970.

Explore the world in one city

Religious organisations and places of worship

Australian Buddhist Mission. The Mission belongs to the Theravada Malaysian tradition. Its president is Gary Chan.
16 Woodhouse Drive, Ambarvale (tel: 4626 7420).

COMMUNITY ORGANISATIONS

MALAY AUSTRALIAN ASSOCIATION OF NSW. The peak organisation for the Sydney Malaysian community.

156 Eastern Avenue, Kingsford
(tel: 9622 4750).

Facts and figures

The Malaysia-born population is one of the largest and fastest-growing Asian communities in the country. The 1991 Census recorded 71,665 Malaysians in Australia – a 54% growth from 1986 – and Sydney, after Melbourne, has the second largest Malaysian community in the country (17,474). The majority of Malaysian immigrants are of Chinese ethnic origin (around 60%). Malaysians have a relatively low citizenship rate (45.1%).

The proportion of Malaysian immigrants with qualifications (52.2%) is considerably higher than the rate for the total Australian population (38.8%). The high level of qualifications is well reflected in the fact that Malaysians form one of the most economically well-off groups in Australia. The number in the highest income brackets is considerably larger than that of Australia-born people. Malaysians in Australia have a median annual income of $16,300, considerably higher than the Australian average. The fact that the proportion of Malaysians owning their own home is slightly lower (67%) than the level of the Australia-born (68.2%) is explained by the proportion of young people in the community.

Chinese languages are the most common spoken by local Malaysians (55.7%), while 8.6% speak Indonesian/Malay, and 1.8% Tamil. In terms of religion – given that the largest majority of Malaysian immigrants are ethnic Chinese and Indians – Christianity and Buddhism are the most popular religions among local Malaysians. Just over 43% of Malaysians identify themselves as Christians, while 17.6% are Buddhists. There is also a small percentage (2.9%) who follow Islam.

The arrival of Malaysian students to Australia – between 1959 and 1976 – marked the beginning of a significant flow of Malaysians to our shores, which has continued to the present.

The Nepalese and Tibetans

The Nepalese-born Tashi Tenzing has reason to be proud. Now an Australian citizen and a Sydney resident, Tashi Tenzing is the grandson of Tenzing Norgay – who in 1953, along with New Zealander Sir Edmund Hillary, was first to climb the world's greatest peak, Mount Everest.

In May 1997, Tashi Tenzing fulfilled his life-long dream to retrace his grandfather's steps. At the age of 31, he reached the summit of the mighty Mount Everest. In a symbolic act Tenzing placed a small Buddhist statue and the flags of Australia and his native Nepal.

The Nepalese

A handful of his fellow Nepalese arrived on Australian shores in the 1970s. Some of them entered as spouses of Australian citizens, while a few Nepalese families with professional backgrounds arrived in Sydney in the 1980s and 1990s under the skilled migrant category. They were later joined by a small number of former *Gurkha* army families who came under the visitor status scheme and were later granted permanent residency status.

About 417 Nepalese were counted in the 1991 Census and it is estimated that around 170 of them have settled in Sydney. According to the secretary of the Gurkha Nepalese Community, Bhoma D Limbu, most Nepalese residents have established themselves in western suburbs such as Campbelltown, while Nepalese students tend to find accommodation in the inner-western suburbs of Marrickville and Strathfield, and some others in the inner-city suburb of Surry Hills.

In 1976 the Nepalese Australian Association was established in Sydney as a non-political and non-profit organisation, and due to the continued flow of immigrants from Nepal, the Gurkha-Nepalese Community Inc. was established in 1996 to assist new Nepalese migrants.

> About 417 Nepalese were counted in the 1991 Census and it is estimated that around 170 of them have settled in Sydney.

The Tibetans

The 1959 Tibetan uprising against Chinese occupation led to more than 80,000 Tibetans searching for refuge in neighbouring countries and overseas. The first Tibetan to arrive on our shores – in 1973 – was Namygel Tsering, the current president of the Tibetan Community Association of New South Wales.

According to Chhime Rigzing, the local representative of the Dalai Lama, today there are about 190 Tibetans Australia-wide and of these about 65 live in our city. They are mainly Buddhists of the Vajrayana tradition.

Restaurants

House of Kathmandu & Nepalese Cuisine. No frills – just an unpretentious spot where you can taste such delicacies as *duku ya la* (goat curry). Average $15, BYO. Open for dinner Tuesday-Sunday 6pm-10.30pm.

423 Cleveland Street, Redfern (tel: 9319 2170).

Kathmandu Ma. A tasty, exotic and inexpensive Nepalese and Tibetan menu. Open for dinner Tuesday-Saturday 5.30pm-10pm, Sunday 5.30pm-10pm. Average $15, BYO.

10 King Street, Newtown (tel: 9557 1425).

Nepali Kitchen. A cosy and authentically Nepalese/Tibetan spot. Try the popular goat curry and meat dumplings (known around the mighty Himalayas as *Ma-ma Cha*).
Open Monday-Sunday 6pm-11pm. Average $15, BYO.

481 Crown Street, Surry Hills (tel: 9319 4264).

Yak & Yeti. One of the best-known in Sydney – the Nepalese/Gurkha/Tibetan menu is good and the vegetarian fare is superb and inexpensive. Average $15, BYO. Open Monday-Sunday 6pm-10.30pm.

41 Glebe Point Road, Glebe (tel: 9552 1220).

Shopping

Au Lion des Neiges. Here you are likely to find fabulous ancient Tibetan cultural objects. It also has a superb collection of antiques from Nepal, Bhutan and Mongolia.

76 Queen Street, Woollahra (tel: 9362 0115).

TIBET GALLERY.

Has a well-earned reputation for showing fine samples of Tibetan artwork, including clothes and graphic rugs woven in Kathmandu.
Open Tuesday-Saturday 11am-5.30pm.

22 Queen Street, Woollahra
(tel: 9363 2588).

The Nepalese Kitchen restaurant in Surry Hills.

Getting to know the Nepalese community

USEFUL NUMBERS FOR VISITORS

NEPALESE CONSULATE:
tel: 9233 6161.

NEPAL TRAVEL CENTRE:
tel: 9299 1111.

Events

Tihar or Dewali.

Every year from October 16-20 the Nepalese community celebrates Tihar – with families gathering together and as a community through cultural functions. During *Tihar* there is a Festival of Lights, worship of *Laxmi* (the Goddess of Prosperity), and offerings made for the crow, the dog and the cow. In the practical Nepalese fashion there is a celebration for the house, property, technical instruments and vehicles that belong to the family. Tihar is also a celebration of *Bhai Tika* ('brothers and sisters day') in which brothers receive special offerings and blessings from their sisters for good health and prosperity.

Viyaya Dashmi.

A national cultural festival of Nepal, it's celebrated during September and October. On this day images of the goddesses *Devi*, *Durga Bhawani*, and *Bhagawati* are worshipped, and family members and relatives visit the houses of their elders to be blessed. In Sydney, the Nepalese community celebrates this festival with a picnic, cultural functions and a fundraising program for 'Eye Camp', part of the Nepal Eye Program, or for victims of natural disasters.

Teej.

A traditional Hindu Nepalese women's festival held in the month of August. Hindu Nepalese women, especially married ones, observe Teej by fasting 24 hours for a long and prosperous life for their husbands.

Dashain, Tihar and Christmas.

An annual festival organised by the Gurkha Nepalese Community on December 28. The event has become an important way to maintain culture and unity among local Nepalese.

Further information: Bhoma D Limbu, Gurkha Nepalese Community (tel: 9564 0461).

Himalayan Culture and Food Festival.

A fundraising festival for the Nepal Eye Program, which runs a training centre for cataract surgeons in the Himalayan region – established by the late Fred Hollows. It's held in October at the Bondi Pavilion, Bondi Beach. The Festival features traditional music and dance, and Nepalese, Tibetan and Indians foods, artefacts and handicrafts.

Further information: 9971 7941 or 9451 4272.

Community organisations

The Australian Nepalese Association.

A non-political and non-profit association established in 1976. The primary objective of the Association is to promote friendship, understanding and goodwill between the people of Australia and Nepal. Activities include social functions and support and assistance to Nepalese visitors and students, and providing information on Nepal to Australians. Membership of the Association is open to any person with an interest in these activities. Meetings are usually held at the Ethnic Affairs Community Centre at 164-174 Liverpool Road, Ashfield.

PO Box 59, Paddington 2121. Further information: Indra Ban (tel: 9331 2970).

Gurkha Nepalese Community Inc NSW.

A welfare organisation that assists Nepalese students and migrants.
31 Woodbury Street, Marrickville. (tel: 9564 0461).

Getting to know the Tibetan community

Events

Losar (Tibetan New Year).

The main festival organised by the Tibetan community, it's celebrated on February 27. Tibetan dancing, singing and food.

Further information: Tibetan Community Association on 9938 1606.

TIBETAN BUDDHIST CENTRES (VAJRAYANA)

AMITABHA CENTRE.
4/1 Lauderdale Avenue, Fairlight. Contact Linda Feldstein (tel: 9907 9774).
AUSTRALIAN INSTITUTE OF TIBETAN HEALING PRACTICES.
2 Karana Place, Chatswood (tel: 9411 2818).
DIAMOND WAY BUDDHIST MEDITATION CENTRE.
99 Gowrie Street, Newtown (tel: 0419 423 939).
DZOG CHEN COMMUNITY.
2/218 Union Street, Erskineville
(tel: 9517 1082).
KARMA KARGYU DO-NGAK CHO-LING.
44 Tindale Road, Artarmon (tel: 9411 1246).
OCEAN OF PEACE.
2nd Floor, The Commonwealth Building, 41 Oxford Street, Darlinghurst (tel: 9283 4804).
THE RIGPA CENTRE.
Level 3, 822 George Street, City (tel: 9555 9952).
SAKYA THARPA LING.
18 Dobroyd Parade Lane, Haberfield (tel: 9716 9710).
SIDDHARTHA'S INTENT – SOUTHERN DOOR.
PO Box 1114, Strawberry Hills (tel: 9398 6048).

Tibet Fair.

Organised by the Australia Tibet Council, this is a showcase of Tibetan art and culture. The Fair is also a reminder of the current political situation of Tibet under Chinese rule.

For venue and dates: Australia Tibet Council (tel: 9283 3466).

Tibetan Buddhist education

Australian Institute of Tibetan Medical Practices.

East meets West here, as the Institute applies Tibetan Buddhist principles to the treatment of health problems: "Tibetans believe that the only way to cure illness, and indeed to extinguish all problems, is by attacking the root cause of a problem in the mind," says the Centre's pamphlet. Classes are held each Wednesday evening at 6.30pm at the University of Technology, Sydney (Level 19, room 1914). No fees are charged for classes.

PO Box 146 Waverley, Sydney 2024 (tel: 9387 3019).

Australian Institute of Buddhist Learning & Practice.

The Centre belongs to the Vajrayana Buddhist tradition. Its headquarters are located in Western Parramatta, only five minutes walk from Toongabbie station.

15 Mettella Road, Toongabbie (tel: 9896 4613).

Community organisations

Australia Tibet Council (ATC).

The Council campaigns for the rights and freedoms of the Tibetan people, including their right to self-determination. It also organises the Tibet Fair in Sydney and major events in other capital cities. The ATC publishes a bimonthly magazine.

Further information: National Office, PO Box 1236 Potts Point, 2011 (tel: 9283 3466).

Tibetan Community Association of NSW.

Provides welfare and social assistance to the Tibetan community.

16/2 Beach Street, South Curl Curl (tel: 9938 1606).

The Pakistanis

"**Paki power!** Paki power! Paki power!" – they know that they're one of the best cricket nations in the world. Paki power is real – it was just a few years ago that the Sydney Cricket Ground saluted the almighty Pakistanis as they smashed their way to the world championship at 10 runs an over. Paki power!

Pakistanis have never emigrated to Australia in large numbers. The 1991 Census counted only 6,000 and the majority came in the late 1960s and early 1970s. An important feature of the Pakistani immigration to Australia is that – in contrast to the immigration to England – most of the Pakistani immigrants are well-educated, urban, fluent in English and from the upper and middle classes. This has certainly made their integration into Australian society very easy.

Only 2,000 Pakistanis currently live in Sydney. They are mainly a multilingual Muslim community that, like the Hindus and Sikhs of India, have been forced to make some minor concessions to their religious practices while remaining largely a homogeneous group with few intermarriages. They speak Urdu, the national language, but they are also able to communicate in *Punjabi, Sindhi* or *Pastho*.

Sydney Pakistani community life has developed around Muslim organisations and social and community associations. One of the key organisations is the Pakistan Association of Australia, located in the western suburb of Lakemba at the heart of the Sydney Muslim community.

The year 1996 was a memorable one for Australian-Pakistanis when Bashir Mirza, a leading Pakistani artist, was appointed as Pakistan's first cultural attache in Australia (also the first such appointment anywhere in the world). Bashir Mirza is an internationally acclaimed painter whose works portray anti-war and anti-nuclear themes and celebrate female beauty through masterful portraiture. He was the founder, in 1965, of the first professional art gallery in Pakistan. The local Pakistanis can hardly hide their pride about this artist cum diplomat.

> An important feature of the Pakistani immigration to Australia is that – in contrast to the immigration to England – most of the Pakistani immigrants are well-educated, urban, fluent in English and from the upper and middle classes.

USEFUL NUMBERS FOR VISITORS

PAKISTANI CONSULATE:
tel: 9267 7066.

PAKISTAN INTERNATIONAL AIRLINES:
tel: 9267 4399.

COMMUNITY ORGANISATIONS

PAKISTAN ASSOCIATION OF AUSTRALIA. Provides social and cultural activities to the Pakistani community.

213 Lakemba Street, Lakemba
(tel: 9745 1672).

Restaurants

For a good Pakistani cuisine experience drop by Geronimo, the Indian restaurant at 106 Curlewis Street, Bondi (tel: 930 2756) or Oh! Calcutta at 251 Victoria Street, Darlinghurst (tel: 9360 3650). Both places are listed in The Indians, page 307.

Mehron Authentic Pakistan Cuisine. Basic, relaxed and friendly – the authentic Pakistani *halal* menu is good. Average $10. Open Monday-Sunday 5.30pm till late.

557 Elizabeth Street, Surry Hills (tel: 9690 2109).

Getting to know the Pakistani community

Events

As a predominantly Muslim community, Sydney Pakistanis celebrate the majority of Muslim events such as *Eid-ul-Qurban* and *Eid-ul-Fitr* and the Holy Prophet Muhammad's birthday (see Muslim Sydney, page 422).

Pakistan's Independence Day.

This is the most significant secular celebration and falls on August 14. It commemorates the day in which Pakistan came into existence as an Islamic Republic in 1947.

Further information: Pakistan Association of Australia (tel: 9745 1672).

Media

Newspapers

Sada-E-Wattan. Published forthnightly, it covers local and international affairs. It has a circulation of 6,000 issues and the editor is Syea Zafar (tel: 9605 5594).

Radio

SBS Radio 2, FM 97.7. News, music and current affairs in Urdu. Sunday 10am-11am.

Television

TV Channel 31. Pakistan Community Network, in Urdu. Friday 10pm-11pm.

The Thais

OK, hands up those who do not like Thai food! With Thai restaurants practically everywhere in Sydney, you would have thought they have been around forever. Not quite. It was on August 26 1976 (to be exact) that the first Thai restaurant made its debut in Sydney – The Siam, which opened in Bondi and later moved to its current location in Paddington (where a small plaque can be seen commemorating its original opening).

Today, Thai restaurants are very much part of Sydney's landscape and green curry chicken has become a kind of national dish.

The first Thai to visit Australia was Butra Mahintra who, in the early 1920s, was commissioned by King Rama VI to purchase a few Australian racehorses. It was also in the 1920s that members of the Thai royal family were sent to study in Australia. One of them was Prince Purachatra, the Prince of Kampaeng and a brother of the King, who led a study tour around Australia. In the 1970s, the current Crown Prince Vajiralongkorn also came to Australia to study.

He spent one year at the prestigious King's School before moving to Canberra where he began his military career at Duntroon. He left Australia in 1975.

Nowadays there are about 6,000 Thai-born people living in our city. Sydney's Thai community has tended to settle in the western suburbs of Ashfield, Fairfield and Cabramatta, but there is also a small pocket in the eastern suburbs of Randwick and Bondi. As 98% of Thais are Theravada Buddhists, their community life mainly revolves around the *wat*, or Buddhist temples. The first Sydney Thai temple, the *Wat* Buddharangsee in Stanmore, was established in 1975, and with the rapid growth of the local Thai population a second and a larger temple, Wat Pa Buddharangsee, was built in the western suburb of Leumeah in 1980. The newest Sydney Buddhist temple – conceived in 1995 – is located at inner-western suburb of Annandale. Currently there are seven Theravada temples across Australia.

> Thai restaurants are very much a part of Sydney's landscape and green curry chicken has become a kind of national dish.

Restaurants

It would not be unlikely that Sydney has the largest number of Thai restaurants per capita than any other city in the world (apart from in Thailand, that is). Even though Thai eateries are widely popular for their wonderful taste and affordable prices, the Sydney food savvies like to whinge that Thai menus are so similar that it has becomes a generic experience going to them. Now, if you're not one of the savvies pick one of the restaurants and just enjoy the food. See also Newtown, page 25.

Sydney has the largest number of Thai restaurants per capita outside Thailand.

Arun Thai. Elegant but not pretentious. A great place to indulge yourself with the timeless *tom kha gai* soup. Average $25, licensed. Open for lunch Wednesday-Monday noon-2.30pm, dinner 6pm-10.30pm.

28 Macleay Street, Potts Point (tel: 9326 9135).

Darley Street Thai. This is serious Thai. The reputation of Thai chef David Thompson is the best guarantee that you're in the right place for an imaginative fare. Ranked as one of Sydney's best, it offers authentic and sophisticated Thai cuisine. Average $45, licensed. Open Monday-Sunday dinner 6.30pm-10.30pm.

28-30 Bayswater Road, Kings Cross (tel: 9358 6530).

George's Thai. In less than a year George's has earned a solid reputation among a large and loyal group of admirers – including Annita Keating, wife of the former Australian Primer Minister Paul Keating. We recommend the trout topped with red curry and leeks. Average $20, BYO. Open for lunch Monday-Saturday noon-3pm, dinner 5pm-10pm.

215 Coogee Bay Road, Coogee (tel: 9665 5077).

Lime and Lemongrass. Stylish decor and a wonderful Thai menu. The hot and sour prawn soup is just perfect. Average $20, licensed. Open for dinner Monday-Sunday 6.30pm-10.30pm.

42 Kellett Street, Kings Cross (tel: 9385 5577).

Phat Boys. One of the most handsomely designed Thai restaurants in Sydney. It has great food, and the delightful presentation is only spoiled by the the use of forks and spoons. Try the grilled octopus marinated in white wine, lemon juice, chilli and garlic. Average $30, licensed. Open for lunch Monday-Friday noon-3pm, dinner Monday-Sunday 6pm-11pm.

118 Crown Street, East Sydney (tel: 9332 3284).

Prasit's Northside Takeaway. First of all it's not a take-away – it's one of the most packed Thai places in town. Yes, we concede it's very small but the quality of the food is so good that bigger premises wouldn't help much. Average $15, BYO. Open for lunch Tuesday-Sunday noon-3pm, dinner 5.30pm-10pm.

395 Crown Street, Surry Hills (tel: 9332 1792).

Sailor's Thai Canteen. David Thompson has done it again (see also Darley Street Thai). He is the mastermind behind this glorious Thai restaurant (downstairs) and noodle bar (ground floor). Average $10 (noodle bar), $20 (restaurant), licensed. The noodle bar is open Monday-Sunday noon-8pm, while the restaurant opens for lunch Monday-Friday noon-3pm, dinner Saturday 6.30 till late.

106 George Street, The Rocks (tel: 9251 2466).

Siam. Thai specialities include a very tasty chilli prawn soup. The food is good and the environment relaxed and friendly. Average $15, BYO. Open for lunch Monday-Saturday noon-3pm, dinner Monday-Sunday 6pm-10pm.

383 Oxford Street, Paddington (tel: 9331 2669).

Silver Spoon. A good place to have dinner after strolling around cosmopolitan Darlo. Try the seafood, it's highly recommended. Average $15, BYO. Open for lunch Monday-Sunday noon-3pm, dinner 6pm-10pm.

203 Oxford Street, Darlinghurst (tel: 9360 4669).

Prasit's Northside on Crown Street, Surry Hills.

Shopping

BKK Supermarket.

If you don't know already, BKK stands for Bangkok. BKK is a bustling grocery with its shelves lined with imported products from Thailand, the Philippines, Indonesia and other Asian countries. Browse here for dried seafood, fresh noodles, confectionery, herbs, cooking utensils and more. Open Monday-Sunday 9am-6pm (till 9pm on Thursday and 4pm on Sunday).

Eastlakes Shopping Centre, Evans Avenue, Eastlakes (tel: 9667 3938) and 53 Park Road, Cabramatta (tel: 9727 8222).

Landmarks and places of interest

Wat Buddharangsee.

A large suburban house was turned into the first Thai Buddhist *Wat* in Australia. Established in 1975, it was the product of a series of requests made by the Sydney Thai Buddhist community to the Thai Government and Buddhist officials. Located in Stanmore (around 15 minutes from the CBD), the *Wat* has played a major role in promoting and disseminating Buddhist beliefs and faith. It is also a focal point for the social life of the Sydney Thai community.

88-90 Stanmore Road, Stanmore (tel: 9557 2039).

Wat Pa Buddharangsee.

Built in 1988, it's known as the 'Forest Monastery'. It's one of the main venues for Sydney Buddhist festivals, including the colourful celebration of the Buddhist new year.

Lot 39 Junction Road, Leumeah (tel: (046) 25 7930).

Buddist Wat in Sydney allow the Thai community to continue their religious traditions.

Getting to know the Thai community

Events

Pha Bha.

This is the name of the monthly event where special prayers are celebrated by Thai Buddhists. On *Pha Bha* people give the monks offerings, including food and new saffron-coloured robes. A very popular venue for this traditional ceremony is the Wat Buddharangsee in Annandale (see religious organisations).

Songkran Festival Day.

Observed also by the Burmese, Laotian and Cambodian community, Songkran is the beginning of a New Solar Year (this is the exact meaning of Songkran). Usually it's celebrated in mid-April (12th-14th) and is organised by the Royal Thai Consulate, the Thai National Office of Culture and the Sydney Thai community. Sydney's Darling Harbour Tumbalong Park has been a recent venue for this festival.

Further information: Thai Consulate (tel: 9241 2542).

Thailand Loy Krathong (Water Festival).

Held on or near November 24 at Parramatta Park (close to Parramatta River), *Loy Krathong* is the main festival in the Sydney Thai calendar. Back in Thailand, it marks the end of the 'wet season'. Some of the many activities during the Sydney Thai festival include floating a '*krathong*' (a kind of boat) with candles, incense and bamboo leaves as a symbol of good luck for the coming season. The Festival also features Thai dancing, a Thai orchestra, food, art and craft stalls, and a spectacular Thai boxing demonstration. Free – all welcome.

Further information: Thai Australian Association of NSW (tel: 9871 5469).

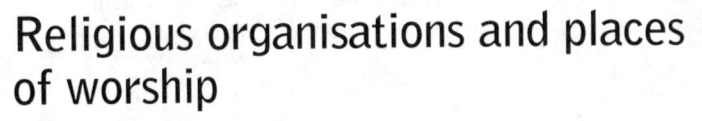

Religious organisations and places of worship

Wat Buddharansee.
88-99 Stanmore Road, Stanmore (tel: 9557 2039).

Wat Mai Buddharangsee.
49 Trafalgar Street, Annandale (tel: 9557 2879).

Community and cultural organisations

Thai National Cultural Council.
Fosters and promotes Thai culture and arts.

PO Box 515, Roselle 2039 (tel: 9744 5635).

Thai Welfare Association.
The Association assists and advises Thai migrants on a wide range of social, cultural and welfare issues.

Suite 3, Level 6, 74 Pitt Street, City (tel: 9232 5386).

Thai Australian Association of NSW. Organises social, cultural and educational activities for the Thai community. It also produces a community newsletter.

PO Box 45, Carlingford 2118 (tel: 9871 5469).

WAT BUDDHASANGSEE DAILY PROGRAM (ANNANDALE)

5am-6am meditation

6am-6.15am morning chanting

6.30am-7pm evening chanting

7am-7.30pm meditation

A gathering Day (Dana) is organised every last Sunday of the month, 10.30am-noon.

Media

Newspapers

Thai Oz News. Published fortnightly, *Thai Oz News* caters also for the Laotian and Cambodian communities. It covers news from Thailand in English. It has a circulation of 5,000. The Advertising Manager is Ratri Doungrutana (tel: 9726 6696).

Radio

SBS Radio 2 FM (97.7). News, current affairs and community announcements. Tuesday 9am-10am, Saturday 8am-9am.

Facts and figures

The majority of the Australian Thai population consists of relatively recent arrivals, with more than half being residents for less than five years, and less than fifth for a decade.

The Thai-born population has been one of the fastest growing groups in Australia since the mid-1970s, more than doubling during each of the last three census periods. According to the 1991 Census, there are 14,023 Thais living in Australia, with 5,982 settled in Sydney. The vast majority of Thais (95%) are Buddhists from the Theravada sect.

The proportion of Thais with a degree or diploma (21.3%) is much greater than that for the Australia-born, partly reflecting a substantial student component in the group. The large presence of students also explains the considerable rate of Thais in the lowest income categories (67.6% earning less than $16,000). The low income also explains the relatively low proportion of Thais (41.6%) who own or are purchasing their own house.

The Vietnamese

"Nhap giang tuy khuc; Nhap gia guy tuc"
"Sailing on a river should depend on its current;
Living in a country must follow its customs"

It's a proverb profoundly entwined in the Vietnamese immigration experience. To follow it hasn't been easy, however. There have been language and cultural obstacles to overcome and old wounds to heal.

The Vietnamese-born Dong Le Quy is no stranger to these obstacles. Hailed as one of the newest and brightest playwrights in the Australian theatre scene, he came in 1994 and had to endure the arduous adjustment to his new country. His pen was replaced by washing machines, packing boxes and forklifts until his first Australian play, *The Request of Spring* was performed in 1996 at Sydney's Belvoir Theatre. For Dong Le Quy it marked a return to his true vocation, and affirmed his belief that you can always start over somewhere.

The earliest Vietnamese presence in Australia was an accidental one: in August 1920 a ship with 38 Vietnamese, part of a group of labourers being shipped between the French colonies of Vietnam and New Caledonia, sought refuge near Townsville in Queensland after being blown off course by a severe storm. More than 30 years elapsed until another group of Vietnamese made their way to Australia, students who arrived in 1958 under the Colombo Plan to undertake university education.

In a little over two decades, Sydney has become the focus of Vietnamese settlement in Australia – *Nguyen* (pronounced N'win), the most common surname in Vietnam, has since 1993 been in the top ten listings in the Sydney White Pages.

The first boat people

The end of the Vietnam war in 1975, with the subsequent takeover of the South by North Vietnam, caused an exodus of over two million Vietnamese refugees, three-quarters of whom managed to escape their war-torn land. The first Vietnamese refugee groups arrived in Sydney in April 1975: 283 orphans and detached children who were adopted by Australian families. They were soon followed by thousands of Vietnamese who, forced into refugee camps in Hong Kong, Singapore and Malaysia, were accepted for resettlement in Australia.

In the last few years the Sydney Vietnamese have moved in to the western suburbs of Fairfield, Bankstown and Marrickville where they have established a vigorous and thriving community (see Marrickville – at the heart of Australian multiculturalism, page 21)

In 1976, just one year after the fall of Saigon, another group of Vietnamese refugees, by-passing both international and Australian refugee procedures, made their way direct from Vietnam to Australia on a frail boat. They were the first 'boat people' to arrive on our shores. Over the next five years, facing the peril of marauding Thai pirates, over 50 more boats with more than 2,000 Vietnamese reached Australian coasts. One of those was the legendary wooden fishing boat *Hong Hai*, captained by Truong Van Soi, which arrived near Darwin in 1980. (The *Hong Hai* can be seen today at Sydney's Australian Maritime Museum, where it is on permanent display). During the decade following 1975 almost all of the 79,000 Vietnamese entering Australia came as refugees, most by plane. A family reunion program in place from the mid-1980s further increased this number by around 45,000.

For the majority of Vietnamese their new life began in migrant hostels, where English classes and orientation programs were available. But when the close-knit community began taking shape and informal social networks to provide mutual support sprang up, they left the hostels and began sharing accommodation. They moved to industrial suburbs where employment was available and rent cheap.

Step aside Chinatown

In a little over two decades, Sydney has become the focus of Vietnamese settlement in Australia. Nguyen (pronounced N'win) is the most common surname in Vietnam and has since 1993 been in the top ten listings in the Sydney White Pages. Today over 47,000 Vietnamese live in Sydney, with a strong presence in the western suburb of Cabramatta where the 25,000-strong community has transformed this area into a thriving showplace of culture and commerce. Every Sunday around 15,000 visitors flow into Cabramatta, making it a serious challenger to Sydney's long-established Chinatown (see Cabramatta, page 263).

Cabramatta is the main centre for Sydney's Vietnamese community.

Apart from Cabramatta, in the last few years Sydney's Vietnamese have poured into the western suburb of Bankstown and Marrickville where they have established a vigorous and thriving community. Marrickville was an old enclave of the Greek community that has relinquished its neighbourhood to the newcomers from Southeast Asia – if you walk along the commercial area of Marrickville you'll see the Greek names of some shops replaced by Vietnamese ones (for more on these areas see Bankstown, page 30, and Marrickville, page 21).

The Vietnamese give great importance to the maintenance of their religious practices. As a mainly Buddhist community, it founded the first Vietnamese-Buddhist society in Sydney in 1979; one year later, the first monk, the Most Venerable Thich Phuoc-Hue, arrived in Australia. The main religious centre for the Buddhist community is at Wetherill Park (see page 343). Catholicism is also well represented in the Vietnamese community (after the Filipinos, the Vietnamese form the most numerous Catholic congregation in Asia). Since 1975, Vietnamese Catholics – over 10% of the Vietnamese community – have been under the religious guidance of Vietnamese priests ordained in either Australia or Vietnam.

Vietnamese people have shown a great deal of determination to succeed and to contribute to their new country. *Quang Tuong* Luu is a good example. A refugee in 1975, Quang Luu is the current head of SBS Radio. Dr Tien Manh Nguyen is another remarkable man who arrived in Australia as one of the boat people and today is a well-known doctor and community leader in Cabramatta – an area that has been, on the other hand, the political stronghold of the very prominent and controversial Vietnamese-born Phuong Ngo. After arriving in Australia as a penniless refugee in 1982, Ngo became a successful businessman and the first Vietnamese to be elected to a political position, a councillor at Fairfield Municipality. An Australian Labour Party powerbroker in the Cabramatta electorate, he came under the spotlight when his political rival in the area John Newman was gunned down in the front of his Cabramatta house in 1995. And how could we forget the very talented Hung Lee – a nine year-old boat person in 1975 – who has become the first high-profile Vietnamese comic in Sydney. "People have never seen a Vietnamese person being funny, all Australians seem to know about our culture is war or restaurants," he once commented. Hung Lee belongs to a generation of Australian Vietnamese who keeps the horrors of the past in mind but looks to the future with hope.

John Street Cabramatta.

The first Sydney Vietnamese community organisations were formed in 1976, providing educational, welfare and legal support for the community. In 1981 an umbrella association, the Council of Vietnamese Organisations in New South Wales, was established with the objective of giving formal direction to the demands of the Vietnamese community, and in 1983 the Vietnamese Education and Culture Committee was created with the aim of maintaining and promoting Vietnamese culture in our city.

Restaurants

Vietnamese cuisine is an amazing experience. There are said to be nearly 500 traditional Vietnamese dishes, and because Buddhism from the Mahayana tradition is strictly vegetarian, *an chay* (vegetarian cooking) is a central part of the Vietnamese cuisine. Also central is *pho*, the noodle soup eaten (at least in Vietnam) at all hours of the day. The following is a selected list of Vietnamese restaurants around inner-city Sydney. If you want to get the full Vietnamese experience take the train and get off at Cabramatta Station (see page 263), or if that sounds too far drop in at Marrickville (see page 21) or Bankstown (see page 30).

Marrickville, Bankstown and Cabramatta are Sydney's main concentrations of Vietnamese-heaven cuisine. Although Vietnamese restaurants are to be found in most Sydney suburbs.

FOR A GOOD RANGE OF VIETNAMESE SHOPS
see Cabramatta, page 263; Bankstown, page 30; and Marrickville, page 21.

Bach Hy. A favourite of inner-city dwellers, it has received the thumbs-up from the specialists. For an entree make sure you try *Goi Guon* (prawn rolls with dipping sauce). Average $15, BYO. Open for lunch Monday-Saturday 11.30am-3pm, dinner 5pm till late, Sunday dinner 5pm till late.

139 Oxford Street, Darlinghurst (tel: 9331 1363)

Chu Bay. Small, with basic decor and a menu that has all the favourites, including the timeless *Goi Guon* (fresh rice paper rolls with shredded pork and prawns served with black bean sauces). Average $15, BYO. Open for dinner Monday-Sunday 5.30pm-11pm.

312A Bourke Street, Darlinghurst (tel: 9331 3386).

Indochina. This is the place to have a hearty bowl of *pho* after a spot of surfing. Average $15, BYO. Open Monday-Sunday 5.30pm-10.30pm.

99 Bondi Road, Bondi (tel: 9387 4081).

Kim. By the look of things, the owners of this small restaurant have put a lot of work into transforming it into a charming and friendly spot. The large menu offers the likes of sweet and sour squid and a delicious asparagus soup with chunks of crab. Average $15, BYO. Open Wednesday-Monday 7pm-10.30pm.

235 Oxford Street, Darlinghurst (tel: 9357 5429).

Old Saigon. You wouldn't be blamed if you felt the beer can helicopters hanging from the ceiling bring back dark memories of the Vietnam War. Your host Carl Robinson, a former war correspondent in Vietnam, knows all about that. He and his Vietnamese wife Kim have done a great job, and this restaurant is one of the highly recommended spots to visit. Average $20, BYO and licensed. Open for lunch Monday-Friday noon-3pm, dinner Tuesday-Sunday 6pm-11pm.

107 King Street, Newtown (tel: 9519 5931).

Viet Nouveau. Personalised service in a super-friendly environment where Vietnam meets France. For the purist, a beginning-to-end Vietnamese menu is available. Average $25, BYO. Open Monday-Sunday 6.30pm-11pm.

731 Military Road, Mosman (tel: 9968 3548).

Landmarks and places of interest
Phuoc Hue Vietnamese Buddhist Temple.
After a decade of community effort and goodwill, the Phuoc Hue Vietnamese

Buddhist Temple was finally inaugurated in November 1991. The construction of the building – covering an area about that of St Mary's Cathedral – was possible thanks to the generosity of architects and site engineers who gave their services free. This impressive temple, where Prince Charles met with religious leaders when he was here, comprises three buildings – a house of worship, a community cultural centre, and a small residential house. The open space and areas that surround the Temple are used for picnics and for other open space activities. The Temple displays an impressive bell tower and a dominant statue of *Kuan Yin*, the Goddess of Peace. Since it opened its door, the Temple has become a place of pilgrimage for Buddhists, and also welcomes visitors (if in groups, it's advisable to call beforehand). Shoes must be removed inside – and don't point the soles of your feet towards other people or Buddhist statues. Open Monday-Saturday 7am-7pm, Sunday 9am-10.30am and then 1-6pm (between 10.30am and noon the main hall is used for prayers).

369 Victoria Street, Wetherill Park (tel: 9725 2324).

Hong Hai, Australian Maritime Museum.

It's a moving and poignant experience to see this 20-metre wooden Vietnamese fishing boat that, under the firm hand of Captain Truong Van Soi, reached the Australian coastline near Darwin in 1980 with 38 Vietnamese refugees on board. (Truong Van Soi still lives in Sydney, by the way.) After some repairs, the frail vessel went on display at Darling Harbour's Australian Maritime Museum. The Museum opens Monday-Sunday 9.30am-5pm. Admission is $7 adults, $4 concession, $18.50 family.

2 Murray Street, Darling Harbour (tel: 9552 7777 Monday-Friday, 9552 7500 Saturday-Sunday, 0055 62002 recorded message).

Getting to know the Vietnamese community

Events

Tet (Vietnamese New Year).

Similar to the Chinese *Xin Nian*, this event marks the beginning of the new year. Usually it consists of three days of festivities starting the first day of the Lunar Year (around February 7) and features Vietnamese

USEFUL NUMBERS FOR VISITORS

VIETNAMESE CONSULATE:
tel: 9327 2539,
9327 1912
(visa enquiries).

VIETNAM AIRLINES:
tel: 9252 3303.

VIETNAM TRAVEL CENTRE:
tel: 9299 2338.

CHILDREN'S FESTIVAL. Various cultural activities for children are organised by the Vietnamese Women's Association. Wiley Park, corner Kingsgrove and Canterbury Roads.

Further information:
tel: 9601 7172.

See also Buddhist Sydney, page 343

PLACES OF WORSHIP

VIETNAMESE BUDDHIST PHAP BAO PAGODA.
148-154 Edensor Road, Smithfield
(tel: 9610 5452).

BUDDHA RELICS TEMPLE.
Abbot: Venerable Thich Minh Thien.
5 Coventry Road, Cabramatta
(tel: 9723 0668).

LIEN HOA TEMPLE.
Abbess: Venerable Thich Nu Tam Lac.
22 O'Hara Street, Marrickville
(tel: 9559 6789).

PHUOC HAU TEMPLE.
292 Cabramatta Road, Cabramatta
(tel: 9754 2092).

BUDDHA RELICS VIHARA TEMPLE.
Belongs to the Mahayana tradition. Abbot: Venerable Thich Minh Thien.
133 John Street, Cabramatta
(tel: 9728 1895).

HUYEN QUANG TEMPLE.
Belongs to the Mahaya tradition. Abbot: Venerable Thich Bon Dien.
188 Chapel Street, South Bankstown
(tel: 9707 3347).

music, food stalls and a display of arts and crafts. A favourite venue for this celebration is Wiley Park, corner Kingsgrove and Canterbury Roads.

Contact the Vietnamese Community Association for additional information (tel: 9796 3794).

Fall of Saigon or 'Day of Shame'.

On April 30 the Sydney Vietnamese community remembers the events of 1975 when the Communist forces of North Vietnam took over Saigon. On this day for the last twenty years, members of the Vietnamese community have travelled to Canberra to hold a political rally demanding democracy for Vietnam.

Further information: Vietnamese Community Association (tel: 9796 8035).

Vu Lan Day or 'Mother's Day'.

This is celebrated on the 5th day of the 7th month of the Solar Calendar (approximately at the end of January). Activities are held in most of the Vietnamese Buddhist temples.

Contact some of the Buddhist temples listed below for further information.

Religious organisations and places of worship

Vietnamese religious life has been shaped by Confucianism, Taoism, Buddhism and Christianity.

Vietnamese Catholic Community.

We have been informed that there are at least 13 masses every week in the Vietnamese language in the Catholic churches of Cabramatta, Lakemba, Granville and other suburbs. Call to get specific information on venues and times of services.

92 The River Road, Revesby (tel: 9773 0733).

Vietnamese Buddhist Society of NSW.

Plays the role of an umbrella body for the Vietnamese Buddhist community.

148 Edensor Road, St Johns Park (tel:9610 5452).

The following is a list of some of the Vietnamese Buddhist temples existing in Sydney. They are usually open 7am-7pm:

Media

Newspapers

Dai Viet. The name can be translated as the 'Great Vietnam Herald'. This paper is published weekly and appears in the newsagencies on Thursday. It costs $1 and has a circulation of 10,000. The current editor is Dan Luu.

PO Box: 514, Cabramatta 2166 (tel: 9728 3385).

Radio

SBS Radio 1, AM 1107. News and current affairs. Monday-Sunday 9am-10am and 7pm-8pm

COMMUNITY ORGANISATIONS

VIETNAMESE COMMUNITY ASSOCIATION. This is the peak community body for the Sydney Vietnamese. It provides welfare and social assistance to Vietnamese immigrants and plays a major role in bridging the cultural gap between Vietnamese and Australians.

Level 2, 300 Chapel Road, Bankstown (tel: 9796 8035).

Facts and figure

Currently there are over 124,000 Vietnamese-born people in Australia. Sydney, with a population of slightly more that 47,000, is the city with the most Vietnamese in the country. Approximately 70% of Vietnamese have taken up Australian citizenship, a rate consistent with the historically high levels among predominantly refugee communities.

Vietnamese are on average not as well off economically as the Australia-born population. Only 2.5% are in the higher income group compared with 11.1% of Australians, and 67% are in the lowest income categories compared with 54.9% of Australian-born. This is in direct relation to their education profile, only 6.8% of adults having a degree or diploma compared to 12.7% for Australian-born. Despite the economic hardships experienced, 52.4% of Vietnamese immigrants own or are purchasing their home.

To obtain reliable statistical information on religious practice has been a major headache since the Vietnamese are involved in several religions. According to the 1991 Australian census, Buddhism is the largest religion among the Vietnamese born, with a further 22.3% identifying themselves as being Catholic (the main Christian religious denomination in Vietnam since the time of French colonisation). Vietnamese is spoken by more than 74% of Vietnamese-born residents, while 22.4% speak Chinese languages.

Significant Vietnamese immigration began following the 1975 reunification of Vietnam. In 1976 there were only 2,498 Vietnam-born people in Australia. However, at the end of the 1970s there was a vast outflow of Vietnamese refugees, most travelling by boat to nearby Asian countries from where they were resettled in third countries such as Australia, Canada and US.

The Afghans

In the middle of last century, hundreds of Afghans were shipped to Australia with their camels and were settled at Marree in Queensland's arid outback. The 'ghans', as they were called, opened up the driest region of the world's driest continent, and played a vital role in the construction of projects such as the rail link between Port Augusta and Alice Springs.

'The Ghan', Australia's most famous train, which runs between Adelaide and Alice Springs, is a fitting tribute to these Afghan pioneers.

These first intrepid 'cameleers' came from the rural provinces of Afghanistan and belonged to the two largest tribal groups, the Pathans and the Baluchis. Dos Mahomet, Botan and Balooch were the names of the first three Afghans who came to Australia, in 1859 (Zainabi Khan, the 80-year-old daughter of Mossha Balooch, still lives in Marree today). They were hired to drive the camels for the expedition of Irishman Robert O'Hara Burke, who was attempting to cross the continent.

In 1866 Sir Thomas Elder of South Australia brought 34 Afghans to manage his 120 imported camels. The Afghans – reliable, hardworking, abstemious and fast – drove their camel caravans across the desert delivering supplies and construction materials for the overland telegraph line between Adelaide and Darwin. Pastoralists, miners and telegraphers owed their survival to the Afghan cameleers' regular supplies of essentials. These early Afghans formed a string of 'ghan towns' along the railway routes, in Broken Hill for example. Mainly Muslims, they built some of the earliest mosques in Australia – no more than humble corrugated-iron constructions with small minarets.

Sadly, the arrival of the motor car around the turn of the century saw the end of the near 50-year desert reign of the skilful Afghan camel drivers (the last surviving driver, Ahmed Medmoosha, 84, lives today in Marree).

The current Afghan immigration dates back to the 1980s, following the civil war and invasion of Afghanistan by the former Soviet Union. Since 1981 the number of Afghan migrants has increased every year. Currently there are 2,724 Afghans living in Australia and the majority (1,390) have settled in Sydney, especially in Blacktown, Ryde, Parramatta and

The current Afghan immigration dates back to the 1980s, following the civil war and invasion of Afghanistan by the former Soviet Union. Since 1981 the number of Afghan migrants has increased every year.

Explore the world in one city

Holroyd. It is a small community which is actively involved with the already-established Muslim organisations, and it is represented by two community bodies, the Afghan Community Support Association and the Australian Afghan Association.

Restaurants

"The staple food of Afghans is *nan* (bread) and *palao* (rice cooked in a variety of ways), and the most popular dish among Afghans is *kabulipalao* – a mix of carrots, sultanas, almonds, dates and meat – fantastic," says the Afghan-born Raz Rashtia, one of the researchers behind this book.

Ariana Afghani Restaurant. As a good intro to this fascinating cuisine try the very popular *murgh dhal* (Tandoori chicken served with tomato souce and lentils). Average $15, BYO.
Open Monday-Saturday from 6pm.

162 Victoria Road, Gladesville (tel: 9879 6557).

You can also try traditional Afghan cuisine at Oh! Calcutta at 251 Victoria Street, Darlinghurst (tel: 9360 3650) – see The Indians, page 305.

Getting to know the Afghan community

Events

As largely a Muslim community, Sydney Afghans participate actively in the majority of the Muslim festivals celebrated in Sydney (see The Sydney Muslims Community, page 422).

Afghan New Year's Day.
This falls on March 21 and is widely celebrated by the Afghan community at various venues.

Further information: Australian Afghan Association (tel: 9451 1663).

Independence Day.
On August 17 1919, Great Britain recognised the independence of Afghanistan. Sydney Afghans, regardless of their political affiliations, come together each year to celebrate this important day at various places around town.

Further information: 9451 1663.

COMMUNITY ORGANISATIONS

AUSTRALIAN AFGHAN ASSOCIATION.
Provides welfare, cultural and social assistance to Sydney Afghans.

4 Miami Place,
Frenchs Forest
(tel: 9451 1663).

AFGHAN COMMUNITY SUPPORT ASSOCIATION OF NSW.
Provides assistance and humanitarian support to Afghan immigrants.

6/16 Main Street,
Blacktown
(tel: 9831 2436).

The Armenians

Consider this startling fact: approximately half of the Armenian population in the world lives outside its homeland. They're part of the surviving generation of the 1915 'Armenian Genocide', when an estimated 1.5 million Armenians were killed by Turkey – the first modern attempt to eliminate an entire population.

Armenians have established communities all over the world, in Greece, India, Iraq, USA, Canada and certainly Australia.

The earliest – although minor – presence of Armenians on our shores dates back to the 1850s goldrush period, but more than a century was to elapse before a more substantial immigration took place. It was in the 1960s, 1970s and mid 1980s when Armenians from more than 40 countries, with over 20 different nationalities and speaking more than 30 different languages, settled here.

> The Sydney Armenian presence is strongly felt in the North Shore suburbs of Willoughby and Chatswood where they have established their own schools, churches, community organisations and businesses.

There are about 10,000 Armenians in Sydney, and their presence is strongly felt in the North Shore suburbs of Willoughby and Chatswood, where they have established their own schools, churches, community organisations and businesses (most of the petrol stations are owned by Armenians). It seems that this North Shore Armenian enclave was started by a group of Armenians who came to the area to work at the refrigerator factory (now closed) that belonged to the late Sir Edward Hallstrom, at Willoughby. The North Shore Armenian community is noted for its self-sufficiency and achievements. It's this community that a few years back raised enough money to buy the Smokey Dawson Ranch for a school music hall – in a truly cross cultural exercise it was renamed The Smokey Dawson Armenian Music Hall.

Although Sydneysiders may know of the Armenian background of the chairman of the New South Wales Ethnic Affairs Commission, Stepan Kerkyasharian (born in Cyprus), it's likely that not many will know of the Armenian ethnic background of the late John Porter (born in Egypt). He was one of the characters of our city – for the past 35 years, John was an ever-present figure at just about every political and social demonstration in Sydney. The Aboriginal land rights campaign, the anti-Hanson protest, the anti-Monorail march. A man of many causes,

John Porter arrived on our shores around 1963 after living in Soviet Armenia. His tireless political commitment and his unmistakable presence – frizzy hair, thick spectacles and a strong accent (which he never lost), transformed him into an icon of the Sydney left. This unique Armenian left this world on July 15 1997; his was a tale of our city.

Restaurants

Arax Basturma Pizzeria. Add a generous portion of *basturma* (salt cured beef) spice it with *sejouk* (a traditional Armenian and Lebanese sauce) and top it with abundant *mozzarella*, and you have an Armenian pizza. Open Tuesday-Sunday 5.30pm-11pm.

670 Willoughby Road, Willoughby (tel: 9958 1518).

Anto's Pizzeria. A serious challenge to the traditional Italian pizzerias, this is another highly recommended place to explore the magic taste of a succulent Armenian pizza. Open for lunch Wednesday-Friday 11am-2pm, dinner Monday-Sunday 5pm-10pm.

321 Penshurst Street, Willoughby (tel: 9417 1266)

ARMENIAN CHRISTMAS. Held on January 7, this is one of the most important and massive festivities celebrated by Sydney Armenians. A wide range of cultural and religious events are organised at Armenian churches and cultural centres.

Further information: Diocese of the Armenian Church of Australia and New Zealand (tel: 9419 6394).

Getting to know the Armenian community

Events

Armenian Martyrs' Day.

On April 24 the Sydney Armenians commemorate the 1915 'Armenian Genocide' where 1.5 million Armenians were killed by Turkey. Churches and cultural centres organise special activities, including a massive open-air mass in Martin Place.

For additional information contact the Armenian community welfare centre on 9419 6394.

Since Armenian community life revolves to a large extent around the church, there are a large number of regular religious celebrations, including the monthly commemoration of religious figures such as St Vartnan's on February 10 and St Mary's Day on August 10 (this coincides with Mother's Day). We suggest contacting the Diocese of the Armenian Church of Australia and New Zealand (see page 388) for information on other Armenian religious festivals.

SHOPPING

DINKUM PIE. At the heart of the Sydney Armenian stronghold of Willoughby, this is the bakery where local Armenians (and Iranians) drop by to get their bread, including Persian *pita*, and sweets and biscuits. Open Monday-Saturday 8am-6pm.

325 Penshurst Street, Willoughby
(tel: 9417 8383).

Religious organisations and places of worship

Diocese of the Armenian Church of Australia and New Zealand.

Established in 1967, this is the peak Armenian religious organisation.

10 Macquarie Street, Chatswood (tel: 9419 6394).

Armenian Evangelical Brethren Church.

Founded in 1972, it holds religious services and prayer meetings each Sunday.

112 Sailors Bay Road, Northbridge (tel: 9412 4851).

Community organisations

Armenian Community Welfare Centre.

This is a community body providing social and welfare assistance to Armenian immigrants. It also has a day centre and an Armenian food service for elderly Armenians.

10 Macquarie Street, Chatswood (tel: 9419 6394).

The Assyrians

Contemporary Assyrians are descendants of the ancient Assyrian people who built the mighty empires of Assyria and Babylon. In Mesopotamia, Assyrians rose to political influence and economic prosperity from about 2,000 to 612 BC. After the fall of their empire, Assyrians were reduced to a small nation scattered in the middle eastern region, where they developed a distinctive historical and cultural identity from that of their neighbours. Assyrians were among the first people to embrace Christianity, and their church – the Church of the East – dates back almost 2,000 years.

Following the end of World War I, the rise of pan-Arabism and the resurgence of Islamic sentiments in the 1940s, Assyrians began seeking a new life in Europe, the US, Canada and Australia. Three families who arrived in Sydney in 1963 were the first recorded Assyrian immigrants in Australia. No official statistics are available on how many Assyrians currently live here, but it is estimated that the community comprises around 11,000 people.

Soon after the arrival of this first group, the community began taking shape under the leadership of the Assyrian Australian Association (AAA). Established in 1969, it is located in Fairfield in Sydney's west, where about 75% of Assyrians now live. Two prominent members of the Fairfield Assyrian community have served on Fairfield City Council, Counsellors Robert Robertson and Anwar Koshaba, who has also served as Deputy Mayor.

The most visible presence of Assyrians in Sydney is the imposing Nineveh Club at Edensor Park. This citadel-like structure is one of the great achievements of the AAA. The Association also played a major role in the establishment in Sydney of the Assyrian Church of the East, and also the Assyrian School, whose Saturday afternoon classes have contributed to the maintenance of Assyrian language and culture among adults and children. Other well-established Assyrian organisations are the Assyrian Sports and Cultural Club, the Assyrian Nations Association and the Assyrian Federation of Australia.

> Three families who arrived in Sydney in 1963 were the first recorded Assyrian immigrants in Australia.

A unique point in the history of Assyrian Australians occurred in December 1996 when the magnificent Assyrian art exhibition – 'Bridging the Gap' – opened in the National Gallery of Victoria. Till January 1997 the exhibition offered a unique opportunity for Australian-Assyrian artists to show their adopted society the richness of a culture that is alive and flourishing.

Landmarks and places of interest

Nineveh Club.

The imposing and lavish Nineveh Club is a matter of pride for Sydney Assyrians. This ambitious project of the Assyrian Australian Association began in 1971 when it purchased a six-acre block of land in Smithfield Road, Edensor Park. In April 1977 a members' meeting was organised in the Cabramatta Civil Hall where $80,000 was committed through donations to the construction of the building that began in November 1978. On November 22 1980, the dream was finally realised. The Nineveh Club building has a distinctive Assyrian design, with two winged lions at its main entrance, complete with chariot, kings and a hunter with spear and arrows. The Club is the focal point for Assyrian community's social, sporting and cultural activities. An extension to the building is under construction and will include a fully licensed restaurant (currently it only has a small bar) – needless to say traditional Assyrian food will be on the menu. Opens Monday-Friday 12.30pm-midnight, Saturday-Sunday 11.30am-midnight.

673-683 Smithfield Road, Edensor Park (tel: 9610 4655).

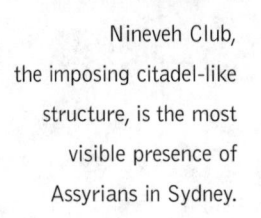

Nineveh Club, the imposing citadel-like structure, is the most visible presence of Assyrians in Sydney.

Getting to know the Assyrian community

Events

Kha B'Neesan (Assyrian New Year).

Neesan means April and represents the beginning of new life with the advent of Spring. The celebration is held on April 1 and the main activities are organised at the Nineveh Club. It features traditional music, art and food.

Further information: 9610 3288.

Shara D'Mar Bhisho-Mar (St Bhisho's Festival).

During September, the Assyrian community comes together to enjoy a day of social and religious activities held at various Assyrian venues in Sydney.

Further information: 9610 3288.

Shara D'Mar Zaia (St Zaid's Festival).

The second religious festival held in September, in which hundreds of Assyrians congregate in churches and cultural clubs. Call some of the given religious organisations for more information.

Community organisations

Assyrian Australian Association.

Established in 1969, the Association serves the social, cultural and sporting needs of the Assyrian community.

673-683 Smithfield Road, Edensor Park (tel: 9610 4655).

Media

SBS Radio 2, FM 97.7. News, music and comment. Friday 8pm-9pm.

Assyrian-language radio programs can also be heard on the following radio stations. Call for information on timeslots:

2GLF FM 89.3. (tel: 9601 4489).

2BCR FM 88.7. (tel: 9724 7877).

RELIGIOUS ORGANISATIONS AND PLACES OF WORSHIP

ASSYRIAN CHURCH OF THE EAST.
25 Edinburgh Road, Cecil Park
(tel: 9822 1132).

ASSYRIAN ANCIENT CHURCH OF THE EAST.
1/11 Hardy Street, Fairfield
(tel: 9725 6708).

KA'LU SULAQUA ('ASCENSION BRIDE'). Celebrated in May, this event is a national day of celebration for young Assyrian girls who – in ancient times – have contributed to the defeat of persecutors and oppressors of Assyrian Christians.

Further information: 9610 3288.

YOUMA D'SAHDEM ATOURAYEH (ASSYRIAN MARTYRS DAY). On August 7 Assyrian devotees honour their martyrs through church services and outdoor festivities. For further information on church services, contact some of the given religious organisations.

The Egyptians

Egyptian-born Sawsan Medina broke two barriers at once. In 1994 she became the first woman and the first person of a non-English-speaking background to head an Australian television network. Her appointment at SBS Television – a position that she held until recently – was rightly hailed as an achievement for Australian multiculturalism.

When Swasan Medina arrived in Australia in 1970, the Egyptian-born population was close to 30,000.

Before World War II the Egyptian community in Sydney was virtually nonexistent. The 1901 Census recorded only 108 Egyptians, and it seems they were of European descent. The major influx of Egyptians into Sydney occurred between 1947 and 1971. They were mainly of Coptic origin and established a small community in the Sydney inner-western suburb of Marrickville, where they built the first Coptic church in Australia. Towards the end of the 1960s, Egyptian Copts began arriving in Australia in large numbers. They had been driven from their homeland – firstly by the pan-Islamic /Arabist policy implemented in 1959 by the Nasser Government (a policy which eventually meant the loss of political and economic influence for the Copts and other minorities), and secondly by the 1967 war against Israel. These two factors caused an explosive growth in the Egyptian population in Australia, from 8,150 in 1954 to more than 28,000 in 1976.

As with the Lebanese, Egyptian Muslims are relative latecomers, arriving in the 1970s and early 1980s. They largely belong to the Sunni sect, and have established close links with the Australian Federation of Islamic Councils. Their religious life revolves around some of the established Sydney mosques.

> The major influx of Egyptians into Sydney occurred between 1947 and 1971. They were mainly of Coptic origin and established a small community in the Sydney inner-western suburb of Marrickville, where they built the first Coptic church in Australia.

The oldest secular organisation of the Sydney Egyptian community is the Institute of Australian Egyptian Culture, established in 1972. Since its foundation, the Institute has shown a strong commitment to the welfare, educational and cultural development of the Egyptian community. On the religious side, the Egyptian Coptic community has experienced a formidable expansion from the late 1960s when Coptic clergy from Egypt began arriving in Australia. Currently there are several Coptic churches in Sydney, and the foundation in 1982 of Sydney's Coptic Theological College has become a major source of inspiration and community cohesion for the Copts.

RELIGIOUS ORGANISATION

POPE SHENOUDA III COPTIC THEOLOGICAL COLLEGE.
72 Wollongong Road, Arncliffe
(tel: 9567 3076).

Restaurants

Egyptian cuisine expresses the cosmopolitan nature of a country where local ingredients have modified Greek, Turkish, Lebanese, Palestinian, and Syrian traditions. The dishes are simple; made with naturally ripened fruits and vegetables and seasoned with fresh spices. If you like this kind of food, then our own cosmopolitan city has a few places that you should visit.

Morris'. Publicised as Sydney's only exclusively Egyptian restaurant, Morri's is a little ripper of a spot. The food is good, hearty and inexpensive, and there are live belly dancing shows every Friday and Saturday. Average $15, BYO. Open Tuesday-Saturday from 6pm.

445 New Canterbury Road, Dulwich Hill (tel: 9560 1346).

The Nile Restaurant. The extensive north African menu (from Morocco, Ethiopia and Sudan) includes unpretentious and well-presented Egyptian fare. Call in on Friday or Saturday for the live music and dance. Average $15, BYO. Open Tuesday-Sunday, 9am-3pm. Dinner 6-11pm.

553 Crown Street, Surry Hills (tel: 9699 4641).

Landmarks and places of interest

St Mary's & St Mina Coptic Orthodox Church.

Founded in 1968, this was the first Coptic Church established in Australia. Located just on the border of the inner-city suburbs of Marrickville and Sydenham, it was the focus of the social and religious life of an early Egyptian community established in that area around the 1960s.

24A Railway Road, Sydenham. Further information: Fr Samuel Guirguis, parish priest (tel: 9519 1706).

The Nile Restaurant at Surry Hills.

USEFUL NUMBERS FOR VISITORS

EGYPTIAN CONSULATE:
tel: 9362 3488.

EGYPTAIR:
tel: 9232 6677.

Getting to know the Egyptian community

Events

National Day (first day of the revolution).

This is an annual commemorative event held on July 23 to mark the abdication of King Farouk in 1952. Less than a year later Egypt proclaimed itself a republic, and under the leadership of Colonel Gamal Abdul Nasser embarked on a complete political and economic reconstruction of the country. In Sydney this event is celebrated annually on July 26 with social and cultural activities, including a night dinner and a ball (it has been held sometimes at the Hilton Hotel, but the venue may change). Politicians, community leaders, and the Egyptian Consul and Ambassador attend this important event.

Further information: Institute of Australian Egyptian Culture, Chairman Dr Mattar (tel: 9790 2068).

Anwar Sadat Memorial.

On October 6 Sydney Egyptians remember the late Anwar Sadat, the first Arab leader to seek agreement with Israel. During the Sadat government, the country changed its name to the Arab Republic of Egypt. Several cultural and social events are held in Sydney to commemorate this day. We suggest you contact the Institute of Australian Egyptian Culture on 9790 2068 or the Egyptian General-Consulate on 9362 3488, for additional information.

Religious organisations and places of worship

Egyptian Islamic Society.
346 Stoney Creek Road, Kingsgrove (tel: 9554 9402).

St Mark Coptic Orthodox Church.
70 Wollongong Road, Arncliffe (tel: 9597 1413).

St George Coptic Orthodox Church.
3A Bowral Street, Kensington (tel: 9599 1702).

St Bakhomious & St Shenouda Coptic Orthodox Church.

Corner Princes Highway and Ellis Street, Sylvania (tel: 9524 6626).

St Mary's & St Mina Coptic Orthodox Church.

24A Railway Road, Sydenham (tel: 9519 1706).

Archangel Michael & St Bishoy Coptic Orthodox Church.

59 Methven Street, Mt. Druitt (tel: 9718 2567).

Community organisations

Institute of Australian Egyptian Culture.

Established in 1972, the Institute has shown a strong commitment to the welfare and educational and cultural development of the Egyptian community.

21/359 Chapel Road North, Bankstown (tel: 9790 2068).

Facts and figures

Currently, of the 33,140 Egyptian-born people in Australia, a little over half (16,226) live in Sydney. With 89.3% of Egyptians taking up Australian citizenship, they have a naturalisation rate substantially higher than that of all persons born in non-English-speaking countries (72.1%). Almost half of all Australian-Egyptians hold educational or occupational qualifications (48.5%), while 20.2% have completed post-secondary studies.

The overwhelming majority of Egyptians living in Australia are Christians (85.4%), and there are small numbers of Muslims (7.3%) and Jews (1.9%). The variety of languages spoken by Australian Egyptians reflects the cosmopolitan and multicultural nature of the Egyptian society — 39.1% of Egyptians in Australia speak Arabic, followed by Greek (16.6%), Italian (12.7%) and French (7.9%).

The variety of languages spoken by post World War II Egyptian immigrants reflects the diverse ethnic and religious character of cosmopolitan cities such as Alexandria and Cairo.

The Jews

Jewish people around the world have never been restricted to the kinds of boundaries that allow most people to define themselves. That the colony's first policeman was a Jew – John Harris – is notable; that he was a former convict is truly remarkable.

Transported for stealing spoons, he was one of sixteen Jewish convicts known to have arrived on the First Fleet in 1788. Eventually he moved to the 'right' side the law, and began a tradition of Jewish involvement in all sectors of Australian life. (He is, by the way, an ancestor of Lord Casey, a former Governor General and Minister in Menzies' government). Also among those sixteen Jewish convicts were five women; of these, Esther Abrahams, a colourful character by all accounts, went on to marry George Johnston, the Lieutenant Governor of New South Wales (who is an ancestor of Admiral Sir David Martin, former Governor of New South Wales).

Outside business and the law – where Australian Jews have shown an extraordinary success– Jews have also made their mark in the arts. There is the pop singer Deborah Conway, comedian Libby Gorr (aka Elle McFeast), the theatre director Barry Kosky and the writer Bernard Cohen.

Establishing the faith

The year 1816 saw the arrival of the first free Jewish settlers, mostly middle class and English-speaking. Sydney's Jewish community life dates back to this group, who in 1817 formed a *'Chevra'* or 'Holy Brotherhood' to perform burials according to Jewish customs. Sporadic Jewish worship, led by a former convict, Joseph Marcus, commenced in the 1820s, and became more regular in 1828 when Philip Joseph Cohen began holding services in his house in George Street. The small congregation of around 400 moved then to a rented premises at 4 Bridge Street, where they established the first Synagogue in Australia, Beth Tephilah, in 1837. Aiming to have a more permanent worship place, the Sydney Jews soon purchased a block of land in York Street – near where Sydney's Town Hall is today – and built the Synagogue Beth Israel. It served the congregation from 1844 until 1878 when the Great Synagogue, located in Elizabeth Street and facing Hyde Park, was consecrated by Rev AB Davis.

Following the assassination of Czar Alexander II in 1881, the Russian government instituted a brutal crackdown against Jews, who were falsely accused of subversive activities. This led to a mass exodus of Jews from Eastern Europe, and while most went to the US some came to Australia, settling mainly in Sydney. These newcomers established congregations in the western suburb of Bankstown, and in the inner-city suburbs of Newtown (1889) and Surry Hills (1912). A few years later Jews from Poland and Russia moved to Bondi, Dover Heights and Bellevue Hill in the eastern suburbs. More Orthodox Jews, on the other hand, settled in the area of Waverley where – by 1914 – there were already three synagogues within walking distance of each other.

Playing a leading role

In terms of numbers, there were just over 15,000 Jews in Australia at the time of Federation. But what was remarkable was the significant number of these who were to fill major positions in the civic, political, economic and social life of Sydney (no wonder that in 1917 the Legislative Assembly had to close on *Yom Kippur* because both the Speaker and Deputy Speaker were Jews). Prominent Sydney Jewish figures of the early years of the twentieth century were Sir Saul Samuels, Sir Julian Salamons and, later, Sir Daniel Levey and Justice Henry Emanuel Cohen.

Several initiatives gave direction to the Sydney Jewish community in the early years of the twentieth century. In 1923 The Council of Jewish Women, the brainchild of Dr Fanny Reading, was founded and in the same year the Maccabean Hall was opened (at the present site of the Sydney Jewish Museum in Darlinghurst). In 1926 the Employment and Welfare Bureau was founded with the aim of assisting new Jewish migrants. These were the years when the comedian Roy 'Mo' Rene, the son of a Dutch-born Jewish migrant, was taking Australia's theatres by storm.

Beyond the Holocaust

With the coming of the Nazis about 10,000 German and Austrian Jewish refugees arrived in Australia, and in the following years another 35,000 Holocaust survivors came, mainly from East and Central Europe. The Sydney Jewish Welfare Society (now the Jewish Community Service), founded in 1937, was stretched to its limit to accommodate the flow. From a small office in Bond Street the Society's 14 full-time employees had to move to bigger premises at the Macabbean Hall. The Society was led by the remarkable Sydney D Einfeld, who remained as its president for 25 years.

The dramatic changes experienced by Sydney's Jewish community in the following years were very much because of these refugees. Central and

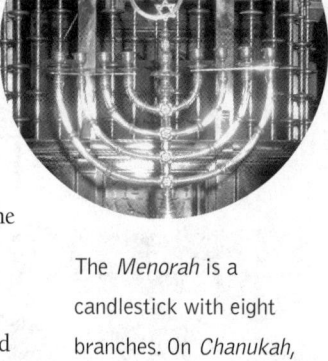

The *Menorah* is a candlestick with eight branches. On *Chanukah*, the Festival of Light, Jewish people light one candle on the first day, two on the second and so forth for eight days.

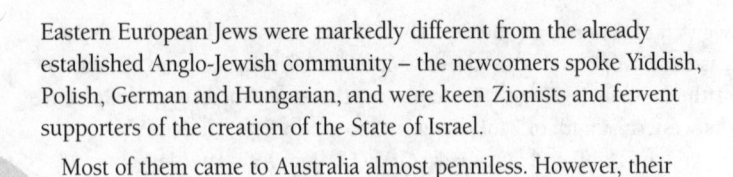

Eastern European Jews were markedly different from the already established Anglo-Jewish community – the newcomers spoke Yiddish, Polish, German and Hungarian, and were keen Zionists and fervent supporters of the creation of the State of Israel.

Most of them came to Australia almost penniless. However, their battered and quickly packed suitcases were full of industrial expertise, skills, education and an enormous desire to start a new life. This generation produced a number of business leaders who are today not only very well known but also very influential – among them Sir Peter Abeles, the transport magnate; Frank Lowy and John Saunders, who established the Westfield shopping chain; and Joseph Brender, who created the immensely successful Katies chain. Many descendants of this generation have also made their mark in business – lipstick queen Poppy King for example – and also in entertainment and the arts – the outrageous Libby Gorr (Elle McFeast), the pop singer Deborah Conway, the theatre director Barry Kosky and the leading writer Bernard Cohen, to name a few.

Dr. Suzanne Rutland is currently Jewish Education Coordinator in the School of Teaching and Curriculum Studies at the University of Sydney. She has published widely in the field of Australian Jewish History, including *Edge of the Diaspora: Two Centuries of Jewish Settlement in Australia* and *Pages of History: A Century of the Australian Jewish Press*.

The Jewish community today

An important number of community, cultural and educational organisations that exist today also owe their existence to the refugees of the 1940s. One of the most important was the Jewish Board of Deputies (1947), which since its establishment has been the official voice of the Jewish community in promoting human rights and combating anti-semitism. Another significant community initiative was the establishment of the Jewish Day Schools, which promote Jewish values and traditions through the study of Jewish history and culture. There are five Jewish Day Schools in Sydney: Masada, Mount Sinai, The Emanuel, Yeshiva and Moriah College.

Further waves of immigration occurred at the end of the 1950s, 1970s and the 1980s when Hungarian, South African, Russian and Israeli Jews arrived in Sydney – reinforcing and expanding the Jewish community in Bondi, Dover Heights and Bellevue Hill. With the growth of the community new places of worship were built so that today there are over 20 Orthodox Synagogues, spread across several suburbs.

With the new arrivals many cultural, sporting and social organisations also emerged, including *B'nai B'rith*, a fraternal service organisation, the NSW

Maccabi, the Folk Centre for Yiddish Culture and the Sydney Hakoah Club which has a membership of over 10,000. The recent and most important event for this vibrant community was the opening in 1992 of the Sydney Jewish Museum. Dedicated to the Holocaust and Australian Jewish history, the Museum has become one of the most important landmarks not only for Jews but for the whole Sydney community.

Cafes

For cafes, restaurants and social clubs see also Bondi beach map, page 408 and Bondi road map, page 15.

Dov Cafe. This warm and friendly corner cafe offers an inexpensive and tasty Israeli-Mediterranean menu. Average $10, BYO. Open Monday-Saturday 6.30am-10.30pm, Sunday 9am-3pm.

252 Forbes Street, Darlinghurst (tel: 9360 9594).

The Bagel House. The owner Simon Furey, has a basic motto – 'if it's not boiled, it's not a bagel'. There's a store in the MLC Centre Food Court.

Martin Place (tel: 9231 1338) and at 2/95 O'Sullivan Road, Rose Bay (tel: 9362 1344).

Shopping

From bagel bakeries to bookshops, from liquor stores to butcheries – Sydney may not yet be New York but it's looking dangerously close.

David Moffat Judaica Gift Shop. Part of the North Shore Temple Emanuel, this small shop offers a huge range of religious articles including candlesticks, *kiddush* cups, *challah* cloths, *Pesach* plates and *matza* covers. Open during the office hours of the Temple, Monday-Friday 9am-5pm (till 3pm on Friday), opens on Sunday by request during Sunday School.

28 Chatswood Avenue, Chatswood (tel: 9419 7011).

Clovelly Liquor Supermarket. The wide selection of local and imported *Kosher* wines and spirits make this liquor supermarket one of the best in town. Open Monday-Wednesday 9am-8.30pm, Thursday-Friday 9am-9pm, Saturday 9am-8pm, Sunday 11am-6pm.

224-226 Clovelly Road, Clovelly (tel: 9665 5088 or 9665 1577).

Gardos & Biro Distribution. Has a large range of *Kosher* meat (minimum order $100). Open Monday-Friday 8am-1pm.

144 McEvoy Street, Alexandria (tel: 9698 4088).

Peter Wertheim, President of the NSW Jewish Board of Deputies – the official roof body of the State's Jewish community

ISRAEL DOWN UNDER

In this unpretentious gift and bookshop you'll find a wide range of products, including candlesticks, ceramics, music and — believe it or not — Dead Sea cosmetics! It also stocks a small range of books of various types — religious, travel, pictorial, historical, nature, Holocaust, cooking and political. Open Tuesday-Saturday 11am-5.30 pm (till late on Thursday), Saturday 10am-4pm.

411 Darling Street, Balmain. (tel: 9818 5247).

Independent Discount Liquor. This is another recommended spot for buying *kosher* wine, spirits and grape juices. Monday-Friday 8.30am-5pm.

9 Brisbane Street, Darlinghurst (tel: 9264 8459).

North Deli. A highly diversified deli, it offers a large variety of *kosher* products, including bagels, bread and groceries. Open Monday-Wednesday 9am-6pm, Thursday 9am-6.30pm, Friday 7.30am-4pm, Sunday 8am-1pm.

360 Pacific Highway. Lindfield (tel: 9416 8288).

Shalom Book and Gift Shop. Has a vast array of Jewish books, gifts, Israeli giftware, religious items and cards. Open Monday-Friday 9am-5pm (till 3pm on Friday).

323 Pacific Highway, Lindfield (tel: 9416 7076).

See also Bondi, page 15

Landmarks and places of interest

The Great Synagogue.

A majestic feature of the Elizabeth Street townscape facing Hyde Park, this is the best-known Jewish building in Australia. It was built under the inspiration of Rev AB Davis (1828-1913), one of the great Jewish religious leaders in Sydney. The Synagogue, designed by Thomas Rowe, an eminent non-Jewish architect of the period, was consecrated on March 4 1878. Modelled on the London Great Synagogue, it is primarily Byzantine in style with French Gothic touches. The tall twin towers on the front are of carved sandstone which was quarried at Pyrmont in Sydney. The interior gives the impression of spaciousness and height with its cast iron columns and panelled and groined ceiling. The plaster decorations on the arches, the stained-glass windows and fine light pendants (originally lit by gas) complete the impressive interior. Free guided tours are available on Tuesday and Thursday at noon. Photography inside is not allowed and head coverings are required.

The Great Synagogue was consecrated on March 4 1878.

Entrance:166 Castlereagh Street, City (tel: 9267 2477).

Rabbi Falk Memorial Library.

Part of the Great Synagogue, this library has a great collection of Judaic and Hebraic literature. Journals, newspapers and rare books are available. As the Falk Library is primarily a reference collection, books must be viewed within the library, however there is an inter-library loan service.

The library also maintains a display of Jewish art work. Open Monday-Thursday 9am-5pm, Friday 9am-2pm.

166 Castlereagh Street, City (tel: 9267 2477).

The Sydney Jewish Museum.

This magnificent museum opened its door in 1992 in what was the original premises of the NSW Jewish War Memorial Maccabean Institute. Visitors to the Museum can explore, on the different levels of the Museum, a chronological and thematic history of the Jewish community. The central part of the museum is dedicated to the Holocaust, where visitors can be given guided tours by survivors of this dramatic chapter of Jewish history – it's a moving experience. Open Monday-Thursday 10am-4pm, Friday 10am-3pm, Sunday 11am-5pm, closed on Jewish holidays. Cost: $6/$4/$3, family $15.

148 Darlinghurst Road, Darlinghurst (tel: 9360 7999).

USEFUL NUMBERS FOR VISITORS

CONSULATE GENERAL OF ISRAEL:
tel: 9264 7933.

ISRAEL AUSTRALIA CHAMBER OF COMMERCE:
tel: 9326 1700.

Getting to know the Jewish community

Events

The Jewish calendar year consists of 12 lunar months, determined by the time of revolution of the moon around the earth; most years consist of 345 days. The following are the major holidays celebrated by the Sydney Jewish community. Festivals commence at sunset. One trait all Jewish holidays have in common is that work, or travelling by car or public transport is prohibited. Jewish students are exempt from attending school on these days.

You can obtain further information about these events by contacting the Jewish Community Services (tel: 9331 5184) or the New South Wales Jewish Board of Deputies (tel: 9360 1600).

Purim (Feast of Lots).

Celebrated on the 14th of Adar (late February and early March) this festival commemorates the occasion when the Jews of the Persian empire were saved from the destruction planned by their enemy, Haman. The main activity of the festival is the reading of the scroll of Esther at the evening service (on the 13th of *Adar*) and the morning service (on the 14th)

Sydney's synagogues are the religious heart of Sydney's Jewish communities

THE JEWS

SHAVUOT (PENTECOST).

Celebrated on the 6th of the month of *Sivan* (May/June), this festival is observed as the anniversary of the giving of the *Matan Torah* (Law) on Mount Sinai. Diverse activities are held in Sydney's synagogues.

SUCCOT (TABERNACLES).

It begins on the 15th and ends on the 22nd of the month of *Tishri* (September/October). It is essentially a festival of thanksgiving marking the gathering of the products from the harvest, and is also a reminder of time spent dwelling in huts by the Jews during their march through the desert (Exodus).

ROSH HASHANAH (JEWISH NEW YEAR).

Falls on the 1st day of the month of *Tishri* (mid-September). It is traditional at this time for Jews to cleanse themselves of sins to usher in the new year.

Pesach (Passover).

This marks the most important moment in Jewish history, the freeing of the Jewish people from slavery in Egypt. This festival, which runs for one week, begins the 15th and ends the 22nd of the month of *Nisan* (March or April). Families get together and symbolic meals are prepared, including fried *gefilte*, *matzo* balls, *charoset* (a wine, nut cinnamon and apple paste), egg, horseradish, chopped liver and fruit salad. During this time it is forbidden to eat or possess *chametz*, a general term for all food and drink made from wheat, barley, rye, oats, spelt or their derivatives. A traditional activity is to listen to the *Haggadah*, the story of the exodus of the Jews from Egypt.

Yom Kippur (Day of Atonement).

This is the holiest day of the Jewish calendar, and is observed on the 10th of the month of *Tishri* (September). It's entirely devoted to fasting, prayer and meditation to symbolically purify the body of past sins. *Yom Kippur* also is a day when Jews formally forgive those against whom they hold a grievance, and ask for God's forgiveness. Services are celebrated in synagogues throughout Sydney. There is also a special appeal held during this time by the Sydney Jewish Community Service (JCS) drawing attention to the social problems of Australia's Jewish community.

Chanukah (Feast of Light).

This festival – which extends from the 25th of Kislev to the 2nd or 3rd of the month of *Tebet* (November/December) – commemorates the victory of the Jewish freedom fighters, the Maccabees over the Greco-Syrian king Antiochus IV (known as Epiphanes) in 165 BC. The struggle culminated in the recapture of the Jewish Temple in Jerusalem and restoration of religious freedom and political sovereignty. At *Chanuka* ('dedication' in Hebrew) Jewish people light the traditional menorah, a candelabra with eight branches.

Public ceremonies are held in various venues, including Guilfoyle Park at Bay Street, Double Bay, and Sydney's Hyde Park.

Other Events

Yom Hashoa (Holocaust Day of Remembrance).

Held in April or May following *Passover*, this day remembers the victims of the Holocaust. Readings, memorial services, candle-lighting ceremonies and community events are held at Jewish schools, temples and synagogues throughout Sydney. The Sydney Jewish Museum usually hosts cultural functions, including films and discussions related to the Holocaust.

Yom Ha'atzmuat (Israel Independence Day).

This annual celebration is held on May 12 to celebrate the founding of the State of Israel in 1948. For further information contact some of the community organisations included in this chapter.

Jewish Film Festival.

Held in November, this festival features the best movies and documentaries made by Jewish film makers around the world. Tickets are $13.

Chauvel Cinema, Paddington Town Hall (tel: 9361 5398).

Religious organisations and places of worship

There are currently more than 20 synagogues in Sydney, belonging to a variety of traditions in the Jewish religious life. The following is a selected list. For a comprehensive directory see the Congregation Guide published in the *Australian Jewish News* ($2.80, from most newsagencies).

Maroubra Synagogue.

Services Monday-Thursday 6.30am, Friday 6pm, Saturday 9am, Sunday 8am.

635 Anzac Parade, Maroubra (tel: 9344 0152).

Newtown Synagogue.

Services Friday 6pm and 9.30pm.

20 Georgina Street, Newtown (tel: 9371 8870).

North Shore Temple Emanuel.

Services Friday 6.30pm, Saturday 10.30am.

28 Chatswood Avenue, Chatswood (tel: 9419 7011).

Parramatta Synagogue.

Services Friday 6.30pm, Saturday 9am.

116 Victoria Road, Parramatta (tel: 9683 5381).

The Congregation of the Temple Emanuel (Kehillat Emanuel).

Services, in Hebrew and English, Friday 6.15pm, Saturday 9.30am, Monday 6.45 am.

7 Ocean Street, Woollahra (tel: 9328 7833).

RELIGIOUS ORGANISATIONS AND PLACES OF WORSHIP

CENTRAL SYNAGOGUE. Services Monday-Friday 6.40am and 7.30pm, Sunday and public holidays 7.30am and 7.30pm.

Hollywood Avenue, corner Ebley Street, Bondi Junction (tel: 9389 5622).

THE GREAT SYNAGOGUE. Services Monday-Tuesday and Thursday 7am and 5.30pm, Friday 5.30pm, Saturday 8.45am. Elizabeth Street (near Park Street); office at 166 Castlereagh Street, City (tel: 9267 2477).

YESHIVA SYNAGOGUE. Has daily services 6.15am, 7.30am and 10 minutes before sunset.

36 Flood Street, Bondi (tel: 9387 3822).

GREAT SYNAGOGUE MUSEUM. This small museum, located in the basement of the Great Synagogue, has changing exhibitions and a sound/light show. Tours, on Tuesday and Thursdays at noon, are free.

166 Castlereagh Street, City (tel: 9267 2477).

Art and Culture

Jewish Arts and Culture Council.

This is an umbrella cultural and artistic organisation that promotes Jewish arts and culture.

146 Darlinghurst Road, Darlinghurst (tel: 9360 1600).

Jewish Folk Centre.

Promotes and preserves Yiddish language and culture, and also maintains a Yiddish library.

23 Saber Street, Woollahra (tel: 9389 3565 or 9327 3832).

Sydney Jewish Choral Society.

The Society fosters and develops choral music, covering the Jewish repertoire and Israeli and secular music.

PO Box 18, Double Bay, 2028 (tel: 9398 3565).

Sydney Jewish Theatre.

A community company providing artistic and theatre space for members of the Jewish community.

PO Box 1099, Double Bay 2028 (tel: 9371 5090 or 9560 8092).

Education

There are more than 12 Jewish educational institutions in Sydney. The following is only a selected list.

MORIAH WAR MEMORIAL COLLEGE. Provides a secular and Jewish education from preschool to matriculation.

Queens Park Road, Bondi Junction (tel: 9387 3555).

Masada College.

The College gives Jewish and secular education from preschool infants to primary and high school.

14a Treatts Road, Lindfield (Primary School), 9-15 Link Road, St Ives (High School) (tel: 9449 3744).

Mount Sinai College.

Provides Jewish education for infants and primary students.

6 Runic Lane, Maroubra (tel: 9349 4877).

Yeshiva Centre.

Established in 1956, it offers Jewish and secular education from preschool to high school as well as *Talmud Torah*, Ladies' Seminary and College of Adult Jewish Education. In 1987 the Yeshiva Centre established a rabbinical college dedicated to the education of new rabbis.

36 Floor Street, Bondi (tel: 9387 3822).

Community organisations

The Jews constitute one of the most highly organised communities in the country. The following is a selected list of community-based organisations.

Australian Jewish Welfare Society.

A non-profit, community-based social work and welfare organisation which provides a range of services to meet the special needs of the Sydney Jewish community.

146 Darlinghurst Road, Darlinghurst (tel: 9331 5184).

NSW Jewish Board of Deputies.

This is the official umbrella organisation of the Sydney Jewish community.

2nd Floor, 146 Darlinghurst Road, Darlinghurst (tel: 9360 1600).

JEWISH COMMUNITY SERVICES. Provides welfare and social services to seniors, migrants, families and children, and to people with intellectual disabilities. Enquiries: Monday-Thursday 9am-5pm.

Level 3 Leyland House, Oxford Street, Bondi (tel: 9369 1400).

Media

Newspapers

The Australian Jewish News. The oldest Jewish newspaper in Australia, the *Australian Jewish News* is a real institution for the Jewish community. This quality weekly, published in English, offers excellent news coverage, intelligent feature stories and interesting opinion pieces. It appears on Friday and costs $2.80. Its Editor in Chief is Sam Lipski, one of the most prestigious journalists in the country. The editor of the Sydney edition is Vic Alhadeff.

146 Darlinghurst Road, Darlinghurst (tel: 9360 5100).

Radio

SBS Radio 1, AM 1107. Broadcasts information, news, comment and current affairs in Hebrew. It can be heard Sunday 11am-noon, and is followed by a radio program in English and Yiddish, noon-1pm. Wednesday and Friday 2-3pm (Hebrew), 3-4pm (Yiddish).

2RES, FM 89.7. The Jewish Week radio program with Robert Teicher can be heard Thursday 3.30pm-4pm.

Bondi: kosher, sand and kites

GETTING THERE

Bondi Junction is at the end of the eastern suburbs train line, from there you can get to Bondi Beach by buses such as the 380, 382 or 389 or alternatively, catch the same buses from Circular Quay.

Along streets such as Hall and Bondi Road, you'll find well stocked *kosher* bakeries, restaurants, butcheries and delicatessens, while the local synagogues – including the Central Synagogue at 19 Hollywood Ave, Bondi Junction and the Yeshiva Synagogue at 36 Flood Street, Bondi – are the main catalysts of Jewish community life.

Apart from the country's highest concentration of models, film-makers, actors and artists of all kinds, Bondi – and the nearby suburb of Bondi Junction – is known as a significant centre for Sydney's Jewish community.

Bondi is also the "natural" home of a small but noisy Brazilian colony that makes itself visible every Sunday around the Bondi Pavilion showing off with soccer balls glued to their feet and with the contagious rhythms of their drums (see The Brazilians, page 475).

Bondi – or "sound of waves breaking on the beach" in Aboriginal language – is located only 7km east of the Sydney CBD. The closest beach to the centre of City. One of the main appeals of Bondi is its cosmopolitan and multi-ethnic nature – the ten largest migrant communities are from the United Kingdom, the former USSR, New Zealand, South Africa, Hungary, Ireland, Poland, Germany and China, and if you hang around long enough it's likely that you'll rate Russian as the second most spoken language in the area.

However, it's the Jewish presence that constitutes the most distinctive "ethnic" aspect of Bondi. Jews have been around Bondi since the early years of the twentieth century when Polish and Russian Jews – who had originally settled in the CBD – began moving to Bondi and the nearby suburbs of North Bondi, Dover Heights and Bellevue Hill, while more orthodox Jews settled in Waverley within a walking distance of the three synagogues that were already built by 1914. The Jewish population in the area was reinforced with the arrival of refugees escaping from the Nazi terror, in the 1930s and with the waves of Jewish immigrants from the former Soviet Union in the 1970s and 1980s. Today, the local Jewish community is solidly established in the area.

The ethnic diversity and cosmopolitanism of Bondi is also visible through a number of events celebrated in the area including the South American Festival (see page 470), the Pacific Wave's – an outdoor music and dance festival featuring Tongan, Torres Strait Islander, Aboriginal, Papua New Guinean, Samoan and Maori artists (more info on 9130 3325), and the Festival of the Winds – hailed as a carnival of kites, multicultural music and dance – held mid September (more info on 9130 3325). There is also the Flickerfest – the International Short Film

Festival – celebrated during the first weeks of January featuring creations of film-makers from all over the world (more info on 9266 7242). Finally, Bondi hosts the very cosmopolitan but infamous "Christmas on Bondi Beach" where young travellers from just about every corner of the world (although the "Pom" contingent is by far the largest) pour into Bondi beach on December 25 in an episode of alcoholic prowess. This latter is highly un-recommended.

Restaurants and Take Away (Bondi Beach).

See map, page 408

1: Tibby's. A *kosher* restaurant and cocktail bar, Tibby's is a bit of an institution in Bondi Beach. At Tibby's, the *kosher* meals are good at a very affordable price. Average $15, licensed. Open Saturday-Thursday from 5pm or after sundown).

Corner Campbell Parade and Francis Street (tel: 9130 5051).

4: Nando's Chickenland. The Portuguese contribution to cosmopolitan Bondi Beach – Nando's is all about chargrilled chicken marinated in hot chilli *piri-piri* sauce, very tasty. Warning, it's very busy particularly over weekends. Open Monday-Friday 11.30am-11.30pm, Saturday-Sunday 11.30am-till late.

Swiss Grand Hotel, Campbell Parade (tel: 9365 7888).

12: Aviv. A good value *kosher* eatery with a strong Israeli accent. The menu has an extensive range of chicken, beef and lamb based dishes. A good selection of salads and *kosher* wine are also available. Average $15, BYO and licensed (*kosher*). Open Sunday-Thursday 10.30am-10pm (closed on Friday and Saturday).

49 Hall Street (tel: 930 8302).

5: Savion. An institution with the Jewish community and a well reputed take away more than anything else, Savion offers good value Israeli *kosher* hot and cold fare. Many "who's who" are regular patrons at Savion, (including the former Prime Minister of Australia, Bob Hawke, we're told). Average $10, no alcohol. Open Sunday-Thursday 9am-10pm, Friday 9am-2pm.

38 Wairoa Avenue (tel: 9130 6357).

What is highly recommended – while in Bondi Beach – is to pay a visit to the Bondi Pavilion Gallery at Queen Elizabeth Drive where some good pieces of alternative art are on display (Monday-Sunday, 10am-5pm, tel: 9130 3325. Free). Optionally you may like to go treasure hunting in the Bondi Beach Market at the Public School, Campbell Parade (Sunday 10am-5pm, tel: 9398 5486), or to take a walk to the North end of Bondi Beach to observe some remarkable Aboriginal carvings found there (more information about this in Indigenous Sydney page 40).

6: Lewis's. One of the most traditional *kosher* eateries in Bondi Beach. The herring and *falafel* are worth a try. Gefilte fish, *matzo* balls, sweet apple *kugel*, salads, cakes and hot dishes to take away are also available. Average $10, no alcohol. Open Sunday-Thursday 9am-9pm, Friday 8.30am-4pm.

2 Curlewis Street (tel: 9365 5421).

BONDI: KOSHER, SAND AND KITES

1. Tibby's.
2. Ravesi's.
3. Gelato Bar.
4. Nando's Chickenland.
5. Savion.
6. Lewis's.
7. Medy's Cakes.
8. Russian Lodge.
9. Stark's Kosher Deli.
10. Hadassa Kosher Butchery.
11. Club Hakoah.
12. Aviv.
13. Roman's Deli.
14. Carmel Cake Shop.
15. Gold Books and Gifts.

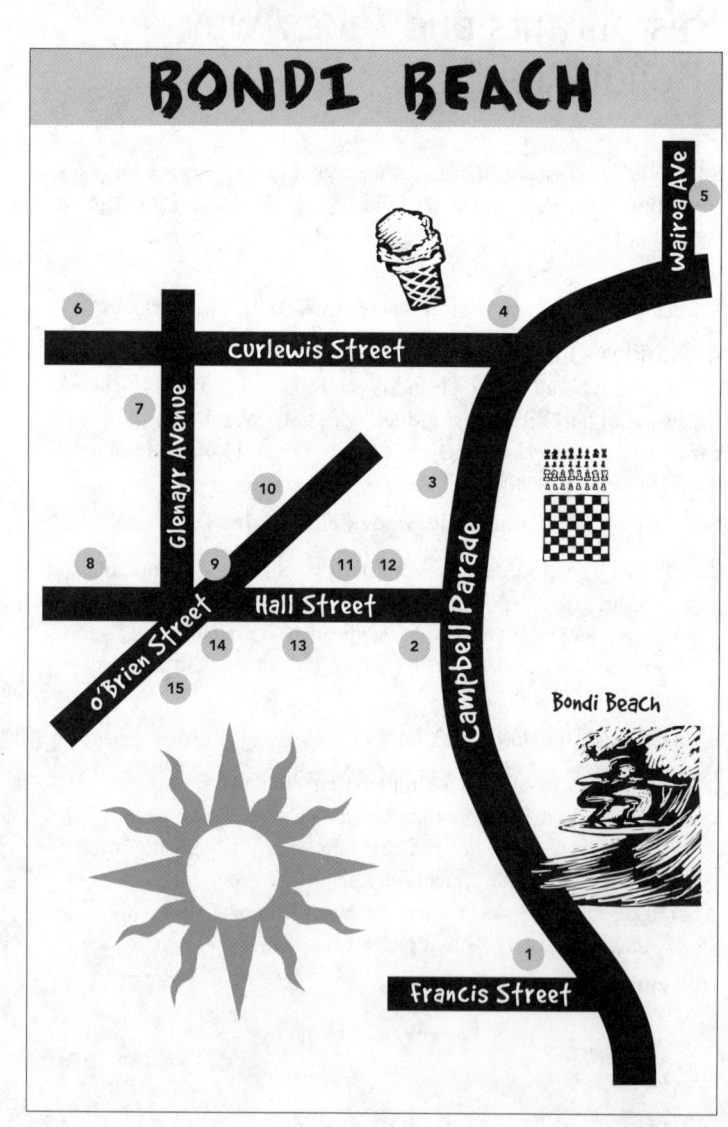

Explore the world in one city

11: Club Hakoah. One of the most popular Jewish social and sports clubs in Sydney. It has a fully licensed restaurant where you can drop by and order a generous and hearty *goulash* or a tasty *matzo* ball soup. Live entertainment is also a regular feature at Hakoah. Average $15, licensed. Open Monday-Sunday from 6pm.

16 Hall Street (tel: 9365 9900).

2: Ravesi's. One of the landmarks in Bondi Beach, Ravesi's has come a long way since an Italian immigrant established a modest corner grocery store (see The Italians, page 155).

3: Gelato Bar. Hungarian cafe. (see The Hungarians, page 149).

140 Campbell Parade (tel: 9130 4033).

8: Russian Lodge. Russian cuisine.(see The Russians, page 213).

113-15 Hall Street (tel: 9365 1997).

The Hakoah Club, Hall Street, Bondi.

Shopping

7: Medy's Cakes. A praised Jewish bakery featuring a complete range of pastries bread and cakes made with potato and *matzo* flour. Try Medy's hazelnut or coconut macaroons. Open Monday-Thursday 8.30am-5pm, Friday 8.30am-5.30pm, Saturday 8.30am-12.30pm.

139 Glenayr Avenue (tel: 9130 3040).

9: Stark's Kosher Deli. It stocks a full line of *kosher* products, including goods imported from the USA, Israel and Eastern Europe. A place to find tinned fish, cheese, sweets, wines and spirits. Open Monday-Thursday 8am-6pm, Friday 7.30am – one hour before Shabbath, Sunday 7.30am-1.30pm.

95 Hall Street (tel: 9130 3872).

10: Hadassa Kosher Butchery. A wide range of *kosher* meats – including preservative-free frankfurts and smallgoods – all prepared by an accomplished *kosher* butcher. Warning: it's a bit hard to find if you're not familiar with the urban puzzle (tucked away in O'Brien Street). Open Monday 7am-1pm, Tuesday-Thursday 7am-6pm, Friday 7am - 2pm, Sunday 7am-1pm.

17 O'Brien Street, Bondi (tel: 9365 4904).

JAKK'S BAGEL AND BREAD COMPANY. A favourite spot for the South African Jewish community, Jakk's isn't just known for its leading bagels but also by its delicious and great range of bread rolls and *foccacias*. Open Monday-Friday 6.30am-5.30pm, Saturday-Sunday 7.30am-1pm.

308 Bronte Road, Waverley (tel: 9389 3588).

13: Roman's Deli. "The Russian connection" according to Bondi's folk, Roman's is one of the best stocked Russian delis in Sydney, here you'll find a range of salted, smoked and marinated fish, Siberian *pelmeni*, *voreniki* and *pirashki* (pie), Russian caviar – needless to say – is also available. Open Monday-Sunday 8.30am-8pm.
78 Hall Street (tel: 9365 7042).

14: Carmel Cake Shop. Easy to miss, (follow the map), it's a Jewish bakery offering some delicious pastries and "real" bagels. Open Tuesday-Thursday 8.30am-5pm, Friday 7am- 5pm (approximately), Sunday 7am-2pm.
14 O'Brien Street (tel: 9130 5797).

15: Gold Books and Gifts. Jewish books, audio and video cassettes (see The Russians, page 213). Open Monday-Thursday 9.30am-5.30pm, Friday 9.30am-3.30pm.
16b O'Brien Street (tel: 9300 0495).

Facts and figures

Despite small congregations in the west and south of Sydney, the majority of Jews are concentrated on the north shore and the eastern suburbs.

According to the 1991 Census there are 74,186 Jews in Australia -- up 7.7% on 1986. However, the real figure is likely to be much higher because the census doesn't take into account Jews who were overseas at the time, nor the 23.4% of Australians who didn't specify their religion. Professor Bill Rubinstein in Judaism in Australia (Bureau of Immigration Multicultural and Population Research, 1996) points out that a figure of about 100,000 to 105,000 Jews in Australia in 1991 seems to be the most accurate - that is, of persons who were Jewish by religion, or were Jewish by ethnicity and practising members of no other religion.'

Sydney has been known as a significant centre of Australia's Jewish community – 39.9% of Australia's Jews live in News South Wales (29,577) and of those 28,544 have settled in Sydney.

Slightly above 45% of Australian Jews were born in Australia, a low figure when compared with 78% for all Australians. Among Jews the second largest birthplace is South Africa (8%), followed by Poland (7.8%), Russia (7.4%) and the United Kingdom (6%).

The Lebanese

A **collective scream** of jubilation was immediately followed by a gasp of disappointment. It was 1989 and proud Lebanese boy Benny Elias had just missed *that* field goal – the one from right in front of the posts that would have clinched the Rugby League Grand Final for battlers Balmain.

But it was not to be, and the Balmain faithful (and most likely all of Sydney's Lebanese, no matter which team they normally supported) suffered with little Benny at that moment. Fortunately, the Lebanese community in Sydney has been successfully 'kicking goals' for many years.

The early years

For the early group of Lebanese who arrived in the 1890s the inner-city suburb of Redfern was their first home. They were Christians from the Bekaa Valley, and were labelled (inaccurately) as 'Syrians' – it was not until the 1950 Census that they were classified as 'Lebanese'. By 1901 this area, especially around Great Buckingham Street between Chalmers and Elizabeth Streets, formed an enclave of some 200 Lebanese working as hawkers, small merchants and importers. Redfern was also the original home of one of the most prominent Lebanese Australians - Sir Nicholas Shehadie, a former mayor of Sydney (and captain of the Australia Rugby Union team between 1947 and 1954). His parents came to Australia before WWI when Sir Nicholas' father an Orthodox priest – migrated here to serve as the first parish priest for the Sydney Lebanese Orthodox Church. (see Cleveland Street, page 17.)

For the early Sydney Lebanese immigrants – Christian Antiochian Orthodox, Melkite and Maronite Catholics – religion was an integral part of their lives. Upon arrival they directed their energies and financial means to the establishment of places of worship. In 1895, the Melkite Catholic community built the first Lebanese church in Australia – St. Michael's Melkite Church – in the inner-city suburb of Waterloo. (This church was established by Archimandrite Silwanos Mansour, the first Lebanese priest to settle in Australia.) Two years later, the Lebanese Maronite congregation founded their own church – St Maroun – in the neighbouring suburb of

The Sydney Lebanese take pride in the achievements and contributions they have made in their new country in all aspects of society. In sport there's Benny Elias of course, while in politics Sir Nicholas Shehadie, a former mayor of Sydney, comes to mind. Leading Australian writer David Malouf was born of Lebanese and English parents; and Zita Antonios has made her mark as the NSW Race Discrimination Commissioner.

The 1970s saw the foundation of perhaps the best-known Arabic language newspaper in Australia, *El Telegraph* (not to be confused with the former Socceroos' colourful coach 'El Tel' Venables). Instrumental in the success of this newspaper was the late Michael Obeid. Born in Matrite, Lebanon, in 1939, he migrated to Australia at the age of 18, and began working as a journalist with *El Telegraph* in 1970, later becoming its director. When he passed away in 1991, more than 2,000 people, including federal MPs, mayors and leaders of the Lebanese community, turned out to his farewell at Our Lady of Lebanon.

Redfern. This same neighbourhood was also saw the first church of the Anthiochian Orthodox community – St George's Orthodox Church – built in 1901 (until then the congregation used to worship in the rather unsuitable top floor of a billiard saloon in Elizabeth Street!).

Not much is known about a Lebanese orchardist – from the Baan village – who established himself in the north-western suburb of Thornleigh in the 1920s and was responsible for the expansion of a Lebanese community in that area. At the beginning of the 1930s, he sponsored over 50 people from his home village to emigrate to Australia and to work on his 300 acres of land. After some time he subdivided his property into small allotments which were purchased by his village employees. Eventually, the Lebanese enclave of Thornleigh grew with the arrival of new Baan villagers who became successful orange growers, market gardeners and farmers.

New arrivals

The three decades after World War II saw a steady growth in Lebanese immigration. During this period, most Lebanese found work in the post-war manufacturing industries, and some of them ventured into their own small businesses, such as milk bars, coffee lounges or taxi driving. By 1954, there were 3,861 Lebanese living in Australia.

With the growing presence of Lebanese immigrants, the need to have more permanent and formal organisations arose. In 1950, the Australian Lebanese Association (ALA) was born, with the aim of providing a non-denominational and non-political venue for Lebanese settlers. At the same time, churches of different denominations continued expanding and were revitalised by the new wave of arrivals.

In 1965 the Maronites refurbished their original building in Redfern and established a primary school attached to the church, and in 1972 – with an enormous economic effort – they built the impressive cathedral Our Lady of Lebanon at Harris Park in the western suburbs (see page 415).
A year later the Antiochian Orthodox community opened their second church, St Nicholas, in the suburb of Punchbowl, south-west of the City.

A rich diversity

Sydney's Muslim Lebanese are latecomers. They began arriving at the end of the 1970s and established a small Sunni Muslim community in the western suburb of Lakemba. They began worshipping in a modest brick suburban house but that has now given way to an enormous modern stone building – known as the Imam Ali Mosque – in Lakemba (see page 423). Lebanese Shi'ite Muslims also arrived around this time.

They established a thriving community in the southern suburb of Arncliffe where in 1985 the Fatima-Al-Zahra Mosque, the largest mosque in Australia, was built.

The Lebanese take pride in the achievements and contributions they have made to their new country in all aspects of society. In sport there's Benny Elias of course, while in politics Sir Nicholas Shehadie, a former mayor of Sydney, comes to mind. Leading Australian writer David Malouf was born of Lebanese and English parents; Zita Antonio has made her mark as the NSW Race Discrimination Commissioner; and Jacques A. Nasser is one of the world's most influential automotive executives. The list goes on, and will continue to do so.

Restaurants and take-aways

Do Sydney Lebanese go to Lebanese restaurants? Sure they do, but it's just that every time you ask a Lebanese friend for advice about a good eating place in Sydney they always come up with the standard answer: "why go out when my Mum cooks such great Lebanese food?" Following are a few tips for those of us who do not have a Lebanese mother. We also recommend dropping by Lakemba (see page 416), or Cleveland Street, (see page 17).

Criterion. Upmarket, with interesting Lebanese and Mediterranean cuisine. Average $50, licensed. Open for lunch Monday-Friday noon-3pm, dinner 6pm-10pm, Saturday 6pm-10pm.
Lobby Level, MLC Centre, corner King and Castlereagh Streets (tel: 9233 1234).

Cafe Libanais. This is a well-established place in charming Glebe Point Road. Try the house speciality, chicken *kebab*. Average $10, BYO. Open Tuesday-Sunday 10am-9pm.
93 Glebe Point Road, Glebe (tel: 9660 3823).

EM Youseff Pizza Bar. Eat in or take away, the enjoyment of having a Lebanese pizza experience will force you to try this place. Select any from the ten different kinds of pizzas and you will not be disappointed. A tip? – try the one with oregano, sesame seeds and *sumac* (*za'atar*). Open Monday-Sunday 5am-8pm.
The Boulevarde, Punchbowl (tel: 9759 2391).

Rockdale Pizza. This place gives ample justification for the rise and rise of Sydney's fascination with Lebanese pizza. Open Monday-Sunday 7am-7pm.
16 Waltz Street, Rockdale (tel: 9597 5212).

CHECK THIS OUT

HABIBI MICHAEL. Cushions on the floor, belly dancers and delicious *kebbee* (spicy lamb) at $14.

147 Oxford Street, Darlinghurst (tel: 9361 5527).

HI JAZI. The large Lebanese community in Arncliffe flock to this spot looking for the most authentic, and cheap Lebanese food in town.

53 Wollongong Road, Arncliffe (tel: 9599 0726).

Summerland Restaurant. Considered one of the best Lebanese restaurants in Sydney, the impressive menu is challenged only by the superb quality of the food. And don't forget the live music and belly dancing. Average $20, BYO and licensed. Open for lunch Tuesday-Friday noon-3pm, dinner Monday-Saturday 5.30pm-11pm (till 3am on Friday and Saturday).

741 Punchbowl Road, Punchbowl (tel: 9708 5107).

Shopping

Abla Pastry. Don't expect a tiny and modest spot. It's not. It's the proper venue for a huge range of those delicious Lebanese sweets that we're already so familiar with: *balourie*, *namoura*, *pistachio* triangles, *bassma*, etc, etc. Also try the local black coffee and the refreshing ice creams.

48 Railway Parade, Granville (tel: 9637 8092).

Banksia Bakery. Among the biscuits and tempting sweet loaves, the traditional Lebanese pizzas are a must. You can get individual mini-pizzas from $1 to $3.50. Open Monday-Sunday 5.30am-7pm.

26 Railway Street, Banksia (tel: 9597 7715).

Belmore Lebanese Bakery. The extensive range of cakes and pasties, especially ones filled with cheese and spinach, deserve a try. You will also find superb Lebanese pizzas. Open Monday-Sunday 5.30am-5.30pm (till later on Friday and till 3pm on Sunday).

339 Burwood Road, Belmore (tel; 9759 2490).

Orion Lebanese Grocery. This is a sweets palace – great *baklawa* and ladies' fingers – with everything fresh and ready to take away: It also has a wide range of products imported from Lebanon, including cheeses, oils, jams and syrups. Open Monday-Saturday 9am-9pm, Sunday 9am-7pm.

327 Penshurst Street, Willoughby (tel: 9417 5493).

See also Cleveland Street, page 17, and Lakemba, page 416.

Nightclubs

Golden Nights. Described by some as the venue for the Lebanese 'who's who', Golden Nights delivers what its name promises. Great restaurant service and a fun and friendly clientele makes this place highly recommended for a Friday and Saturday night out. Open Friday and Saturday 9pm-4am.

10-12 Restwell Street, Bankstown (tel: 9790 5555).

El Samir Nightclub. To experience a Sydney Lebanese night in all its glory, this is the place to go. At *El Samir* the options are various and attractive. You can have dinner from the set menu (which is good and not expensive), get a few pastries from downstairs, attend the live show with belly dancers and singers (upstairs) or just hop to the dance floor and shake your hips. The party starts at 10pm and rolls on till 4am.

425 New Canterbury Road, Dulwich Hill (tel: 9560 9500).

Landmarks and places of interest

Our Lady of Lebanon Church.

Our Lady of Lebanon is considered the most visually impressive of all churches built by the Lebanese in Australia. The Sydney Maronite community paid over one million dollars for this magnificent building. On top of the church there is a ten metre tall statue of the Virgin Mary wearing an oatmeal-coloured robe, blue cloak and white veil and showing a gesture of welcoming and motherhood. The representation of the Virgin Mary is the second largest in the southern hemisphere with the face alone weighing over 180 kilograms. Our Lady of Lebanon is regularly open Monday-Saturday 9am-7pm; we have been advised if you want to visit inside the Church call beforehand.

40 Alice Street, Harris Park (tel: 9689 2899).

GETTING THERE

By train, City/Lakemba Station.

Lakemba, "Little Lebanon"

Lakemba - within the Municipality of Canterbury – has been the heartland of the Sydney Muslim community since the late 1960s.

The Muslim presence in the area was reinforced in the 1970s with the arrival of Muslims from Lebanon following the civil war, and by the construction of the imposing Lakemba Mosque in 1974 (most of the Lebanese living in Lakemba are from the north of the country).

Located 15 km south-west of the Sydney CBD, Lakemba, like the whole municipality of Canterbury, was until the end of War World II a predominately Anglo-Irish enclave (there were also Chinese market gardeners in the area at the time of Federation). The post-war period saw an increasing number and diversity of people from non-English-speaking backgrounds settling in the area. According to the latest figures, 43.2 per cent of Canterbury's residents were born in non-English-speaking countries, and although 47.6 per cent of them came from four major sources – Lebanon, Greece, Vietnam and China – there are as many as 120 other source countries in the area.

Lakemba, especially along Haldon Street, boasts some unpretentious Lebanese eateries where you can eat cheaply and well. An interesting day to visit the area is on Friday when the streets are alive with the faithful walking to and from the Lakemba Mosque which regularly accommodates around 4,000 worshippers. The end of Ramadan – when the streets of the area are packed with joyful Muslims – is also a good time to explore the uniqueness of this suburb.

La Roche Lebanese restaurant, Lakemba.

Restaurants and Take Away

4: El-Manara. This praised *halal* restaurant offers good and inexpensive Lebanese fare including *tabouli*, *falafel*, *hommos* and minced lamb. Open Monday-Sunday 8am-10pm. Average $10, no alcohol.
143 Haldon Street (tel: 9740 6762).

7: La Roche. Don't be put off by appearances – the food is fresh, tasty and very cheap. Go for the highly recommended *sharwarma* (grilled lamb). Average $10, BYO.
Open Monday-Friday 8am-9.30pm, Sunday 8am-6pm.
Corner Haldon Street and the Boulevard (tel: 9759 9257).

"LITTLE LEBANON" – LAKEMBA

1. Middle East Book Store.
2. Star Spices & Nuts.
3. Youseff Sweets.
4. El-Manara.
5. Patisserie Arja.
6. Paradise bakery.
7. La Roche.
8. Jasmin.

أهلاً و سهلاً

THE LEBANESE

L8: Jasmin. This tiny and plain Lebanese restaurant offers some of the most traditional and sought after dishes – including spicy lamb, *kebab*, *hommos* and the timeless *falafel*. On Friday after the prayer, Jasmin is all busy and buzzy. Average $10, BYO.
Open Monday-Sunday 8am-10pm.
30 Haldon Street (tel: 9740 3589).

Shopping

5: Patisserie Arja. Sweets, gelato and coffee – all with a strong Lebanese accent. Open Monday-Sunday 9am-11.30pm.
129 Haldon Street (tel: 9740 8320).

1: Middle East Book Store. Religious books and videos.
184 Haldon Street (tel: 9750 2779).

2: Star Spices & Nuts. Lebanese grocery.
60A Haldon Street (tel: 9740 9891).

3: Youseff Sweets. Lebanese sweets and cakes.
158 Haldon Street (tel: 9740 3249).

6: Paradise bakery. Lebanese breads, spices and groceries.
117 Haldon Street (tel: 9759 1142).

Labanese shops sell a great variety of Lebanese merchandise and food ingredients.

Zita Antonios

RACE DISCRIMINATION COMMISSIONER

Hers is the quintessential second-generation migrant success story. Her father – a goat herder in his native village of Bann in the north of Lebanon – emigrated to Australia looking for a better life.

Born in Sydney, she attended Sydney University to study social welfare. Shortly after graduating she began working as a Research Officer with the NSW Bureau of Crime, Statistics and Research. After occupying several positions as a state government policy adviser, she was appointed to the Social Policy Unit of the Premier's Department, before becoming a conciliator with the Human Rights Commission. In October 1994, Zita Antonios was appointed Race Discrimination Commissioner.

Explore the world in one city

Getting to know the Lebanese community

Events

Australian Lebanese Association Youth Award.

Established in 1991, this annual award celebrates the achievements of Lebanese-Australian youth who have excelled in sport, art, drama, music and education.

Further information: 9564 3506.

St Maroun.

On January 9 Lebanese Catholics celebrate the memory of St Maroun, who lived as a hermit on the Syria's Oronte River until his death in 410. St Maroun was a wise man followed by thousands, and his tomb became the site of a monastery from which the Maronite Church was founded.

Further information: The Lebanese Maronite Order of Monks (tel: 9750 6000).

Saint Charbel's Feast Day.

On the third Sunday of July, the Lebanese Maronite Order celebrates the memory of its Patron Saint, Saint Charbel. The venue for this annual feast is the Saint Charbel's Church and Monastery at 142 Highclere Avenue, Punchbowl. Additional information on the above number.

For Lebanese Muslim festivals see Sydney Muslim Community, page 420, and Multicultural Arabic Events, see page 424.

Religious organisations and places of worship

The Lebanese Maronite Order of Monks.

A religious organisation with a strong commitment to social and educational issues. The main activities of the Order are held at the Saint Charbel's Monastery and College at 142 Highclere Avenue, Punchbowl (tel: 9759 7470).

USEFUL NUMBER FOR VISITORS

LEBANESE CONSULATE:
tel: 9361 5449.

CEDARS OF LEBANON FOLKLORIC GROUP.
The best-known Sydney Lebanese folkloric group. It performs and teaches Lebanese folkloric '*Dabki*' dance.

62 Christian Road, Punchbowl
(tel: 9750 0134).

LEBANESE COMMUNITY COUNCIL. Organises and conducts diverse activities in the field of community development, including social research and youth work.

Level 2/85 Highclere Avenue, Punchbowl (tel: 9740 3600).

St George Antiochian Orthodox Cathedral.

Has regular weekday and Sunday services.

Corner Walker & Cooper Streets, Redfern (tel: 9319 4456).

Our Lady of Lebanon Church.

Holds regular religious services at 40 Alice Street, Harris Park (tel: 9689 2899).

For Lebanese Muslim organisations and places of worship, see page 423.

Community organisations

Australian Lebanese Association of NSW.

The peak Lebanese community body in Sydney. It deals with a broad range of social and cultural issues.

Suite 3, 554 Marrickville Road, Dulwich Hill (tel: 9564 3506).

Lebanese Welfare Centre.

The Centre provides social and welfare assistance to the Lebanese community.

66 Payten Avenue, Roselands (tel: 9750 6588).

Media

Newspapers and magazines

Al-Bairak. This paper, with a circulation of 35,000, is published three times a week, appearing in the newsagencies on Tuesday, Thursday and Saturday. The editor is Joseph George Khoury.

Further information: 9660 2033.

El Telegraph. The largest Lebanese and Arab language newspaper in the country, it's published three times a week – on Monday, Wednesday and Friday. It covers political, social, economic and cultural news and has a circulation of 100,000 issues. Its editor is Anwar Harb.

Further information: 9740 7711.

Lebanon DownUnder Magazine. Published entirely in English, this is a welcome cool drink in the quality media drought of our city. For those interested in the state of affairs in the Middle East, this is a good source of information. It costs $4 and can be found in most City and suburban newsagencies. Its editor is Joe Doueihi.

1021 Canterbury Road, Lakemba (tel: 9740 7711).

Lebanon DownUnder Magazine.

Radio

Radio Lebanon Abroad. This the first 24-hour and seven-days-a-week Lebanese radio station. The deal is very straightforward: you have to purchase the radio ($85) from this private business and then you get news, music and current affairs.

Further information: 9750 6022.

SBS Radio 2, FM 97.7. News and current affairs. Monday-Sunday 7am-8am and 7pm-8pm.

2SER, FM 107.3. Community news. Sunday 3pm-4pm.

Television

SBS Television. News services every Sunday 8am-8.55am.

For information on other Arabic television programs, contact the Arabic Community Television (CBR) (tel: 9740 4900).

Facts and figures

By the 1991 Census there were 68,787 Lebanese-born people living in Australia. Sydney is the city with by far the largest concentration of these – 49,858. The Lebanese have shown a great desire to identify themselves as Australians, with a high proportion (88%) taking up Australian citizenship.

Just under 25% of Lebanon-born persons have some type of educational or vocational qualifications, a figure considerably lower than that for the total Australia population (38.8%). Lebanese also have a lower level of post-secondary qualification (4.5%) compared with the Australian average (12.8%). The low level of qualifications may explain the lower median annual income ($11,300) when compared to that of the total Australian population ($14,200). Their lower rate of house ownership (59.2%) is also a direct result of these factors.

Regarding religion, 55.0% of Lebanese immigrants are Christians and a substantial proportion follow Islam (37.0%). The overwhelming majority of Lebanese immigrants speak Arabic, including Lebanese, at home (93.2%), while a small proportion speak Armenian (1.6%).

Through hard work, entrepreneurial drive and the help of their families, Sydneys Lebanese have established successful businesses, most notably in the clothing and food industries. Many clothing factories established by Lebanese span three generations.

THE LEBANESE

The Sydney Muslim Community

Soon after the death of the prophet Mohammed in 632 AD the Muslims became divided over who should succeed him and two opposing groups were formed, the *Sunnis* and the *Shi'ites*.

Both groups have a presence in Australia today. In Sydney, the Sydney *Sunni Muslim* community tends to concentrate in the suburb of Lakemba where the Imam Ali Mosque was built, and the *Shi'ite* Muslims have settled around Arncliffe and built their own Mosque, Al-Zahra.

It is estimated that currently just over 200,000 Muslims live in Australia, with almost 78,000 having settled in our State. They have come mainly from Lebanon (24.5%) and from Turkey (11.4%). The peak organisation of the Muslim community is the Federation of Islamic Councils, which is made up of representatives from the Islamic Councils of the states and territories. Its main role is to represent the broader Muslim community.

Australian Muslims

Festivals

Lakemba in Sydney's west is the centre of the Islamic community, and during the festival season it's a great place to be. The friendly athmosphere, the restaurants and sweets shops in the main drag and the joyful scenes are an invitation to drop by and enjoy the cultural and religious tradition of Australian Muslims. A time to learn.

Id-ul-Fither or Ramadan. *Sawm*, or fasting between dawn and dusk for the month of *Ramadan*, is one of the five basic tenets of Islam. *Ramadan* begins with the sighting of the new moon in the 9th month of the Islamic calendar (approximately January 8). At sunset a special meal known as *iftar* is eaten and people meet in the streets after evening prayers. It is customary on this day to visit friends and relatives, especially the elders in the community, and to give presents to children. One of the focal points for this celebration is the Imam Ali Mosque at 65-67 Wangee Road, Lakemba.

Further information: 9750 6833.

Hajj (Annual Islamic pilgrimage to Mecca). This is celebrated on April 16. Every adult Muslim is expected to perform a pilgrimage to Mecca (the birthplace of the prophet Muhammed) at least once in their life. Wearing the simple garb of white cloth to denote a state of ritual purification, pilgrims congregate in the Great Mosque to perform a series of holy rites. A direct airline service between Australia

Explore the world in one city

and Mecca was inaugurated in 1992 to cater for the large number of Muslim Australians visiting the holy site every year.

Eid-ul-Adha (Festival of the Sacrifice). This festival marks the end of the *Hajj* and recalls Abraham's test of obedience when God ordered him to sacrifice his son, Ismail. It is celebrated according to the Islamic lunar year on the 10th day of the 12th month (approximately mid April). Muslims offer special prayers at mosques in the morning soon after the sun rises. Special celebrations are held at Mosques and streets in the Sydney western suburb of Lakemba.

Isra'a-wal-mi'raj. On the 27th day of the 7th month of the Islamic lunar calendar the Muslim community remembers the miraculous ascent of the Prophet Muhammad from Mecca to heaven where he was instructed by God on matters pertaining to Islamic worship. A large celebration is held at the Imam Ali Mosque in Lakemba.

Hijra (Islamic New Year). On the 1st day of the 1st month of the Islamic lunar calendar (around May), Muslims celebrate the day when the Prophet Muhammad migrated from Mecca to Madinah, where the first Islamic state was established.

Prophet Muhammad's Birthday. On the 12th day of the 3rd month of the Islamic lunar calendar, Muslims from all over Sydney visit mosques to celebrate the birthday of the Prophet Muhammad. Al-Zahara Mosque at 1 Wollongong Street, Arncliffe is one of the important venues for this event.

Juma'a Salaat. This is the midday Friday prayer called by the *muezzin* (the call, however, it's not amplified as it would be in Lebanon). If you're in Lakemba – the heart of the Muslim community – by this day, you will note that the main drag of this suburb, Haldon Street, is practically empty at midday as the faithful pray and hear sermons from the Imam at the local Mosque.

Landmarks and places of interest

Lakemba Mosque.

Known as the Imam Ali Mosque and established by the Sydney *Sunni* Muslim community in 1976, this is a large, modern stone building consisting of a very large carpeted room. Do not expect to see any visual representations of God, people or animals inside – this is strictly forbidden by Islamic law. However, its enormous size makes the Mosque an impressive building and one worthwhile seeing. Shower rooms are attached to the

SYDNEY MOSQUES

AUBURN CAMII MOSQUE.
15 North Parade, Auburn
(tel: 9646 5972).

DAWN OF ISLAM MOSQUE.
177 Commonwealth Street, Surry Hills
(tel: 9281 0440).

FATIMA-AL-ZAHRA MOSQUE.
1 Wollongong Road, Arncliffe
(tel: 9567 4332).

IMAM ALI MOSQUE.
65 Wangee Road, Lakemba
(tel: 9750 6833).

REDFERN MOSQUE.
328 Cleveland Street, Redfern
(tel: 9698 4149).

SYDNEY MOSQUE.
13 John Street, Ernskineville
(tel: 9516 3039).

COMMUNITY ORGANISATIONS

AUSTRALIAN ARABIC WELFARE COUNCIL.
A peak Arabic language community body, it deals with social and cultural issues.
7 Leonard Street, Bankstown
(tel: 9709 4333).

MULTICULTURAL EID FESTIVAL AND FAIR (MEFF). Even though this festival has no fixed date, it's an annual event which takes place usually on the weekend following the end of the fasting month of Ramadan. The Festival, involving Muslims from Africa, Asia, Middle East and Europe, features a wide range of activities including theatre, dance and live music. It is also a time to show off some soccer skills. This one-day event at Fairfield Show Ground kicks off at 9am and finishes at around 5pm. By the way, no alcohol, smoking or gambling allowed. $2.50 adults, 50c children.
Further information: Zasar Siddiqui, President of the MEFF
(tel: 9610 0164).

premises where the faithful cleanse themselves before worship according to Muslim custom. There are also offices attached, occupied by the Lebanese Muslim Association. The Mosque is open 24 hours a day, seven days a week. Inside you must behave soberly, take your shoes off and avoid wearing shorts. You can get there by train, as it's near Lakemba station.

65 Wangee Road, Lakemba. Further information: 9750 6833 Monday-Friday 9am-5pm.

The Arabic-speaking community

The Australian Arabic community is the second largest ethnic group in Australia – slightly above 100,000 people (and this number excludes those from an Arabic background that do not speak Arabic). The peak Arabic organisation is the Australian Arabic Council.

Events
Arabic Day Carnivale.

The first Arabic Day Carnivale was held in Sydney in 1983 and it has now become the second largest carnival-style gathering in Sydney, surpassed only by the Sydney Festival. This event has become a venue for education and awareness campaigns, information, market research – even business! Until 1996, the Carnivale was held around mid-October but lately it has been subject to some changes. So we suggest you call for information on dates and venues.

Further information: **Australian Arabic Welfare Council** (tel: 9709 4333).

Media
Newspapers

The Arab World. Published in English and Arabic, it has a good coverage of political issues concerning the Middle Eastern region. It appears on Friday and costs 50c. Its editor is Sam Meguid.

172A Burwood Road, Belmore (tel: 9740 7000).

The Iranians

They come from the land of the 1,001 Nights, the land of Omar Khayyam – Persia, now Iran. The 1979 Iranian Revolution (considered one of the major social revolutions of the twentieth century) is a clear line dividing the two waves of Iranian immigration to our shores.

Before 1979 a group of Iranians, mainly of Assyrian and Armenian origin entered the country. They came as free immigrants looking for a new home. Among them there was also a small group of Iranian *Baha'is* (the *Baha'is* constitute the largest religious minority in Iran and the religion was born there).

After the overthrow of the Shah of Iran in 1979, the steady flow of free immigration was joined by a group of political exiles and by a considerable number of Baha'is, who were subject – by the new authorities – to systematic persecution. In Sydney, *Baha'is* constitute a well-established, sound community whose religious and cultural life revolve around the magnificent *Baha'i Temple* in the northern suburb of Mona Vale (for more about the Baha'is and the Temple see page 428).

Sydney Iranians – around 6,000 – are scattered throughout the western suburbs of Fairfield and Parramatta. The headquarters of the main community body of Sydney Iranians – the Iranian Community Organisation – is in Parramatta. It was established in 1985, and since then has played a crucial role in the settlement process of a considerable number of Iranian refugees.

> Before 1979 a group of Iranians, mainly of Assyrian and Armenian origin entered the country. They came as free immigrants looking for a new home.

Restaurants

Iranian culinary tradition goes back to the first recipes written 4,000 years ago in a cuneiform script on clay tablets. In the Iranian tradition, rice is considered the jewel of Persian cooking, and is combined with meat, fowl, fish, vegetables, fruits and herbs in what is a celebration of colour, taste and balance.

CHECK THIS OUT ALSO...

CAFE MAXIM. The Iranian-born owner Sept Zangenech offers a small Iranian menu that is winning the hearts of many. Open Monday-Friday 8am-5.30pm.

395 Church Street, North Parramatta (tel: 9890 9600).

Chattanooga (Persia at Night). Don't go just straight for the *kebabs*, enjoy the smell of onions and garlic cooking, and the captivating aroma of mint. Average $15, BYO and licensed. Open dinner Tuesday-Sunday 5.30-10pm (till midnight on Friday and Saturday), lunch and dinner Sunday noon-10pm.

308 Military Road, Cremorne (tel: 9953 8775).

Shiraz. This is a place where an ordinary chicken *kebab* reaches a new high. Try also the barbecued marinated meat kebab. Average $15, BYO. Open Monday-Saturday 10am-10pm (till 1am on Friday and Saturday), Sunday noon-10pm.

380 Military Road, Cremorne (tel: 9953 7926).

Shopping

Darya Deli. This is the place where the Middle East meets the West. You'll find aromatic mint, *nan-e barbari* (the traditional Iranian crusty flat bread), roasted nuts, *hummus* and a huge range of imported products from Iran and its regional neighbours. Open Monday-Sunday 9am-9pm.

331 Penshurst Street, Willoughby (tel: 9417 2035).

Landmarks and places of interest

Bas-Relief of Cyrus the Great.

Located at Sydney's Bicentennial Park, right beside Homebush Bay (the site for the Sydney 2000 Olympic Games), this is a replica of a bas-relief found in Pasagarde, the capital city of Persia, depicting Cyrus the Great (580-529 BC). Cyrus was the first Achaemenian Emperor of Persia and his political vision and statements have been hailed as the first declaration of rights. His original decree, inscribed on a clay cylinder (discovered in 1879) is preserved at the British Museum in London, and a copy of it is found at the headquarters of the United Nations in New York. The Bicentennial Park's bas-relief was made by the Sydney artist Lewis Batros and was unveiled in 1994. It symbolises the celebration of living in a city where people from different ethnic backgrounds cohabit in peace and harmony. Every September, this monument is the focal point for the annual *Persian Festival of Mehregan*. Free admission. Open daily sunrise to sunset. You can get there by taking a train to Strathfield, then the 401 bus.

Bicentennial Park, Australia Avenue, Homebush (tel: 9763 1844).

Getting to know the Iranian community

Events

Norouz (Iranian New Year).

The name *Norouz* means 'new day' and it refers to the day the sun reenters the sign of Aries. Held in January, it's a celebration of the beginning of spring (in the northern hemisphere). On *Norouz* eve Iranian families gather for a feast, around candle-lit tables, which includes the seven S's or '*Haftsin*', seven dishes that begins with the letter S in Farsi, the Iranian language (seven has been a sacred number in Iran since the ancient times). The dishes represent the seven virtues of life: rebirth, health, happiness, joy, prosperity, patience, and beauty. During this time Iranians eat the traditional festivity meal *Sabzi Polo* (rice mixed with green herbs and served with fish). On the thirteenth day of the festival, Iranian families leave their homes to have a picnic; it's believed that staying home the thirteenth day brings bad luck.

Further information: 9890 9439.

Mehregan (Annual Persian Festival of Autumn).

Held in September at the site of the Cyrus the Great bas-relief at Sydney's Bicentennial Park, this festival is celebrated annually to mark the beginning of Autumn (in the northern hemisphere). This colourful event has been celebrated as a harvest festival by Persians for thousands of years where food and fodder was to be stored and fruit trees were to be pruned. In Sydney, this Persian festival features food, music, cultural dances, arts and crafts and kids' entertainment. All are welcome.

Further information: 9823 4371.

Community organisations

Iranian Community Organisation.

Established in 1985, it provides information, advice and assistance to the Iranian community on welfare and immigration issues.

1a Victoria Road, Parramatta (tel: 9890 9439).

RELIGIOUS ORGANISATIONS AND PLACES OF WORSHIP

IRANIAN ANGLICAN CHURCH.

Holds regular religious services in Farsi.

West Ryde
(tel: 9858 4843).

Media

Radio

SBS Radio 2, FM 97.7. News and current affairs in Farsi. Saturday 2pm-3pm.

The Sydney Baha'i Community

According to the 1996 Australian Census, there are 2,889 *Baha'is* living in New South Wales, the vast majority of whom live in Sydney. The *Baha'i* community is spread across our city, with a strong presence in the areas of Baulkham Hills, Blacktown, Fairfield, Hornsby, Kuring-gai, Parramatta and Ryde.

Of Sydney's *Baha'is* 36% are born in Australia, while the remainder were born chiefly in Iran (44%) but also in other countries including Canada, China, Croatia, Egypt, Fiji, France, Germany, Hong Kong, India, Indonesia, Italy, Laos, Lebanon, Malaysia, Mauritius, New Zealand, the Philippines, Singapore, South Africa, Sri Lanka, Taiwan, Turkey, United Kingdom, USA and Vietnam.

BAHA'I TEMPLE. This is the main centre for the religious activities of *Baha'i* followers. Mona Vale Road, Ingleside (tel: 9931 2771). For more information about *Baha'is* dial 0055 11334 for recorded information. *Baha'i* communities are located in various suburbs including at **3 Timberline Avenue, Baulkham Hills,** (tel: 9872 3887), and **37 Epping Road, Lane Cove** (tel: 9427 0632).

The current figures reflect a significant increase over the past 15 years, due mainly to the influx of *Baha'i* refugees from Iran, where followers of this religion suffer permanent persecution. Some 1,500 or 52% of the *Baha'is* in Sydney have arrived since 1980, including 15% over the past five years. The overwhelming majority are now Australian citizens.

Place of interest and landmarks

The Baha'i House of Worship.

Located in superb natural surroundings, at Mona Vale Road, Ingleside, the *Baha'i House of Worship* – one of only seven in the world – was dedicated in 1961. This well-kept building has nine sides with nine entrances, symbolising the fact that it welcomes all people irrespective of race, religion, nation or class. The seats in the auditorium face the Holy Land in Israel where *Baha'u'llah*, the Prophet of the *Baha'i* faith, passed away. Above the heads of the worshippers, in the apex of the dome, is a calligraphic rendering of an invocation to God: 'O Glory of the All-Glorious'.

The Baha'i house of worship at Mona Vale Road.

The *Baha'i House of Worship* is open daily to the public for prayer and meditation between 9am and 5pm. On Sunday at 11am a service is held with readings selected from scriptures of all the world religions.

Further information: Baha'i National Office (tel: 9913 2771).

The Fijians

An early contact between Australia and Fiji was made by escaped convicts looking for refugee in the some of Fijian islands. One of those was Patrick O'Connor, an Irishman who reached Kadavu in 1804. He made a living raising cattle and married a chief's daughter. Descendants of Patrick O'Connor still live on the Island running a small tourist business.

Fijian immigrants have been arriving in Australia since the late nineteenth century. By the turn of the twentieth century there were just 585, and by the mid-1950s they reached the mark of 2,000. Migration from Fiji to Australia began to grow in the early 1970s due to economic and population pressures at home, and to the easing of restrictive immigration policies regarding non-Europeans in Australia. The political instability back in Fiji in the 1980s, including military coups, has pushed migration even higher.

Sports and religious activities have played a central part in the development of the Sydney Fijian community. They love rugby and cricket, and are actively involved in Christian churches and welfare organisations. Fijians of Indian descent, on the other hand, have tended to join existing Hindu or Muslim-based groups instead of establishing their own community organisations. Sydney Fijians have mostly settled in the western suburbs of Blacktown, Fairfield and Parramatta. There is also a small group living in the inner-western suburb of Marrickville. However, the most visible urban presence of Fijians is found along the multi-ethnic King Street, in the inner-western suburb of Newtown, where the legendary shop Fiji Markets is located. Here you're able to find Fijian products virtually nonexistent elsewhere in Australia. (see Newtown, page 25).

> By the turn of the twentieth century there were just 585, and by the mid-1950s they reached the mark of 2,000. Migration from Fiji to Australia began to grow in the early 1970s due to economic and population pressures at home, and to the easing of restrictive immigration policies regarding non-Europeans in Australia.

SHOPPING

PACIFIC FOOD CENTRE. A multi-purpose grocery, it offers a wide range of fresh and imported Fijian products. Naturally, Fijian curry and other spices are available. Videos and newspapers from back home can also be found. Open Saturday - Wednesday 10am-6.30pm (till 8.30pm on Thursday and Friday).

3/5 Patrick Street, Blacktown
(tel: 9831 2214).

See also Newtown, page 25.

Restaurants

Curry Shop. A very good ambassador for the island cuisine, this is the place to try meat and poultry in a Fijian curry. Average $10, BYO. Open Monday-Saturday 9am-4pm (till 8.30pm on Thursday).

Lower Ground Floor, Grace Bros, Chatswood (tel: 9412 0318).

Getting to know the Fijian community

Events

Fiji National Day.

Celebrated on October 10, it brings together the Sydney Fijian community in a celebration of national self-determination.

For information about activities and venues: Fiji-Australian Community Council (tel: 9740 3126).

Religious organisations and places of worship

Fijians, like other Pacific Islanders, are serious about religion. Back home, even in the most remote and small town, you'll always find a church. Sydney Fijians are no exception.

Fijian Assembly of God.

Holds regular religious services and biblical studies.

42 George Street, Rockdale (tel: 9567 4770).

Fijian National Council (Assemblies of God in Australia).

The Council plays the role of an umbrella organisation for Fijian churches associated with the Assemblies of God.

Further information: Rev Tevita Vuli, 35 Trevenar Street, Ashfield (tel: 9798 7208).

Community organisations

Fiji Australia Association of NSW.
A peak organisation, it organises cultural and social activities, including charitable fundraising events.
PO Box 222, Canterbury 2193 (tel: 9799 4861).

Fiji Australian Community Council.
A lobby group representing Fijians living in Australia.
Further information: William Pawa (the current president)
PO Box 363 Lakemba 2195 (tel: 9740 3126).

Media
Radio
SBS Radio 1, AM 1107. News and current affairs.
Saturday 3pm-4pm

A FIJIAN RADIO PROGRAM can also be heard on 2RSR FM (88.9). Call 9550 9552 for the information on timeslots.

Facts and figures

With approximately 30,000 people, the Fijian-born in Australia are a small community when compared to other ethnic groups. Currently there are around 17,000 Fijians living in Sydney. Approximately half of the Fijians (52.8%) living in Australian have taken up Australian citizenship.

The English language is widely spoken by Fijians and their proficiency is relatively high. Other languages extensively spoken are Hindi (45.5%) and Fijian (15.5%). The high level of Hindi language is due to the large number of Fijians of Indian origin who have settled here.

In educational terms, 43.1% of Fiji-born have completed some form of educational or vocational education, more than the national average (38.8%).

The median annual income of Fijian-born people ($17,000) is also higher than the median annual income of the total Australian population ($14,200). Fijians have a fairly low rate of home purchasing (37.7%).

Fijians are mostly Christians (39.7%), but also there is a considerable number of Hindus (37.0%) and Muslims (11.4%).

The Papua New Guineans

Australia has certainly produced its share of top sopranos but Papua New Guinea is not a country that comes to mind when one talks opera. But in Australia at the moment we have not one but two budding soprano stars.

The New Guinea-born sisters Clare and Miriam Gormley, two of the five children of a Papuan woman and an Australian man, are making the Australian opera scene sit up and take notice, and making all Australian-Papua New Guineans very proud. In 1991, Clare became the first Australian in 26 years to win New York's Metropolitan Opera auditions, and Miriam has been the recipient of an endless list of scholarships to study in some of the most prestigious music academies, including Covent Garden, home of Britain's Royal Opera Company, and the Vienna State Opera.

One can hardly call Sydney's PNG-born residents 'immigrants', since the majority of them are children of Australians who went to Papua New Guinea during the 1960s and 1970s, when PNG was receiving Australian investment and training in the years prior to independence in 1975. This explains why the largest percentage of the current 5,000 or so PNG-born residents are 'non-indigenous' Papua New Guineans.

The presence of 'indigenous' Papua New Guineans (now only 9% of the PNG-born population) dates back to the mid 1880s when just over 3,000 labourers were recruited to work in the sugar fields of Queensland. Most of them returned, but a handful remained indefinitely among the Pacific Islander community in Queensland. Papuans were also numerous in the pearl-fishing industry, representing the second largest immigrant group after the Japanese.

In Sydney the small community of indigenous PNG immigrants established its first and only community organisation, the Papua New Guinea Australian Association, in 1989.

> In Sydney the small community of indigenous PNG immigrants established its first and only community organisation, the Papua New Guinea Australian Association, in 1989.

Places of interest

Sydney, along with Paris and New York, has become one of the world centres for tribal art. For those wanting to purchase pieces of tribal art, the prestigious Sotheby's tribal art specialist organises an annual auction in November (tel: 9332 3500 or (03) 9509 2900). A similar auction is also held every year by The Lawson Gallery (tel: 9241 3511).

Further information: Oceanic Art Society, PO Box 678, Woollahra, NSW 2025.

Aboriginal Art and Tribal Centre.

The Centre has a very good display of contemporary paintings and tribal art pieces, with a strong emphasis on Papua New Guinean art. Open Monday-Sunday 10am-5pm.

117 George Street, The Rocks (tel: 9247 9025).

Getting to know the Papua New Guinean community

Events

Papua New Guinea Independence Day.

PNG became an autonomous nation in 1975, and the PNG Australian Association organises a dinner/dance on the Saturday closest to December 16 to commemorate this historic moment. In previous years this celebration has been held at the University of New South Wales but we have been told that a new venue has been suggested for future celebrations – the Auburn RSL Club, 33 Northumberland Road, Auburn.

Further information: Mr Henry, Secretary (tel: 9983 9502).

Community organisations

PNG (Sydney) Australian Association.

Represents the interests of the Sydney PNG community.

Further information contact Mr. Henry on 9983 9502.

USEFUL NUMBER FOR VISITORS

PNG CONSULATE:
tel: 9299 5151.

NEW GUINEAN PRIMITIVE ART.
Established in the early 1970s, this tribal art gallery has an extensive collection of art, tools, and weaponry from New Guinea and Melanesia. Stone carvings, wooden gables, fine hand-made baskets and other types of tribal art makes this gallery a fascinating place to visit. Open Monday-Friday 9am-6pm.

Dymock's Building
428, George Street, City
(tel: 9232 4737).

The Mauritians

When the Australia II team achieved their historic triumph in the 1983 America's Cup, there was Mauritian blood in the crew – David Rees, the great-great-grandson of Lion Burguez (1830-87), a Mauritian immigrant who in the 1870s became involved in the Queensland sugar industry.

Lion Burguez belonged to a group of Mauritians who came to Australia as early as 1856. They were sugar experts with pioneering ideas for the local sugar industry. Such was the case of Jerome Thomy de Keating, who arrived in Sydney in January 1865 and became a strong promoter of large-scale sugar growing in northern New South Wales. Equally influential was Paul Laurent Edmond Icery, who in the second half of the nineteenth century was a leader in sugar refining technology, and Albert Jules Alexis Giraud, a Sorbonne-trained agronomist, who undertook several research projects on sugar-growing prospects in the Northern Rivers District of New South Wales.

Among the earliest Mauritian immigrants to Australia was a woman – Genevieve Sornay – who married Francis Nicolas Rossi, one of the first police superintendents in New South Wales. She arrived in the first half of the 1800s, a period in which a substantial number of convicts from Mauritius also came. Between 1817 and 1840 more than 100 were transported, and after completing their sentences very few of them went back to their homeland. Later the goldrush of the 1850s tempted many Mauritians to try their luck in the goldfields of eastern Australia, but luck was elusive and the way back home was walked by many.

By the 1901 Census there were some 744 Mauritian immigrants in Australia. This number fell dramatically over the next four decades, reaching an all-time low in 1947 with just 236. It was not until the beginning of the 1960s that the Mauritian community began experiencing significant growth. These were the years in which the independence movement began undermining the social and economic privileges of the long-standing colonial European elite. It was a time of social dislocation, communal riots and ethnic tensions. From around 1,500 Mauritians living in Australia by the early 1960s, the number grew to more around 10,500 at the beginning of the 1980s.

The contemporary Sydney Mauritian community, around 6,000, is fanned across the western suburbs of Blacktown and Campbelltown. Community life, with a strong Catholic influence, has developed around the Australian Mauritian Association (AMA).

Restaurants

Katkoko Cafe Creole. The savvy of the Mauritian-born host, Alain Albert, will take you on an exotic trip to the heart of Creole cuisine – a unique fusion of African, Indian, Chinese and French. Average $25, BYO. Open Wednesday-Sunday 6pm-11pm.
62 Enmore Road, Newtown (tel: 9519 7816).

Places of interest and landmarks
Father Jacques Laval Shrine.

For many Catholic Mauritians the trip of up to two hours to the charming historic town of Berrima, in the Southern Highlands, is not a bother. At Berrima, in the Penrose Park Catholic Monastery, there is small shrine dedicated to the revered Father Jacques Laval, whose miracles and work among liberated Mauritian slaves have led to his imminent canonisation. He will become the first Mauritian saint in history (at a time when Australia is also receiving its first, Mary Mackillop). For people wanting to visit the shrine, trains to the Southern Highlands depart from Sydney's Central Station regularly (call the Public Transport Infoline, 13 1500, for details).

Getting to know the Mauritian community

Events
Father Laval Commemorative Mass.

Every year in September the Sydney Catholic Mauritian community comes together for a church service in honour of Father Jacques Disiri Laval (see above). The religious service, attended by several thousand Mauritians, is conducted in French.

Further information: Danielle Perombelon, President of the Australian Mauritian Association (tel: 9825 1897 (H), or 9829 2200 (W)).

USEFUL NUMBERS FOR VISITORS

MAURITIAN CONSULATE:
tel: 9522 7027.

AIR MAURITIUS:
tel: 9241 5300 or 9247 1444.

Community organisations

Australian Mauritian Association.

The Association is recognised by the state and federal governments as the voice of the Sydney Mauritian community. It develops cultural, social and sporting activities, and is currently in the process of establishing a nursing home for the elderly Mauritians. For information call Danielle Perombelon (see above).

Media

Newspapers

Mauritian in Australia. A small monthly publication covering community news and news from Mauritius. Its editor is Silvio Belcourt.

Further information: 9632 8451.

For French-language newspapers see The French, page 118.

Radio

News and current affairs segments about Mauritius can be heard on the French-language program at SBS Radio, see The French, page 119.

The Samoans

When Ano Sei arrived in Sydney at the end of the 1960s he remembers there was a grand total of seven Samoans living in the city. Like him, they were students sponsored by the Australian government under the Colombo Plan.

Despite contact between Samoa and Australia dating back to the early years of Australia's white settlement, Samoan migration to Australia has always been limited. The earliest connection between the two countries was established by the French explorer La Perouse, who arrived in Botany Bay from Samoa shortly after the arrival of the First Fleet in 1788.

Further 'connections' were also made by convicts who escaped from the penal colony and sought refuge in the Samoan islands. Samoa was in the headlines of the *Sydney Morning Herald* on December 19, 1894 due to the tragic death of the writer Robert Louis Stevenson, who settled there and helped the Samoans resist German colonisers. Venerated by the Samoans as a national hero, Stevenson visited Sydney several times (Stevenson's pictures, *artefacts* and manuscripts are displayed at the Australian National Maritime Museum, the Powerhouse Museum and the State Library of NSW).

Some of the first Samoans to arrive in Sydney were Methodist pastors who came to receive theological training in the 1850s. Similar visits were organised by Australia's Catholic Marist missionaries working in Samoa from 1845. In 1863, 14 Samoans were in Sydney studying for the priesthood at the Catholic Seminar at Clydesdale, near the western suburb of Richmond.

Ano Sei comments that "The first large group of Samoan immigrants arrived in Sydney in the mid-1970s and early 1980s; it was a group of Samoan Seventh Day Adventists from Auckland, New Zealand." This group settled in the inner western suburbs of Ashfield and Five Dock, and eventually built a church in Drummoyne.

Even today, the largest group of Samoan immigrants currently living in Sydney, around 3,000, have come not from Samoa however, but from New Zealand. They are semiskilled or unskilled workers whose difficult

Some of the first Samoans to arrive in Sydney were Methodist pastors who came to receive theological training in the 1850s.

USEFUL NUMBERS FOR VISITORS

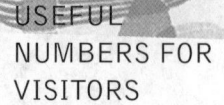

WESTERN SAMOA CONSULATE:
tel: 9331 7120.

WESTERN SAMOA VISITORS BUREAU:
tel: 9238 6113.

settlement in Australia has been eased to some extent by the advice and assistance received from the Samoan Advisory Council, where Ano now works as the community development worker. Established in 1986, the Council has helped to link Sydney's Samoan residents culturally and socially through a diverse range of community activities. Of equal importance is the role played by the more than 60 Samoan-based churches scattered throughout Sydney. For Samoans, the church is like a surrogate village. It is their community, and their cultural and social centre.

Getting to know the Samoan community

Events

Western Samoan National Day.

By far the largest and most important community event, held annually by the Sydney Samoan community to celebrate its independence in 1962. The celebrations start on the first Friday in June with a formal ball held in a venue around the western suburbs of Liverpool or Bankstown. Approximately 400 Samoans and friends attend this ball.

Further information: Samoan Advisory Council (tel: 9718 3555 or 9789 3744).

Samoan Sport Carnival.

Held on the second weekend in June (Queen's Birthday long weekend), this is a massive and hugely popular sporting event among Sydney Samoans. The sports included are golf, athletics, cricket, rugby and volleyball. Because of the high number of teams participating, there is an elimination process that begins in May. The main venues for the Carnival are the University of Western Sydney's Milperra Campus Sports Ground and the Ashbury Athletic Field. Food stalls with typical Samoan dishes can be found at both venues.

Further information: Samoan Advisory Council (tel: 9718 3555 or 9789 3744).

Sydney has a vibrant Pacific Islander community.

Community organisations

Samoan Advisory Council.
This is the peak body for Samoan organisations in Sydney, especially the churches. The Council organises major events and co-ordinates community activities as well as providing advice to the Samoan people in Sydney.

Further information: Ano Sei. 139 Beamish Street, Campsie (tel: 9718 3555 or 9789 3744).

Sporting Clubs

Sydney Samoan Social Golf Association.
The Association operates on a membership basis. It currently has 50 members.

Further information from Ano Sei (see above).

Sydney Samoan Rugby Organisation.
Samoans have a proud Rugby tradition. The Sydney Samoan rugby Organisation sends teams to compete in a 7-a-side and a 15-a-side competition in Samoa. The Samoan national team is chosen from these competitions and there are several Sydney-based players who have made the national team.

Further information: Ano Sei (see above).

Media

Radio
SBS Radio 1, AM 1107. Community news and music.
Sunday 9-10pm.

2SER FM, 107.3. Community information and music.
Sunday 5.30-6.30pm.

RELIGIOUS ORGANISATIONS AND PLACES OF WORSHIP

There are over 60 Samoan-based churches in Sydney. The following are just a few of them. Times of the services tend to vary, so ring for further information.

SAMOAN METHODIST CHURCH
116 Dwyer Road,
Leppington
(tel: 9606 5949).

SAMOAN CONGREGATIONAL CHURCH
391 Cabramatta Road,
Cabramatta
(tel: 9600 7537).

SAMOAN CATHOLIC CHURCH
54 Northern Avenue,
Bankstown Central
(tel: 9790 2859).

SAMOAN ASSEMBLY OF GOD
23 Rea Street,
Greenacre
(tel: 9642 5616).

SAMOAN UNITING CHURCH
5 Melville Street,
Ashbury
(tel: 9798 9927).

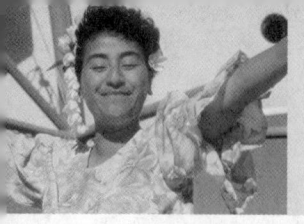

The Tongans

If you want the job done, get a Tongan. This must have been the thinking of the Australian Rugby selectors when they appointed the awesome Willie Ofahengaue to the national team for its toughest test, the 1991 World Cup. Born in Tonga in 1968, Ofahengaue arrived in Sydney in 1988 after living a few years in New Zealand. 'Willie O' delivered the goods of course (along with another 'ethnic', Italian-Australian David Campese) as he helped his new country to win the Cup.

Until the mid-1970s, when Tongans began arriving in Sydney in large numbers seeking better economic opportunities, the small Tongan presence was limited to a group of students, most of them attending the private Newington College and the University of Sydney. Both institutions have traditionally been chosen by wealthy Tongan families for their children's education. It seems this was a trend inaugurated by the King of Tonga, Taufa'ahau Tupou IV, who was himself educated at Newington in the late 1940s, and at the University of Sydney in the early 1950s where he graduated with a Bachelor of Laws (during his time at the University of Sydney he boarded at Wesley College where he was a member of the rowing team). These institutions have also become a kind of 'tourist attraction' for many Tongans, who like to visit the places where the King was educated.

Since the mid-1970s thousands of Tongans have emigrated to Australia. A large number arrived from New Zealand following the end of its contract worker scheme in 1975. In the early 1980s, with the establishment of the first Australian Embassy in Tonga – making the immigration application process easier – Tongan immigration grew even further, mainly under the family reunion program.

The 4,000-strong Sydney Tongan community has developed a very strong church-oriented life. Tongan parishes of the Methodist Church are prominent in Sydney and scattered throughout New South Wales, from Toukley on the Central Coast to Port Kembla in the Illawarra region. In 1985 the parish of the Free Wesleyan Church of Tonga was formally established, providing another community venue for Sydney Tongans.

> The 4,000-strong Sydney Tongan community has developed a very strong church-oriented life. Tongan parishes of the Methodist Church are prominent in Sydney and scattered throughout New South Wales, from Toukley on the Central Coast to Port Kembla in the Illawarra region.

The Church of Tonga – which has been in Sydney since 1987 – also has a strong presence, mainly around the western suburb of Emerton, where the church has recently purchased a property. Catholic Tongans, on the other hand, are regular attendants at the Tongan language services celebrated at Auburn's Catholic Church in Sydney's west. As singing is a central part of religious expression for Tongans, their choirs are both numerous and impressive.

Secular community initiatives have also helped Tongans to ease the hardship of settlement in Australia. The Tongan Association of Sydney, through its different branches – sport, education, welfare and art – has performed a valuable job. Likewise the Tongan Housing Project Association, founded in 1990, whose settlement services are highly regarded by the Tongan community. An important role has also been played by the Tongan media, which comprises regular radio programs and a newspaper, *Fetu'u Tonga* (Tongan Star).

Embracing Tongan music and dance with gusto.

Getting to know the Tongan community

Events

Tongan Independence Day.

A celebration of self determination held every June 4. A well-attended religious service, followed by a cocktail party, is organised in Canberra by the local Tongan Association. In Sydney, the same Association organises similar activities, including a festival.

Further information: Inoke Huakan, Tongan Association of Sydney (tel: 9799 4518, home).

Education Sunday.

As part of Education Week in New South Wales, churches and community organisations celebrate Education Sunday. This is widely practised back in the homeland and replicated by Tongans in Sydney during February or March. Community organisations or individuals get together to discuss and promote general educational issues.

Further information: contact the Tongan Association.

USEFUL NUMBERS FOR VISITORS

TONGAN CONSULATE:
tel: 9929 8794.

TONGA VISITOR BUREAU:
tel: 9550 4711.

TONGA ISLANDS TOURIST CENTRE:
tel: 9262 6555.

FACTS AND FIGURES

Approximately 4,000 Tongan-born people live in New South Wales, and the largest majority are Christians (94.2%). In terms of education, only 3.3% have obtained a degree or diploma, and 4.3% have some skilled and basic vocational training.

Religious organisations and places of worship

Church of Tonga.

With its head branch in Tonga, the Church has been in Sydney since 1987. It organises regular services and biblical studies.

1 Heine Avenue, Emerton.

Tongan parish of the Methodist Church.

Operates out of the Presbyterian Church of Sydney. It has more 20 than branches in New South Wales.

27 Arthur Street, Ashfield.

A Catholic service in the Tongan language is organised every Sunday at 8am and 10am at the Auburn Catholic Church.

Further information: Amaloni Tuakalau (tel: 9646 5039).

Community organisations

Tongan Association of Sydney.

An umbrella body for Tongan organisations and individuals, it has four branches, dedicated to welfare, education, sport and traditional performing arts.

The current president is Inoke Huakan (tel: 9799 4518, home).

Media

Newspapers

Fetu'u Tonga (Tongan Star). A newcomer, established in 1997. It's published twice a week, and covers local community issues and news from Tonga. It has a circulation of 1,000 and its current editor is Lisiate Akau (tel: 9809 7450).

Radio

SBS Radio 1, AM 1107. Music, news and current affairs, Monday and Saturday 4pm-5pm.

2RSR, FM 88.9. News, community announcements and a good range of Tongan traditional and modern music, Thursday 6pm-7pm.

Explore the world in one city

Getting to know the African Sydney

"**The power of** the black culture." This is the Afro-Brazilian meaning of *Azeviche* – from which the well-known Sydney African dance workshop takes its name – and Sydney is feeling the power. Black African music and dance, the arts, the food and clothing is here and we love it. Great vibes! Although African culture isn't new to Sydney, it's only in the last few years that we have begun embracing it with passion.

The African population in Sydney is small. There are approximately 2,000 who have settled here. The majority comes from South Africa, Somalia, Zimbabwe and Kenya. It's a young community where more than three-quarters aren't yet 40. While the Africans are fanned across Sydney suburbs, it is in the inner city, especially Newtown, where they are visible through the presence of African shops, restaurants and art galleries (see Newtown, page 25).

Cafes & restaurants

Afro. A welcoming place specialising in North and South African food. Average $30, licensed (wine by glass). Open lunch Friday noon-3pm, dinner Monday-Saturday 6-11pm.
118 Crown Street, East Sydney (tel: 9332 1648).

Cafe Kutubia. Marrakech decor and sofas of bright colours add an extra touch to this relative newcomer on the Sydney scene. The highlights of the menu are the traditional Moroccan *couscous*, marinated vegetables and platters of fruit and *tagine*. On Friday and Saturday nights belly dancing keeps the patrons dreaming of Marrakech. Average $15, BYO. Open lunch Tuesday-Saturday noon-3pm, dinner Monday-Saturday 6pm-till late.
7 Stanley Street, Darlinghurst (tel: 9380 9193).

Cafe Tunis. Praised by the critics, this is the only Tunisian restaurant in town and it's doing pretty well. Recommended: lamb casserole with *melokhia*. Average $25, BYO and licensed. Open Monday-Sunday 7am-10.30pm.
30 South Steyne, Manly (tel: 9976 2805).

> While the Africans are fanned across Sydney suburbs, it is in the inner city, especially Newtown, where they are visible through the presence of African shops, restaurants and art galleries.

THE MOSQUITO BAR. The house specialities include the splendid *Moroccan Marrakech brochette lamb* and the timeless *couscous*. Average $12, BYO. Open Monday-Saturday 6-10pm.

Shop 5, 142 Spit Road, Mosman.
(tel: 9968 1801).

THE NILE RESTAURANT. Specialises in Egyptian, Ethiopian, Moroccan and Sudanese cuisine. Tuesday and Sunday there are special African vegetarian dishes. Live entertainment included on Friday and Saturday. Average $12, BYO. Open Tuesday-Sunday, 9am-3pm, dinner 6-11pm.

553 Crown Street, Surry Hills
(tel: 9699 4641).

Dar Essalem Casablanca. A very colourful place with excellent food, and live entertainment on Fridays and Saturdays. Try the fantastic fresh grilled sardine, the delicious *bissara* dip of broad beans, garlic and cumin, and don't leave without having a Moroccan mint tea. Average $25, licensed. Open lunch Thursday and Friday 12.30-3pm, dinner Sunday-Thursday 6-9.30pm, Friday-Saturday 6-10.30pm.

Pitwatter Road, Manly (tel: 9977 2890).

Downtown Marrakech. A Moroccan restaurant with a talented Moroccan cook, Abdul Bertah. Marrakech is a cosy place where the three little alcoves of low tables, cushions and rugs are rapidly taken by the agile and adventurous. The menu includes *harika* (chickpea and lentil soup), *bissara* (a puree of dried broad beans) and a tasty Moroccan style *couscous* (a combination of couscous, beef and vegetables). Average $25, BYO. Open dinner 6pm till late.

13 O'Brien Street, Bondi (tel: 9365 7135).

Fez Cafe. Food and environment for the soul – traditional North African and Middle Eastern fare, including treats such as a wonderful lamb dish served with vegetable *couscous*, and feta and tomato omelettes. For lunch try the vegie *couscous bidaoui* (traditional Moroccan-style spiced vegies on steamed *couscous*). Average $15, BYO and licensed. Open for breakfast, lunch and dinner, Monday-Saturday 7am-10.30pm, Sunday 8am-10.30pm.

247 Victoria Street, Darlinghurst (tel: 9360 9581).

Radio Cairo. A food tour throughout Africa with several stopovers – South African marinated lamb, Mozambican marinated and grilled prawn, Sudanese bean dips, Moroccan salads and also influences from Sri Lanka and the Caribbean. If you're unable to book a table, drop by Cafe Cairo, just over the road. Average $20, BYO. Open lunch Thursday-Friday noon-2.30pm, dinner Monday-Saturday 6-10pm.

Corner Military Road and Spofforth Street, Cremorne
(tel: 9953 0822).

Sirocco. This is an inspiring place to sit and enjoy traditional North African and French fare. Average $50, licensed (wine by glass). Open lunch Thursday-Friday noon-2.30pm, dinner Monday-Saturday 6.30-10.30pm.

23 Craigend Street, Darlinghurst (tel: 9332 4495).

Shopping

Earth Chat.
Has an extensive variety of African and Australian Aboriginal musical instruments, including African tribal drums. It also has a good collection of African music. Open Tuesday-Saturday 11am-6pm.

205 Bondi Road, Bondi (tel: 9369 4770).

Gye Nyme (Except God).
African fashion, traditional African clothing, embroidery, hand printed clothes. Open Tuesday-Saturday 10am-6pm.

139 Enmore Road, Enmore (tel: 9519 7507 during business hours, 9564 0546 after hours).

Macondo.
A great range of African artefacts and clothing. Open Monday-Saturday 10am-6pm, Sunday 11am-5pm.

Shop 13, 135 Glebe Point Road, Glebe (tel: 9566 2135).

Out of Africa.
Offers a wide range of African arts and crafts, including ceremonial masks, bags and jewellery. Open Monday-Friday 10am-7.30pm, Saturday-Sunday 9.30-8pm.

Shop 427 Harbourside, Darling Harbour (tel: 9212 7035).

Arts

Inyaka, African Art Gallerie.
Specialists in traditional African artefacts sourced throughout Africa. Open by appointment.

264 Glenmore Road, Paddington (tel: 9361 0295).

Thomas Thorpe Collector Gallery.
It has a well-earned reputation for showing fine tribal collections throughout the world, including African arts. 'Out of Africa', an impressive collection of 100 pieces representing the art of the Congo and South and West Africa, was exhibited here not long ago.
Open Tuesday-Sunday 11am-6pm.

2 Cascade Street, Paddington (tel: 9331 8302).

SIMBA WA AFRIKA.
Here you'll find mainly African arts & crafts, drums, batik, carvings, pottery and other African artefacts. Open Monday-Friday 11am-6pm.

158 Enmore Road, Enmore
(tel: 9519 3746).

SOUL CITY.
Robert Kaleel, Sydney's best-known 'soul man', has been in the Sydney music scene for more than 25 years and his new venture is a very well-stocked music shop at Bankstown. Check out the latest in Afro, reggae, jazz and Latin music. Open Monday-Saturday 10am-5.30pm.

Shop 82 Old Town Centre (across from the train station), Bankstown
(tel: 9708 0818).

USEFUL NUMBER FOR VISITORS

AFRICA TRAVEL CENTRE:
tel: 9267 3048.

WORKSHOPS

AZEVICHE DANCE WORKSHOPS. Ralph and Izabel Silva-Lidsey are the organisers of these workshops designed to achieve personal growth and spiritual renewal through communal African dance and music. The workshops attract hundreds of people of all ages.

Further information: Ralph or Izabel (tel: 9499 4084).

Live music

Lansdowne Hotel. One of the oldest pubs in Sydney, the Lansdowne makes room for the vibes of some of Sydney's best African and reggae bands, including *Caribbean Soul*, *Badema* and *Bac tu Africa*. Be ready and dress super light for the conga lines and the limbo competition.
No cover charge. Saturday nights 9.30pm till late.
2-6 City Road, Broadway (tel: 9211 2325).

Reggae Club. Nothing here is fancy – the decor is what you would call basic but the Afro-Caribbean ambience is good. The green metallic door opens every Friday and Saturday from 10pm to very enthusiastic and loyal habitues. Dress in red, yellow and green! $5 gets you in.
150 Elizabeth Street, City (no telephone available, sorry).

Tailors On Central. Every Saturday from 9pm this venue makes space for the spiritual rhythms of *reggae* and *soukous*. Check out upcoming African nights by giving them a call. Cover is $7.
84 Mary Street, Surry Hills (tel: 9281 4178).

Getting to know the African community

African events

African Freedom Day.

This has been described by Sydney Africans as a festival of 'de-colonisation'. Usually held in May, African Freedom Day celebrates those African countries that have shaken off colonisation and gained independence. It has regularly been celebrated at the Coogee-Randwick RSL, Carr Street, Coogee.

Further information: Tredwell Lukondeh, President of the Zambian Association (tel: 9385 5214 or 9314 5483).

Afro-Caribbean Carnivale.

Held for the first time in 1996, this event is a showcase of the best cultural expressions of the African and West Indian communities of

Explore the world in one city

Sydney. It includes live music and performances, workshops, traditional and contemporary dance, visual arts, crafts and clothing stalls, African and Caribbean food and an evening concert. In 1997 the Festival was held on September 14 at the Addison Road Community Centre at Marrickville.

Further information: Victor Mannie, African Communities' Council (tel: 9876 1918).

Religious organisations and places of worship

Africa Inland Mission.

This is an interdenominational charitable mission working in East and Central Africa.

37 Hercules, Chastwood (tel: 9412 2303).

Music

Baraka Community Singers. If you come to hear this singing group you will not only be treated to wonderful music, you'll be helping raise funds to support humanitarian projects for the needy in Africa. All welcome.

Further information: Frederick (tel: 9564 6790).

Community organisations

African Communities Council (ACC).

The aim of the ACC is to act as an umbrella organisation to unite Sydney's African communities and individuals. Meetings are held on the second Saturday of every month.

221 Cope Street, Waterloo (tel: 9716 5593).

Media

The African. A small but very informative newsletter edited by Caroline Brem. It is published monthly by the African Communities Council and has a circulation of 2,000.

Further information: tel 9716 5593.

See also The South Africans, page 456.

CHECK ALSO

The African Night/Out of Africa parties usually advertised in some of the Sydney's free mags such as *Sydney City Hub*, *Drum Media*, *On The Street*. and the Metro section every Friday in the *Sydney Morning-Herald*.

Sydney's Afro-Caribbean community move to the rythmic beat of Bob Marley's reggae music.

Radio Programs

SBS Radio 2, FM 97.7. The best of African music. Sunday 11-midnight.

2MBS FM, 102.5. *Eardrum*, a wide and good selection of African rhythms. Wednesday midnight-1am. *World Vibrations*, the best of world reggae and Afro beats. Wednesday 1-3am.

2RSR FM, 88.9. *African Connexions*, news and groovy music. Sunday 11am-2pm.

Kinky Afro with Clue and Adrian. Tuesday 9-10pm.

Black Routes Blues, a great selection of blues and black gospel. Thursday 9-10pm.

Intensified Jamaican Sound. Thursday 10-11.30pm.

2RDJ FM, 88.1. The latest in Afro, reggae, Latin and jazz with Robert 'Soul Man' Kaleel. Monday 10pm-midnight.

Reggae and African Nights with MC Maurice. Wednesday 9pm-midnight.

2RES FM, 89.7. *Black & Blue*, reggae, soul and blues. Monday 6-7.30pm.

Cool Runnings, Caribbean and Afro music. Tuesday 6-7.30pm.

Facts and figures

There are approximately 2,000 people in the Sydney African community.

There are approximately 2,000 people in the Sydney African community. In terms of education, 61.7% have no formal qualifications, although this includes those African immigrants whose qualifications haven't been recognised in Australia. Of the rest, 9.3% have tertiary studies, while 6.4% have obtained some skilled or vocational training.

About 26% of African speakers have an annual income of $25,000 or below, while about 10% have an income of $60,000 or more.

Sydney Africans are mainly Christians. Slightly over 20% are Catholic and 7% are Anglicans, while 47% belong to other Christian denominations. Among the non-Christians, 7% follow Islam and an even smaller percentage are Buddhists and Hindus (1%).

The Ethiopians

In the heart of Sisay Bezabeh there was pain and fear. It was during the 1996 Sydney World Junior Championship that this young Ethiopian athlete defected from his troubled homeland and made Sydney his new home. One of the new crop of African runners, Bezabeh is considered of world class in the 5,000 and 10,000 metres.

A world away from his family and friends and from the hills where he used to train, Sisay Bezabeth is one of the latest Ethiopians to seek refuge from a land devastated by civil conflict and hunger. He now wants to represent Australia at the Sydney 2000 Olympic Games.

The first large group of Ethiopian refugees arrived in Australia in the late 1980s and early 1990s. By then, the television cameras of the world had already revealed the terrible scenes of the mid-1980s famine that caused the death of more than one million Ethiopians. Then, it was the civil war – more death and more refugees. Some of them arrived in Australia under the Special Humanitarian Program, others – a small group – finished as illegal immigrants in Sydney's Villawood Detention Centre. A small number still are waiting to be considered as refugees.

For the Ethiopians, the arduous adjustment to a new country has been eased by a small but effective network of community organisations. One of the most outstanding works in this regard has been developed by the Ethiopian Women's Association in Sydney (EWAIS). Instrumental in the foundation of the EWAIS was the tireless Zewditu Tadesse. Zed, as she likes to be called, arrived in Sydney along with her three young daughters as refugees in 1985, after losing her husband – brutally murdered during the war. Equally important has been the spiritual guidance provided to Ethiopians by St Mary's Ethiopian Orthodox Tewhdo Church, in the western suburb of Auburn.

> For the Ethiopians, the arduous adjustment to a new country has been eased by a small but effective network of community organisations. One of the groups that has carried out outstanding work in this area is the Ethiopian Women's Association.

Getting to know the Ethiopian community

USEFUL NUMBER FOR VISITORS

CONSULATE GENERAL (IN MELBOURNE):
tel: (03) 9417 3419.

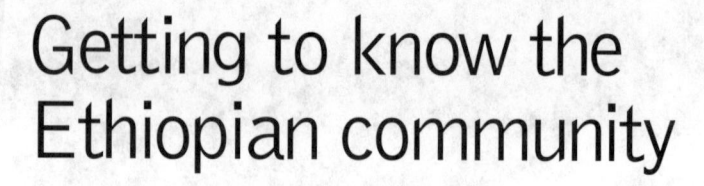

RELIGIOUS ORGANISATIONS AND PLACES OF WORSHIP

ST MARY'S ETHIOPIAN ORTHODOX TEWHDO CHURCH.
Organises regular religious services in Ethiopian language.
Further information: Anteneh Bayou (tel: 9749 2491).

For media see African Sydney, page 447.

Events

Ethiopian New Year.

This is the largest and most important event on the Sydney Ethiopian calendar. Held on September 11, the Ethiopian New Year is celebrated with a night of poetry, traditional dance, music and food. Ethiopian children sing traditional songs that tell that the darkness of the night is going and the light of a new year will shine. Flowers are given to the everyone and candles are lit to signify the light of the new year. The venue for this event changes annually, so it is advisable to call for details.

Further information: Zewditu Tadesse, Ethiopian Women's Group (tel: 9715 8091).

Ethiopian Christmas.

Held on January 7, this is when Sydney Ethiopians get together to celebrate the children of the community, with presents, traditional dances and song.

Further information: Ethiopian Women's Group (see above).

Community organisations

Ethiopian Women's Association.

Established in 1986, the Association provides support and advice to Ethiopian women to help them overcome isolation and language problems. It also organises Ethiopian language classes for Ethiopian children.

Further information: Zewditu Tadesse (tel: 9715 8091).

Ethiopian Project.

Supports a part-time Ethiopian community worker based at the Liverpool Migrant Resource Centre.

1st Floor 179-183 Northumberland Street, Liverpool (tel: 9601 3788).

The Ghanaians

Ghana in the 1970s was a land pockmarked by successive military coups. In the '80s it was a land in the grip of great economic hardships. When in 1984 Australia began taking – for the first time – a regular intake of black African refugees there was a handful of Ghanaians among them, fleeing their troubled home.

Paralleling other African communities, the Sydney Ghanaian community began establishing itself in the early 1970s. At the time, they were mainly students attending the University of New South Wales. They formed the Ghana Student Association that eventually – with the increasing number of Ghanaians entering the country in the following decades – became the Ghana Association of NSW, the main representative body for the Ghanaian immigrants in Sydney.

The Ghanaians who came in the 1970s, established a small community around the eastern suburbs of Kensington and Randwick, near the local university. However, the later-arriving Ghanaians have tended to settle in the western suburbs of Sydney, where accommodation is more affordable. Ghanaian community life in Sydney revolves around the cultural and social activities organised by the Ghana Association. There is also a Ghanaian Pentecostal community that meets every Sunday at the Sefton High School in Sydney's west. Ghanaians have enriched the Sydney music scene with several Ghanaian-African musical bands that have been in the local scene since the end of 1970s. They have followed the tradition inaugurated by *Afrijah*, the first Ghanaian band in Australia, formed in 1979.

Getting to know the Ghanaian community

USEFUL NUMBER FOR VISITORS

GHANA CONSULATE:
tel: 9223 5151.

THE GHANA ASSOCIATION OF NSW, an umbrella organisation, provides welfare and social assistance to new arrivals from Ghana.

149 Oxford Street, Cambridge Park (tel: 9638 1451)

Events

Ghana Independence Day.

On March 5 the Sydney Ghanaian community celebrates the peaceful 1956 transfer of power from Britain, when the Gold Coast (not the one in Queensland!) became Ghana and its red, green and gold flag replaced the Union Jack. Organised by the Ghana Association of NSW, this celebration has been traditionally held at the University of New South Wales' Round House with traditional Ghanaian food, music and dance.

Further information: Sam Amayke Adjei, President of the Ghana Association of NSW (tel: 9638 1451).

Religious organisations and places of worship

Ghanaian Community Church (Pentecostal).

Meets every Sunday from 9.30am-12.30pm and 6.30pm-8.30pm at the Sefton High School, 41-43 Hector Street, Sefton (tel: 9644 4800 – school reception). You also can contact this group by writing to the Ghanaian Community Church, PO Box 5006, Minto 2566.

The Nigerians

In the urban kaleidoscope of Newtown's King Street, the record shop Blackstarr is a temple for black music. Its owner, the Nigerian-born and UK-grown Sam Mbakwe, is the priest. The uncompromising gospel is authentic black music – reggae, jazz, soul, African, spirituals and acid jazz. "They are good for the spirit," says Sam, who came to Sydney in 1995.

The earliest Nigerians in Sydney were tertiary students who came at the end of the 1960s and early 1970s. One of them was Henry Enahora, who, after completing his studies went back to his homeland to become one of the most prominent academics. Years later, Professor Enahora eventually moved back to Sydney with his Australian wife and his young family.

Nigerians, like Ghanaians, began arriving in groups during the first half of the 1980s. They were mainly students, academics and professionals in the fields of science and engineering who entered Australia under the skilled immigration program. In the late 1980s and in early 1990s they were joined by an increasing number of refugees fleeing from the political and social instability in their homeland.

Originally, Nigerians settled in the eastern and inner-west suburbs of Sydney. However, in the last few years there has been a movement to the outer western suburbs where accommodation prices are lower. The community body of the Sydney Nigerians is the Nigerian Association of NSW, which has played a central role as a community outreach agency and organises the annual Nigerian Independence Day event that highlights the hard struggle for African self-determination.

> Nigerians began arriving in groups during the first half of the 1980s. They were mainly students, academics and professionals in the fields of science and engineering who entered Australia under the skilled immigration program.

USEFUL NUMBER FOR VISITORS

NIGERIAN HIGH COMMISSION:
tel: (06) 286 1322.

Getting to know the Nigerian community

Events

Nigerian Independence Day.

By far the most populous of African Nations, Nigeria achieved its independence from Britain on October 1 1960. Traditionally, the Sydney Nigerian community has celebrated this day with a picnic at Centennial Park where traditional food is served and Nigerian bands perform the best of African music. Expect to see Sam Mbakwe there.

Community organisations

Nigerian Association of NSW.

This is the main community organisation for Sydney Nigerians. It meets on the last Sunday of every month at the NSW Ethnic Affairs Commission.

161-164 Liverpool Road, Ashfield (tel: 9980 7685).

Media

Newspapers

The Nigerian. A newsletter published monthly by the Nigerian Association of NSW covering mainly community events.

Further information: the Association (tel: 9980 7685).

The Sierra Leoneans

Of the twelve or so ethnic groups existing in Sierra Leone, six of them are represented in Sydney. The two largest are Mendes and Temnes. When a Mendes meets a Temnes they speak to each other in the Anglo-African hybrid Krio – Sierra Leone's *lingua franca*.

In the late 1970s and early 1980s there was just a handful of students from Sierra Leone living in Sydney. In the following years, especially from the late 1980s, the political and economic instability of the post-independence movement forced a large number of Sierra Leoneans to immigrate to the US and Europe. A few came to Australia, and the majority of these settled in Sydney.

Because of its large number of Muslims, the Sierra Leonean community is mainly found around the largest mosques, located in Auburn and Lakemba. Here they are close to friends, family and the community support of the local Islamic community. There is also a small Christian community, mainly Anglicans and Catholics.

Established in 1982, the Sierra Leone Association in Australia is the main social and cultural organisation for Sierra Leone's immigrants. It assists with settlement issues and promotes Sierra Leone's culture and traditions.

Getting to know the Sierra Leonean community

Events

Independence Day.

This is the major event for Sierra Leone's community. It is held on April 27 and commemorates independence from Britain in 1961. Each year the community gets together for an 'African night' party, seasoned with traditional food, music and dances. There is no permanent venue, however the event is always held near the Auburn/Lakemba area.

Further information: Alhajie Sesay, President of the Sierra Leonean Association in Australia (tel: 9688 1153).

The South Africans

Sydneysiders still remember with emotion President Nelson Mandela standing on the steps of the Sydney Opera House, back in 1990. It was one of the greatest moments for the city. Nelson Mandela had recently walked to freedom after 27 years of prison, and South Africa had begun its long-awaited transition to a non-racist democratic society.

The lyric of *Nkosi Sikelel' iAfrica* – the South African national anthem - filled Sydney's landscape with a message of struggle and freedom. It was an unforgettable moment.

Many South Africans came to Australia during the years of the infamous apartheid. They were not a homogeneous group, needless to say. For a considerable number of white South Africans who feared a black power takeover and the loss of privileges, Australia was a safe haven. There were, on the other hand, a group of white, liberal, professional and English-speaking South Africans who left their homeland in the mid-1970s and 1980s fed up with living in an embarrassing racist system.

There were also the black South Africans, those who had suffered the most. Many came fearing for their lives, while others were searching for a land where their children could grow up in freedom and with opportunities. One of those was a young black South African call Mangala Munsami. In 1976 he was the youngest lifesaver to be banned from South Africa for opposing apartheid in sport. When Mangala came to Sydney he was able to break our own racist barriers: between 1991 and 1993 he was the first black captain of Bondi Surf Club, a national icon in Australia.

Contact between South Africa and Australia dates back to the early days of Sydney's establishment when the Cape of Good Hope, founded in 1652 by Dutch explorers, became a supply centre for food and other goods for the newly created colony. In the second half of the nineteenth century, the discovery of gold in Australia attracted a considerable number of South Africans and, similarly, the 1880s South African goldrush in the Transvaal attracted a large contingent of Australian diggers. Further contact was established at the time of the Boer War

> In 1976, Mangala Munsami was the youngest lifesaver to be banned from South Africa for opposing apartheid in sport. When Mangala came to Sydney he was able to break our own racist barriers: between 1991 and 1993 he was the first black captain of Bondi Surf Club, a national icon in Australia.

(1899-1902) when many of the 16,000 volunteers who served in the Australian contingents remained in South Africa after their discharge.

When Nelson Mandela was elected president in 1994, many of Australia's South Africans contemplated returning to their homeland. However, the economic hardship and still unresolved political problems back in their country convinced them that there was no way back, at least not for now. In many respects they have assimilated and planted solid roots in Australia.

South Africans – depending very much upon financial, ethnic and religious factors – have established small communities in a number of Sydney's suburbs. There is a very visible South African community in St Ives, on the upper North Shore, whose similarities to some of the areas of Johannesburg, and the presence of the Jewish school, Masada, has attracted a thriving community. "There is also a small community of black South Africans, mainly tradespeople, who have settled in the newly developing suburbs, around Sydney, where they have found work in the construction industry," explains Victor Mannie, President of the South African Association of Sydney. He also tells that a South African Muslim community has been established in the western suburbs of Lakemba and Auburn, where they have been welcomed by the long-settled Muslim community. Sydney is also home to an even smaller Hindu South African community – around 1,000 people – whose community life revolves around the Cultural Advancement Society of Australia, a religious and cultural organisation. Since 1976 the number of South Africans in Australia has increased by an average of around 2,500 each year and South Africa is today one of Australia's top ten sources of immigrants.

The immensely famous Bryce Courtenay, author of *The Power of One, The Potato Factory* and other celebrated novels, was born in Johannesburg in 1933. He arrived in Australia in 1958 and his books are worldwide bestsellers.

From Courtenay to Lubambo

Many South Africans have left their mark here. Certainly, one of the best known is the writer Bryce Courtenay, who came to Australia in 1958. However, there are also those South Africans who are probably less well-known but whose struggle in Australia made an enormous contribution to the downfall of apartheid. We still remember with emotion the late John Brink -- the white South African and anti-apartheid activist who, after sharing a cell with the late Joe Slovo (who later served as a minister in Nelson Mandela's first government) migrated with his family to Australia in 1961. Here, in the 1960s he founded the South African Defence and Aid Fund (SADAF), put out a monthly newsletter and ran campaigns against companies that traded with South Africa. He died on Christmas Eve in 1997. Equally unforgettable are Eddie Funde, the ANC Chief Representative for Australasia between 1983 and 1990; Ndumiso Ntshinga, who succeeded

USEFUL NUMBERS FOR VISITORS

SOUTH AFRICAN HIGH COMMISSION:
tel: (06) 2732 424.

SOUTH AFRICAN AIRLINES:
tel: 9223 4402 (reservations)

SOUTH AFRICAN TOURISM BOARD:
tel: 9261 3424.

SOUTH AFRICAN TRAVEL CENTRE:
tel: 9299 8444.

Eddie Funde in 1990 and today works in the South African Embassy in Washington; and Siphiwe Lubambo, the young ex-ANC army combatant who was responsible for training the choir that performed on that unforgettable day in 1990 when Nelson Mandela spoke to us about a new South Africa.

Getting to know the South African community

Events

South Africa Freedom Day.

On April 27 the South African community commemorates the first non-racial democratic election in South African history (in 1994) in which the ANC obtained a clear majority.

Further information: Victor Mannie, South African Association of Sydney (tel: 9698 5820).

Community and cultural organisations

South African Association of Sydney.

Holds informal social and cultural gatherings for the South African community.

Further information: as above.

Cultural Advancement Society of Australia.

The Society promotes South African culture and Hindu religion among Hindu South Africans. It meets for prayer sessions on the first Friday of every month.

Further information: Aroo Govender (tel: 9873 3943).

Media

Newspapers

The Star & SA Times. A weekly covering several South African newspapers, including the *Star*, *Cape Argus*, *Cape Times*, *Pretoria News*, *The Sowetan* and the *Natal Mercury*. This 32-page paper – published by the Australian Provincial Newspapers publishing group – includes general news, political news, finance and sport. The paper is available through selected newsagencies for $2.95.

Further information: tel 9936 8700.

For radio programs see African Sydney, page 448.

Facts and Figures

Between 1986 and 1991 the number of South Africans living in Australia increased by more than one-third (34.5%). Currently there are just over 49,000 in Australia, with Sydney home to more than 16,000.

About 72% of South African-born immigrants have taken out Australian citizenship – higher than the average (61.4%).

In terms of education, 55.2% of South African immigrants have some type of educational or occupational qualifications, a percentage considerably higher than for the total Australian population (around 38%). The proportion with post-secondary qualifications (about 29%) is also considerably higher than the Australian average.

Slightly higher than 13 per cent of South Africans have received some skilled or basic vocational training.

The median annual income of the South African-born, $18,900, is well above that of Australian average of $14,200. According to the 1991 Census, 25% of all South African-born living in Australia own their home, while a further 39% were purchasing their place.

The majority of South-African born are Anglicans (23%). They are followed by Catholics (18%) and other Christians (22%). Among non-Christian religions (17.7%), Judaism is the largest religious group (12%). Around 88 % of South Africans speak English at home, while only 7% speak Afrikaans.

Most of the South African immigrants living in Australia are white, highly educated, and from large cities. In Sydney they tend to live in Ku-ring-gai and Waverley.

The Sudanese

Sudanese and Egyptians do not only share the life-giving Nile back in their homeland in northern Africa, they also have a common religious heritage. So when they came to Australia, in the mid-1960s, the Sudanese and Egyptians soon merged into one community under the auspices of the Coptic Orthodox Church.

Sudanese began emigrating to Australia as a direct consequence of the serious ethnic conflicts and warfare facing modern Sudan. The country is deeply divided between the mainly Sunni Muslim peoples, of the northern and central regions, and the southern tribes which are mainly either non-religious or are Christian converts. The largest number of Sudanese immigrants in Australia are Christians who fled Sudan to escape religious persecution by the current Muslim government. Due to the escalation of the Sudanese internal conflict, the Australian government established in 1992 a 'special assistance category' for Sudanese. That year 155 Sudanese refugees entered the country, and since then an estimated 300 have been allowed into Australia every year.

In Sydney there are two main pockets of Sudanese settlement. The Coptic Sudanese community has tended to settle in Sydney's western suburbs, especially around Mt Druitt and Blacktown, where the Archangel Michael and St Bishoy Coptic Orthodox Church and the Coptic Cultural Association are located (see The Egyptians, page 392). The Syrian Sudanese community, on the other hand, is found mainly in the Sydney eastern suburbs of Mascot and Eastlakes, where the Sudanese Cultural and Social Organisation operates. There is also a small group of Sudanese Muslims whose community life thrives around the long-established Sydney Muslim community.

> The largest number of Sudanese immigrants in Australia are Christians who fled Sudan to escape religious persecution.

Getting to know the Sudanese community

Events

Sudan Day.

The Sudan was under Anglo-Egyptian rule from 1899 until its independence on January 1 1956. The Sydney Sudanese community does not have regular festivities on this day, but at the end of the year a Sudanese art and craft exhibition, and a traditional food, music and dance festival is held at the Ukrainian Cultural & Social Club, 11-15 Church Street, Lidcombe. This event is organised by the Sudanese Ethnic Group of NSW.

Further information: Abdullah Monsour, president (tel: 9740 3791).

Community and cultural organisations

Sudanese Cultural and Social Organisation.

Provides cultural and social activities for Syrian Sudanese.

Further information: Michael Hakim (tel: 9585 8646).

Australian Coptic Welfare Association.

The Association provides social and welfare assistance to Sydney Sudanese.

Further information: Magdi Zaki (tel: 9831 0734).

Media

Newspapers

The Sudanese community has just began circulating *Tabaldi*, a newspaper published with the assistance of the Blacktown Migrant Resource Centre.

Further information: 9621 6633.

Sudanese community news is regularly published in the fortnightly Coptic newspaper, *The Egyptian*.

Further information: Mr Habashi, editor (tel: 9625 8184).

SUDANESE ETHNIC GROUP.
This is an umbrella social, cultural and welfare organisation for the Sydney Sudanese community.
4 Maddock Avenue, Moorebank.
(tel: 9740 3791).

The North Americans

The recipe for American pumpkin pie or what the temperature it will be in San Francisco in October are some of the odd bits of information regularly requested from The American Society – the oldest American association in Sydney (needless to say, more relevant information is also requested). It was in October 1922 – when five American businessman residing in our city got together – that the American Society was conceived. In November of the same year, the first luncheon was held and the first officers of the Society were elected. By that year there were over 6,000 Americans living in Australia.

Early pioneers

The American presence spans back to the 1770s and James Cook's *Endeavour* – which had a Virginian, John Gore, and a New Yorker of Italian background, Mario Matra, on board. Their legacy and pioneer presence remains in the names of the Sydney suburbs of Gore Hill and Matraville.

Another important American pioneer of the early years was Eber Bunker, a native from Massachusetts who – as the captain of the whaler the *William and Ann*, carrying 181 convicts and a company of soldiers – sailed with the Third Fleet and arrived in Port Jackson in August 1791. In Sydney he bought 100 acres of land at Bunaming, near Petersham Hill, and named it Bunker's Farm; years later it would become a centre for fresh meat supply for Government stores. Bunker became a prominent member of Liverpool society in western Sydney; he died in 1836 and his headstone lies in the Liverpool Pioneers' Memorial Park.

From the ship *Philadelphia* – the first trade vessel of any country to call in to Sydney, in 1792 – to the current managing director of Westpac – Bob Joss – Americans have brought to our shores their economic acumen, entreprenurial skills and industry know-how. During the 1800s American experts came to Australia to work in agriculture, railway, construction and mining. One those experts was a mining engineer by

Many Americans who call Australia home bear familiar and famous names such as the entertainer Don Lane, singer Marcia Hines, and acting superstar Mel Gibson.

the name of Herbert Hoover – who in 1896 came to Australia to manage the Gwalia mine about 100 miles north of Kalgoorlie. Years later he would become President of the United States.

Into the twentieth century

At the time of the 1901 Census there were 7,448 American citizens living in Australia, and one of the most prominent to live in Sydney during the first decades of the century was the architect Walter Burley Griffin. He came to Australia in 1913 after winning the worldwide competition launched in 1911 to find a design for a new federal capital – Canberra. His work in Canberra ended in 1920 but he remained in Sydney a few more years, a period in which he developed Castlecrag – the north shore suburb that overlooks Middle Harbour. Griffin was a devoted theosophist and the design of this must-visit suburb followed these principles.

The first years of this century – especially during the 1920s – also witnessed a real explosion of American companies investing in Australia – Mobil Oil, General Electric, Ford and household names such as Kellogg's, Colgate-Palmolive and Johnson & Johnson.

During these years, The American Society in Sydney was actively trying to make American soldiers feel at home. It established and ran the American Center, in Elizabeth Street, which provided hospitality, meals and entertainment (when Eleanor Roosevelt came to Sydney in 1943 she dropped in).

In 1947 – the year in which the still very much active American Club was established in Sydney – the Minister for Immigration, Arthur Calwell, sent a message to the United States that Australia would like to see "at least one million Americans immigrating" (read 'white' Americans). His pledge was heard but the number of American immigrants was a bit more modest than he expected.

Many Americans who call Australia home – though most haven't taken up citizenship – have succeeded in many aspects of Australian life. Look no further than entertainer Don Lane, singer Marcia Hines, and acting superstar Mel Gibson to prove it. A special mention is needed for the American-born Hayes Gordon, who was an inspirational theatre mentor for many generations of Australian actors. He arrived in 1952 with a production of *Kiss Me Kate* and began teaching acting and the principles of performance to the theory-starved Australian actors of the time.
In 1958, along with a group of his devoted students, he founded the Ensemble Theatre, now one of the longest-standing professional theatres in the country.

By the outbreak of the World War II, the number of Americans in Australia was steady at 6,000, a number that rose dramatically though temporarily with the presence of approximately one million United States servicemen from 1941-1945.

During 1945-1960 around 18,000 American immigrants arrived on our shores, and steady but moderate growth has continued till today. Currently there are more than 43,000 Americans Australia-wide, with Sydney home to around 14,000.

See also Rockerfellers, page 34.

Restaurants

Until recently, saying "let's go out to have American food" would have sounded a bit odd to say the least. Of course we *do* have McDonald's and the rest but now you can taste 'real' American cuisine in Sydney – an ecletic treat of *Tex-Mex*, *Cajun*, and *Creole*.

Cafe Gueville. A strong *Cajun* accent – in the attractive menu you'll find the all-time New Orleans favorites. Try the Cajun pork fillet and *jambalaya* (a rice-based dish). Average $25, BYO. Open for lunch Tuesday-Friday noon-2.30pm, dinner Monday-Saturday 6pm-10.30pm.

105 Longeville Road, Lane Cove (tel: 9428 1007).

Coyotes on Crown. Again the *Cajun* cuisine is the star in this well-known spot. The food is good, the portions are huge and the Margaritas are not bad at all. Average $25, BYO and licensed. Open Monday-Sunday 6.30-11pm.

294 Crown Street, Darlinghurst (tel: 9361 4935).

Rattlesnake Grill. For the neophyte this is the place to go – you'll get fully introduced to an attractive and intriguing menu. Get a carafe of frozen margarita and tuck into a superb Santa Fe *mezze* plate or the seafood *fajitas*. Average $30, licensed. Open for lunch Sunday 11.30am-3pm, dinner Monday-Saturday from 6pm.

130 Military Road, Neutral Bay (tel: 9953 4789).

Yipiyiyo. One of the best-known *Tex-Mex* spots in Sydney. The quality and variety of the food and the friendly environment keep regulars coming back here. Average $25, BYO. Open for dinner Monday-Saturday from 6.30pm.

90 Crown Street, Surry Hills (tel: 9332 3114).

Shopping

Four Winds Gallery. For those who are serious about Native American art, this is the place to go – 16 years in the business goes a long way towards making this gallery one for connoisseurs of Sioux and Navajo jewellery and art. Drop by and browse through the beautiful and extensive collection of primitive timber furniture, alabaster, bronze and marble scultptures, lithographs and fetish effigies.
Open Monday-Sunday 10am-5pm.

Shop 11, Bay Village, 28-34 Cross Street, Double Bay (tel: 9328 7951).

Pandarra Country & Western. The place where city slickers buy the right stuff to conquer the wild urban prairie – from cowboy boots to JR-style hats, all the right gear is here. Open Monday-Friday 10am-5.45pm (later on Thursday), Saturday 10am-6pm, Sunday 11am-4pm.
96 Oxford Street, **Darlinghurst** (tel: 9361 5785).

Snakenavel. Tucked away in The Rocks, this place specialises in authentic Native American arts and crafts, jewellery, artefacts, pendleton blankets and other stuff. Open Monday-Sunday 10am-6pm.
23 Playfair Street, The Rocks, City (tel: 9569 3813).

Places of interest and landmarks

Linked by the Sea: USA Gallery (National Maritime Museum).

Located in the 'sea level' of the National Maritime Museum, Linked by the Sea Gallery honours and remembers the long-lasting friendship between USA and our country. In the past many American traders stopped off in Australia while navigating to China. Open Monday-Sunday 9.30am-5pm. Admission $7 adults; $4 concessions; $18.50 family ticket.
2 Murray Street, Darling Harbour (tel: 9552 7777 on Monday-Friday; 9552 75000 on Saturday-Sunday).

Getting to know the American community

Events

Independence Day.

The American Society is behind this most important American annual event. On July 4 an informal dinner dance is organised at the Royal Agricultural Showgrounds and is attended by the American Consul in Sydney (as the Showground will be redeveloped by Fox Studios into a film studio, the venue will change).

For additional information call 9247 8529. The American Club also holds a lunch for members and guests (tel: 9251 2016).

USEFUL NUMBER FOR VISITORS

AMERICAN CONSULATE:
tel: 9373 9200.

CLUBS

THE AMERICAN CLUB.
This is where the who's who of Sydney's American and Australian business community meet. Established in 1947, it's a quintessential business social club (interestingly enough you won't hear any telephones ringing inside since mobile phones must be switched off or left at reception). The Club, which acts as a the venue for theatre nights, American celebrations and corporate functions, has a good and fully licensed restaurant open for lunch between noon-3pm and dinner from 4.30pm.

131 Macquarie Street, City (tel: 9241 2015).

Halloween.
'Trick or treating' – and the American Society is behind it. Recently the event – on October 31 – has been held at the Mosman Community Centre but don't drop by without calling beforehand since the venue changes every year (tel: 9247 8529).

Thanksgiving Day.
An unlucky turkey and the very American pumpkin pie, cranberry sauce and vegies, plus a Thanksgiving message from the US President set the scene for this traditional celebration held around November 28.

Further information: The American Society (tel: 9247 8529).

Community organisations

The American Society. Established in 1922, this is a non-profit organisation that provides social, cultural activities for Americans living in Sydney (just read the information above to see how hard they work!). It also organises diverse fundraising activities throughout the year.

89 Macquarie Street, City (tel: 9247 8529).

The Eagle
The Newsletter of The American Club of Sydney   May 1997

Explore the world in one city

The Latin Americans

When the Latinos arrived in Sydney they brought with them the music that *hace hasta los muertos bailar* (makes even the dead dance) – the sensuality of the *ritmos calientes* of Tito Puentes or Celia Cruz, Sierra Maestra – whose sound inundated the vintage walls of the Basement – and Gloria Estefan – whose contagious rhythm even brought out the soul in the soulless Entertainment Centre. Even the 'anglos' are moving those stiff hips to the rhythm (well at least trying!). And the latest Latin invasion of Sydney comes from Cuba, in the way of aromatic cigars, whose popularity has been increasing across Sydney for the past three or four years. (If you can afford it, go for the Cohiba Esplendids, Fidel Castro's favourites, at $58 a stick.)

Nightlife

Forget 'El Niño'. *Rumba*, *cha cha* and *mambo* are popping up all over the place. Sydneysiders are feeling the sensual and romantic Latin soul and on Fridays and Saturdays are taking the local Spanish and Latin American nightclubs by storm. Here the fun and the good music from talented local bands, such as the Afro-Peruvian *Cumana* or the superb Afro-Cuban *Sandunga*, is guaranteed. And if you feel that your hips are not moving quite right, take advantage of the club's free classes (call to check times and venues). After you've done some classes you can drop by the club on a Friday or Saturday, have dinner, then hop on the dance floor and show off what you've learnt!

See also: La Campana, page 234.

La Viña. Arguably the premier Latin dance venue in Sydney, La Viña moved a few years ago from Parramatta Road to the inner city. A small bar area makes way for a small dance floor with a gigantic television screen at the back showing exotic images of Rio and Copacabana (on a rainy Sydney day you're going to hate it). Some of the best Sydney South American bands – including *Sonora Galaxia*, *Caliente la Banda* or the *Tropical Brothers* with Maria Cuevas – perform here live on Fridays and

> *Rumba*, *cha cha* and *mambo* are popping up all over the place. Sydneysiders are feeling the sensual and romantic Latin soul and on Fridays and Saturdays are taking the local Spanish and Latin American nightclubs by storm.

RESTAURANTS

CASAPUEBLO.
Diana, from Uruguay, and Zulma, from Peru, have done a good job here. The ambience is warm and inviting and the owners attend to every detail in this charming restaurant, featuring dishes from Colombia, Peru, Brazil, Uruguay. We ordered the recommended spicy chicken with walnut and it's just sensational. Average $15, BYO. Open dinner only, Tuesday-Saturday 6.30-10.30pm.

**650 Bourke Street, Redfern
(tel: 9319 6377).**

Other than Casapueblo – and despite a large number of Mexican and Spanish places around town – you need to look a bit wider to get good South American food. The national social clubs (see The Chileans, page 477; and The Argentinians, page 473) are good places to find cheap and great homemade traditional South American food, and don't forget Gaucho Grill, see page 474. which has a strong Argentinian accent and offers a range of South American dishes.

Saturdays. A restaurant service is also available. Free dancing classes on Wednesdays and Thursdays from 7.30pm. A small $6 cover charge gets you in. Open Wednesday-Thursday 6pm-midnight; Friday and Saturday 6pm-3am.

504 Elizabeth Street (tel: 9319 0423).

Vivaz. American actress Brooke Shields and our very own Kerri-Anne Kennerley from Channel 9's *Midday Show* have been caught here moving their hips to the rhythm of the *lambada* and *salsa* pumped out by Latin Soul, the resident band. The colourful decor, the live Latin music and a fun clientele give this venue an authentic carnival atmosphere. Vivaz also has a restaurant service with an exotic buffet-style menu ($26). Chilean and Australian wines available. A $8 cover charge gets you in if you are not dining there. Open Friday and Saturday from 6.30pm.

80 George Street (tel: 9251 4467).

La Havana. This is a Cold War connection – a Cuban Latin Club (La Havana) operating in a Russian restaurant (The Russian Coachman). Every Thursday the irresistible Cuban rhythms of the *cha cha*, *mambo*, *rumba* and *salsa* invade the Russians, and the party starts rolling from 8pm onwards. Free Afro-Cuban dance classes at 7.30pm. Cover $7 after 8pm.

763 Bourke Street, Surry Hills (tel: 9400 4661).

The Olive. No it's not a Spanish deli, it's a place where you can taste the flavour of Latin Music every Friday. Regular visitors like to describe it as 'glamorous' – and the staircase certainly lives up to the description. Escaping from the sweaty and crowded dancefloor, you will find people still hitting their hips out in William Street. Surreal. Cover charge $10. The party goes from 8 till late.

108 William Street, Woolloomooloo (tel: 9368 1855).

Shopping

Confiteria La Torre. After more than 20 years at the heart of the Sydney Spanish speaking community – in the area of Fairfield – La Torre is a well-known bakery and cake shop with a strong emphasis on South American products. Apart from a huge array of delicious and highly diet-threatening cakes, La Torre specialises in the super sweet *torta merengue*, a meringue-cake used traditionally for birthday parties. Open Tuesday-Friday 6am-6pm, Saturday 6am-4pm and Sunday 6am-noon.

Shop 1/9 Nelson Street, Fairfield (tel: 9724 4565).

Eddie's Brighton Butchery. Following the tradition of South American shops, it isn't only meat that you'll find here, but a huge array of traditional goods, such as *mate* (the traditional tea-like infusion so popular among Uruguayans and Argentinians), *dulces de leche* (brown milk fudge) and Argentinian mayonnaise. And in term of meats this is where South Americans drop by for the right 'Rio de la plata' cut for a South American *asado* (barbecue). Don't leave without getting a good portion of *matambre* (rolled meat filled with egg and spinach) or spicy fresh sausage. Open Monday-Friday 7am-6pm; Saturday 7am-1pm.

309 Bay Street, corner of Trafalgar, Brighton Le Sands (tel: 9567 1816).

Rodriguez Hermanos Butchery. This is the kingdom of the delicious *morcillas* (sweet and sour black pudding), tasty *chorizos* (spicy sausages) and the right ribs and beef cuts needed for a Buenos Aires-style *parrillada* (*asado*, or barbecue). Open Monday-Friday 7.30am-5.30pm (till 6.30 on Thursday), Saturday 7.30am-3pm; Sunday 7.30am-noon.

485 Hume Highway, Yagoona (tel: 9796 8903).

La Paula. Ask any Chilean where to find good *empanadas* and they will tell you '*anda a La Paula*'. This bakery is a real institution among Sydney South Americans. Here you can get the two well-known versions of *empanadas* – beef mince or cheese - and they are both delicious. The bread and pastries all have a strong Chilean accent. Open Tuesday-Sunday 8am-6pm (till 4pm on Sunday).

118 Gardeners Road, Kingsford (tel: 9663 1041). Also at Shop 1, 9 Barbara Street, Fairfield (tel: 9726 2379) – open Tuesday-Sunday 9am-7pm (till 9pm on Thursday and 5pm on Sunday).

Martinez Brothers. The *'hermanos* Martinez' have transformed this delicatessen into a must-go place when a South American-style party is happening. The range of goods is huge but the prices are anything but huge. You will find organically grown *mate* and also sausages, *empanadas* filled with beef onion, herbs, olives and the much sought-after *matambre*. Open Monday-Friday 8.30am-5.30pm, Saturday 8am-1.20pm.

33 Spencer Street, Fairfield (tel: 9724 5509).

When the 'Latinos' arrived in Sydney they brought with them the music that makes even the dead dance

COMMUNITY ORGANISATIONS

SPANISH & LATIN AMERICAN ASSOCIATION FOR SOCIAL ASSISTANCE (SLASA).
This is arguably the most important Spanish-speaking welfare organisation in Sydney. It provides a wide range of social and welfare services, including advice and counselling.

Cabramatta Railway Parade, corner McBurney Road (tel: 9724 2220).

CUBAN FESTIVAL.
An annual event that has been traditionally held at the end of November at the Marrickville Community Centre, 142 Addison Road, Marrickville. This day-long festival, organised by the Australia-Cuba Friendship Society, is a celebration of Latin American music, dance, poetry, art and food. Admission is only $3 and the money collected goes to social, cultural and health projects in Cuba. 10am-10pm.

Further information: the Australia-Cuba Friendship Society (tel: 9388 2181).

Getting to know the Latin American community

The Sydney Latin American community has been able to recreate their wonderful culture in several annual festivals. The geographical borders of Latin Americans – the reason for more than a few wars back in their homeland – fall down and they get together along with a huge contingent of non-Latinos. The objective: to have a great time.

The South American Music Festival.

Formerly known as the Festival del Sol, this festival is traditionally celebrated in mid-February at the Bondi Pavilion, Bondi Beach. Established in 1979, it is now one of the highlights of the entire Sydney annual festival calendar. The four-week extravaganza features Latin films, social and political forums, dance, music, theatre and, of course, food.

Further information: 9130 3325.

Latina Film Festival.

This twice-yearly event, featuring the best of the Latin American cinema, is held in mid-September at the Museum of Contemporary Art and the Mandolin Cinema, 150 Elizabeth Street. Over two weekends the festival features movies, documentaries and experimental shorts from Chile, Peru, Argentina and also from Central America. Will Raul Ruiz be there next time? We hope so!

Further information: 9252 4033.

Fiesta.

Head down to Darling Harbour between 4-6 October and be seduced by this colourful annual three-day celebration of Latin American and Spanish culture. There's food, music, and workshops featuring top Spanish and Latin performers.

Further information: 9281 3999.

Rio at the Rocks.

Expect to see Brazil Beat, the legendary Roddy Montez and his Copacabana, and the group Capoiera Brazil. Naturally, there is food available as well. Saturday-Sunday 11am-5pm..

For information on dates, programs and venues: 9255 1788.

Hispanoamerica Live.

More than 1000 artists, representing around 15 countries from Latin America and Spain, perform traditional dances and music at this annual festival held at the beginning of May. The venue is the Fairfield Showground at Smithfield Road, Prairiewood. Entry $7 adults, $2 children.

Further information: 9726 8724 or 015 015 609.

Arts and culture

Amaru.

Formed at the beginning of the 1990s, *Amaru* is considered one of the most important music groups in Sydney. *Amaru* – which in the Aymare language means "rainbow" – consists of five musician who recreate a wide range of rhythms from the Latin American folklore tradition.

Further information: 9789 1682

Latin American Cultural Centre.

The Centre organises cultural activities, including classes in guitar and Spanish language, from its base at the Newtown Neighbourhood Centre,.

1 Bedford Street, Newtown (tel: 9519 4874).

Grupo de Teatro Las Tablas.

A very successful Spanish community theatre group, *Las Tablas* has staged the works of some of the most celebrated Latin American playwrights. Upcoming productions are usually advertised in the Spanish-speaking media. As the plays are in Spanish they're a great way to get to know some of the best Latin American authors in their authentic form, and to practise your Spanish. Entry $20.

Further information: 9313 6920.

Papalote.

Founded in 1979, this is one of the oldest and most respected Latin American groups on the Sydney music scene. *Papalote* combines the haunting and ancient sounds of the Andean Indian flutes and pan pipes, the intricate guitar and *charango* rhythms and the irresistible syncopated dance beat of the African drums of the Caribbean. In fact, it's a rhythmic journey through Latin America, showcasing a huge array of instruments and styles.

Further information: 9698 1330.

RELIGIOUS ORGANISATIONS AND PLACES OF WORSHIP

MISIÓN CATÓLICA HISPANA.
Organises regular religious services and educational activities.

Further information:
Father Josi Marma Enedaguila.
16 Vine Street,
Fairfield
(tel: 9724 3846).

Formed at the beginning of the 1990s, Amaru is one of the most important music groups in Sydney.

RADIO

SBS RADIO 2 FM, 97.7. NEWS, community information and a good selection of Latin American and Spanish music. Monday, Wednesday and Friday 1-2pm and 10-11pm; Tuesday, Thursday, Saturday and Sunday 1-2pm.

Radio programs in Spanish can also be heard in most of the Sydney community radio stations; call them to get the latest timelots.

RADIO AUSTRAL FM, 87.8
(tel: 9717 7102).

2BCR FM, 88.7
(tel: 9724 7877 or 9726 8233).

2GLF FM, 89.3
(tel: 9601 4489).

2MWM FM, 92.1/93.7.
(tel: 9913 8986).

2NBC FM, 90.1.
(tel: 9534 2778).

2RDJ FM, 88.1
(tel: 9744 3284 or 9744 0881).

2RES FM, 89.7
(tel: 9331 3000).

2RRR FM, 88.5
(tel: 9816 2988).

2RSR FM, 88.9
(tel: 9550 9552)

Media

Sydney's Spanish speakers don't suffer any shortage of media outlets. Spanish language newspapers – some closer to the right and some closer to the left – have been around for a long time. Radio community programs have also been extremely important, and lately SBS Television has added two news services in Spanish.

Newspapers

El Español en Australia. Published weekly, *El Español* can be found on Tuesdays in selected newsagencies. It has a circulation of 9,000 and offers a good coverage of Spanish and Latin American issues. It also has a section dedicated to community news. The cost is $1.50. Its current editor is Juan Arrua.

P.O.Box 675 Hurtsville, NSW 2220 (tel: 9585 9669).

Extra Informativo. Published nationally, this is a weekly newspaper covering national and international issues. It appears on newsstands on Wednesdays and costs $2. It has a circulation of 25,000 and the current editor is Eduardo Gonzalez Cristobal.

Suite 6-9 William Street, Fairfield (tel: 9727 7102).

Spanish Herald. Provides a very good overview of national, Spanish and Latin American events – it's the only Spanish local newspaper with any real editorial analysis. It's published three times a week, on Tuesday, Thursday and Saturday, has a circulation of 50,000 and costs $1.30. The current editor is Santiago Poso.

7 Garners Avenue, Marrickville (tel: 9562 0500).

Television

SBS Television. Esta Semana – a summary of weekly news from Chilean state television. Sunday, 9.30-10am.

Community Channel 31. 'Quedate con Nosotros' – community news and music. Wednesday 10pm.

The Argentinians

The Argentinian presence in Australia dates back to the 1880s when a number of missions were sent out by the government of the Province of Buenos Aires to learn about the successful Australian rural export industry of the time. One of these missions was headed by Ricardo Newton, who in 1883 travelled extensively throughout New South Wales and Victoria studying the booming Australian meat market.

This was a time in which both countries, with predominantly rural economies, began seeing each other as competitors in the international market.

A mere 249 Argentinians were counted as living here in the early years of the twentieth century, and it was not until the 1970s that Argentinians began arriving in large numbers. The twin causes of this immigration were economic deterioration and military dictatorship. By 1981, there were just over 8,000 Argentinian-born people in Australia.

Today, there are a little more than 5,000 Argentinians living in Sydney. The largest number have settled in the western suburb of Fairfield, where their main community organisation, the Argentinian Association of Sydney, was established. In general, Argentinian organisations have been scarce and short lived. The first founded in Sydney was the Argentinian Centre of New South Wales, in 1977, and it closed seven years later. A recently established organisation is the Argentinian Folkloric Group Dance and Friendship that performs and conducts workshops on Argentinian dance and culture. Two of the most familiar Argentinian names to Sydneysiders are former Rugby Union player, Enrique 'Topo' Rodriguez, and Socceroo assistant coach, Raul Blanco.

In the 1980s, the Argentinian-born Enrique 'Topo' Rodriguez became something of a Rugby legend in Australia. In 1984, soon after emigrating to Australia, he began playing for Warringah Rugby Club, where his performance was rewarded with his elevation to the New South Wales team, and then to the national squad, the Wallabies.

USEFUL NUMBERS FOR VISITORS

ARGENTINIAN CONSULATE:
tel: 9251 3402.

AEROLINEAS ARGENTINAS:
tel: 9283 3660.
(reservations),
9317 3018
(Sydney Airport).

SOCIAL CLUBS

ARGENTINIAN LIDCOMBE UNITED.
On Saturday nights, the Club is the place for that Argentinian flavour.
If you're interested in the melancholy and sensual rhythm of the tango, this is the place to learn to dance. Triglav Club, 80-94 Brisbane Road, St. Johns Park.

Restaurants

Gaucho Grill. Nobody would argue that the most famous Argentinian presence in Sydney is the superb steakhouse Gaucho Grill – known until recently as Rancho Amigo. Established in 1979 as El Rancho Argentino, this Argentinian-style steakhouse is where you'll come closest to having those worldwide famous "*asados*" (barbecues) only found in Buenos Aires. Traditional dishes from Uruguay and Brazil are also on the menu. Average $30, licensed. Open lunch Thursday and Friday noon-3.30pm; dinner Monday-Saturday 6.30pm till late.

164 Parramatta Road, Stanmore (tel: 9519 6019)

Getting to know the Argentinian community

Events

National Day.
On May 25 1810, the Argentinians ridded their country of their Spanish rulers. Every year Sydney Argentinians get together in various venues to celebrate this historic event.

Community Organisations

Argentinean Association of Sydney.
Provides welfare and social assistance to Argentinian immigrants.
PO Box 659, Fairfield 2165

Explore the world in one city

The Brazilians

Ten, eleven, twelve, thirteen... thirty-one, thirty-two, thirty-three... How long can they keep going before that soccer ball finally hits the sand? Stroll down to Bondi Beach on any weekend and you can't help but marvel at the deft touch of the Brazilian boys – showing some of the skill that has made their country the indisputable world champions.

On the sandy beach Brazilians also like to showcase the sensuous rhythms of their drums, drawing a crowd whenever they play. There are about 1,000 Brazilians currently living in Sydney, and Bondi Beach is often singled out as the main Brazilian enclave. The Bondi Pavilion Community Cultural Centre at Queen Elizabeth Drive, Bondi Beach, runs workshops and classes in Brazilian music and dance throughout the year, and welfare and settlement assistance to Brazilian immigrants is provided by the Brazilian Community Council of Australia.

The Brazilian community in Sydney is the only non-Spanish-speaking Latin American group in this city; it's the second largest Portuguese-speaking community in the country. Although a small community, some Brazilians were already in Australia during the 1901 census, when 105 Brazilian-born people were counted. It's also likely that some Brazilians migrated to Australia during last century on some of the English ships that called at Rio de Janeiro on their way to Sydney. This early contact between the two countries has been maintained until today, and is demonstrated by the fact that Brazil is currently Australia's largest trading partner in Latin America, with a two-way trade in 1990-91 of A$445 million.

Restaurants

Rio's Churrascaria. If you show up on Friday and Saturday you'll probably find they've added an extra touch to the Brazilian menu: live music and dance in the form of *samba* and *capoeira*. Rio's is a restaurant fully committed to showing Sydney the richness and taste of Brazilian cuisine. Average $20 ($38 full menu), licensed. Open for dinner Friday-Saturday 7.30pm-3am.

128 Pyrmont Bridge Road, Camperdown (tel: 9557 1371).

USEFUL NUMBERS FOR VISITORS

BRAZILIAN CONSULATE:
tel: 9267 4414.

BRAZIL-AUSTRALIA CHAMBER OF COMMERCE:
tel: 9969 6846.

COMMUNITY ORGANISATION

BRAZILIAN COMMUNITY COUNCIL OF AUSTRALIA.
The Council provides social and welfare assistance to Brazilian immigrants.

PO Box 43,
Cherrybrook 2126
(tel: 9716 6508).

Sydneysiders aren't immune to the Brazilian rhythm of capoeira

Shopping

Brazilian Coffee and Nut Factory.

A terrific place to find imported and fresh roasted coffee blends from Brazil, Colombia, Costa Rica, Nicaragua and Indonesia. Drop by the cafe attached to the shop for a cup of Brazil's finest. Open Monday-Friday 8am-6pm (till 9pm on Thursday), Saturday 8am-3pm, Sunday 10am-4pm.

34 Victoria Road, Marrickville (tel: 9519 4984).

Brazil Galeria.

It has a very tasteful selection of beautiful indigenous art and handmade artefacts made by Brazil natives. Open Wednesday-Sunday 2pm-7pm (or by appointment).

278 Unwins Bridge Road, Sydenham (tel: 9519 4986).

Dance classes

Brazilian Latin Dance Co.

Established nine years ago, this is the place where the long road to becoming a true Brazilian/Latin dancer starts. Classes on Brazilian rhythms, including *salsa*, *samba* and *lambada*, are held at 128 Pyrmont Bridge Road, Camperdown (in the venue of Rio's Churrascaria) on Wednesday at 7pm. The cost is only $10.

Further information: 9365 2378.

Getting to know the Brazilian community

Regular events involving Brazilian music, dance and classes on drums and samba are run throughout the year in what has become a traditional Brazilian meeting place, The Bondi Pavilion Community Cultural Centre at Queen Elizabeth Drive (just in front of the beach).

Further information: call the Pavilion (tel: 9130 3325).

The Chileans

Chileans never miss the opportunity to remind you that the first Labor Prime Minister of Australia, John Watson, was Chilean. Well, not quite. It is true that Watson, who held the position of Prime Minister between April and August 1904, was born in 1867 in the Chilean port of Valparaiso while his parents were on their way from Britain to New Zealand.

Valparaiso was also the departure point for Australia's first Chilean political exile. He was General Ramón Freire, a deposed president who arrived in Sydney on June 26 1837. He stayed only briefly in Sydney before going back to Chile.

Chilean immigration to Australia dates back to the 1850s when around 50 families came to South Australia to work for the Australian Copper Company. After a few years they returned to Chile. Though small, there was also a group of Chileans that made their way to the Bendigo and Bathurst goldfields – in the early 1850s '16 Chilean miners' were mentioned in a story published in the *Bathurst Free Press*. By the end of the nineteenth century there were about 50 Chileans living in New South Wales.

It was not until the political and economic crisis of the 1970s and the 1980s that Chileans began arriving on our shores in significant numbers. During the political uncertainties of the Socialist government of Dr Salvador Allende, from 1970 to 1973, 2,000 Chileans arrived here. They were joined by a large wave of people who fled the country after the bloody military coup in 1973 that deposed Allende's government. The failure of the 1980s economic policies of Pinochet's dictatorship and a renewed process of political repression against dissidents pushed more Chileans to lodge immigration applications in the Australian embassy in Santiago.

At present, the Chilean-born population is the largest Spanish-speaking community in Australia. Sydney is by far the most popular city, with a strong concentration in the outer western suburbs of Fairfield, Liverpool, Campbelltown and Blacktown.

USEFUL NUMBER FOR VISITORS

CHILEAN CONSULATE:
tel: 9299 2533.

SOCIAL CLUBS

COLO COLO CLUB.
Named after a 'Mapuche' Indian leader who fought against the Spanish conquistadors, the Club is a traditional gathering venue for the numerous Chileans and other Spanish-speaking immigrants living in the western suburbs. The Club has a kitchen service operating every Friday after 6pm. The home-made food, including the timeless *empanadas* (a sort of pie filled with cheese or beef mince) and *humitas* (mashed corn parcel wrapped in corn cob leaves) are always available. On Sunday, the Club is open for the *'Almuerzos Familiares'* (family lunch) from noon-3pm.

**55 Smart Street, Fairfield
(tel: 9726 3333).**

The 1970s saw the foundation in Sydney of several sporting, cultural and humanitarian organisations. Two of the oldest are the Club Colo Colo in the west, and Trasandinos in the eastern suburbs. Both clubs shelter soccer clubs, social and folkloric groups. They also organise the main Chilean annual event, the 'Fiestas Patrias' (National Day) held on September 18.

Arguably the best-known Australian-Chilean is the acclaimed artist – one of the 'bad boys' of Australian contemporary art – Juan Davila. He came to Australia in 1974 and his paintings have been exhibited, among other places, at the Australian National Gallery and the New York Museum of Modern Art.

Getting to know the Chilean community

Events
Fiestas Patrias (National Independence Day).

A celebration of national pride, it's celebrated the weekend closest to September 18. On this day in 1818 Chile gained its independence from Spain. In Sydney, there are two venues where the very well attended celebrations are held: one is at the showground in Fairfield – at the heart of the Chilean community – and the other at Botany Swimming Pool, in Botany. The day-long events feature traditional dances, music and food stalls.

For further information on the event held in Fairfield, contact Colo-Colo Club (tel: 9726 3333), and in Botany contact the Club Trasandino (tel: 9554 8373).

Art and culture
Ballet Folkloric Peulla.

This is a quite successful folk ballet whose performances attract not only Chileans but a wide range of people. The ballet is also a good place to learn the first steps in the very lively South American traditional dances. Rehearsals are held at the Trasandinos Club

418 Gardeners Road, Rosebery; PO Box 8755, Sydney 2000.

Los Chilenos.

Since its establishment in 1971, this Chilean cultural and dance folk group has played a major role in maintaining Chilean folkoric and musical traditions. The director and choreographer is Andres Alarcon.
27 Blight Street, Villawood (tel: 9728 7310).

Community organisations

Chilean Community Services Network.

Provides assistance and advice to new Chilean migrants.
c/o Cabramatta Community Centre, corner McBurney Road and Railway Parade, Cabramatta (tel: 9727 0477).

The Chilean-born painter Juan Davila is considered one of the 'bad boys' of Australian contemporary art. Responding to this reputation a few years back, he almost caused an international conflict between Venezuela and his native Chile. His painting of Venezuela's national hero, Simón Bolivar semi-naked, wearing earings and make-up, and sticking his middle finger up did not amuse Venezuela's government. Juan Davila has been living in Australia since 1974.

Facts and figures

Currently there are about 24,000 Chilean-born people in Australia. This makes Chileans the largest Spanish-speaking community, and also the largest South American community, in Australia. Of these, 49% have settled in Sydney.

The latest figures show that 52.8% of Chilean immigrants had taken out Australian citizenship; in general the largest percentage of them have done it after spending 15 years or more living here. In terms of education, 45.4% of Chilean immigrants have some educational or vocational qualifications, which is higher than for the general Australian population (38.8%). In terms of income, Chileans have a slightly higher median income ($15,500) than that for all Australians ($14,200). However, they are far less likely to own their own houses (45.8%).

Chileans are very proud about their culture. Spanish is spoken at home by 92.9 % of the first generation Chilean-Australians, while it is also the 'home language' spoken by 69.3% of the second generation. Most Chileans are Catholics (72.2%).

In the 1990s Chilean migration to Australia slowed markedly, possibly reflecting the return of a civilian, democratic government in Chile in 1989.

The Mexicans

"**It seems that** the first Mexican in Sydney was the late *Señor* Carlos Zalapa who arrived in Sydney in 1925 and was later appointed Honorary Consul," says the very informative Adriana Rojas, from Mexican Consulate in Sydney. "*Señor* Zalapa was a resourceful man," Mrs Rojas adds. Apparently he opened the first Mexican restaurant in Australia, *La Bodega* in Paddington. He had six children, and one of them, Ricardo Zalapa, is the current Commercial Adviser for the Australian Embassy in Spain.

"I'm the oldest survivor," says Manuel Nila and, he's proud of it. Mr. Nila, a Mexican-American, came to Australia in 1972 and the next year he began operating a small Mexican food manufacturing business – Señor Nila in Brookvale. He remembers that back then there were a few similar manufacturers in Queensland and Melbourne but they soon went broke. Señor Nila (the shop and the man) survived. Today, it is the oldest remaining business of its kind in Australia, and has expanded successfully in the last few years. Mr Nila, who was born in Los Angeles, says that his grocery supplies almost 60 per cent of the Mexican restaurants in Sydney. His is a story of success in the very small Mexican community in Sydney (there are not more than 600 in the whole of Australia).

The Mexican Festival, a month long event held in September, is already a traditional fixture in the Sydney festival scene. One of the highlights of this event is the excellent festival of Mexican cinema.

Restaurants

In contrast to Mexican restaurants in the US, our local ones are still trying to find ways to show Australians real Mexican food, and anyone who has been in the land of Carlos Fuentes and Comandante Marcos always complains about the difficulty of finding authentic Mexican cuisine in Sydney. Some are trying, nonetheless.

Vera Cruz. Not your trad suburban Mexican spot – Vera Cruz is an innovative and refreshing place where you can try the very traditional Mexican *mole* (a poultry dish with a sauce prepared with smoky chillies) and a generous plate of lamb *fajitas*. Average $15, BYO.
Open Monday-Sunday 6pm-10.30pm.
Military Road, Cremorne (tel: 9904 5818).

Juanita's. Located in the rapidly growing Indonesian/Malaysian Sydney enclave of Kensington, Juanita's has given an authentic Mexican touch to its menu. Average $15, BYO. Open Monday-Sunday from 6pm.
180 Anzac Parade, Kensington (tel: 9663 5013).

Newtons Cocina. With a strong accent in modern Mexican cuisine, it has an extensive menu with a very attractive bill. *Fajitas* and char-grilled chicken are highly recommended. South American wine and beers are available. Average $15, BYO and licensed. Open lunch Thursday-Sunday from noon, dinner Monday-Sunday (closed Tuesdays) 5.30-10pm.
403 King Street, Newtown (tel: 9519 8211).

Poco's Cantina. Although it has a special emphasis on Tex-Mex, some of the traditional Mexican dishes such as *burritos* and *tacos* are good. Average $20, BYO. Open Monday-Sunday from 5.30pm.
52 St Pauls Street, Randwick (tel: 9314 7447).

Casa Mexicana. Casual atmosphere, affordable and fine Mexican cuisine. Average $15, BYO. Open 6pm till late.
306 Oxford Street, Bondi Junction (tel: 9389 9945).

Azteca's. Owned by the Mexican-born Jose Cruz, this restaurant surprises its patrons with such innovations as *fajitas* with kangaroo meat. Average $20, BYO. Open Tuesday-Friday from 6pm.
137 Avoca Street, Randwick (tel: 9398 1020).

Shopping
Mexico
Art and craft pieces for the home with typical Mexican designs. It also has some lively art works in silver. Open Monday-Friday 10.30am-6pm, Saturday 10am-5pm and Sunday noon-4pm.
92 Oxford Street, Paddington (tel:9360 7283).

Señor Nila.
The place to buy fresh Mexican products, such as *tortillas* and corn chips. Imported products, like *jalapeño* and some of the deadliest chilli sauces, are also available. Open Monday-Thursday 8am-4.30pm, Friday 8am-3.30pm.
1/6 Grosvenor Place, Brookvale. (tel: 9938 2274).

USEFUL NUMBERS FOR VISITORS

MEXICAN CONSULATE:
tel: 9326 1311.

AEROMEXICO:
tel: 9959 3922.

TOWN & COUNTRY LIVING.

If you're planning to go Mexican with the house decor, this is the place where you can find the renowned Segusino look in furniture. Born in the Spanish Haciendas of the 16th to 19th centuries, the Segusino furniture is handcrafted in Mexico from a blend of new and recycled timbers. Well worth a look.
Open Monday-Friday 9am-5.30pm (till 9pm on Thursday), Sunday 10am-5.30pm

420 Pacific Highway, Crows Nest (tel: 9436 0133).

Getting to know the Mexican community

Events

The Sydney Mexican Festival.

Organised by the Mexican Cultural Fund since 1992, this month-long event, held in September, is an annual celebration of Mexican dance, music, art, theatre, tourism and cuisine, with the renowned Mexican chef, Susanna Palazuelos. As the president of the Cultural Fund, Gina Castañeda, explains that the Festival coincides with the Mexican National Day on September 15. One of the highlights is the excellent Mexican Film Festival.

Further information: Mexican Cultural Fund on 9362 4270.

Art and culture

Mexican Cultural Fund.

A non-profit organisation intended to enhance and develop the knowledge of Mexican culture in Australia. The Fund has the responsibility of organising the annual Sydney Mexican Festival, held in September.

PO Box 545, Edgecliff 2027 (tel: 9362 4270).

Xochipilli Mexican Dancers.

A dance company that promotes dances from many different regions of Mexico through live performances and workshops. Its director and choreographer is Rolando Cano.

2/6 Alfred Street, Mascot (tel: 9693 1469).

Community organisations

Australian-Mexican Welfare Association.

The peak Mexican welfare society in Sydney, it provides support and social assistance to Mexican immigrants. It also organises an annual mass dedicated to the Virgin of Guadalupe, the patron of Mexico.

Further information: Julieta Morabito (tel: 9874 7275).

The Peruvians

Peru gave Sydney one of its most gifted artists, Ernesto Arrisueño. A leading Australian contemporary painter, Arrisueño has been described as an artist who takes us into a world of sharp but dreamy exaggerations. His representations of boats – his recurrent subject – speak of a man who travels other lands in search of inspiration and the magic of real life.

Peruvians form the fourth largest Latin American community in Sydney, with approximately 4,000 people. Carlos Llanos, a Peruvian-born writer, explains that the main flow of Peruvians to Australia occurred during the mid-1960s and the beginning of 1970s when a large number of Peruvians, especially single young women, made use of an assisted passage to come to Australia. Carlos, who is currently researching the Peruvian settlement in Sydney, argues that the peculiar immigration of Peruvian women, aged between 20 and 24 years, was supported by Australian Catholic nuns. As soon as they arrived in Sydney they were accommodated in an inner-city YMCA youth hostel. Most of the women had clerical and secretarial skills and as soon they mastered the language were employed as secretaries. "This is why there are so many Peruvian-born women doing clerical work, for example in the public service," explains Carlos.

In the last few years the Peruvian Consulate has played an important role in the development of the Sydney Peruvian community. After almost six years as an honorary diplomatic mission it has recently been upgraded with the appointment, in April 1996, of the new consul Ricardo Morote. As he explains, this is "a recognition of the growth in the bilateral trade relationship between Australia and Peru."

USEFUL NUMBER FOR VISITORS

PERUVIAN CONSULATE:
tel: 9262 6464.

Born in Lima, Peru, in 1957, painter Ernesto Arrisueño is an artist able to recreate objects – usually with a sentimental meaning - in perfect representation and then play with the image and expose it to completely absurd or ironic situations. Boats are his favourite subject.
The works of Ernesto Arrisueño are usually displayed at the Wagner Gallery, Monday-Saturday 10.30am-6pm. Free.

39 Gurner Street, Paddington
tel: (9360 6069).

Restaurants

Inca Food. This cheap and low key spot offers a generous menu featuring some of the most traditional Peruvian dishes (some regular South American patrons suggest that the menu has also a strong Chilean influence). To start with, try the *ceviche mixto* - a succulent plate of seafood cooked in lemon juice with onions, corn and sweet potato, and for main course, the *adobo a la arequipeña* is worth a try. Average $18, BYO. Open lunch and dinner, Monday-Friday 4-10.30pm; Saturday-Sunday 2-10.30pm.

92 Enmore Road, Enmore (tel: 9550-4709).

Getting to know the Peruvian community

Events

Peruvian National Day.

Organised by the Sporting Peru Social and Cultural Club, this is the day the Sydney Peruvian community gets together at the premises of the Ukrainian Association of Sydney at 59-63 Joseph Street, Lidcombe, to commemorate the National Day, on July 28. The event is a feast of music, food, poetry and dance.

Further information: Peruvian Consulate General (tel: 9262 6464).

The New Zealanders

Last but not least, the 'Kiwis' – the only immigrants out of one million applicants world wide who don't have to queue up with everyone else to face the points test to decide who gets selected to come to Australia. In 1997 New Zealand overtook the United Kingdom to become the biggest source of Australia's immigrants for the first time. Like Australians, New Zealanders are a diverse lot: white New Zealanders (pakaha) – mainly of British and European origins – indigenous Maoris and Pacific Islander immigrants to New Zealand.

Sydneysiders have always had a funny love/hate relationship with Kiwis. We love them when prominent New Zealanders in the arts community decide to live in Sydney and become famous, but we hate them when they beat us at sport. We appropriate their best and brightest as our own if they use Sydney or other Australian cities as a launch-pad to international acclaim (put it this way: if we can't beat you, we'll steal you).

Take Jane Campion, the brilliant New Zealand born film director of *The Piano* and other great films, who has been a long-time resident of Sydney. The hearts of Sydneysiders swelled with pride when her obvious talent was recognised on the world film stage. Our media call Campion and the New Zealand born actors Sam Neil and Russell Crowe "Australians". We treated musicians Tim and Neil Finn as our own, and were proud when Crowded House decided to end it all with a concert – beamed across the globe – on the steps of the Sydney Opera House.

After all New Zealand is so much like Australia. New Zealand shares a British colonial history with Australia, while both countries are Down Under. Both countries have indigenous peoples who resisted white invasion, though New Zealand Maoris are a much larger proportion of the NZ population (about 8%) than Aboriginals (about 2% of the Australian population). Both countries had diverse post-war immigration.

We also share a love of sports bequeathed to us from our English history, particularly rugby union, rugby league and cricket, but also netball. But

MARTIN BROWNE FINE ART. A well known Sydney art dealer gallery where you can find a good selection of the works by contemporary New Zealand artists. Open Tuesday-Sunday 10am-6pm. Free entry.

13 Macdonald Street, Paddington (tel: 9360 2051).

GLASS ARTIST' GALLERY. It displays an impressive selection of handcrafted and original works by New Zealand glassblowers and designers. Open Tuesday-Saturday 10am-6pm, Sunday 1-5pm.

70 Glebe Point Road, Glebe (tel: 9552 1552).

the rivalry is sharp and intense, particularly around the Bledisloe Cup, the annual trophy for rugby supremacy between the Australian *Wallaby* and the New Zealand *All Blacks*. But at least we tend to win the rugby league, netball, soccer and the cricket.

Kiwis

Sydney has always been the preferred Australian city for Kiwis. In 1991, there were 85,000 first generation and 60,000 second generation New Zealanders living in NSW. Most of these live in Sydney. Traditionally many New Zealanders headed for Bondi Beach after arriving in our city. The pubs in Bondi Beach – especially the Champions Bar at the legendary Bondi Beach Hotel were synonymous with Kiwis, particularly Maoris. But Kiwis are scattered across Sydney suburbs, adding to their relative "invisibility" on the Sydney landscape.

Overall, the new Zealand-born have an occupational profile very similar to the Australian-born but tend to have higher education qualifications than the Australian-born. Other than on the sporting field or the arts, New Zealanders do not appear to have made much of a visible mark on Sydney. The most important New Zealander cultural celebrations centre around the *Maori Haka* that is performed before the All Blacks rugby matches. Many New Zealand born players play for Sydney rugby union and rugby league teams, while the Sydney Kiwis RUFC enlivened the sub-district rugby union competition.

This is not to say that some prominent New Zealanders have had a substantial impact on Sydney. R J Heffron, who was a Premier of New South Wales from 1959 to 1964, was born in New Zealand. So to was Sir William Hudson, the creator of the Snowy Mountains Scheme, and Sir Frederick White, a chairman of the Commonwealth Scientific and Industrial Research Organisation. Other New Zealanders have made their mark of the Sydney business and medical communities, and in the horse racing industry.

The Maoris

While many of the people in Sydney's Pacific Islander communities have arrived via New Zealand, Maoris are the largest of all Pacific Islander communities in Sydney. Maori history in Sydney is as long as white settlement itself. Maoris were involved in shipping and trade with the Sydney ever since first settlement in 1788. In 1800, Maori Te Pahi and his son visited Sydney as guests of Governor King. Te Pahi later established a close relationship with the Rev. Samuel Marsden, the "hanging parson". Maoris were excluded from the sanctions of the White

Australia policy because they were British citizens, but there were only 257 Maoris in the whole of Australia by 1954. From the mid 1970s, Maori immigration doubled.

In 1986 – the only year that ethnicity data was collected – there were 9,000 Maoris living in Sydney. Maori settlement has been concentrated in Sydney, particularly in the southeastern municipalities such as Waverley, Rockdale and Randwick: many still rent flats around Bondi. The Astra Hotel in Bondi, which sponsored a Maori Rugby team, was a key hang for Maoris before it closed.

The most important organised Maori activity in Sydney is the *Maori Arohanui*. Fellowship, a division of the Anglican Home Mission Society of Sydney. The Fellowship was headed by Archdeacon Kingi Ihaka, whose arrival from New Zealand in 1984 was celebrated by a *hui* (gathering) at Blacktown. The chaplaincy was established at the Church of the Holly Spirit, *Te Wairua Tapu*, in Elizabeth Street Redfern in October 1985.

USEFUL NUMBERS FOR VISITORS

NZ Consulate:
tel: 9247 1999.

NZ Tourism Board:
1902 260 558 (enquiries)

NZ NATURAL ICE CREAM is one of Sydney's most well known chain of ice cream parlours with branches throughout Sydney. Kiwis should note that the NZ Natural Ice Cream shop does serve *hokey pokey*. Check out the one at Bondi Beach, 178 Campbell Parade.

Getting to know the Kiwi & Maori community

Events

Waitangi Day.

Celebrated on February 6, it remembers the Treaty of Waitangi between the Maori and the British. The NZ Consulate occasionally holds celebrations on this day. However many Maori – who consider that the treaty marks the day when the Maori people were dispossed of their land- don't join the celebration.

Further information on possible activities contact the NZ Consulate on 9247 1999

Maori Cultural Festival.

Held mid January, this colourful festival includes traditional dances and music and a *hangi*. In 1997 the festival was held at the International Rangers Association, University of Western Sydney, Penrith Campus, but the venue may change.

THE NEW ZEALANDERS

Religious organisations and places of worship

Te Wairua Tapu Church.
Maoris from all over Sydney attend the religious service holds every Sunday at 10.30am at 587 Elizabeth Street, Redfern..

For additional information contact Rev. Ngarahu Katene on 9743 6409.

Media

Newspapers

The Kiwi News Overseas. A widely read Kiwi tabloid, it hits the stands every two weeks and costs $2.50. It covers a diverse range of stories coming from New Zealand: from crime to rugby, from obituaries to fashion. Information on kiwis expat also included. *The Kiwi News Overseas* can be found in most Sydney's news agencies.

For further information: tel 9415 2940 (Editorial)

The New Zealander. Widely available in Sydney news agencies, it's weekly newspaper providing a very good overview of events happening back in New Zealand. It costs $3.50.

For further information: tel 9955 8658 (Sydney Master Agent)

Radio

SBS Radio 1, AM 1107. Maori radio program, Thursday 12noon-1pm.

Radio Skid Row, FM 88.9. *Te Whanau Puoro O Poihakena*, Saturday 6am-9am.

2RRR, FM 88.5. NZ On Air In Australia, Sunday 10am-11pm.

2RES, FM 89.7. NZ musician Julian Lee Radio, Friday 9am-12noon.

2SSR, FM 99.7. Sutherland Shire, Huhana Rare Maori & youth issues, Sunday 7-9am.

Transport

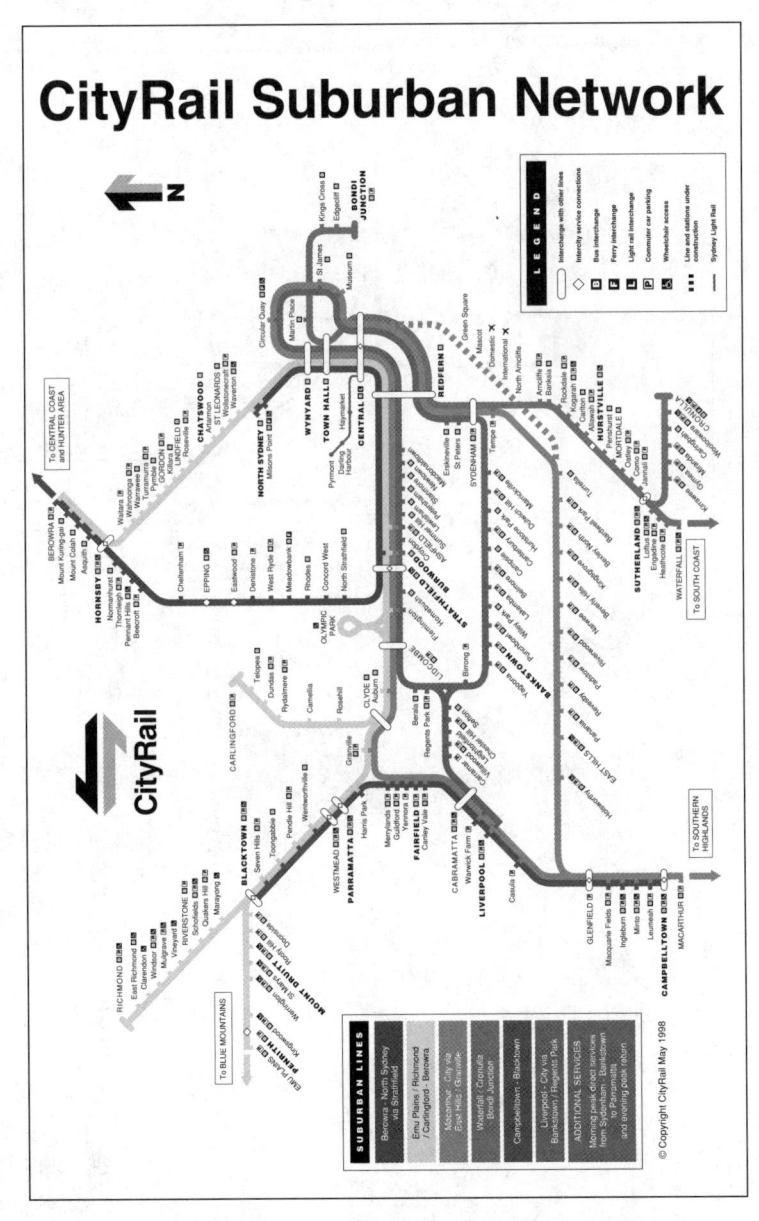

CityRail Suburban Network

Sydney Ferries

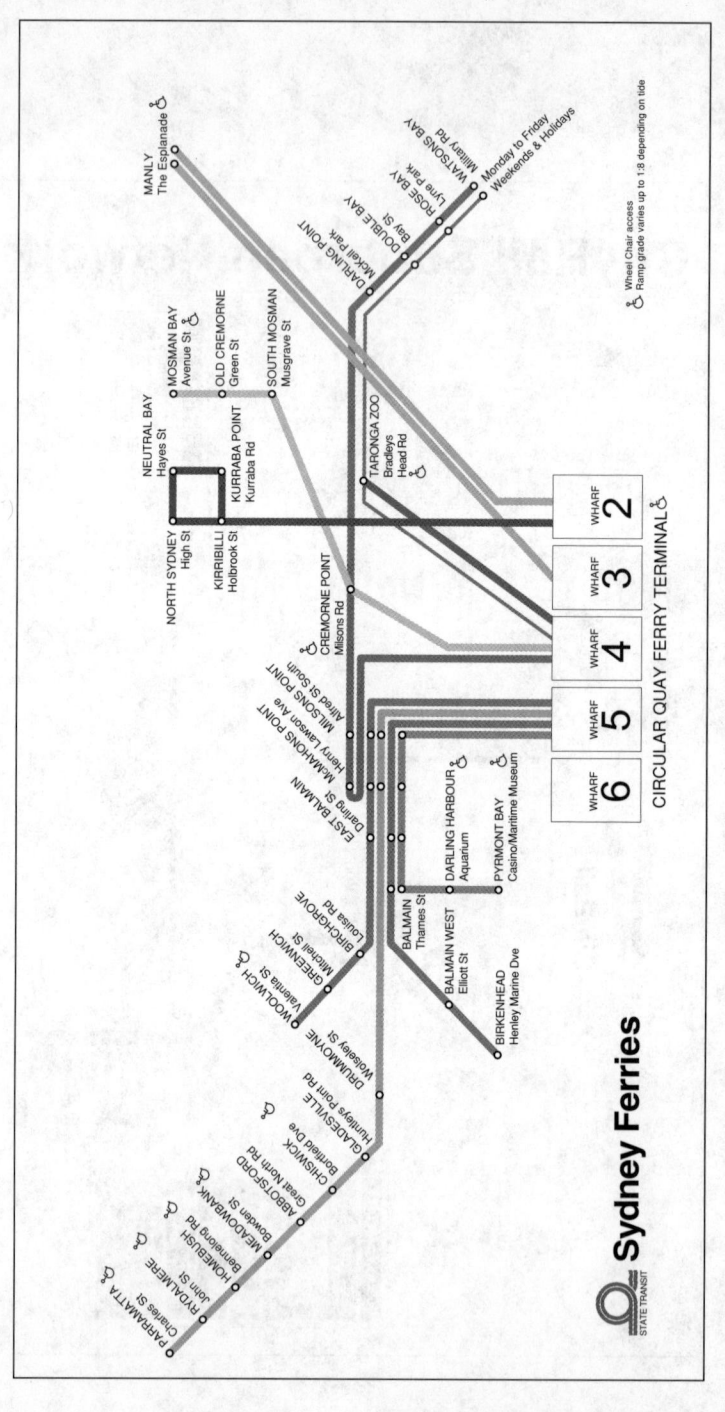

Explore the world in one city

Circular Quay Ferry Terminal

- WHARF 2
- WHARF 3
- WHARF 4
- WHARF 5
- WHARF 6

Stops

- MANLY – The Esplanade
- WATSONS BAY – Military Rd
- ROSE BAY – Lyne Park
- DOUBLE BAY – Bay St
- DARLING POINT – McKell Park
- MOSMAN BAY – Avenue St
- OLD CREMORNE – Green St
- SOUTH MOSMAN – Musgrave St
- NEUTRAL BAY – Hayes St
- KURRABA POINT – Kurraba Rd
- NORTH SYDNEY – High St
- KIRRIBILLI – Holbrook St
- TARONGA ZOO – Bradleys Head Rd
- CREMORNE POINT – Milsons Rd
- MILSONS POINT – Alfred St South
- McMAHONS POINT – Henry Lawson Ave
- EAST BALMAIN – Darling St
- DARLING HARBOUR – Aquarium
- PYRMONT BAY – Casino/Maritime Museum
- BALMAIN – Thames St
- BIRCHGROVE – Louisa Rd
- GREENWICH – Mitchell St
- BALMAIN WEST – Elliot St
- WOOLWICH – Valentia St
- DRUMMOYNE – Wolseley St
- BIRKENHEAD – Henley Marine Dve
- GLADESVILLE – Trumneys Point Rd
- CHISWICK – Burtkead Dve
- ABBOTSFORD – Great North Rd
- MEADOWBANK – Bowden St
- HOMEBUSH – Bennelong Rd
- RYDALMERE – John St
- PARRAMATTA – Charles St

Monday to Friday
Weekends & Holidays

♿ Wheel Chair access
♿ Ramp grade varies up to 1:8 depending on tide

STATE TRANSIT

490

Readers' Feedback

Let us know....

Sydney is a dynamic global city which changes relentlessly. This is the natural fate of a city that is always in the making. Restaurants close, organisations change their address and telephone numbers and community events may change their dates and venues. Also important community historical information may have been omitted or new cultural events develop. So please let us know if there is information you think we should add next time. Help us make the next edition – the Sydney Olympic Games edition – even more useful.

Cosmopolitan Melbourne on the way!

Cosmopolitan Melbourne is already in the making and Pluto Press is requesting Melbournians to send their ideas for information to include. We'll ensure that every morsel of information finds its way to the authors.

Send information to:

Tony Moore
Publisher
Pluto Press Australia
Locked Bag 199 Annandale, NSW 2038, Australia
Tel 61 2 95193299
Fax 61 2 95198940
Email tmoore@socialchange.net.au

Order **Cosmopolitan Sydney** while stocks last!

☐ Yes, I would like ____ copies
of **Cosmopolitan Sydney** $24.95

Explore Australia further through these bestselling books

☐ **Migrant Hands in Distant Lands** $24.95
by Jock Collins

A human story of consecutive waves of Australian immigration providing a blueprint for the future

☐ **A Shop Full of Dreams** $24.95
by Jock Collins, Katherine Gibson, Stephen Castles, David Tait and Carlone Alcorso

The story of the immigrants who set up the restaurants, grocery stores and corner shops of Australia

☐ **Mistaken Identity** $24.95
by Stephen Castles, Mary Kalantzis, Bill Cope and Michael Morrissey

Multiculturalism and the Demise of Nationalism in Australia – a groundbreaking exposure of the ethnic diversity that lies at Australia's heart

☐ **Productive Diversity** $24.95
by Bill Cope and Mary Kalantzis

A New Australian Model For Work and Management – shows how ethic diversity at work is an economic advantage in the global market place.

Order summary

Total number of books ____

Total order value $ ____

+Total postage costs $ ____

= Total payment $ ____

Postage: $4 for the first book, $1.20 for each book thereafter. Outside Australia cost is $9 per order.

Name
____

Postal address
____
postcode

Phone / fax
____

Email address
____

☐ I have included a cheque/money order.
☐ Please charge to my:
   ☐ Bankcard   ☐ Mastercard   ☐ Visa card   ☐ Amex

Card number
____

Expiry date   Today's date
__ / __   __ / __ / __

Signature
____

Order **Now** • **Fill in** the form above and:

- FAX to 61 2 95198940
- Phone your order to 61 2 95193299
- Post orders to Pluto Press, locked bag 199, Annandale 2038
- Buy books ONLINE at http://www.socialchange.net.au/pluto/